BRITISH PARLIAMENTARY ELECTION RESULTS 1832–1885

OTHER BOOKS IN THIS SERIES
Compiled and Edited by F.W.S. Craig

British Parliamentary Election Results 1885–1918
British Parliamentary Election Results 1918–1949
British Parliamentary Election Results 1950–1970
British Electoral Facts 1885–1975
Boundaries of Parliamentary Constituencies 1885–1972
Minor Parties at British Parliamentary Elections 1885–1974
British General Election Manifestos 1900–1974
The Most Gracious Speeches to Parliament 1900–1974

BRITISH PARLIAMENTARY ELECTION RESULTS 1832–1885

Compiled and Edited by

F.W.S. CRAIG

M

First published 1977 by
THE MACMILLAN PRESS LTD
London and Basingstoke
Associated companies in New York
Dublin Melbourne Johannesburg and Madras

ISBN 0333 17153 5

Typeset by
LITHOSET
Chichester

Printed in Great Britain by
The Scolar Press, Ilkley, West Yorkshire

To the pioneers in the compilation of parliamentary election results this book is dedicated:

Charles Roger Phipps Dodd (later Dod), 1793–1855
Henry Stooks Smith, 1808–1881
James Acland, 1799–1876

CONTENTS

PREFACE ix

ABBREVIATIONS and SYMBOLS xi

INTRODUCTORY NOTES xiii

ENGLAND

London Boroughs 1

Provincial Boroughs 23

Counties 349

WALES and MONMOUTHSHIRE:

Boroughs 495

Counties 515

SCOTLAND:

Burghs 533

Counties 565

UNIVERSITIES 609

TABLES

1 Candidates at General Elections 621

2 Members Elected at General Elections 622

3 Electorate 623

4 Uncontested Constituencies 624

5 The Illiterate Vote 625

6 Spoilt Ballot Papers 625

7 Seats in the House of Commons 626

8 General Election Time-Table 627

9 Contested and Uncontested By-Elections 628

10 Reasons for By-Elections 629

11 Analysis of Constituencies 630

12 Election Petitions 631

APPENDICES

1	Representation of Irish Constituencies 1832-1880	635
2	Boroughs Disfranchised for Corruption	640
3	Double and Treble Elections	641
4	Double and Treble Returns	642
5	British Governments and Prime Ministers, 1830-1885	643
6	Reasons for Holding General Elections	644
7	Select Bibliography	645

INDEX to CANDIDATES 649

INDEX to CONSTITUENCIES 685

INDEX to PLACES of ELECTION 691

PREFACE

This fourth and final volume of parliamentary election results follows the layout and presentation adopted in the earlier volumes but omits percentage figures and majorities. To have included such figures for the 1832-85 period would have been pointless for reasons which are explained in the Introductory Notes.

As with the earlier volumes in this series, I have received the most willing help and co-operation of very many people and I would especially like to thank John Palmer, an Assistant Librarian, House of Commons Library; David Johnson, Assistant Clerk of the Records, House of Lords Record Office; Frank Simmons, Royal Courts of Justice; Dr. James Kellas of the Department of Politics, University of Glasgow; Geoffrey Block of the Conservative Research Department; George Awdry, formerly Librarian of the Gladstone Library; Dr. Brian Walker of Queen's University, Belfast, and the Royal Irish Academy, Dublin.

The research work was principally carried out at the British Library (Reference Division), Bloomsbury and Colindale; the Public Record Office; the Gladstone Library of the National Liberal Club; Westminster Central Reference Library; the Guildhall Library; the House of Lords Record Office; Chichester Public Library. The helpfulness and co-operation of librarians and staff was gratifying and it was heartening to note a very considerable improvement in the service provided by the British Library. Gone for good, I hope, are the days of frequent delays and incivility.

Although the typescript and proof-pages were subjected to very thorough checking, it is inevitable that some errors will have gone undetected and I must again ask readers to bring these to my attention so that future reprints can be corrected.

This volume brings to a close a series which was commenced some eight years ago and now provides a unique reference source to parliamentary election results during the past 140 years.

Parliamentary Research Services
18 Lincoln Green
Chichester
West Sussex

March 1977

F.W.S. CRAIG
Compiler and Editor

ABBREVIATIONS AND SYMBOLS

PARTIES

C	Conservative or Tory
Ch	Chartist
Conf	Irish Confederate
HR	Home Ruler (Ireland)
Ind	Independent
Ind Op	Independent (Irish) Opposition
L	Liberal or Radical or Whig
L/Lab	Liberal/Labour (see Introductory Notes)
R	Irish Repealer

MISCELLANEOUS

Bt.	Baronet
H.M.	His/Her Majesty
Hon.	Honourable
Junr.	Junior
MP	Member of Parliament
Senr.	Senior
Unopp.	Unopposed

SYMBOLS

† before the name of a candidate in 1832 indicates a member of the previous Parliament at the time of Dissolution.

† following an electorate indicates a boundary change.

* following an electorate indicates that no figure was available for that election and the total shown represents the number of electors on an earlier register.

* before the name of a candidate indicates that he *was elected* as the result of an election petition.

** before the name of a candidate indicates that he was found *not to have been elected* as the result of an election petition.

INTRODUCTORY NOTES

General Note The name of the constituency at the top of each page is followed, within square brackets, by a constituency reference number which is used in the indexes to candidates and constituencies. This number should not be confused with the folio number which appears in small type at the foot of each page.

Under the name of each constituency are five columns with the following headings:

Election The year of each General Election and the date of any intervening by-election.

Electors The number of electors on the Register in force at the time of the election.

Candidate The initials and surname of the candidate[1].

Party The party affiliation of the candidate.

Votes The number of votes polled by the candidate.

BY-ELECTIONS These are denoted by the year followed by the date (day/month) within round brackets. The dates are those given in the official *Return of Members of Parliament* (House of Commons Papers, 1878 (69–1), lxii and 1890-91 (169), lxii, 281). This Return was compiled from the indentures and writs preserved in the Public Record Office and refer to (prior to the Ballot Act of 1872) the date of the indenture which was normally the day on which the Returning Officer declared the result. From July 1872 the date given was that on which the endorsed writ was received at the Crown Office which could be a few days (or in rare cases several days) after polling had taken place.

The cause of the by-election is shown within square brackets above the year, and if the MP was elevated or succeeded to the Peerage, his new title is given.

Under the provisions of the Succession to the Crown Act, 1707 and a number of subsequent Acts, MPs appointed to certain ministerial and legal offices were required to seek re-election. For a list of offices which if accepted by an MP were held to vacate his seat but did not debar him from seeking re-election see *A Complete Dictionary of the Law and Practice of Elections* by J.D. Chambers (pp. 211-216, London, 1837).

Apart from by-elections caused through ministerial or legal appointments, vacancies could only occur for one of the following reasons: (1) death; (2) elevation or succession to the Peerage; (3) acceptance of an office of profit under the Crown (including certain nominal offices to which MPs who wish to resign are appointed); (4) bankruptcy; (5) lunacy; (6) election petition; (7) expulsion from the House of Commons; (8) sitting or voting in the House of Commons without taking the oath or affirmation of allegiance; (9) disqualification from having been elected to the House of Commons.

CONSTITUENCY BOUNDARIES Details of the area included within constituency boundaries in England and Wales will be found in the *Parliamentary Boundary Act, 1832,* the *Representation of the People Act, 1867* and the *Parliamentary Boundary Act, 1868.* For constituencies in Scotland the relative Acts are the *Representation of the People (Scotland) Act, 1832* and the *Representation of the People (Scotland) Act, 1868.*

Other than changes caused through the disfranchisement of certain boroughs (see Appendix 2) the only boundary changes during the period took place at the General Election of 1868.

Maps showing constituency boundaries in detail were included with the Boundary Commission report published in 1868.

ELECTION PETITIONS These are briefly recorded in footnotes to the constituency pages and are summarised in Table 12, p. 631.

For a list of reports on election petitions, see *Select List of British Parliamentary Papers 1833-1899* by P. & G. Ford, pp. 135-143 (Oxford, 1953).

ELECTORATE STATISTICS The figures of electors at General Elections and by-elections have been taken from official Returns wherever possible. In the relatively few cases where I was unable to obtain official figures, I have relied upon the reference books of Charles Dod and Henry Stooks Smith. At the General Election of 1865, no electorate figures, either official or unofficial were available (except for county constituencies) and for the boroughs I have used the figures of the 1865-66 Register instead of 1864-65.

Due to the system of registration during the period, it was common for some electors to have their names recorded more than once in the same electoral register. They were however only entitled to vote once in the same constituency and many of the official Returns published during the period gave no indication as to the number of duplicates. The electorate figures must therefore be regarded as only approximate and, especially in Scotland, the registers published in the 1830's and 1840's were not subject to revision and contained a large number of names of electors who had died or moved from the constituency.

A rise or fall in the electorate of a constituency may merely indicate that duplicate entries had been included or excluded from a particular set of figures.

For the above reasons it is not possible to calculate turnout with any degree of accuracy and prior to the Ballot Act of 1872, it was possible for a candidate to withdraw and the poll to be closed before the normal time.

The date on which the annual electoral registers came into effect were as follows:

ENGLAND and WALES:	1 November 1832 to 31 October 1833 and annually
	1 December 1843 to 30 November 1844 and annually
	1 January 1868 to 31 October 1868
	1 November 1868 to 31 December 1869
	1 January 1870 to 31 December 1870 and annually
	1 January 1885 to 18 November 1885
SCOTLAND:	15 October 1832 to 14 September 1833
	15 September 1833 to 14 September 1834 and annually
	15 September 1855 to 31 October 1856 (burghs only)
	1 November 1856 to 31 October 1857 (burghs only) and annually
	15 September 1861 to 31 October 1862 (counties only)
	1 November 1862 to 31 October 1863 and annually

GENERAL ELECTION POLLING DATES For a detailed time-table of each General Election see Table 8, p. 627.

IRELAND As in previous volumes in this series, detailed constituency results in Ireland (prior to the creation of Northern Ireland in 1921) are not included. However, the statistics of elections in Ireland have been included in the Tables and Appendices, and Appendix 1 (pp. 635-639) summarises the party representation in the House of Commons after each General Election. I am grateful to Dr. Brian M. Walker and the editors of a New History of Ireland for permitting me to make use of a typescript of the first volume of a definitive reference work on Irish elections *Parliamentary Election Results in Ireland 1801-1922* which will be published later this year by the Royal Irish Academy, Dublin.

LIBERAL CONSERVATIVES This was the name given to the followers of Sir Robert Peel after he broke with the Conservative Party in 1846 over the repeal of the Corn Laws. Some of these free-trade Conservatives returned to the official wing of the Conservative Party after a period of independence while others became Liberals. The problems in defining Liberal Conservatives at the General Elections from 1847 to 1859 are immense and no two sources of reference agree. The term more or less went out of use just after the General Election of 1859 when many of the Liberal Conservatives joined with the Whigs and Radicals to defeat the minority Conservative Government. From then on it was fairly simple to decide whether an MP should be classed as a Conservative or a Liberal.

Throughout the book Liberal Conservatives have been classed as Conservatives until such time as they appear to have severed all links with that party and become Liberals.

For a detailed study of the Peelites or Liberal Conservatives see J.B. Conacher's *The Aberdeen Coalition 1852-1855* (Cambridge, 1968) and *The Peelites and the Party System 1846-52* (Newton Abbot, 1972).

LIBERAL/LABOUR CANDIDATES These candidates were in most cases nominees of local Liberal and Radical associations but campaigned mainly on trade union and labour issues. A number of them were sponsored by trade unions and at the General Election of 1874 thirteen candidates were supported by the Labour Representation League.

MULTIPLE CANDIDATURES With polling at General Elections spread over several weeks it was possible for candidates to contest more than one constituency at the same election and there were a number of cases of candidates being returned for more than one constituency. See Appendix 3, p. 641.

PARTY DESIGNATIONS The party designations of candidates have been extensively cross-checked against numerous contemporary reference books and discrepancies subjected to further research. The party designation of each MP was verified by checking the biographical entry in *Dod's Parliamentary Companion.*

During a period when party ties were often tenuous and changes of party allegiance after election were frequent and rarely reported in the national press, there is no doubt that some errors will have occurred, but these are unavoidable. There were always a number of candidates who could equally well have been classed as Liberal or Conservative.

POLLING The number of days and the hours of polling were as follows:

ENGLISH and WELSH BOROUGHS:	From 1832 until 24 August, 1835, polling was held on two consecutive days, the poll being open from 9.0 a.m. to 4.0 p.m. on the first day and from 8.0 a.m. to 4.0 p.m. on the second day. From 25 August, 1835 polling was restricted to one day between the hours of 8.0.a.m. and 4.0.p.m. From 25 February, 1878 polling in the London boroughs was altered to 8.0 a.m. to 8.0 p.m. and from 28 July, 1884 this later closing of the poll was extended to other boroughs in the United Kingdom with an electorate of over 3,000.

ENGLISH and WELSH COUNTIES.	From 1832 until 1 October, 1853 polling was held on two consecutive days the poll being open from 9.0 a.m. to 4.0 p.m. on the first day and from 8.0 a.m. to 4.0 p.m. on the second day. From 2 October, 1853 polling was restricted to one day between the hours of 8.0 a.m. and 5.0 p.m.
SCOTTISH BURGHS:	From 1832 until 8 September, 1835 polling was held on two consecutive days the poll being open from 9.0 a.m. to 4.0 p.m. on the first day and from 8.0 a.m. to 4.0 p.m. on the second day. From 9 September, 1835 polling was restricted to one day between the hours of 8.0 a.m. and 4.0 p.m.
SCOTTISH COUNTIES:	From 1832 until 13 June, 1853 polling was held on two consecutive days the poll being open from 9.0 a.m. to 4.0 p.m. on the first day and from 8.0 a.m. to 4.0 p.m. on the second day. From 14 June, 1853 polling was restricted to one day (except in Orkney and Shetland) between the hours of 8.0 a.m. and 4.0 p.m.
UNIVERSITIES:	Prior to 1853 the Universities polled over a period of between 8 and 15 days. From 15 August, 1853 polling was restricted to a maximum of 5 days.

SURNAMES and INITIALS The surname and initials of candidates have been cross-checked against various contemporary reference books and local histories. It is impossible to be certain of complete accuracy, especially with unsuccessful candiates, but every effort has been made to verify the numerous discrepancies which came to light.

VOTING STATISTICS The number of votes cast for candidates have been taken from official Returns wherever possible and in other cases the figures have been cross-checked against the principal contemporary reference books. Numerous discrepancies were noted and these were further researched in local newspaper files. Prior to the introduction of the secret ballot in 1872 it must be remembered that it was perfectly possible for discrepancies to occur in subsequently published figures. At the close of polling, figures were normally issued by the candidates' agents (and these often varied slightly) before the official declaration, which might not take place until the following day or even later. The unofficial figures were used by the national press who frequently did not wait until the Returning Officer had counted the votes recorded in the poll-books. The subsequent publication of privately printed pollbooks sometimes produced yet another set of figures.

During the checking, a number of polls were found which are not recorded in the contemporary reference books and I feel fairly confident that all the elections recorded as unopposed were in fact uncontested.

It was not infrequent for a candidate to withdraw on the eve of a poll and sometimes the Returning Officer insisted on formally opening the poll and then closing it after a few electors had voted. This explains some of the polls recorded in this book which show a contest with only a few votes recorded. A candidate could (and often did) withdraw after polling commenced and the poll would then close early. Although candidates were nominated on the hustings prior to 1872 when written nomination was introduced, it was possible for a person to become a candidate during the actual poll if he was nominated at a polling station by some electors. There was also no requirement that a candidate proposed on the hustings had to consent to his nomination or be present and there were several cases of an absent candidate being proposed without his knowledge or consent.

All these circumstances and the large number of two-member seats make the study of voting figures hazardous and turnout impossible to accurately calculate. I have therefore not included percentage figures either for turnout or votes cast for candidates. These figures have little value prior to 1885.

It should be noted that from the General Election of 1868, electors in constituencies returning three MPs were only allowed to vote for two candidates. In the City of London constituency which returned four MPs, electors were only allowed to vote for three candidates.

WRITS SUSPENDED A form of punishment for corrupt constituencies was the suspension of the writ which should have been issued when a vacancy occurred. This was used fairly frequently during the period and all instances of writs being suspended for a considerable time are recorded in the footnotes on petitions. There were numerous other cases of writs being suspended for short peiods or subject to divisions in the House of Commons.

1 Where a candidate changed his surname or acquired a courtesy title after being elected this is shown in italic type within brackets.

ENGLAND ---- LONDON BOROUGHS

CHELSEA [1]
(Two Seats)

Election	Electors	Candidate	Party	Votes
1868	17,408	C.W. Dilke	L	7,374
		Sir H.A. Hoare, Bt.	L	7,183
		W.H. Russell	C	4,177
		C.J. Freake	C	3,929
1874	23,560	Sir C.W. Dilke, Bt.	L	7,217
		W. Gordon	C	7,172
		Sir H.A. Hoare, Bt.	L	6,701
		G.M. Kiell	L	1,967
1880	30,951	Sir C.W. Dilke, Bt.	L	12,406
		J.F.B. Firth	L	12,046
		Lord Inverurie	C	9,666
		W.J. Browne	C	9,488

[Appointment of Dilke as President of the Local Government Board]

Election	Electors	Candidate	Party	Votes
1883 (11/1)		Sir C.W. Dilke, Bt.	L	Unopp.

CITY of LONDON [2]
(Four Seats)

Election	Electors	Candidate	Party	Votes
1832	18,584	G. Grote	L	8,412
		†M. Wood	L	7,488
		†R. Waithman	L	7,452
		Sir J. Key, Bt.	L	6,136
		G. Lyall	C	5,112
		M. Scales	L	569
[Death of Waithman]				
1833 (27/2)	18,584	G. Lyall	C	5,569
		W. Venables	L	4,527
[Resignation of Key]				
1833 (12/8)	18,584	W. Crawford	L	4,041
		F. Kemble	C	2,004
1835	18,288	M. Wood	L	6,418
		J. Pattison	L	6,050
		W. Crawford	L	5,961
		G. Grote	L	5,955
		G. Lyall	C	4,599
		W. Ward	C	4,559
		T. Wilson	C	4,514
1837	19,678	M. Wood	L	6,517
		W. Crawford	L	6,071
		J. Pattison	L	6,070
		G. Grote	L	5,879
		J.H. Palmer	C	5,873
1841	19,068	J. Masterman	C	6,339
		Sir M. Wood, Bt.	L	6,315
		G. Lyall	C	6,290
		Lord John Russell	L	6,221
		M.W. Attwood	C	6,212
		J. Pattison	L	6,070
		W. Crawford	L	6,065
		J. Pirie	C	6,017
[Death of Wood]				
1843 (20/10)	20,030	J. Pattison	L	6,532
		T. Baring	C	6,367
[Appointment of Russell as Prime Minister and First Lord of the Treasury]				
1846 (8/7)		Lord John Russell	L	Unopp.
1847	20,057	Lord John Russell	L	7,137
		J. Pattison	L	7,030
		Baron L.N. de Rothschild	L	6,792
		J. Masterman	C	6,722
		Sir G.G. de H. Larpent, Bt.	L	6,719
		R.C.L. Bevan	C	5,268
		J. Johnson	C	5,069
		J.W. Freshfield	C	4,704
		W. Payne	L	513

CITY of LONDON [2] (Cont.)
(Four Seats)

Election	Electors	Candidate	Party	Votes
[Rothschild seeks re-election after rejection of the Jewish Disabilities Bill]				
1849 (4/7)	21,270	Baron L.N. de Rothschild	L	6,017
		Lord John Manners	C	2,814
[Death of Pattison				
1849 (27/7)		Sir J. Duke	L	Unopp.
1852	20,728	J. Masterman	C	6,195
		Lord John Russell	L	5,537
		Sir J. Duke, Bt.	L	5,270
		Baron L.N. de Rothschild	L	4,748
		R.W. Crawford	L	3,765
[Appointment of Russell as Secretary of State for Foreign Affairs]				
1853 (3/1)		Lord John Russell	L	Unopp.
[Appointment of Russell as Lord President of the Council]				
1854 (14/6)		Lord John Russell	L	Unopp.
[Appointment of Russell as Secretary of State for the Colonies]				
1855 (3/3)		Lord John Russell	L	Unopp.
1857	19,115	Sir J. Duke, Bt.	L	6,664
		Baron L.N. de Rothschild	L	6,398
		Lord John Russell	L	6,308
		R.W. Crawford	L	5,808
		R. Currie	L	4,519
[Rothschild seeks re-election after rejection of the Jewish Disabilities Bill]				
1857 (28/7)		Baron L.N. de Rothschild	L	Unopp.
1859	19,026	Sir J. Duke, Bt.	L	Unopp.
		Baron L.N. de Rothschild	L	Unopp.
		Lord John Russell	L	Unopp.
		R.W. Crawford	L	Unopp.
[Appointment of Russell as Secretary of State for Foreign Affairs]				
1859 (27/6)		Lord John Russell	L	Unopp.
[Elevation of Russell to the Peerage — Earl Russell]				
1861 (29/7)	18,562*	W. Wood	L	5,747
		W. Cubitt	C	5,241

CITY of LONDON [2] (Cont.)

(Four Seats)

Election	Electors	Candidate	Party	Votes
[Death of Wood]				
1863 (2/6)		G.J. Goschen	L	Unopp.
1865	15,534	G.J. Goschen	L	7,102
		R.W. Crawford	L	7,086
		W. Lawrence	L	6,637
		Baron L.N. de Rothschild	L	6,525
		G. Lyall	C	4,197
		R.N. Fowler	C	4,086
[Appointment of Goschen as Chancellor of the Duchy of Lancaster]				
1866 (26/2)		G.J. Goschen	L	Unopp.
1868	20,185	G.J. Goschen	L	6,520
		R.W. Crawford	L	6,258
		W. Lawrence	L	6,215
		C. Bell	C	6,130
		P. Twells	C	6,099
		S.J. Gibbons	C	6,013
		Baron R.N. de Rothschild	L	5,995
[Appointment of Goschen as President of the Poor Law Board]				
1868 (21/12)		G.J. Goschen	L	Unopp.
[Death of Bell]				
1869 (22/2)		Baron L.N. de Rothschild	L	Unopp.
1874	22,626	W.J.R. Cotton	C	8,397
		P. Twells	C	8,330
		J.G. Hubbard	C	8,210
		G.J. Goschen	L	6,787
		W. Lawrence	L	6,654
		Baron R.N. de Rothschild	L	6,490
1880	24,042	W.J.R. Cotton	C	10,326
		R.N. Fowler	C	10,274
		J.G. Hubbard	C	10,256
		W. Lawrence	L	5,950
		R.B. Martin	L	5,837
		W. Morrison	L	5,743

Petitions:—

1837: Dismissed
1849: Withdrawn
(4/7)

FINSBURY [3]
(Two Seats)

Election	Electors	Candidate	Party	Votes
1832	10,309	†R. Grant	L	4,278
		R. Spankie	C	2,842
		C. Babbage	L	2,311
		T. Wakley	L	2,151
		C. Temple	L	787
[Resignation of Grant on appointment as Governor of Bombay]				
1834 (2/7)	9,294	T.S. Duncombe	L	2,514
		H. Pownall	C	1,915
		T. Wakley	L	695
		C. Babbage	L	379
1835	10,299	T.S. Duncombe	L	4,497
		T. Wakley	L	3,359
		R. Spankie	C	2,332
		H.W. Hobhouse	L	1,817
1837	12,264	T. Wakley	L	4,957
		T.S. Duncombe	L	4,895
		D.M. Perceval	C	2,470
1841	12,974*	T.S. Duncombe	L	Unopp.
		T. Wakley	L	Unopp.
1847	15,921	T.S. Duncombe	L	Unopp.
		T. Wakley	L	Unopp.
1852	20,025	T. Challis	L	7,504
		T.S. Duncombe	L	6,678
		J. Wyld	L	2,010
1857	20,626	T.S. Duncombe	L	6,922
		W. Cox	L	4,110
		J.H. Parry	L	3,954
		J.H. Reed	L	2,378
1859	21,951	T.S. Duncombe	L	8,538
		Sir S.M. Peto, Bt.	L	8,174
		W. Cox	L	4,556
[Death of Duncombe]				
1861 (17/12)	22,556	W. Cox	L	4,884
		J.R. Mills	L	4,848
1865	25,461	W.T.M. Torrens	L	8,480
		A. Lusk	L	7,959
		W. Cox	L	5,100
		W. Phillips	C	866
		T.W. Perfitt	L	316

FINSBURY [3] (Cont.)
(Two Seats)

Election	Electors	Candidate	Party	Votes
1868	33,601†	W.T.M. Torrens	L	13,159
		A. Lusk	L	12,503
		P.F. O'Malley	C	6,137
		W. Cox	L	1,238
1874	36,804	W.T.M. Torrens	L	10,099
		A. Lusk	L	9,713
		C.W. Randolph	C	7,737
		B. Lucraft	L/Lab	3,205
1880	44,955	Sir A. Lusk, Bt.	L	16,128
		W.T.M. Torrens	L	15,247
		F. Duncan	C	12,800

Petitions:-

1852: Withdrawn (Challis only)
1857: Withdrawn (Cox only)

GREENWICH [4]
(Two Seats)

Election	Electors	Candidate	Party	Vote
1832	2,714	J.W.D. Dundas	L	1,633
		E.G. Barnard	L	1,442
		J. Angerstein	L	1,033
		F.G. Hammond	L	15
1835	2,516	J. Angerstein	L	1,826
		E.G. Barnard	L	1,102
		M.W. Attwood	C	1,063
1837	3,107	M.W. Attwood	C	1,368
		E.G. Barnard	L	1,194
		C. Napier	L	1,158
1841	3,811	J.W.D. Dundas	L	1,747
		E.G. Barnard	L	1,592
		Sir G. Cockburn	C	1,274
[Appointment of Dundas as a Lord Commissioner of the Admiralty]				
1846 (13/7)		J.W.D. Dundas	L	Unopp.
1847	5,187	J.W.D. Dundas	L	2,409
		E.G. Barnard	L	1,511
		D. Salomons	L	1,236
[Death of Barnard]				
1851 (28/6)	6,022	D. Salomons	L	2,165
		D.W. Wire	L	1,278
[Resignation of Dundas on appointment as Commander of the Mediterranean Fleet]				
1852 (11/2)	6,308	H. Stewart	L	2,956
		M. Chambers	L	1,211
1852	6,308	P. Rolt	C	2,415
		M. Chambers	L	2,360
		H. Stewart	L	2,026
		D. Salomons	L	1,102
[Resignation of Rolt]				
1857 (9/2)	7,888	Sir W.J. Codrington	L	2,975
		B.W.A. Sleigh	L	1,543
1857	7,888	Sir W.J. Codrington	L	2,985
		J. Townsend	L	2,784
		M. Chambers	L	2,065
[Resignation of Townsend following bankruptcy and suspension from the House of Commons]				
1859 (16/2)	7,942	D. Salomons	L	3,444
		W. Angerstein	L	2,523

GREENWICH [4] (Cont.)
(Two Seats)

Election	Electors	Candidate	Party	Votes
1859	7,942	D. Salomons	L	3,873
		W. Angerstein	L	3,520
		M. Chambers	L	1,718
		Sir J.H. Maxwell, Bt.	C	1,031
1865	9,805	D. Salomons	L	4,499
		Sir C.T. Bright	L	3,691
		Sir J.H. Maxwell, Bt.	C	2,328
		J.B. Langley	L	190
		D. Harris	C	116
1868	15,588†	D. Salomons	L	6,684
		W.E. Gladstone	L	6,386
		Sir H.W. Parker	C	4,704
		Viscount Mahon	C	4,372
[Appointment of Gladstone as Prime Minister and First Lord of the Treasury]				
1868 (21/12)		W.E. Gladstone	L	Unopp.
[Death of Salomons]				
1873 (4/8)	15,990	T.W. Boord	C	4,525
		J.B. Langley	L	2,379
		W. Angerstein	L	1,064
		Sir J. Bennett	L	324
		R. Coningsby	C	27
		W. Pook	C	27
1874	17,599	T.W. Boord	C	6,193
		W.E. Gladstone	L	5,968
		J.E. Liardet	C	5,561
		J.B. Langley	L	5,255
1880	22,161	T.W. Boord	C	9,243
		Baron de Worms	C	9,240
		J.E. Saunders	L	8,152
		W.H. Stone	L	8,141

HACKNEY [5]
(Two Seats)

Election	Electors	Candidate	Party	Votes
1868	40,613	C. Reed	L	14,785
		J. Holms	L	12,243
		C.S. Butler	L	6,825
		C.L. Webb	C	2,633
		L.S. Dickson	L	2,575
		J.J. Homer	L	2,021
1874	40,870	J. Holms	L	6,968
		C. Reed	L	6,893
		W.J. Gill	C	6,310
[Election declared void on petition]				
1874 (25/4)	40,870	J. Holms	L	10,905
		H. Fawcett	L	10,476
		W.J. Gill	C	8,994
1880	43,773	H. Fawcett	L	18,366
		J. Holms	L	16,997
		G.C.F. Bartley	C	10,322
[Appointment of Fawcett as Postmaster-General and Holms as a Lord Commissioner of the Treasury]				
1880 (7/5)		H. Fawcett	L	Unopp.
		J. Holms	L	Unopp.
[Death of Fawcett]				
1884 (20/11)	48,076	J. Stuart	L	14,540
		A. MacAlister	C	8,543

Petition :—

1874: Void election

LAMBETH [6]
(Two Seats)

Election	Electors	Candidate	Party	Votes
1832	4,768	†C. Tennyson	L	2,716
		B. Hawes	L	2,166
		D. Wakefield	L	819
		J. Moore	L	155
1835	4,435	B. Hawes	L	2,008
		C. Tennyson *(D'Eyncourt)*	L	1,995
		C. Farebrother	C	931
1837	7,040	B. Hawes	L	2,934
		C.T. D'Eyncourt	L	2,811
		C. Baldwin	C	1,624
1841	7,731	B. Hawes	L	2,601
		C.T. D'Eyncourt	L	2,568
		C. Baldwin	C	1,999
		T. Cabbell	C	1,763
1847	13,885	C. Pearson	L	4,614
		C.T. D'Eyncourt	L	3,708
		B. Hawes	L	3,344
[Resignation of Pearson]				
1850 (7/8)	16,284	W. Williams	L	3,834
		Sir C. Napier	L	1,182
		J.H. Palmer	L	585
1852	18,131	W.A. Wilkinson	L	4,752
		W. Williams	L	4,022
		C.T. D'Eyncourt	L	3,829
1857	20,276	W. Roupell	L	9,318
		W. Williams	L	7,648
		W.A. Wilkinson	L	3,234
1859	21,737	W. Roupell	L	Unopp.
		W. Williams	L	Unopp.
[Resignation of Roupell]				
1862 (5/5)	23,542	F. Doulton	L	5,124
		W.C. Sleigh	C	754
		W.A. Wilkinson	L	347
[Death of Williams]				
1865 (9/5)		J.C. Lawrence	L	Unopp.
1865	27,754	T. Hughes	L	6,373
		F. Doulton	L	6,280
		J.C. Lawrence	L	4,743
		J. Haig	C	514

LAMBETH [6] (Cont.)
(Two Seats)

Election	Electors	Candidate	Party	Votes
1868	33,377	J.C. Lawrence	L	15,051
		W. McArthur	L	14,553
		J.M. Howard	C	7,043
1874	40,103	Sir J.C. Lawrence, Bt.	L	12,175
		W. McArthur	L	11,788
		J.M. Howard	C	11,201
1880	50,541	Sir J.C. Lawrence, Bt.	L	19,315
		W. McArthur	L	18,983
		J.M. Howard	C	16,701

Petition :—

1857: Dismissed (Roupell only)

MARYLEBONE [7]
(Two Seats)

Election	Electors	Candidate	Party	Votes
1832	8,901	†E.B. Portman	L	4,317
		†Sir W. Horne	L	3,320
		Sir S. St. S.B. Whalley	L	2,185
		T. Murphy	L	913
		L.G. Jones	L	316
[Resignation of Portman]				
1833 (20/3)	8,901	Sir S. St. S.B. Whalley	L	2,869
		H.T. Hope	C	2,055
		Hon. C.A. Murray	L	791
		T. Murphy	L	172
1835	7,752	Sir S. St. S.B. Whalley	L	2,956
		H.L.E. Bulwer	L	2,781
		Sir W. Horne	L	1,862
		G.A. Young	L	378
1837	10,843	B. Hall	L	3,512
		Sir S. St. S.B. Whalley	L	3,350
		Lord Teignmouth	C	2,952
		G.A. Young	L	764
		Sir W. Horne	L	662
[Election of Whalley declared void on petition]				
1838 (3/3)	11,799	Lord Teignmouth	C	4,166
		W. Ewart	L	3,762
		T.P. Thompson	L	186
1841	11,570	Sir B. Hall, Bt.	L	4,661
		Sir C. Napier	L	4,587
		B.B. Cabbell	C	3,410
		Sir J.J. Hamilton, Bt.	C	3,383
		W.V. Sankey	L	61
1847	15,662	Lord Dudley Stuart	L	5,367
		Sir B. Hall, Bt.	L	5,343
		Sir J.J. Hamilton, Bt.	C	3,677
		W. Shee	L	662
		R. Owen	Ch	1
1852	19,710	Sir B. Hall, Bt.	L	Unopp.
		Lord Dudley Stuart	L	Unopp.
[Appointment of Hall as President of the General Board of Health]				
1854 (16/8)		Sir B. Hall, Bt.	L	Unopp.
[Death of Stuart]				
1854 (20/12)	19,892*	Viscount Ebrington	L	6,919
		J. Bell	L	4,166

(Two Seats)

Election	Electors	Candidate	Party	Votes
[Appointment of Hall as First Commissioner of Works and Public Buildings]				
1855 (28/7)		Sir B. Hall, Bt.	L	Unopp.
1857	20,851	Viscount Ebrington	L	Unopp.
		Sir B. Hall, Bt.	L	Unopp.
[Resignation of Ebrington]				
1859 (25/2)	20,490	E.J. James	L	6,803
		F. Romilly	L	3,354
1859	20,490	E.J. James	L	5,029
		Sir B. Hall, Bt.	L	4,663
		Lord Stanley	C	1,102
[Elevation of Hall to the Peerage — Lord Llanover]				
1859 (7/7)	20,490	Lord Fermoy	L	4,219
		W. Lyon	L	2,318
		L.S. Dickson	L	1,083
[Resignation of James]				
1861 (19/4)	21,022*	J.H. Lewis	L	5,269
		Sir R.W. Carden	C	2,612
		G.W. Cooke	L	2,369
		J.C. Marshman	L	65
		H. Twelvetrees	L	1
1865	23,588	J.H. Lewis	L	7,159
		T. Chambers	L	6,488
		Lord Fermoy	L	4,121
1868	35,575	J.H. Lewis	L	9,782
		T. Chambers	L	9,444
		H. Sandwith	L	5,591
		D. Grant	L	4,058
		Sir T.G.A. Parkyns, Bt.	C	3,989
1874	30,740	W. Forsyth	C	9,849
		Sir T. Chambers	L	8,251
		D. Grant	L	7,882
		T. Hughes	L	294
1880	35,535	D. Grant	L	14,147
		Sir T. Chambers	L	14,003
		Lord Headley	C	11,890
		F.S. Hunt	C	11,888

Petition:—

1837: Election of Whalley declared void

SOUTHWARK [8]
(Two Seats)

Election	Electors	Candidate	Party	Votes
1832	4,775	†W. Brougham	L	2,264
		J. Humphery	L	1,708
		L.B. Allen	L	1,040
1835	5,249	D.W. Harvey	L	Unopp.
		J. Humphery	L	Unopp.
1837	5,477	J. Humphery	L	1,941
		D.W. Harvey	L	1,927
		J. Richards	C	847
		B. Harrison	C	2
[Appointment of Harvey as Registrar of Metropolitan Public Carriages]				
1839 (27/2)		D.W. Harvey	L	Unopp.
[Resignation of Harvey on appointment as Commissioner of Police for the City of London]				
1840 (24/1)	5,047	B. Wood	L	2,059
		J. Walter	C	1,535
1841	5,124	J. Humphery	L	Unopp.
		B. Wood	L	Unopp.
[Death of Wood]				
1845 (12/9)	5,353*	Sir W. Molesworth, Bt.	L	1,943
		J. Pilcher	C	1,182
		E. Miall	L	352
1847	7,989	J. Humphery	L	Unopp.
		Sir W. Molesworth, Bt.	L	Unopp.
1852	9,458	Sir W. Molesworth, Bt.	L	3,941
		A. Pellatt	L	3,887
		G. Scovell	L	2,909
[Appointment of Molesworth as First Commissioner of Works and Public Buildings]				
1853 (1/1)		Sir W. Molesworth, Bt.	L	Unopp.
[Appointment of Molesworth as Secretary of State for the Colonies]				
1855 (27/7)		Sir W. Molesworth, Bt.	L	Unopp.
[Death of Molesworth]				
1855 (20/11)		Sir C. Napier	L	Unopp.
1857	10,170	Sir C. Napier	L	3,991
		J. Locke	L	3,647
		A. Pellatt	L	2,499

SOUTHWARK [8] (Cont.)
(Two Seats)

Election	Electors	Candidate	Party	Votes
1859	10,606	Sir C. Napier	L	4,446
		J. Locke	L	4,255
		A. Pellatt	L	2,730
[Death of Napier]				
1860 (12/12)	11,278*	A.H. Layard	L	4,572
		G. Scovell	L	3,377
[Appointment of Locke as Recorder of Brighton]				
1861 (24/4)		J. Locke	L	Unopp.
1865	11,631	A.H. Layard	L	Unopp.
		J. Locke	L	Unopp.
1868	17,703	J. Locke	L	6,027
		A.H. Layard	L	5,908
		W.J.R. Cotton	C	2,495
[Appointment of Layard as First Commissioner of Works and Public Buildings]				
1868 (21/12)		A.H. Layard	L	Unopp.
[Resignation of Layard on appointment as United Kingdom Ambassador to Spain]				
1870 (17/2)	17,703*	M. Beresford	C	4,686
		G. Odger	L/Lab	4,382
		Sir S.H. Waterlow	L	2,966
1874	20,419	J. Locke	L	5,901
		M. Beresford	C	5,716
		G. Odger	L/Lab	3,496
		A. Dunn	L	3,121
[Death of Locke]				
1880 (14/2)	23,472	E.G. Clarke	C	7,683
		A. Dunn	L	6,830
		G. Shipton	L/Lab	799
1880	23,472	A. Cohen	L	9,693
		J.E.T. Rogers	L	9,521
		E.G. Clarke	C	8,163
		M. Cattley	C	7,674

TOWER HAMLETS [9]
(Two Seats)

Election	Electors	Candidate	Party	Votes
1832	9,906	†S. Lushington	L	3,978
		W. Clay	L	3,751
		Hon. L. Stanhope	L	2,952
		F. Marryat	L	1,934
1835	9,462	W. Clay	L	2,779
		S. Lushington	L	2,580
		J.R. Burton	C	465
1837	13,318	W. Clay	L	Unopp.
		S. Lushington	L	Unopp.
[Appointment of Lushington as a Judge of the High Court of Admiralty]				
1839 (11/2)		S. Lushington	L	Unopp.
1841	13,842	W. Clay	L	4,706
		C.R. Fox	L	4,096
		G.R. Robinson	C	2,183
		A.K. Hutchinson	L	1,775
		T.E.P. Thompson	L	831
[Appointment of Fox as Surveyor-General of the Ordnance]				
1846 (11/7)		C.R. Fox	L	Unopp.
1847	18,748	G. Thompson	L	6,268
		Sir W. Clay, Bt.	L	3,839
		C.R. Fox	L	2,622
1852	23,534	Sir W. Clay, Bt.	L	7,728
		C.S. Butler	L	7,718
		G. Thompson	L	4,568
		A.S. Ayrton	L	2,792
		W. Newton	L	1,095
1857	27,980	A.S. Ayrton	L	7,813
		C.S. Butler	L	7,297
		Sir W. Clay, Bt.	L	6,654
1859	28,843	A.S. Ayrton	L	Unopp.
		C.S. Butler	L	Unopp.
1865	34,115	A.S. Ayrton	L	Unopp.
		C.S. Butler	L	Unopp.
1868	32,546†	A.S. Ayrton	L	9,839
		J.D'A Samuda	L	7,849
		O.E. Coope	C	7,446
		E. Beales	L	7,160
		W. Newton	L/Lab	2,890

TOWER HAMLETS [9] (Cont.)
(Two Seats)

Election	Electors	Candidate	Party	Votes
[Appointment of Ayrton as First Commissioner of Works and Public Buildings]				
1869 (8/11)		A.S. Ayrton	L	Unopp.
1874	32,937	C.T. Ritchie	C	7,228
		J.D'A Samuda	L	5,900
		E.H. Currie	L	5,022
		A.S. Ayrton	L	3,202
		F.A. Maxse	L	2,992
1880	41,042	J. Bryce	L	12,020
		C.T. Ritchie	C	11,720
		J.D'A Samuda	L	10,384
		B. Lucraft	L/Lab	5,103

WESTMINSTER [10]
(Two Seats)

Election	Electors	Candidate	Party	Votes
1832	11,576	†Sir F. Burdett, Bt.	L	3,248
		†Sir J.C. Hobhouse, Bt.	L	3,214
		†G. De L. Evans	L	1,076
[Appointment of Hobhouse as Chief Secretary to the Lord Lieutenant of Ireland]				
1833 (4/4)		Sir J.C. Hobhouse, Bt.	L	Unopp.
[Hobhouse seeks re-election after his resignation from the Government on the issue of the House and Window taxes]				
1833 (11/5)	11,576	G. De L. Evans	L	2,027
		Sir J.C. Hobhouse, Bt.	L	1,835
		B. Escott	C	738
1835	13,268	Sir F. Burdett, Bt.	L	2,747
		G. De L. Evans	L	2,588
		Sir T.J. Cochrane	C	1,528
[Burdett seeks re-election as a Conservative]				
1837 (12/5)	15,262	Sir F. Burdett, Bt.	C	3,567
		J.T. Leader	L	3,052
1837	15,262	J.T. Leader	L	3,793
		G. De L. Evans	L	3,715
		Sir G. Murray	C	2,620
1841	13,767	Hon. H.J. Rous	C	3,338
		J.T. Leader	L	3,281
		Sir G. De L. Evans	L	3,258
[Appointment of Rous as a Lord Commissioner of the Admiralty]				
1846 (19/2)	14,801*	Sir G. De L Evans	L	3,843
		Hon. H.J. Rous	C	2,906
1847	14,572	Sir G. De L. Evans	L	3,139
		C. Lushington	L	2,831
		C. Cochrane	L	2,819
		Viscount Mandeville	C	1,985
1852	14,883	Sir J.V. Shelley, Bt.	L	4,199
		Sir G. De L. Evans	L	3,756
		Viscount Maidstone	C	3,373
		W. Coningham	L	1,716
1857	13,182	Sir G. De L. Evans	L	Unopp.
		Sir J.V. Shelley, Bt.	L	Unopp.
1859	13,801	Sir G. De L. Evans	L	Unopp.
		Sir J.V. Shelley, Bt.	L	Unopp.

WESTMINSTER [10] (Cont.)
(Two Seats)

Election	Electors	Candidate	Party	Votes
1865	12,546	Hon. R.W. Grosvenor	L	4,534
		J.S. Mill	L	4,525
		W.H. Smith	C	3,824
1868	18,879	W.H. Smith	C	7,648
		Hon. R.W. Grosvenor	L	6,584
		J.S. Mill	L	6,284
1874	19,845	W.H. Smith	C	9,371
		Sir C. Russell, Bt.	C	8,681
		Sir T.F. Buxton, Bt.	L	4,749
		Sir W.J. Codrington	L	3,435
[Appointment of Smith as First Lord of the Admiralty]				
1877 (11/8)		W.H. Smith	C	Unopp.
1880	21,081	W.H. Smith	C	9,093
		Sir C. Russell, Bt.	C	8,930
		J. Morley	L	6,564
		Sir A. Hobhouse	L	6,443
[Resignation of Russell]				
1882 (10/2)		Lord Algernon Percy	C	Unopp.
[Appointment of Smith as Secretary of State for the War Department]				
1885 (29/6)		W.H. Smith	C	Unopp.

Petition:—

1868: Dismissed (Smith only)

Note:—

1833: (11/5) Hobhouse had abstained in a vote in the House of Commons on the repeal of the House and Window taxes. He resigned as Chief Secretary to the Lord Lieutenant of Ireland and decided to seek re-election in order to give his constituents an opportunity to endorse his actions.

ENGLAND —— PROVINCIAL BOROUGHS

ABINGDON [11]

Election	Electors	Candidate	Party	Votes
1832	300	T. Duffield	C	157
		†W.L. Maberly	L	43
		T. Bowles	L	1
1835	292	T. Duffield	C	Unopp.
1837	306	T. Duffield	C	Unopp.
1841	321	T. Duffield	C	Unopp.
[Resignation]				
1844 (11/5)		F. Thesiger	C	Unopp.
[Appointed Attorney-General]				
1845 (9/7)	315*	Sir F. Thesiger	C	156
		J. Caulfeild	L	126
1847	339	Sir F. Thesiger	C	153
		J. Caulfeild	L	151
[Appointed Attorney-General]				
1852 (5/3)		Sir F. Thesiger	C	Unopp.
1852	312	J. Caulfeild	L	Unopp.
[Death]				
1852 (3/12)	312	Lord Norreys	L	153
		D.H.D. Burr	C	129
[Succession to the Peerage – Earl of Abingdon]				
1854 (13/12)	389*	J.H. Reed	L	125
		J.T. Norris	L	117
1857	323	J.T. Norris	L	Unopp.
1859	320	J.T. Norris	L	144
		J.G.B. Hudson	C	119
1865	304	Hon. C.H. Lindsay	C	137
		J.T. Norris	L	116
[Appointed a Groom in Waiting to Her Majesty]				
1866 (6/8)		Hon. C.H. Lindsay	C	Unopp.

Election	Electors	Candidate	Party	Votes
1868	801†	Hon. C.H. Lindsay	C	397
		G. Lushington	L	324
1874	860	J.C. Clarke	L	439
		Hon. C.H. Lindsay	C	333
1880	890	J.C. Clarke	L	428
		A.G.H. Gibbs	C	386

Petition:—

1847: Withdrawn

ANDOVER [12]
(Two seats until 1868; one seat from 1868)

Election	Electors	Candidate	Party	Votes
1832	246	†H.A.W. Fellowes	L	Unopp.
		†R. Etwall	L	Unopp.
1835	240	R. Etwall	L	149
		Sir J.W. Pollen, Bt.	C	108
		E. Nightingale	L	100
		E.R. Tunno	C	35
1837	265	R. Etwall	L	Unopp.
		Sir J.W. Pollen, Bt.	C	Unopp.
1841	234	R. Etwall	L	131
		Lord William Paget	L	112
		Sir J.W. Pollen, Bt.	C	105
1847	243	H.B. Coles	C	134
		W. Cubitt	C	121
		I.N. Fellowes	L	107
		T.C. Smith	L	60
1852	241	W. Cubitt	C	140
		H.B. Coles	C	121
		J. Curling	L	20
1857	233	W. Cubitt	C	143
		Hon. D.F. Fortescue	L	120
		H.B. Coles	C	102
1859	239	W. Cubitt	C	153
		Hon. D.F. Fortescue	L	120
		R.W. Johnson	C	114
[Resignation of Cubitt in order to contest the City of London]				
1861 (29/7)		H.B. Coles	C	Unopp.
[Death of Coles]				
1862 (17/12)		W. Cubitt	C	Unopp.
[Death of Cubitt]				
1863 (18/11)	244	W.H. Humphery	C	130
		J.C. Hawkshaw	L	83
1865	255	Hon. D.F. Fortescue	L	Unopp.
		W.H. Humphery	C	Unopp.
[Resignation of Humphery]				
1867 (11/2)		Sir J.B. Karslake	C	Unopp.

ANDOVER [12] (Cont.)
(Two seats until 1868; one seat from 1868)

Election	Electors	Candidate	Party	Votes
[Appointment of Karslake as Attorney-General]				
1867 (22/7)		Sir J.B. Karslake	C	Unopp.
1868	775	Hon. D.F. Fortescue	L	377
		H. Wellesley	C	307
1874	764	H. Wellesley	C	395
		Hon. D.F. Fortescue	L	259
1880	833	F.W. Buxton	L	405
		H. Wellesley	C	364

Petition:—

1847: Withdrawn

ARUNDEL [13]

Election	Electors	Candidate	Party	Votes
1832	351	†Lord Dudley Stuart	L	Unopp.
1835	360	Lord Dudley Stuart	L	Unopp.
1837	322	Lord Fitzalan	L	176
		Lord Dudley Stuart	L	105
1841	261*	Lord Fitzalan *(Earl of Arundel and Surrey)*	L	Unopp.
1847	221	Earl of Arundel and Surrey	L	Unopp.
[Resignation]				
1851 (16/7)		E. Strutt	L	Unopp.
1852	208	Lord Edward Howard	L	Unopp.
1857	199	Lord Edward Howard	L	Unopp.
1859	196	Lord Edward Howard	L	Unopp.
1865	174	Lord Edward Howard	L	Unopp.

This constituency ceased to return a Member of Parliament in 1868 and was incorporated into the county constituency of Sussex, Western.

ASHBURTON [14]

Election	Electors	Candidate	Party	Votes
1832	198	†W.S. Poyntz	L	Unopp.
1835	190	C. Lushington	L	89
		J.H. Palmer	C	71
1837	226	C. Lushington	L	98
		U. Browne	C	87
1841	280	W. Jardine	L	Unopp.
[Death]				
1843	270	J. Matheson	L	141
(8/3)		J.H. Palmer	C	96
1847	262	T. Matheson	L	Unopp.
1852	236	G. Moffatt	L	Unopp.
1857	182	G. Moffatt	L	Unopp.
1859	196	J.H. Astell	C	91
		G. Moffatt	L	90
1865	350	R. Jardine	L	Unopp.

This constituency ceaed to return a Member of Parliament in 1868 and was incorporated into the county constituency of Devon, Eastern.

Petition:—

1859: Dismissed

ASHTON-UNDER-LYNE [15]

Election	Electors	Candidate	Party	Votes
1832	433	G. Williams	L	176
		C. Hindley	L	163
		T.W. Helps	C	33
1835	515	C. Hindley	L	212
		T.W. Helps	C	105
		G. Williams	L	63
1837	603	C. Hindley	L	237
		J. Wood	C	201
		J.R. Stephens	Ch	19
1841	713	C. Hindley	L	303
		J. Harrop	C	254
1847	871	C. Hindley	L	Unopp.
1852	937	C. Hindley	L	Unopp.
1857	1,085	C. Hindley	L	Unopp.
[Death]				
1857 (14/12)	1,085*	T.M. Gibson	L	522
		B. Mason	C	390
1859	1,081	T.M. Gibson	L	Unopp.
[Appointed President of the Poor Law Board]				
1859 (27/6)		T.M. Gibson	L	Unopp.
[Appointed President of the Board of Trade]				
1859 (9/7)		T.M. Gibson	L	Unopp.
1865	967	T.M. Gibson	L	Unopp.
1868	4,822†	T.W. Mellor	C	2,318
		T.M. Gibson	L	2,109
1874	5,471	T.W. Mellor	C	2,612
		A. Buckley	L	2,432
1880	5,901	H. Mason	L	2,966
		J.R. Coulthart	C	2,586

AYLESBURY [16]
(Two Seats)

Election	Electors	Candidate	Party	Votes
1832	1,654	†W. Rickford	L	1,076
		†H. Hanmer	C	657
		T.B. Hobhouse	L	602
1835	1,544	W. Rickford	L	855
		H. Hanmer	C	586
		T.B. Hobhouse	L	508
		J. Lee	L	269
1837	1,414	W. Rickford	L	865
		W.M. Praed	C	657
		Lord Nugent	L	540
[Death of Praed]				
1839 (31/7)	1,416*	C.J.B. Hamilton	C	620
		J.I. Lockhart	L	72
		Lord Nugent	L	3
1841	1,624	R.R. Clayton	C	Unopp.
		C.J.B. Hamilton	C	Unopp.
1847	1,513	J.P. Deering	C	687
		Lord Nugent	L	620
		R.R. Clayton	C	546
[Election of Deering declared void on petition]				
1848 (29/3)	1,513	Q. Quick	C	614
		J. Houghton	L	345
[Death of Nugent]				
1850 (27/12)	1,512	F. Calvert	L	499
		J. Houghton	L	147
[Election declared void on petition]				
1851 (11/4)	1,512	R. Bethell	L	544
		W.B. Ferrand	C	518
1852	1,417	A.H. Layard	L	558
		R. Bethell	L	525
		A.F. Bayford	C	447
		J.T. West	C	435
[Appointment of Bethell as Solicitor-General]				
1853 (6/1)		R. Bethell	L	Unopp.
[Appointment of Bethell as Attorney-General]				
1857 (9/2)		Sir R. Bethell	L	Unopp.

(Two Seats)

Election	Electors	Candidate	Party	Votes
1857	1,266	T.T. Bernard	C	546
		Sir R. Bethell	L	501
		A.H. Layard	L	439
1859	1,304	T.T. Bernard	C	552
		*S.G. Smith	C	535
		**T.V. Wentworth	L	535
1865	1,225	N.M. de Rothschild	L	Unopp.
		S.G. Smith	C	Unopp.
1868	3,602†	N.M. de Rothschild	L	1,772
		S.G. Smith	C	1,468
		G. Howell	L/Lab	942
1874	4,064	N.M. de Rothschild	L	1,761
		S.G. Smith	C	1,624
		G. Howell	L/Lab	1,144
1880	4,228	Sir N.M. de Rothschild, Bt.	L	2,111
		G.W.E. Russell	L	1,919
		S.G. Smith	C	1,511
[Elevation of Rothschild to the Peerage — Lord Rothschild]				
1885 (18/7)	4,473*	Baron F.J. de Rothschild	L	2,353
		W. Graham	C	1,416

Petitions:—

1847: Election of Deering declared void. Petition against Nugent dismissed

1850: Void election

1851: Withdrawn

1859: Treble return. On scrutiny one vote was struck of Wentworth's total and his election declared void. Petitions against Bernard and Smith dismissed.

BANBURY [17]

Election	Electors	Candidate	Party	Votes
1832	329	H.W. Tancred	L	Unopp.
1835	368	H.W. Tancred	L	205
		E.L. Williams	L	45
1837	343	H.W. Tancred	L	181
		H. Tawney	C	75
1841	385	H.W. Tancred	L	124
		H. Holbech	C	100
		H. Vincent	Ch	51
1847	465	H.W. Tancred	L	226
		J. McGregor	C	164
1852	491	H.W. Tancred	L	Unopp.
1857	538	H.W. Tancred	L	216
		E. Yates	L	58
[Resignation]				
1859 (9/2)	672	B. Samuelson	L	177
		J. Hardy	C	176
		E. Miall	L	118
1859	672	Sir C.E. Douglas	L	235
		B. Samuelson	L	199
1865	614	B. Samuelson	L	206
		C. Bell	C	165
		Sir C.E. Douglas	L	160
1868	1,524	B. Samuelson	L	772
		G. Stratton	C	397
1874	1,906	B. Samuelson	L	760
		J.J. Wilkinson	C	676
1880	1,848	B. Samuelson	L	1,018
		T.G. Bowles	C	583

Petition:—

1865: Dismissed

BARNSTAPLE [18]
(Two Seats)

Election	Electors	Candidate	Party	Votes
1832	720	†J.P.B. Chichester	L	519
		C. St. J. Fancourt	C	349
		T. Northmore	L	225
		Lord George Hervey	L	129
1835	790	J.P.B. Chichester	L	542
		C. St.J. Fancourt	C	528
		J. Stewart	L	134
		J. Woolley	C	3
1837	794	J.P.B. Chichester	L	387
		F. Hodgson	C	356
		Hon. W.S. Best	C	348
1841	807	F. Hodgson	C	360
		M. Gore	C	349
		Hon. J.W. Fortescue	L	346
		Sir J.P.B. Chichester, Bt.	L	343
1847	781	R. Bremridge	C	464
		Hon. J.W. Fortescue	L	396
		F. Hodgson	C	356
1852	771	Sir W.A. Fraser, Bt.	C	406
		R. Bremridge	C	393
		Viscount Ebrington	L	332
[Election declared void on petition]				
1854 (25/8)	784	J. Laurie	C	333
		R.S. Guinness	C	323
		W. Tite	L	286
[Election of Laurie declared void on petition]				
1855 (10/3)		G.S. Buck	C	Unopp.
1857	742	Sir W.A. Fraser, Bt.	C	344
		J. Laurie	C	252
		J. Taylor	L	180
		G. Potts	L	179
		H.T. Prinsep	C	36
1859	693	J.D.F. Davie	L	348
		G. Potts	L	266
		Sir G.S. Stucley, Bt.	C	210
		Sir W.A. Fraser, Bt.	C	199
[Death of Potts]				
1863 (20/10)	738	**T. Lloyd	L	305
		*R. Bremridge	C	284

BARNSTAPLE [18] (Cont.)
(Two Seats)

Election	Electors	Candidate	Party	Votes
1865	715	Sir G.S. Stucley, Bt.	C	364
		T. Cave	L	331
		H. Gwyn	C	302
		H. Hawkins	L	262
1868	1,596†	T. Cave	L	791
		C.H. Williams	C	788
		W.H. Evans	L	667
1874	1,591	T. Cave	L	757
		S.D. Waddy	L	675
		J. Fleming	C	622
		J. Holt	C	580
[Resignation of Waddy in order to contest Sheffield]				
1880 (12/2)	1,646	Viscount Lymington	L	817
		Sir R.W. Carden	C	721
1880	1,646	Sir R.W. Carden	C	856
		Viscount Lymington	L	811
		H.R. Grenfell	L	720

Petitions:—

1841: Withdrawn

1852: Void election

1854: Election of Laurie declared void. Petition against Guinness dismissed

1859: Withdrawn

1863: Election of Lloyd declared void. Brembridge duly elected after scrutiny

1865: Withdrawn

1874: Dismissed

BATH [19]
(Two Seats)

Election	Electors	Candidate	Party	Votes
1832	2,853	†C. Palmer	L	1,492
		J.A. Roebuck	L	1,138
		H.W. Hobhouse	L	1,040
1835	2,764	C. Palmer	L	1,097
		J.A. Roebuck	L	1,042
		H. Daubeney	C	706
1837	2,994	Viscount Powerscourt	C	1,087
		W.H.L. Bruges	C	1,024
		C. Palmer	L	962
		J.A. Roebuck	L	910
1841	2,985	Viscount Duncan	L	1,223
		J.A. Roebuck	L	1,157
		W.H.L. Bruges	C	930
		Viscount Powerscourt	C	926
1847	2,825	Lord Ashley	C	1,278
		Viscount Duncan	L	1,228
		J.A. Roebuck	L	1,093
[Succession of Ashley to the Peerage — Earl of Shaftesbury]				
1851 (25/6)	3,130	G.T. Scobell	L	1,110
		W. Sutcliffe	C	1,041
1852	3,278	G.T. Scobell	L	1,332
		T. Phinn	L	1,290
		W. Whateley	C	1,253
[Resignation of Phinn on appointment as Assistant Secretary to the Admiralty]				
1855 (5/6)	3,155*	W. Tite	L	1,176
		W. Whateley	C	1,129
1857	3,144	Sir A.H. Elton, Bt.	L	1,243
		W. Tite	L	1,200
		A.E. Way	C	1,197
1859	3,185	W. Tite	L	1,349
		A.E. Way	C	1,339
		T. Phinn	L	1,198
1865	2,960	J.M. Hogg	C	Unopp.
		W. Tite	L	Unopp.
1868	5,024†	W. Tite	L	2,478
		D. Dalrymple	L	2,187
		J.M. Hogg	C	2,024

BATH [19] (Cont.)
(Two Seats)

Election	Electors	Candidate	Party	Votes
[Death of Tite]				
1873	5,182	Viscount Chelsea	C	2,251
(7/5)		J. Murch	L	1,991
[Succession of Chelsea to the Peerage – Earl Cadogan]				
1873	5,182	Viscount Grey de Wilton	C	2,194
(28/6)		A.D. Hayter	L	2,143
		J.C. Cox	L	15
[Death of Dalrymple]				
1873	5,182	A.D. Hayter	L	2,210
(9/10)		W. Forsyth	C	2,071
		C. Thompson	L	57
1874	5,454	A.D. Hayter	L	2,520
		N.G.P. Bousfield	C	2,397
		Lord John Hervey	L	2,391
		Viscount Grey de Wilton	C	2,348
1880	5,534	Sir A.D. Hayter, Bt.	L	2,712
		E.R. Wodehouse	L	2,700
		R. Hardy	C	2,359
		T.J. Smyth	C	2,241
[Appointment of Hayter as a Lord Commissioner of the Treasury]				
1880		Sir A.D. Hayter, Bt.	L	Unopp.
(8/5)				

Petitions:—

1832: Dismissed (Roebuck only)

1857: Dismissed (Tite only)

BEDFORD [20]
(Two Seats)

Election	Electors	Candidate	Party	Votes
1832	1,572	†W.H. Whitbread	L	599
		S. Crawley	L	486
		†F. Polhill	C	483
1835	1,252	F. Polhill	C	490
		S. Crawley	L	403
		W.H. Whitbread	L	383
1837	1,192	F. Polhill	C	467
		**H. Stuart	C	419
		*S. Crawley	L	412
1841	826	F. Polhill	C	433
		H. Stuart	C	421
		W.H. Whitbread	L	410
1847	1,073	Sir H. Verney, Bt.	L	453
		H. Stuart	C	432
		F. Polhill	C	392
1852	910	H. Stuart	C	517
		S. Whitbread	L	435
		T.C. Anstey	L	252
[Death of Stuart]				
1854 (6/12)	913*	W. Stuart	C	422
		J.S. Trelawny	L	331
1857	879	S. Whitbread	L	452
		T. Barnard	L	435
		W. Stuart	C	376
		E.T. Smith	C	176
1859	927	S. Whitbread	L	455
		W. Stuart	C	449
		T. Barnard	L	427
		F.C.P. Turner	C	427
[Appointment of Whitbread as a Civil Lord of the Admiralty]				
1859 (28/6)	927	S. Whitbread	L	441
		F.C.P. Turner	C	389
1865	1,106	S. Whitbread	L	574
		W. Stuart	C	476
		M. Chambers	L	345
1868	2,127	J. Howard	L	1,311
		S. Whitbread	L	1,242
		F.C.P. Turner	C	769
		E.L. O'Malley	C	491
1874	2,213	S. Whitbread	L	1,155
		F.C.P. Turner	C	1,010
		C. Magniac	L	1,006

BEDFORD [20] (Cont.)
(Two Seats)

Election	Electors	Candidate	Party	Votes
1880	2,603	S. Whitbread	L	1,470
		C. Magniac	L	1,333
		F.C.P. Turner	C	1,053

Petitions:—

1832 Dismissed (Crawley only)

1837: Election of Stuart declared void. Crawley duly elected after scrutiny

BERWICK-UPON-TWEED [21]
(Two Seats)

Election	Electors	Candidate	Party	Votes
1832	705	Sir R.S. Donkin	L	371
		†Sir F. Blake, Bt.	L	357
		†M. Beresford	C	345
1835	688	J. Bradshaw	C	410
		Sir R.S. Donkin	L	350
		Sir F. Blake, Bt.	L	337

[Appointment of Donkin as Surveyor-General of the Ordnance]

Election	Electors	Candidate	Party	Votes
1835 (27/4)		Sir R.S. Donkin	L	Unopp.
1837	706	R. Hodgson	C	357
		W. Holmes	C	354
		Sir R.S. Donkin	L	328
1841	714	M. Forster	L	394
		R. Hodgson	C	343
		T. Weeding	C	335
1847	888	M. Forster	L	484
		J.C. Renton	C	463
		W.H. Miller	C	151
1852	781	M. Forster	L	412
		J. Stapleton	L	335
		J.C. Renton	C	251
		R. Hodgson	C	210

[Election declared void on petition]

Election	Electors	Candidate	Party	Votes
1853 (14/5)	853	D.C. Marjoribanks	L	473
		J. Forster	L	385
		J.C. Renton	C	196
		R. Hodgson	C	157
1857	805	J. Stapleton	L	339
		D.C. Marjoribanks	L	271
		C.W. Gordon	C	269
		M. Forster	L	250
1859	790	C.W. Gordon	C	366
		R.A. Earle	C	348
		D.C. Marjoribanks	L	330
		J. Stapleton	L	257

[Resignation of Earle]

Election	Electors	Candidate	Party	Votes
1859 (20/8)	790	D.C. Marjoribanks	L	305
		R. Hodgson	C	304

BERWICK-UPON-TWEED [21] (Cont.)
(Two Seats)

Election	Electors	Candidate	Party	Votes
[Death of Gordon]				
1863	799	W.W. Cargill	C	328
(29/6)		A. Mitchell	L	310
1865	731	D.C. Marjoribanks	L	396
		A. Mitchell	L	367
		W.W. Cargill	C	295
		J. Hubback	C	268
1868	1,415	Viscount Bury	L	669
		J. Stapleton	L	609
		G.W. Carpenter	C	508
		R. Hodgson	C	424
1874	1,313	Sir D.C. Marjoribanks, Bt.	L	617
		D.M. Home	C	533
		J. Stapleton	L	418
		Viscount Bury	L	330
1880	1,443	Sir D.C. Marjoribanks, Bt.	L	687
		Hon. H. Strutt	L	614
		W.M. Macdonald	C	552
		D.M. Home	C	457
[Succession of Strutt to the Peerage — Lord Belper]				
1880	1,443	D.M. Home	C	584
(21/7)		J. McLaren	L	582
[Elevation of Marjoribanks to the Peerage — Lord Tweedmouth]				
1881	1,989	H.E.H. Jerningham	L	1,046
(28/10)		H.J. Trotter	C	529

Petitions:—

1837: Withdrawn

1852: Void election

1857: Withdrawn

1859: Withdrawn

1859: (20/8) Dismissed

1863: Dismissed

1880: (21/7) Dismissed

BEVERLEY [22]

(Two Seats)

Election	Electors	Candidate	Party	Votes
1832	1,011	Hon. C. Langdale	L	516
		†H. Burton	L	490
		C. Winn	C	464
1835	1,042	J.W. Hogg	C	523
		H. Burton	L	497
		J. Sykes	L	314
1837	1,062	J.W. Hogg	C	622
		G.L. Fox	C	582
		J. Clay	L	380
		G. Rennie	L	347
[Resignation of Fox]				
1840 (24/1)	1,053	S.W.L. Fox	C	556
		T.L. Murray	L	410
1841	1,073	J. Towneley	L	531
		J.W. Hogg	C	529
		S.W.L. Fox	C	489
1847	1,357	J. Towneley	L	543
		S.W.L. Fox	C	542
		Sir I.L. Goldsmid, Bt.	L	257
1852	1,405	Hon. F.C. Lawley	L	611
		W. Wells	L	584
		E.A. Glover	L	497
[Resignation of Lawley]				
1854 (31/7)	1,333	Hon. A.H. Gordon	L	493
		G.W. Hastings	C	192
1857	1,136	Hon. W.H.F. Denison	L	566
		E.A. Glover	L	537
		W. Wells	L	492
[Election of Glover declared void on petition]				
1857 (11/8)	1,136	H. Edwards	C	579
		W. Wells	L	401
1859	1,210	R. Walters	L	605
		H. Edwards	C	539
		J.R. Walker	C	439
		E.A. Glover	L	54
[Election of Walters declared void on petition]				
1860 (31/1)	1,213	J.R. Walker	C	599
		H.G. Gridley	L	473

BEVERLEY [22] (Cont.)

(Two Seats)

Election	Electors	Candidate	Party	Votes
1865	1,239	H. Edwards	C	689
		C. Sykes	C	637
		D. Keane	L	495
1868	2,672	Sir H. Edwards, Bt.	C	1,132
		E.H. Kennard	C	986
		Hon. M.C. Maxwell	L	895
		A. Trollope	L	740

Writ suspended. Royal Commission appointed which found proof of extensive bribery and as a result the borough lost its right to return a Member of Parliament and was incorporated into the county constituency of Yorkshire, East Riding, from July 4, 1870

Petitions:—

1857:	Election of Glover declared void. Petition against Denison withdrawn
1857: (11/8)	Withdrawn
1859:	Election of Walters declared void. Petition against Edwards dismissed
1860:	Dismissed
1865:	Withdrawn
1868:	Void election

BEWDLEY [23]

Election	Electors	Candidate	Party	Votes
1832	337	†Sir T.E. Winnington, Bt.	L	Unopp.
1835	414	Sir T.E. Winnington, Bt.	L	Unopp.
1837	400	Sir T.E. Winnington, Bt.	L	Unopp.
1841	411	Sir T.E. Winnington, Bt.	L	173
		R. Monteith	C	168
1847	379	T.J. Ireland	C	160
		Sir T.E. Winnington, Bt.	L	158
[Election declared void on petition]				
1848 (18/4)	394	Viscount Mandeville	C	171
		Hon. S. Lyttelton	L	156
1852	390	Sir T.E. Winnington, Bt.	L	169
		J. Sandars	C	151
1857	370	Sir T.E. Winnington, Bt.	L	Unopp.
1859	386	Sir T.E. Winnington, Bt.	L	Unopp.
1865	356	Sir T.E. Winnington, Bt.	L	Unopp.
1868	1,043†	Sir R.A. Glass	C	518
		T. Lloyd	L	418
[Election declared void on petition]				
1869 (11/3)	1,043	**J.C.P. Cunliffe	C	477
		*Hon. A.H.A. Anson	L	463
1874	1,082	C. Harrison	L	504
		S. Leighton	C	405
		G. Griffith	L	1
1880	1,228	C. Harrison	L	598
		R.E. Webster	C	530
[Election declared void on petition]				
1880 (13/7)	1,228	E. Baldwin	L	611
		W.N. Marcy	C	491

Petitions:—

1841: Withdrawn
1847: Void election
1868: Void election
1869: Election of Cunliffe declared void. Anson duly elected after scrutiny
1880: Void election

BIRKENHEAD [24]

Election	Electors	Candidate	Party	Votes
[New constituency created]				
1861	3,489	J. Laird	C	1,643
(11/12)		T. Brassey	L	1,296
1865	4,563	J. Laird	C	2,108
		H.M. Jackson	L	1,073
1868	5,892	J. Laird	C	2,921
		S. Osborn	L	2,039
1874	7,458	J. Laird	C	3,692
		J. Samuelson	L	1,580
[Death]				
1874	7,458	D. MacIver	C	3,421
(26/11)		S. Stitt	L	2,474
1880	9,127	D. MacIver	C	4,025
		A.J. Williams	L	3,658

BIRMINGHAM [25]

(Two seats until 1868; three seats from 1868)

Election	Electors	Candidate	Party	Votes
1832	4,309	T. Attwood	L	Unopp.
		J. Scholefield	L	Unopp.
1835	3,681	T. Attwood	L	1,718
		J. Scholefield	L	1,660
		R. Spooner	C	915
1837	5,236	T. Attwood	L	2,145
		J. Scholefield	L	2,114
		A.G. Stepleton	C	1,046
[Resignation of Attwood]				
1840 (25/1)	4,619	G.F. Muntz	L	1,458
		Sir C. Wetherell	C	917
1841	5,870	G.F. Muntz	L	2,176
		J. Scholefield	L	1,963
		R. Spooner	C	1,825
[Death of Scholefield]				
1844 (15/7)	6,129*	R. Spooner	C	2,095
		W. Scholefield	L	1,735
		J. Sturge	L	346
1847	7,081	G.F. Muntz	L	2,830
		W. Scholefield	L	2,824
		R. Spooner	C	2,302
		R. Allen	L	89
1852	7,936	G.F. Muntz	L	Unopp.
		W. Scholefield	L	Unopp.
1857	9,074	G.F. Muntz	L	Unopp.
		W. Scholefield	L	Unopp.
[Death of Muntz]				
1857 (10/8)		J. Bright	L	Unopp.
1859	9,222	W. Scholefield	L	4,425
		J. Bright	L	4,282
		T.D. Acland	C	1,544
1865	14,997	J. Bright	L	Unopp.
		W. Scholefield	L	Unopp.
[Death of Scholefield]				
1867 (23/7)	14,997*	G. Dixon	L	5,819
		S.S. Lloyd	C	4,214

BIRMINGHAM [25] (Cont.)
(Two seats until 1868; three seats from 1868)

Election	Electors	Candidate	Party	Votes
1868	42,042	G. Dixon	L	15,198
		P.H. Muntz	L	14,614
		J. Bright	L	14,601
		S.S. Lloyd	C	8,700
		S. Evans	C	7,061
[Appointment of Bright as President of the Board of Trade]				
1868 (21/12)		J. Bright	L	Unopp.
[Appointment of Bright as Chancellor of the Duchy of Lancaster]				
1873 (20/10)		J. Bright	L	Unopp.
1874	51,361	J. Bright	L	Unopp.
		G. Dixon	L	Unopp.
		P.H. Muntz	L	Unopp.
[Resignation of Dixon]				
1876 (27/6)		J. Chamberlain	L	Unopp.
1880	63,398	P.H. Muntz	L	22,969
		J. Bright	L	22,079
		J. Chamberlain	L	19,544
		F.G. Burnaby	C	15,735
		Hon. A.C.G. Calthorpe	C	14,308
[Appointments of Bright as Chancellor of the Duchy of Lancaster and Chamberlain as President of the Board of Trade]				
1880 (8/5)		J. Bright	L	Unopp.
		J. Chamberlain	L	Unopp.

BLACKBURN [26]
(Two Seats)

Election	Electors	Candidate	Party	Votes
1832	626	W. Feilden	L	376
		W. Turner	L	346
		J. Bowring	L	334
1835	761	W. Turner	L	432
		W. Feilden	L	316
		J. Bowring	L	303
1837	842	W. Turner	L	515
		W. Feilden	L	416
		J.B. Smith	L	9
1841	906	W. Feilden	C	441
		J. Hornby	C	427
		W. Turner	L	426
1847	1,121	J. Hornby	C	641
		J. Pilkington	L	602
		W. Hargreaves	L	392
		W.P. Roberts	Ch	68
1852	1,258	J. Pilkington	L	846
		W. Eccles	L	580
		J. Hornby	C	509
[Election of Eccles declared void on petition]				
1853 (24/3)	1,325	M.J. Feilden	L	631
		W.H. Hornby	C	574
1857	1,518	W.H. Hornby	C	Unopp.
		J. Pilkington	L	Unopp.
1859	1,617	W.H. Hornby	C	832
		J. Pilkington	L	750
		J.P. Murrough	L	567
1865	1,894	W.H. Hornby	C	1,053
		J. Feilden	C	938
		J. Pilkington	L	744
		J.G. Potter	L	577
1868	9,183†	W.H. Hornby	C	4,907
		J. Feilden	C	4,826
		J.G. Potter	L	4,399
		M.J. Feilden	L	4,164
[Election declared void on petition]				
1869 (30/3)	9,183	E.K. Hornby	C	4,738
		H.M. Feilden	C	4,697
		J.G. Potter	L	3,964
		J. Morley	L	3,804

BLACKBURN [26] (Cont.)
(Two Seats)

Election	Electors	Candidate	Party	Votes
1874	11,195	H.M. Feilden	C	5,532
		W.E. Briggs	L	5,338
		D. Thwaites	C	5,323
		R. Shackleton	L	4,851
[Death of Feilden]				
1875 (2/10)	11,721	D. Thwaites	C	5,792
		J.T. Hibbert	L	4,832
1880	13,062	W.E. Briggs	L	6,349
		W. Coddington	C	6,207
		D. Thwaites	C	6,088
		G.B.G.F.R.P. Molesworth	L	5,760

Petitions:—

1837:	Withdrawn (Feilden only)
1841:	Dismissed (Hornby only)
1852:	Election of Eccles declared void
1853:	Withdrawn
1868:	Void election

BODMIN [27]

(Two seats until 1868; one seat from 1868)

Election	Electors	Candidate	Party	Votes
1832	252	W. Peter	L	171
		S.T. Spry	L	114
		C.C. Vivian	L	106
1835	313	C.C. Vivian	L	170
		Sir S.T. Spry	L	138
		Lord Eliot	C	118
1837	333	C.C. Vivian	L	200
		Sir S.T. Spry	C	130
		C.W.J. Ellis	L	98
1841	368	Hon. C.C. Vivian	L	224
		Earl of Leicester *(J.D. Gardner)*	C	142
		Sir S.T. Spry	C	135
[Succession of Vivian to the Peerage — Lord Vivian]				
1843 (9/2)	405	Sir S.T. Spry	C	165
		C.B.G. Sawle	L	161
1847	401	J. Wyld	L	297
		H.C. Lacy	L	259
		Sir S.T. Spry	C	117
1852	367	W. Michell	L	273
		C.B.G. Sawle	L	157
		W. Henderson	C	149
		J.C. Whitehurst	L	82
		H. Carr	C	54
1857	390	Hon. J.C.W. Vivian	L	244
		J. Wyld	L	190
		W. Michell	L	169
		J.H. Lewis	L	31
1859	390	Hon. E.F.L. Gower	L	215
		W. Michell	C	198
		J. Wyld	L	167
[Resignation of Michell]				
1859 (13/8)		J. Wyld	L	Unopp.
1865	397	Hon. E.F.L. Gower	L	263
		J. Wyld	L	238
		C.L. Webb	C	114
1868	886	Hon. E.F.L. Gower	L	424
		J. Wyld	L	334

BODMIN [27] (Cont.)

(Two seats until 1868; one seat from 1868)

Election	Electors	Candidate	Party	Votes
1874	959	Hon. E.F.L. Gower	L	464
		C.E. Sergeant	L	230
		C.L. Webb	C	113
1880	903	Hon. E.F.L. Gower	L	418
		J.R. Farquharson	L	375

Petitions:—

1847: Dismissed

1857: Withdrawn (Wyld only)

1859: Withdrawn (Michell only)

1868: Dismissed

Note:—

1841: Leicester claimed to be the eldest son of the third Marquess of Townshend but in 1843 it was proved that he was an illegitimate son and not entitled to use the courtesy title of Earl of Leicester. For a short time he reverted to his real name of John Townshend but subsequently changed this by Royal License to John Dunn Gardner.

BOLTON [28]
(Two Seats)

Election	Electors	Candidate	Party	Votes
1832	1,040	†R. Torrens	L	627
		W. Bolling	C	492
		J.A. Yates	L	482
		W. Eagle	L	107
1835	1,001	W. Bolling	C	633
		P. Ainsworth	L	590
		R. Torrens	L	343
1837	1,340	P. Ainsworth	L	615
		W. Bolling	C	607
		A. Knowles	L	538
1841	1,471*	P. Ainsworth	L	669
		J. Bowring	L	614
		P. Rothwell	C	536
		W. Bolling	C	441
1847	1,479	W. Bolling	C	714
		J. Bowring	L	652
		J. Brooks	L	645
[Death of Bolling]				
1848 (12/9)		S. Blair	C	Unopp.
[Resignation of Bowring on appointment as Consul-General at Canton, China]				
1849 (9/2)	1,437	Sir J. Walmsley	L	621
		T.R. Bridson	C	568
1852	1,671	T. Barnes	L	745
		J. Crook	L	727
		S. Blair	C	717
		P. Ainsworth	L	346
1857	1,933	W. Gray	C	930
		J. Crook	L	895
		T. Barnes	L	832
1859	2,050	J. Crook	L	Unopp.
		W. Gray	C	Unopp.
[Resignation of Crook]				
1861 (11/2)		T. Barnes	L	Unopp.
1865	2,186	W. Gray	C	1,022
		T. Barnes	L	979
		S. Pope	L	864
		W. Gibb	C	727

BOLTON [28] (Cont.)
(Two Seats)

Election	Electors	Candidate	Party	Votes
1868	12,650†	J. Hick	C	6,062
		W. Gray	C	5,848
		T. Barnes	L	5,451
		S. Pope	L	5,436
1874	12,595	J. Hick	C	5,987
		J.K. Cross	L	5,782
		W. Gray	C	5,650
		J. Knowles	L	5,440
1880	13,956	J.K. Cross	L	6,964
		J.P. Thomasson	L	6,673
		T.L. Rushton	C	6,540
		Hon. F.C. Bridgeman	C	6,415

Petitions:—

1835: Withdrawn (Ainsworth only)

1837: Withdrawn (Bolling only)

1847: Dismissed (Bolling only)

1848: Withdrawn

1852: Dismissed

1874: Dismissed (Cross only)

BOSTON [29]
(Two Seats)

Election	Electors	Candidate	Party	Votes
1832	869	†J. Wilks	L	509
		B. Handley	L	433
		J.S. Brownrigg	C	353
1835	938	J.S. Brownrigg	C	532
		J. Wilks	L	356
		B. Handley	L	321
1837	955	J.S. Brownrigg	C	459
		Sir J. Duke	L	442
		B. Handley	L	350
		W.R. Collett	C	156
1841	1,146	J.S. Brownrigg	C	527
		Sir J. Duke	L	515
		C.A. Wood	C	466
1847	1,083	Sir J. Duke	L	590
		B.B Cabbell	C	466
		D.W. Wire	L	339
[Resignation of Duke in order to contest the City of London]				
1849 (2/8)	963	Hon. D.A. Pelham	L	422
		D.W. Wire	L	321
[Death of Pelham]				
1851 (22/4)	967	J.W. Freshfield	C	368
		D.W. Wire	L	251
1852	987	G.H. Heathcote	L	547
		B.B. Cabbell	C	490
		J.A. Hankey	L	437
		T. Hankey	L	148
		W.H. Adams	C	18
[Resignation of Heathcote in order to contest Rutlandshire]				
1856 (7/3)	1,003	H. Ingram	L	521
		W.H. Adams	C	296
1857	1,057	W.H. Adams	C	Unopp.
		H. Ingram	L	Unopp.
[Appointment of Adams as Recorder of Derby]				
1859 (3/2)		W.H. Adams	C	Unopp.
1859	1,078	H. Ingram	L	621
		M. Staniland	L	593
		J.H. Hollway	C	452

BOSTON [29] (Cont.)
(Two Seats)

Election	Electors	Candidate	Party	Votes
[Death of Ingram]				
1860 (30/10)	1,019	J.W. Malcolm	C	533
		G.P. Tuxford	L	303
1865	1,090	J.W. Malcolm	C	646
		**T. Parry	L	465
		*M. Staniland	L	453
[Resignation of Staniland]				
1867 (16/3)		T. Parry	L	Unopp.
1868	2,527	J.W. Malcolm	C	1,306
		T. Collins	C	1,119
		M. Staniland	L	1,029
		T.M. Jones	L	926
1874	2,651	W.J. Ingram	L	1,572
		**T. Parry	L	1,347
		*J.W. Malcolm	C	996
		T. Collins	C	679
[Resignation of Malcolm in order to contest Argyll]				
1878 (12/8)		T. Garfit	C	Unopp.
1880	3,094	T. Garfit	C	1,412
		W.J. Ingram	L	1,367
		G.F. Rowley	C	1,350
		S.C. Buxton	L	1,182

Petitions:—

1852: Withdrawn

1865: Election of Parry declared void. Staniland duly elected after scrutiny

1868: Withdrawn

1874: Election of Parry declared void. Malcolm duly elected after scrutiny. Petition against Ingram dismissed.

1880: Void election. Writ suspended

BRADFORD [30]

(Two Seats)

Election	Electors	Candidate	Party	Votes
1832	1,139	E.C. Lister	L	650
		J. Hardy	L	471
		G. Banks	L	402
1835	1,225	J. Hardy	C	611
		E.C. Lister	L	589
		G. Hadfield	L	392
1837	1,347	E.C. Lister	L	635
		W. Busfeild (1)	L	621
		J. Hardy	C	443
		W. Busfeild (2)	C	383
1841	1,398	J. Hardy	C	612
		W.C. Lister	L	540
		W. Busfeild (1)	L	536
[Death of Lister]				
1841 (16/9)	1,398	W. Busfeild (1)	L	526
		W. Wilberforce	C	522
1847	2,083	W. Busfeild (1)	L	937
		T.P. Thompson	L	926
		H.W. Wickham	C	860
		G. Hardy	C	812
[Death of Busfeild]				
1851 (21/10)		R. Milligan	L	Unopp.
1852	2,683	R. Milligan	L	1,266
		H.W. Wickham	C	1,159
		T.P. Thompson	L	1,153
1857	3,279	T.P. Thompson	L	Unopp.
		H.W. Wickham	L	Unopp.
1859	3,599	H.W. Wickham	L	2,076
		T. Salt	L	1,727
		A. Harris	C	1,229
[Resignation of Salt]				
1861 (11/2)		W.E. Forster	L	Unopp.
1865	5,189	W.E. Forster	L	Unopp.
		H.W. Wickham	C	Unopp.

(Two Seats)

Election	Electors	Candidate	Party	Votes
[Death of Wickham]				
1867 (16/10)	5,189*	M.W. Thompson	L	2,210
		E. Miall	L	1,807
1868	21,518	W.E. Forster	L	9,646
		H.W. Ripley	L	9,347
		E. Miall	L	8,768
[Appointment of Forster as Vice-President of the Committee of the Privy Council for Education]				
1868 (21/12)		W.E. Forster	L	Unopp.
[Election of Ripley declared void on petition]				
1869 (12/3)	21,518	E. Miall	L	9,243
		M.W. Thompson	L	7,806
1874	24,331	W.E. Forster	L	11,945
		H.W. Ripley	C	10,223
		J.V. Godwin	L	8,398
		J. Hardaker	L/Lab	8,115
1880	27,049	W.E. Forster	L	14,245
		A. Illingworth	L	12,922
		H.W. Ripley	C	9,018
[Appointment of Forster as Chief Secretary to the Lord Lieutenant of Ireland]				
1880 (8/5)		W.E. Forster	L	Unopp.

Petitions:—

1852: Withdrawn

1868: Election of Ripley declared void. Petition against Forster dismissed

BRIDGNORTH [31]

(Two seats until 1868; one seat from 1868)

Election	Electors	Candidate	Party	Votes
1832	746	R. Pigot	C	Unopp.
		T.C. Whitmore	C	Unopp.
1835	791	T.C. Whitmore	C	490
		R. Pigot	C	423
		H.H. Tracy	L	353
1837	790	T.C. Whitmore	C	429
		H.H. Pracy	L	371
		R. Pigot	C	367
[Resignation of Tracy]				
1838 (20/2)		R. Pigot	C	Unopp.
1841	810	T.C. Whitmore	C	496
		Sir R. Pigot, Bt.	C	475
		F.J. Howard	L	225
		N. Throckmorton	L	66
1847	838	T.C. Whitmore	C	611
		Sir R. Pigot, Bt.	C	388
		Sir J. Easthope, Bt.	L	368
1852	717	H. Whitmore	C	443
		Sir R. Pigot, Bt.	C	360
		Hon. F.W. Cadogan	L	283
[Election of Pigot declared void on petition]				
1853 (22/3)		J. Pritchard	C	Unopp.
1857	678	J. Pritchard	C	Unopp.
		H. Whitmore	C	Unopp.
[Appointment of Whitmore as a Lord Commissioner of the Treasury]				
1858 (3/3)		H. Whitmore	C	Unopp.
1859	708	J. Pritchard	C	Unopp.
		H. Whitmore	C	Unopp.
1865	614	J. Pritchard	C	299
		**Sir J.E.E.D. Acton, Bt.	L	289
		*H. Whitmore	C	288
[Appointment of Whitmore as a Lord Commissioner of the Treasury]				
1866 (21/7)		H. Whitmore	C	Unopp.

BRIDGNORTH [31] (Cont.)
(Two seats until 1868; one seat from 1868)

Election	Electors	Candidate	Party	Votes
1868	1,279	H. Whitmore	C	548
		Sir J.E.E.D. Acton, Bt.	L	497
[Resignation]				
1870 (16/2)		W.H. Foster	L	Unopp.
1874	1,267	W.H. Foster	L	701
		G. Barbour	C	275
1880	1,224	W.H. Foster	C	641
		E.R. Vyvyan	L	321

Petitions:—

1837: Withdrawn

1852: Election of Pigot declared void. Petition against Whitmore dismissed

1865: Election of Acton declared void. Whitmore duly elected after scrutiny

BRIDGWATER [32]
(Two Seats)

Election	Electors	Candidate	Party	Votes
1832	484	W. Tayleur	L	Unopp.
		†C.K.K. Tynte	L	Unopp.
1835	430	C.K.K. Tynte	L	234
		J.T. Leader	L	208
		H. Broadwood	C	190
		T.M. Martin	C	162

[Resignation of Leader in order to contest Westminster]

Election	Electors	Candidate	Party	Votes
1837 (16/5)	558	H. Broadwood	C	279
		R.B. Sheridan	L	221
1837	558	H. Broadwood	C	279
		P. Courtenay	C	277
		Sir T.B. Lethbridge, Bt.	L	5
		R.B. Sheridan	L	2
1841	595	H. Broadwood	C	280
		T.S. Forman	C	276
		E.S. Drewe	L	247
		A. Robinson	L	242
1847	529	C.J.K. Tynte	L	395
		H. Broadwood	C	265
		S. Gaselee	L	196
1852	688	C.J.K. Tynte	L	271
		B.S. Follett	C	244
		J.C. Mansell	L	177
		Lord Henley	L	149
		A.W. Kinglake	L	101
1857	589	C.J.K. Tynte	L	330
		A.W. Kinglake	L	301
		B.S. Follett	C	203
1859	614	C.J.K. Tynte	L	290
		A.W. Kinglake	L	279
		H. Padwick	C	230
		H. Westropp	C	208
1865	644	H. Westropp	C	328
		A.W. Kinglake	L	257
		Sir J.V. Shelley, Bt.	L	237

[Election of Westropp declared void on petition]

Election	Electors	Candidate	Party	Votes
1866 (7/6)	644	G. Patton	C	301
		W. Bagehot	L	293

BRIDGWATER [32] (Cont.)
(Two Seats)

Election	Electors	Candidate	Party	Votes
[Appointment of Patton as Lord Advocate]				
1866 (12/7)	644	P. Vanderbyl	L	312
		G. Patton	C	275
1868	1,499†	A.W. Kinglake	L	731
		P. Vanderbyl	L	725
		H. Westropp	C	681
		C.W. Gray	C	650

Writ suspended. Royal Commission appointed which found proof of extensive bribery and as a result the borough lost its right to return a Member of Parliament and was incorporated into the county constituency of Somerset, Western, from July 4, 1870.

Petitions:—

1837: (16/5) Lapsed on Dissolution of Parliament

1837: Withdrawn

1859: Withdrawn

1865: Election of Westropp declared void. Petition against Kinglake dismissed

1868: Void election

BRIDPORT [33]
(Two seats until 1868; one seat from 1868)

Election	Electors	Candidate	Party	Votes
1832	425	†H. Warburton	L	271
		J. Romilly	L	219
		R.W. Astell	C	182
1835	420	H. Warburton	L	244
		H. Twiss	C	207
		J. Romilly	L	199
1837	505	H. Warburton	L	283
		S. Jervis	L	232
		H. Baillie	C	212
1841	557	H. Warburton	L	304
		T.A. Mitchell	L	282
		A.D.R.W.B. Cochrane	C	244
[Resignation of Warburton]				
1841 (15/9)		A.D.R.W.B. Cochrane	C	Unopp.
[Cochrane seeks re-election as a supporter of free trade]				
1846 (7/3)	571*	**A.D.R.W.B. Cochrane	C	240
		*J. Romilly	L	239
1847	663	A.D.R.W.B. Cochrane	C	276
		T.A. Mitchell	L	267
		Hon. E.R. Petre	L	222
		R.M. Martin	C	11
1852	524	T.A. Mitchell	L	366
		J.P. Murrough	L	249
		J. Rolt	C	191
1857	478	T.A. Mitchell	L	330
		K.D. Hodgson	L	290
		W.U. Heygate	C	109
1859	501	T.A. Mitchell	L	334
		K.D. Hodgson	L	290
		H.H.N. Bankes	C	170
1865	472	K.D. Hodgson	L	Unopp.
		T.A. Mitchell	L	Unopp.
1868	1,027	T.A. Mitchell	L	Unopp.
1874	1,045	T.A. Mitchell	L	Unopp.

BRIDPORT [33] (Cont.)

(Two seats until 1868; one seat from 1868)

Election	Electors	Candidate	Party	Votes
[Death]				
1875 (31/3)	1,011	P. Ralli	L	620
		Sir C. Whetham	C	189
1880	1,085	C.N. Warton	C	468
		P. Ralli	L	459

Petitions:—

1841:	Withdrawn (Mitchell only)
1841: (15/9)	Withdrawn
1846:	Election of Cochrane declared void. Romilly duly elected after scrutiny
1857:	Withdrawn

BRIGHTON [34]
(Two Seats)

Election	Electors	Candidate	Party	Votes
1832	1,649	I.N. Wigney	L	873
		G. Faithful	L	722
		G.R.B. Pechell	L	613
		W. Crawford	L	391
		†Sir A.J. Dalrymple, Bt.	C	32
1835	1,535	G.R.B. Pechell	L	961
		I.N. Wigney	L	523
		Sir A.J. Dalrymple, Bt.	C	483
		G. Faithful	L	467
1837	1,968	G.R.B. Pechell	L	1,083
		Sir A.J. Dalrymple, Bt.	C	819
		I.N. Wigney	L	801
		G. Faithful	L	183
1841	2,403	G.R.B. Pechell	L	1,443
		I.N. Wigney	L	1,235
		Sir A.J. Dalrymple, Bt.	C	872
		C. Brooker	L	19
[Resignation of Wigney]				
1842 (5/5)	2,533*	Lord Alfred Hervey	C	1,277
		S. Harford	L	640
		C. Brooker	L	16
1847	2,776	G.R.B. Pechell	L	1,571
		Lord Alfred Hervey	C	1,239
		W. Coningham	L	886
1852	3,675	Sir G.R.B. Pechell, Bt.	L	1,924
		Lord Alfred Hervey	C	1,431
		J.S. Trelawny	L	1,173
		J. Fooks	L	119
[Appointment of Hervey as a Lord Commissioner of the Treasury]				
1853 (4/1)		Lord Alfred Hervey	C	Unopp.
1857	3,936	Sir G.R.B. Pechell, Bt.	L	2,278
		W. Coningham	L	1,900
		Lord Alfred Hervey	C	1,080
1859	4,277	Sir G.R.B. Pechell, Bt.	L	2,322
		W. Coningham	L	2,106
		Sir A. MacNab, Bt.	C	1,327
[Death of Pechell]				
1860 (16/7)	4,786	J. White	L	1,588
		H. Moor	C	1,242
		F.D. Goldsmid	L	548

BRIGHTON [34] (Cont.)
(Two Seats)

Election	Electors	Candidate	Party	Votes
[Resignation of Coningham]				
1864	5,434	H. Moor	C	1,663
(16/2)		H. Fawcett	L	1,468
		J. Goldsmid	L	775
		F.K. Dumas	L	246
		E. Harper	Ind	82
1865	5,978	J. White	L	3,065
		H. Fawcett	L	2,665
		H. Moor	C	2,134
1868	8,661†	J. White	L	3,342
		H. Fawcett	L	3,081
		J.L. Ashbury	C	2,917
		H. Moor	C	1,232
		W. Coningham	L	432
1874	10,228	J.L. Ashbury	C	4,393
		C.C. Shute	C	3,995
		J. White	L	3,351
		H. Fawcett	L	3,130
1880	12,454	J.R. Hollond	L	4,913
		W.T. Marriott	L	4,904
		J.L. Ashbury	C	4,739
		E. Field	C	4,664
[Marriott seeks re-election as a Conservative]				
1884	13,340	W.T. Marriott	C	5,478
(3/3)		R. Romer	L	4,021
[Appointment of Marriott as Judge-Advocate General]				
1885		W.T. Marriott	C	Unopp.
(10/7)				

Petition:—

1842: Withdrawn

BRISTOL [35]

(Two Seats)

Election	Electors	Candidate	Party	Votes
1832	10,315	†Sir R.R. Vyvyan, Bt.	C	3,697
		†J.E. Baillie	L	3,159
		†E. Protheroe	L	3,030
		†J. Williams	L	2,741
1835	10,100	P.J. Miles	C	3,709
		Sir R.R. Vyvyan, Bt.	C	3,313
		J.E. Baillie	L	2,518
		Sir J.C. Hobhouse, Bt.	L	1,808
1837	9,992	P.W.S. Miles	C	3,839
		F.H.F. Berkeley	L	3,212
		W. Fripp	C	3,156
1841	11,150	P.W.S. Miles	C	4,193
		F.H.F. Berkeley	L	3,739
		W. Fripp	C	3,684
1847	11,032	F.H.F. Berkeley	L	4,381
		P.W.S. Miles	C	2,595
		W. Fripp	C	2,476
		A. Pellatt	L	171
1852	12,548	F.H.F. Berkeley	L	4,681
		W.H.G. Langton	L	4,531
		F.A. McGeachy	C	3,632
1857	12,612	F.H.F. Berkeley	L	Unopp.
		W.H.G. Langton	L	Unopp.
1859	12,929	F.H.F. Berkeley	L	4,432
		W.H.G. Langton	L	4,285
		F.W. Slade	C	4,205
1865	11,303	F.H.F. Berkeley	L	5,296
		Sir S.M. Peto, Bt.	L	5,228
		T.F. Fremantle	L	4,269
[Resignation of Peto]				
1868 (30/4)	11,303*	J.W. Miles	C	5,173
		S. Morley	L	4,977
1868	21,153	F.H.F. Berkeley	L	8,759
		S. Morley	L	8,714
		J.W. Miles	C	6,694
[Death of Berkeley]				
1870 (29/3)	21,153*	E.S. Robinson	L	7,882
		S.V. Hare	C	7,062

BRISTOL [35] (Cont.)
(Two Seats)

Election	Electors	Candidate	Party	Votes
[Election declared void on petition]				
1870	21,153*	K.D. Hodgson	L	7,816
(27/6)		S.V. Hare	C	7,238
1874	22,867	K.D. Hodgson	L	8,888
		S. Morley	L	8,732
		S.V. Hare	C	8,552
		G.H. Chambers	C	7,626
[Resignation of Hodgson]				
1878	24,851	L. Fry	L	9,342
(16/12)		Sir I.B. Guest, Bt.	C	7,795
1880	23,229	S. Morley	L	10,704
		L. Fry	L	10,070
		Sir I.B. Guest, Bt.	C	9,395
		E.S. Robinson	L	4,100

Petitions:—

1832:	Dismissed
1837:	Dismissed (Berkeley only)
1868: (30/4)	Void election
1870: (29/3)	Void election

BUCKINGHAM [36]

(Two seats until 1868; one seat from 1868)

Election	Electors	Candidate	Party	Votes
1832	300	Sir H. Verney, Bt.	L	175
		†Sir T.F. Fremantle, Bt.	C	156
		G. Morgan	L	138
1835	351	Sir T.F. Fremantle, Bt.	C	Unopp.
		Sir H. Verney, Bt.	L	Unopp.
1837	341	Sir T.F. Fremantle, Bt.	C	236
		Sir H. Verney, Bt.	L	157
		Sir J. Chetwode, Bt.	C	138
1841	396	Sir J. Chetwode, Bt.	C	Unopp.
		Sir T.F. Fremantle, Bt.	C	Unopp.
[Appointment of Fremantle as Secretary at War]				
1844 (25/5)		Sir T.F. Fremantle, Bt.	C	Unopp.
[Appointment of Fremantle as Chief Secretary to the Lord Lieutenant of Ireland]				
1845 (10/2)		Sir T.F. Fremantle, Bt.	C	Unopp.
[Death of Chetwode]				
1846 (20/1)		J. Hall	C	Unopp.
[Resignation of Fremantle]				
1846 (11/2)		Marquess of Chandos	C	Unopp.
1847	388	Marquess of Chandos	C	Unopp.
		J. Hall	C	Unopp.
[Appointment of Chandos as a Lord Commissioner of the Treasury]				
1852 (5/3)		Marquess of Chandos	C	Unopp.
1852	349	Marquess of Chandos	C	Unopp.
		J. Hall	C	Unopp.
1857	354	Sir H. Verney, Bt.	L	193
		J. Hall	C	151
		Hon. R. Cavendish	L	134
		P. Box	C	82
1859	364	Sir H. Verney, Bt.	L	198
		J.G. Hubbard	C	196
		Hon. G.W. Barrington	C	147

BUCKINGHAM [36] (Cont.)
(Two seats until 1868; one seat from 1868)

Election	Electors	Candidate	Party	Votes
1865	391	J.G. Hubbard	C	Unopp.
		Sir H. Verney, Bt.	L	Unopp.
1868	948	Sir H. Verney, Bt.	L	463
		J.G. Hubbard	C	338
1874	1,118	E. Hubbard	C	589
		Sir H. Verney, Bt.	L	391
1880	1,149	Sir H. Verney, Bt.	L	528
		E. Hubbard	C	520

BURNLEY [37]

Election	Electors	Candidate	Party	Votes
1868	6,417	R. Shaw	L	2,620
		Hon. Sir J.Y. Scarlett	C	2,238
1874	6,607	R. Shaw	L	3,065
		W.A. Lindsay	C	2,490
[Death]				
1876 (14/2)	7,127	P. Rylands	L	3,520
		W.A. Lindsay	C	3,077
1880	7,614	P. Rylands	L	3,943
		Lord Edmund Talbot	C	3,217

BURY [38]

Election	Electors	Candidate	Party	Votes
1832	535	R. Walker	L	306
		E. Grundy	L	153
1835	526	R. Walker	L	Unopp.
1837	637	R. Walker	L	251
		J.P. Cobbett	L	96
		R. Spankie	C	87
1841	768	R. Walker	L	325
		H. Hardman	C	288
1847	868	R. Walker	L	Unopp.
1852	959	F. Peel	L	472
		Viscount Duncan	L	410
1857	1,218	R.N. Philips	L	565
		F. Peel	L	530
1859	1,289	F. Peel	L	641
		T. Barnes	L	478
1865	1,352	R.N. Philips	L	595
		F. Peel	L	572
1868	5,587	R.N. Philips	L	2,830
		Viscount Chelsea	C	2,264
1874	6,236	R.N. Philips	L	3,016
		O.O. Walker	C	2,500
1880	6,835	R.N. Philips	L	Unopp.

Petitions:—

1857: Dismissed

1859: Dismissed

BURY ST. EDMUNDS [39]

(Two Seats)

Election	Electors	Candidate	Party	Votes
1832	620	†Lord Charles Fitzroy	L	344
		†Earl Jermyn	C	272
		F.K. Eagle	L	238
1835	633	Earl Jermyn	C	317
		Lord Charles Fitzroy	L	312
		C.J.F. Bunbury	L	287
[Appointment of Fitzroy as Vice-Chamberlain of H.M. Household]				
1835 (26/6)		Lord Charles Fitzroy	L	Unopp.
1837	640	Lord Charles Fitzroy	L	289
		Earl Jermyn	C	277
		C.J.F. Bunbury	L	275
		Hon. F.G. Calthorpe	C	248
[Appointment of Jermyn as Treasurer of H.M. Household]				
1841 (14/9)		Earl Jermyn	C	Unopp.
1841	713	Earl Jermyn	C	341
		Lord Charles Fitzroy	L	310
		H. Twiss	C	298
		R.G. Alston	L	256
1847	751	Earl Jermyn	C	390
		E.H. Bunbury	L	327
		H. Twiss	C	264
1852	741	Earl Jermyn	C	493
		J. Stuart	C	328
		E.H. Bunbury	L	319
[Resignation of Stuart on appointment as a Vice-Chancellor]				
1852 (4/12)	713	J.H.P. Oakes	C	324
		J.A. Hardcastle	L	316
1857	702	Earl Jermyn	C	344
		J.A. Hardcastle	L	320
		J.H.P. Oakes	C	266
[Succession of Jermyn to the Peerage — Marquess of Bristol]				
1859 (7/3)		Lord Alfred Hervey	C	Unopp.
1859	695	Lord Alfred Hervey	C	418
		J.A. Hardcastle	L	307
		Sir R.J. Buxton, Bt.	C	284

BURY ST. EDMUNDS [39] (Cont.)
(Two Seats)

Election	Electors	Candidate	Party	Votes
1865	676	J.A. Hardcastle	L	331
		E. Greene	L	300
		Lord Alfred Hervey	C	266
1868	1,505	E. Greene	C	714
		J.A. Hardcastle	L	703
		E.H. Bunbury	L	593
1874	1,919	E. Green	C	1,004
		Lord Francis Hervey	C	914
		J.A. Hardcastle	L	707
		C. Lamport	L	628
1880	2,122	J.A. Hardcastle	L	1,110
		E. Greene	C	850
		Lord Francis Hervey	C	803

Petitions:—

1832:	Withdrawn (Fitzroy only)
1837:	Withdrawn
1852: (4/12)	Dismissed
1857:	Dismissed (Hardcastle only)
1880:	Withdrawn (Hardcastle only)

CALNE [40]

Election	Electors	Candidate	Party	Votes
1832	191	Earl of Kerry	L	Unopp.
1835	178	Earl of Kerry	L	Unopp.
[Death]				
1836 (28/9)		Hon. J.G.C.F. Strangways	L	Unopp.
1837	186	Earl of Shelburne	L	Unopp.
1841	176	Earl of Shelburne	L	Unopp.
1847	154	Earl of Shelburne	L	Unopp.
[Appointed a Lord Commissioner of the Treasury]				
1847 (27/12)		Earl of Shelburne	L	Unopp.
1852	160	Earl of Shelburne	L	Unopp.
[Resignation]				
1856 (9/7)		Sir W.F. Williams, Bt.	L	Unopp.
1857	164	Sir W.F. Williams, Bt.	L	Unopp.
1859	174	R. Lowe	L	103
		T.L. Henly	C	35
[Appointed Vice-President of the Committee of the Privy Council for Education]				
1859 (27/6)		R. Lowe	L	Unopp.
1865	174	R. Lowe	L	Unopp.
1868	590	Lord Edmond Fitzmaurice	L	Unopp.
1874	687	Lord Edmond Fitzmaurice	L	Unopp.
1880	795	Lord Edmond Fitzmaurice	L	518
		U.R. Burke	C	116

CAMBRIDGE [41]

(Two Seats)

Election	Electors	Candidate	Party	Votes
1832	1,499	G. Pryme	L	979
		†T.S. Rice	L	709
		†Sir E.B. Sugden	C	540

[Appointment of Rice as Secretary of State for War and the Colonies]

Election	Electors	Candidate	Party	Votes
1834 (13/6)	1,456	T.S. Rice	L	615
		Sir E.B. Sugden	C	590
1835	1,482	T.S. Rice	L	736
		G. Pryme	L	693
		J.L. Knight	C	688

[Appointment of Rice as Chancellor of the Exchequer]

Election	Electors	Candidate	Party	Votes
1835 (27/4)		T.S. Rice	L	Unopp.
1837	1,698	T.S. Rice	L	690
		G. Pryme	L	678
		J.L. Knight	C	614
		Hon. J.H.T.M. Sutton	C	599

[Elevation of Rice to the Peerage — Lord Monteagle of Brandon]

Election	Electors	Candidate	Party	Votes
1839 (6/9)	1,698*	Hon. J.H.T.M. Sutton	C	717
		T.M. Gibson	L	617

[Election declared void on petition]

Election	Electors	Candidate	Party	Votes
1840 (23/5)	1,857	Sir A.C. Grant, Bt.	C	736
		T. Starkie	L	657
1841	1,940	Hon. J.H.T.M. Sutton	C	758
		Sir A.C. Grant, Bt.	C	722
		R. Foster	L	695
		Lord Cosmo Russell	L	656

[Resignation of Grant]

Election	Electors	Candidate	Party	Votes
1843 (21/3)	1,904	F. Kelly	C	713
		R. Foster	L	680

[Appointment of Kelly as Solicitor-General]

Election	Electors	Candidate	Party	Votes
1845 (16/7)	1,904*	F. Kelly	C	746
		R.A.S. Adair	L	729
1847	1,834	R.A.S. Adair	L	811
		Hon. W.F. Campbell	L	727
		Hon. J.H.T.M. Sutton	C	465
1852	1,984	K. Macaulay	C	821
		J.H. Astell	C	803
		R.A.S. Adair	L	737
		F. Mowatt	L	673

CAMBRIDGE [41] (Cont.)
(Two Seats)

Election	Electors	Candidate	Party	Votes
[Election declared void on petition]				
1854 (18/8)	1,977	R.A.S. Adair	L	758
		F. Mowatt	L	733
		Viscount Maidstone	C	708
		F.W. Slade	C	696
1857	1,878	K. Macaulay	C	770
		A. Steuart	C	735
		R.A.S. Adair	L	729
		J.T. Hibbert	L	702
1859	1,797	K. Macaulay	C	753
		A. Steuart	C	750
		Hon. E.T.B. Twistleton	L	683
		F. Mowatt	L	669
[Resignation of Steuart]				
1863 (12/2)	1,831	F.S. Powell	C	708
		H. Fawcett	L	627
1865	1,769	W. Forsyth	C	762
		F.S. Powell	C	760
		R.R. Torrens	L	726
		W.D. Christie	L	725
[Election of Forsyth declared void on petition]				
1866 (24/4)	1,769	J.E. Gorst	C	774
		R.R. Torrens	L	755
1868	4,000†	R.R. Torrens	L	1,879
		W. Fowler	L	1,857
		F.S. Powell	C	1,436
		J.E. Gorst	C	1,389
1874	4,428	A.G. Marten	C	1,856
		P.B. Smollett	C	1,794
		W. Fowler	L	1,774
		Sir R.R. Torrens	L	1,738
1880	4,806	W. Fowler	L	2,386
		H. Shield	L	2,326
		A.G. Marten	C	2,003
		P.B. Smollett	C	1,902

Petitions:—

1839: Void election
1843: Dismissed
1852: Void election
1854: Withdrawn
1857: Dismissed (Steuart only)
1865: Election of Forsyth declared void
1868: Withdrawn

CANTERBURY [42]

(Two Seats)

Election	Electors	Candidate	Party	Votes
1832	1,511	†Hon. R. Watson	L	834
		†Viscount Fordwich	L	802
		Sir W.P.H. Courtenay	L	375
1835	1,467	Lord Albert Conygham	L	755
		**F. Villiers	L	660
		*S.R. Lushington	C	658
1837	1,835	J. Bradshaw	C	761
		Lord Albert Conygham	L	755
		H.P. Gipps	C	751
		F. Villiers	L	698
[Resignation of Conygham]				
1841 (3/2)	1,918	Hon. G.A.F.P.S. Smythe	C	772
		J.W.H. Wilson	L	628
		T.T. Hodges	L	17
1841	1,918	Hon. G.A.F.P.S. Smythe	C	823
		J. Bradshaw	C	729
		T.T. Hodges	L	720
[Death of Bradshaw]				
1847 (15/3)		Lord Albert Conygham	L	Unopp.
1847	2,010	Lord Albert Conygham *(Denison)*	L	808
		Hon. G.A.F.P.S. Smythe	C	782
		J. Vance	C	643
		Lord Thomas Pelham-Clinton	C	641
[Elevation of Denison to the Peerage — Lord Londesborough]				
1850 (4/3)		F. Romilly	L	Unopp.
1852	1,874	H.P. Gipps	C	766
		Hon. H.B. Johnstone	C	758
		Sir W.M. Somerville, Bt.	L	570
		F. Romilly	L	533
		Hon. G.A.F.P.S. Smythe	C	7
[Election declared void on petition]				
1854 (18/8)	1,973	C.M. Lushington	C	727
		Sir W.M. Somerville, Bt.	L	699
		Hon. C.L. Butler	C	671
		C.P. Cooper	L	406
		E.A. Glover	L	41
1857	1,876	Hon. H.B. Johnstone	C	815
		Sir W.M. Somerville, Bt.	L	759
		C.P. Cooper	L	477

CANTERBURY [42] (Cont.)

(Two Seats)

Election	Electors	Candidate	Party	Votes
1859	1,831	Hon. H.B. Johnstone *(Lord Athlumney)*	C	Unopp.
		Sir W.M. Somerville, Bt.	L	Unopp.
[Resignation of Johnstone]				
1862 (6/3)	1,850	H.A.M.B. Johnstone	C	694
		W. Lyon	L	691
1865	1,603	H.A.M.B. Johnstone	C	767
		J.W. Huddleston	C	737
		W. Lyon	L	643
		R.A.S. Adair	L	614
1868	3,001	H.A.M.B. Johnstone	C	1,453
		T.H. Brinckman	L	1,236
		J.W. Huddleston	C	1,157
		H.J.L. Warner	C	709
1874	3,103	H.A.M.B. Johnstone	C	1,488
		L.A. Majendie	C	1,406
		T.H. Brinckman	L	934
		R.J. Biron	L	873
[Resignation of Johnstone]				
1878 (2/3)		Hon. A.E.G. Hardy	C	Unopp.
[Resignation of Majendie]				
1879 (8/5)	3,089	R.P. Laurie	C	1,159
		C. Edwards	L	1,103
1880	3,671	Hon. A.E.G. Hardy	C	1,467
		R.P. Laurie	C	1,425
		C. Edwards	L	1,294
		H.A.M.B. Johnstone	L	1,218

Petitions:—

1835:	Election of Villiers declared void. Lushington duly elected after scrutiny. A petition was subsequently presented against Lushington but this was dismissed
1837:	Withdrawn
1841: (3/2)	Dismissed
1852	Void election
1865:	Withdrawn
1880:	Void election. Writ suspended

CARLISLE [43]
(Two Seats)

Election	Electors	Candidate	Party	Votes
1832	977	†W. James	L	477
		†P.H. Howard	L	472
		†Sir J. Malcolm	C	124
1835	946	P.H. Howard	L	Unopp.
		W. Marshall	L	Unopp.
1837	1,012	P.H. Howard	L	Unopp.
		W. Marshall	L	Unopp.
1841	751	P.H. Howard	L	419
		W. Marshall	L	345
		E. Goulburn	C	296
1847	1,054	J. Dixon	L	479
		W.N. Hodgson	C	471
		P.H. Howard	L	440
[Election declared void on petition]				
1848 (14/3)	1,067	W.H. Hodgson	C	477
		P.H. Howard	L	414
		J. Dixon	L	328
		P.M. McDouall	Ch	55
1852	1,134	Sir J.R.G. Graham, Bt.	L	525
		J. Ferguson	L	512
		W.N. Hodgson	C	419
[Appointment of Graham as First Lord of the Admiralty]				
1853 (1/1)		Sir J.R.G. Graham, Bt.	L	Unopp.
1857	1,223	W.N. Hodgson	C	529
		Sir J.R.G. Graham, Bt.	L	502
		J. Ferguson	L	469
1859	1,253	Sir J.R.G. Graham, Bt.	L	538
		W. Lawson	L	516
		W.N. Hodgson	C	475
[Death of Graham]				
1861 (26/11)	1,195*	E. Potter	L	536
		W.N. Hodgson	C	533
1865	1,304	W.N. Hodgson	C	616
		E. Potter	L	604
		W. Lawson	L	586

CARLISLE [43] (Cont.)
(Two Seats)

Election	Electors	Candidate	Party	Votes
1868	4,537	Sir W. Lawson, Bt.	L	2,043
		E. Potter	L	1,971
		W.N. Hodgson	C	1,957
		W. Slater	L	71
1874	4,693	R. Ferguson	L	2,154
		Sir W. Lawson, Bt.	L	2,051
		W.F. Ecroyd	C	1,741
		W. Banks	C	1,551
1880	5,550	R. Ferguson	L	2,802
		Sir W. Lawson, Bt.	L	2,691
		M.W. Mattinson	C	1,968

Petitions:—

1847: Void election

1859: Dismissed

CHATHAM [44]

Election	Electors	Candidate	Party	Votes
1832	677	†W.L. Maberly	L	363
		T.E. Perry	L	248
[Resignation on appointment as a Commissioner of Customs]				
1834 (26/6)	676	G.S. Byng	L	262
		W. Ching	C	192
1835	672	Sir J.P. Beresford, Bt.	C	323
		G.S. Byng	L	298
1837	785	Hon. G.S. Byng	L	Unopp.
1841	862	Hon. G.S. Byng	L	457
		Lord Dufferin and Claneboye	C	234
1847	1,145	Hon. G.S. Byng *(Viscount Enfield)*	L	Unopp.
1852	1,371	Sir J.M.F. Smith	C	636
		Sir J. Stirling	L	482
[Election declared void on petition]				
1853 (23/6)	1,339	L.V. Vernon	C	610
		Sir J. Stirling	L	598
1857	1,463	Sir J.M.F. Smith	C	672
		W.G. Romaine	L	643
1859	1,544	Sir J.M.F. Smith	C	713
		A.J. Otway	L	652
1865	2,104	A.J. Otway	L	986
		G. Elliot	C	704
1868	4,518†	A.J. Otway	L	2,042
		G. Elliot	C	1,858
1874	4,468	G. Elliot	C	2,132
		A.J. Otway	L	1,476
[Resignation]				
1875 (16/2)	4,935	J.E. Gorst	C	2,173
		W.H. Stone	L	1,958
1880	5,548	J.E. Gorst	C	2,499
		Hon. H.C. Glyn	L	2,398

Election	Electors	Candidate	Party	Votes
[Appointed Solicitor-General]				
1885 (11/7)		J.E. Gorst	C	Unopp.

Petitions:—

1852: Void election
1853: Withdrawn
1857: Withdrawn
1859: Withdrawn

CHELTENHAM [45]

Election	Electors	Candidate	Party	Votes
1832	919	Hon. C.F. Berkeley	L	Unopp.
1835	960	Hon. C.F. Berkeley	L	411
		W.P. Gaskell	L	25
1837	1,324	Hon. C.F. Berkeley	L	632
		J. Peel	C	298
1841	2,003	Hon. C.F. Berkeley	L	764
		J.A. Gardner	C	655
		T.P. Thompson	L	4
1847	2,345	Sir W. Jones, Bt.	C	1,015
		Hon. C.F. Berkeley	L	907
		E.C. Smith	C	4
[Election declared void on petition]				
1848 (29/6)	2,345	Hon. C.F. Berkeley	L	1,024
		J.A. Gardner	C	848
[Election declared void on petition]				
1848 (4/9)	2,345	C.L.G. Berkeley	L	986
		B. Escott	C	835
1852	2,400	Hon. C.F. Berkeley	L	999
		Sir W. Jones, Bt.	C	869
[Death]				
1855 (14/7)	2,147*	C.L.G. Berkeley	L	760
		W. Ridler	C	178
[Resignation on appointment as a Commissioner of Customs]				
1856 (8/5)	2,170*	F.W.F. Berkeley	L	841
		E.G. Hallewell	C	655
1857	2,170	F.W.F. Berkeley	L	Unopp.
1859	2,171	F.W.F. Berkeley	L	922
		C. Schreiber	C	910
1865	2,793	C. Schreiber	C	1,157
		Hon. F.W.F. Berkeley	L	1,129
1868	3,536†	H.B. Samuelson	L	1,646
		J.T.A. Gardner	C	1,458

Election	Electors	Candidate	Party	Votes
1874	4,438	J.T.A. Gardner	C	2,121
		H.B. Samuelson	L	1,842
1880	5,018	Baron De Ferrières	L	2,318
		J.T.A. Gardner	C	2,297

Petitions:—

1847:	Void election
1848: (29/6)	Void election
1859:	Dismissed
1865:	Dismissed
1868:	Dismissed
1880:	Dismissed

CHESTER [46]
(Two Seats)

Election	Electors	Candidate	Party	Votes
1832	2,028	†Lord Robert Grosvenor	L	1,166
		J. Jervis	L	1,053
		†J.F. Maddock	L	499
1835	2,053	Lord Robert Grosvenor	L	Unopp.
		J. Jervis	L	Unopp.
1837	2,298	Lord Robert Grosvenor	L	1,282
		J. Jervis	L	1,109
		Hon. F.D. Ryder	C	352
1841	2,445*	Lord Robert Grosvenor	L	Unopp.
		J. Jervis	L	Unopp.
[Appointment of Jervis as Solicitor-General]				
1846 (11/7)		J. Jervis	L	Unopp.
[Appointment of Grosvenor as Treasurer of H.M. Household]				
1846 (8/8)		Lord Robert Grosvenor	L	Unopp.
[Resignation of Grosvenor in order to contest Middlesex]				
1847 (30/1)		Earl Grosvenor	L	Unopp.
1847	2,450	Earl Grosvenor	L	Unopp.
		Sir J. Jervis	L	Unopp.
[Resignation of Jervis on appointment as Chief Justice of the Court of Common Pleas]				
1850 (22/7)	2,529	Hon. W.O. Stanley	L	986
		E.C. Egerton	C	645
1852	2,524	Earl Grosvenor	L	Unopp.
		Hon. W.O. Stanley	L	Unopp.
1857	2,428	Earl Grosvenor	L	1,244
		E.G. Salisbury	L	924
		H.R. Grenfell	L	786
1859	2,502	Earl Grosvenor	L	1,464
		P.S. Humberston	C	1,110
		E.G. Salisbury	L	708
1865	2,274	Earl Grosvenor	L	1,284
		W.H. Gladstone	L	860
		W. Fenton	C	565
		H.C. Raikes	C	533

CHESTER [46] (Cont.)
(Two Seats)

Election	Electors	Candidate	Party	Votes
1868	6,062†	Earl Grosvenor	L	2,270
		H.C. Raikes	C	2,198
		E.G. Salisbury	L	1,283
		R. Hoare	L	1,071
[Succession of Grosvenor to the Peerage — Marquess of Westminster]				
1869 (4/12)		Hon. N. Grosvenor	L	Unopp.
1874	6,268	H.C. Raikes	C	2,356
		J.G. Dodson	L	2,134
		Sir T.G. Frost	L	2,125
1880	7,611	J.G. Dodson	L	3,204
		Hon. B. Lawley	L	3,147
		H.C. Raikes	C	2,056
		T.M. Sandys	C	1,961
		F.L. Malgarini	Ind	16
[Appointment of Dodson as President of the Local Government Board]				
1880 (8/5)		J.G. Dodson	L	Unopp.

Petition:—

1880: Void election. Writ suspended

CHICHESTER [47]

(Two seats until 1868; one seat from 1868)

Election	Electors	Candidate	Party	Votes
1832	852	†Lord Arthur Lennox	L	707
		†J.A. Smith	L	456
		W.P. Carter	L	263
1835	958	Lord Arthur Lennox	L	486
		J.A. Smith	L	421
		J.M. Cobbett	L	121
1837	885	J.A. Smith	L	490
		Lord Arthur Lennox	L	387
		J.M. Cobbett	L	252
1841	829*	Lord Arthur Lennox	C	Unopp.
		J.A. Smith	L	Unopp
[Appointment of Lennox as a Lord Commissioner of the Treasury]				
1844 (27/5)		Lord Arthur Lennox	C	Unopp.
[Appointment of Lennox as Clerk of the Ordnance]				
1845 (12/8)		Lord Arthur Lennox	C	Unopp.
[Resignation of Lennox]				
1846 (10/2)		Lord Henry Gordon-Lennox	C	Unopp.
1847	799	Lord Henry Gordon-Lennox	C	Unopp.
		J.A. Smith	L	Unopp.
[Appointment of Gordon-Lennox as a Lord Commissioner of the Treasury]				
1852 (4/3)		Lord Henry Gordon-Lennox	C	Unopp.
1852	757	Lord Henry Gordon-Lennox	C	Unopp.
		J.A. Smith	L	Unopp.
1857	638	Lord Henry Gordon-Lennox	C	Unopp.
		J.A. Smith	L	Unopp.
[Appointment of Gordon-Lennox as a Lord Commissioner of the Treasury]				
1858 (6/3)		Lord Henry Gordon-Lennox	C	Unopp.
1859	624	H.W. Freeland	L	300
		Lord Henry Gordon-Lennox	C	288
		J.A. Smith	L	282

CHICHESTER [47] (Cont.)
(Two seats until 1868; one seat from 1868)

Election	Electors	Candidate	Party	Votes
[Resignation of Freeland]				
1863 (21/2)		J.A. Smith	L	Unopp.
1865	562	Lord Henry Gordon-Lennox	C	Unopp.
		J.A. Smith	L	Unopp.
1868	1,195†	Lord Henry Gordon-Lennox	C	603
		J.A. Smith	L	433
1874	1,240	Lord Henry Gordon-Lennox	C	Unopp.
[Appointed First Commissioner of Works and Public Buildings]				
1874 (13/3)		Lord Henry Gordon-Lennox	C	Unopp.
1880	1,279	Lord Henry Gordon-Lennox	C	602
		F.W. Gibbs	L	467

CHIPPENHAM [48]

(Two seats until 1868; one seat from 1868)

Election	Electors	Candidate	Party	Votes
1832	208	†J. Neeld	C	139
		W.H.F. Talbot	L	132
		J.T. Mayne	L	40
1835	217	H.G. Boldero	C	Unopp.
		J. Neeld	C	Unopp.
1837	239	H.G. Boldero	C	Unopp.
		J. Neeld	C	Unopp.
1841	267	J. Neeld	C	165
		H.G. Boldero	C	128
		W.J. Lysley	L	96
[Appointment of Boldero as Clerk of the Ordnance]				
1841 (14/9)		H.G. Boldero	C	Unopp.
1847	303	H.G. Boldero	C	Unopp.
		J. Neeld	C	Unopp.
1852	300	H.G. Boldero	C	Unopp.
		J. Neeld	C	Unopp.
[Death of Neeld]				
1856 (9/4)		R.P. Nisbet	C	Unopp.
1857	334	H.G. Boldero	C	174
		R.P. Nisbet	C	150
		W.J. Lysley	L	132
1859	387	R.P. Long	C	Unopp.
		W.J. Lysley	L	Unopp.
1865	392	Sir J. Neeld, Bt.	C	208
		G. Goldney	C	201
		W.J. Lysley	L	172
1868	972	G. Goldney	C	418
		Sir G. Young, Bt.	L	359
1874	979	G. Goldney	C	530
		H. Cossham	L	304
1880	1,031	G. Goldney	C	478
		S. Butler	L	455

CHRISTCHURCH [49]

Election	Electors	Candidate	Party	Votes
1832	206	G.W. Tapps	C	Unopp.
1835	354	G.W. Tapps *(Gervis)*	C	Unopp.
1837	271	Sir G.H. Rose	C	116
		G. Cameron	L	106
1841	300	Sir G.H. Rose	C	Unopp.
[Resignation]				
1844 (28/3)	331*	Hon. E.A.J. Harris	C	180
		W. Tice	L	84
1847	301	Hon. E.A.J. Harris	C	Unopp.
1852	313	J.E. Walcott	C	Unopp.
1857	328	J.E. Walcott	C	Unopp.
1859	339	J.E. Walcott	C	Unopp.
1865	419	J.E. Walcott	C	211
		E.H. Burke	L	143
1868	1,329	E.H. Burke	L	609
		Sir H.D. Wolff	C	560
1874	1,831	Sir H.D. Wolff	C	978
		C. Milward	L	607
1880	2,555	H. Davey	L	1,185
		J.E.E. Moss	C	1,117

Petition:—

1868: Withdrawn

CIRENCESTER [50]

(Two seats until 1868; one seat from 1868)

Election	Electors	Candidate	Party	Votes
1832	604	†Lord Apsley	C	Unopp.
		†J. Cripps	C	Unopp.
[Succession of Apsley to the Peerage — Earl Bathurst]				
1834 (6/8)		Lord Robert Somerset	C	Unopp.
1835	615	J. Cripps	C	494
		Lord Robert Somerset	C	405
		T.D. Whatley	L	91
1837	585	J. Cripps	C	Unopp.
		T.W.C. Master (Senr.)	C	Unopp.
1841	552*	W. Cripps	C	Unopp.
		T.W.C. Master (Senr.)	C	Unopp.
[Resignation of Master]				
1844 (2/8)		Viscount Villiers	C	Unopp.
[Appointment of Cripps as a Lord Commissioner of the Treasury]				
1845 (14/8)		W. Cripps	C	Unopp.
1847	485	W. Cripps	C	Unopp.
		Viscount Villiers	C	Unopp.
[Death of Cripps]				
1848 (24/5)	478	J.R. Mullings	C	262
		Hon. C.F.A.C. Ponsonby	L	130
1852	434	J.R. Mullings	C	235
		Hon. A.G.J. Ponsonby	L	218
		Viscount Villiers	C	214
1857	423	A.A. Bathurst	C	307
		J.R. Mullings	C	200
		Hon. A.G.J. Ponsonby	L	188
1859	421	A.A. Bathurst	C	273
		Hon. A.G.J. Ponsonby	L	190
		B.S. Follett	C	182
1865	464	A.A. Bathurst	C	296
		Hon. R.H. Dutton	C	222
		J. Goldsmid	L	172

CIRENCESTER [50] (Cont.)
(Two seats until 1868; one seat from 1868)

Election	Electors	Candidate	Party	Votes
1868	1,076†	A.A. Bathurst	C	629
		F.A. Inderwick	L	284
1874	1,101	A.A. Bathurst	C	Unopp.

[Succession of Bathurst to the Peerage — Earl Bathurst]

Election	Electors	Candidate	Party	Votes
1878 (13/3)	1,128	T.W.C. Master (Junr.)	C	698
		Hon. A.G.J. Ponsonby	L	347
1880	1,145	T.W.C. Master (Junr.)	C	Unopp.

Petition:—

1852: Dismissed (Ponsonby only)

CLITHEROE [51]

Election	Electors	Candidate	Party	Votes
1832	306	J. Fort	L	157
		†J. Irving	C	124
1835	351	J. Fort	L	Unopp.
1837	368	J. Fort	L	164
		W. Whalley	C	155
1841	387	**M. Wilson	L	175
		*E. Cardwell	C	170
1847	504	M. Wilson	L	Unopp.
1852	448	M. Wilson	L	221
		J.T.W. Aspinall	C	187
[Election declared void on petition]				
1853 (28/5)	456	J.T.W. Aspinall	C	215
		R. Fort	L	208
[Election declared void on petition]				
1853 (23/8)	456	Le G.N. Starkie	L	216
		J. Peel	C	205
1857	457	J.T. Hopwood	L	Unopp.
1859	469	J.T. Hopwood	L	Unopp.
1865	438	R. Fort	L	Unopp.
[Death]				
1868 (13/7)		R. Assheton	C	Unopp.
1868	1,595	R. Assheton	C	760
		C.S. Roundell	L	693
1874	1,790	R. Assheton	C	896
		E.E. Kay	L	804
1880	2,068	R. Fort	L	1,078
		R. Assheton	C	882

Petitions:—

1841:	Election of Wilson declared void. Cardwell duly elected after scrutiny
1852:	Void election
1853: (28/5)	Void election

COCKERMOUTH [52]
(Two seats until 1868; one seat from 1868)

Election	Electors	Candidate	Party	Votes
1832	305	F.L.B. Dykes	L	187
		H.A. Aglionby	L	153
		A. Green	L	125
1835	328	H.A. Aglionby	L	192
		F.L.B. Dykes	L	145
		E. Horsman	L	113
[Resignation of Dykes]				
1836 (15/2)		E. Horsman	L	Unopp.
1837	297	H.A. Aglionby	L	169
		E. Horsman	L	122
		R. Benson	L	111
[Appointment of Horsman as a Lord Commissioner of the Treasury]				
1840 (1/6)	288	E. Horsman	L	117
		H. Wyndham	C	91
1841	293	H.A. Aglionby	L	129
		E. Horsman	L	127
		H. Wyndham	C	100
1847	319	H.A. Aglionby	L	Unopp.
		E. Horsman	L	Unopp.
1852	355	H. Wyndham	C	160
		H.A. Aglionby	L	154
		E. Horsman	L	147
[Death of Aglionby]				
1854 (9/8)		J. Steel	L	Unopp.
1857	408	Lord Naas	C	Unopp.
		J. Steel	L	Unopp.
[Appointment of Naas as Chief Secretary to the Lord Lieutenant of Ireland]				
1858 (3/3)		Lord Naas	C	Unopp.
1859	412	Lord Naas	C	Unopp.
		J. Steel	L	Unopp.
1865	336	Lord Naas	C	Unopp.
		J. Steel	L	Unopp.

COCKERMOUTH [52] (Cont.)
(Two seats until 1868; one seat from 1868)

Election	Electors	Candidate	Party	Votes
[Appointment of Naas as Chief Secretary to the Lord Lieutenant of Ireland]				
1866 (11/7)		Lord Naas *(Earl of Mayo)*	C	Unopp.
[Death of Steel]				
1868 (27/4)	336*	A.G. Thompson	C	171
		I. Fletcher	L	144
1868	1,074	I. Fletcher	L	620
		Hon. H.L. Bourke	C	388
1874	1,077	I. Fletcher	L	506
		J.H. Fawcett	C	388
[Death]				
1879 (18/4)	1,102	W. Fletcher	L	557
		D. Rapley	C	366
1880	1,094	E. Waugh	L	582
		R.G. Webster	C	380

Petition:—

1852: Dismissed

COLCHESTER [53]
(Two Seats)

Election	Electors	Candidate	Party	Votes
1832	1,099	R. Sanderson	C	648
		†D.W. Harvey	L	411
		†W. Mayhew	L	272
1835	1,152	R. Sanderson	C	637
		Sir G.H. Smyth, Bt.	C	568
		H. Tufnell	L	505
1837	1,175	R. Sanderson	C	472
		Sir G.H. Smyth, Bt.	C	435
		J.R. Todd	L	306
1841	1,206*	R. Sanderson	C	Unopp.
		Sir G.H. Smyth, Bt.	C	Unopp.
1847	1,258	Sir G.H. Smyth, Bt.	C	678
		J.A. Hardcastle	L	596
		R. Sanderson	C	531
[Resignation of Smyth]				
1850 (9/2)	1,250	Lord John Manners	C	622
		G.W. Cooke	L	389
[Appointment of Manners as First Commissioner of Works and Public Buildings]				
1852 (4/3)		Lord John Manners	C	Unopp.
1852	1,258	W.W. Hawkins	C	686
		Lord John Manners	C	615
		J.A. Hardcastle	L	468
		H.T. Prinsep	C	98
[Resignation of Manners in order to contest Leicestershire, Northern]				
1857 (24/2)	1,282	J.G. Rebow	L	563
		T.J. Miller	C	462
		W.R. Havens	L	7
1857	1,282	T.J. Miller	C	599
		J.G. Rebow	L	581
		W.R. Havens	L	48
1859	1,257	T.J. Miller	C	651
		P.O. Papillon	C	598
		J.G. Rebow	L	518
1865	1,405	J.G. Rebow	L	691
		T.J. Miller	C	640
		P.O. Papillon	C	561

COLCHESTER [53] (Cont.)
(Two Seats)

Election	Electors	Candidate	Party	Votes
[Resignation of Miller]				
1867 (15/2)	1,405*	E.K. Karslake	C	675
		W. Brewer	L	598
1868	2,970	J.G. Rebow	L	1,467
		W. Brewer	L	1,417
		E.K. Karslake	C	1,284
		A. Learmonth	C	1,217
[Death of Rebow]				
1870 (3/11)	3,145*	A. Learmonth	C	1,363
		Sir H.K. Storks	L	853
1874	3,183	A. Learmonth	C	1,515
		H.B.M. Praed	C	1,407
		W. Brewer	L	1,279
		R.K. Causton	L	1,218
1880	3,713	R.K. Causton	L	1,738
		W. Willis	L	1,650
		A. Learmonth	C	1,648
		F.H. Jeune	C	1,529

Petitions:—

1847: Withdrawn

1880: Withdrawn (Willis only). As the result of a recount there were found to be 1,641 undisputed votes for Learmonth and 1,640 for Willis. Twenty-three ballot papers were reserved for judgement on scrutiny but the Conservatives decided to withdraw the petition giving as their reason the costs involved. It would seem more likely that the real reason was that they considered that Willis was certain to maintain or increase his majority over Learmonth after the disputed ballot-papers had been dealt with.

COVENTRY [54]
(Two Seats)

Election	Electors	Candidate	Party	Votes
1832	3,285	†E. Ellice	L	1,613
		†H.L.E. Bulwer	L	1,607
		T.B. Fyler	C	371
		M.D. Thomas	C	366
[Appointment of Ellice as Secretary at War]				
1833 (12/4)	3,285	E. Ellice	L	1,502
		M.D. Thomas	C	1,208
		J.M. Cobbett	L	89
1835	3,577	W. Williams	L	1,865
		E. Ellice	L	1,601
		M.D. Thomas	C	1,566
1837	3,662	E. Ellice	L	1,778
		W. Williams	L	1,748
		M.D. Thomas	C	1,511
		J.D.H. Hill	C	1,392
		J. Bell	Ch	43
1841	3,789	W. Williams	L	1,870
		E. Ellice	L	1,829
		T. Weir	C	1,290
1847	4,043	E. Ellice	L	2,901
		G.J. Turner	C	1,754
		W. Williams	L	1,633
[Resignation of Turner on appointment as Vice-Chancellor]				
1851 (8/4)	4,223	C. Geach	L	1,669
		E. Strutt	L	1,104
1852	4,502	E. Ellice	L	Unopp.
		C. Geach	L	Unopp.
[Death of Geach]				
1854 (2/12)		Sir J. Paxton	L	Unopp.
1857	4,982	E. Ellice	L	2,810
		Sir J. Paxton	L	2,384
		J. Mellor	L	703
		M.D. Treherne	C	599
		R.J. Phillimore	L	356
1859	5,363	E. Ellice	L	3,107
		Sir J. Paxton	L	2,409
		M.D. Treherne	C	1,928

COVENTRY [54] (Cont.)
(Two Seats)

Election	Electors	Candidate	Party	Votes
[Death of Ellice]				
1863 (8/10)	5,206	M.D. Treherne	C	2,263
		A.W. Peel	L	2,129
[Death of Paxton]				
1865 (21/6)	4,967	H.W. Eaton	C	2,395
		T.M. Jones	L	2,142
1865	4,967	H.W. Eaton	C	2,489
		M.D. Treherne	C	2,401
		E.F. Flower	L	2,342
		T.M. Jones	L	2,259
[Death of Treherne]				
1867 (23/7)	4,967*	H.M. Jackson	L	2,429
		W.B. Ferrand	C	2,123
[Election declared void on petition]				
1868 (26/3)	4,967*	S. Carter	L	2,415
		A.S. Hill	C	2,134
1868	7,925†	H.W. Eaton	C	3,781
		A.S. Hill	C	3,761
		H.M. Jackson	L	3,594
		S. Carter	L	3,576
1874	8,027	H.W. Eaton	C	3,823
		H.M. Jackson	L	3,799
		S. Carter	L	3,662
		F. Du P. Thornton	C	3,628
1880	9,208	Sir H.M. Jackson, Bt.	L	4,184
		W.H. Wills	L	4,105
		H.W. Eaton	C	4,008
		A. Kekewich	C	3,715
[Resignation of Jackson on appointment as a Judge of the Queen's Bench Division of the High Court of Justice]				
1881 (14/3)	8,263	H.W. Eaton	C	4,011
		Sir U.J.K. Shuttleworth, Bt.	L	3,568

Petitions:—

1832: Dismissed

1867: Void election

1868: Dismissed

CRICKLADE [55]
(Two Seats)

Election	Electors	Candidate	Party	Votes
1832	1,534	†T. Calley	L	Unopp.
		†R. Gordon	L	Unopp.
1835	1,633	R. Gordon	L	Unopp.
		J. Neeld	C	Unopp.
1837	1,687	J. Neeld	C	833
		A. Goddard	C	734
		Hon. H.T. Howard	L	720
1841	1,663	Hon. H.T. Howard	L	Unopp.
		J. Neeld	C	Unopp.
1847	1,659	A.L. Goddard	C	Unopp.
		J. Neeld	C	Unopp.
1852	1,647	A.L. Goddard	C	Unopp.
		J. Neeld	C	Unopp.
1857	1,682	J. Neeld	C	778
		A.L. Goddard	C	770
		C.J. Monk	L	633
1859	1,692	A.L. Goddard	C	745
		Lord Ashley	L	743
		Sir J. Neeld, Bt.	C	712
1865	2,029	A.L. Goddard	C	978
		D. Gooch	C	879
		Lord Eliot	L	772
1868	5,825	Hon. F.W. Cadogan	L	2,844
		Sir D. Gooch, Bt.	C	2,452
		A.L. Goddard	C	2,009
1874	6,325	Sir D. Gooch, Bt.	C	2,624
		A.L. Goddard	C	2,231
		Hon. F.W. Cadogan	L	2,092
		H. Tucker	L	1,578
		W. Morris	L/Lab	497
		J. Arkell	L	40
1880	7,473	M.H.N.S. Maskelyne	L	4,350
		Sir D. Gooch, Bt.	C	2,441
		A.W. Neeld	C	1,748

DARLINGTON [56]

Election	Electors	Candidate	Party	Votes
1868	3,057	E. Backhouse	L	1,789
		H.K. Spark	L	875
1874	4,073	E. Backhouse	L	1,625
		H.K. Spark	L	1,607
		T.G. Bowles	C	305
1880	4,966	T. Fry	L	2,772
		H.K. Spark	L	1,331

DARTMOUTH [57]

Election	Electors	Candidate	Party	Votes
1832	243	J.H. Seale	L	Unopp.
1835	240	J.H. Seale	L	Unopp.
1837	257	J.H. Seale	L	Unopp.
1841	276	Sir J.H. Seale, Bt.	L	Unopp.
[Death]				
1844 (27/12)	282*	J. Somes	C	125
		G. Moffatt	L	118
[Death]				
1845 (3/7)	282*	G. Moffatt	L	125
		H.T. Prinsep	C	111
1847	376	G. Moffatt	L	Unopp.
1852	302	Sir T. Herbert	C	146
		W.S. Lindsay	L	135
1857	269	J. Caird	L	127
		C.S. Hayne	L	94
1859	257	E.W.H. Schenley	L	123
		Sir T. Herbert	C	116
[Election declared void on petition]				
1859 (8/8)		J. Dunn	C	Unopp.
[Death]				
1860 (3/11)	246	J. Hardy	C	112
		C.S. Hayne	L	110
1865	282	J. Hardy	C	Unopp.

This constituency ceased to return a Member of Parliament in 1868 and was incorporated into the county constituency of Devon, Southern.

Petitions:—

1844: Dismissed

1852: Dismissed

1859: Void election

DERBY [58]
(Two Seats)

Election	Electors	Candidate	Party	Votes
1832	1,384	†E. Strutt	L	884
		†H.F.C. Cavendish	L	716
		Sir C. Colvile	C	430
1835	1,478	E. Strutt	L	903
		Hon. J.G.B. Ponsonby	L	724
		Hon. F. Curzon	C	525
1837	1,751	E. Strutt	L	836
		Hon. J.G.B. Ponsonby	L	791
		Hon. F. Curzon	C	525
		C.R. Colvile	C	456
1841	1,906	E. Strutt	L	875
		Hon. J.G.B. Ponsonby *(Viscount Duncannon)*	L	784
		E.S.C. Pole	C	587
[Appointment of Strutt as Chief Commissioner of Railways]				
1846 (4/9)	2,022*	E. Strutt	L	835
		Sir D. Mackworth, Bt.	C	559
[Succession of Duncannon to the Peerage—Earl of Bessborough]				
1847 (16/6)		Hon. E.F.L. Gower	L	Unopp.
1847	2,177	E. Strutt	L	881
		Hon. E.F.L. Gower	L	852
		H. Raikes	C	820
		P. McGrath	Ch	216
[Election declared void on petition]				
1848 (2/9)	2,177	M.T. Bass	L	956
		L. Heyworth	L	912
		J.W. Freshfield	C	778
		J. Lord	C	760
1852	2,448	M.T. Bass	L	1,252
		**T.B. Horsfall	C	1,025
		*L. Heyworth	L	1,018
1857	2,479	M.T. Bass	L	884
		S. Beale	L	846
		W.F. Mackenzie	C	430
1859	2,513	M.T. Bass	L	1,260
		S. Beale	L	902
		W.M. James	L	736
		H.C. Raikes	C	648

DERBY [58] (Cont.)
(Two Seats)

Election	Electors	Candidate	Party	Votes
1865	2,450	W.T. Cox	C	1,096
		M.T. Bass	L	1,063
		S. Plimsoll	L	691
		S. Beale	L	608
1868	9,777†	M.T. Bass	L	4,995
		S. Plimsoll	L	4,677
		W.T. Cox	C	2,492
1874	11,316	M.T. Bass	L	5,579
		S. Plimsoll	L	4,938
		W.T. Cox	C	3,642
1880	13,006	M.T. Bass	L	8,864
		S. Plimsoll	L	7,758
		T. Collins	C	2,730
[Resignation of Plimsoll]				
1880 (26/5)		Sir W.G.G.V.V. Harcourt	L	Unopp.
[Resignation of Bass]				
1883 (12/6)		T. Roe	L	Unopp.

Petitions:—

1847: Void election

1852: Election of Horsfall declared void. Heyworth duly elected after scrutiny. Petition against Bass dismissed

DEVIZES [59]

(Two seats until 1868; one seat from 1868)

Election	Electors	Candidate	Party	Votes
1832	315	W. Locke	L	216
		M. Gore	L	166
		Sir P.C.H. Durham	C	94
[Resignation of Gore on becoming a Conservative]				
1834 (17/2)		Sir P.C.H. Durham	C	Unopp.
1835	311	W. Locke	L	240
		Sir P.C.H. Durham	C	154
		Hon. P.P. Bouverie	L	96
[Death of Locke]				
1835 (25/11)	343	T.H.S.B. Estcourt	C	157
		J.W.D. Dundas	L	145
[Resignation of Durham]				
1836 (10/2)		J.W.D. Dundas	L	Unopp.
1837	341	J.W.D. Dundas	L	Unopp.
		T.H.S.B. Estcourt *(Sotheron)*	C	Unopp.
[Appointment of Dundas as Clerk of the Ordnance]				
1838 (26/3)	266	**J.W.D. Dundas	L	109
		*G.H.W. Heneage	C	102
1841	375*	G.H.W. Heneage	C	Unopp.
		T.H.S. Sotheron	C	Unopp.
[Resignation of Sotheron in order to contest Wiltshire, Northern]				
1844 (7/2)	385*	W.H.L. Bruges	C	202
		C. Temple	L	67
1847	389	W.H.L. Bruges	C	Unopp.
		G.H.W. Heneage	C	Unopp.
[Resignation of Bruges]				
1848 (25/2)		J.B.B. Estcourt	C	Unopp.
1852	373	J.N. Gladstone	C	Unopp.
		G.H.W. Heneage	C	Unopp.
1857	319	S.W. Taylor	L	230
		C.D. Griffith	C	159
		J.N. Gladstone	C	118

DEVIZES [59] (Cont.)

(Two seats until 1868; one seat from 1868)

Election	Electors	Candidate	Party	Votes
1859	314	J.N. Gladstone	C	171
		C.D. Griffith	C	167
		S.W. Taylor	L	148
[Death of Gladstone]				
1863 (18/2)	331	Hon. W.W. Addington	C	170
		J.W. Probyn	L	88
		I. Abrahams	L	6
[Succession of Addington to the Peerage — Viscount Sidmouth]				
1864 (18/4)		Sir T. Bateson, Bt.	C	Unopp.
1865	359	Sir T. Bateson, Bt.	C	181
		C.D. Griffith	C	152
		J. Curling	L	0
1868	858	Sir T. Bateson, Bt.	C	385
		J.W. Probyn	L	321
		C.D. Griffith	C	34
1874	902	Sir T. Bateson, Bt.	C	396
		C.D. Griffith	C	364
		S.F.K. Sloper	Ind	2
1880	913	Sir T. Bateson, Bt.	C	446
		A.C.M. Thompson	L	388

Petitions:—

1838: Election of Dundas declared void. Heneage duly elected after scrutiny

1844: Withdrawn

DEVONPORT [60]

(Two Seats)

Election	Electors	Candidate	Party	Votes
1832	1,777	Sir G. Grey, Bt.	L	1,178
		Sir E. Codrington	L	891
		G. Leach	L	575
1835	1,870	Sir E. Codrington	L	1,114
		Sir G. Grey, Bt.	L	956
		G.R. Dawson	C	764
1837	2,145	Sir E. Codrington	L	Unopp.
		Sir G. Grey, Bt.	L	Unopp.
[Appointment of Grey as Judge-Advocate General]				
1839 (20/2)		Sir G. Grey, Bt.	L	Unopp.
[Resignation of Codrington]				
1840 (24/1)	2,121	H. Tufnell	L	974
		G.R. Dawson	C	750
1841	2,131	H. Tufnell	L	966
		Sir G. Grey, Bt.	L	932
		G.R. Dawson	C	780
[Appointment of Grey as Secretary of State for the Home Department]				
1846 (10/7)		Sir G. Grey, Bt.	L	Unopp.
1847	2,343	H. Tufnell	L	1,136
		J. Romilly	L	1,022
		J. Sandars	C	842
[Appointment of Romilly as Solicitor-General]				
1848 (3/4)		J. Romilly	L	Unopp.
[Appointment of Romilly as Attorney-General]				
1850 (17/7)		Sir J. Romilly	L	Unopp.
[Appointment of Romilly as Master of the Rolls]				
1851 (2/4)		Sir J. Romilly	L	Unopp.
1852	2,407	H. Tufnell	L	1,079
		Sir G.H.F. Berkeley	C	1,056
		Sir J. Romilly	L	1,046
		Sir J.H. Maxwell, Bt.	C	1,032

DEVONPORT [60] (Cont.)

(Two Seats)

Election	Electors	Candidate	Party	Votes
[Resignation of Tufnell]				
1854 (11/5)	2,417	Sir T.E. Perry	L	1,091
		Sir J.H. Maxwell, Bt.	C	689
1857	2,628	Sir T.E. Perry	L	Unopp.
		J. Wilson	L	Unopp.
1859	2,759	J. Wilson	L	1,216
		Sir T.E. Perry	L	1,198
		W.B. Ferrand	C	1,075
		A. Peel	C	1,039
[Appointment of Wilson as Vice-President of the Board of Trade]				
1859 (27/6)		J. Wilson	L	Unopp.
[Resignation of Perry on appointment as a Member of the Council of India]				
1859 (9/8)	2,759	Sir M. Seymour	L	1,096
		W.B. Ferrand	C	1,047
[Resignation of Wilson]				
1859 (17/8)	2,759	Sir A.W. Buller	L	1,189
		W.B. Ferrand	C	1,114
[Resignation of Seymour]				
1863 (12/2)	2,758	W.B. Ferrand	C	1,234
		Hon. F.W. Grey	L	1,204
[Resignation of Buller in order to contest Liskeard]				
1865 (22/6)	2,820	T. Brassey	L	1,264
		J. Fleming	C	1,208
1865	2,820	J. Fleming	C	1,307
		W.B. Ferrand	C	1,290
		T. Brassey	L	1,279
		T. Phinn	L	1,243
[Election declared void on petition]				
1866 (22/5)	2,820	Lord Eliot	L	1,275
		M. Chambers	L	1,269
		H.C. Raikes	C	1,216
		Hon. R.C.E. Abbot	C	1,215
1868	3,374	J.D. Lewis	L	1,541
		M. Chambers	L	1,519
		W.B. Ferrand	C	1,370
		W. Palliser	C	1,365

DEVONPORT [60] (Cont.)
(Two Seats)

Election	Electors	Candidate	Party	Votes
1874	3,348	J.H. Puleston	C	1,525
		G.E. Price	C	1,483
		J.D. Lewis	L	1,327
		G.S. Symons	L	1,250
1880	3,790	J.H. Puleston	C	1,753
		G.E. Price	C	1,746
		J.D. Lewis	L	1,509
		A.C. Sellar	L	1,476

Petitions:—

1859: (9/8)	Withdrawn
1865: (22/6)	Lapsed on Dissolution of Parliament
1865:	Void election
1866:	Withdrawn

DEWSBURY [61]

Election	Electors	Candidate	Party	Votes
1868	7,072	J. Simon	L	3,392
		H. Cossham	L	2,923
1874	8,803	J. Simon	L	3,706
		J.C. Cox	L	3,272
		W.H. Colbeck	C	26
1880	9,960	J. Simon	L	3,599
		W. Hoyle	L	3,254
		A. Austin	C	1,586

DORCHESTER [62]

(Two seats until 1868; one seat from 1868)

Election	Electors	Candidate	Party	Votes
1832	322	†Hon. A.H.A. Cooper	C	Unopp.
		†R. Williams (Senr.)	C	Unopp.
1835	318	Hon. A.H.A. Cooper	C	Unopp.
		R. Williams (Junr.)	C	Unopp.
1837	397	Hon. A.H.A. Cooper	C	Unopp.
		R. Williams (Junr.)	C	Unopp.
1841	367	Hon. A.H.A. Cooper	C	Unopp.
		Sir J.R.G. Graham, Bt.	C	Unopp.
[Appointment of Graham as Secretary of State for the Home Department]				
1841 (13/9)		Sir J.R.G. Graham, Bt.	C	Unopp.
1847	405	Hon. G.L.D. Damer	C	Unopp.
		H.G. Sturt	C	Unopp.
1852	432	R.B. Sheridan	L	235
		H.G. Sturt	C	215
		Hon. G.L.D. Damer	C	186
[Resignation of Sturt in order to contest Dorset]				
1856 (22/7)		C.N. Sturt	C	Unopp.
1857	451	R.B. Sheridan	L	Unopp.
		C.N. Sturt	C	Unopp.
1859	442	R.B. Sheridan	L	Unopp.
		C.N. Sturt	C	Unopp.
1865	432	C.N. Sturt	C	268
		R.B. Sheridan	L	255
		Sir H.D. Wolff	C	103
1868	628	C.N. Sturt	C	Unopp.
1874	688	W.E. Brymer	C	353
		F.F. Head	L	233
1880	817	W.E. Brymer	C	374
		Hon. A.W.F. Greville	L	332

DOVER [63]
(Two Seats)

Election	Electors	Candidate	Party	Votes
1832	1,651	†C.P. Thomson	L	713
		Sir J.R. Reid, Bt.	C	644
		J. Halcomb	C	523
		†R.H. Stanhope	L	498
[Thomson elects to sit for Manchester]				
1833 (7/3)	1,651	J. Halcomb	C	734
		R.H. Stanhope	L	665
1835	1,564	J.M. Fector	C	908
		Sir J.R. Reid, Bt.	C	782
		E.R. Rice	L	761
1837	1,677	E.R. Rice	L	854
		Sir J.R. Reid, Bt.	C	829
		J.M. Fector	C	742
1841	1,857	Sir J.R. Reid, Bt.	C	1,000
		E.R. Rice	L	960
		J. Halcomb	C	536
		A. Galloway	L	281
1847	2,060	E.R. Rice	L	1,104
		Sir G. Clerk, Bt.	C	932
		H.T. Prinsep	C	897
1852	2,064	Viscount Chelsea	C	1,097
		E.R. Rice	L	898
		Sir G. Clerk, Bt.	C	781
1857	2,024	R.B. Osborne	L	989
		Sir W. Russell, Bt.	L	958
		Sir G. Clerk, Bt.	C	695
		G.W. Hope	C	574
1859	2,038	Sir H.J. Leeke	C	931
		W. Nicol	C	902
		Sir W. Russell, Bt.	L	788
		R.B. Osborne	L	752
1865	2,318	A.G. Dickson	C	1,026
		C.K. Freshfield	C	1,012
		Viscount Bury	L	903
		T.E. Smith	L	892
1868	3,392	A.G. Dickson	C	1,461
		G. Jessel	L	1,435
		C.K. Freshfield	C	1,387
		I. Abrahams	L	35

DOVER [63] (Cont.)
(Two Seats)

Election	Electors	Candidate	Party	Votes
[Appointment of Jessel as Solicitor-General]				
1871	3,443	G. Jessel	L	1,235
(25/11)		E.W. Barnett	C	1,144
[Resignation of Jessel on appointment as Master of the Rolls]				
1873	3,563	E.W. Barnett	C	1,415
(23/9)		J.S. Forbes	L	1,089
1874	3,714	C.K. Freshfield	C	1,595
		A.G. Dickson	C	1,316
		C. Weguelin	L	1,118
		F.A. Inderwick	L	1,062
1880	4,239	C.K. Freshfield	C	1,734
		A.G. Dickson	C	1,701
		Hon. P.J. Stanhope	L	1,607
		W.C. Walker	L	1,506

Petitions:—

1833: Dismissed

1857: Withdrawn

1859: Dismissed

1865: Withdrawn

1868: Dismissed (Dickson only)

DROITWICH [64]

Election	Electors	Candidate	Party	Votes
1832	243	†J.H.H. Foley	L	Unopp.
1835	285	J. Barneby	C	128
		J.H.H. Foley	L	125
1837	341	J.S. Pakington	C	Unopp.
1841	347	J.S. Pakington	C	Unopp.
1847	346	Sir J.S. Pakington, Bt.	C	Unopp.
[Appointed Secretary of State for War and the Colonies]				
1852 (4/3)		Sir J.S. Pakington, Bt.	C	Unopp.
1852	367	Sir J.S. Pakington, Bt.	C	Unopp.
1857	371	Sir J.S. Pakington, Bt.	C	Unopp.
[Appointed First Lord of the Admiralty]				
1858 (3/3)		Sir J.S. Pakington, Bt.	C	Unopp.
1859	394	Sir J.S. Pakington, Bt.	C	Unopp.
1865	400	Sir J.S. Pakington, Bt.	C	Unopp.
[Appointed First Lord of the Admiralty]				
1866 (11/7)		Sir J.S. Pakington, Bt.	C	Unopp.
[Appointed Secretary of State for the War Department]				
1867 (13/3)		Sir J.S. Pakington, Bt.	C	Unopp.
1868	1,532†	Sir J.S. Pakington, Bt.	C	790
		J. Corbett	L	603
1874	1,377	J. Corbett	L	787
		Sir J.S. Pakington, Bt.	C	401
1880	1,408	J. Corbett	L	857
		G.H. Allsopp	C	348
		E.B.A. Jones	L	5

Petition:—

1835: Dismissed

DUDLEY [65]

Election	Electors	Candidate	Party	Votes
1832	670	†Sir J. Campbell	L	318
		†Sir H.D.C. St. Paul, Bt.	C	229
[Appointed Attorney-General]				
1834 (28/2)	715	T. Hawkes	C	322
		Sir J. Campbell	L	254
1835	727	T. Hawkes	C	360
		J. Forbes	L	279
1837	844	T. Hawkes	C	385
		M.M. Turner	L	289
1841	971	T. Hawkes	C	436
		W.A. Smith	L	189
[Resignation]				
1844 (8/8)	911*	J. Benbow	C	388
		W. Rawson	L	175
1847	791	J. Benbow	C	Unopp.
1852	912	J. Benbow	C	400
		J. Baldwin	L	231
[Death]				
1855 (8/3)	907*	Sir S.H. Northcote, Bt.	C	346
		J. Baldwin	L	3
1857	884	H.B. Sheridan	L	Unopp.
1859	992	H.B. Sheridan	L	432
		Viscount Monck	C	361
1865	1,358	H.B. Sheridan	L	526
		F.W. Truscott	C	275
1868	11,847†	H.B. Sheridan	L	Unopp.
1874	14,593	H.B. Sheridan	L	5,149
		F.S. Shenstone	C	4,181
[Election declared void on petition]				
1874 (21/5)	14,593	H.B. Sheridan	L	5,607
		B. Hingley	C	4,889

Election	Electors	Candidate	Party	Votes
1880	15,000	H.B. Sheridan	L	6,948
		A. Waterman	C	4,163

Petition:—

1874: Void election

DURHAM [66]
(Two Seats)

Election	Electors	Candidate	Party	Votes
1832	806	W.C. Harland	L	440
		†W.R.C. Chaytor	L	404
		†Hon. A. Trevor	C	383
1835	892	Hon. A. Trevor	C	473
		W.C. Harland	L	433
		T.C. Granger	L	350
1837	949	Hon. A. Trevor *(Viscount Dungannon)*	C	465
		W.C. Harland	L	373
		T.C. Granger	L	371
1841	1,022	R. Fitzroy	C	Unopp.
		T.C. Granger	L	Unopp.
[Resignation of Fitzroy on appointment as Governor of New Zealand]				
1843 (5/4)	1,106	Viscount Dungannon	C	507
		J. Bright	L	405
[Election declared void on petition]				
1843 (16/7)	1,106	J. Bright	L	488
		T. Purvis	C	410
1847	1,161	T.C. Granger	L	595
		H.J. Spearman	L	519
		D.E. Wood	C	450
1852	1,157	T.C. Granger	L	571
		W. Atherton	L	510
		Lord Adolphus Vane	C	506
[Death of Granger]				
1852 (3/12)	1,094	Lord Adolphus Vane	C	545
		H. Fenwick	L	496
[Election declared void on petition]				
1853 (25/6)	1,094	J.R. Mowbray	C	529
		Sir C.E. Douglas	L	444
1857	1,184	W. Atherton	L	Unopp.
		J.R. Mowbray	C	Unopp.
[Appointment of Mowbray as Judge-Advocate General]				
1858 (17/3)		J.R. Mowbray	C	Unopp.
1859	1,147	W. Atherton	L	Unopp.
		J.R. Mowbray	C	Unopp.

DURHAM [66] (Cont.)
(Two Seats)

Election	Electors	Candidate	Party	Votes
[Appointment of Atherton as Solicitor-General]				
1860 (9/1)		W. Atherton	L	Unopp.
[Appointment of Atherton as Attorney-General]				
1861 (8/7)		Sir W. Atherton	L	Unopp.
[Death of Atherton]				
1864 (9/2)		J. Henderson	L	Unopp.
1865	1,056	J. Henderson	L	Unopp.
		J.R. Mowbray	C	Unopp.
[Appointment of Mowbray as Judge-Advocate General]				
1866 (11/7)		J.R. Mowbray	C	Unopp.
1868	1,756†	J. Henderson	L	823
		J.R. Davison	L	784
		J.L. Wharton	C	732
[Appointment of Davison as Judge-Advocate General]				
1871 (14/1)		J.R. Davison	L	Unopp.
[Death of Davison]				
1871 (28/4)	1,946	J.L. Wharton	C	814
		T.C. Thompson	L	776
1874	2,059	T.C. Thompson	L	924
		J. Henderson	L	879
		J.L. Wharton	C	846
[Election declared void on petition]				
1874 (13/6)	2,059	F. Herschell	L	930
		Sir A.E. Monck *(Middleton)*, Bt.	L	918
		F. Duncan	C	752
		F.L. Barrington	C	742
1880	2,352	T.C Thompson	L	1,237
		F. Herschell	L	1,152
		J.L. Wharton	C	1,058

DURHAM [66] (Cont.)
(Two Seats)

Election	Electors	Candidate	Party	Votes
[Appointment of Herschell as Solicitor-General]				
1880 (10/5)		F. Herschell	L	Unopp.

Petitions:—

1837:	Dismissed (Harland only)
1843: (5/4)	Void election
1843: (26/7)	Withdrawn
1852:	Withdrawn
1852: (3/12)	Void election
1874:	Void election

EAST RETFORD [67]
(Two Seats)

Election	Electors	Candidate	Party	Votes
1832	2,312	†G.H. Vernon	L	1,311
		†Viscount Newark	L	1,153
		†Sir J. Beckett, Bt.	C	970
1835	2,459	G.H. Vernon	L	1,286
		Hon. A. Duncombe	C	1,252
		Lord Charles Clinton	C	1,164
1837	2,680	Hon. A. Duncombe	C	1,372
		G.H. Vernon	C	1,352
		W. Mason	L	1,234
1841	2,785*	Hon. A. Duncombe	C	Unopp.
		G.H. Vernon	C	Unopp.
[Appointment of Duncombe as a Groom in Waiting to Her Majesty]				
1841 (2/10)		Hon. A. Duncombe	C	Unopp.
1847	2,654	Hon. A. Duncombe	C	Unopp.
		Viscount Galway	C	Unopp.
[Resignation of Duncombe in order to contest Yorkshire, East Riding]				
1852 (11/2)		Hon. W.E. Duncombe	C	Unopp.
[Appointment of Galway as a Lord in Waiting to Her Majesty]				
1852 (19/3)		Viscount Galway	C	Unopp.
1852	2,710	Hon. W.E. Duncombe	C	Unopp.
		Viscount Galway	C	Unopp.
1857	2,646	F.J.S. Foljambe	L	Unopp.
		Viscount Galway	C	Unopp.
1859	2,621	F.J.S. Foljambe	L	Unopp.
		Viscount Galway	C	Unopp.
1865	2,489	F.J.S. Foljambe	L	Unopp.
		Viscount Galway	C	Unopp.
1868	7,510	F.J.S. Foljambe	L	Unopp.
		Viscount Galway	C	Unopp.
1874	7,768	F.J.S. Foljambe	L	Unopp.
		Viscount Galway	C	Unopp.

EAST RETFORD [67] (Cont.)
(Two Seats)

Election	Electors	Candidate	Party	Votes
[Death of Galway]				
1876	8,131	W.B. Denison	C	3,538
(25/2)		H.F. Bristowe	L	3,351
1880	8,278	F.J.S. Foljambe	L	4,333
		F.T. Mappin	L	4,134
		W.B. Denison	C	3,021
		H. Eyre	C	2,776

EVESHAM [68]
(Two seats until 1868; one seat from 1868)

Election	Electors	Candidate	Party	Votes
1832	359	†Sir C. Cockerell, Bt.	L	234
		†T. Hudson	L	212
		P. Borthwick	C	126
1835	338	P. Borthwick	C	Unopp.
		Sir C. Cockerell, Bt.	L	Unopp.
[Death of Cockerell]				
1837 (4/2)	354	G. Rushout	C	165
		Lord Marcus Hill	L	140
1837	354	G. Rushout	C	168
		**P. Borthwick	C	166
		*Lord Marcus Hill	L	156
1841	335	Lord Marcus Hill	L	188
		P. Borthwick	C	161
		G. Rushout	C	137
[Appointment of Hill as Comptroller of H.M. Household]				
1846 (11/7)		Lord Marcus Hill	L	Unopp.
1847	355	Lord Marcus Hill	L	195
		Sir H.P. Willoughby, Bt.	C	172
		Sir R. Howard, Bt.	L	131
1852	349	Sir H.P. Willoughby, Bt.	C	189
		C.L.G. Berkeley	L	170
		C. Wilkins	L	87
[Resignation of Berkeley in order to contest Cheltenham]				
1855 (11/7)		E. Holland	L	Unopp.
1857	330	Sir H.P. Willoughby, Bt.	C	172
		E. Holland	L	170
		H.R. Addison	L	61
1859	338	Sir H.P. Willoughby, Bt.	C	188
		E. Holland	L	149
		E. Chadwick	L	49
[Death of Willoughby]				
1865 (4/4)		J. Bourne	C	Unopp.
1865	337	J. Bourne	C	175
		E. Holland	L	124
		J. Harris	L	29

EVESHAM [68] (Cont.)

(Two seats until 1868; one seat from 1868)

Election	Electors	Candidate	Party	Votes
1868	769	J. Bourne	C	347
		T.S. Richardson	L	303
1874	744	J. Bourne	C	346
		J.N. Higgins	L	299
1880	827	D.R. Ratcliff	L	382
		A. Borthwick	C	373
[Election declared void on petition]				
1880 (9/7)	827	**F. Lehmann	L	378
		*F.D.D. Hartland	C	376

Petitions:—

1837: Election of Borthwick declared void. Hill duly elected after scrutiny. Petition against Rushout dismissed

1880: Void election

1880: (9/7) Election of Lehmann declared void. Hartland duly elected after scrutiny

EXETER [69]
(Two Seats)

Election	Electors	Candidate	Party	Votes
1832	2,952	†J.W. Buller	L	1,615
		E. Divett	L	1,121
		W.W. Follett	C	985
1835	3,239	Sir W.W. Follett	C	1,425
		E. Divett	L	1,176
		J.W. Buller	L	1,029
1837	3,488	E. Divett	L	Unopp.
		Sir W.W. Follett	C	Unopp.
1841	3,698	Sir W.W. Follett	C	1,302
		E. Divett	L	1,192
		Lord Lovaine	C	1,119
[Appointment of Follett as Solicitor-General]				
1841 (13/9)		Sir W.W. Follett	C	Unopp.
[Appointment of Follett as Attorney-General]				
1844 (20/4)	3,728*	Sir W.W. Follett	C	1,293
		J. Briggs	L	529
[Death of Follett]				
1845 (7/7)	3,728*	Sir J.T.B. Duckworth, Bt.	C	1,258
		J. Briggs	L	588
1847	3,798	E. Divett	L	Unopp.
		Sir J.T.B. Duckworth, Bt.	C	Unopp.
1852	2,501	Sir J.T.B. Duckworth, Bt.	C	1,210
		E. Divett	L	1,191
		G.S. Buck	C	1,111
1857	3,162	E. Divett	L	Unopp.
		R.S. Gard	C	Unopp.
1859	3,216	E. Divett	L	Unopp.
		R.S. Gard	C	Unopp.
[Death of Divett]				
1864 (4/8)	2,564	Lord Courtenay	C	1,096
		J.D. Coleridge	L	1,070
1865	3,088	J.D. Coleridge	L	Unopp.
		Lord Courtenay	C	Unopp.

EXETER [69] (Cont.)
(Two Seats)

Election	Electors	Candidate	Party	Votes
1868	6,156†	J.D. Coleridge	L	2,317
		E.A. Bowring	L	2,247
		Sir J.B. Karslake	C	2,218
		A. Mills	C	2,026
[Appointment of Coleridge as Solicitor-General]				
1868 (21/12)		Sir J.D. Coleridge	L	Unopp.
[Resignation of Coleridge on appointment as Chief Justice of the Court of Common Pleas]				
1873 (11/12)	6,206	A. Mills	C	2,346
		Sir E.W. Watkin	L	2,025
1874	6,337	A. Mills	C	2,523
		J.G. Johnson	C	2,330
		E.A. Bowring	L	2,264
		E. Johnson	L	2,053
1880	7,361	E. Johnson	L	3,038
		H.S. Northcote	C	2,590
		A. Mills	C	2,545

Petition:—

1873: Lapsed on Dissolution of Parliament

EYE [70]

Election	Electors	Candidate	Party	Votes
1832	253	†Sir E. Kerrison, Bt.	C	Unopp.
1835	282	Sir E. Kerrison, Bt.	C	Unopp.
1837	301	Sir E. Kerrison, Bt.	C	Unopp.
1841	342	Sir E. Kerrison, Bt.	C	Unopp.
1847	322	Sir E. Kerrison, Bt.	C	Unopp.
1852	356	E.C. Kerrison	C	Unopp.
1857	359	Sir E.C. Kerrison, Bt.	C	Unopp.
1859	342	Sir E.C. Kerrison, Bt.	C	Unopp.
1865	339	Sir E.C. Kerrison, Bt.	C	Unopp.
[Resignation in order to contest Suffolk, Eastern]				
1866 (27/7)		Hon. G.W. Barrington (*Viscount Barrington*)	C	Unopp.
1868	1,198	Viscount Barrington	C	Unopp.
1874	1,163	Viscount Barrington	C	Unopp.
[Appointed Vice-Chamberlain of H.M. Household]				
1874 (19/3)	1,163	Viscount Barrington	C	656
		C. Easton	L	386
1880	1,081	E.A. Bartlett	C	540
		C. Easton	L	478
[Appointed a Civil Lord of the Admiralty]				
1885 (2/7)	983*	E.A. Bartlett	C	473
		M.L. Hawkes	L	336

FROME [71]

Election	Electors	Candidate	Party	Votes
1832	322	T. Sheppard	L	163
		Sir T.S.M. Champneys	L	100
1835	285	T. Sheppard	C	100
		M. Bridges	L	78
		Sir C. Boyle	L	51
1837	291	T. Sheppard	C	124
		Sir C. Boyle	L	120
1841	340	T. Sheppard	C	154
		W.J. Sturch	L	129
1847	412	Hon. R.E. Boyle	L	Unopp.
1852	383	Hon. R.E. Boyle	L	Unopp.
[Election declared void on petition]				
1853 (7/3)		Hon. R.E. Boyle	L	Unopp.
[Death]				
1854 (24/10)	365	Viscount Dungarvan	L	181
		D. Nicoll	L	129
[Succession to the Peerage – Earl of Cork and Orrery]				
1856 (23/7)	366	Hon. W.G. Boyle	L	158
		Lord Edward Thynne	C	157
1857	363	D. Nicoll	L	162
		Hon. W.G. Boyle	L	92
		Lord Edward Thynne	C	72
1859	385	Lord Edward Thynne	C	194
		D. Nicoll	L	147
1865	414	Sir H.C. Rawlinson	L	206
		J.W.D.T. Wickham	C	183
1868	1,267	T. Hughes	L	571
		W.C. Sleigh	C	476
1874	1,327	H.C. Lopes	C	642
		W.H. Willans	L	557
[Resignation on appointment as a Judge of the Common Pleas Division of the High Court of Justice]				
1876 (24/11)	1,351	H.B. Samuelson	L	661
		Sir J. Fergusson, Bt.	C	568

Election	Electors	Candidate	Party	Votes
1880	1,383	H.B. Samuelson	L	Unopp.

Petitions:—

1852: Void election
1859: Withdrawn
1865: Withdrawn

GATESHEAD [72]

Election	Electors	Candidate	Party	Votes
1832	454	C. Rippon	L	Unopp.
1835	506	C. Rippon	L	Unopp.
1837	534	C. Rippon	L	236
		J.W. Williamson	L	151
1841	554	W. Hutt	L	Unopp.
1847	656	W. Hutt	L	Unopp.
1852	711	W. Hutt	L	270
		Hon. A.F.O. Liddell	C	190
		R. Walters	L	136
1857	895	W. Hutt	L	Unopp.
1859	913	W. Hutt	L	Unopp.
[Appointed Vice-President of the Board of Trade]				
1860 (13/2)		W. Hutt	L	Unopp.
1865	1,165	W. Hutt	L	Unopp.
1868	5,578	Sir W. Hutt	L	2,442
		W. Arbuthnot	C	1,406
1874	9,782	W.H. James	L	4,250
		R. Forster	C	1,396
		W. Arbuthnot	C	12
1880	11,551	W.H. James	L	5,749
		G. Bruce	C	1,570

GLOUCESTER [73]

(Two Seats)

Election	Electors	Candidate	Party	Votes
1832	1,427	†M.F.F. Berkeley	L	684
		J. Phillpotts	L	658
		†H.T. Hope	C	549
[Appointment of Berkeley as a Lord Commissioner of the Admiralty]				
1833 (9/4)	1,427	H.T. Hope	C	566
		M.F.F. Berkeley	L	457
1835	1,523	M.F.F. Berkeley	L	708
		H.T. Hope	C	621
		J. Phillpotts	L	598
		W. Cother	C	402
1837	1,674	H.T. Hope	C	727
		J. Phillpotts	L	710
		M.F.F. Berkeley	L	630
[Hope seeks re-election after election petition against him had been dismissed]				
1838 (21/5)	1,674	H.T. Hope	C	685
		E. Webb	L	579
1841	1,876	J. Phillpotts	L	753
		M.F.F. Berkeley	L	732
		H.T. Hope	C	646
		Viscount Loftus	C	510
[Appointment of Berkeley as a Lord Commissioner of the Admiralty]				
1846 (11/7)		M.F.F. Berkeley	L	Unopp.
1847	1,631*	M.F.F. Berkeley	L	Unopp.
		H.T. Hope	C	Unopp.
1852	1,621	W.P. Price	L	831
		M.F.F. Berkeley	L	786
		H.T. Hope	C	760
[Appointment of Berkeley as a Lord Commissioner of the Admiralty]				
1853 (4/1)	1,652	M.F.F. Berkeley	L	761
		H.T. Hope	C	670
[Price seeks re-election]				
1855 (31/3)		W.P. Price	L	Unopp.
1857	1,743	Sir R.W. Carden	C	742
		W.P. Price	L	717
		Sir M.F.F. Berkeley	L	710

GLOUCESTER [73] (Cont.)

(Two Seats)

Election	Electors	Candidate	Party	Votes
1859	1,721	W.P. Price	L	807
		C.J. Monk	L	779
		Sir R.W. Carden	C	595
[Election declared void on petition]				
1862 (26/2)	1,742	Hon. C.P.F. Berkeley	L	761
		J.J. Powell	L	716
		R. Potter	C	687
[Appointment of Powell as Recorder of Wolverhampton]				
1864 (25/5)		J.J. Powell	L	Unopp.
1865	1,715	W.P. Price	L	854
		C.J. Monk	L	774
		A.S. Kennard	C	726
1868	4,437†	W.P. Price	L	1,933
		C.J. Monk	L	1,922
		W.N. Lees	C	1,520
		E.J. Brennan	C	1,504
[Resignation of Price on appointment as a Railway Commissioner]				
1873 (8/5)	4,737	W.K. Wait	C	1,850
		T. Robinson	L	1,767
1874	4,838	W.K. Wait	C	2,132
		C.J. Monk	L	2,070
		J.J. Powell	L	1,990
		Sir J.J.T. Lawrence, Bt.	C	1,865
1880	5,583	T. Robinson	L	2,797
		C.J. Monk	L	2,680
		W.K. Wait	C	2,304
		B. St.J. Ackers	C	1,898

Petitions:—

1837: Dismissed (Hope only)

1841: Withdrawn

1852: Withdrawn (Price only)

1857: Dismissed

1859: Void election

1868: Withdrawn

1873: Dismissed

1880: Election of Robinson declared void. Petition against Monk dismissed. Writ suspended

Note:—

1855: Price resigned and then sought re-election after he had accepted a Government contract in the Crimea which would have disqualified him from remaining a Member of the House of Commons.

GRANTHAM [74]

(Two Seats)

Election	Electors	Candidate	Party	Votes
1832	698	Hon. A.G. Tollemache	C	388
		†G.E. Welby	C	303
		Sir M.J. Cholmeley, Bt.	L	241
1835	667	Hon. A.G. Tollemache	C	351
		G.E. Welby	C	351
		G.F. Holt	L	149
1837	669	G.E. Welby	C	398
		Hon. F.J. Tollemache	C	308
		R. Turner	L	291
1841	691*	Hon. F.J. Tollemache	C	Unopp.
		G.E. Welby	C	Unopp.
1847	760	Hon. F.J. Tollemache	C	Unopp.
		G.E. Welby	C	Unopp.
1852	774	G.E. Welby	C	483
		Lord William Graham	C	375
		Hon. F.J. Tollemache	C	329
1857	740	W.E. Welby	C	472
		Hon. F.J. Tollemache	L	393
		Lord William Graham	C	308
1859	743	Hon. F.J. Tollemache	L	Unopp.
		W.E. Welby	C	Unopp.
1865	755	J.H. Thorold	C	432
		W.E. Welby	C	404
		Hon. F.J. Tollemache	L	315
[Resignation of Welby in order to contest Lincolnshire, Parts of Kesteven and Holland]				
1868 (27/4)	755*	E. Turnor	C	374
		H.A.H. Cholmeley	L	299
1868	2,018	H.A.H. Cholmeley	L	Unopp.
		Hon. F.J. Tollemache	L	Unopp.
1874	2,199	Sir H.A.H. Cholmeley, Bt.	L	1,055
		H.F.C. Cust	C	965
		J.W. Mellor	L	899
1880	2,390	J.W. Mellor	L	1,329
		C.S. Roundell	L	1,304
		H.F.C. Cust	C	915
		C.B. Marlay	C	835

GRAVESEND [75]

Election	Electors	Candidate	Party	Votes
1868	2,722	Sir C.J. Wingfield	L	1,237
		B.C.T. Pim	C	1,069
1874	2,856	B.C.T. Pim	C	1,355
		Sir C.J. Wingfield	L	1,142
1880	3,286	T. Bevan	L	1,544
		Sir F.W. Truscott	C	1,422
[Election declared void on petition]				
1880	3,286	Sir S.H. Waterlow, Bt.	L	1,504
(2/7)		Sir R. Peel, Bt.	C	1,284

Petition:—

1880: Void election

GREAT GRIMSBY [76]

Election	Electors	Candidate	Party	Votes
1832	656	W. Maxfield	L	297
		†Lord Loughborough	C	158
1835	592	E. Heneage (1)	L	260
		Sir A.C. Grant, Bt.	C	227
1837	590	E. Heneage (1)	L	Unopp.
1841	573	E. Heneage (1)	L	Unopp.
1847	619	E. Heneage (1)	L	Unopp.
1852	861	Earl Annesley	C	347
		E. Heneage (1)	L	286
1857	888	Lord Worsley	L	Unopp.
1859	920	Lord Worsley	L	526
		C.W. Parker	L	51
[Succession to the Peerage — Earl of Yarborough]				
1862 (14/2)	1,062	J. Chapman	C	458
		G.F. Heneage	L	446
1865	1,273	J. Fildes	L	571
		J. Chapman	C	485
1868	4,348	G. Tomline	L	1,548
		J. Fildes	L	1,337
1874	5,091	J. Chapman	C	1,534
		E. Heneage (2)	L	1,393
[Death]				
1877 (3/8)	5,235	A.M. Watkin	L	1,699
		P.K. Seddon	C	1,315
		P. Sayle	L	97
1880	6,562	E. Heneage (2)	L	3,054
		G.M. Hutton	C	2,002

Petition:—

1862: Dismissed

GREAT MARLOW [77]
(Two seats until 1868; one seat from 1868)

Election	Electors	Candidate	Party	Votes
1832	457	†W.R. Clayton	L	Unopp.
		†T.P. Williams	C	Unopp.
1835	373	Sir W.R. Clayton, Bt.	L	201
		T.P. Williams	C	185
		W. Carpenter	L	34
1837	369	Sir W.R. Clayton, Bt.	L	Unopp.
		T.P. Williams	C	Unopp.
1841	369	T.P. Williams	C	233
		**Sir W.R. Clayton, Bt.	L	170
		*R. Hampden	C	169
1847	371	T.P. Williams	C	238
		B.W. Knox	C	178
		Sir W.R. Clayton, Bt.	L	161
1852	354	T.P. Williams	C	242
		B.W. Knox	C	198
		J. Bell	L	96
1857	343	B.W. Knox	C	Unopp.
		T.P. Williams	C	Unopp.
1859	340	T.P. Williams	C	229
		B.W. Knox	C	175
		J.W. Probyn	L	120
1865	349	B.W. Knox	C	Unopp.
		T.P. Williams	C	Unopp.
1868	760	T.O. Wethered	C	345
		E.H. Verney	L	314
1874	856	T.O. Wethered	C	Unopp.
1880	941	O.L.C. Williams	C	505
		J.O. Griffits	L	355

Petitions:—

1841: Election of Clayton declared void. Hampden duly elected after scrutiny

1847: Dismissed

GREAT YARMOUTH [78]

(Two Seats)

Election	Electors	Candidate	Party	Votes
1832	1,683	†C.E. Rumbold	L	837
		†Hon. G. Anson	L	828
		A. Colville	C	750
1835	1,615	T. Baring	C	772
		W.M. Praed	C	768
		Hon. G. Anson	L	680
		C.E. Rumbold	L	675
1837	1,740	C.E. Rumbold	L	790
		W. Wilshere	L	779
		T. Baring	C	699
		C.S. Gambier	C	685
[Resignation of Wilshere]				
1838 (23/8)	1,719	W. Wilshere	L	735
		T. Baring	C	702
1841	1,930	W. Wilshere	L	945
		C.E. Rumbold	L	943
		T. Baring	C	501
		J. Somes	C	494
1847	1,877	Lord Arthur Lennox	C	834
		O.E. Coope	C	813
		C.E. Rumbold	L	729
		F.H. Goldsmid	L	698
[Election declared void on petition]				
1848 (8/7)	1,877	J. Sandars	C	416
		C.E. Rumbold	L	384
		R.J. Bagshaw	L	300
1852	1,249	Sir E.H.K. Lacon, Bt.	C	611
		C.E. Rumbold	L	547
		W.T. McCullagh	L	521
		Sir C. Napier	L	486
1857	1,308	W.T. McCullagh	L	609
		E.W. Watkin	L	590
		Sir E.H.K. Lacon, Bt.	C	521
		Hon. C.S. Vereker	C	451
[Election declared void on petition]				
1857 (10/8)		J. Mellor	L	Unopp.
		A.W. Young	L	Unopp.
1859	1,326	Sir E.H.K. Lacon, Bt.	C	699
		Sir H.J. Strachey, Bt.	C	659
		E.W. Watkin	L	568
		A.W. Young	L	536

GREAT YARMOUTH [78] (Cont.)

(Two Seats)

Election	Electors	Candidate	Party	Votes
1865	1,645	Sir E.H.K. Lacon, Bt.	C	828
		J. Goodson	C	784
		A. Brogden	L	634
		P. Vanderbyl	L	589

Royal Commission appointed which found proof of extensive bribery and as a result the borough lost its right to return a Member of Parliament and was incorporated into the county constituencies of Norfolk, Northern, and Suffolk, Eastern, from the Dissolution.

Petitions:—

1837: Dismissed

1847: Void election

1857: Void election

1859: Dismissed

1865: Dismissed

Note:—

1838: During the hearing of the 1837 election petition, a compromise was reached between the Liberal and Conservative parties. It was agreed that at the end of the Parliamentary session Wilshere should resign and allow Baring to be elected without opposition. Although Wilshere did keep to the agreement and resigned, his supporters nominated him without his consent (he was abroad at the time) and he was re-elected.

GUILDFORD [79]

(Two seats until 1868; one seat from 1868)

Election	Electors	Candidate	Party	Votes
1832	342	†J. Mangles	L	299
		†C.B. Wall	C	180
		†Hon. C.F. Norton	L	138
1835	537	J. Mangles	L	299
		C.B. Wall	C	214
		H.A.C. Austen	L	131
1837	425	C.B. Wall	C	252
		Hon. J.Y. Scarlett	C	188
		J. Mangles	L	159
1841	486	R.D. Mangles	L	242
		C.B. Wall	L	221
		Hon. J.Y. Scarlett	C	177
		H. Currie	C	161
1847	585	H. Currie	C	336
		R.D. Mangles	L	242
		T.L. Thurlow	C	184
1852	648	R.D. Mangles	L	370
		J. Bell	L	251
		T.L. Thurlow	C	244
1857	666	R.D. Mangles	L	349
		W. Bovill	C	338
		J. Bell	L	167
[Resignation of Mangles on appointment as a Member of the Council of India]				
1858 (22/10)	666*	G.J.H.M.E. Onslow	L	268
		W.J. Evelyn	C	239
1859	677	W. Bovill	C	Unopp.
		G.J.H.M.E. Onslow	L	Unopp.
1865	667	G.J.H.M.E. Onslow	L	333
		W. Bovill	C	318
		W.W. Pocock	L	228
[Appointment of Bovill as Solicitor-General]				
1866 (11/7)	667	W. Bovill	C	316
		H.L. Long	L	11
[Appointment of Bovill as Chief Justice of the Court of Common Pleas]				
1866 (17/12)	667*	R. Garth	C	339
		W.W. Pocock	L	301
1868	1,219†	G.J.H.M.E. Onslow	L	536
		R. Garth	C	515

GUILDFORD [79] (Cont.)
(Two seats until 1868; one seat from 1868)

Election	Electors	Candidate	Party	Votes
1874	1,306	D.R. Onslow	C	673
		G.J.H.M.E. Onslow	L	430
1880	1,406	D.R. Onslow	C	705
		T.R. Kemp	L	571

Petitions:—

1852: Dismissed

1868: Dismissed

HALIFAX [80]

(Two Seats)

Election	Electors	Candidate	Party	Votes
1832	531	R. Briggs	L	242
		†C. Wood	L	235
		M. Stocks	L	186
		Hon. J.A.S. Wortley	C	174
1835	648	C. Wood	L	336
		Hon. J.A.S. Wortley	C	308
		E. Protheroe	L	307
1837	970	E. Protheroe	L	496
		C. Wood	L	487
		Hon. J.A.S. Wortley	C	308
1841	899	E. Protheroe	L	409
		C. Wood	L	383
		Sir G. Sinclair, Bt.	C	320
[Appointment of Wood as Chancellor of the Exchequer]				
1846 (9/7)		C. Wood	L	Unopp.
1847	1,022	H. Edwards	C	511
		Sir C. Wood, Bt.	L	507
		E. Miall	L	349
		E.C. Jones	Ch	280
1852	1,200	Sir C. Wood, Bt.	L	596
		F. Crossley	L	573
		H. Edwards	C	521
		E.C. Jones	Ch	37
[Appointment of Wood as President of the Board of Control for the Affairs of India]				
1853 (5/1)	1,218	Sir C. Wood, Bt.	L	592
		H. Edwards	C	526
[Appointment of Wood as First Lord of the Admiralty]				
1855 (3/3)		Sir C. Wood, Bt.	L	Unopp.
1857	1,488	F. Crossley	L	830
		Sir C. Wood, Bt.	L	714
		H. Edwards	C	651
1859	1,521	J. Stansfeld	L	Unopp.
		Sir C. Wood, Bt.	L	Unopp.
[Appointment of Wood as Secretary of State for India]				
1859 (28/6)		Sir C. Wood, Bt.	L	Unopp.

HALIFAX [80] (Cont.)
(Two Seats)

Election	Electors	Candidate	Party	Votes
[Appointment of Stansfeld as a Civil Lord of the Admiralty]				
1863 (28/4)		J. Stansfeld	L	Unopp.
1865	1,771	E. Akroyd	L	Unopp.
		J. Stansfeld	L	Unopp.
1868	9,328†	J. Stansfeld	L	5,278
		E. Akroyd	L	5,141
		E.O. Greening	L/Lab	2,802
[Appointment of Stansfeld as a Lord Commissioner of the Treasury]				
1868 (21/12)		J. Stansfeld	L	Unopp.
[Appointment of Stansfeld as President of the Poor Law Board]				
1871 (13/3)		J. Stansfeld	L	Unopp.
1874	11,282	J. Crossley	L	5,563
		J. Stansfeld	L	5,473
		H.C. McCrea	C	3,927
[Resignation of Crossley]				
1877 (21/2)	11,737	J.D. Hutchinson	L	5,750
		R.W. Gamble	C	3,624
1880	11,728	J. Stansfeld	L	6,392
		J.D. Hutchinson	L	6,364
		W. Barber	C	3,452
[Resignation of Hutchinson]				
1882 (21/8)		T. Shaw	L	Unopp.

Petition:—

1835: Withdrawn

THE HARTLEPOOLS [81]

Election	Electors	Candidate	Party	Votes
1868	3,922	R.W. Jackson	C	1,550
		T. Richardson	L	1,547
1874	4,524	T. Richardson	L	2,308
		R.W. Jackson	C	1,390
[Resignation]				
1875 (29/7)	4,820	I.L. Bell	L	1,982
		W.J. Young	C	1,464
		A.L. Kenealy	L	259
1880	6,681	T. Richardson	L	1,965
		I.L. Bell	L	1,717
		T.H. Tristram	C	1,597

Petition:—

1868: Withdrawn

HARWICH [82]

(Two seats until 1868; one seat from 1868)

Election	Electors	Candidate	Party	Votes
1832	214	†J.C. Herries	C	97
		C.T. Tower	L	93
		†N.P. Leader	C	90
		J. Disney	L	89
1835	156	J.C. Herries	C	97
		F.R. Bonham	C	78
		R.N. Verner	L	35
1837	162	J.C. Herries	C	75
		A. Ellice	L	75
		C.T. Tower	L	74
		F.R. Bonham	C	66
1841	186	J. Attwood	C	94
		W. Beresford	C	94
		J. Bagshaw	L	84
		D. Le Marchant	L	73
1847	295	J. Bagshaw	L	213
		J. Attwood	C	184
		W. Knight	C	65
		Sir D.St.L. Hill	C	2
[Election of Attwood declared void on petition]				
1848 (1/4)	294	Sir J.C. Hobhouse, Bt.	L	131
		Hon. J.H.T.M. Sutton	C	127
[Elevation of Hobhouse to the Peerage — Lord Broughton]				
1851 (5/3)	289	H.T. Prinsep	C	135
		R.W. Crawford	L	130
[Election declared void on petition]				
1851 (28/5)	289	R.W. Crawford	L	133
		H.T. Prinsep	C	127
[Election declared void on petition]				
1852 (10/4)		Sir F. Kelly	C	Unopp.
[Resignation of Kelly in order to contest Suffolk, Eastern]				
1852 (8/5)		I. Butt	C	Unopp.
1852	272	G.M.W. Peacocke	C	135
		D. Waddington	C	134
		J. Bagshaw	L	125
		G.D. Warburton	L	110

HARWICH [82] (Cont.)
(Two seats until 1868; one seat from 1868)

Election	Electors	Candidate	Party	Votes
[Election of Peacocke declared void on petition				
1853 (21/6)	299	J. Bagshaw	L	140
		Sir W.A. Fraser, Bt.	C	115
1857	313	J. Bagshaw	L	173
		G.D. Warburton	L	147
		H.J.W. Jervis	C	113
		B.B. Greene	C	98
[Death of Warburton]				
1857 (9/12)	313*	R.J. Bagshaw	L	162
		A. Arcedeckne	L	69
[Resignation of Bagshaw]				
1859 (18/3)	334	H.J.W. Jervis	C	145
		Hon. W.F. Campbell	L	134
1859	334	H.J.W. Jervis	C	156
		Hon. W.F. Campbell	L	155
		Hon. R.T. Rowley	C	152
		J.C. Marshman	L	144
[Succession of Campbell to the Peerage — Lord Stratheden and Campbell]				
1860 (24/4)	317	Hon. R.T. Rowley	C	146
		S.A. Donaldson	L	116
1865	386	H.J.W. Jervis	C	209
		J. Kelk	C	194
		M. Wills	L	117
		J.F. Stephen	L	77
1868	622	H.J.W. Jervis	C	328
		D.J. Jenkins	L	141
1874	712	H.J.W. Jervis	C	Unopp.
1880	759	Sir H.W. Tyler	C	368
		G. Tomline	L	310

Petitions:—

1841:	Withdrawn
1847:	Election of Attwood declared void
1848:	Withdrawn
1851: (5/3)	Void election
1851: (28/5)	Void election
1852: (10/4)	Withdrawn upon resignation of Kelly
1852:	Election of Peacocke declared void. Petition against Waddington dismissed
1853:	Withdrawn
1859: (18/3)	Withdrawn
1865:	Dismissed
1880:	Dismissed

HASTINGS [83]
(Two Seats)

Election	Electors	Candidate	Party	Votes
1832	574	†F. North	L	356
		†J.A. Warre	L	239
		H. Elphinstone	L	212
1835	673	F. North	L	374
		H. Elphinstone	L	291
		J. Planta	C	159
		M. Brisco	C	157
1837	924	J. Planta	C	401
		R. Hollond	L	382
		M. Brisco	C	312
1841	952	R. Hollond	L	Unopp.
		J. Planta	C	Unopp.
[Resignation of Planta]				
1844 (30/3)	899*	M. Brisco	C	513
		R.R.R. Moore	L	174
1847	909	R. Hollond	L	423
		M. Brisco	C	407
		J.A. Warre	L	387
		P.F. Robertson	C	348
		W.D. Bruce	C	0
1852	1,090	P.F. Robertson	C	501
		M. Brisco	C	487
		J.A. Warre	L	477
		J. Locke	L	386
[Resignation of Brisco]				
1854 (10/5)		F. North	L	Unopp.
1857	1,199	F. North	L	Unopp.
		P.F. Robertson	C	Unopp.
1859	1,235	F. North	L	613
		Lord Harry Vane	L	557
		P.F. Robertson	C	429
		W.D.L. Shadwell	C	230
[Succession of Vane to the Peerage – Duke of Cleveland]				
1864 (6/10)	1,613	Hon. G.W. Leslie	L	645
		P.F. Robertson	C	616
1865	1,871	Hon. G.W. Leslie	L	746
		P.F. Robertson	C	737
		F. North	L	728
		J.E. Gorst	C	591

HASTINGS [83] (Cont.)
(Two Seats)

Election	Electors	Candidate	Party	Votes
1868	2,801†	T. Brassey	L	1,508
		F. North	L	1,446
		Hon. S.G. Calthorpe	C	967
		C.A. Thruston	C	873
[Death of North]				
1869 (18/11)	2,801	U.J.K. Shuttleworth	L	1,218
		P.F. Robertson	C	1,084
1874	3,082	T. Brassey	L	1,721
		U.J.K. Shuttleworth	L	1,495
		P.F. Robertson	C	1,244
		R. Nicholson	C	945
1880	3,905	C.J. Murray	C	1,873
		T. Brassey	L	1,838
		Sir U.J.K. Shuttleworth, Bt.	L	1,702
[Appointment of Brassey as a Civil Lord of the Admiralty]				
1880 (10/5)		T. Brassey	L	Unopp.
[Resignation of Murray]				
1883 (2/7)	4,743	H.B. Ince	L	2,138
		J.H.B. Warner	C	2,101

Petition:—

1868: Dismissed

HELSTON [84]

Election	Electors	Candidate	Party	Votes
1832	341	†S.W.L. Fox	C	Unopp.
1835	356	Lord James Townshend	C	Unopp.
1837	366	Viscount Cantelupe	C	160
		A.W. Buller	L	125
[Resignation in order to contest Lewes]				
1840 (12/3)		J. Bassett	C	Unopp.
1841	398	Sir R.R. Vyvyan, Bt.	C	159
		W.R. Vigors	L	133
1847	385	Sir R.R. Vyvyan, Bt.	C	Unopp.
1852	317	Sir R.R. Vyvyan, Bt.	C	Unopp.
1857	309	C. Trueman	L	Unopp.
1859	318	J.J. Rogers	C	158
		C. Trueman	L	128
1865	348	A.W. Young	L	154
		S.M. Grylls	C	144
[Election declared void on petition]				
1866 (1/5)	348	**R. Campbell	L	154
		*W.B. Brett	C	153
[Appointed Solicitor-General]				
1868 (19/2)		W.B. Brett	C	Unopp.
1868	1,029	A.W. Young	L	494
		Hon. T.C. Bruce	C	374
1874	1,040	A.W. Young	L	473
		N. Lees	C	420

Election	Electors	Candidate	Party	Votes
1880	1,063	W.N.M. St. Aubyn	C	466
		A.W. Young	L	429

Petitions:—

1865: Void election

1866: The candidates had polled 153 votes each but the Returning Officer (who had voted for Campbell and was the father of Campbell's election agent) had given a casting vote to the Liberal candidate. A petition was lodged and the Committee decided that the Returning Officer had no right to a casting vote and should have returned both candidates. On scrutiny one vote was struck off Campbell's total and his election declared void. Brett declared duly elected. As a result of this case the House of Commons (July 26, 1866) resolved "that according to the law and usage of Parliament it is the duty of the sheriff or other returning officer in England, in the case of an equal number of votes being polled for two or more candidates at an election, to return all such candidates". The House decided to take no action against the Returning Officer who was the 75-year-old Mayor of Helston and said to be in poor health. He had failed to appear before the Committee hearing the petition but subsequently wrote to the Speaker claiming that he had consulted a legal textbook which indicated that he could give a casting vote.

HEREFORD [85]
(Two Seats)

Election	Electors	Candidate	Party	Votes
1832	920	†E.B. Clive	L	392
		R. Biddulph	L	380
		R. Blakemore	C	245
1835	891	E.B. Clive	L	457
		R. Biddulph	L	435
		R. Blakemore	C	426
1837	909	E.B. Clive	L	444
		D.H.D. Burr	C	430
		R. Biddulph	L	420
1841	961	E.B. Clive	L	531
		H.W. Hobhouse	L	500
		D.H.D. Burr	C	308
[Resignation of Hobhouse]				
1841 (5/10)	961	R. Pulsford	L	442
		E. Griffiths	C	297
[Death of Clive]				
1845 (31/7)		Sir R. Price, Bt.	L	Unopp.
1847	1,061	H.M. Clifford	L	Unopp.
		Sir R. Price, Bt.	L	Unopp.
1852	1,013	Sir R. Price, Bt.	L	458
		H.M. Clifford	L	452
		A.W.H. Meyrick	C	292
[Resignation of Price]				
1857 (14/2)	832	G. Clive	L	399
		K. Davies	C	230
1857	832	H.M. Clifford	L	Unopp.
		G. Clive	L	Unopp.
1859	971	H.M. Clifford	L	Unopp.
		G. Clive	L	Unopp.
1865	1,215	R. Baggallay	C	510
		G. Clive	L	499
		H.M. Clifford	L	483
1868	2,380	G. Clive	L	1,055
		J.W.S. Wyllie	L	1,015
		R. Baggallay	C	983
		G. Arbuthnot	C	872

(Two Seats)

Election	Electors	Candidate	Party	Votes
[Election declared void on petition]				
1869	2,380	E.H. Clive	L	1,064
(30/3)		C.W. Hoskyns	L	1,033
		Sir R. Baggallay	C	871
		G. Arbuthnot	C	826
[Resignation of Clive]				
1871	2,298	G. Arbuthnot	C	946
(28/2)		A.D. Hayter	L	678
1874	2,340	E. Pateshall	C	978
		G. Clive	L	921
		G. Arbuthnot	C	903
		J. Pulley	L	902
[Resignation of Pateshall]				
1878	2,631	G. Arbuthnot	C	1,110
(14/3)		J. Pulley	L	1,066
1880	2,837	J. Pulley	L	1,505
		R.T. Reid	L	1,321
		G. Arbuthnot	C	1,099
		F.D.D. Hartland	C	1,041

Petitions:—

1852:	Withdrawn
1865:	Dismissed
1868:	Void election
1880:	Withdrawn

HERTFORD [86]

(Two seats until 1868; one seat from 1868)

Election	Electors	Candidate	Party	Votes
1832	700	†Viscount Ingestre	C	432
		†Viscount Mahon	C	381
		†T.S. Duncombe	L	329
		J.E. Spalding	L	186
1835	633	Viscount Mahon	C	359
		Hon. W.F. Cowper	L	327
		Viscount Ingestre	C	321
1837	631	Hon. W.F. Cowper	L	378
		Viscount Mahon	C	306
		J. Currie	L	297
[Appointment of Cowper as a Commissioner of Greenwich Hospital]				
1839 (20/5)	619*	Hon. W.F. Cowper	L	297
		Sir W.M.T. Farquhar, Bt.	C	278
1841	614*	Hon. W.F. Cowper	L	Unopp.
		Viscount Mahon	C	Unopp.
[Appointment of Cowper as a Civil Lord of the Admiralty]				
1846 (11/7)		Hon. W.F. Cowper	L	Unopp.
1847	567	Hon. W.F. Cowper	L	Unopp.
		Viscount Mahon	C	Unopp.
1852	685	Hon. W.F. Cowper	L	301
		T. Chambers	L	235
		Viscount Mahon	C	213
		C.J. Dimsdale	C	182
[Appointment of Cowper as a Civil Lord of the Admiralty]				
1853 (1/1)		Hon. W.F. Cowper	L	Unopp.
[Appointment of Cowper as President of the General Board of Health]				
1855 (14/8)		Hon. W.F. Cowper	L	Unopp.
[Appointment of Cowper as Vice-President of the Committee of the Privy Council for Education]				
1857 (9/2)		Hon. W.F. Cowper	L	Unopp.
1857	620	Hon. W.F. Cowper	L	301
		Sir W.M.T. Farquhar, Bt.	C	273
		T. Chambers	L	235
1859	530	Hon. W.F. Cowper	L	Unopp.
		Sir W.M.T. Farquhar, Bt.	C	Unopp.

HERTFORD [86] (Cont.)
(Two seats until 1868; one seat from 1868)

Election	Electors	Candidate	Party	Votes
[Appointment of Cowper as Vice-President of the Board of Trade]				
1859 (19/8)	530	Hon. W.F. Cowper	L	281
		R. Dimsdale	C	204
[Appointment of Cowper as First Commissioner of Works and Public Buildings]				
1860 (13/2)		Hon. W.F. Cowper	L	Unopp.
1865	543	Hon. W.F. Cowper	L	Unopp.
		Sir W.M.T. Farquhar, Bt.	C	Unopp.
[Death of Farquhar]				
1866 (30/6)		R. Dimsdale	C	Unopp.
1868	922†	R. Dimsdale	C	434
		F.W. Gibbs	L	345
1874	1,041	A.J. Balfour	C	Unopp.
1880	1,081	A.J. Balfour	C	564
		E.E. Bowen	L	400
[Appointed President of the Local Government Board]				
1885 (30/6)		A.J. Balfour	C	Unopp.

Petition:—

1832: Void election. Writ suspended

HONITON [87]

(Two Seats)

Election	Electors	Candidate	Party	Votes
1832	511	†Viscount Villiers	C	360
		J.R. Todd	L	302
		J.P. Cockburn	C	110
1835	471	H.D. Baillie	C	332
		A. Chichester	C	226
		J.R. Todd	L	221
1837	460	H.D. Baillie	C	294
		J. Stewart	L	225
		Sir A.C. Grant, Bt.	C	203
1841	440	H.D. Baillie	C	Unopp.
		F.A. MacGeachy	C	Unopp.
1847	446	Sir J.W. Hogg, Bt.	C	Unopp.
		J. Locke	L	Unopp.
1852	287	J. Locke	L	166
		Sir J.W. Hogg, Bt.	C	152
		R.S. Gard	C	123
1857	264	J. Locke	L	214
		Hon. A.H.P.S.S. Wortley	C	119
		Sir J.W. Hogg, Bt.	C	117
1859	287	A.D.R.W.B. Cochrane	C	Unopp.
		J. Locke	L	Unopp.
[Death of Locke]				
1860 (22/10)		G. Moffatt	L	Unopp
1865	267	F.D. Goldsmid	L	171
		A.D.R.W.B. Cochrane	C	140
		E.M. Richards	L	88
[Death of Goldsmid]				
1866 (28/3)		J. Goldsmid	L	Unopp.

This constituency ceased to return a Member of Parliament in 1868 and was incorporated into the county constituency of Devon, Eastern.

Petition:—

1837: Withdrawn (Stewart only)

HORSHAM [88]

Election	Electors	Candidate	Party	Votes
1832	257	R.H. Hurst (Senr.)	L	114
		†E. Blount	L	74
1835	280	R.H. Hurst (Senr.)	L	127
		T. Broadwood	C	124
1837	319	R.H. Hurst (Senr.)	L	147
		T. Broadwood	C	145
1841	377	Hon. R.C. Scarlett	C	Unopp.
[Succession to the Peerage — Lord Abinger]				
1844 (1/5)		R.H. Hurst (Senr.)	L	Unopp.
1847	341	J. Jervis	L	164
		W.R.S.V. Fitzgerald	C	155
[Election declared void on petition]				
1848 (28/6)	351	**W.R.S.V. Fitzgerald	C	182
		*Lord Edward Howard	L	115
1852	350	W.R.S.V. Fitzgerald	C	Unopp.
1857	350	W.R.S.V. Fitzgerald	C	173
		J. Scott	L	117
1859	387	W.R.S.V. Fitzgerald	C	Unopp.
1865	400	R.H. Hurst (Junr.)	L	164
		W.R.S.V. Fitzgerald	C	159
1868	799	**J. Aldridge	C	380
		*R.H. Hurst (Junr.)	L	380
1874	955	Sir W.R.S.V. Fitzgerald	C	520
		R.H. Hurst (Junr.)	L	310
[Resignation on appointment as Chief Charity Commissioner for England and Wales]				
1875 (17/12)	992	R.H. Hurst (Junr.)	L	437
		J. Aldridge	C	424
		T. Richardson	L	5
[Election declared void on petition]				
1876 (29/2)	1,007	J.C. Brown	L	478
		Sir H.S. Giffard	C	424

Election	Electors	Candidate	Party	Votes
1880	1,214	Sir H. Fletcher, Bt.	C	605
		J.C. Brown	L	504

[Appointed a Groom in Waiting to Her Majesty]

1885 (16/7)		Sir H. Fletcher, Bt.	C	Unopp.

Petitions:—

1835:	Dismissed
1847:	Void election
1848:	Election of Fitzgerald declared void. Howard duly elected after scrutiny
1865:	Dismissed
1868:	Double return. Petitions were lodged against both Aldridge and Hurst but were withdrawn after Aldridge decided not to defend his claim to the seat and allow Hurst to be declared duly elected
1875:	Void election
1880:	Withdrawn

HUDDERSFIELD [89]

Election	Electors	Candidate	Party	Votes
1832	608	L. Fenton	L	263
		J. Wood	L	152
[Death]				
1834 (9/1)	604	J. Blackburne	L	234
		M.T. Sadler	C	147
		J. Wood	L	108
1835	671	J. Blackburne	L	241
		W.A. Johnson	L	109
[Death]				
1837 (8/5)	800	E. Ellice	L	340
		R. Oastler	C	290
1837	800	W.R.C. Stansfield	L	323
		R. Oastler	C	301
1841	1,003	W.R.C. Stansfield	L	Unopp.
1847	1,142	W.R.C. Stansfield	L	525
		J. Cheetham	L	488
1852	1,364	W.R.C. Stansfield	L	625
		W. Willans	L	590
[Election declared void on petition]				
1853 (22/4)	1,415	Viscount Goderich	L	675
		J. Starkey	L	593
1857	1,552	E. Akroyd	L	823
		R. Cobden	L	590
1859	1,660	E.A. Leatham	L	779
		E. Akroyd	L	760
1865	2,138	T.P. Crosland	L	1,019
		E.A. Leatham	L	787
[Death]				
1868 (20/3)	2,138*	E.A. Leatham	L	1,111
		W.C. Sleigh	C	789
1868	11,242†	E.A. Leatham	L	Unopp.
1874	11,917	E.A. Leatham	L	5,668
		T. Brooke	C	4,985

Election	Electors	Candidate	Party	Votes
1880	13,386	E.A. Leatham	L	7,008
		W.A. Lindsay	C	4,486

Petitions:—

1852:	Void election
1859:	Dismissed
1865:	Dismissed

HUNTINGDON [90]

(Two seats until 1868; one seat from 1868)

Election	Electors	Candidate	Party	Votes
1832	327	†J. Peel	C	177
		†F. Pollock	C	171
		J. Duberley	L	128
		E.H. Maltby	L	94
1835	380	J. Peel	C	Unopp.
		Sir F. Pollock	C	Unopp.
1837	356	J. Peel	C	Unopp.
		Sir F. Pollock	C	Unopp.
1841	416	J. Peel	C	Unopp.
		Sir F. Pollock	C	Unopp.
[Appointments of Peel as Surveyor-General of the Ordnance and Pollock as Attorney-General]				
1841 (14/9)		J. Peel	C	Unopp.
		Sir F. Pollock	C	Unopp.
[Resignation of Pollock on appointment as Chief Justice of the Court of the Exchequer]				
1844 (22/4)		T. Baring	C	Unopp.
1847	373	T. Baring	C	Unopp.
		J. Peel	C	Unopp.
1852	390	T. Baring	C	Unopp.
		J. Peel	C	Unopp.
1857	382	T. Baring	C	Unopp.
		J. Peel	C	Unopp.
[Appointment of Peel as Secretary of State for the War Department]				
1858 (4/3)		J. Peel	C	Unopp.
1859	378	T. Baring	C	Unopp.
		J. Peel	C	Unopp.
1865	383	T. Baring	C	Unopp.
		J. Peel	C	Unopp.
[Appointment of Peel as Secretary of State for the War Department]				
1866 (11/7)		J. Peel	C	Unopp.
1868	976	T. Baring	C	Unopp.

HUNTINGDON [90] (Cont.)
(Two seats until 1868; one seat from 1868)

Election	Electors	Candidate	Party	Votes
[Death]				
1873 (20/12)	1,008	Sir J.B. Karslake A. Arnold	C L	499 341
1874	1,049	Sir J.B. Karslake	C	Unopp.
[Appointed Attorney-General]				
1874 (16/3)		Sir J.B. Karslake	C	Unopp.
[Resignation]				
1876 (16/2)		Viscount Hinchingbrooke	C	Unopp.
1880	1,052	Viscount Hinchingbrooke	C	Unopp.
[Succession to the Peerage — Earl of Sandwich]				
1884 (22/3)	3,658	Sir R. Peel, Bt. C. Veasey	C L	455 446

Petition:—

1847: Withdrawn

HYTHE [91]

Election	Electors	Candidate	Party	Votes
1832	469	†S. Marjoribanks	L	226
		W. Fraser	C	198
1835	477	S. Marjoribanks	L	Unopp.
[Resignation]				
1837 (16/5)		Viscount Melgund	L	Unopp.
1837	476	Viscount Melgund	L	243
		Hon. W.H. Beresford	C	136
1841	513	S. Marjoribanks	L	Unopp.
1847	485	E.D. Brockman	L	211
		Baron M.A. de Rothschild	L	189
1852	856	E.D. Brockman	L	512
		R.S. Motte	L	98
1857	998	Sir J.W. Ramsden, Bt.	L	490
		A. Hankey	C	258
[Resignation]				
1859 (15/2)		Baron M.A. de Rothschild	L	Unopp.
1859	997	Baron M.A. de Rothschild	L	Unopp.
1865	1,291	Baron M.A. de Rothschild	L	Unopp.
1868	2,275	Baron M.A. de Rothschild	L	1,268
		A. Nugent	C	521
1874	2,445	Sir E.W. Watkin	L	1,347
		M. Merryweather	L	300
1880	2,893	Sir E.W. Watkin, Bt.	L	Unopp.

IPSWICH [92]

(Two Seats)

Election	Electors	Candidate	Party	Votes
1832	1,219	†J. Morrison	L	599
		†R. Wason	L	593
		E. Goulburn	C	303
		F. Kelly	C	267
		C. Mackinnon	C	94
1835	1,209	F. Kelly	C	557
		R.A. Dundas	C	555
		R. Wason	L	531
		J. Morrison	L	516
[Election declared void on petition]				
1835 (19/6)	1,209	J. Morrison	L	542
		R. Wason	L	533
		H.G. Broke	C	454
		W. Holmes	C	434
1837	1,418	T.M. Gibson	C	601
		**H. Tufnell	L	595
		*F. Kelly	C	593
		R. Wason	L	593
[Gibson seeks re-election as a Liberal]				
1839 (15/7)	1,418*	Sir T.J. Cochrane	C	621
		T.M. Gibson	L	615
1841	1,587	R. Wason	L	659
		G. Rennie	L	657
		F. Kelly	C	611
		J.C. Herries	C	604
[Election declared void on petition]				
1842 (3/6)	1,619*	Earl of Desart	C	680
		T. Gladstone	C	673
		T. Gisborne	L	543
		G. Moffatt	L	541
		T. Nicholson	L	3
[Election declared void on petition]				
1842 (17/8)	1,619*	J.N. Gladstone	C	651
		S.W.L. Fox	C	641
		G. Thornbury	L	548
		H. Vincent	Ch	473
		T. Nicholson	L	2
1847	1,714	J.C. Cobbold	C	829
		H.E. Adair	L	708
		J.N. Gladstone	C	661
		H. Vincent	Ch	546
1852	1,838	J.C. Cobbold	C	809
		H.E. Adair	L	782
		T.B. Hobhouse	L	725
		S.S. Bateson	C	725

IPSWICH [92] (Cont.)
(Two Seats)

Election	Electors	Candidate	Party	Votes
1857	1,891	J.C. Cobbold	C	780
		H.E. Adair	L	759
		J.C. Marshman	L	738
		H.J. Selwin	C	709
1859	1,914	J.C. Cobbold	C	918
		H.E. Adair	L	864
		H.J. Selwin	C	842
		J. King	L	388
1865	2,118	H.E. Adair	L	992
		J.C. Cobbold	C	910
		H.W. West	L	904
		W. Tidmas	C	774
1868	5,352	H.E. Adair	L	2,321
		H.W. West	L	2,195
		J.C. Cobbold	C	2,044
1874	6,619	J.P. Cobbold	C	3,059
		J.R. Bulwer	C	2,827
		H.E. Adair	L	2,506
		H.W. West	L	2,322
[Death of Cobbold]				
1876 (1/1)	6,789	T.C. Cobbold	C	2,213
		W. Newton	L/Lab	1,607
1880	7,406	T.C. Cobbold	C	3,142
		J. Collings	L	3,074
		H.W. West	L	3,025
		J.R. Bulwer	C	2,979
[Death of Cobbold]				
1883 (14/12)	7,914	H.W. West	L	3,266
		Sir W.T. Charley	C	2,816

Petitions:—

1835:	Void election
1837:	Election of Tufnell declared void. Kelly duly elected after scrutiny. Petition against Gibson dismissed
1839:	Dismissed
1841:	Void election
1842: (3/6)	Void election
1857:	Dismissed

KENDAL [93]

Election	Electors	Candidate	Party	Votes
1832	327	†J. Brougham	L	Unopp.
[Death]				
1834 (17/2)		J. Barham	L	Unopp.
1835	344	J. Barham	L	Unopp.
1837	321	G.W. Wood	L	Unopp.
1841	353	G.W. Wood	L	Unopp.
[Death]				
1843 (9/11)	368	H. Warburton	L	182
		G.W.P. Bentinck	C	119
1847	397	G.C. Glyn	L	Unopp.
1852	382	G.C. Glyn	L	Unopp.
1857	402	G.C. Glyn	L	Unopp.
1859	432	G.C. Glyn	L	Unopp.
1865	439	G.C. Glyn	L	Unopp.
1868	1,884	J. Whitwell	L	Unopp.
1874	1,859	J. Whitwell	L	1,061
		W.A.F. Saunders	C	470
1880	1,917	J. Whitwell	L	1,118
		A. Harris	C	541
[Death]				
1880 (17/12)	1,917	J. Cropper	L	953
		A. Harris	C	653

KIDDERMINSTER [94]

Election	Electors	Candidate	Party	Votes
1832	390	†R. Godson	L	172
		†G.R. Philips	L	159
1835	383	G.R. Philips	L	197
		R. Godson	C	124
1837	440	R. Godson	C	198
		J. Bagshaw	L	157
1841	482	R. Godson	C	212
		S. Ricardo	L	200
1847	548	R. Godson	C	Unopp.
[Death]				
1849 (5/9)	494	J. Best	C	217
		T. Gisborne	L	200
1852	495	R. Lowe	L	246
		J. Best	C	152
[Appointment as Vice-President of the Board of Trade]				
1855 (14/8)		R. Lowe	L	Unopp.
1857	502	R. Lowe	L	234
		W. Boycott	C	146
1859	487	A.R. Bristow	L	216
		J.W. Huddleston	C	207
[Resignation]				
1862 (27/5)	493	Hon. L. White	L	229
		J.G. Talbot	C	219
1865	612	A. Grant	C	285
		Hon. L. White	L	270
1868	2,323†	T. Lea	L	1,262
		W.T. Makins	C	802
1874	3,394	A. Grant	C	1,509
		T. Lea	L	1,398
[Election declared void on petition]				
1874 (1/8)	3,394	Sir W.A. Fraser, Bt.	C	1,651
		G.H. Lea	L	1,318

Election	Electors	Candidate	Party	Votes
1880	3,606	J. Brinton	L	1,795
		A. Grant	C	1,472
[Seeks re-election]				
1880 (8/5)		J. Brinton	L	Unopp.

Petitions:—

1849:	Dismissed
1852:	Withdrawn
1859:	Withdrawn
1865:	Withdrawn
1874:	Void election

Note:—

1880: (8/5) Immediately following the election, Brinton discovered that his election agent had been reported for bribery at a previous municipal election and to avoid the possibility of an election petition being brought against him, he decided to resign his seat and seek re-election.

KING'S LYNN [95]
(Two Seats)

Election	Electors	Candidate	Party	Votes
1832	836	†Lord George Bentinck	C	Unopp.
		†Lord William Lennox	L	Unopp.
1835	865	Lord George Bentinck	C	531
		Sir S. Canning	C	416
		Sir J.S. Lillie	L	238
1837	885	Lord George Bentinck	C	468
		Sir S. Canning	C	382
		Hon. G.T. Keppel	L	369
1841	1,144*	Lord George Bentinck	C	Unopp.
		Sir S. Canning	C	Unopp.
[Resignation of Canning on appointment as United Kingdom Ambassador to Turkey]				
1842 (10/2)		Viscount Jocelyn	C	Unopp.
1847	1,157	Lord George Bentinck	C	Unopp.
		Viscount Jocelyn	C	Unopp.
[Death of Bentinck]				
1848 (22/12)		Hon. E.H. Stanley (*Lord Stanley*)	C	Unopp.
1852	1,176	Viscount Jocelyn	C	641
		Lord Stanley	C	559
		R. Pashley	L	390
[Death of Jocelyn]				
1854 (16/9)		J.H. Gurney	L	Unopp.
1857	1,055	J.H. Gurney	L	Unopp.
		Lord Stanley	C	Unopp.
[Appointment of Stanley as Secretary of State for the Colonies]				
1858 (4/3)		Lord Stanley	C	Unopp.
[Appointment of Stanley as President of the Board of Control for the Affairs of India]				
1858 (5/6)		Lord Stanley	C	Unopp.
1859	1,019	J.H. Gurney	L	Unopp.
		Lord Stanley	C	Unopp.

KING'S LYNN [95] (Cont.)
(Two Seats)

Election	Electors	Candidate	Party	Votes
1865	852	Lord Stanley	C	445
		Sir T.F. Buxton, Bt.	L	401
		Hon. F. Walpole	C	339
[Appointment of Stanley as Secretary of State for Foreign Affairs]				
1866 (11/7)		Lord Stanley	C	Unopp.
1868	2,514†	Lord Stanley	C	1,265
		Hon. R. Bourke	C	1,125
		Sir T.F. Buxton, Bt.	L	1,012
[Succession of Stanley to the Peerage — Earl of Derby]				
1869 (9/12)	2,514	Lord Claud Hamilton	C	1,051
		R. Young	L	1,032
1874	2,450	Hon. R. Bourke	C	1,163
		Lord Claud Hamilton	C	1,093
		Sir W.H.B. Ffolkes, Bt.	L	999
		E.R. Wodehouse	L	895
1880	2,779	Sir W.H.B. Ffolkes, Bt.	L	1,286
		Rt. Hon. R. Bourke	C	1,257
		Lord Claud Hamilton	C	1,192
		F. Lockwood	L	1,151

Petitions:—

1865: Withdrawn (Buxton only)

1868: Dismissed (Bourke only)

KINGSTON UPON HULL [96]

(Two Seats)

Election	Electors	Candidate	Party	Votes
1832	3,863	M.D. Hill	L	1,674
		W. Hutt	L	1,610
		D. Carruthers	C	1,429
		J. Acland	L	433
1835	4,244	D. Carruthers	C	1,836
		W. Hutt	L	1,536
		M.D. Hill	L	1,371
[Death of Carruthers]				
1835 (20/6)	4,244	T.P. Thompson	L	1,428
		H. St.J. Mildmay	C	1,423
1837	4,222	**W. Wilberforce	C	1,514
		Sir W.C. James, Bt.	C	1,505
		*W. Hutt	L	1,497
		B. Wood	L	1,430
1841	4,862	Sir J. Hanmer, Bt.	C	1,843
		Sir W.C. James, Bt.	C	1,830
		J. Clay	L	1,761
		T.P. Thompson	L	1,645
1847	4,618	M.T. Baines	L	2,168
		J. Clay	L	2,135
		J. Brown	L	1,705
[Appointment of Baines as President of the Poor Law Board]				
1849 (7/2)		M.T. Baines	L	Unopp.
1852	5,221	J. Clay	L	2,246
		Viscount Goderich	L	2,242
		J.B. Moore	C	1,815
		Hon. C.L. Butler	C	1,626
[Election declared void on petition]				
1854 (18/8)	4,572	W.D. Seymour (1)	L	1,820
		W.H. Watson	L	1,806
		S.A. Dickson	C	1,600
[Resignation of Watson on appointment as a Judge of the Court of the Exchequer]				
1857 (11/2)		J. Clay	L	Unopp.
1857	5,494	J. Clay	L	2,365
		Lord Ashley	L	2,303
		Lord William Compton	L	1,392
		W.D. Seymour (2)	L	434

KINGSTON UPON HULL [96] (Cont.)
(Two Seats)

Election	Electors	Candidate	Party	Votes
1859	5,526	J. Clay	L	2,445
		J. Hoare	C	2,269
		J.H. Lewis	L	1,959
[Election of Hoare declared void on petition]				
1859 (20/8)	5,526	J. Somes	C	2,068
		J.H. Lewis	L	1,579
1865	5,566	J. Clay	L	2,583
		C.M. Norwood	L	2,547
		J. Somes	C	1,910
		J. Hoare	C	1,374
1868	17,146†	C.M. Norwood	L	7,282
		J. Clay	L	6,874
		H.J. Atkinson	C	6,383
		R. Baxter	C	5,444
[Death of Clay]				
1873 (24/10)	20,947	J.W. Pease	C	6,873
		E.J. Reed	L	6,594
1874	22,026	C.H. Wilson	L	8,886
		C.M. Norwood	L	8,549
		J.W. Pease	C	7,706
1880	26,193	C.M. Norwood	L	12,071
		C.H. Wilson	L	11,837
		J.B. Pope	C	6,767
		H.J. Atkinson	C	6,067

Petitions:—

1835: (20/6)	Dismissed
1837:	Election of Wilberforce declared void. Hutt duly elected after scrutiny. Petition against James dismissed.
1852:	Void election
1857: (11/2)	Lapsed on Dissolution of Parliament
1859:	Election of Hoare declared void. Petition against Clay withdrawn
1868:	Withdrawn

KNARESBOROUGH [97]

(Two seats until 1868; one seat from 1868)

Election	Electors	Candidate	Party	Votes
1832	278	J. Richards	L	187
		B. Rotch	L	116
		H. Rich	L	96
		A. Lawson	C	76
1835	264	A. Lawson	C	179
		J. Richards	L	134
		H. Rich	L	111
		Sir G.A. Lewin	C	20
1837	271	H. Rich	L	172
		Hon. C. Langdale	L	124
		A. Lawson	C	118
1841	241	A. Lawson	C	150
		W.B. Ferrand	C	122
		C. Sturgeon	L	85
1847	242	W.S.S. Lascelles	L	158
		J.P. Westhead *(J.P.B. Westhead)*	L	128
		A. Lawson	C	114
[Death of Lascelles]				
1851 (12/7)	217	T. Collins	C	95
		A. Lawson	C	64
1852	242	**J.P.B. Westhead	L	113
		*J.D. Dent	L	113
		*B.T. Woodd	C	113
		T. Collins	C	107
1857	270	B.T. Woodd	C	174
		T. Collins	C	138
		R. Campbell	L	100
1859	286	B.T. Woodd	C	173
		T. Collins	C	140
		H.S. Thompson	L	127
1865	272	B.T. Woodd	C	156
		I. Holden	L	127
		T. Collins	C	123
1868	769	A. Illingworth	L	362
		A.S. Lawson	C	347
1874	770	B.T. Woodd	C	397
		Sir A. Fairbairn	L	309
1880	762	Sir H.M.M. Thompson, Bt.	L	357
		B.T. Woodd	C	341

(Two seats until 1868; one seat from 1868)

Election	Electors	Candidate	Party	Votes
[Election declared void on petition]				
1881	758	T. Collins	C	374
(13/5)		C.G.M. Gaskell	L	333
[Death]				
1884	651	R. Gunter	C	319
(10/12)		A. Holden	L	267

Petitions:—

1832: Withdrawn (Rotch only)

1852: Treble return. On scrutiny one vote was struck off Westhead's total and his election declared void. Petitions against Dent and Woodd dismissed

1880: Void election

LANCASTER [98]

(Two Seats)

Election	Electors	Candidate	Party	Votes
1832	1,109	†T. Greene	C	Unopp.
		†P.M. Stewart	L	Unopp.
1835	1,207	T. Greene	C	Unopp.
		P.M. Stewart	L	Unopp.
1837	1,161	T. Greene	C	614
		G. Marton	C	527
		P.M. Stewart	L	453
		W.R. Greg	L	347
1841	1,296	T. Greene	C	699
		G. Marton	C	594
		J. Armstrong	L	572
1847	1,377	S. Gregson	L	724
		T. Greene	C	721
		E.D. Salisbury	C	621
[Election of Gregson declared void on petition]				
1848 (9/3)	1,377	R.B. Armstrong	L	636
		Hon. E.H. Stanley	C	620
1852	1,393	S. Gregson	L	699
		R.B. Armstrong	L	690
		T. Greene	C	509
		J. Ellis	C	432
[Election of Armstrong declared void on petition]				
1853 (12/4)	1,420	T. Greene	C	686
		J. Armstrong	L	554
1857	1,328	S. Gregson	L	827
		W.J. Garnett	C	773
		R. Gladstone	C	537
1859	1,288	W.J. Garnett	C	660
		S. Gregson	L	641
		W.A.F. Saunders	C	509
		E.M. Fenwick	L	459
[Resignation of Garnett]				
1864 (13/4)	1,394	E.M. Fenwick	L	682
		W.A.F. Saunders	C	525
[Death of Gregson]				
1865 (20/2)		H.W. Schneider	L	Unopp.

LANCASTER [98] (Cont.)

(Two Seats)

Election	Electors	Candidate	Party	Votes
1865	1,465	E.M. Fenwick	L	713
		H.W. Schneider	L	687
		E. Lawrence	C	665

Writ suspended. Royal Commission appointed which found proof of extensive bribery and as a result the borough lost its right to return a Member of Parliament and was incorporated into the county constituency of Lancashire, Northern, from the Dissolution.

Petitions:—

1847:	Election of Gregson declared void
1848:	Dismissed
1852:	Election of Armstrong declared void
1853:	Withdrawn
1865:	Void election

LAUNCESTON [99]

Election	Electors	Candidate	Party	Votes
1832	243	†Sir H. Hardinge	C	115
		D. Howell	L	108
1835	323	Sir H. Hardinge	C	163
		D. Howell	L	84
1837	353	Sir H. Hardinge	C	Unopp.
1841	342	Sir H. Hardinge	C	Unopp.
[Appointed Secretary at War]				
1841 (15/9)		Sir H. Hardinge	C	Unopp.
[Resignation on appointment as Governor-General of India]				
1844 (20/5)		W. Bowles	C	Unopp.
1847	369	W. Bowles	C	Unopp.
1852	361	Hon. J.W. Percy	C	Unopp.
1857	438	Hon. J.W. Percy	C	Unopp.
1859	438	T.C. Haliburton	C	Unopp.
1865	371	A.H. Campbell	C	Unopp.
[Resignation]				
1868 (9/4)		H.C. Lopes	C	Unopp.
1868	749	H.C. Lopes	C	Unopp.
1874	790	J.H. Deakin (Senr.)	C	453
		H.C. Drinkwater	L	216
[Election declared void on petition]				
1874 (3/7)	790	J.H. Deakin (Junr.)	C	417
		J. Dingley	L	233
		H.S. Giffard	C	1
[Resignation]				
1877 (3/3)	826	Sir H.S. Giffard	C	392
		R. Collier	L	274

Election	Electors	Candidate	Party	Votes
1880	842	Sir H.S. Giffard	C	439
		R. Collier	L	334

[Resignation on appointment as Lord Chancellor and elevation to the Peerage — Lord Halsbury]

1885	853*	R.E. Webster	C	417
(4/7)		W. Pethick	L	374

Petition:—

1874: Void election

LEEDS [100]

(Two seats until 1868; three seats from 1868)

Election	Electors	Candidate	Party	Votes
1832	4,171	J. Marshall	L	2,012
		†T.B. Macaulay	L	1,984
		†M.T. Sadler	C	1,596
[Resignation of Macaulay on appointment as a Member of the Council of India]				
1834 (17/2)	5,062	E. Baines (Senr.)	L	1,951
		Sir J. Beckett, Bt.	C	1,917
		J. Bower	L	24
1835	4,774	Sir J. Beckett, Bt.	C	1,941
		E. Baines (Senr.)	L	1,803
		W. Brougham	L	1,665
		J.P. Tempest	C	4
1837	5,579	E. Baines (Senr.)	L	2,028
		Sir W. Molesworth, Bt.	L	1,880
		Sir J. Beckett, Bt.	C	1,759
1841	6,316	W. Beckett	C	2,076
		W. Aldam	L	2,043
		J. Hume	L	2,033
		Viscount Jocelyn	C	1,926
1847	6,300	W. Beckett	C	2,529
		J.G. Marshall	L	2,172
		J. Sturge	L	1,978
1852	6,406	Sir G. Goodman	L	2,344
		M.T. Baines	L	2,311
		R. Hall	C	1,132
		T. Sidney	C	1,089
[Appointment of Baines as President of the Poor Law Board]				
1853 (3/1)		M.T. Baines	L	Unopp.
[Appointment of Baines as Chancellor of the Duchy of Lancaster]				
1856 (6/2)		M.T. Baines	L	Unopp.
1857	6,204	M.T. Baines	L	2,329
		R. Hall	C	2,237
		J.R. Mills	L	2,143
[Death of Hall]				
1857 (5/6)	6,204	G.S. Beecroft	C	2,070
		J.R. Mills	L	2,064
1859	5,945	E. Baines (Junr.)	L	2,343
		G.S. Beecroft	C	2,302
		W.E. Forster	L	2,280

LEEDS [100] (Cont.)

(Two seats until 1868; three seats from 1868)

Election	Electors	Candidate	Party	Votes
1865	7,217	G.S. Beecroft	C	3,223
		E. Baines (Junr.)	L	3,045
		Viscount Ambereley	L	2,902
1868	39,244	E. Baines (Junr.)	L	15,941
		R.M. Carter	L	15,105
		W. St.J. Wheelhouse	C	9,437
		Sir A. Fairbairn	L	5,658
		Hon. A. Duncombe	C	5,621
1874	45,991	R.M. Carter	L	15,390
		W.St.J. Wheelhouse	C	14,864
		R. Tennant	C	13,194
		E. Baines (Junr.)	L	11,850
		F.R. Lees	L	5,954
[Resignation of Carter]				
1876 (15/8)	48,313	J. Barran	L	16,672
		W.L. Jackson	C	13,774
1880	49,000	W.E. Gladstone	L	24,622
		J. Barran	L	23,647
		W.L. Jackson	C	13,331
		W.St.J. Wheelhouse	C	11,965
[Gladstone elects to sit for Edinburghshire]				
1880 (10/5)		H.J. Gladstone	L	Unopp.
[Appointment of Gladstone as a Lord Commissioner of the Treasury]				
1881 (24/8)		H.J. Gladstone	L	Unopp.

LEICESTER [101]
(Two Seats)

Election	Electors	Candidate	Party	Votes
1832	3,063	†W. Evans	L	1,663
		†W. Ellis	L	1,527
		J.W.B. Leigh	C	1,266
1835	3,049	E. Goulburn	C	1,484
		T. Gladstone	C	1,475
		W. Evans	L	1,352
		W. Ellis	L	1,314
1837	3,569	S. Duckworth	L	1,816
		J. Easthope	L	1,816
		E. Goulburn	C	1,454
		T. Gladstone	C	1,453
[Resignation of Duckworth on appointment as a Master of the Court of Chancery]				
1839 (22/3)	3,581*	W. Ellis	L	1,666
		C.H. Frewen	C	1,371
1841	3,687*	J. Easthope	L	Unopp.
		W. Ellis	L	Unopp.
1847	4,241	Sir J. Walmsley	L	1,671
		R. Gardner	L	1,621
		J. Parker	C	1,421
[Election declared void on petition]				
1848 (2/9)		J. Ellis	L	Unopp.
		R. Harris	L	Unopp.
1852	3,853	Sir J. Walmsley	L	1,673
		R. Gardner	L	1,673
		J.P. Wilde	L	1,116
		G. Palmer	L	1,114
[Death of Gardner]				
1856 (18/6)		J. Biggs	L	Unopp.
1857	4,162	J.D. Harris	L	1,618
		J. Biggs	L	1,603
		Sir J. Walmsley	L	1,440
1859	4,207	J. Biggs	L	1,584
		J.W. Noble	L	1,496
		W.U. Heygate	C	1,476
		J.D. Harris	L	1,397
[Death of Noble]				
1861 (7/2)	3,965*	W.U. Heygate	C	1,596
		J.D. Harris	L	1,033
		P.A. Taylor	L	977

LEICESTER [101] (Cont.)
(Two Seats)

Election	Electors	Candidate	Party	Votes
[Resignation of Biggs]				
1862 (17/2)		P.A. Taylor	L	Unopp.
1865	4,762	J.D. Harris	L	2,295
		P.A. Taylor	L	2,199
		W.U. Heygate	C	1,945
1868	15,161	P.A. Taylor	L	7,148
		J.D. Harris	L	6,876
		J.B. Greene	L	2,494
1874	17,069	P.A. Taylor	L	7,408
		A. McArthur	L	7,283
		J.H.B. Warner	C	5,615
1880	18,808	P.A. Taylor	L	10,675
		A. McArthur	L	10,438
		W. Winterton	C	4,186
		J.H.B. Warner	C	3,820
[Resignation of Taylor]				
1884 (27/6)		J.A. Picton	L	Unopp.

Petitions:—

1837:	Dismissed
1847:	Void election
1852:	Dismissed

LEOMINSTER [102]
(Two seats until 1868; one seat from 1868)

Election	Electors	Candidate	Party	Votes
1832	779	T. Bish	L	Unopp.
		†Lord Hotham	C	Unopp.
1835	694	T. Bish	L	Unopp.
		Lord Hotham	C	Unopp.
1837	671	Lord Hotham	C	395
		C. Greenaway	L	364
		J. Wigram	C	266
1841	619	C. Greenaway	L	Unopp.
		J. Wigram	C	Unopp.
[Resignation of Wigram on appointment as Vice-Chancellor]				
1842 (8/2)		G. Arkwright	C	Unopp.
[Resignation of Greenaway]				
1845 (26/4)		H. Barkly	C	Unopp.
1847	631	G. Arkwright	C	Unopp.
		H. Barkly	C	Unopp.
[Resignation of Barkly on appointment as Governor of British Guiana]				
1849 (6/2)		F. Peel	C	Unopp.
1852	551	G. Arkwright	C	260
		J.G. Phillimore	L	206
		J.P. Willoughby	C	190
[Death of Arkwright]				
1856 (19/2)	387	G. Hardy	C	179
		J. Campbell	L	101
1857	370	G. Hardy	C	Unopp.
		J.P. Willoughby	C	Unopp.
[Resignation of Willoughby on appointment as a Member of the Council of India]				
1858 (22/10)		Hon. C.S.B. Hanbury	C	Unopp.
1859	392	G. Hardy	C	Unopp.
		Hon. C.S.B. Hanbury (*Lennox*)	C	Unopp.
1865	367	A. Walsh	C	214
		G. Hardy	C	208
		J. Hindmarch	L	137

LEOMINSTER [102] (Cont.)
(Two seats until 1868; one seat from 1868)

Election	Electors	Candidate	Party	Votes
[Hardy elects to sit for Oxford University]				
1866 (26/2)		R. Arkwright	C	Unopp.
[Resignation of Walsh in order to contest Radnorshire]				
1868 (27/4)		Viscount Mahon	C	Unopp.
1868	882	R. Arkwright	C	432
		T. Spinks	L	174
1874	905	R. Arkwright	C	Unopp.
[Resignation]				
1876 (16/2)	927	T. Blake	L	434
		Hon. C.S.B.H.K. Lennox	C	349
1880	900	J. Rankin	C	457
		T. Blake	L	355

Petitions:—

1852: Withdrawn (Phillimore only)

1880: Withdrawn

LEWES [103]
(Two seats until 1868; one seat from 1868)

Election	Electors	Candidate	Party	Votes
1832	878	†Sir C.R. Blunt, Bt.	L	Unopp.
		†T.R. Kemp	L	Unopp.
1835	761	Sir C.R. Blunt, Bt.	L	511
		T.R. Kemp	L	382
		Hon. H. Fitzroy	C	359
[Resignation of Kemp]				
1837 (21/4)	842	Hon. H. Fitzroy	C	397
		J. Easthope	L	371
1837	842	Sir C.R. Blunt, Bt.	L	413
		Hon. H. Fitzroy	C	401
		Hon. T. Brand	L	398
		W. Lyon	C	343
[Death of Blunt]				
1840 (9/3)		Viscount Cantelupe	C	Unopp.
1841	853	**S. Harford	L	411
		H. Elphinstone	L	409
		*Hon. H. Fitzroy	C	407
		Viscount Cantelupe	C	388
[Appointment of Fitzroy as a Civil Lord of the Admiralty]				
1845 (17/2)		Hon. H. Fitzroy	C	Unopp.
[Resignation of Elphinstone]				
1847 (17/3)		R. Perfect	L	Unopp.
1847	866	Hon. H. Fitzroy	C	457
		R. Perfect	L	402
		J.G.B. Hudson	C	207
		Lord Henry Loftus	C	143
1852	713	Hon. H.B.W. Brand	L	Unopp.
		Hon. H. Fitzroy	C	Unopp.
[Appointment of Brand as a Lord Commissioner of the Treasury]				
1855 (5/4)		Hon. H.B.W. Brand	L	Unopp.
1857	724	Hon. H.B.W. Brand	L	Unopp.
		H. Fitzroy	L	Unopp.

LEWES [103] (Cont.)
(Two seats until 1868; one seat from 1868)

Election	Electors	Candidate	Party	Votes
1859	697	H. Fitzroy	L	339
		Hon. H.B.W. Brand	L	338
		R.P. Amphlett	C	200
		Sir C.W. Blunt, Bt.	C	189
[Appointment of Fitzroy as First Commissioner of Works and Public Buildings]				
1859 (27/6)		H. Fitzroy	L	Unopp.
[Death of Fitzroy]				
1860 (16/1)		J.G. Blencowe	L	Unopp.
1865	676	H.B.W. Brand	L	325
		Lord Pelham	L	324
		W.L. Christie	C	292
		Sir A.F.A. Slade, Bt.	C	232
1868	1,350†	Lord Pelham	L	601
		W.L. Christie	C	587
1874	1,430	W.L. Christie	C	772
		A. Cohen	L	500
1880	1,459	W.L. Christie	C	717
		Sir W.J. Codrington	L	580

Petitions:—

1841: Election of Harford declared void. Fitzroy duly elected after scrutiny. Petition against Elphinstone dismissed

1865: Withdrawn

LICHFIELD [104]
(Two seats until 1868; one seat from 1868)

Election	Electors	Candidate	Party	Votes
1832	861	†Sir E.D. Scott, Bt.	L	497
		†Sir G. Anson	L	373
		F. Finch	L	167
1835	695	Sir G. Anson	L	490
		Sir E.D. Scott, Bt.	L	414
		F. Finch	L	232
1837	901	Sir G. Anson	L	Unopp.
		Lord Alfred Paget	L	Unopp.
1841	646	Sir G. Anson	L	381
		Lord Alfred Paget	L	289
		R. Dyott	C	281
[Resignation of Anson]				
1841 (15/9)		Lord Leveson	L	Unopp.
[Succession of Leveson to the Peerage – Earl Granville]				
1846 (31/1)		Hon. E.M.L. Mostyn	L	Unopp.
[Appointment of Paget as Chief Equerry and Clerk Marshal to Her Majesty]				
1846 (15/7)		Lord Alfred Paget	L	Unopp.
1847	947	Viscount Anson	L	Unopp.
		Lord Alfred Paget	L	Unopp.
1852	836	Viscount Anson	L	369
		Lord Alfred Paget	L	320
		R.B. Follett	C	224
[Appointment of Paget as Chief Equerry and Clerk Marshal to Her Majesty]				
1853 (5/1)		Lord Alfred Paget	L	Unopp.
[Succession of Anson to the Peerage – Earl of Lichfield]				
1854 (9/5)		Lord Waterpark	L	Unopp.
[Resignation of Waterpark]				
1856 (30/5)		Viscount Sandon	C	Unopp.
1857	600	Lord Alfred Paget	L	Unopp.
		Viscount Sandon	L	Unopp.

(Two seats until 1868; one seat from 1868)

Election	Electors	Candidate	Party	Votes
1859	737	Hon. A.H.A. Anson	L	Unopp.
		Lord Alfred Paget	L	Unopp.

[Appointment of Paget as Chief Equerry and Clerk Marshal to Her Majesty]

1859 (6/7)		Lord Alfred Paget	L	Unopp.
1865	564	Hon. A.H.A. Anson	L	302
		R. Dyott	C	257
		Lord Alfred Paget	L	209
1868	1,320	R. Dyott	C	525
		Hon. A.H.A. Anson	L	474
1874	1,312	R. Dyott	C	571
		C. Simpson	L	440
1880	1,374	R. Dyott	C	553
		Sir J. Swinburne, Bt.	L	537

[Election delcared void on petition]

1880 (19/7)	1,374	T.J. Levett	C	578
		Sir J. Swinburne, Bt.	L	544

Petitions:—

1841:	Dismissed (Paget only)
1865:	Withdrawn (Dyott only)
1868:	Dismissed
1880:	Void election

LINCOLN [105]

(Two Seats)

Election	Electors	Candidate	Party	Votes
1832	1,043	†G.F. Heneage	L	543
		†E.G.E.L. Bulwer	L	490
		†C.D.W. Sibthorp	C	402
1835	1,124	C.D.W. Sibthorp	C	565
		E.G.E.L. Bulwer	L	406
		Hon. C.B. Phipps	L	335
1837	1,041	C.D.W. Sibthorp	C	514
		E.G.E.L. Bulwer	L	436
		Hon. H. Ellis	C	392
		C.H. Churchill	L	330
1841	1,064*	C.D.W. Sibthorp	C	541
		W.R. Collett	C	481
		Sir E.G.E.L. Bulwer, Bt.	L	443
		C. Seely	L	340
1847	1,271	C.D.W. Sibthorp	C	659
		C. Seely	L	518
		Sir E.G.E.L.B. Lytton, Bt.	L	436
		W.R. Collett	C	278
[Election of Seely declared void on petition]				
1848 (16/3)	1,271	T.B. Hobhouse	L	552
		L.C. Humfrey	C	505
1852	1,363	C.D.W. Sibthorp	C	840
		G.F. Heneage	C	661
		C. Seely	L	478
[Death of Sibthorp]				
1856 (16/1)		G.T.W. Sibthorp	C	Unopp.
1857	1,405	G.T.W. Sibthorp	C	829
		G.F. Heneage	L	641
		J.H. Palmer	L	541
1859	1,435	G.T.W. Sibthorp	C	740
		G.F. Heneage	L	658
		J.H. Palmer	L	629
[Death of Sibthorp]				
1861 (9/11)		C. Seely	L	Unopp.
[Resignation of Heneage]				
1862 (12/2)	1,490	J.B. Moore	C	715
		J.H. Palmer	L	690

(Two Seats)

Election	Electors	Candidate	Party	Votes
1865	1,713	C. Seely	L	878
		E. Heneage	L	870
		J.B. Moore	C	765
1868	4,243	J.H. Palmer	L	Unopp.
		C. Seely	L	Unopp.
1874	4,689	E. Chaplin	C	2,107
		C. Seely	L	1,907
		J.H. Palmer	L	1,784
1880	6,402	C. Seely	L	3,401
		J.H. Palmer	L	3,128
		E. Chaplin	C	2,190
[Death of Palmer]				
1884 (16/6)	6,769	J. Ruston	L	3,234
		R. Hall	C	2,263

Petitions:—

1832 : Dismissed (Bulwer only)

1847: Election of Seely declared void

1865: Withdrawn

LISKEARD [106]

Election	Electors	Candidate	Party	Votes
1832	218	C. Buller	L	Unopp.
1835	216	C. Buller	L	114
		S.T. Kekewich	C	64
1837	248	C. Buller	L	113
		S.T. Kekewich	C	95
1841	296	C. Buller	L	Unopp.
[Appointed Judge-Advocate General]				
1846 (15/7)		C. Buller	L	Unopp.
1847	349	C. Buller	L	170
		W.C. Curteis	C	117
[Appointed President of the Poor Law Board]				
1847 (14/12)		C. Buller	L	Unopp.
[Death]				
1849 (3/1)		R.B. Crowder	L	Unopp.
1852	343	R.B. Crowder	L	Unopp.
[Resignation on appointment as a Judge of the Court of Common Pleas]				
1854 (29/3)	352	R.W. Grey	L	138
		J.S. Trelawny	L	119
		J.H. Reed	L	11
1857	373	R.W. Grey	L	174
		Hon. A.H. Gordon	L	124
1859	395	R.W. Grey	L	164
		W.H.P. Carew	C	160
[Resignation on appointment as a Commissioner of Customs]				
1859 (19/8)		R.B. Osborne	L	Unopp.
[Resignation]				
1865 (21/6)		Sir A.W. Buller	L	Unopp.
1865	434	Sir A.W. Buller	L	Unopp.

Election	Electors	Candidate	Party	Votes
1868	881	Sir A.W. Buller	L	Unopp.
[Death]				
1869 (11/5)	881	E. Horsman	L	368
		Sir F. Lycett	L	285
1874	811	E. Horsman	L	334
		L.H. Courtney	L	329
[Death]				
1876 (22/12)	777	L.H. Courtney	L	388
		J.B. Sterling	C	281
1880	736	L.H. Courtney	L	370
		E.P. Bouverie	L	301

LIVERPOOL [107]
(Two seats until 1868; three seats from 1868)

Election	Electors	Candidate	Party	Votes
1832	11,283	†W. Ewart	L	4,931
		†Viscount Sandon (Senr.)	C	4,260
		T. Thornely	L	4,096
		Sir H. Douglas, Bt.	C	3,249
1835	12,492	Viscount Sandon (Senr.)	C	4,407
		W. Ewart	L	4,075
		Sir H. Douglas, Bt.	C	3,869
		J. Morris	L	3,627
1837	11,179	Viscount Sandon (Senr.)	C	4,786
		C. Cresswell	C	4,652
		W. Ewart	L	4,381
		H. Elphinstone	L	4,206
1841	15,539	Viscount Sandon (Senr.)	C	5,979
		C. Cresswell	C	5,792
		Sir J. Walmsley	L	4,647
		Viscount Palmerston	L	4,431
[Resignation of Cresswell on appointment as a Judge of the Court of Common Pleas]				
1842 (8/2)		Sir H. Douglas, Bt.	C	Unopp.
1847	17,004	E. Cardwell	C	5.581
		Sir T.B. Birch, Bt.	L	4,882
		Sir D. Mackworth, Bt.	C	4,089
		Lord John Manners	C	2,413
1852	17,433	C. Turner	C	6,693
		W.F. Mackenzie	C	6,367
		E. Cardwell	C	5,247
		J.C. Ewart	L	4,910
[Election declared void on petition]				
1853 (9/7)	16,182	T.B. Horsfall	C	6,034
		Hon. H.T. Liddell	C	5,543
		Sir T.E. Perry	L	4,673
		J.B. Moore	C	1,274
[Succession of Liddell to the Peerage — Lord Ravensworth]				
1855 (29/3)	17,795*	J.C. Ewart	L	5,718
		Sir S.G. Bonham, Bt.	C	4,262
1857	18,314	T.B. Horsfall	C	7,566
		J.C. Ewart	L	7,121
		C. Turner	C	6,316
1859	18,779	J.C. Ewart	L	Unopp.
		T.B. Horsfall	C	Unopp.

LIVERPOOL [107] (Cont.)
(Two seats until 1868; three seats from 1868)

Election	Electors	Candidate	Party	Votes
1865	20,618	T.B. Horsfall	C	7,866
		S.R. Graves	C	7,500
		J.C. Ewart	L	7,160
1868	39,645	S.R. Graves	C	16,766
		Viscount Sandon (Junr.)	C	16,222
		W. Rathbone	L	15,337
		W.N. Massey	L	15,017
[Death of Graves]				
1873 (10/2)	52,912	J. Torr	C	18,702
		W.S. Caine	L	16,790
1874	54,952	Viscount Sandon (Junr.)	C	20,206
		J. Torr	C	19,763
		W. Rathbone	L	16,706
		W.S. Caine	L	15,801
		W.S. Simpson	L/Lab	2,435
[Appointment of Sandon as Vice-President of the Committee of the Privy Council for Education]				
1874 (14/3)		Viscount Sandon (Junr.)	C	Unopp.
[Death of Torr]				
1880 (6/2)	63,946	E. Whitley	C	26,106
		Lord Ramsay	L	23,885
1880	63,946	Lord Ramsay	L	Unopp.
		Viscount Sandon (Junr.)	C	Unopp.
		E. Whitley	C	Unopp.
[Succession of Ramsay to the Peerage — Earl of Dalhousie]				
1880 (9/8)	63,946	Lord Claud Hamilton	C	21,019
		S. Plimsoll	L	19,118
[Succession of Sandon to the Peerage — Earl of Harrowby]				
1882 (11/12)	62,039	S. Smith	L	18,198
		A.B. Forwood	C	17,889

Petitions:—

1852: Void election

1853: Withdrawn

LUDLOW [108]

(Two seats until 1868; one seat from 1868)

Election	Electors	Candidate	Party	Votes
1832	359	†Viscount Clive	C	198
		E. Romilly	L	185
		†Hon. R.H. Clive	C	169
		W. Davies	L	115
1835	360	Viscount Clive	C	234
		E.L. Charlton	C	159
		E. Romilly	L	154
1837	375	Viscount Clive	C	193
		H. Salwey	L	188
		T. Alcock	L	158
[Succession of Clive to the Peerage — Earl of Powis]				
1839 (6/6)	404	T. Alcock	L	186
		H. Clive	C	182
[Election declared void on petition]				
1840 (23/5)	422	B. Botfield	C	194
		G.G. de H. Larpent	L	160
1841	415	B. Botfield	C	222
		J. Ackers	C	219
		H. Salwey	L	156
1847	452	H.B. Clive	C	207
		H. Salwey	L	206
		B. Botfield	C	183
1852	450	R. Clive	C	250
		Lord William Powlett	C	214
		H. Salwey	L	157
[Resignation of Clive in order to contest Shropshire, Southern]				
1854 (7/2)		Hon. P.E. Herbert	C	Unopp.
1857	407	B. Botfield	C	Unopp.
		Hon. P.E. Herbert	C	Unopp.
1859	394	B. Botfield	C	Unopp.
		Hon. P.E. Herbert	C	Unopp.
[Resignation of Herbert]				
1860 (4/9)		Hon. G.H.W.W. Clive	C	Unopp.
[Death of Botfield]				
1863 (28/8)		Sir W.A. Fraser, Bt.	C	Unopp.

LUDLOW [108] (Cont.)

(Two seats until 1868; one seat from 1868)

Election	Electors	Candidate	Party	Votes
1865	400	Hon. G.H.W.W. Clive	C	236
		J.E. Severne	C	209
		Sir W. Yardley	L	137
1868	789	Hon. G.H.W.W. Clive	C	428
		Sir W. Yardley	L	170
1874	840	Hon. G.H.W.W. Clive	C	Unopp.
1880	989	Hon. G.H.W.W. Clive	C	525
		E.L. Glyn	L	343

Petition:—

1839: Void election

LYME REGIS [109]

Election	Electors	Candidate	Party	Votes
1832	222	W. Pinney	L	79
		Lord Burghersh	C	60
		J. Melville	L	44
1835	250	W. Pinney	L	Unopp.
1837	243	W. Pinney	L	121
		R. Hampden	C	87
1841	277	**W. Pinney	L	123
		*T. Hussey	C	110
1847	326	T.N. Abdy	L	146
		Sir F. Kelly	C	143
1852	309	W. Pinney	L	145
		Sir P. Hornby	C	126
1857	263	W. Pinney	L	144
		Sir T.G. Hesketh, Bt.	C	53
1859	264	W. Pinney	L	116
		J.W. Treeby	C	115
1865	250	J.W. Treeby	C	116
		J.C. Hawkshaw	L	107

This constituency ceased to return a Member of Parliament in 1868 and was incorporated into the county constituency of Dorset.

Petitions:—

1841: Election of Pinney declared void. Hussey duly elected after scrutiny

1847: Dismissed

1859: Withdrawn

LYMINGTON [110]

(Two seats until 1868; one seat from 1868)

Election	Electors	Candidate	Party	Votes
1832	249	Sir H.B. Neale, Bt.	C	158
		J. Stewart	C	128
		J. Blakiston	L	77
1835	294	W.A. Mackinnon (Senr.)	C	Unopp.
		J. Stewart	C	Unopp.
1837	296	J. Stewart	C	161
		W.A. Mackinnon (Senr.)	C	138
		S. Gregson	L	97
1841	307	J. Stewart	C	170
		W.A. Mackinnon (Senr.)	C	149
		Hon. G.T. Keppel	L	106
1847	318	Hon. G.T. Keppel	L	162
		W.A. Mackinnon (Senr.)	C	146
		J. Stewart	C	120
[Resignation of Keppel]				
1850 (30/4)	287	E.J. Hutchins	L	121
		A. Stewart	C	103
1852	338	Sir J.R. Carnac, Bt.	C	201
		E.J. Hutchins	L	158
		W.A. Mackinnon (Senr.)	L	139
1857	323	W.A. Mackinnon (Junr.)	L	194
		Sir J.R. Carnac, Bt.	C	187
		W. Peacocke	C	83
		P.F.C. Johnstone	L	11
1859	326	W.A. Mackinnon (Junr.)	L	157
		Sir J.R. Carnac, Bt.	C	140
		J.B. Moore	C	125
[Resignation of Carnac]				
1860 (24/5)	330	Lord George Gordon-Lennox	C	147
		H.R. Grenfell	L	123
1865	347	W.A. Mackinnon (Junr.)	L	192
		Lord George Gordon-Lennox	C	174
		T. Norton	L	25
1868	662	Lord George Gordon-Lennox	C	330
		D. Pratt	L	199
1874	714	E.H. Kennard	C	449
		W.C. West	L	158

LYMINGTON [110] (Cont.)
(Two seats until 1868; one seat from 1868)

Election	Electors	Candidate	Party	Votes
1880	778	E.H. Kennard	C	432
		H.S. Smith	L	239

Petition:—

1857: Withdrawn (Mackinnon only)

MACCLESFIELD [111]

(Two Seats)

Election	Electors	Candidate	Party	Votes
1832	718	J. Ryle	C	433
		J. Brocklehurst	L	402
		T. Grimsditch	C	186
1835	895	J. Ryle	C	464
		J. Brocklehurst	L	424
		T. Grimsditch	C	342
1837	975	J. Brocklehurst	L	546
		T. Grimsditch	C	471
		R.H. Greg	L	292
1841	894	J. Brocklehurst	L	534
		T. Grimsditch	C	410
		S. Stocks	L	327
1847	946	J. Brocklehurst	L	598
		J. Williams	L	500
		T. Grimsditch	C	428
1852	1,058	J. Brocklehurst	L	628
		E.C. Egerton	C	530
		J. Williams	L	468
1857	1,106	J. Brocklehurst	L	637
		E.C. Egerton	C	556
		T. Huggins	L	9
1859	1,073	J. Brocklehurst	L	Unopp.
		E.C. Egerton	C	Unopp.
1865	943	E.C. Egerton	C	471
		J. Brocklehurst	L	469
		D. Chadwick	L	421
1868	4,737†	W.C. Brocklehurst	L	2,812
		D. Chadwick	L	2,509
		W.M. Eaton	C	2,321
1874	6,224	W.C. Brocklehurst	L	3,173
		D. Chadwick	L	2,792
		W.M. Eaton	C	2,750
		J. Croston	C	2,250
1880	5,304	W.C. Brocklehurst	L	2,946
		D. Chadwick	L	2,744
		W.M. Eaton	C	2,678
		J.C. Whitehorne	C	2,188

Writ suspended. Royal Commission appointed which found proof of extensive bribery and as a result the borough lost its right to return a Member of Parliament and was incorporated into the county constituency of Cheshire, Eastern, from June 25, 1885.

Petition:— 1880: Void election

MAIDSTONE [112]
(Two Seats)

Election	Electors	Candidate	Party	Votes
1832	1,108	†A.W. Robarts	L	500
		†C.J. Barnett	L	469
		W. Lewis	C	422
1835	1,234	W. Lewis	C	529
		A.W. Robarts	L	398
		C.J. Barnett	L	333
		M.P. Lucas	C	5
		E. Hildyard	C	3
1837	1,399	W. Lewis	C	782
		B. Disraeli	C	668
		T.P. Thompson	L	559
		T.E. Perry	L	25
[Death of Lewis]				
1838 (28/3)	1,484	J.M. Fector	C	708
		A.W. Robarts	L	583
[Election declared void on petition]				
1838 (15/6)	1,484	J.M. Fector	C	707
		A.W. Robarts	L	512
1841	1,660	A.J.B. Hope	C	765
		G. Dodd	C	725
		D. Salomons	L	418
1847	1,741	G. Dodd	C	Unopp.
		A.J.B. Hope	C	Unopp.
1852	1,751	J. Whatman	L	848
		G. Dodd	C	709
		W. Lee	L	584
[Election of Dodd delcared void on petition]				
1853 (16/5)	1,814	W. Lee	L	748
		C.W. Martin	L	738
1857	1,611	A.J.B.B. Hope	C	801
		E. Scott	C	759
		W. Lee	L	689
		H.F. St. J. Mildmay	L	655
1859	1,848	W. Lee	L	776
		C. Buxton	L	776
		J. Wardlaw	C	751
		E.V. Harcourt	C	749
1865	1,817	W. Lee	L	869
		J. Whatman	L	867
		E.L. Betts	C	838
		J. Wardlaw	C	801

MAIDSTONE [112] (Cont.)
(Two Seats)

Election	Electors	Candidate	Party	Votes
1868	3,420	W. Lee	L	1,569
		J. Whatman	L	1,546
		W.F. White	C	1,412
		G. Parbury	C	1,369
1870 (25/2)	3,214*	Sir J. Lubbock, Bt.	L	1,504
		W.F. White	C	1,402
1874	3,517	Sir J. Lubbock, Bt.	L	1,558
		Sir S.H. Waterlow, Bt.	L	1,491
		A.H. Ross	C	1,414
		Hon. J.C. Stanley	C	1,365
1880	3,878	A.H. Ross	C	1,965
		J.E.E. Aylmer	C	1,832
		Sir J. Lubbock, Bt.	L	1,725
		Sir S.H. Waterlow, Bt.	L	1,624

Petitions:—

1838: (28/3)	Void election
1838: (15/6)	Dismissed
1852:	Election of Dodd declared void. Petition against Whatman withdrawn
1857:	Dismissed
1859:	Dismissed
1865:	Dismissed

MALDON [113]

(Two seats until 1868; one seat from 1868)

Election	Electors	Candidate	Party	Votes
1832	716	†T.B. Lennard	L	448
		†Q. Dick	C	416
		P.L. Wright	L	277
1835	789	Q. Dick	C	441
		T.B. Lennard	L	407
		H. St.J. Mildmay	C	356
1837	876	Q. Dick	C	420
		J. Round	C	407
		T.B. Lennard	L	395
1841	855	Q. Dick	C	472
		J. Round	C	446
		T.N. Abdy	L	413
1847	951	D. Waddington	C	461
		T.B. Lennard	L	443
		Q. Dick	C	427
1852	845	C. Du Cane	C	370
		T.J. Miller	C	357
		T.B. Lennard	L	351
		Q. Dick	C	330
[Election declared void on petition]				
1854 (17/8)	968	G.M.W. Peacocke	C	406
		J.B. Moore	C	399
		T.B. Lennard	L	335
		T. McEnteer	L	217
		Q. Dick	C	34
1857	879	T.S. Western	L	427
		J.B. Moore	C	405
		G.M.W. Peacocke	C	360
1859	1,071	G.M.W. Peacocke	C	503
		T.S. Western	L	431
		A.W.H. Meyrick	C	427
1865	859	G.M.W. Peacocke *(Sandford)*	C	461
		R.A. Earle	C	420
		T.S. Western	L	394
1868	1,397	E.H. Bentall	L	657
		G.M.W. Sandford	C	504
1874	1,522	G.M.W. Sandford	C	632
		Sir J. Bennett	L	519

MALDON [113] (Cont.)

(Two seats until 1868; one seat from 1868)

Election	Electors	Candidate	Party	Votes
[Resignation]				
1878 (12/12)	1,534	G. Courtauld	L	671
		Sir W.N. Abdy, Bt.	C	530
1880	1,564	G. Courtauld	L	679
		Sir W.N. Abdy, Bt.	C	651

Petitions:—

1837: Dismissed (Round only)

1847: Withdrawn (Lennard only)

1852: Void election

1857: Dismissed

MALMESBURY [114]

Election	Electors	Candidate	Party	Votes
1832	291	Viscount Andover, Senr.	L	Unopp.
1835	292	Viscount Andover, Senr.	L	Unopp.
1837	260	Viscount Andover, Senr.	L	112
		I. Salter	C	95
1841	315	Hon. J.K. Howard	L	125
		L.A. Burton	C	105
1847	320	Hon. J.K. Howard	L	Unopp.
1852	309	T. Luce	L	137
		P.A. Lovell	C	128
1857	315	T. Luce	L	Unopp.
1859	343	Viscount Andover, Junr.	L	Unopp.
1865	329	Viscount Andover, Junr.	L	157
		J.G. Talbot	C	136
1868	785	W. Powell	C	337
		Viscount Andover, Junr	L	314
1874	1,053	W. Powell	C	Unopp.
1880	1,079	W. Powell	C	602
		A.G. Kitching	L	310
[Death]				
1882 (8/3)	1,066	C.W. Miles	C	491
		C.R. Luce	L	435

MALTON [115]
(Two seats until 1868; one seat from 1868)

Election	Electors	Candidate	Party	Votes
1832	667	Hon. W.C.W. Fitzwilliam *(Viscount Milton)*	L	Unopp.
		†C.C. Pepys	L	Unopp.

[Resignation of Milton in order to contest Northamptonshire, Northern]

1833 (8/3)		J.C. Ramsden	L	Unopp.

[Appointment of Pepys as Solicitor-General]

1834 (4/3)		Sir C.C. Pepys	L	Unopp.

1835	616	Sir C.C. Pepys	L	Unopp.
		J.C. Ramsden	L	Unopp.

[Appointment of Pepys as First Lord Commissioner for the Custody of the Great Seal]

1835 (19/5)		Sir C.C. Pepys	L	Unopp.

[Resignation of Pepys on appointment as Lord Chancellor and elevation to the Peerage — Lord Cottenham]

1836 (12/2)		J.W. Childers	L	Unopp.

[Death of Ramsden]

1837 (27/1)		Viscount Milton	L	Unopp.

1837	603	J.W. Childers	L	Unopp.
		Viscount Milton	L	Unopp.

1841	572	J.W. Childers	L	Unopp.
		J.E. Denison	L	Unopp.

[Resignation of Childers]

1846 (15/4)		Viscount Milton	L	Unopp.

1847	535	J.W. Childers	L	Unopp.
		J.E. Denison	L	Unopp.

1852	539	J.E. Denison	L	Unopp.
		Hon. C.W.W. Fitzwilliam	L	Unopp.

1857	594	J. Brown	L	Unopp.
		Hon. C.W.W. Fitzwilliam	L	Unopp.

1859	595	J. Brown	L	Unopp.
		Hon. C.W.W. Fitzwilliam	L	Unopp.

MALTON [115] (Cont.)

(Two seats until 1868; one seat from 1868)

Election	Electors	Candidate	Party	Votes
1865	600	J. Brown	L	Unopp.
		Hon. C.W.W. Fitzwilliam	L	Unopp.
1868	1,218	Hon. C.W.W. Fitzwilliam	L	Unopp.
1874	1,240	Hon. C.W.W. Fitzwilliam	L	603
		R.H. Bower	C	474
1880	1,379	Hon. C.W.W. Fitzwilliam	L	809
		Sir W.C. Worsley, Bt.	C	445

MANCHESTER [116]

(Two seats until 1868; three seats from 1868)

Election	Electors	Candidate	Party	Votes
1832	6,726	M. Phillps	L	2,923
		†C.P. Thomson	L	2,068
		S.J. Loyd	L	1,832
		†J.T. Hope	C	1,560
		W. Cobbett	L	1,305
1835	8,432	C.P. Thomson	L	3,355
		M. Philips	L	3,163
		B. Braidley	C	2,535
		Sir C. Wolseley, Bt.	L	583
[Appointment of Thomson as President of the Board of Trade]				
1835 (30/4)	8,432	C.P. Thomson	L	3,205
		B. Braidley	C	1,839
1837	11,185	C.P. Thomson	L	4,158
		M. Philips	L	3,759
		W.E. Gladstone	C	2,224
[Resignation of Thomson on appointment as Governor-General of Canada]				
1839 (7/9)	11,185*	R.H. Greg	L	3,421
		Sir G. Murray	C	3,156
1841	10,818	M. Philips	L	3,695
		T.M. Gibson	L	3,575
		Sir G. Murray	C	3,115
		W. Entwisle	C	2,692
[Appointment of Gibson as Vice-President of the Board of Trade]				
1846 (13/7)		T.M. Gibson	L	Unopp.
1847	12,841	J. Bright (1)	L	Unopp.
		T.M. Gibson	L	Unopp.
1852	13,921	T.M. Gibson	L	5,762
		J. Bright (1)	L	5,475
		G. Loch	L	4,364
		Hon. J. Denman	L	3,969
1857	18,044	Sir J. Potter	L	8,368
		J.A. Turner	L	7,854
		T.M. Gibson	L	5,588
		J. Bright (1)	L	5,458
[Death of Potter]				
1858 (17/11)		T. Bazley	L	Unopp.

MANCHESTER [116] (Cont.)
(Two seats until 1868; three seats from 1868)

Election	Electors	Candidate	Party	Votes
1859	18,334	T. Bazley	L	7,545
		J.A. Turner	L	7,300
		A. Heywood	L	5,448
		Hon. J. Denman	L	5,201
1865	21,542	T. Bazley	L	7,909
		E. James	L	6,698
		J. Bright (2)	L	5,562
		A. Heywood	L	4,242
[Death of James]				
1867 (27/11)	21,542*	J. Bright (2)	L	8,160
		J.M. Bennett	C	6,420
		M. Henry	L	643
1868	48,256	H. Birley	C	15,486
		T. Bazley	L	14,192
		J. Bright (2)	L	13,514
		J. Hoare	C	12,684
		E.C. Jones	L	10,662
		M. Henry	L	5,236
1874	60,222	H. Birley	C	19,984
		W.R. Callender	C	19,649
		Sir T. Bazley, Bt.	L	19,325
		J. Bright (2)	L	18,727
[Death of Callender]				
1876 (19/2)	62,074	J. Bright (2)	L	22,770
		F.S. Powell	C	20,985
1880	61,234	J. Slagg	L	24,959
		J. Bright (2)	L	24,789
		H. Birley	C	20,594
		W.H. Houldsworth	C	20,268
[Death of Birley]				
1883 (6/10)	52,831	W.H. Houldsworth	C	18,188
		R.M. Pankhurst	L	6,216

Petition:—

1868: Dismissed (Birley only)

MARLBOROUGH [117]

(Two seats until 1868; one seat from 1868)

Election	Electors	Candidate	Party	Votes
1832	240	Lord Ernest Bruce	C	135
		†H.B. Baring	C	118
		Sir A.C. Malet, Bt.	L	73
1835	280	H.B. Baring	C	Unopp.
		Lord Ernest Bruce	C	Unopp.
1837	280	H.B. Baring	C	Unopp.
		Lord Ernest Bruce	C	Unopp.
1841	282	H.B. Baring	C	Unopp.
		Lord Ernest Bruce	C	Unopp.

[Appointments of Baring as a Lord Commissioner of the Treasury and of Bruce as Vice-Chamberlain of H.M. Household]

Election	Electors	Candidate	Party	Votes
1841 (14/9)		H.B. Baring	C	Unopp.
		Lord Ernest Bruce	C	Unopp.
1847	262	H.B. Baring	C	Unopp.
		Lord Ernest Bruce	C	Unopp.
1852	271	H.B. Baring	C	Unopp.
		Lord Ernest Bruce	C	Unopp.

[Appointment of Bruce as Vice-Chamberlain of H.M. Household]

Election	Electors	Candidate	Party	Votes
1853 (4/1)		Lord Ernest Bruce	L	Unopp.
1857	242	Lord Ernest Bruce	L	184
		H.B. Baring	L	125
		W.D. Lewis	C	51
1859	281	H.B. Baring	L	Unopp.
		Lord Ernest Bruce	L	Unopp.
1865	275	H.B. Baring	L	Unopp.
		Lord Ernest Bruce	L	Unopp.
1868	616	Lord Ernest Bruce	L	Unopp.
1874	659	Lord Ernest Bruce	L	Unopp.

[Succession to the Peerage — Marquess of Ailesbury]

Election	Electors	Candidate	Party	Votes
1878 (31/1)		Lord Charles Bruce	L	Unopp.

MARLBOROUGH [117] (Cont.)
(Two seats until 1868; one seat from 1868)

Election	Electors	Candidate	Party	Votes
1880	668	Lord Charles Bruce	L	333
		Lord Henry Bruce	C	239

[Appointed Vice-Chamberlain of H.M. Household]

1880 (8/5)		Lord Charles Bruce	L	Unopp.

Petition:—

1857: Dismissed (Baring only)

MIDDLESBROUGH [118]

Election	Electors	Candidate	Party	Votes
1868	5,196	H.W.F. Bolckow	L	Unopp.
1874	8,862	H.W.F. Bolckow	L	3,719
		J. Kane	L/Lab	1,541
		W.R.J. Hopkins	C	996
[Death]				
1878	11,824	I. Wilson	L	5,307
(5/7)		S.A. Sadler	C	2,415
1880	10,641	I. Wilson	L	4,515
		S.A. Sadler	C	1,626
		E.D. Lewis	L/Lab	1,171

MIDHURST [119]

Election	Electors	Candidate	Party	Votes
1832	252	†Hon. F. Spencer	L	Unopp.
1835	246	W.S. Poyntz	L	Unopp.
1837	248	W.S. Poyntz	L	Unopp.
[Resignation]				
1837 (12/12)		Hon. F. Spencer	L	Unopp.
1841	289	Sir H.B. Seymour	C	Unopp.
[Resignation in order to contest Antrim]				
1846 (30/1)		S.H. Walpole	C	Unopp.
1847	304	S.H. Walpole	C	Unopp.
[Appointed Secretary of State for the Home Department]				
1852 (5/3)		S.H. Walpole	C	Unopp.
1852	279	S.H. Walpole	C	Unopp.
[Resignation]				
1856 (7/2)		S. Warren	C	Unopp.
1857	411	S. Warren	C	Unopp.
[Resignation on appointment as a Master in Lunacy]				
1859 (3/3)		J. Hardy	C	Unopp.
1859	429	W.T. Mitford	C	Unopp.
1865	309	W.T. Mitford	C	Unopp.
1868	1,007	W.T. Mitford	C	375
		D.A. Lange	L	262
1874	1,009	C.G.J. Perceval	C	530
		W.T. Mitford	C	185
		J.P. Murrough	L	60

Election	Electors	Candidate	Party	Votes
[Succession to the Peerage — Earl of Egmont]				
1874 (23/9)		Sir H.T. Holland, Bt.	C	Unopp.
1880	1,042	Sir H.T. Holland, Bt.	C	501
		C.W. Wallis	L	283

MORPETH [120]

Election	Electors	Candidate	Party	Votes
1832	321	Hon. F.G. Howard	L	Unopp.
[Death]				
1833 (31/12)		Hon. E.G.G. Howard	L	Unopp.
1835	336	Hon. E.G.G. Howard	L	Unopp.
[Resignation]				
1837 (8/2)		Lord Leveson	L	Unopp.
1837	360	Lord Leveson	L	Unopp.
[Resignation]				
1840 (22/2)		Hon. E.G.G. Howard	L	Unopp.
1841	392	Hon. E.G.G. Howard	L	Unopp.
1847	440	Hon. E.G.G. Howard	L	Unopp.
1852	415	Hon. E.G.G. Howard	L	Unopp.
[Resignation]				
1853 (1/1)		Sir G. Grey, Bt.	L	Unopp.
[Appointed Secretary of State for the Colonies]				
1854 (17/6)		Sir G. Grey, Bt.	L	Unopp.
1857	391	Sir G. Grey, Bt.	L	Unopp.
1859	408	Sir G. Grey, Bt.	L	Unopp.
[Appointed Chancellor of the Duchy of Lancaster]				
1859 (27/6)		Sir G. Grey, Bt.	L	Unopp.
[Appointed Secretary of State for the Home Department]				
1861 (31/7)		Sir G. Grey, Bt.	L	Unopp.
1865	448	Sir G. Grey, Bt.	L	Unopp.

Election	Electors	Candidate	Party	Votes
1868	2,006†	Sir G. Grey, Bt.	L	Unopp.
1874	4,912	T. Burt	L/Lab	3,332
		F. Duncan	C	585
1880	5,458	T. Burt	L/Lab	Unopp.

NEWARK-ON-TRENT [121]
(Two Seats)

Election	Electors	Candidate	Party	Votes
1832	1,575	W.E. Gladstone	C	887
		†W.F. Handley	C	798
		T. Wilde	L	726
1835	1,273	W.E. Gladstone	C	Unopp.
		T. Wilde	L	Unopp.
1837	1,221	W.E. Gladstone	C	Unopp.
		T. Wilde	L	Unopp.
[Appointment of Wilde as Solicitor-General]				
1840 (25/1)	1,130	T. Wilde	L	541
		F. Thesiger	C	532
1841	1,116	W.E. Gladstone	C	633
		Lord John Manners	C	630
		T.B. Hobhouse	L	394
[Appointment of Gladstone as Vice-President of the Board of Trade and Master of the Mint]				
1841 (14/9)		W.E. Gladstone	C	Unopp.
[Appointment of Gladstone as Secretary of State for War and the Colonies]				
1846 (29/1)		J. Stuart	C	Unopp.
1847	951	J.H.M. Sutton	C	614
		J. Stuart	C	487
		G.H. Packe	C	443
1852	867	G.E.H. Vernon	C	545
		J.H.M. Sutton	C	479
		M.M. Turner	L	362
1857	763	J. Handley	L	Unopp.
		Earl of Lincoln	L	Unopp.
1859	763	G. Hodgkinson	L	489
		J. Handley	L	435
		Earl of Lincoln	L	416
1865	710	Lord Arthur Clinton	L	Unopp.
		G. Hodgkinson	L	Unopp.
1868	1,803	G. Hodgkinson	L	1,089
		E. Denison	L	1,017
		P.H. Handley	L	826

(Two Seats)

Election	Electors	Candidate	Party	Votes
[Death of Denison]				
1870 (1/4)	1,803*	S.B. Bristowe	L	827
		W.C. Sleigh	C	653
		Sir G. Grey	L	52
1874	1,974	T. Earp	L	973
		S.B. Bristowe	L	912
		E. Field	C	824
		H. Eyre	C	813
1880	2,297	T. Earp	L	1,073
		W.N. Nicholson	C	993
		Hon. M.E.G.F. Hatton	C	985
		S.B. Bristowe	L	982

Note:—

1846: Gladstone, a supporter of Sir Robert Peel, decided not to seek re-election due to opposition from the Duke of Newcastle who had considerable influence in the constituency.

NEWCASTLE-UNDER-LYME [122]
(Two Seats)

Election	Electors	Candidate	Party	Votes
1832	973	†W.H. Miller	C	607
		†Sir H.P. Willoughby, Bt.	C	587
		†E. Peel	C	478
1835	987	E. Peel	C	689
		W.H. Miller	C	494
		Sir H.P. Willoughby, Bt.	C	397
1837	991	W.H. Miller	C	669
		S.H. De Horsey	C	635
		R. Badnall	L	292
1841	1,038	E. Buckley (1)	C	721
		J.Q. Harris	L	565
		W.H. Miller	C	417
[Election of Harris declared void on petition]				
1842 (14/6)	1,038*	**J.Q. Harris	L	499
		*J.C. Colquhoun	C	479
1847	1,074	S. Christy	C	571
		W. Jackson	L	565
		Viscount Brackley	C	522
		W. Greig	L	101
[Christy seeks re-election]				
1847 (15/12)	1,074	S. Christy	C	546
		T. Ross	L	367
1852	1,090	W. Jackson	L	622
		S. Christy	C	585
		T. Ross	L	252
1857	997	S. Christy	C	654
		W. Jackson	L	413
		J. Riley	L	113
1859	994	W. Jackson	L	Unopp.
		W. Murray	C	Unopp.
1865	1,077	W.S. Allen	L	520
		E. Buckley (2)	C	494
		J.A. Wise	L	166
1868	2,849	E. Buckley (2)	C	1,423
		W.S. Allen	L	1,081
		H.T. Salmon	L	744

NEWCASTLE-UNDER-LYME [122] (Cont.)

(Two Seats)

Election	Electors	Candidate	Party	Votes
1874	2,999	Sir E. Buckley, Bt.	C	1,173
		W.S. Allen	L	1,116
		H.T. Davenport	C	1,037
[Resignation of Buckley]				
1878 (26/8)	3,396	S.R. Edge	L	1,330
		C.D. Hudson	C	990
1880	3,235	C.D. Hudson	C	1,484
		W.S. Allen	L	1,252
		S.R. Edge	L	1,175

Petitions:—

1837: Dismissed (Miller only)

1841: Election of Harris declared void

1842: Election of Harris declared void owing to disqualification. Colquhoun duly elected

1847: Withdrawn (Jackson only)

1857: Withdrawn

Note:—

1847 (15/12) Christy resigned and then sought re-election in order to forestall the possibility of an election petition being brought against him. At the time of the General Election he had held a Government contract which was a disqualification from being elected.

NEWCASTLE UPON TYNE [123]
(Two Seats)

Election	Electors	Candidate	Party	Votes
1832	3,905	†Sir M.W. Ridley, Bt.	L	2,112
		†J. Hodgson	C	1,686
		C.M. Attwood	L	1,092
1835	4,054	W. Ord	L	1,843
		Sir M.W. Ridley, Bt.	L	1,499
		J. Hodgson	C	1,254
		J. Aytoun	L	988
[Death of Ridley]				
1836 (27/7)	4,110	J. Hodgson *(Hinde)*	C	1,576
		C. Blackett	L	1,528
1837	4,582	W. Ord	L	1,792
		J.H. Hinde	C	1,701
		C.J. Bigge	L	1,187
		J.B. Coulson	C	1,127
		A.H. Beaumont	Ch	290
1841	5,124	J.H. Hinde	C	Unopp.
		W. Ord	L	Unopp.
1847	5,245	W. Ord	L	2,196
		T.E. Headlam	L	2,068
		R. Hodgson	C	1,680
1852	5,269	J.F.B. Blackett	L	2,418
		T.E. Headlam	L	2,172
		W.H. Watson	L	1,795
[Resignation of Blackett]				
1856 (5/2)		G. Ridley	L	Unopp.
1857	5,962	G. Ridley	L	2,445
		T.E. Headlam	L	2,133
		P. Carstairs	C	1,673
1859	6,008	T.E. Headlam	L	2,688
		G. Ridley	L	2,679
		P.A. Taylor	L	462
[Appointment of Headlam as Judge-Advocate General]				
1859 (28/6)	6,008	T.E. Headlam	L	2,153
		W. Cuthbert	C	1,086
[Resignation of Ridley on appointment as a Copyhold, Inclosure, and Tithe Commissioner]				
1860 (7/12)	5,475*	S.A. Beaumont	L	2,346
		P. Carstairs	L	1,500

NEWCASTLE UPON TYNE [123] (Cont.)
(Two Seats)

Election	Electors	Candidate	Party	Votes
1865	6,630	J. Cowen	L	2,941
		T.E. Headlam	L	2,477
		S.A. Beaumont	L	2,060
1868	18,557	J. Cowen	L	7,057
		T.E. Headlam	L	6,674
		C.F. Hamond	C	2,725
[Death of Cowen]				
1874 (17/1)	21,407	J. Cowen	L	7,356
		C.F. Hamond	C	6,353
1874	21,407	J. Cowen	L	8,464
		C.F. Hamond	C	6,479
		T.E. Headlam	L	5,807
1880	23,800	J. Cowen	L	11,766
		A.W. Dilke	L	10,404
		C.F. Hamond	C	5,271
[Resignation of Dilke]				
1883 (26/2)	26,305	J. Morley	L	9,443
		G. Bruce	C	7,187

NEWPORT [124]

(Two seats until 1868; one seat from 1868)

Election	Electors	Candidate	Party	Votes
1832	421	†J.H. Hawkins	L	216
		W.H. Ord	L	216
		Sir J.W. Gordon, Bt.	C	161
1835	500	W.H. Ord	L	233
		J.H. Hawkins	L	230
		Sir J.W. Gordon, Bt.	C	229
		W.J. Hamilton	C	205
[Appointment of Ord as a Lord Commissioner of the Treasury]				
1835 (27/4)		W.H. Ord	L	Unopp.
1837	633	J.H. Hawkins	L	265
		W.J. Blake	L	263
		C.W. Martin	C	244
		W.J. Hamilton	C	236
1841	750	C.W. Martin	C	254
		W.J. Hamilton	C	252
		T. Gisborne	L	229
		W.J. Blake	L	226
1847	646	W.H.C. Plowden	C	262
		C.W. Martin	C	252
		W.J. Blake	L	250
		C. Crompton	L	238
1852	707	W. Biggs	L	310
		W.N. Massey	L	306
		C.W. Martin	C	257
		W.H.C. Plowden	C	257
[Resignation of Biggs]				
1857 (11/2)	654	R.W. Kennard	C	289
		C. Seely	L	243
1857	654	C.E. Mangles	L	305
		C. Buxton	L	294
		R.W. Kennard	C	283
		W.A. Rose	C	257
1859	647	R.W. Kennard	C	319
		P.L. Powys	C	312
		R. Charles	L	228
1865	643	C.W. Martin	L	309
		R.W. Kennard	C	307
		Hon. A.E.W.M. Herbert	C	230
1868	965†	C.W. Martin	L	Unopp.

(Two seats until 1868; one seat from 1868)

Election	Electors	Candidate	Party	Votes
[Death]				
1870 (23/11)	965*	C.C. Clifford	L	437
		H.M. Kennard	C	351
1874	1,166	C.C. Clifford	L	522
		H.R. Twyford	C	475
1880	1,362	C.C. Clifford	L	618
		H.R. Twyford	C	560

Petitions:—

1841: Withdrawn

1857: (11/2) Lapsed on Dissolution of Parliament

1857: Withdrawn

NORTHALLERTON [125]

Election	Electors	Candidate	Party	Votes
1832	232	J.G. Boss	L	108
		†W.B. Wrightson	L	97
1835	261	W.B. Wrightson	L	Unopp.
1837	278	W.B. Wrightson	L	Unopp.
1841	281	W.B. Wrightson	L	129
		Hon. E. Lascelles	C	114
1847	269	W.B. Wrightson	L	Unopp.
1852	281	W.B. Wrightson	L	Unopp.
1857	272	W.B. Wrightson	L	129
		Hon. E.W. Lascelles	C	126
1859	283	W.B. Wrightson	L	138
		C.H. Mills	C	136
1865	442	C.H. Mills	C	239
		J.W. Johns	L	190
[Election declared void on petition]				
1866 (10/5)	442	Hon. E.W. Lascelles	C	224
		W.B. Wrightson	L	201
1868	808	J. Hutton	C	386
		J.W. Johns	L	372
1874	829	G.W. Elliot	C	387
		W.B. Wrightson	L	378
1880	912	G.W. Elliot	C	483
		A.O. Rutson	L	383

Petitions:—

1865: Void election

1868: Dismissed

NORTHAMPTON [126]
(Two Seats)

Election	Electors	Candidate	Party	Votes
1832	2,497	†R.V. Smith	L	1,321
		†C. Ross	C	1,275
		G. Bainbridge	L	1,191
		†Hon. H. Fitzroy	C	958
1835	2,178	R.V. Smith	L	1,119
		C. Ross	C	1,111
		C. Hill	L	951
1837	2,079	R.V. Smith	L	1,095
		R. Currie	L	1,033
		C. Ross	C	925
1841	1,997	R.V. Smith	L	990
		R. Currie	L	970
		Sir H.P. Willoughby, Bt.	C	897
		P.M. McDouall	Ch	176
1847	1,867	R. Currie	L	897
		R.V. Smith	L	841
		L.C. Humfrey	C	652
		A.F. Bayford	C	607
		J. Epps	Ch	141
[Appointment of Smith as Secretary at War]				
1852 (11/2)	2,263	R.V. Smith	L	823
		C. Markham	C	480
1852	2,263	R.V. Smith	L	855
		R. Currie	L	825
		G.W. Hunt	C	745
		J.I. Lockhart	Ch	106
[Appointment of Smith as President of the Board of Control for the Affairs of India]				
1855 (5/3)		R.V. Smith	L	Unopp.
1857	2,375	R.V. Smith	L	1,079
		C. Gilpin	L	1,011
		G.W. Hunt	C	815
1859	2,526	C. Gilpin	L	1,151
		R.V. Smith	L	1,143
		J.T. Mackenzie	C	832
		R. Hart	L	27
[Elevation of Smith to the Peerage — Lord Lyveden]				
1859 (5/7)		Lord Henley	L	Unopp.

NORTHAMPTON [126] (Cont.)

(Two Seats)

Election	Electors	Candidate	Party	Votes
1865	2,620	Lord Henley	L	1,269
		C. Gilpin	L	1,250
		G.F. Holroyd	C	1,029
		S.G. Stopford	C	950
1868	6,621†	C. Gilpin	L	2,691
		Lord Henley	L	2,154
		C.G. Merewether	C	1,634
		W.E. Lendrick	C	1,396
		C. Bradlaugh	L	1,086
		F.R. Lees	L	492
1874	6,829	P. Phipps	C	2,690
		C. Gilpin	L	2,310
		C.G. Merewether	C	2,175
		Lord Henley	L	1,796
		C. Bradlaugh	L	1,653

[Death of Gilpin]

Election	Electors	Candidate	Party	Votes
1874 (7/10)	6,829	C.G. Merewether	C	2,171
		W. Fowler	L	1,836
		C. Bradlaugh	L	1,766
1880	8,189	H. Labouchere	L	4,158
		C. Bradlaugh	L	3,827
		P. Phipps	C	3,152
		C.G. Merewether	C	2,826

[Unseating of Bradlaugh for voting in the House of Commons before taking the Oath]

Election	Electors	Candidate	Party	Votes
1881 (12/4)	8,185	C. Bradlaugh	L	3,437
		E. Corbett	C	3,305

[Explusion of Bradlaugh from the House of Commons]

Election	Electors	Candidate	Party	Votes
1882 (4/3)	8,361	C. Bradlaugh	L	3,796
		E. Corbett	C	3,688

[Bradlaugh seeks re-election following resolution to exclude him from the precints of the House of Commons]

Election	Electors	Candidate	Party	Votes
1884 (21/2)	8,886	C. Bradlaugh	L	4,032
		H.C. Richards	C	3,664

NORWICH [127]

(Two Seats)

Election	Electors	Candidate	Party	Votes
1832	4,238	†Viscount Stormont	C	2,016
		†Sir J. Scarlett	C	1,962
		†R.H. Gurney	L	1,809
		H.C.B. Ker	L	1,765
1835	4,102	Viscount Stormont	C	1,892
		Hon. R.C. Scarlett	C	1,878
		Hon. E.V. Harbord	L	1,592
		F.O. Martin	L	1,582
1837	4,390	**Hon. R.C. Scarlett	C	1,865
		Marquess of Douro	C	1,863
		*B. Smith	L	1,843
		M. Nurse	L	1,831
1841	4,334*	Marquess of Douro	C	Unopp.
		B. Smith	L	Unopp.
1847	4,976*	S.M. Peto	L	2,448
		Marquess of Douro	C	1,727
		J.H. Parry	L	1,572
1852	5,390	S.M. Peto	L	2,190
		E. Warner	L	2,145
		Marquess of Douro	C	1,592
		L.S. Dickson	C	1,465
[Resignation of Peto]				
1854 (29/12)	5,911*	Sir S. Bignold	C	1,899
		A. Hamond	L	1,629
1857	6,175	H.W. Schneider	L	2,247
		Viscount Bury	L	2,238
		Sir S. Bignold	C	1,636
1859	5,058	Viscount Bury	L	2,154
		H.W. Schneider	L	2,134
		Sir S. Bignold	C	1,966
		C.M. Lushington	C	1,900
[Appointment of Bury as Treasurer of H.M. Household]				
1859 (28/6)	5,058	Viscount Bury	L	1,922
		Sir S. Bignold	C	1,561
		H.G. Boldero	C	39
[General Election and By-Election declared void on petition]				
1860 (28/3)	5,381	E. Warner	L	2,083
		Sir W. Russell, Bt.	L	2,045
		W. Forlonge	C	1,636
		W.D. Lewis	C	1,631

NORWICH [127] (Cont.)
(Two Seats)

Election	Electors	Candidate	Party	Votes
1865	4,817	Sir W. Russell, Bt.	L	1,845
		E. Warner	L	1,838
		A. Goldsmid	C	1,466
		R.E.C. Waters	C	1,363
1868	13,296	Sir H.J. Stracey, Bt.	C	4,521
		Sir W. Russell, Bt.	L	4,509
		J.H. Tillett	L	4,364
[Election of Stracey declared void on petition]				
1870 (13/7)	13,296*	J.H. Tillett	L	4,236
		J.W. Huddleston	C	3,874
[Election declared void on petition]				
1871 (22/2)	12,338	J.J. Colman	L	4,637
		Sir C. Legard, Bt.	C	3,389
1874	15,166	J.J. Colman	L	6,138
		J.W. Huddleston	C	5,823
		J.H. Tillett	L	5,776
		Sir H.J. Stracey, Bt.	C	5,290
[Resignation of Huddleston on appointment as a Judge of the Court of Common Pleas]				
1875 (6/3)	14,953	J.H. Tillett	L	5,877
		J.J. Wilkinson	C	5,079
1880	15,349	J.J. Colman	L	6,549
		J.H. Tillett	L	6,512
		H. Harben	C	5,242
		Hon. W.F.B.M. Mainwaring	C	5,032

Petitions:—

1832:	Dismissed
1837:	Election of Scarlett declared void. Smith duly elected after scrutiny. Petition against Douro dismissed
1852:	Withdrawn
1859:	Void election
1859: (28/6)	Void election
1860:	Withdrawn
1868:	Election of Stracey declared void
1870:	Void election
1875:	Void election. Writ suspended

NOTTINGHAM [128]
(Two Seats)

Election	Electors	Candidate	Party	Votes
1832	5,220	†Sir R.C. Ferguson	L	2,399
		†Viscount Duncannon	L	2,349
		J.E. Gordon	C	976

[Resignation of Duncannon on appointment as Secretary of State for the Home Department and called to the House of Lords as Lord Duncannon]

1834	5,166	Sir J.C. Hobhouse, Bt.	L	1,591
(25/7)		W. Eagle	L	566
1835	4,454	Sir R.C. Ferguson	L	Unopp.
		Sir J.C. Hobhouse, Bt.	L	Unopp.

[Appointment of Hobhouse as President of the Board of Control for the Affairs of India]

1835		Sir J.C. Hobhouse, Bt.	L	Unopp.
(24/4)				
1837	5,475	Sir R.C. Ferguson	L	2,056
		Sir J.C. Hobhouse, Bt.	L	2,052
		W.H.C. Plowden	C	1,397
		H. Twiss	C	1,396

[Death of Ferguson]

1841	4,678	J. Walter (Senr.)	C	1,983
(26/4)		G.G. de H. Larpent	L	1,745
1841	4,678	G.G. de H. Larpent	L	529
		Sir J.C. Hobhouse, Bt.	L	527
		J. Walter (Senr.)	C	144
		T.B. Charlton	C	142

[Resignation of Larpent]

1842	5,436*	J. Walter (Senr.)	C	1,885
(4/8)		J. Sturge	L	1,801

[Election declared void on petition]

1843	5,172	T. Gisborne	L	1,839
(5/4)		J. Walter (Junr.)	C	1,728

[Appointment of Hobhouse as President of the Board of Control for the Affairs of India]

1846		Sir J.C. Hobhouse, Bt.	L	Unopp.
(8/7)				
1847	5,148*	J. Walter (Junr.)	C	1,683
		F. O'Connor	Ch	1,257
		T. Gisborne	L	999
		Sir J.C. Hobhouse, Bt.	L	893
1852	5,260	E. Strutt	L	1,960
		J. Walter (Junr.)	L	1,863
		C. Sturgeon	Ch	512

NOTTINGHAM [128] (Cont.)

(Two Seats)

Election	Electors	Candidate	Party	Votes
[Appointment of Strutt as Chancellor of the Duchy of Lancaster]				
1853 (1/1)		E. Strutt	L	Unopp.
[Elevation of Strutt to the Peerage — Lord Belper]				
1856 (30/7)		C. Paget	L	Unopp.
1857	5,650	C. Paget	L	2,393
		J. Walter (Junr.)	L	1,836
		E.C. Jones	Ch	614
1859	6,012	C. Paget	L	2,456
		J. Mellor	L	2,181
		T. Bromley	C	1,836
		E.C. Jones	Ch	151
[Resignation of Mellor on appointment as a Judge of the Queen's Bench Division of the High Court of Justice]				
1861 (26/12)	6,533	Sir R.J. Clifton, Bt.	L	2,513
		Earl of Lincoln	L	1,122
1865	5,934	S. Morley	L	2,393
		Sir R.J. Clifton, Bt.	L	2,352
		C. Paget	L	2,327
		A.G. Marten	C	2,242
[Election declared void on petition]				
1866 (11/5)	5,934	R.B. Osborne	L	2,518
		Viscount Amberley	L	2,494
		Sir G.S. Jenkinson, Bt.	C	2,411
		H. Cossham	L	2,307
		D. Faulkner	L	3
1868	14,168	Sir R.J. Clifton, Bt.	L	5,285
		C.I. Wright	C	4,591
		C. Seely	L	4,004
		P.W. Clayden	L	2,716
		R.B. Ocborne	L	2,031
[Death of Clifton]				
1869 (16/6)	14,168	C. Seely	L	4,627
		W.D. Seymour	L	4,517
[Resignation of Wright]				
1870 (24/2)	14,168*	Hon. A.E.W.M. Herbert	L	4,971
		W.D. Seymour	L	4,675

(Two Seats)

Election	Electors	Candidate	Party	Votes
1874	16,154	W.E. Denison	C	5,268
		S. Isaac	C	4,790
		R. Laycock	L	3,732
		H. Labouchere	L	3,545
		D.W. Heath	L	2,752
		R. Birkin	L	1,074
1880	18,699	C. Seely	L	8,499
		J.S. Wright	L	8,055
		S. Isaac	C	5,575
		W.J. Gill	C	5,052
[Death of Wright]				
1880 (8/5)		A. Morley	L	Unopp.

Petitions:—

1841: Dismissed

1842: Void election

1843: Dismissed

1847: Withdrawn (O'Connor only)

1865: Void election

1869: Dismissed

1880: Withdrawn following death of Wright

OLDHAM [129]
(Two Seats)

Election	Electors	Candidate	Party	Votes
1832	1,131	J. Fielden	L	677
		W. Cobbett	L	645
		B.H. Bright	L	150
		†W. Burge	C	101
		G. Stephen	L	3
1835	1,029	W. Cobbett	L	Unopp.
		J. Fielden	L	Unopp.
[Death of Cobbett]				
1835 (8/7)	1,029	J.F. Lees	C	394
		J.M. Cobbett	L	381
		F. O'Connor	L	34
1837	1,372	W.A. Johnson	L	545
		J. Fielden	L	541
		J. Jones	C	315
		J.F. Lees	C	279
1841	1,467	J. Fielden	L	Unopp.
		W.A. Johnson	L	Unopp.
1847	1,691	W.J. Fox	L	726
		J. Duncuft	C	696
		J.M. Cobbett	L	624
		J. Fielden	L	612
1852	1,890	J.M. Cobbett	L	957
		J. Duncuft	C	868
		W.J. Fox	L	777
[Death of Duncuft]				
1852 (3/12)	1,978	W.J. Fox	L	895
		J. Heald	C	783
1857	2,098	J.M. Cobbett	L	949
		J. Platt	L	934
		W.J. Fox	L	898
[Death of Platt]				
1857 (19/10)		W.J. Fox	L	Unopp.
1859	2,151	W.J. Fox	L	1,039
		J.M. Cobbett	L	966
		J.T. Hibbert	L	955
[Resignation of Fox]				
1862 (5/5)		J.T. Hibbert	L	Unopp.

OLDHAM [129] (Cont.)
(Two Seats)

Election	Electors	Candidate	Party	Votes
1865	2,285	J.T. Hibbert	L	1,104
		J. Platt	L	1,075
		J.M. Cobbett	L	899
		F.L. Spinks	C	846
1868	13,454†	J.T. Hibbert	L	6,140
		J. Platt	L	6,122
		J.M. Cobbett	C	6,116
		F.L. Spinks	C	6,084
[Death of Platt]				
1872 (5/6)	16,063	J.M. Cobbett	C	7,278
		Hon. E.L. Stanley	L	6,984
1874	18,560	F.L. Spinks	C	8,582
		J.M. Cobbett	C	8,541
		J.T. Hibbert	L	8,397
		Hon. E.L. Stanley	L	8,360
[Death of Cobbett]				
1877 (1/3)	20,249	J.T. Hibbert	L	9,542
		T.E. Lees	C	8,831
1880	21,084	J.T. Hibbert	L	10,630
		Hon. E.L. Stanley	L	10,409
		F.L. Spinks	C	8,982
		S.T. Whitehead	C	8,593

Petition:—

1868: Dismissed

OXFORD [130]
(Two Seats)

Election	Electors	Candidate	Party	Votes
1832	2,312	†J.H. Langston	L	1,260
		T. Stonor	L	953
		†W.H. Hughes	L	919
		†Sir C. Wetherell	C	523
[Election of Stonor declared void on petition]				
1833 (18/3)	2,312	W.H. Hughes	L	803
		C. Towneley	L	702
		D. Maclean	C	462
1835	2,436	W.H. Hughes	C	1,394
		D. Maclean	C	1,217
		T. Stonor	L	1,022
1837	2,424	D. Maclean	C	1,348
		W. Erle	L	1,217
		W.H. Hughes	C	897
1841	2,786	J.H. Langston	L	1,349
		D. Maclean	C	1,238
		N. Malcolm	C	1,041
1847	2,819	J.H. Langston	L	Unopp.
		W.P. Wood	L	Unopp.
[Appointment of Wood as Solicitor-General]				
1851 (3/4)		W.P. Wood	L	Unopp.
1852	2,818	J.H. Langston	L	Unopp.
		Sir W.P. Wood	L	Unopp.
[Resignation of Wood on appointment as Vice-Chancellor]				
1853 (4/1)		E. Cardwell	C	Unopp.
1857	2,656	J.H. Langston	L	1,671
		C. Neate	L	1,057
		E. Cardwell	L	1,016
		S. Gaselee	L	245
[Election of Neate declared void on petition]				
1857 (21/7)	2,656	E. Cardwell	L	1,085
		W.M. Thackeray	L	1,018
1859	2,731	E. Cardwell	L	Unopp.
		J.H. Langston	L	Unopp.

OXFORD [130] (Cont.)

(Two Seats)

Election	Electors	Candidate	Party	Votes
[Appointment of Cardwell as Chief Secretary to the Lord Lieutenant of Ireland]				
1859 (27/6)		E. Cardwell	L	Unopp.
[Appointment of Cardwell as Chancellor of the Duchy of Lancaster]				
1861 (30/7)		E. Cardwell	L	Unopp.
[Death of Langston]				
1863 (7/11)		C. Neate	L	Unopp.
[Appointment of Cardwell as Secretary of State for the Colonies]				
1864 (9/4)		E. Cardwell	L	Unopp.
1865	2,594	E. Cardwell	L	Unopp.
		C. Neate	L	Unopp.
1868	5,328†	E. Cardwell	L	2,765
		W.G.G.V.V. Harcourt	L	2,636
		J.P. Deane	C	1,225
[Appointment of Cardwell as Secretary of State for the War Department]				
1868 (22/12)		E. Cardwell	L	Unopp.
[Appointment of Harcourt as Solicitor-General]				
1873 (6/12)		W.G.G.V.V. Harcourt	L	Unopp.
1874	5,680	Sir W.G.G.V.V. Harcourt	L	2,332
		E. Cardwell	L	2,281
		A.W. Hall	C	2,198
[Elevation of Cardwell to the Peerage - Viscount Cardwell]				
1874 (16/3)	5,680	A.W. Hall	C	2,554
		J.D. Lewis	L	2,092
1880	6,163	Sir W.G.G.V.V. Harcourt	L	2,771
		J.W. Chitty	L	2,669
		A.W. Hall	C	2,659
[Appointment of Harcourt as Secretary of State for the Home Department]				
1880 (10/5)	6,163	A.W. Hall	C	2,735
		Sir W.G.G.V.V. Harcourt	L	2,681

Petitions:—

1832: Election of Stone declared void

1857: Election of Neate declared void

1880 (10/5): Void election. Writ suspended

PENRYN and FALMOUTH [131]
(Two Seats)

Election	Electors	Candidate	Party	Votes
1832	875	R.M. Rolfe	L	490
		†Lord Tullamore	C	428
		†J.W. Freshfield	C	338
		†C. Stewart	C	83
1835	811	J.W. Freshfield	C	464
		R.M. Rolfe	L	424
		Lord Tullamore	C	397
[Appointment of Rolfe as Solicitor-General]				
1835 (28/4)	811	R.M. Rolfe	L	348
		Lord Tullamore	C	326
1837	888	Sir R.M. Rolfe	L	523
		J.W. Freshfield	C	434
		J.H. Plumridge	L	363
[Resignation of Rolfe on appointment as a Judge of the Court of the Exchequer]				
1840 (23/1)	885	E.J. Hutchins	L	462
		W. Carne	C	238
1841	884	Hon. J.C.W. Vivian	L	462
		J.H. Plumridge	L	432
		H. Gwyn	C	381
		E.J. Sartoris	C	240
1847	863	H. Gwyn	C	548
		F. Mowatt	L	377
		P. Borthwick	C	87
1852	906	H. Gwyn	C	464
		J.W. Freshfield	C	435
		T.G. Baring	L	339
1857	856	T.G. Baring	L	Unopp.
		S. Gurney	L	Unopp.
[Appointment of Baring as a Civil Lord of the Admiralty]				
1857 (27/5)		T.G. Baring	L	Unopp.
1859	831	T.G. Baring	L	389
		S. Gurney	L	373
		H. Gwyn	C	324
		J.F.L. Foster	C	200
1865	837	T.G. Baring	L	Unopp.
		S. Gurney	L	Unopp.

PENRYN and FALMOUTH [131] (Cont.)
(Two Seats)

Election	Electors	Candidate	Party	Votes
[Succession of Baring to the Peerage — Lord Northbrook]				
1866	837	J. Smith	L	376
(15/10)		R.N. Fowler	C	313
1868	1,808†	R.N. Fowler	C	732
		E.B. Eastwick	C	683
		J. Smith	L	611
		K.D. Hodgson	L	597
1874	1,860	D.J. Jenkins	L	851
		H.T. Cole	L	784
		R.N. Fowler	C	743
		E.B. Eastwick	C	646
1880	2,202	D.J. Jenkins	L	1,176
		R.B. Brett	L	1,071
		Sir J. Vogel	C	882
		J.D. Mayne	C	765

Petitions:—

1835: (28/4)	Dismissed
1841:	Dismissed (Plumridge only)
1868:	Dismissed

PETERBOROUGH [132]
(Two Seats)

Election	Electors	Candidate	Party	Votes
1832	773	†Sir R. Heron, Bt.	L	Unopp.
		†J.N. Fazakerley	L	Unopp.
1835	685	J.N. Fazakerley	L	412
		Sir R. Heron, Bt.	L	358
		W. Ferrand	C	281
1837	552	J.N. Fazakerley	L	311
		Sir R. Heron, Bt.	L	288
		W.E. Surtees	C	234
1841	576	Hon. G.W. Fitzwilliam	L	317
		Sir R. Heron, Bt.	L	255
		T. Gladstone	C	244
1847	553	W.G. Cavendish	L	Unopp.
		Hon. G.W. Fitzwilliam	L	Unopp.
1852	518	Hon. G.W. Fitzwilliam	L	260
		Hon. R. Watson	L	229
		J.T. Clifton	C	210
[Death of Watson]				
1852 (6/12)	526	G.H. Whalley	L	233
		G.C. Lewis	L	218
[Election declared void on petition]				
1853 (25/6)	526	**G.H. Whalley	L	236
		*T. Hankey	L	215
1857	542	Hon. G.W. Fitzwilliam	L	321
		T. Hankey	L	266
		G.H. Whalley	L	181
1859	568	T. Hankey	L	275
		G.H. Whalley	L	253
		J.H.L. Wingfield	C	195
		J.P. Wilde	L	187
1865	641	G.H. Whalley	L	340
		T. Hankey	L	320
		W. Wells	L	303
1868	2,461†	W. Wells	L	1,282
		G.H. Whalley	L	1,122
		T. Hankey	L	834
		W. Green	L	204
		H.T. Wrenfordsley	C	167

PETERBOROUGH [132] (Cont.)
(Two Seats)

Election	Electors	Candidate	Party	Votes
1874	3,056	T. Hankey	L	1,135
		G.H. Whalley	L	1,105
		H.T. Wrenfordsley	C	666
		G. Potter	L/Lab	562
		N. Goodman	L	323
		R.M. Kerr	L	71
[Death of Whalley]				
1878 (29/10)	3,340	Hon. W.J.W. Fitzwilliam	L	1,360
		J.C. Lawrance	C	671
		J.H. Raper	L	653
		G. Potter	L	8
1880	3,393	Hon. W.J.W. Fitzwilliam	L	1,615
		G.H. Whalley	L	1,257
		R. Tennant	C	987
		T. Hankey	L	841
[Resignation of Whalley]				
1883 (23/6)	3,589	S.C. Buxton	L	1,438
		J.A. Fergusson	C	1,106

Petitions:—

1852: (6/12)	Void election
1853:	Election of Whalley declared void owing to disqualification. Hankey duly elected.
1857:	Withdrawn
1859:	Petition against Whalley dismissed. Petition against Hankey withdrawn

PETERSFIELD [133]

Election	Electors	Candidate	Party	Votes
1832	234	**J.G.S. Lefevre	L	101
		†*W.G.H. Jolliffe	C	100
1835	287	C.J. Hector	L	103
		Sir W.G.H. Jolliffe, Bt.	C	87
1837	320	**Sir W.G.H. Jolliffe, Bt.	C	125
		*C.J. Hector	L	124
1841	352	Sir W.G.H. Jolliffe, Bt.	C	Unopp.
1847	380	Sir W.G.H. Jolliffe, Bt.	C	Unopp.
1852	353	Sir W.G.H. Jolliffe, Bt.	C	Unopp.
1857	331	Sir W.G.H. Jolliffe, Bt.	C	Unopp.
1859	332	Sir W.G.H. Jolliffe, Bt.	C	Unopp.
1865	296	Sir W.G.H. Jolliffe, Bt.	C	Unopp.
[Elevation to the Peerage — Lord Hylton]				
1866 (23/7)		W. Nicholson	L	Unopp.
1868	774	W. Nicholson	L	370
		F. Du P. Thornton	C	222
1874	870	Hon. W.S.H. Jolliffe	C	372
		W. Nicholson	L	361
1880	801	W. Nicholson	L	406
		Hon. W.S.H. Jolliffe	C	320

Petitions:—

1832: Election of Lefevre declared void. Jolliffe duly elected after scrutiny

1837: Election of Jolliffe declared void. Hector duly elected after scrutiny

1874: Dismissed

PLYMOUTH [134]
(Two Seats)

Election	Electors	Candidate	Party	Votes
1832	1,415	T.B. Bewes	L	Unopp.
		J. Collier	L	Unopp.
1835	1,571	J. Collier	L	720
		T.B. Bewes	L	687
		Sir G. Cockburn	C	667
1837	1,811	J. Collier	L	780
		T.B. Bewes	L	772
		Sir G. Cockburn	C	551
		Hon. P. Blackwood	C	466
1841	1,903	T. Gill	L	821
		Viscount Ebrington	L	787
		J. Johnson	C	552
[Appointment of Ebrington as a Lord Commissioner of the Treasury]				
1846 (11/7)	1,944*	Viscount Ebrington	L	716
		H. Vincent	Ch	188
1847	2,174	Viscount Ebrington	L	921
		R. Palmer	C	837
		C.B. Calmady	L	769
1852	2,482	C.J. Mare	C	1,036
		R.P. Collier	L	1,004
		G.T. Braine	L	906
		B. Escott	L	372
[Election of Mare declared void on petition]				
1853 (2/6)	2,508	R. Palmer	C	944
		G.T. Braine	L	876
1857	2,604	R.P. Collier	L	1,167
		J. White	L	1,106
		J. Hardy	C	622
1859	2,706	Viscount Valletort	C	1,153
		R.P. Collier	L	1,086
		J. White	L	964
[Succession of Valletort to the Peerage – Earl of Mount Edgcumbe]				
1861 (31/10)	2,781*	W. Morrison	L	1,179
		Hon. W.W. Addington	C	984
[Appointment of Collier as Solicitor-General]				
1863 (17/10)		R.P. Collier	L	Unopp.

PLYMOUTH [134] (Cont.)
(Two Seats)

Election	Electors	Candidate	Party	Votes
1865	2,944	Sir R.P. Collier	L	1,299
		W. Morrison	L	1,218
		R.S. Lane	C	1,147
1868	4,840†	Sir R.P. Collier	L	2,086
		W. Morrison	L	2,065
		R.S. Lane	C	1,506
[Appointment of Collier as Attorney-General]				
1868 (21/12)		Sir R.P. Collier	L	Unopp.
[Appointment of Collier as Recorder of Bristol]				
1870 (15/8)		Sir R.P. Collier	L	Unopp.
[Resignation of Collier on appointment as a Judge of the Court of Common Pleas]				
1871 (22/11)	4,671	E. Bates	C	1,753
		A. Rooker	L	1,511
1874	4,728	E. Bates	C	2,045
		S.S. Lloyd	C	2,000
		Sir G. Young, Bt.	L	1,714
		W. Morrison	L	1,700
1880	5,552	E. Bates	C	2,442
		P.S. Macliver	L	2,406
		Sir G. Young, Bt.	L	2,402
		S.S. Lloyd	C	2,384
[Election of Bates declared void on petition]				
1880 (10/7)	5,552	E.G. Clarke	C	2,449
		Sir G. Young, Bt.	L	2,305

Petitions:—

1852: Election of Mare declared void. Petition against Collier dismissed

1880: Election of Bates declared void

PONTEFRACT [135]

(Two Seats)

Election	Electors	Candidate	Party	Votes
1832	956	J. Gully	L	Unopp.
		†Hon. H.V.S. Jerningham	L	Unopp.
1835	862	J. Gully	L	509
		Viscount Pollington	C	498
		A. Raphael	L	478
1837	795	R.M. Milnes	C	507
		W.M. Stanley	L	403
		Sir C.E. Smith, Bt.	L	123
		H. Gompertz	C	0
1841	712	Viscount Pollington	C	464
		R.M. Milnes	C	433
		J. Gully	L	253
1847	685	S. Martin	L	415
		R.M. Milnes	C	365
		T.H. Preston	C	346
[Resignation of Martin on appointment as a Judge of the Court of the Exchequer]				
1851 (13/2)	675	Hon. B.R. Lawley	L	427
		Viscount Pollington	C	115
1852	684	R.M. Milnes	C	433
		B. Oliveira	L	338
		W.D. Lewis	C	313
1857	705	R.M. Milnes	L	439
		W. Wood	L	374
		B. Oliveira	L	319
1859	701	R.M. Milnes	L	497
		W. Overend	C	306
		H.C.E. Childers	L	296
[Resignation of Overend]				
1860 (31/1)	689	H.C.E. Childers	L	320
		S. Waterhouse	C	257
[Elevation of Milnes to the Peerage – Lord Houghton]				
1863 (3/8)		S. Waterhouse	C	Unopp.
[Appointment of Childers as a Civil Lord of the Admiralty]				
1864 (20/4)		H.C.E. Childers	L	Unopp.
1865	699	H.C.E. Childers	L	359
		S. Waterhouse	C	330
		W. McArthur	L	288

PONTEFRACT [135] (Cont.)
(Two Seats)

Election	Electors	Candidate	Party	Votes
1868	1,910	H.C.E. Childers	L	913
		S. Waterhouse	C	900
		C.G.M. Gaskell	L	680
[Appointment of Childers as First Lord of the Admiralty]				
1868 (21/12)		H.C.E. Childers	L	Unopp.
[Appointment of Childers as Chancellor of the Duchy of Lancaster]				
1872 (17/8)	1,941	H.C.E. Childers	L	658
		Viscount Pollington	C	578
1874	2,038	H.C.E. Childers	L	934
		S. Waterhouse	C	861
		Viscount Pollington	C	709
1880	2,429	H.C.E. Childers	L	1,154
		S. Woolf	L	1,029
		E. Green	C	904
		J. Shaw	C	627
[Appointment of Childers as Secretary of State for the War Department]				
1880 (8/5)		H.C.E. Childers	L	Unopp.

Petitions:—

1852: Withdrawn
1857: Dismissed (Wood only)
1859: Withdrawn (Overend only)
1860: Withdrawn

Note:—

1872: The first election by secret ballot.

POOLE [136]

(Two seats until 1868; one seat from 1868)

Election	Electors	Candidate	Party	Votes
1832	412	†B.L. Lester	L	284
		†Sir J. Byng	L	186
		C.A. Tulk	L	168
1835	450	Sir J. Byng	L	230
		C.A. Tulk	L	199
		J. Irving	C	119
		T. Bonar	C	46
[Elevation of Byng to the Peerage — Lord Strafford]				
1835 (21/5)	450	G.S. Byng	L	199
		Sir C. Grant	C	174
1837	645	Hon. C.F.A.C. Ponsonby	L	278
		G.R. Philips	L	259
		Sir H.P. Willoughby, Bt.	C	242
		Sir J.B. Walsh, Bt.	C	222
1841	469	Hon. C.F.A.C. Ponsonby	L	231
		G.R. Philips	L	211
		G.P. Rose	C	189
1847	522	G.R. Robinson	C	240
		G.R. Philips	L	220
		E.J. Hutchins	L	203
		M.M. Turner	L	52
[Death of Robinson]				
1850 (24/9)	498	H.D. Seymour	L	187
		I. Savage	C	167
1852	508	G.W. Franklyn	C	Unopp.
		H.D. Seymour	L	Unopp.
1857	539	H.D. Seymour	L	211
		G.W. Franklyn	C	189
		W.T. Haly	L	98
1859	553	G.W. Franklyn	C	208
		H.D. Seymour	L	193
		W.T. Haly	L	143
1865	521	H.D. Seymour	L	258
		C. Waring	L	248
		S. Lewin	C	178
1868	1,256	A.E. Guest	C	623
		C. Waring	L	563

POOLE [136] (Cont.)
(Two seats until 1868; one seat from 1868)

Election	Electors	Candidate	Party	Votes
1874	1,526	C. Waring	L	705
		A.E. Guest	C	580
[Election declared void on petition]				
1874 (26/5)	1,526	Hon. A.E.M. Ashley	L	631
		Sir I.B. Guest, Bt.	C	622
1880	1,911	C. Schreiber	C	854
		C. Waring	L	848
[Death]				
1884 (19/4)	1,983	W.J. Harris	C	877
		T.C. Clarke	L	815

Petitions:—

1837:	Withdrawn
1874:	Void election
1874: (26/5)	Withdrawn

PORTSMOUTH [137]
(Two Seats)

Election	Electors	Candidate	Party	Votes
1832	1,295	†J.B. Carter	L	826
		†F.T. Baring	L	707
		C. Napier	L	258
1835	1,340	J.B. Carter	L	643
		F.T. Baring	L	571
		Sir C. Rowley	C	557
		C. Napier	L	335
1837	1,561	F.T. Baring	L	635
		J.B. Carter	L	630
		Sir G. Cockburn	C	518
		Vicount Fitzharris	C	438
[Death of Carter]				
1838 (26/2)		Sir G.T. Staunton, Bt.	L	Unopp.
[Appointment of Baring as Chancellor of the Exchequer]				
1839 (30/8)		F.T. Baring	L	Unopp.
1841	1,834	F.T. Baring	L	Unopp.
		Sir G.T. Staunton, Bt.	L	Unopp.
1847	2,068	F.T. Baring	L	Unopp.
		Sir G.T. Staunton, Bt.	L	Unopp.
[Appointment of Baring as First Lord of the Admiralty]				
1849 (6/2)		F.T. Baring	L	Unopp.
1852	3,332	Sir F.T. Baring, Bt.	L	Unopp.
		Viscount Monck	L	Unopp.
[Appointment of Monck as a Lord Commissioner of the Admiralty]				
1855 (14/3)	3,439*	Viscount Monck	L	1,478
		S. Gaselee	L	473
1857	3,671	Sir J.D.H. Elphinstone, Bt.	C	1,522
		Sir F.T. Baring, Bt.	L	1,496
		Viscount Monck	L	1,476
1859	3,821	Sir J.D.H. Elphinstone, Bt.	C	1,640
		Sir F.T. Baring, Bt.	L	1,574
		Hon. T.C. Bruce	C	1,447
		Hon. Sir H. Keppel	L	1,386
1865	4,670	W.H. Stone	L	2,164
		S. Gaselee	L	2,103
		Sir J.D.H. Elphinstone, Bt.	C	1,677
		Hon. T.C. Bruce	C	1,559

(Two Seats)

Election	Electors	Candidate	Party	Votes
1868	11,597	Sir J.D.H. Elphinstone, Bt.	C	5,306
		W.H. Stone	L	3,785
		S. Gaselee	L	3,687
1874	14,931	Sir J.D.H. Elphinstone, Bt.	C	5,927
		Hon. T.C. Bruce	C	5,879
		W.H. Stone	L	4,644
		W.S. Portal	L	4,588
[Appointment of Elphinstone as a Lord Commissioner of the Treasury]				
1874 (16/3)		Sir J.D.H. Elphinstone, Bt.	C	Unopp.
1880	16,463	Hon. T.C. Bruce	C	6,683
		Sir H.D. Wolff	C	6,593
		J.F. Norris	L	6,040
		E.H. Verney	L	6,023

Petitions:—

1857: Withdrawn

1865: Withdrawn

PRESTON [138]
(Two Seats)

Election	Electors	Candidate	Party	Votes
1832	6,352	P.H. Fleetwood	C	3,372
		Hon. H.T. Stanley	L	3,273
		†H. Hunt	L	2,054
		J. Forbes	L	1,926
		C. Crompton	L	118
1835	3,734	P.H. Fleetwood	C	2,165
		Hon. H.T. Stanley	L	2,092
		T.P. Thompson	L	1,385
		T. Smith	L	789
1837	3,656	P.H. Fleetwood	C	2,726
		R.T. Parker	C	1,821
		J. Crawfurd	L	1,562
1841	3,371	Sir P.H. Fleetwood, Bt.	L	1,655
		Sir G. Strickland, Bt.	L	1,629
		R.T. Parker	C	1,270
		C. Swainson	C	1,255
1847	3,044	Sir G. Strickland, Bt.	L	1,404
		C.P. Grenfell	L	1,378
		R.T. Parker	C	1,361
1852	2,854	R.T. Parker	C	1,335
		Sir G. Strickland, Bt.	L	1,253
		C.P. Grenfell	L	1,127
		J. German	L	692
1857	2,793	C.P. Grenfell	L	1,503
		R.A. Cross	C	1,433
		Sir G. Strickland, Bt.	L	1,094
1859	2,657	R.A. Cross	C	1,542
		C.P. Grenfell	L	1,208
		J.T. Clifton	C	1,168
[Resignation of Cross]				
1862 (4/4)	2,773	Sir T.G. Hesketh, Bt.	C	1,527
		G. Melly	L	1,014
1865	2,562	Sir T.G. Hesketh, Bt. *(Sir T.G.F. Hesketh, Bt.)*	C	Unopp.
		Hon. F.A. Stanley	C	Unopp.
1868	10,763†	E. Hermon	C	5,803
		Sir T.G.F. Hesketh, Bt.	C	5,700
		J.F. Leese	L	4,741
		Lord Edward Howard	L	4,663

PRESTON [138] (Cont.)
(Two Seats)

Election	Electors	Candidate	Party	Votes
[Death of Hesketh]				
1872 (16/9)	10,214	J. Holker	C	4,542
		J. German	L	3,824
1874	12,073	E. Hermon	C	6,512
		J. Holker	C	5,211
		T. Mottershead	L/Lab	3,756
[Appointment of Holker as Solicitor-General]				
1874 (24/4)		J. Holker	C	Unopp.
1880	12,108	E. Hermon	C	6,239
		Sir J. Holker	C	5,641
		G.W. Bahr	L	5,355
[Death of Hermon]				
1881 (23/5)	11,748	W.F. Ecroyd	C	6,004
		H.Y. Thompson	L	4,340
[Resignation of Holker on appointment as a Lord Justice of Appeal]				
1882 (4/2)	12,978	H.C. Raikes	C	6,045
		W.S. Simpson	L/Lab	4,212
[Resignation of Raikes in order to contest Cambridge University]				
1882 (25/11)	12,978	W.E.M. Tomlinson	C	6,351
		R.W. Hanbury	C	4,167

Petitions:—

1859: Dismissed

1868: Withdrawn

READING [139]
(Two Seats)

Election	Electors	Candidate	Party	Votes
1832	1,001	†C.F. Palmer	L	Unopp.
		†C. Russell	C	Unopp.
1835	1,002	T.N. Talfourd	L	643
		C. Russell	C	441
		B. Oliveira	L	384
1837	1,035	T.N. Talfourd	L	468
		C.F. Palmer	L	457
		C. Russell	C	448
1841	1,194	C. Russell	C	570
		Viscount Chelsea	C	564
		T. Mills	L	410
		W. Tooke	L	397
1847	1,251	F. Pigott	L	614
		T.N. Talfourd	L	596
		C. Russell	C	521
		Viscount Chelsea	C	376
[Resignation of Talfourd on appointment as a Judge of the Court of Common Pleas]				
1849 (8/8)	1,309	J.F. Stanford	C	507
		G. Bowyer	L	364
		T. Norton	L	107
1852	1,399	F. Pigott	L	753
		H.S. Keating	L	631
		S.A. Dickson	C	518
1857	1,431	H.S. Keating	L	Unopp.
		F. Pigott	L	Unopp.
[Appointment of Keating as Solicitor-General]				
1857 (2/6)		H.S. Keating	L	Unopp.
1859	1,451	F. Pigott	L	761
		Sir H.S. Keating	L	666
		R.A. Benson	C	544
[Appointment of Keating as Solicitor-General]				
1859 (27/6)		Sir H.S. Keating	L	Unopp.
[Resignation of Keating on appointment as a Judge of the Court of Common Pleas]				
1860 (11/1)	1,506	Sir F.H. Goldsmid, Bt.	L	661
		R.A. Benson	C	551

READING [139] (Cont.)

(Two Seats)

Election	Electors	Candidate	Party	Votes
[Resignation of Pigott on appointment as Governor of the Isle of Man]				
1860 (21/11)	1,506	G. Pigott	L	586
		E. Walter	C	435
[Resignation of Pigott on appointment as a Judge of the Court of the Exchequer]				
1863 (17/10)		G.J.S. Lefevre	L	Unopp.
1865	1,769	Sir F.H. Goldsmid, Bt.	L	727
		G.J.S. Lefevre	L	714
		S. Tucker	C	444
[Appointment of Lefevre as a Civil Lord of the Admiralty]				
1866 (5/5)		G.J.S. Lefevre	L	Unopp.
1868	3,228	Sir F.H. Goldsmid, Bt.	L	1,629
		G.J.S. Lefevre	L	1,618
		Sir R.W. Carden	C	979
1874	4,118	G.J.S. Lefevre	L	1,794
		Sir F.H. Goldsmid, Bt.	L	1,791
		R. Attenborough	C	1,652
		W.D. Mackenzie	C	1,631
[Death of Goldsmid]				
1878 (18/5)	4,721	G. Palmer	L	2,223
		R. Attenborough	C	1,565
1880	5,107	G. Palmer	L	2,513
		G.J.S. Lefevre	L	2,286
		A.G. Sandeman	C	2,067
[Appointment of Lefevre as First Commissioner of Works and Public Buildings]				
1880 (15/12)		G.J.S. Lefevre	L	Unopp.

Petitions:—

1837: Dismissed (Palmer only)

1841: Dismissed

REIGATE [140]

Election	Electors	Candidate	Party	Votes
1832	152	†Viscount Eastnor	C	101
		Lord Garvagh	L	0
1835	165	Viscount Eastnor	C	85
		J. Moore	L	14
1837	205	Viscount Eastnor	C	Unopp.
[Succession to the Peerage — Earl Somers]				
1841 (3/2)		Viscount Eastnor	C	Unopp.
1841	199	Viscount Eastnor	C	106
		J. Bedford	Ch	9
1847	182	T.S. Cocks	C	Unopp.
1852	228	T.S. Cocks	C	100
		H.M. Parratt	L	76
1857	442	W. Hackblock	L	228
		Sir H.C. Rawlinson	L	127
[Death]				
1858 (6/2)	442*	Sir H.C. Rawlinson	L	212
		F. Doulton	L	116
		Hon. W.J. Monson	L	95
[Resignation on appointment as a Member of the Council of India]				
1858 (23/10)	442*	Hon. W.J. Monson	L	225
		W.A. Wilkinson	L	210
1859	548	Hon. W.J. Monson	L	260
		W.A. Wilkinson	L	161
[Succession to the Peerage — Lord Monson]				
1863 (6/2)	737	G.W.G.L. Gower	L	346
		W.A. Wilkinson	L	333
1865	920	G.W.G.L. Gower	L	473
		Hon. E.J. Monson	L	276
		G.G. Richardson	C	11

Writ suspended. Royal Commission appointed which found proof of extensive bribery and as a result the borough lost its right to return a Member of Parliament and was incorporated into the county constituency of Surrey, Mid, from the Dissolution.

Petitions:—

1863: Withdrawn

1865: Void election

RICHMOND [141]

(Two seats until 1868; one seat from 1868)

Election	Electors	Candidate	Party	Votes
1832	273	†Hon. J.C. Dundas	L	Unopp.
		†Sir R.L. Dundas	L	Unopp.
1835	278	Hon. T. Dundas	L	Unopp.
		A. Speirs	L	Unopp.
1837	272	Hon. T. Dundas *(Lord Dundas)*	L	Unopp.
		A. Speirs	L	Unopp.
[Succession of Dundas to the Peerage — Earl of Zetland]				
1839 (12/3)	284*	Hon. Sir R.L. Dundas	L	162
		M.T. Stapleton	C	80
[Resignation of Speirs]				
1841 (16/2)		Hon. G.W. Fitzwilliam	L	Unopp.
1841	289*	Hon. W.N.R. Colborne	L	Unopp.
		Hon. J.C. Dundas	L	Unopp.
[Death of Colborne]				
1846 (8/4)		H. Rich	L	Unopp.
[Appointment of Rich as a Lord Commissioner of the Treasury]				
1846 (13/7)		H. Rich	L	Unopp.
1847	283	H. Rich	L	Unopp.
		M. Wyvill	L	Unopp.
1852	243	H. Rich	L	Unopp.
		M. Wyvill	L	Unopp.
1857	342	H. Rich	L	Unopp.
		M. Wyvill	L	Unopp.
1859	327	H. Rich	L	Unopp.
		M. Wyvill	L	Unopp.
[Resignation of Rich]				
1861 (9/7)		R. Palmer	L	Unopp.
[Appointment of Palmer as Attorney-General]				
1863 (17/10)		Sir R. Palmer	L	Unopp.

(Two seats until 1868; one seat from 1868)

Election	Electors	Candidate	Party	Votes
1865	316	Hon. J.C. Dundas	L	Unopp.
		Sir R. Palmer	L	Unopp.
[Death of Dundas]				
1866 (6/3)	316	M. Wyvill	L	213
		W.H. Roberts	L	13
1868	650†	Sir R. Palmer	L	375
		W.H. Roberts	L	87
[Resignation on appointment as Lord Chancellor and elevation to the Peerage — Lord Selborne]				
1872 (7/11)	682	L. Dundas	L	314
		C.E.B. Cooke	C	228
[Succession to the Peerage — Earl of Zetland]				
1873 (27/5)		Hon. J.C. Dundas	L	Unopp.
1874	706	Hon. J.C. Dundas	L	313
		C.E.B. Cooke	L	259
1880	696	Hon. J.C. Dundas	L	447
		G.S. King	C	143

RIPON [142]

(Two seats until 1868; one seat from 1868)

Election	Electors	Candidate	Party	Votes
1832	341	T.K. Staveley	L	168
		J.S. Crompton	L	168
		Sir J.C. Dalbiac	C	162
		W. Markham	C	159
1835	383	Sir J.C. Dalbiac	C	246
		T. Pemberton	C	235
		T.K. Staveley	L	125
1837	424	T. Pemberton	C	Unopp.
		Sir E.B. Sugden	C	Unopp.
1841	373	T. Pemberton	C	Unopp.
		Sir E.B. Sugden	C	Unopp.
[Resignation of Sugden on appointment as Lord Chancellor of Ireland]				
1841 (27/9)		Sir G. Cockburn	C	Unopp.
[Resignation of Pemberton]				
1843 (18/3)		T.B.C. Smith	C	Unopp.
[Resignation of Smith on appointment as Master of the Rolls in Ireland]				
1846 (2/2)		Hon. E. Lascelles	C	Unopp.
1847	350	Sir J.R.G. Graham, Bt.	C	Unopp.
		Hon. E. Lascelles	C	Unopp.
1852	353	W. Beckett	C	266
		Hon. E. Lascelles	C	202
		A. Newton	L	75
1857	339	J. Greenwood	L	Unopp.
		J.A. Warre	L	Unopp.
1859	337	J. Greenwood	L	223
		J.A. Warre	L	205
		A.B. Richards	L	31
[Death of Warre]				
1860 (22/12)	343*	R.A. Vyner	L	187
		F.R. Lees	Ch	0
1865	348	Sir C. Wood, Bt.	L	215
		R. Kearsley	L	189
		J. Greenwood	L	173

RIPON [142] (Cont.)

(Two seats until 1868; one seat from 1868)

Election	Electors	Candidate	Party	Votes
[Elevation of Wood to the Peerage — Viscount Halifax]				
1866 (26/2)		Lord John Hay	L	Unopp.
[Appointment of Hay as a Lord Commissioner of the Admiralty]				
1866 (28/3)		Lord John Hay	L	Unopp.
1868	1,132	Lord John Hay	L	554
		G.A. Cayley	C	408
[Appointed a Lord Commissioner of the Admiralty]				
1868 (21/12)		Lord John Hay	L	Unopp.
[Resignation]				
1871 (15/2)	1,035	Sir H.K. Storks	L	522
		G.A. Cayley	C	302
1874	1,025	Earl de Grey	L	Unopp.
1880	1,087	G.J. Goschen	L	591
		F. Darwin	C	362

Petition:—

1832: Dismissed

ROCHDALE [143]

Election	Electors	Candidate	Party	Votes
1832	687	J. Fenton	L	277
		J. Entwisle	C	246
		J. Taylor	L	109
1835	746	J. Estwisle	C	369
		J. Fenton	L	326
[Death]				
1837 (19/4)	857	J. Fenton	L	383
		C. Royds	C	339
1837	857	J. Fenton	L	374
		A. Ramsay	C	349
1841	1,016	W.S. Crawford	L	399
		J. Fenton	L	335
1847	1,026	W.S. Crawford	L	Unopp.
1852	1,160	E. Miall	L	529
		Sir A. Ramsay, Bt.	C	375
1857	1,255	Sir A. Ramsay, Bt.	L	532
		E. Miall	L	488
1859	1,340	R. Cobden	L	Unopp.
[Death]				
1865 (15/4)	1,358	R.B. Potter	L	646
		W.B. Brett	C	496
1865	1,358	T.B. Potter	L	Unopp.
1868	9,280†	T.B. Potter	L	4,455
		W.W. Schofield	C	3,270
1874	10,352	T.B. Potter	L	4,498
		R.W. Gamble	C	3,998
1880	11,172	T.B. Potter	L	5,614
		R.W. Gamble	C	3,716

Petition:—

1857: Dismissed

ROCHESTER [144]
(Two Seats)

Election	Electors	Candidate	Party	Votes
1832	973	†R. Bernal	L	354
		†J. Mills	C	350
		G.L.N. Collingwood	L	293
1835	967	R. Bernal	L	502
		T.T. Hodges	L	443
		Lord Charles Wellesley	C	442
1837	1,015	R. Bernal	L	489
		T.B. Hobhouse	L	473
		J.D.S. Douglas	C	445
		Hon. T. Best	C	412
1841	1,139	J.D.S. Douglas	C	541
		W.H. Bodkin	C	499
		Viscount Melgund	L	497
		F. Dashwood	L	489
1847	1,451	R. Bernal	L	637
		T.T. Hodges	L	617
		W.H. Bodkin	C	464
		J.D.S. Douglas	C	462
1852	1,269	Hon. F.J.R. Villiers	C	584
		Sir T.H. Maddock	C	581
		R. Bernal	L	514
		T.T. Hodges	L	507
[Resignation of Villiers]				
1856 (8/2)	1,170	P.W. Martin	L	560
		W.H. Bodkin	C	499
1857	1,180	J.A. Kinglake	L	Unopp.
		P.W. Martin	L	Unopp.
1859	1,419	P.W. Martin	L	665
		J.A. Kinglake	L	662
		G.H. Money	C	505
		G. Mitchell	C	493
1865	1,458	P.W. Martin	L	855
		J.A. Kinglake	L	792
		A. Smee	C	414
1868	2,569	P.W. Martin	L	1,458
		J.A. Kinglake	L	1,305
		A. Smee	C	703
[Death of Kinglake]				
1870 (19/7)	2,571*	J. Goldsmid	L	987
		C.J. Fox	C	550

Election	Electors	Candidate	Party	Votes
1874	2,676	P.W. Martin	L	1,206
		J. Goldsmid	L	1,144
		A. Smee	C	835
[Death of Martin]				
1878 (14/6)	2,832	A.J. Otway	L	1,284
		W.S.S. Karr	C	1,004
1880	3,026	A.J. Otway	L	1,497
		R. Leigh	C	1,393
		W.S.S. Karr	C	1,312
		Sir J. Goldsmid, Bt.	L	1,294

Petitions:—

1835: Dismissed (Hodges only)

1841: Withdrawn

1856: Dismissed

RYE [145]

Election	Electors	Candidate	Party	Votes
1832	422	E.B. Curteis	L	162
		†G. De L. Evans	L	128
1835	471	E.B. Curteis	L	211
		T.G. Monypenny	C	101
1837	523	T.G. Monypenny	C	Unopp.
1841	572	H.B. Curteis	L	262
		C.H. Frewen	C	108
1847	574	H.B. Curteis	L	239
		B.B. Williams	C	113
[Death]				
1847 (23/12)		H.M. Curteis	L	Unopp.
[Election declared void on petition]				
1848 (6/4)		H.M. Curteis	L	Unopp.
1852	562	W.A. Mackinnon, Junr.	L	240
		R.C. Pomfret	C	208
[Election delcared void on petition]				
1853 (23/5)	508	W.A. Mackinnon, Senr.	L	216
		R.C. Pomfret	C	184
1857	462	W.A. Mackinnon, Senr.	L	Unopp.
1859	470	W.A. Mackinnon, Senr.	L	Unopp.
1865	373	L.B. Mackinnon	L	180
		W.M. Macdonald	C	172
1868	1,208	J.S. Hardy	C	513
		W.J. Loyd	L	499
1874	1,287	J.S. Hardy *(J.S.G. Hardy)*	C	597
		A. Fytche	L	539
1880	1,389	F.A. Inderwick	L	626
		Hon. J.S.G. Hardy	C	618

Petitions:—

1847: (23/12)	Void election	1865:	Dismissed
1852	Void election		

ST. ALBANS [146]
(Two Seats)

Election	Electors	Candidate	Party	Votes
1832	657	†Sir F. Vincent, Bt.	L	392
		H.G. Ward	L	373
		W. Turner	C	345
1835	544	Hon. E.H. Grimston	C	362
		H.G. Ward	L	284
		Hon. W.H. Beresford	C	237
1837	595	Hon. E.H. Grimston	C	361
		G.A. Muskett	L	347
		B.B. Cabbell	C	219
[Resignation of Grimston]				
1841 (9/2)	500	Earl of Listowel	L	252
		B.B. Cabbell	C	205
1841	500	G.W.J. Repton	C	288
		Earl of Listowel	L	258
		H.T. Worley	C	251
		G.A. Muskett	L	150
[Appointment of Listowel as a Lord in Waiting to Her Majesty]				
1846 (11/8)	541*	B.B. Cabbell	C	264
		Earl of Listowel	L	149
1847	532	A. Raphael	L	295
		G.W.J. Repton	C	276
		J. Wilks	L	230
		Hon. F.K. Craven	L	126
[Death of Raphael]				
1850 (24/12)	483	J. Bell	L	276
		Sir R.W. Carden	C	147

Royal Commission appointed which found proof of extensive bribery and as a result the borough lost its right to return a Member of Parliament and was incorporated into the county constituency of Hertfordshire, from May 3, 1852.

Petitions:—

1841: (9/2) Dismissed

1846: Withdrawn

1850: Dismissed

ST. IVES [147]

Election	Electors	Candidate	Party	Votes
1832	584	†J. Halse	C	302
		†W.M. Praed	C	168
		H.L. Stephens	C	39
1835	599	J. Halse	C	Unopp.
1837	579	J. Halse	C	272
		W.T. Praed	C	223
[Death]				
1838 (24/5)	566	W.T. Praed	C	256
		F.H. Stephens	C	248
1841	600	W.T. Praed	C	272
		E. Ley	C	268
[Death]				
1846 (21/7)		Lord William Powlett	C	Unopp.
1847	594	Lord William Powlett	C	262
		P. Borthwick	C	141
1852	578	R.M. Laffan	C	256
		H. Paull	C	218
		R.E. Barnes	L	18
1857	536	H. Paull	C	Unopp.
1859	522	H. Paull	C	257
		G. Geissler	L	130
1865	486	H. Paull	C	233
		E. Vivian	L	177
1868	1,398	C. Magniac	L	Unopp.
1874	1,430	E.G. Davenport	C	751
		J.B. Bolitho	L	432
[Death]				
1874 (30/12)	1,430	C.T. Praed	C	617
		Sir F. Lycett	L	552
[Election declared void on petition]				
1875 (8/3)	1,410	C.T. Praed	C	658
		Sir F. Lycett	L	550

Election	Electors	Candidate	Party	Votes
1880	1,135	Sir C. Reed	L	487
		C.C. Ross	C	439
[Death]				
1881 (13/4)	1,012	C.C. Ross	C	462
		W.C. Pendarves	L	360

Petitions:—

1841: Withdrawn

1874: (30/12) Void election

SALFORD [148]

(One seat until 1868; two seats from 1868)

Election	Electors	Candidate	Party	Votes
1832	1,497	J. Brotherton	L	712
		W. Garnett	C	518
1835	2,336	J. Brotherton	L	795
		J. Dugdale	C	572
1837	2,628	J. Brotherton	L	890
		W. Garnett	C	888
1841	2,443	J. Brotherton	L	991
		W. Garnett	C	873
1847	2,605	J. Brotherton	L	Unopp.
1852	2,950	J. Brotherton	L	Unopp.
[Death]				
1857 (2/2)		E.R. Langworthy	L	Unopp.
1857	4,028	W.N. Massey	L	1,880
		Sir E. Armitage	L	1,264
1859	4,222	W.N. Massey	L	1,919
		H. Ashworth	L	1,787
[Resignation on appointment as a Member of the Council of India]				
1865 (13/2)		J. Cheetham	L	Unopp.
1865	5,397	J. Cheetham	L	Unopp.
1868	15,862	C.E. Cawley	C	6,312
		W.T. Charley	C	6,181
		J. Cheetham	L	6,141
		H. Rawson	L	6,018
1874	19,177	C.E. Cawley	C	7,003
		W.T. Charley	C	6,987
		J. Kay	L	6,827
		H. Lee	L	6,709
[Death of Cawley]				
1877 (19/4)	22,041	O.O. Walker	C	8,642
		J. Kay	L	8,372

(One seat until 1868; two seats from 1868)

Election	Electors	Candidate	Party	Votes
1880	23,334	B. Armitage	L	11,116
		A. Arnold	L	11,110
		Sir W.T. Charley	C	8,400
		O.O. Walker	C	8,302

Petitions:—

1837: Dismissed

1868: Dismissed

SALISBURY [149]
(Two Seats)

Election	Electors	Candidate	Party	Votes
1832	576	W.B. Brodie	L	392
		†**W. Wyndham	C	268
		†*Hon. D.P. Bouverie	L	265
1835	650	W.B. Brodie	L	Unopp.
		W. Wyndham	C	Unopp.
1837	707	W.B. Brodie	L	Unopp.
		W. Wyndham	C	Unopp.
1841	613	W. Wyndham	C	366
		W.B. Brodie	L	293
		Hon. J.A. Ashley	C	234
[Resignation of Brodie]				
1843 (4/5)	724	A. Hussey	C	252
		Hon. E.P. Bouverie	L	188
[Death of Wyndham]				
1843 (24/11)	724	J.H. Campbell *(Wyndham)*	C	317
		Hon. E.P. Bouverie	L	270
[Resignation of Hussey]				
1847 (25/1)		W.J. Chaplin	L	Unopp.
1847	708	W.J. Chaplin	L	490
		C.B. Wall	C	374
		J. Smith	C	170
1852	680	W.J. Chaplin	L	381
		C.B. Wall	L	331
		F.W. Slade	C	173
		D.H.D. Burr	C	131
[Death of Wall]				
1853 (15/11)	680	E.P. Buckley	L	255
		J. Roberts	C	88
1857	650	E.P. Buckley	L	Unopp.
		M.H. Marsh	L	Unopp.
1859	687	E.P. Buckley	L	370
		M.H. Marsh	L	326
		J. Chapman	C	262
1865	691	M.H. Marsh	L	367
		E.W.T. Hamilton	L	312
		J. Chapman	C	252

SALISBURY [149] (Cont.)
(Two Seats)

Election	Electors	Candidate	Party	Votes
1868	1,461†	J.A. Lush	L	748
		E.W.T. Hamilton	L	679
		G.R. Ryder	C	623
[Resignation of Hamilton]				
1869 (5/8)	1,461	A. Seymour	L	562
		G.R. Ryder	C	549
		M.H. Marsh	L	82
1874	1,829	G.R. Ryder	C	835
		J.A. Lush	L	800
		A.S. Kennard	C	783
		A. Seymour	L	759
1880	1,969	W.H. Grenfell	L	961
		J.P. Edwards	L	958
		C.J. Kennard	C	841
		Hon. R.H. Dutton	C	828
[Appointment of Grenfell as a Groom in Waiting to Her Majesty]				
1882 (21/11)	2,061	C.J. Kennard	C	955
		W.H. Grenfell	L	852

Petitions:—

1832:	Election of Wyndham declared void. Bouverie duly elected after scrutiny
1852:	Withdrawn
1868:	Dismissed (Hamilton only)
1880:	Dismissed
1882:	Dismissed

SANDWICH [150]
(Two Seats)

Election	Electors	Candidate	Party	Votes
1832	916	†J. Marryat	L	495
		†Sir E.T. Troubridge, Bt.	L	485
		S.G. Price	C	361
		Sir E.W.C.R. Owen	C	265
1835	934	S.G. Price	C	551
		Sir E.T. Troubridge, Bt.	L	405
		Sir E.W.C.R. Owen	C	389
[Appointment of Troubridge as a Lord Commissioner of the Admiralty]				
1835 (27/4)		Sir E.T. Troubridge, Bt.	L	Unopp.
1837	911	Sir E.T. Troubridge, Bt.	L	416
		Sir J.R. Carnac, Bt.	L	401
		S.G. Price	C	370
		Sir B.W. Bridges, Bt.	C	330
[Resignation of Carnac on appointment as Governor of Bombay]				
1839 (12/2)		Sir R.S. Donkin	L	Unopp.
[Death of Donkin]				
1841 (11/5)	952	H.H. Lindsay	C	406
		C.R. Fox	L	360
1841	952	H.H. Lindsay	C	Unopp.
		Sir E.T. Troubridge, Bt.	L	Unopp.
1847	943	Lord Clarence Paget	L	459
		C.W. Grenfell	L	437
		Lord Charles Clinton	C	392
[Resignation of Grenfell in order to contest Windsor]				
1852 (28/5)	960	Lord Charles Clinton	C	460
		J.T.W. French	L	257
1852	960	Lord Charles Clinton	C	Unopp.
		J. McGregor	C	Unopp.
1857	1,008	E.H.K. Hugessen	L	547
		Lord Clarence Paget	L	503
		J. McGregor	C	322
		J. Lang	L	24
1859	1,030	E.H.K. Hugessen	L	497
		Lord Clarence Paget	L	458
		Sir J. Fergusson, Bt.	C	404
		W.D. Lewis	C	328

SANDWICH [150] (Cont.)
(Two Seats)

Election	Electors	Candidate	Party	Votes
[Appointment of Hugessen as a Lord Commissioner of the Treasury]				
1859 (28/6)	1,030	E.H.K. Hugessen	L	463
		Sir J. Fergusson, Bt.	C	283
1865	1,054	E.H.K. Hugessen	L	494
		Lord Clarence Paget	L	477
		C. Capper	C	413
[Resignation of Paget]				
1866 (8/5)	1,054	C. Capper	C	466
		T. Brassey	L	458
1868	1,906	E.H.K. Hugessen	L	933
		H.A. Brassey	L	923
		H. Worms	C	710
1874	2,046	H.A. Brassey	L	1,035
		E.H.K. Hugessen	L	1,006
		F.C.H. Hallett	C	764
		H.S. Baillie	C	611
1880	2,115	H.A. Brassey	L	Unopp.
		E.H.K. Hugessen	L	Unopp.
[Elevation of Hugessen to the Peerage — Lord Brabourne]				
1880 (19/5)	2,115	C.H.C. Roberts	C	1,145
		Sir J. Goldsmid, Bt.	L	705

Writ suspended. Royal Commission appointed which found proof of extensive bribery and as a result the borough lost its right to return a Member of Parliament and was incorporated into the county constituency of Kent, Eastern, from June 25, 1885.

Petitions:—

1857:	Withdrawn
1859:	Withdrawn
1865:	Withdrawn
1880: (19/5)	Void Election

SCARBOROUGH [151]
(Two Seats)

Election	Electors	Candidate	Party	Votes
1832	431	†Sir J.V.B. Johnstone, Bt.	L	285
		Sir G. Cayley, Bt.	L	255
		†Sir F.W. Trench	C	145
1835	412	Sir F.W. Trench	C	176
		Sir J.V.B. Johnstone, Bt.	L	161
		Sir G. Cayley, Bt.	L	122
1837	488	Sir F.W. Trench	C	225
		Sir T.C. Style, Bt.	L	211
		Sir J.V.B. Johnstone, Bt.	C	192
1841	564	Sir J.V.B. Johnstone, Bt.	C	296
		Sir F.W. Trench	C	253
		Hon. C.B. Phipps	L	237
1847	670	Sir J.V.B. Johnstone, Bt.	C	Unopp.
		Earl of Mulgrave	L	Unopp.
[Appointment of Mulgrave as Comptroller of H.M. Household]				
1851 (19/7)	743	G.F. Young	C	314
		Earl of Mulgrave	L	281
1852	805	Sir J.V.B. Johnstone, Bt.	C	422
		Earl of Mulgrave	L	387
		G.F. Young	C	313
[Appointment of Mulgrave as Treasurer of H.M. Household]				
1853 (1/1)		Earl of Mulgrave	L	Unopp.
1857	934	Sir J.V.B. Johnstone, Bt.	L	540
		Earl of Mulgrave	L	508
		A.F. Bayford	C	275
[Resignation of Mulgrave on appointment as Lieutenant-Governor of Nova Scotia]				
1857 (14/12)	934*	J.D. Dent	L	373
		G.J. Cayley	C	280
1859	967	Hon. W.H.F. Denison	L	562
		Sir J.V.B. Johnstone, Bt.	L	540
		J.D. Dent	L	428
		G.J. Cayley	C	66
[Succession of Denison to the Peerage — Lord Londesborough]				
1860 (1/2)	1,078	J.D. Dent	L	472
		J.M. Caulfeild	L	340
1865	1,351	Sir J.V.B. Johnstone, Bt.	L	932
		J.D. Dent	L	674
		G.J. Cayley	C	441

SCARBOROUGH [151] (Cont.)
(Two Seats)

Election	Electors	Candidate	Party	Votes
1868	2,964	Sir J.V.B. Johnstone, Bt.	L	1,826
		J.D. Dent	L	1,678
		G.J. Cayley	C	742
[Death of Johnstone]				
1869 (12/3)		Sir H.V.B. Johnstone, Bt.	L	Unopp.
1874	3,631	Sir C. Legard, Bt.	C	1,280
		Sir H.V.B. Johnstone, Bt.	L	1,103
		J.D. Dent	L	799
		J.E.T. Rogers	L	772
1880	4,302	Sir H.V.B. Johnstone, Bt.	L	2,157
		W.S. Caine	L	2,065
		J.C.F. Cookson	C	1,581
		Sir C. Legard, Bt.	C	1,562
[Resignation of Johnstone]				
1880 (31/7)	4,302	J.G. Dodson	L	1,828
		A. Duncombe	C	1,606
[Elevation of Dodson to the Peerage – Lord Monk Bretton]				
1884 (5/11)	4,167	R.F. Steble	L	1,895
		Sir G.R. Sitwell, Bt.	C	1,606
[Appointment of Caine as a Civil Lord of the Admiralty]				
1884 (28/11)	4,167	W.S. Caine	L	1,832
		Sir G.R. Sitwell, Bt.	C	1,639

SHAFTESBURY [152]

Election	Electors	Candidate	Party	Votes
1832	634	J.S. Poulter	L	318
		†E. Penrhyn	L	210
1835	554	J.S. Poulter	L	237
		Hon. W.S. Best	C	148
1837	496	**J.S. Poulter	L	224
		*G.B. Mathew	C	219
1841	497	Lord Howard	L	219
		G.B. Mathew	C	202
[Succession to the Peerage — Earl of Effingham]				
1845 (5/3)		R.B. Sheridan	L	Unopp.
1847	484	R.B. Sheridan	L	213
		R. Bethell	C	176
1852	509	Hon. W.H.B. Portman	L	Unopp.
1857	540	G.G. Glyn	L	Unopp.
1859	515	G.G. Glyn	L	Unopp.
1865	461	G.G. Glyn	L	Unopp.
1868	1,311	G.G. Glyn	L	Unopp.
[Succession to the Peerage — Lord Wolverton]				
1873 (30/8)	1,311	V.F.B. Stanford	C	603
		H.D. Seymour	L	534
1874	1,286	V.F.B. Stanford	C	591
		H.D. Seymour	L	562
1880	1,388	Hon. S.C. Glyn	L	652
		V.F.B. Stanford	C	618

Petitions:—

1837: Election of Poulter declared void. Mathew duly elected after scrutiny

SHEFFIELD [153]
(Two Seats)

Election	Electors	Candidate	Party	Votes
1832	3,308	J. Parker	L	1,515
		J.S. Buckingham	L	1,498
		T.A. Ward	L	1,210
		S. Bailey	L	813
1835	3,587	J. Parker	L	1,607
		J.S. Buckingham	L	1,554
		S. Bailey	L	1,434
[Appointment of Parker as a Lord Commissioner of the Treasury]				
1836 (22/8)	3,903	J. Parker	L	414
		J. Bell	L	0
1837	4,028	J. Parker	L	2,186
		H.G. Ward	L	1,976
		J. Thornely	C	655
1841	4,347	J. Parker	L	1,849
		H.G. Ward	L	1,805
		D. Urquhart	C	503
		W. Sheppard	C	457
1847	4,934	J. Parker	L	1,125
		H.G. Ward	L	1,110
		T. Clark	Ch	326
[Resignation of Ward on appointment as Lord High Commissioner to the Ionian Islands]				
1849 (3/5)		J.A. Roebuck	L	Unopp.
1852	5,322	J.A. Roebuck	L	2,092
		G. Hadfield	L	1,853
		J. Parker	L	1,580
		W. Overend	C	1,180
1857	6,874	J.A. Roebuck	L	3,200
		G. Hadfield	L	2,871
		W. Overend	C	2,059
1859	7,381	G. Hadfield	L	Unopp.
		J.A. Roebuck	L	Unopp.
1865	8,557	J.A. Roebuck	L	3,410
		G. Hadfield	L	3,348
		Hon. J.F.S. Wortley	C	2,626
		T.C. Foster	L	1,576
1868	29,955	G. Hadfield	L	14,793
		A.J. Mundella	L	12,212
		J.A. Roebuck	L	9,571
		E.P. Price	C	5,272

SHEFFIELD [153] (Cont.)
(Two Seats)

Election	Electors	Candidate	Party	Votes
1874	36,701	J.A. Roebuck	L	14,193
		A.J. Mundella	L	12,858
		J. Chamberlain	L	11,053
		J. Allott	L	621
[Death of Roebuck]				
1879 (21/12)	39,270	S.D. Waddy	L	14,062
		C.B.S. Wortley	C	13,584
1880	42,794	A.J. Mundella	L	17,217
		C.B.S. Wortley	C	16,546
		S.D. Waddy	L	16,506
[Appointment of Mundella as Vice-President of the Committee of the Privy Council for Education]				
1880 (8/5)		A.J. Mundella	L	Unopp.

SHOREHAM [154]
(Two Seats)

Election	Electors	Candidate	Party	Votes
1832	1,925	†Sir C.M. Burrell, Bt.	C	785
		H.D. Goring	L	774
		G.F. Jones	C	406
1835	1,910	Sir C.M. Burrell, Bt.	C	Unopp.
		H.D. Goring	L	Unopp.
1837	1,940	H.D. Goring	L	850
		Sir C.M. Burrell, Bt.	C	773
		D. Salomons	L	619
1841	1,918	Sir C.M. Burrell, Bt.	C	959
		C. Goring	C	856
		Lord Edward Howard	L	673
1847	1,864	Sir C.M. Burrell, Bt.	C	Unopp.
		C. Goring	C	Unopp.
[Death of Goring]				
1849 (28/12)		Lord Alexander Gordon-Lennox	C	Unopp.
1852	1,865	Sir C.M. Burrell, Bt.	C	Unopp.
		Lord Alexander Gordon-Lennox	C	Unopp.
1857	1,800	Sir C.M. Burrell, Bt.	C	991
		Lord Alexander Gordon-Lennox	C	806
		H.W. Pemberton	L	487
1859	1,843	Sir C.M. Burrell, Bt.	C	Unopp.
		S. Cave	C	Unopp.
[Death of Burrell]				
1862 (5/2)		Sir P. Burrell, Bt.	C	Unopp.
1865	1,978	S. Cave	C	972
		Sir P. Burrell, Bt.	C	891
		J. Hannen	L	592
[Appointment of Cave as Vice-President of the Board of Trade]				
1866 (14/7)		S. Cave	C	Unopp.
1868	4,774	Sir P. Burrell, Bt.	C	Unopp.
		S. Cave	C	Unopp.
1874	4,998	Sir P. Burrell, Bt.	C	2,527
		S. Cave	C	2,414
		W. Lyon	L	896

Election	Electors	Candidate	Party	Votes
[Appointment of Cave as Judge-Advocate General and Paymaster-General]				
1874 (13/3)		S. Cave	C	Unopp.
[Death of Burrell]				
1876 (5/8)	5,129	Sir W.W. Burrell, Bt.	C	2,152
		W.E. Hubbard	L	1,394
1880	5,480	Sir W.W. Burrell, Bt.	C	2,445
		R. Loder	C	2,195
		W.E. Hubbard	L	2,059

SHREWSBURY [155]
(Two Seats)

Election	Electors	Candidate	Party	Votes
1832	1,714	Sir J. Hanmer, Bt.	C	808
		†R.A. Slaney	L	797
		†J.C. Pelham	C	634
1835	1,270	Sir J. Hanmer, Bt.	C	761
		J.C. Pelham	C	629
		R.A. Slaney	L	578
1837	1,473	R. Jenkins	C	700
		R.A. Slaney	L	697
		J.C. Pelham	C	655
		F. Dashwood	L	537
1841	1,564	G. Tomline	C	793
		B. Disraeli	C	785
		Sir L.P.J. Parry	L	605
		C. Temple	L	578
1847	1,805	E.H. Baldock	C	769
		R.A. Slaney	L	743
		G. Tomline	C	732
1852	1,666	G. Tomline	L	1,159
		E.H. Baldock	C	736
		A. Robinson	L	438
1857	1,617	G. Tomline	L	706
		R.A. Slaney	L	695
		J.W. Huddleston	C	548
		R. Phibbs	C	484
1859	1,635	R.A. Slaney	L	Unopp.
		G. Tomline	L	Unopp.
[Death of Slaney]				
1862 (2/6)	1,506	H. Robertson	L	671
		R.B. Oakeley	C	361
		H. Atkins	C	10
1865	1,533	W.J. Clement	L	Unopp.
		G. Tomline	L	Unopp.
1868	3,381	W.J. Clement	L	1,840
		J. Figgins	C	1,751
		R. Crawford	L	685
[Death of Clement]				
1870 (21/9)	3,381*	D. Straight	C	1,291
		C.C. Cotes	L	1,253

SHREWSBURY [155] (Cont.)
(Two Seats)

Election	Electors	Candidate	Party	Votes
1874	3,620	C.C. Cotes	L	1,672
		H. Robertson	L	1,561
		J. Figgins	C	1,388
		D. Straight	C	1,328
1880	3,846	C.C. Cotes	L	1,945
		H. Robertson	L	1,884
		A.R. Scoble	C	1,622
		Viscount Newry	C	1,568

[Appointment of Cotes as a Lord Commissioner of the Treasury]

1880 (10/5)		C.C. Cotes	L	Unopp.

Petitions:—

1841: Withdrawn

1868: Withdrawn (Figgins only)

1870: Dismissed

SOUTHAMPTON [156]
(Two Seats)

Election	Electors	Candidate	Party	Votes
1832	1,403	†A. Atherley	L	645
		**J.B. Hoy	C	604
		†*J.S. Penleaze	L	594
		†J. Mackillop	C	249
1835	1,172	J.B. Hoy	C	508
		A.R. Dottin	C	492
		J. Easthope	L	423
		P. Bingham	L	371
1837	1,433	A.R. Dottin	C	587
		Viscount Duncan	L	564
		C.C. Martyn	C	543
		Lord Clarence Paget	L	509
1841	1,563	Lord Bruce *(Earl of Elgin)*	C	648
		C.C. Martyn	C	645
		E.J. Hutchins	L	556
		C.E. Mangles	L	554
[Election declared void on petition]				
1842 (9/8)	1,463*	H. St. J. Mildmay	C	685
		G.W. Hope	C	682
		Lord Nugent	L	535
		G. Thompson	L	532
1847	2,258	A.J.E. Cockburn	L	Unopp.
		B.M. Willcox	L	Unopp.
[Appointment of Cockburn as Solicitor-General]				
1850 (17/7)		A.J.E. Cockburn	L	Unopp.
[Appointment of Cockburn as Attorney-General]				
1851 (2/4)		Sir A.J.E. Cockburn	L	Unopp.
1852	2,419	B.M. Willcox	L	1,062
		Sir A.J.E. Cockburn	L	1,017
		A.D.R.W.B. Cochrane	C	797
		A.A. Vansittart	C	767
[Appointment of Cockburn as Attorney-General]				
1853 (7/1)	2,576	Sir A.J.E. Cockburn	L	1,098
		A.D.R.W.B. Cochrane	C	596
[Appointment of Cockburn as Recorder of Bristol]				
1854 (12/4)		Sir A.J.E. Cockburn	L	Unopp.

(Two Seats)

Election	Electors	Candidate	Party	Votes
[Resignation of Cockburn on appointment as Chief Justice of the Court of Common Pleas]				
1857 (11/2)	3,508	T.M. Weguelin	L	994
		Sir E. Butler	C	962
		R. Andrews	L	726
1857	3,508	T.M. Weguelin	L	Unopp.
		B.M. Willcox	L	Unopp.
1859	3,730	W.D. Seymour	L	1,331
		B.M. Willcox	L	1,204
		T.M. Weguelin	L	1,012
[Death of Willcox]				
1862 (6/12)	4,124	W.A. Rose	C	1,715
		C.E. Mangles	L	1,647
1865	4,189	R. Gurney	C	1,565
		G. Moffatt	L	1,527
		W.A. Rose	C	1,422
		T.M. Mackay	L	1,388
		W.D. Seymour	L	447
1868	5,696	R. Gurney	C	2,393
		P.M. Hoare	C	2,178
		G. Moffatt	L	2,161
		F.A. Maxse	L	1,947
1874	6,537	Sir F. Perkins	L	2,724
		R. Gurney	C	2,534
		G. Moffatt	L	2,345
		J.R. Engledue	C	2,103
[Death of Gurney]				
1878 (17/6)	7,021	A. Giles	C	2,552
		H.M. Bompas	L	2,304
1880	7,394	H. Lee	L	3,051
		C.P. Butt	L	3,023
		A. Giles	C	2,972
		Sir J.E. Commerell	C	2,902
[Resignation of Butt on appointment as a Judge of the Probate, Divorce and Admiralty Division of the High Court of Justice]				
1883 (7/4)		A. Giles	C	Unopp.

Petitions:—

1832:	Election of Hoy declared void. Penleaze duly elected after scrutiny
1841:	Void election
1852:	Dismissed
1853:	Withdrawn
1857: (11/2)	Withdrawn
1868:	Dismissed

SOUTH SHIELDS [157]

Election	Electors	Candidate	Party	Votes
1832	475	R. Ingham	L	205
		G. Palmer	C	108
		W. Gowan	L	104
		R. Bowlby	L	2
1835	518	R. Ingham	L	273
		R. Bowlby	L	128
1837	644	R. Ingham	C	Unopp.
1841	676	J.T. Wawn	L	240
		R. Ingham	C	207
		G. Fyler	C	34
1847	744	J.T. Warn	L	333
		W. Whateley	C	176
1852	925	R. Ingham	L	430
		Hon. H.T. Liddell	C	249
1857	1,079	R. Ingham	L	Unopp.
1859	1,126	R. Ingham	L	506
		J.T. Warn	L	300
1865	1,113	R. Ingham	L	Unopp.
1868	6,208	J.C. Stevenson	L	2,582
		C.M. Palmer	L	2,277
1874	8,870	J.C. Stevenson	L	Unopp.
1880	9,893	J.C. Stevenson	L	4,435
		H.B.H. Hamilton	C	1,486

STAFFORD [158]
(Two Seats)

Election	Electors	Candidate	Party	Votes
1832	1,176	W.F. Chetwynd	L	739
		R.H. Gronow	L	526
		W. Blount	L	476
1835	1,117	F.L.H. Goodricke	C	605
		W.F. Chetwynd	L	456
		R. Farrand	C	312
		R.H. Gronow	L	246
		Sir C. Wolseley, Bt.	L	29
[Resignation of Goodricke in order to contest Staffordshire, Southern]				
1837 (21/2)		R. Farrand	C	Unopp.
1837	1,246	W.F. Cheywynd	L	565
		R. Farrand	C	504
		Hon. W.B. Baring	C	464
		W. Blount	L	348
1841	1,154	Hon. S.T. Carnegie	C	681
		E. Buller	L	587
		W. Holmes	C	339
[Appointment of Carnegie as a Lord Commissioner of the Treasury]				
1846 (13/3)	1,257*	Hon. S.T. Carnegie	C	733
		W.W. Sleigh	L	25
1847	1,272	D. Urquhart	C	754
		T. Sidney	C	516
		Hon. S.T. Carnegie	C	271
		J. Lea	L	6
		J.A. Gordon	L	1
1852	1,246	J.A. Wise	L	801
		A.J. Otway	L	501
		J. Bourne	C	458
		J.C. Evans	L	39
		E. Hopkinson	C	1
1857	1,252	J.A. Wise	L	993
		Viscount Ingestre	C	745
		Hon. F.W. Cadogan	L	286
1859	1,364	J.A. Wise	L	911
		T. Salt	C	624
		T. Sidney	L	366
		H.R. Addison	L	181
[Resignation of Wise]				
1860 (3/8)	1,390	T. Sidney	L	716
		Viscount Sandon	C	326

STAFFORD [158] (Cont.)
(Two Seats)

Election	Electors	Candidate	Party	Votes
1865	1,540	M.A. Bass	L	1,091
		W. Meller	C	658
		H.D. Pochin	L	598
1868	3,152†	H.D. Pochin	L	1,189
		W. Meller	C	1,124
		R.C. Chawner	L	1,107
[Election declared void on petition]				
1869 (7/6)	3,152	T. Salt	C	1,206
		Hon. R.A.J. Talbot	C	1,130
		T.W. Evans	L	954
		B. Whitworth	L	943
1874	3,440	T. Salt	C	1,238
		A. Macdonald	L/Lab	1,183
		Hon. F.C. Bridgeman	C	947
		H.D. Pochin	L	903
1880	3,699	C.B.B. McLaren	L	1,498
		A. Macdonald	L/Lab	1,345
		T. Salt	C	1,230
		G.F. Talbot	C	1,149
[Death of Macdonald]				
1881 (21/11)	3,344	T. Salt	C	1,482
		G. Howell	L/Lab	1,185

Petitions:—

1832: Withdrawn (Gronow only)

1841: Withdrawn (Buller only)

1847: Withdrawn (Urquhart only)

1868: Void election

Note:—

1837: (21/2) Goodricke resigned in May 1835 but the issue of a new writ was suspended. It was finally issued in February 1837 after a Division resulted in a majority of one vote in favour of the writ being issued.

STALYBRIDGE [159]

Election	Electors	Candidate	Party	Votes
1868	5,338	J. Sidebottom	C	2,405
		N. Buckley	L	2,078
[Death]				
1871 (1/3)	4,918	N. Buckley	L	2,198
		F.S. Powell	C	2,033
1874	5,129	T.H. Sidebottom	C	2,378
		N. Buckley	L	2,220
1880	5,606	W. Summers	L	2,706
		T.H. Sidebottom	C	2,542

Petition:—

1868: Dismissed

STAMFORD [160]

(Two seats until 1868; one seat from 1868)

Election	Electors	Candidate	Party	Votes
1832	851	T. Chaplin	C	526
		G. Finch	C	463
		A.F. Gregory	L	296
1835	755	T. Chaplin	C	Unopp.
		G. Finch	C	Unopp.
1837	684	T. Chaplin	C	201
		Marquess of Granby	C	200
		Lord Langford	L	1
[Resignation of Chaplin]				
1838 (1/5)		Sir G. Clerk, Bt.	C	Unopp.
1841	661	Sir G. Clerk, Bt.	C	Unopp.
		Marquess of Granby	C	Unopp.
[Appointment of Clerk as Master of the Mint]				
1845 (10/2)		Sir G. Clerk, Bt.	C	Unopp.
1847	616	Marquess of Granby	C	349
		J.C. Herries	C	288
		J. Rolt	C	236
[Appointment of Herries as President of the Board of Control for the Affairs of India]				
1852 (6/3)		J.C. Herries	C	Unopp.
1852	566	J.C. Herries	C	Unopp.
		Sir F. Thesiger	C	Unopp.
[Resignation of Herries]				
1853 (22/8)		Lord Robert Cecil	C	Unopp.
1857	529	Lord Robert Cecil	C	Unopp.
		Sir F. Thesiger	C	Unopp.
[Resignation of Thesiger on appointment as Lord Chancellor and elevation to the Peerage — Lord Chelmsford]				
1858 (3/3)		J. Inglis	C	Unopp.
[Resignation of Inglis on appointment as Lord Justice Clerk — Lord Glencorse]				
1858 (17/7)		Sir S.H. Northcote, Bt.	C	Unopp.

STAMFORD [160] (Cont.)
(Two seats until 1868; one seat from 1868)

Election	Electors	Candidate	Party	Votes
1859	539	Lord Robert Cecil *(Viscount Cranborne)*	C	Unopp.
		Sir S.H. Northcote, Bt.	C	Unopp.
1865	512	Viscount Cranborne	C	Unopp.
		Sir S.H. Northcote, Bt.	C	Unopp.

[Resignation of Northcote in order to contest Devon, Northern]

1866 (8/5)		Sir J.C.D. Hay, Bt.	C	Unopp.

[Appointments of Cranborne as Secretary of State for India and of Hay as a Lord Commissioner of the Admiralty]

1866 (12/7)		Viscount Cranborne	C	Unopp.
		Sir J.C.D. Hay, Bt.	C	Unopp.

[Succession of Cranborne to the Peerage — Marquess of Salisbury]

1868 (4/5)		Viscount Ingestre	C	Unopp.

[Succession of Ingestre to the Peerage — Earl of Shrewsbury]

1868 (24/6)		W.U. Heygate	C	Unopp.
1868	1,094†	Sir J.C.D. Hay, Bt.	C	Unopp.
1874	1,183	Sir J.C.D. Hay, Bt.	C	557
		M.C. Buszard	L	411
1880	1,255	M.C. Buszard	L	601
		Sir J.C.D. Hay, Bt.	C	551

STOCKPORT [161]
(Two Seats)

Election	Electors	Candidate	Party	Votes
1832	1,012	T. Marsland	C	551
		J.H. Lloyd	L	444
		H. Marsland	L	431
		E.D. Davenport	L	237
1835	922	H. Marsland	L	582
		T. Marsland	C	482
		E.D. Davenport	L	361
1837	1,192	H. Marsland	L	467
		T. Marsland	C	467
		R. Cobden	L	412
1841	1,238	H. Marsland	L	571
		R. Cobden	L	541
		T. Marsland	C	346
1847	1,108	R. Cobden	L	643
		J. Heald	C	570
		J. Kershaw	L	537
		J. West	Ch	14
[Cobden elects to sit for Yorkshire, West Riding]				
1847 (16/12)	1,205	J. Kershaw	L	545
		T. Marsland	C	518
1852	1,341	J. Kershaw	L	725
		J.B. Smith	L	622
		J. Heald	C	549
1857	1,417	J. Kershaw	L	834
		J.B. Smith	L	606
		W. Gibb	C	557
1859	1,389	J. Kershaw	L	769
		J.B. Smith	L	641
		W. Gibb	C	594
[Death of Kershaw]				
1864 (9/5)		E.W. Watkin	L	Unopp.
1865	1,348	E.W. Watkin	L	736
		J.B. Smith	L	664
		W. Tipping	C	601
1868	5,702	W. Tipping	C	2,714
		J.B. Smith	L	2,658
		Sir E.W. Watkin	L	2,598
		W. Ambrose	C	2,475

STOCKPORT [161] (Cont.)

(Two Seats)

Election	Electors	Candidate	Party	Votes
1874	7,814	C.H. Hopwood	L	3,628
		F. Pennington	L	3,538
		W. Tipping	C	3,406
		P. Mitford	C	3,372
1880	8,353	C.H. Hopwood	L	4,232
		F. Pennington	L	4,103
		G.A. Fernley	C	3,873
		H. Bell	C	3,685

Petitions:—

1847: Withdrawn (Heald only)

1868: Withdrawn

1874: Withdrawn

STOCKTON-ON-TEES [162]

Election	Electors	Candidate	Party	Votes
1868	4,492	J. Dodds	L	2,476
		Lord Ernest Vane-Tempest	C	867
1874	5,961	J. Dodds	L	3,223
		F.L. Barrington	C	1,425
1880	8,333	J. Dodds	L	4,991
		W.D. Seymour	C	1,452

STOKE-ON-TRENT [163]
(Two Seats)

Election	Electors	Candidate	Party	Votes
1832	1,349	J. Wedgwood	L	822
		J. Davenport	C	625
		R.E. Heathcote	L	588
		G.M. Mason	L	247
1835	1,266	J. Davenport	C	Unopp.
		R.E. Heathcote	L	Unopp.
[Resignation of Heathcote]				
1836 (15/2)		Hon. G. Anson	L	Unopp.
1837	1,475	W.T. Copeland	C	683
		J. Davenport	C	670
		M. Bridges	L	472
		R.B. Sheridan	L	469
1841	1,682	J.L. Ricardo	L	870
		W.T. Copeland	C	606
		Hon. F.D. Ryder	C	486
1847	1,695	J.L. Ricardo	L	954
		W.T. Copeland	C	819
		T.P. Healey	L	384
1852	1,778	J.L. Ricardo	L	921
		Hon. E.F.L. Gower	L	848
		W.T. Copeland	C	769
1857	2,115	W.T. Copeland	C	1,261
		J.L. Ricardo	L	822
		Hon. E.F.L. Gower	L	764
1859	2,221	J.L. Ricardo	L	1,258
		W.T. Copeland	C	1,074
		S. Pope	L	569
[Death of Ricardo]				
1862 (23/9)	2,461	H.R. Grenfell	L	1,089
		A.J.B.B. Hope	C	918
		W. Shee	L	32
1865	3,189	A.J.B.B. Hope	C	1,463
		H.R. Grenfell	L	1,373
		G. Melly	L	1,277
[Resignation of Hope in order to contest Cambridge University]				
1868 (20/2)	3,189*	G. Melly	L	1,489
		C.M. Campbell	C	1,420

STOKE-ON-TRENT [163] (Cont.)
(Two Seats)

Election	Electors	Candidate	Party	Votes
1868	16,199†	G. Melly	L	Unopp.
		W.S. Roden	L	Unopp.
1874	19,129	G. Melly	L	6,700
		R. Heath	C	6,180
		W.S. Roden	L	5,369
		A.A. Walton	L/Lab	5,198
[Resignation of Melly]				
1875 (18/2)	19,548	E.V.H. Kenealy	Ind	6,110
		A.A. Walton	L/Lab	4,168
		H.T. Davenport	C	3,901
1880	19,976	W. Woodall	L	12,130
		H. Broadhurst	L/Lab	11,379
		R. Heath	C	5,126
		E.V.H. Kenealy	Ind	1,091

Petition:—

1852: Withdrawn

STROUD [164]
(Two Seats)

Election	Electors	Candidate	Party	Votes
1832	1,247	W.H. Hyett	L	985
		D. Ricardo	L	585
		G.P. Scrope	L	562
[Resignation of Ricardo]				
1833 (27/5)		G.P. Scrope	L	Unopp.
1835	1,305	G.P. Scrope	L	866
		C.R. Fox	L	708
		J.C. Symons	L	187
[Resignation of Fox]				
1835 (19/5)		Lord John Russell	L	Unopp.
1837	1,340	G.P. Scrope	L	698
		Lord John Russell	L	681
		J. Adams	C	297
1841	1,224	W.H. Stanton	L	594
		G.P. Scrope	L	527
		Sir W.L. Wraxall, Bt.	C	377
1847	1,210	W.H. Stanton	L	563
		G.P. Scrope	L	541
		M.M. Turner	L	176
1852	1,328	G.P. Scrope	L	565
		Lord Moreton	L	528
		S. Baker	C	488
		J. Norton	L	316
[Succession of Moreton to the Peerage — Earl Ducie]				
1853 (28/6)		E. Horsman	L	Unopp.
[Appointment of Horsman as Chief Secretary to the Lord Lieutenant of Ireland]				
1855 (6/3)		E. Horsman	L	Unopp.
1857	1,287	E. Horsman	L	Unopp.
		G.P. Scrope	L	Unopp.
1859	1,320	E. Horsman	L	Unopp.
		G.P. Scrope	L	Unopp.
1865	1,356	E. Horsman	L	687
		G.P. Scrope	L	685
		Hon. A.G.J. Ponsonby	L	287

(Two Seats)

Election	Electors	Candidate	Party	Votes
[Resignation of Scrope]				
1867 (20/8)	1,356*	H.S.P. Winterbotham	L	580
		J.E. Dorington	C	508
1868	5,642†	S.S. Dickinson	L	2,907
		H.S.P. Winterbotham	L	2,805
		J.E. Dorington	C	2,096
[Death of Winterbotham]				
1874 (8/1)	5,942	J.E. Dorington	C	2,817
		Sir H.M. Havelock, Bt.	L	2,426
1874	5,942	W.J. Stanton	L	2,798
		S.S. Dickinson	L	2,794
		J.E. Dorington	C	2,763
		G. Holloway	C	2,467
[Election declared void on petition]				
1874 (18/5)	5,942	J.E. Dorington	C	2,796
		A.J. Stanton	L	2,722
		H.R. Brand	L	2,677
		G. Holloway	C	2,582
[Election of Dorington declared void on petition]				
1874 (27/7)	5,942	H.R. Brand	L	2,695
		J.T. Stanton	C	2,613
[Election declared void on petition]				
1875 (22/2)	6,046	S.S. Marling	L	2,783
		Viscount Bury	C	2,577
1880	6,376	W.J. Stanton	L	3,098
		H.R. Brand	L	3,081
		G. Holloway	C	2.810
		J.E. Dorington	C	2,722

Petitions:—

1874:	Void election
1874: (18/5)	Election of Dorington declared void. Petition against Stanton dismissed
1874: (27/7)	Void election
1880:	Withdrawn

SUDBURY [165]

(Two Seats)

Election	Electors	Candidate	Party	Votes
1832	509	M.A. Taylor	L	263
		†Sir J.B. Walsh, Bt.	C	253
		†D.C. Wrangham	C	234
		J. Bagshaw	L	46
[Death of Taylor]				
1834 (25/7)	547	Sir E. Barnes	C	264
		J. Bagshaw	L	263
1835	554	J. Bagshaw	L	285
		B. Smith	L	251
		Sir E. Barnes	C	241
		S.L. Stephens	C	227
1837	599	Sir E. Barnes	C	372
		Sir J.J. Hamilton, Bt.	C	342
		W.A. Smith	L	151
		T.E.M. Turton	L	19
[Resignation of Hamilton]				
1837 (12/12)	602	J. Bailey	C	303
		J. Morrison	L	255
[Death of Barnes]				
1838 (27/3)	602	Sir J.B. Walsh, Bt.	C	293
		J. Bagshaw	L	266
[Resignation of Walsh in order to contest Radnorshire]				
1840 (5/6)		G. Tomline	C	Unopp.
1841	603	F.M. Villiers	L	284
		D.O.D. Sombre	L	281
		D. Jones	C	274
		C. Taylor	C	274

Writ suspended. Royal Commission appointed which found proof of extensive bribery and as a result the borough lost its right to return a Member of Parliament and was incorporated into the county constituency of Suffolk, Western, from July 29, 1844.

Petitions:—

1834: Lapsed on Dissolution of Parliament. (The candidates had polled 263 votes each but the Returning Officer had given a casting vote to Barnes. A similar case arose at Helston in 1866 and as a result the House of Commons resolved that the Returning Officer did not have the right of a casting vote and it was his duty to return all candidates who polled equal votes).

1838: Withdrawn

1840: Dismissed

1841: Void election

SUNDERLAND [166]

(Two Seats)

Election	Electors	Candidate	Party	Votes
1832	1,378	Sir W. Chaytor, Bt.	L	697
		Hon. G. Barrington	L	525
		D. Barclay	L	404
		†W. Thompson	C	392
[Resignation of Barrington]				
1833 (4/4)	1,378	W. Thompson	C	574
		D. Barclay	L	556
1835	1,359	W. Thompson	C	844
		D. Barclay	L	709
		Sir W. Chaytor, Bt.	L	389
1837	1,532	W. Thompson	C	688
		A. White	L	628
		D. Barclay	L	591
1841	1,691	D. Barclay	L	Unopp.
		W. Thompson	C	Unopp.
[Resignation of Thompson in order to contest Westmorland]				
1841 (17/9)	1,691	Viscount Howick	L	706
		M.W. Attwood	C	462
[Succession of Howick to the Peerage – Earl Grey]				
1845 (15/8)	1,681*	G. Hudson	C	627
		T.P. Thompson	L	498
1847	1,693	G. Hudson	C	879
		D. Barclay	L	642
		W.A. Wilkinson	L	568
[Resignation of Barclay]				
1847 (22/12)	1,692	Sir H. Williamson, Bt.	L	705
		W.A. Wilkinson	L	576
1852	1,973	G. Hudson	C	868
		W.D. Seymour	L	814
		H. Fenwick	L	654
[Appointment of Seymour as Recorder of Newcastle upon Tyne]				
1855 (2/1)	2,176*	H. Fenwick	L	956
		W.D. Seymour	L	646
1857	2,493	H. Fenwick	L	1,123
		G. Hudson	C	1,081
		R. Walters	L	863

(Two Seats)

Election	Electors	Candidate	Party	Votes
1859	2,729	H. Fenwick	L	1,527
		W.S. Lindsay	L	1,292
		G. Hudson	C	790
1865	3,468	H. Fenwick	L	1,826
		J. Hartley	C	1,355
		J. Candlish	L	1,307
[Appointment of Fenwick as a Civil Lord of the Admiralty]				
1866 (28/2)	3,468	J. Candlish	L	1,430
		H. Fenwick	L	1,294
1868	11,364†	J. Candlish	L	6,237
		E.T. Gourley	L	4,901
		T.C. Thompson	L	3,596
1874	14,008	E.T. Gourley	L	6,172
		Sir H.M. Havelock, Bt. *(Allan)*	L	5,920
		L.R. Bailey	C	3,781
1880	15,021	E.T. Gourley	L	7,639
		Sir H.M.H. Allan, Bt.	L	6,995
		E. Brooke	C	4,262
[Resignation of Allan]				
1881 (12/4)		S. Storey	L	Unopp.

Petitions:—

1841: (17/9) Withdrawn

1857: Withdrawn (Hudson only)

TAMWORTH [167]
(Two Seats)

Election	Electors	Candidate	Party	Votes
1832	586	†Sir R. Peel, Bt.	C	Unopp.
		†Lord Charles Townshend	L	Unopp.
1835	505	Sir R. Peel, Bt.	C	Unopp.
		W.Y. Peel	C	Unopp.
1837	497	Sir R. Peel, Bt.	C	387
		E.H. A'Court	C	245
		J. Townshend	L	185
1841	485	Sir R. Peel, Bt.	C	365
		E.H. A'Court	C	241
		J. Townshend	L	147
[Appointment of Peel as Prime Minister and First Lord of the Treasury]				
1841 (13/9)		Sir R. Peel, Bt.	C	Unopp.
1847	393	Sir R. Peel, Bt.	C	Unopp.
		W.Y. Peel	C	Unopp.
[Resignation of W.Y. Peel]				
1847 (18/12)		J. Townshend	L	Unopp.
[Death of Peel]				
1850 (19/7)		Sir R. Peel, Bt.	C	Unopp.
1852	382	Sir R. Peel, Bt.	C	Unopp.
		J. Townshend	L	Unopp.
[Appointment of Peel as a Civil Lord of the Admiralty]				
1855 (14/3)		Sir R. Peel, Bt.	C	Unopp.
[Succession of Townshend to the Peerage — Marquess of Townshend]				
1856 (7/2)		Viscount Raynham	L	Unopp.
1857	419	Sir R. Peel, Bt.	L	Unopp.
		Viscount Raynham	L	Unopp.
1859	465	Sir R. Peel, Bt.	L	341
		Viscount Raynham	L	285
		W.T.S. Daniel	C	80

TAMWORTH [167] (Cont.)
(Two Seats)

Election	Electors	Candidate	Party	Votes
[Appointment of Peel as Chief Secretary to the Lord Lieutenant of Ireland]				
1861 (31/7)		Sir R. Peel, Bt.	L	Unopp.
[Succession of Raynham to the Peerage — Marquess of Townshend]				
1863 (12/10)	463	J. Peel	L	224
		Hon. H.F. Cowper	L	167
1865	532	Sir R. Peel, Bt.	L	416
		J. Peel	L	287
		W.T.S. Daniel	C	103
1868	1,753	Sir R. Peel, Bt.	L	1,136
		Sir H.L.E. Bulwer	L	827
		J. Peel	L	798
[Elevation of Bulwer to the Peerage — Lord Dalling and Bulwer]				
1871 (28/3)		J. Peel	L	Unopp.
[Death of J. Peel]				
1872 (16/4)	1,747	R.W. Hanbury	C	946
		Sir R.S. Robinson	L	323
1874	1,850	Sir R. Peel, Bt.	L	1,089
		R.W. Hanbury	C	1,086
		H. Hawkes	L	448
		C.P. Butt	L	209
[Resignation of Hanbury in order to contest Staffordshire, Northern]				
1878 (25/4)	2,096	H.A. Bass	L	1,186
		Hon. F.C. Bridgeman	C	607
1880	2,368	H.A. Bass	L	1,409
		J.S. Balfour	L	1,074
		W.H. Worthington	C	920

Petitions:—

1837: Dismissed (A'Court only)

1868: Dismissed

TAUNTON [168]
(Two Seats)

Election	Electors	Candidate	Party	Votes
1832	949	†E.T. Bainbridge	L	Unopp.
		†H. Labouchere	L	Unopp.
1835	920	E.T. Bainbridge	L	Unopp.
		H. Labouchere	L	Unopp.
[Appointment of Labouchere as Vice-President of the Board of Trade and Master of the Mint]				
1835 (29/4)	920	H. Labouchere	L	452
		B. Disraeli	C	282
1837	943	H. Labouchere	L	469
		E.T. Bainbridge	L	414
		R.N. Lee	C	409
1841	856	H. Labouchere	L	430
		E.T. Bainbridge	L	409
		W. Wilberforce	C	381
		J. Hall	C	218
[Resignation of Bainbridge]				
1842 (11/2)	1,010*	Sir T.E. Colebrooke, Bt.	L	394
		J. Hall	C	337
[Appointment of Labouchere as Chief Secretary to the Lord Lieutenant of Ireland]				
1846 (10/7)		H. Labouchere	L	Unopp.
1847	911	H. Labouchere	L	543
		Sir T.E. Colebrooke, Bt.	L	388
		A. Mills	C	376
1852	790	H. Labouchere	L	430
		A. Mills	C	361
		Sir T.E. Colebrooke, Bt.	L	358
[Election of Mills declared void on petition]				
1853 (4/5)	886	Sir J.W. Ramsden, Bt.	L	372
		H. Badcock	C	367
[Appointment of Labouchere as Secretary of State for the Colonies]				
1856 (5/2)		H. Labouchere	L	Unopp.
1857	887	H. Labouchere	L	442
		A. Mills	C	401
		Hon. W.F. Campbell	L	366

TAUNTON [168] (Cont.)
(Two Seats)

Election	Electors	Candidate	Party	Votes
1859	832	A. Mills	C	415
		H. Labouchere	L	388
		G.A.F.C. Bentinck	C	325
		W. Beadon	L	255

[Elevation of Labouchere to the Peerage — Lord Taunton]

Election	Electors	Candidate	Party	Votes
1859 (9/8)	832	G.A.F.C. Bentinck	C	382
		A.C. Barclay	L	337
1865	839	A.C. Barclay	L	478
		Lord William Hay	L	470
		E.W. Cox	C	292
		A. Austin	C	260
1868	1,977†	A.C. Barclay	L	1,105
		**E.W. Cox	C	988
		*H. James	L	890

[Appointment of James as Solicitor-General]

Election	Electors	Candidate	Party	Votes
1873 (14/10)	1,913	H. James	L	899
		Sir A.F.A. Slade, Bt.	C	812
1874	1,999	A.C. Barclay	L	Unopp.
		Sir H. James	L	Unopp.
1880	2,225	Sir W. Palliser	C	1,084
		Sir H. James	L	1,000
		W.W. Cargill	C	971
		R. Eykyn	L	968

[Appointment of James as Attorney-General]

Election	Electors	Candidate	Party	Votes
1880 (8/5)		Sir H. James	L	Unopp.

[Death of Palliser]

Election	Electors	Candidate	Party	Votes
1882 (17/2)	2,362	S.C. Allsopp	C	1,144
		Viscount Kilcoursie	L	917

Petitions:—

1837: Dismissed (Bainbridge only)

1852: Void election (Mills only)

1853: Dismissed

1857: Withdrawn (Mills only)

1865: Withdrawn

1868: Election of Cox declared void. James duly elected after scrutiny. Two petitions against Barclay were withdrawn. A petition was subsequently lodged against James but the Court ruled that a petitioner who had been seated on petition could not afterwards be petitioned against.

1873: Dismissed

TAVISTOCK [169]

(Two seats until 1868; one seat from 1868)

Election	Electors	Candidate	Party	Votes
1832	247	Lord Russell	L	159
		†C.R. Fox	L	129
		Sir F. Knowles	L	64
1835	289	Lord Russell	L	167
		J. Rundle	L	145
		Sir F. Knowles	L	5
1837	329	J. Rundle	L	Unopp.
		Lord Russell (*Marquess of Tavistock*)	L	Unopp.
1841	275	J. Rundle	L	Unopp.
		Lord Edward Russell	L	Unopp.
[Resignation of Rundle]				
1843 (16/3)	264	J.S. Trelawny	L	113
		H. Vincent	Ch	69
1847	315	Hon. E.S. Russell	L	153
		J.S. Trelawny	L	150
		R.J. Phillimore	L	86
		S. Carter	L	56
[Trelawny seeks re-election]				
1852 (28/4)	349	S. Carter	L	115
		J.S. Trelawny	L	89
		R.J. Phillimore	L	80
1852	349	Hon. G.H.C. Byng	L	220
		**S. Carter	L	169
		*R.J. Phillimore	L	104
1857	395	Hon. G.H.C. Byng	L	242
		Sir J.S. Trelawny, Bt.	L	198
		S. Carter	L	130
[Resignation of Byng]				
1857 (4/9)	395	A.J.E. Russell	L	164
		E. Miall	L	120
1859	414	A.J.E. Russell	L	Unopp.
		Sir J.S. Trelawny, Bt.	L	Unopp.
1865	426	A.J.E. Russell	L	330
		J.D'A. Samuda	L	179
		S. Carter	L	119
		J. Rummens	C	93
		T.A. Blakely	L	8

TAVISTOCK [169] (Cont.)

(Two seats until 1868; one seat from 1868)

Election	Electors	Candidate	Party	Votes
1868	802	A.J.E. Russell	L	Unopp.
1874	805	Lord Arthur Russell	L	362
		R.H.W. Biggs	L	273
1880	847	Lord Arthur Russell	L	Unopp.

Petition:—

1852: Election of Carter declared void owing to disqualification. Phillimore duly elected.

Note:—

1852: (28/4) Trelawny's reasons for resigning and then becoming a candidate at the by-election are not entirely clear but local press reports suggest that it was probably the result of him having failed to support the more radical policies advocated by the local Liberals. Although he declared he was not seeking re-election, he made it clear that he would be prepared to take his seat in the House of Commons if re-elected and as a result he was nominated by his supporters.

TEWKESBURY [170]
(Two seats until 1868; one seat from 1868)

Election	Electors	Candidate	Party	Votes
1832	386	†C.H. Tracy	L	210
		J. Martin (1)	L	195
		W. Dowdeswell	C	184
1835	396	W. Dowdeswell	C	195
		C.H. Tracy	L	195
		J. Martin (1)	L	192
1837	404	W. Dowdeswell	C	219
		J. Martin (1)	L	192
		J. Peel	C	169
1841	507	W. Dowdeswell	C	193
		J. Martin (1)	L	189
		J. Easthope	L	181
1847	409	H. Brown	L	43
		J. Martin (1)	L	43
		Viscount Lascelles	C	0
1852	370	H. Brown	L	205
		J. Martin (1)	L	189
		E.W. Cox	C	147
1857	371	Hon. F. Lygon	C	200
		J. Martin (1)	L	169
		H. Brown	L	127
		E.W. Cox	C	25
[Appointment of Lygon as a Civil Lord of the Admiralty]				
1859 (8/3)	341	Hon. F. Lygon	C	171
		H. Brown	L	0
1859	341	Hon. F. Lygon	C	Unopp.
		J. Martin (2)	L	Unopp.
[Resignation of Lygon in order to contest Worcestershire, Western]				
1864 (9/2)		J.R. Yorke	C	Unopp.
1865	325	W.E. Dowdeswell	C	195
		J.R. Yorke	C	182
		J. Martin (2)	L	150
[Resignation of Dowdeswell in order to contest Worcestershire, Western]				
1866 (20/3)	325	Sir E.A.H. Lechmere, Bt.	C	151
		J. Martin (2)	L	147

TEWKESBURY [170] (Cont.)

(Two seats until 1868; one seat from 1868)

Election	Electors	Candidate	Party	Votes
1868	745	W.E. Price	L	355
		Sir E.A.H. Lechmere, Bt.	C	279
1874	730	W.E. Price	L	350
		Sir E.A.H. Lechmere, Bt.	C	323
1880	733	W.E. Price	L	350
		J.A. Fowler	C	341
[Election declared void on petition]				
1880	733	R.B. Martin	L	380
(12/7)		J.A. Fowler	C	298

Petitions:—

1857: Dismissed (Martin only)

1880: Void election

THETFORD [171]
(Two Seats)

Election	Electors	Candidate	Party	Votes
1832	146	F. Baring	C	Unopp.
		†Lord James Fitzroy	L	Unopp.
[Death of Fitzroy]				
1834 (8/8)		Earl of Euston (Senr.)	L	Unopp.
1835	160	F. Baring	C	Unopp.
		Earl of Euston (Senr.)	L	Unopp.
1837	161	Hon. F. Baring	C	Unopp.
		Earl of Euston (Senr.)	L	Unopp.
1841	156	Hon. W.B. Baring	C	86
		**Earl of Euston (Senr.)	L	71
		*Sir J. Flower, Bt.	C	71
[Appointment of Baring as Paymaster-General]				
1845 (24/2)		W.B. Baring	C	Unopp.
1847	214	W.B. Baring	C	Unopp.
		Earl of Euston (Junr.)	L	Unopp.
[Succession of Baring to the Peerage – Lord Ashburton]				
1848 (3/8)		Hon. F. Baring	C	Unopp.
1852	200	Hon. F. Baring	C	Unopp.
		Earl of Euston (Junr.)	L	Unopp.
1857	218	Hon. F. Baring	C	Unopp.
		Earl of Euston (Junr.)	L	Unopp.
[Resignation of Baring]				
1857 (9/12)		A.H. Baring	L	Unopp.
1859	231	A.H. Baring	L	Unopp.
		Earl of Euston (Junr.)	L	Unopp.
[Succession of Euston to the Peerage – Duke of Grafton]				
1863 (21/4)	232	Lord Frederick Fitzroy	L	93
		R.J.H. Harvey	C	81
1865	224	R.J.H. Harvey	C	193
		Hon. A.H. Baring	L	137
		A.T. Dakin	L	69

THETFORD [171] (Cont.)
(Two Seats)

Election	Electors	Candidate	Party	Votes
[Resignation of Baring]				
1867 (2/12)		E.S. Gordon	C	Unopp.

This constituency ceased to return a Member of Parliament in 1868 and was incorporated into the county constituency of Norfolk, Western.

Petition:—

1841: Treble return. On scrutiny one vote was struck off Euston's total and his election declared void. Flower duly elected

THIRSK [172]

Election	Electors	Candidate	Party	Votes
1832	254	†Sir R. Frankland, Bt.	L	Unopp.
[Resignation]				
1834 (21/3)		S. Crompton	L	Unopp.
1835	267	S. Crompton	L	Unopp.
1837	283	S. Crompton	L	Unopp.
1841	328	J. Bell	L	Unopp.
1847	332	J. Bell	L	Unopp.
[Death]				
1851 (21/3)		Sir W.P. Gallwey, Bt.	C	Unopp.
1852	357	Sir W.P. Gallwey, Bt.	C	Unopp.
1857	398	Sir W.P. Gallwey, Bt.	C	Unopp.
1859	414	Sir W.P. Gallwey, Bt.	C	Unopp.
1865	380	Sir W.P. Gallwey, Bt.	C	Unopp.
1868	902	Sir W.P. Gallwey, Bt.	C	416
		H.V.B. Johnstone	L	390
1874	935	Sir W.P. Gallwey, Bt.	C	410
		H.M. Stapylton	L	409
1880	1,014	Hon. L.P. Dawnay	C	485
		H.M. Stapylton	L	422
		Sir W.A. Frankland, Bt.	C	10

Petitions:—

1868: Withdrawn

1880: Dismissed

TIVERTON [173]
(Two Seats)

Election	Electors	Candidate	Party	Votes
1832	462	J. Heathcoat	L	376
		J. Kennedy	L	265
		B. Wood	L	55
		C. Chichester	L	40
[Election of Kennedy declared void on petition]				
1833 (24/5)	462	J. Kennedy	L	214
		B. Wood	L	95
1835	473	J. Heathcoat	L	366
		J. Kennedy	L	184
		C. Chichester	L	134
		J. Langmead	C	62
[Resignation of Kennedy]				
1835 (1/6)		Viscount Palmerston	L	Unopp.
1837	498	J. Heathcoat	L	323
		Viscount Palmerston	L	246
		B.B. Dickinson	C	180
1841	478	J. Heathcoat	L	Unopp.
		Viscount Palmerston	L	Unopp.
[Appointment of Palmerston as Secretary of State for Foreign Affairs]				
1846 (10/7)		Viscount Palmerston	L	Unopp.
1847	445	J. Heathcoat	L	148
		Viscount Palmerston	L	127
		G.J. Harney	Ch	0
1852	461	J. Heathcoat	L	Unopp.
		Viscount Palmerston	L	Unopp.
[Appointment of Palmerston as Secretary of State for the Home Department]				
1853 (3/1)		Viscount Palmerston	L	Unopp.
[Appointment of Palmerston as Prime Minister and First Lord of the Treasury]				
1855 (12/2)		Viscount Palmerston	L	Unopp.
1857	482	J. Heathcoat	L	Unopp.
		Viscount Palmerston	L	Unopp.
1859	506	Hon. G. Denman	L	Unopp.
		Viscount Palmerston	L	Unopp.

TIVERTON [173] (Cont.)

(Two Seats)

Election	Electors	Candidate	Party	Votes
[Appointment of Palmerston as Prime Minister and First Lord of the Treasury]				
1859 (27/6)		Viscount Palmerston	L	Unopp.
[Appointment of Palmerston as Constable of Dover Castle and Warden Keeper of the Cinque Ports]				
1861 (28/3)		Viscount Palmerston	L	Unopp.
1865	465	Viscount Palmerston	L	261
		J.W. Walrond	L	220
		Hon. G. Denman	L	217
[Death of Palmerston]				
1866 (28/2)	465	Hon. G. Denman	L	232
		Sir J.C.D. Hay, Bt.	C	186
1868	1,155	J.H.H. Amory	L	Unopp.
		Hon. G. Denman	L	Unopp.
[Resignation of Denman on appointment as a Judge of the Court of Common Pleas]				
1872 (6/11)	1,258	W.N. Massey	L	577
		J.W. Walrond	C	547
1874	1,294	J.H.H. Amory	L	677
		W.N. Massey	L	629
		J.W. Walrond	C	605
1880	1,320	Sir J.H.H. Amory, Bt.	L	743
		W.N. Massey	L	699
		J.W. Walrond	C	590
[Death of Massey]				
1881 (15/11)	1,405	Viscount Ebrington	L	705
		R.F. Loosemore	C	453

Petitions:—

1832: Election of Kennedy declared void

1866: Withdrawn

TOTNES [174]
(Two Seats)

Election	Electors	Candidate	Party	Votes
1832	217	J. Cornish	L	127
		J. Parrott	L	127
		Viscount Boringdon	C	66
[Resignation of Cornish]				
1834 (17/2)	277	Lord Seymour	L	153
		J.T. Mayne	L	73
1835	259	J. Parrott	L	Unopp.
		Lord Seymour	L	Unopp.
[Appointment of Seymour as a Lord Commissioner of the Treasury]				
1835 (24/4)		Lord Seymour	L	Unopp.
1837	318	Lord Seymour	L	192
		J. Parrott	L	159
		Sir G.P. Adams	C	121
[Resignation of Parrott]				
1839 (26/7)	297*	C.B. Baldwin	C	142
		W. Blount	L	142
[Election delcared void on petition]				
1840 (21/4)	341	C.B. Baldwin	C	158
		T. Gisborne	L	151
1841	391	C.B. Baldwin	C	Unopp.
		Lord Seymour	L	Unopp.
1847	378	Lord Seymour	L	280
		C.B. Baldwin	C	154
		S. Ricardo	L	153
[Appointment of Seymour as Commissioner of Woods, Forests, Land Revenues, Works, and Buildings]				
1850 [30/3)		Lord Seymour	L	Unopp.
1852	371	Lord Seymour	L	263
		T. Mills	L	154
		C.B. Baldwin	C	141
[Succession of Seymour to the Peerage — Duke of Somerset]				
1855 (5/11)		Earl of Gifford	L	Unopp.
1857	315	Earl of Gifford	L	171
		T. Mills	L	150
		J.T. Mackenzie	L	118
		J. Gregory	C	57

TOTNES [174] (Cont.)
(Two Seats)

Election	Electors	Candidate	Party	Votes
1859	341	Earl of Gifford	L	180
		T. Mills	L	152
		J. Dunn	C	135
[Death of Mills]				
1862 (9/12)	357	J. Pender	L	171
		J. Dent	C	5
[Death of Gifford]				
1863 (20/1)	357	A. Seymour	L	165
		J. Dent	C	157
1865	382	J. Pender	L	210
		A. Seymour	L	204
		W.G. Dawkins	C	162
		B.C.T. Pim	C	147

Writ suspended. Royal Commission appointed which found proof of extensive bribery and as a result the borough lost its right to return a Member of Parliament and was incorporated into the county constituency of Devon, Southern, from the Dissolution.

Petitions:—

1839: Double return. The election was declared void on a technicality — the Returning Officer having failed to give proper notice of the poll

1852: Dismissed (Mills only)

1857: Withdrawn

1865: Election of Pender declared void. Petition against Seymour dismissed

TRURO [175]
(Two Seats)

Election	Electors	Candidate	Party	Votes
1832	405	Sir R.H. Vivian, Bt.	L	291
		W. Tooke	L	203
		J.E. Vivian	C	196
1835	510	J.E. Vivian	C	316
		W. Tooke	L	274
		Sir R.H. Vivian, Bt.	L	176
1837	579	E. Turner	L	393
		J.E. Vivian	C	254
		W. Tooke	L	226
1841	622	E. Turner	L	Unopp.
		J.E. Vivian	C	Unopp.
1847	627	E. Turner	L	Unopp.
		J.E. Vivian	C	Unopp.
[Death of Turner]				
1849 (11/1)	586	H. Willyams	L	240
		M.E. Smith	C	224
1852	607	H.H. Vivian	L	267
		J.E. Vivian	C	263
		A. Smith	L	255
		M.E. Smith	C	229
1857	646	A. Smith	L	Unopp.
		E.W.B. Willyams	L	Unopp.
1859	647	M.E. Smith	C	303
		A. Smith	L	225
		Hon. J.C.W. Vivian	L	213
[Resignation of M.E. Smith on appointment as a Judge of the Court of Common Pleas]				
1865 (14/2)	567	F.M. Williams	C	249
		Hon. J.C.W. Vivian	L	220
1865	567	Hon. J.C.W. Vivian	L	Unopp
		F.M. Williams	C	Unopp
1868	1,435	F.M. Williams	C	731
		Hon. J.C.W. Vivian	L	683
		J.P. Edwards	L	406
[Appointment of Vivian as a Lord Commissioner of the Treasury]				
1868 (21/12)		Hon. J.C.W. Vivian	L	Unopp.

TRURO [175] (Cont.)
(Two Seats)

Election	Electors	Candidate	Party	Votes
[Resignation of Vivian on appointment as Permanent Under-Secretary of State for War]				
1871 (13/9)	1,442	J.M. Hogg	C	605
		E. Jenkins	L	436
1874	1,582	Sir F.M. Williams, Bt.	C	798
		J.M. Hogg *(J.M.M. Hogg)*	C	723
		H.R. Grenfell	L	565
		J. Graham	L	455
[Death of Williams]				
1878 (26/9)	1,578	A. Tremayne	C	656
		E.W.B. Willyams	L	611
1880	1,542	Sir J.M.M. Hogg, Bt.	C	781
		E.W.B. Willyams	L	754
		J. Chester	C	181

TYNEMOUTH and NORTH SHIELDS [176]

Election	Electors	Candidate	Party	Votes
1832	760	G.F. Young	L	326
		S. Ilderton	L	264
1835	660	G.F. Young	L	Unopp.
1837	704	**G.F. Young	L	269
		*Sir C.E. Grey	L	253
1841	709	H. Mitcalfe	L	295
		W. Chapman	C	213
1847	789	R.W. Grey	L	Unopp.
1852	883	H. Taylor	C	340
		R.W. Grey	L	328
[Election declared void on petition]				
1854 (30/3)	908	W.S. Lindsay	L	357
		P. Dickson	C	340
1857	1,048	W.S. Lindsay	L	Unopp.
1859	1,049	H. Taylor	C	Unopp.
[Resignation]				
1861 (23/4)	1,064*	R. Hodgson	C	421
		A.J. Otway	L	374
1865	1,271	G.O. Trevelyan	L	494
		R. Hodgson	C	438
1868	2,601	T.E. Smith	L	1,098
		H.J. Trotter	C	710
1874	4,898	T.E. Smith	L	Unopp.
1880	5,736	T.E. Smith	L	2,844
		H.J. Trotter	C	1,397

Petitions:—

1837: Election of Young declared void. Grey duly elected after scrutiny

1852: Void election

WAKEFIELD [177]

Election	Electors	Candidate	Party	Votes
1832	726	D. Gaskell	L	Unopp
1835	617	D. Gaskell	L	277
		Hon. W.S.S. Lascelles	C	220
1837	702	Hon. W.S.S. Lascelles	C	307
		D. Gaskell	L	281
1841	750	**J. Holdsworth	L	328
		*Hon. W.S.S. Lascelles	C	300
1847	682	G. Sandars	C	392
		G.W. Alexander	L	258
1852	766	G. Sandars	C	359
		W.H. Leatham	L	326
1857	906	J.C.D. Charlesworth	C	Unopp.
1859	882	W.H. Leatham	L	406
		J.C.D. Charlesworth	C	403
[Election declared void on petition]				
1862 (28/2)	1,030	Sir J.C.D. Hay, Bt.	C	455
		R. Smethurst	L	426
1865	1,086	W.H. Leatham	L	507
		Sir J.C.D. Hay, Bt.	C	457
1868	3,627†	S.A. Beaumont	L	1,557
		T.K. Sanderson	C	1,512
1874	3,889	E. Green	C	1,779
		R.B. Mackie	L	1,600
[Election declared void on petition]				
1874 (6/5)	3,889	T.K. Sanderson	C	1,814
		R.B. Mackie	L	1,627
1880	4,430	R.B. Mackie	L	2,194
		T.K. Sanderson	C	1,796
[Death]				
1885 (4/7)	4,026*	E. Green	C	1,918
		W.H. Lee	L	1,661

Petitions:—

1841: Election of Holdsworth declared void owing to disqualification Lascelles duly elected
1859: Void election
1862: Withdrawn
1865: Dismissed
1874: Void election

WALLINGFORD [178]

Election	Electors	Candidate	Party	Votes
1832	453	W.S. Blackstone	C	202
		C. Eyston	L	165
1835	366	W.S. Blackstone	C	Unopp.
1837	333	W.S. Blackstone	C	159
		T. Teed	L	118
1841	386	W.S. Blackstone	C	Unopp.
1847	398	W.S. Blackstone	C	166
		A. Morrison	L	154
1852	428	R. Malins	C	174
		A. Morrison	L	168
1857	371	R. Malins	C	149
		A. Sartoris	L	135
1859	381	R. Malins	C	Unopp.
1865	357	Sir C.W. Dilke, Bt.	L	158
		R. Malins	C	132
1868	942	S. Vickers	C	453
		Sir C.W. Dilke, Bt.	L	358
[Death]				
1872 (9/3)		E. Wells	C	Unopp.
1874	1,141	E. Wells	C	575
		E. Jones	L	437
1880	1,226	W. Wren	L	582
		E. Wells	C	541
[Election declared void on petition]				
1880 (1/7)	1,226	P. Ralli	L	567
		R.W. Hanbury	C	548

Petitions:-

1868:	Dismissed
1880:	Void election
1880: (1/7)	Dismissed

WALSALL [179]

Election	Electors	Candidate	Party	Votes
1832	597	C.S. Forster	C	304
		G. de B. Attwood	L	231
1835	578	C.S. Forster	C	Unopp.
1837	746	F. Finch	L	316
		C.S. Forster	C	296
[Resignation]				
1841 (2/2)	808	J.N. Gladstone	C	362
		J.B. Smith	L	335
1841	808	R. Scott	L	334
		J.N. Gladstone	C	312
1847	856	Hon. E.R. Littleton	L	289
		C. Forster	L	282
		W.H. Cooke	C	124
1852	1,026	C. Forster	L	Unopp.
1857	1,188	C. Forster	L	Unopp.
1859	1,092	C. Forster	L	495
		C. Bagnall	C	383
1865	1,296	C. Forster	L	Unopp.
1868	6,047†	C. Forster	L	Unopp.
1874	8,684	C. Forster	L	3,364
		W.M. Bell	C	1,731
1880	9,537	Sir C. Forster, Bt.	L	Unopp.

Petitions:—

1837: Dismissed

1841 (2/2): Dismissed

1847: Withdrawn

WAREHAM [180]

Election	Electors	Candidate	Party	Votes
1832	339	J.H. Calcraft	C	175
		J.S.W.S.E. Drax	L	140
1835	339	J.H. Calcraft	C	Unopp.
1837	368	J.H. Calcraft	C	170
		J.S.W.S.E. Drax	L	155
1841	438	J.S.W.S.E. Drax	L	211
		J.H. Calcraft	C	187
1847	442	J.S.W.S.E. Drax	L	Unopp.
1852	418	J.S.W.S.E. Drax	C	Unopp.
1857	312	J.H. Calcraft	L	143
		J.S.W.S.E. Drax	C	140
1859	342	J.S.W.S.E. Drax	C	Unopp.
1865	273	J.H.M. Calcraft	L	125
		J.S.W.S.E. Drax	C	109
1868	894	J.H.M. Calcraft	L	314
		J.S.W.S.E. Drax	C	301
		T.F. Fremantle	C	68
[Death]				
1868 (23/12)	894	J.S.W.S.E. Drax	C	374
		W.M. Calcraft	L	305
1874	953	J.S.W.S.E. Drax	C	502
		M.J. Guest	L	310
		S.H. Emmens	C	26
1880	987	M.J. Guest	L	451
		J.S.W.S.E. Drax	C	416

Petitions:—

1841: Withdrawn

1857: Dismissed

1865: Withdrawn

WARRINGTON [181]

Election	Electors	Candidate	Party	Votes
1832	456	E.G. Hornby	L	203
		J.I. Blackburne	C	176
1835	557	J.I. Blackburne	C	148
		C. Hindley	L	130
1837	635	J.I. Blackburne	C	278
		E.D. Davenport	L	254
1841	633*	J.I. Blackburne	C	Unopp.
1847	699	G. Greenall	C	327
		W. Allcard	L	298
1852	701	G. Greenall	C	Unopp.
1857	720	G. Greenall	C	Unopp.
1859	723	G. Greenall	C	Unopp.
1865	768	G. Greenall	C	Unopp.
1868	4,470	P. Rylands	L	1,984
		G. Greenall	C	1,957
1874	5,022	G. Greenall	C	2,381
		P. Rylands	L	2,201
1880	5,919	J.G. McMinnies	L	3,002
		Sir G. Greenall, Bt.	C	2,473

Petition:—

1868: Dismissed

WARWICK [182]
(Two Seats)

Election	Electors	Candidate	Party	Votes
1832	1,340	Hon. Sir C.J. Greville	C	701
		†E.B. King	L	553
		†J. Tomes	L	463
1835	971	Hon. Sir C.J. Greville	C	564
		E.B. King	L	478
		J. Halcomb	C	416
[Resignation of Greville]				
1836 (23/8)	1,046	Hon. C.J. Canning	C	463
		H.W. Hobhouse	L	434
[Succession of Canning to the Peerage — Viscount Canning]				
1837 (28/3)	1,013	W. Collins	L	457
		J. Adams	C	422
1837	1,013	W. Collins	L	498
		Sir C.E. Douglas	C	468
		E.B. King	L	439
1841	957	W. Collins	L	Unopp.
		Sir C.E. Douglas	C	Unopp.
[Appointment of Douglas as a Commissioner of Greenwich Hospital]				
1845 (13/8)		Sir C.E. Douglas	C	Unopp.
1847	770	W. Collins	L	443
		Sir C.E. Douglas	C	407
		H. Roberts	L	30
1852	723	G.W.J. Repton	C	383
		E. Greaves	C	348
		J. Mellor	L	327
1857	734	E. Greaves	C	Unopp.
		G.W.J. Repton	C	Unopp.
1859	721	E. Greaves	C	Unopp.
		G.W.J. Repton	C	Unopp.
1865	690	G.W.J. Repton	C	342
		A.W. Peel	L	315
		E. Greaves	C	297
1868	1,688	A.W. Peel	L	873
		E. Greaves	C	863
		W.R. Cremer	L/Lab	260

WARWICK [182] (Cont.)
(Two Seats)

Election	Electors	Candidate	Party	Votes
1874	1,664	G.W.J. Repton	C	836
		A.W. Peel	L	783
		A.F. Godson	C	740
		W.R. Cremer	L/Lab	180
1880	1,758	A.W. Peel	L	981
		G.W.J. Repton	C	768
		A.F. Godson	C	676

Petition:—

1832: Election of Greville declared void. Writ suspended

Note:—

1880: Peel was Speaker of the House of Commons from February 1884 until April 1895

WEDNESBURY [183]

Election	Electors	Candidate	Party	Votes
1868	14,277	A. Brogden	L	6,129
		T.E. Walker	C	3,779
		E.V.H. Kenealy	Ind	969
1874	20,357	A. Brogden	L	7,530
		R. Mills	C	5,813
1880	20,035	A. Brogden	L	6,912
		F.W. Isaacson	C	207

WELLS [184]
(Two Seats)

Election	Electors	Candidate	Party	Votes
1832	338	N. Lamont	L	169
		†J.L. Lee	L	167
		†N.W.R. Colborne	L	164
		†J.E. Vaughan	C	59
[Death of Lamont]				
1834 (5/5)		N.W.R. Colborne	L	Unopp.
1835	377	N.W.R. Colborne	L	Unopp.
		J.L. Lee	L	Unopp.
1837	402	R. Blakemore	C	Unopp.
		W.G. Hayter	L	Unopp.
1841	346	R. Blakemore	C	Unopp.
		W.G. Hayter	L	Unopp.
1847	375	R. Blakemore	C	Unopp.
		W.G. Hayter	L	Unopp.
[Appointment of Hayter as Judge-Advocate General]				
1847 (27/12)		W.G. Hayter	L	Unopp.
1852	325	R.C. Tudway	C	187
		W.G. Hayter	L	175
		J.A. Kinglake	L	101
[Death of Tudway]				
1855 (21/11)	380*	H.H. Jolliffe	C	146
		J.A. Kinglake	L	121
1857	343	W.G. Hayter	L	Unopp.
		H.H. Jolliffe	C	Unopp.
1859	327	Sir W.G. Hayter, Bt.	L	Unopp.
		H.H. Jolliffe	C	Unopp.
1865	274	A.D. Hayter	L	Unopp.
		Hon. H.H. Jolliffe	C	Unopp.

This constituency ceased to return a Member of Parliament in 1868 and was incorporated into the county constituency of Somerset, Mid.

WENLOCK [185]

(Two Seats)

Election	Electors	Candidate	Party	Votes
1832	691	†Hon. G.C.W. Forester	C	448
		J.M. Gaskell	C	330
		M. Bridges	L	308
1835	809	Hon. G.C.W. Forester	C	519
		J.M. Gaskell	C	422
		Sir W.M. Somerville, Bt.	L	323
1837	906	Hon. G.C.W. Forester	C	Unopp.
		J.M. Gaskell	C	Unopp.
1841	961	Hon. G.C.W. Forester	C	Unopp.
		J.M. Gaskell	C	Unopp.
[Appointment of Gaskell as a Lord Commissioner of the Treasury]				
1841 (14/9)		J.M. Gaskell	C	Unopp.
1847	857	Hon. G.C.W. Forester	C	Unopp.
		J.M. Gaskell	C	Unopp.
[Appointment of Forester as Comptroller of H.M. Household]				
1852 (3/3)		G.C.W. Forester	C	Unopp.
1852	905	G.C.W. Forester	C	Unopp.
		J.M. Gaskell	C	Unopp.
1857	871	G.C.W. Forester	C	Unopp.
		J.M. Gaskell	C	Unopp.
[Appointment of Gaskell as Comptroller of H.M. Household]				
1858 (3/3)		G.C.W. Forester	C	Unopp.
1859	881	G.C.W. Forester	C	Unopp.
		J.M. Gaskell	C	Unopp.
1865	961	G.C.W. Forester	C	Unopp.
		J.M. Gaskell	C	Unopp.
1868	3,445	A.H. Brown	L	Unopp.
		G.C.W. Forester	C	Unopp.
1874	3,541	G.C.W. Forester	C	1,708
		A.H. Brown	L	1,575
		C.G.M. Gaskell	C	846

WENLOCK [185] (Cont.)
(Two Seats)

Election	Electors	Candidate	Party	Votes
[Succession of Forester to the Peerage — Lord Forester]				
1874 (16/11)	3,541	C.T.W. Forester	C	1,720
		Hon. B. Lawley	L	1,401
1880	3,481	A.H. Brown	L	2,058
		C.T.W. Forester	C	1,358
		R.A. Benson	C	1,013

WESTBURY [186]

Election	Electors	Candidate	Party	Votes
1832	185	†Sir R. Lopes, Bt.	L	Unopp.
1835	192	Sir R. Lopes, Bt.	L	Unopp.
1837	213	J.I. Briscoe	L	98
		Sir R. Lopes, Bt.	C	96
1841	291*	Sir R. Lopes, Bt.	C	Unopp.
1847	342	J. Wilson	L	170
		M. Higgins	C	149
1852	314	J. Wilson	L	145
		L.M. Lopes	C	138
1857	342	Sir L.M. Lopes, Bt.	C	Unopp.
1859	328	Sir L.M. Lopes, Bt.	C	Unopp.
1865	300	Sir L.M. Lopes, Bt.	C	Unopp.
1868	1,046	J.L. Phipps	C	492
		A. Laverton	L	465
[Election declared void on petition]				
1869 (27/2)	1,046	C.P. Phipps	C	499
		A. Laverton	L	488
1874	1,123	A. Laverton	L	540
		C.P. Phipps	C	518
1880	1,125	C.N.P. Phipps	C	559
		A. Laverton	L	505

Petitions:—

1847: Withdrawn

1868: Void election

1880: Dismissed

WEYMOUTH and MELCOMBE REGIS [187]
(Two Seats)

Election	Electors	Candidate	Party	Votes
1832	475	†T.F. Buxton	L	238
		Sir F.G. Johnstone, Bt.	C	215
		W.W. Burdon	L	214
		†G. Bankes	C	175
1835	518	T.F. Buxton	L	268
		W.W. Burdon	L	239
		Viscount Villiers	C	150
1837	589	Viscount Villiers	C	291
		G.W. Hope	C	268
		T.F. Buxton	L	211
		G. Stephen	L	151
1841	598	**Viscount Villiers	C	259
		**G.W. Hope	C	257
		*R. Bernal	L	254
		*W.D. Christie	L	251
1847	625	W.D. Christie	L	274
		W.L. Freestun	L	274
		Hon. F.W.C. Villiers	C	272
		G.M. Butt	C	271
[Resignation of Christie]				
1847 (15/12)		Hon. F.W.C. Villiers	C	Unopp.
1852	679	G.M. Butt	C	386
		W.L. Freestun	L	336
		A.H. Oswald	L	283
1857	681	W.L. Freestun	L	446
		R.J.R. Campbell	L	349
		G.M. Butt	C	272
1859	748	R. Brooks	C	341
		Viscount Grey de Wilton	C	340
		W.L. Freestun	L	311
		R.J.R. Campbell	L	297
1865	906	R. Brooks	C	381
		H.G. Gridley	L	378
		Viscount Grey de Wilton	C	28
		H. Edwards	L	14
[Resignation of Gridley]				
1867 (11/6)		H. Edwards	L	Unopp.

WEYMOUTH and MELCOMBE REGIS [187] (Cont.)
(Two Seats)

Election	Electors	Candidate	Party	Votes
1868	1,343	C.J.T. Hambro	C	750
		H. Edwards	L	701
		J.J. Powell	L	452
1874	1,467	H. Edwards	L	944
		Sir F.J.W. Johnstone, Bt.	C	504
		C.J.T. Hambro	C	452
1880	1,612	H. Edwards	L	1,156
		Sir F.J.W. Johnstone, Bt.	C	807
		A.C. Wylie	L	653

Petitions:—

1832: Withdrawn

1841: Election of Villiers and Hope declared void. Bernal and Christie duly elected after scrutiny

1857: Dismissed

1859: Dismissed

WHITBY [188]

Election	Electors	Candidate	Party	Votes
1832	422	A. Chapman	C	217
		R. Moorsom	L	139
1835	432	A. Chapman	C	Unopp.
1837	458	A. Chapman	C	Unopp.
1841	424	A. Chapman	C	Unopp.
1847	403	R. Stephenson	C	Unopp.
1852	454	R. Stephenson	C	218
		Hon. E. Phipps	L	109
1857	532	R. Stephenson	C	Unopp.
1859	647	R. Stephenson	C	Unopp.
[Death]				
1859 (23/11)	647	H.S. Thompson	L	229
		T. Chapman	C	190
1865	703	C. Bagnall	C	305
		H.S. Thompson	L	282
1868	2,058	W.H. Gladstone	L	894
		W.C. Worsley	C	518
[Appointed a Lord Commissioner of the Treasury]				
1869 (18/11)	2,058	W.H. Gladstone	L	779
		W.C. Worsley	C	596
1874	2,069	W.H. Gladstone	L	873
		C. Bagnall	C	754
1880	2,163	A. Pease	L	1,072
		R.G.C. Mowbray	C	699

WHITEHAVEN [189]

Election	Electors	Candidate	Party	Votes
1832	458	†M. Attwood	C	210
		I. Littledale	L	174
1835	460	M. Attwood	C	Unopp.
1837	476	M. Attwood	C	Unopp.
1841	558	M. Attwood	C	Unopp.
1847	543	R.C. Hildyard	C	Unopp.
1852	512	R.C. Hildyard	C	Unopp.
1857	555	R.C. Hildyard	C	Unopp.
[Death]				
1857 (17/12)		G. Lyall	C	Unopp.
1859	571	G. Lyall	C	Unopp.
1865	648	G.A.F.C. Bentinck	C	Unopp.
1868	2,495	G.A.F.C. Bentinck	C	1,125
		A.B. Steward	L	771
1874	2,431	G.A.F.C. Bentinck	C	Unopp.
[Appointed Judge-Advocate General]				
1875 (18/12)	2,599	G.A.F.C. Bentinck	C	1,503
		C. Thompson	L	313
1880	2,622	G.A.F.C. Bentinck	C	1,204
		W.C. Gully	L	1,072

WIGAN [190]
(Two Seats)

Election	Electors	Candidate	Party	Votes
1832	483	†R. Thicknesse	L	302
		R. Potter	L	296
		J. Whittle	L	212
		†J.H. Kearsley	C	174
1835	495	J.H. Kearsley	C	296
		R. Potter	L	191
		C.S. Standish	L	166
1837	539	C.S. Standish	L	249
		R. Potter	L	245
		J.H. Kearsley	C	229
		P. Greenall	C	211
[Resignation of Potter]				
1839 (9/3)	551*	W. Ewart	L	261
		J.H. Kearsley	C	259
1841	586	P. Greenall	C	273
		**T.B. Crosse	C	268
		*C.S. Standish	L	264
		C.P. Grenfell	L	263
[Death of Greenall]				
1845 (16/10)	517*	Hon. J. Lindsay	C	274
		R.A. Thicknesse	L	211
1847	637	Hon. J. Lindsay	C	Unopp.
		R.A. Thicknesse	L	Unopp.
1852	718	R.A. Thicknesse	L	366
		Hon. J. Lindsay	C	356
		F.S. Powell	C	324
[Death of Thicknesse]				
1854 (3/10)	788	J. Acton	L	339
		F.S. Powell	C	334
1857	797	F.S. Powell	C	492
		H. Woods	L	447
		Hon. J. Lindsay	C	309
1859	835	Hon. J. Lindsay	C	500
		H. Woods	L	476
		F.S. Powell	C	273
1865	863	Hon. J. Lindsay	C	Unopp.
		H. Woods	L	Unopp.

Election	Electors	Candidate	Party	Votes
[Resignation of Lindsay]				
1866 (27/3)	863	N. Eckersley	C	411
		J. Lancaster	L	349
1868	3,939	H. Woods	L	2,219
		J. Lancaster	L	2,166
		N. Eckersley	C	1,920
		J. Pearson	C	1,875
1874	5,062	Lord Lindsay	C	2,493
		T. Knowles	C	2,401
		J. Lancaster	L	1,883
		W. Pickard	L/Lab	1,134
		H. Woods	L	1,029
1880	6,120	Lord Lindsay	C	2,946
		T. Knowles	C	2,913
		J. Lancaster	L	2,880
		G. McCorquodale	L	2,653
[Succession of Lindsay to the Peerage — Earl of Crawford and Balcarres]				
1881 (20/1)	5,937	F.S. Powell	C	3,005
		J. Lancaster	L	2,536
[Election declared void on petition]				
1882 (4/12)	6,097	Hon. A.F. Egerton	C	2,867
		W. Wren	L	2,243
[Death of Knowles]				
1883 (21/12)		N. Eckersley	C	Unopp.

Petitions:—

1839:	Dismissed
1841:	Election of Crosse declared void. Standish duly elected after scrutiny. Petition against Greenall dismissed
1845:	Dismissed
1868:	Dismissed
1881:	Void election

WILTON [191]

Election	Electors	Candidate	Party	Votes
1832	204	†J.H. Penruddocke	C	Unopp.
1835	203	J.H. Penruddocke	C	Unopp.
1837	210	E. Baker	C	Unopp.
1841	194	Viscount Fitzharris	C	Unopp.
[Succession to the Peerage — Earl of Malmesbury]				
1841 (6/10)		Viscount Somerton	C	Unopp.
1847	216	Viscount Somerton	C	Unopp.
1852	219	C.H.W. A'Court	L	125
		J.G.J. Greene	C	26
[Resignation on appointment as a Special Commissioner of Property and Income Tax in Ireland]				
1855 (28/3)		E. Antrobus	L	Unopp.
1857	251	E. Antrobus	L	Unopp.
1859	258	E. Antrobus	L	Unopp.
1865	265	E. Antrobus	L	Unopp.
1868	931†	E. Antrobus	L	Unopp.
1874	1,040	Sir E. Antrobus, Bt.	L	Unopp.
[Resignation]				
1877 (21/2)	1,087	Hon. S. Herbert	C	751
		J.F. Norris	L	187
1880	1,401	Hon. S. Herbert	C	819
		J. Arch	L/Lab	397
[Appointed a Lord Commissioner of the Treasury]				
1885 (2/7)		Hon. S. Herbert	C	Unopp.

Petition:—

1880: Withdrawn

WINCHESTER [192]
(Two Seats)

Election	Electors	Candidate	Party	Votes
1832	531	†P.St.J. Mildmay	L	351
		W.B. Baring	L	263
		†J.B. East	C	151
1835	515	J.B. East	C	254
		W.B. Baring	L	176
		P.St.J. Mildmay	L	123
1837	585	J.B. East	C	258
		P.St.J. Mildmay	L	242
		B. Escott	C	216
1841	567	J.B. East	C	320
		B. Escott	C	292
		R.B. Crowder	L	191
		F. Pigott	L	166
1847	684	J.B. Carter	L	363
		Sir J.B. East, Bt.	C	315
		B. Escott	L	243
1852	788	J.B. Carter	L	376
		Sir J.B. East, Bt.	C	269
		W.W. Bulpett	L	288
1857	842	J.B. Carter	L	398
		Sir J.B. East, Bt.	C	384
		W.S. Portal	L	253
1859	866	Sir J.B. East, Bt.	C	402
		J.B. Carter	L	349
		T.W. Fleming	C	341
		G.J.S. Lefevre	L	231
[Resignation of East]				
1864 (10/2)		T.W. Fleming	C	Unopp.
1865	963	J.B. Carter	L	459
		W.B. Simonds	C	367
		T.W. Fleming	C	336
[Appointment of Carter as a Lord Commissioner of the Treasury]				
1866 (4/6)	963	J.B. Carter	L	361
		C. Lempriere	C	46
1868	1,621	W.B. Simonds	C	830
		J.B. Carter	L	690
		A.J. Scott	L	529

WINCHESTER [192] (Cont.)
(Two Seats)

Election	Electors	Candidate	Party	Votes
1874	1,793	W.B. Simonds	C	949
		A.R. Naghten	C	793
		J.B. Carter	L	657
1880	2,011	Viscount Baring	L	979
		R. Moss	C	808
		W.B. Simonds	C	773

WINDSOR [193]
(Two seats until 1868; one seat from 1868)

Election	Electors	Candidate	Party	Votes
1832	507	†J. Ramsbottom	L	408
		Sir S.J.B. Pechell, Bt.	L	230
		Sir J.E. de Beauvoir	L	205
1835	504	J. Ramsbottom	L	353
		**Sir J.E. de Beauvoir	L	239
		*Sir J. Elley	C	231
1837	703	J. Ramsbottom	L	326
		R. Gordon	L	292
		Sir J.E. de Beauvoir	L	182
		T. Bulkeley	C	140
1841	642	J. Ramsbottom	L	316
		R. Neville	C	311
		W.F. Fergusson	L	265
		Sir J.E. de Beauvoir	L	130
[Death of Ramsbottom]				
1845 (8/11)		G.A. Reid	C	Unopp.
[Appointment of Neville as a Lord Commissioner of the Treasury]				
1846 (14/3)		R. Neville	C	Unopp.
1847	728	Lord John Hay	L	Unopp.
		G.A. Reid	C	Unopp.
[Resignation of Hay]				
1850 (6/2)		J. Hatchell	L	Unopp.
[Appointment of Hatchell as Attorney-General for Ireland]				
1851 (10/2)		J. Hatchell	L	Unopp.
[Death of Reid]				
1852 (22/5)	712	C.W. Grenfell	L	330
		A. Vansittart	C	230
1852	712	Lord Charles Wellesley	C	241
		C.W. Grenfell	L	224
		S. Ricardo	L	210
		T. Bulkeley	C	107
[Resignation of Wellesley]				
1855 (14/2)		S. Ricardo	L	Unopp.

WINDSOR [193] (Cont.)
(Two seats until 1868; one seat from 1868)

Election	Electors	Candidate	Party	Votes
1857	642	W. Vansittart	C	325
		C.W. Grenfell	L	289
		S. Ricardo	L	286
1859	609	W. Vansittart	C	325
		G.W. Hope	C	269
		C.W. Grenfell	L	246
[Death of Hope]				
1863 (4/11)	619	R.H.R.H. Vyse	C	287
		A.D. Hayter	L	236
1865	651	Sir H.A. Hoare, Bt.	L	324
		H. Labouchere	L	323
		W. Vansittart	L	291
		R.H.R.H. Vyse	C	251
[Election declared void on petition]				
1866 (9/5)		C. Edwards	L	Unopp.
		R. Eykyn	L	Unopp.
1868	1,777†	R. Eykyn	L	803
		R.R. Gardner	C	795
1874	1,951	R.R. Gardner	C	1,064
		R. Eykyn	L	618
1880	2,122	R.R. Gardner	C	995
		V.W.B. Van de Weyer	L	824

Petitions:—

1835:	Election of Beauvoir declared void. Elley duly elected after scrutiny
1841:	Withdrawn
1852:	Dismissed (Wellesley only)
1859:	Withdrawn
1865:	Void election
1868:	Dismissed
1874:	Dismissed

WOLVERHAMPTON [194]
(Two Seats)

Election	Electors	Candidate	Party	Votes
1832	1,700	†W.W. Whitmore	L	850
		R. Fryer	L	810
		F. Holyoake	C	615
		J. Nicholson	L	358
1835	1,839	C.P. Villiers	L	776
		T. Thornely	L	776
		D. Fereday	C	658
		J. Nicholson	L	374
1837	2,170	C.P. Villiers	L	1,068
		T. Thornely	L	1,024
		J.R. Burton	C	623
		J. Benbow	C	613
1841	2,571	T. Thornely	L	Unopp.
		Hon. C.P. Villiers	L	Unopp.
1847	2,692	T. Thornely	L	Unopp.
		Hon. C.P. Villiers	L	Unopp.
1852	3,587	T. Thornely	L	Unopp.
		Hon. C.P. Villiers	L	Unopp.
[Appointment of Villiers as Judge-Advocate General]				
1853 (4/1)		C.P. Villiers	L	Unopp.
1857	3,611	T. Thornely	L	Unopp.
		C.P. Villiers	L	Unopp.
1859	3,821	Sir R. Bethell	L	Unopp.
		C.P. Villiers	L	Unopp.
[Appointment of Bethell as Attorney-General]				
1859 (27/6)		Sir R. Bethell	L	Unopp.
[Appointment of Villiers as President of the Poor Law Board]				
1859 (9/7)		C.P. Villiers	L	Unopp.
[Resignation of Bethell on appointment as Lord Chancellor and elevation to the Peerage — Lord Westbury]				
1861 (3/7)	4,110†	T.M. Weguelin	L	1,363
		S. Griffiths	L	772
		A.S. Hill	C	665

WOLVERHAMPTON [194] (Cont.)
(Two Seats)

Election	Electors	Candidate	Party	Votes
1865	4,830	C.P. Villiers	L	1,623
		T.M. Weguelin	L	1,519
		T. Thorneycroft	C	47
1868	15,772	C.P. Villiers	L	Unopp.
		T.M. Weguelin	L	Unopp.
1874	23,257	C.P. Villiers	L	10,358
		T.M. Weguelin	L	10,036
		W. Williams	C	3,628
1880	22,821	C.P. Villiers	L	12,197
		H.H. Fowler	L	11,606
		A. Hickman	C	5,874

Petition:—

1861: Withdrawn

WOODSTOCK [195]

Election	Electors	Candidate	Party	Votes
1832	317	Marquess of Blandford	C	Unopp.
1835	306	Lord Charles Churchill	C	Unopp.
1837	330	H. Peyton	C	126
		Lord Charles Churchill	C	117
[Resignation]				
1838	385	Marquess of Blandford	C	160
(11/5)		Lord John Churchill	L	155
[Succession to the Peerage – Duke of Marlborough]				
1840 (20/3)		F. Thesiger	C	Unopp.
1841	356	F. Thesiger	C	Unopp.
[Resignation on appointment as Solicitor-General and decision to contest Abingdon]				
1844 (22/4)		Marquess of Blandford	C	Unopp.
[Resignation]				
1845 (1/5)		Viscount Loftus	C	Unopp.
[Succession to the Peerage – Marquess of Ely]				
1845 (18/12)		Lord Alfred Churchill	C	Unopp.
1847	404	Marquess of Blandford	C	Unopp.
1852	347	Marquess of Blandford	C	Unopp.
1857	336	Marquess of Blandford	C	Unopp.
[Succession to the Peerage – Duke of Marlborough]				
1857 (24/7)		Lord Alfred Churchill	C	Unopp.
1859	310	Lord Alfred Churchill	C	Unopp.
1865	286	H. Barnett	C	143
		M. Henry	L	119
1868	1,127	H. Barnett	C	502
		Hon. G.C. Brodrick	L	481

Election	Electors	Candidate	Party	Votes
1874	1,071	Lord Randolph Churchill	C	569
		Hon. G.C. Brodrick	L	404
1880	1,060	Lord Randolph Churchill	C	512
		W. Hall	L	452
[Appointed Secretary of State for India]				
1885 (6/7)	1,084*	Lord Randolph Churchill	C	532
		C. Grant	L	405

Petitions:—

1837: Withdrawn

1838: Dismissed

WORCESTER [196]
(Two Seats)

Election	Electors	Candidate	Party	Votes
1832	2,366	†T.H.H. Davies	L	Unopp.
		†G.R. Robinson	L	Unopp.
1835	2,400	G.R. Robinson	L	1,611
		J. Bailey	C	1,154
		T.H.H. Davies	L	1,137
1837	3,238	J. Bailey	C	Unopp.
		T.H.H. Davies	L	Unopp.
1841	3,037	Sir T. Wilde	L	1,187
		J. Bailey	C	1,173
		R. Hardy	L	875
[Resignation of Wilde on appointment as Attorney-General]				
1846 (8/7)		Sir D. Le Marchant, Bt.	L	Unopp.
1847	2,518	O. Ricardo	L	1,168
		F. Rufford	C	1,141
		R. Hardy	L	932
[Resignation of Rufford]				
1852 (28/4)		W. Laslett	L	Unopp.
1852	2,290	W. Laslett	L	1,212
		O. Ricardo	L	1,164
		J.W. Huddleston	C	661
1857	2,530	W. Laslett	L	1,137
		O. Ricardo	L	1,003
		T. Sidney	L	615
1859	2,563	W. Laslett	L	Unopp.
		O. Ricardo	L	Unopp.
[Resignation of Laslett]				
1860 (12/3)		R. Padmore	L	Unopp.
1865	2,309	A.C. Sherriff	L	1,255
		R. Padmore	L	1,033
		J. Levick	C	978
1868	5,542†	W. Laslett	C	2,439
		A.C. Sherriff	L	2,063
		T.R. Hill	L	1,586
		Sir F. Lycett	L	1,269

(Two Seats)

Election	Electors	Candidate	Party	Votes
1874	5,578	A.C. Sherriff	L	2,284
		T.R. Hill	L	2,164
		J.D. Allcroft	C	1,958
		W. Laslett	C	1,672
[Death of Sherriff]				
1878 (28/3)	6,290	J.D. Allcroft	C	2,609
		Sir F. Lycett	L	2,155
1880	6,422	T.R. Hill	L	2,716
		A.J. McIntyre	L	2,511
		J.D. Allcroft	C	2,502

Petitions:—

1835: Dismissed (Bailey only)

1837: Withdrawn

1880: Dismissed

Note:—

1846: A few days after becoming Attorney-General, Wilde was appointed Chief Justice of the Court of Common Pleas.

WYCOMBE [197]

(Two seats until 1868, one seat from 1868)

Election	Electors	Candidate	Party	Votes
1832	298	†Hon. R.J. Smith	L	179
		†Hon. C. Grey	L	140
		B. Disraeli	C	119
1835	309	Hon. R.J. Smith	L	289
		Hon. C. Grey	L	147
		B. Disraeli	C	128
1837	387	G.H. Dashwood	L	Unopp.
		Hon. R.J. Smith	L	Unopp.
[Succession of Smith to the Peerage — Lord Carrington]				
1838 (23/10)		G.R. Smith	L	Unopp.
1841	388	G.H. Dashwood	L	189
		R. Bernal (*Osborne*)	L	159
		J.W. Freshfield	C	130
		R. Alexander	C	86
1847	335	G.H. Dashwood	L	Unopp.
		M.T. Smith	L	Unopp.
1852	346	Sir G.H. Dashwood, Bt.	L	262
		M.T. Smith	L	208
		W. Simpson	L	116
1857	390	Sir G.H. Dashwood, Bt.	L	Unopp.
		M.T. Smith	L	Unopp.
1859	392	Sir G.H. Dashwood, Bt.	L	Unopp.
		M.T. Smith	L	Unopp.
[Death of Dashwood]				
1862 (18/3)	423	J.R. Mills	L	220
		D. Cameron	C	158
1865	551	Hon. C.R. Carington	L	Unopp.
		J.R. Mills	L	Unopp.
[Succession of Carington to the Peerage — Lord Carrington]				
1868 (11/4)		Hon. W.H.P. Carington	L	Unopp.
1868	1,338	Hon. W.H.P. Carington	L	701
		J.R. Mills	L	500

WYCOMBE [197] (Cont.)
(Two seats until 1868, one seat from 1868)

Election	Electors	Candidate	Party	Votes
1874	1,599	Hon. W.H.P. Carington	L	953
		H. Broadhurst	L/Lab	415
		F. Charsley	C	19
1880	1,865	Hon. W.H.P. Carington	L	Unopp.
[Appointed a Groom in Waiting to Her Majesty]				
1880 (26/5)		Hon. W.H.P. Carington	L	Unopp.
[Resignation]				
1883 (12/3)	2,062	G. Smith	L	1,105
		J.S. Carson	C	557

YORK [198]
(Two Seats)

Election	Electors	Candidate	Party	Votes
1832	2,873	†Hon. E.R. Petre	L	1,505
		†S.A. Bayntun	L	1,140
		†J.H. Lowther	C	884
		†Hon. T. Dundas	L	872
[Death of Bayntun]				
1833 (11/11)	2,890	Hon. T. Dundas	L	1,337
		J.H. Lowther	C	846
1835	2,890	J.H. Lowther	C	1,499
		Hon. J.C. Dundas	L	1,301
		C.F. Barkley	L	919
1837	2,829	J.H. Lowther	C	1,461
		Hon. J.C. Dundas	L	1,276
		D.F. Atcherley	C	1,180
1841	3,507	J.H. Lowther	C	1,625
		H.G.R. Yorke	L	1,552
		D.F. Atcherley	C	1,456
1847	4,047	J.G. Smyth	C	Unopp.
		H.G.R. Yorke	L	Unopp.
[Death of Yorke]				
1848 (24/5)	4,178	W.M.E. Milner	L	1,505
		H. Vincent	Ch	860
		C. Wilkins	L	57
1852	4,133	J.G. Smyth	C	1,870
		W.M.E. Milner	L	1,831
		H. Vincent	Ch	886
1857	4,236	J.P.B. Westhead	L	1,548
		J.G. Smyth	C	1,530
		M. Lewin	L	1,006
1859	4,355	J.P.B. Westhead	L	1,875
		J.G. Smyth	C	1,805
		A.H. Layard	L	1,706
1865	4,277	J. Lowther	C	2,079
		G. Leeman	L	1,854
		J.P.B. Westhead	L	1,792
1868	9,088	J. Lowther	C	3,735
		J.P.B. Westhead	L	3,279
		J.H. Gladstone	L	3,038

(Two Seats)

Election	Electors	Candidate	Party	Votes
[Resignation of Westhead]				
1871 (14/2)		G. Leeman	L	Unopp.
1874	9,744	G. Leeman	L	3,880
		J. Lowther	C	3,371
		Hon. L.P. Dawnay	C	2,830
[Appointment of Lowther as Chief Secretary to the Lord Lieutenant of Ireland]				
1878 (20/2)		J. Lowther	C	Unopp.
1880	10,971	R. Creyke	L	4,505
		J.J. Leeman	L	4,413
		J. Lowther	C	3,959
[Death of Leeman]				
1883 (23/11)	11,395	Sir F.G. Milner, Bt.	C	3,948
		F. Lockwood	L	3,927

Petition:—

1868: Withdrawn

ENGLAND —— COUNTIES

BEDFORDSHIRE [199]

(Two Seats)

Election	Electors	Candidate	Party	Votes
1832	3,966	Lord Charles Russell	L	1,937
		W. Stuart (Senr.)	C	1,871
		†Sir P. Payne, Bt.	L	1,756
1835	4,015	Viscount Alford	C	Unopp.
		Lord Charles Russell	L	Unopp.
1837	4,134	Viscount Alford	C	Unopp.
		Lord Charles Russell	L	Unopp.
1841	4,333	Viscount Alford	C	Unopp.
		W. Astell	C	Unopp.
[Death of Astell]				
1847 (30/3)		Lord Charles Russell	L	Unopp.
1847	4,339	Viscount Alford	C	Unopp.
		F.C.H. Russell	L	Unopp.
[Death of Alford]				
1851 (24/2)	4,071	R.T. Gilpin	C	1,562
		J. Houghton	L	558
1852	4,513	R.T. Gilpin	C	Unopp.
		F.C.H. Russell	L	Unopp.
1857	4,231	F.C.H. Russell	L	1,564
		R.T. Gilpin	C	1,374
		W.B. Higgins	L	1,343
		W. Stuart (Junr.)	C	1,246
1859	4,701	R.T. Gilpin	C	2,027
		F.C.H. Russell	L	1,837
		W.B. Higgins	L	1,583
1865	4,845	R.T. Gilpin	C	Unopp.
		F.C.H. Russell	L	Unopp.
1868	6,680	R.T. Gilpin	C	Unopp.
		F.C.H. Russell	L	Unopp.
[Succession of Russell to the Peerage — Duke of Bedford]				
1872 (27/6)	6,580	F. Bassett	L	2,450
		W. Stuart (Junr.)	C	2,250
1874	6,874	F. Bassett	L	Unopp.
		R.T. Gilpin	C	Unopp.

(Two Seats)

Election	Electors	Candidate	Party	Votes
[Resignation of Bassett]				
1875 (28/4)		Marquess of Tavistock	L	Unopp.
1880	7,133	J. Howard	L	3,143
		Marquess of Tavistock	L	3,088
		W. Stuart (Junr.)	C	2,500

BERKSHIRE [200]

(Three Seats)

Election	Electors	Candidate	Party	Votes
1832	5,582	†R. Palmer	C	2,942
		†R.G. Throckmorton	L	2,774
		J. Walter (Senr.)	L	2,479
		†P. Pusey	C	2,440
1835	5,632	R. Palmer	C	Unopp.
		P. Pusey	C	Unopp.
		J. Walter (Senr.)	L	Unopp.
1837	5,599	R. Palmer	C	2,556
		Viscount Barrington	C	2,360
		P. Pusey	C	2,312
		E.G.C. East	L	1,302
1841	5,685	Viscount Barrington	C	Unopp.
		R. Palmer	C	Unopp.
		P. Pusey	C	Unopp.
1847	5,241	Viscount Barrington	C	Unopp.
		R. Palmer	C	Unopp.
		P. Pusey	L	Unopp.
1852	5,129	G.H. Vansittart	C	1,741
		R. Palmer	C	1,705
		Viscount Barrington	C	1,636
		J. Walter (Junr.)	L	155
1857	4,884	R. Palmer	C	1,802
		Hon. P.P. Bouverie	L	1,524
		G.H. Vansittart	C	1,494
		L.V. Vernon	C	1,360
1859	4,791	Hon. P.P. Bouverie	L	Unopp.
		L.V. Vernon	C	Unopp.
		J. Walter (Junr.)	L	Unopp.
[Death of Vernon]				
1860 (2/5)		R. Benyon	C	Unopp.
1865	5,066	R.J.L. Lindsay	C	2,227
		R. Benyon	C	2,192
		Sir C. Russell, Bt.	C	2,117
		J. Walter (Junr.)	L	1,813
		Viscount Uffington	L	1,809
		Hon. E.P. Bouverie	L	1,583
1868	7,647†	R.J.L. Lindsay	C	3,231
		R. Benyon	C	3,171
		J. Walter (Junr.)	L	2,747
		Hon. A.E.W.M. Herbert	L	2,450

BERKSHIRE [200] (Cont.)
(Three Seats)

Election	Electors	Candidate	Party	Votes
1874	7,745	R. Benyon	C	Unopp.
		R.J.L. Lindsay	C	Unopp.
		J. Walter (Junr.)	L	Unopp.
[Resignation of Benyon]				
1876 (24/2)	7,721	P. Wroughton	C	3,454
		C.D. Griffith	C	1,149
1880	8,061	R.J.L. Lindsay	C	3,294
		P. Wroughton	C	3,272
		J. Walter (Junr.)	L	1,794
		T. Rogers	L	1,696

BUCKINGHAMSHIRE [201]
(Three Seats)

Election	Electors	Candidate	Party	Votes
1832	5,306	†Marquess of Chandos	C	2,856
		†J. Smith	L	2,402
		G.H. Dashwood	L	1,647
		C.R.S. Murray	C	1,536
1835	5,371	Marquess of Chandos	C	3,094
		Sir W.L. Young, Bt.	C	2,394
		J.B. Praed	C	2,179
		G.H. Dashwood	L	1,672
		J. Lee	L	1,365
[Death of Praed]				
1837 (20/2)	5,760	G.S. Harcourt	C	2,233
		G.H. Dashwood	L	982
1837	5,760	Marquess of Chandos	C	2,993
		G.S. Harcourt	C	2,704
		Sir W.L. Young, Bt.	C	2,633
		G.R. Smith	L	2,071
[Succession of Chandos to the Peerage – Duke of Buckingham and Chandos]				
1839 (18/2)		C.G. Du Pré	C	Unopp.
1841	6,156	Sir W.L. Young, Bt.	C	2,578
		C.G. Du Pré	C	2,572
		C.R.S. Murray	C	2,547
		J. Lee	L	495
		H.M. Vane	L	450
[Death of Young]				
1842 (15/7)		Hon. W.E. Fitzmaurice	C	Unopp.
[Resignation of Murray]				
1845 (21/2)		C. Tower	C	Unopp.
1847	5,798	Hon. C.C. Cavendish	L	Unopp.
		B. Disraeli	C	Unopp.
		C.G. Du Pré	C	Unopp.
[Appointment of Disraeli as Chancellor of the Exchequer]				
1852 (12/3)		B. Disraeli	C	Unopp.
1852	5,659	C.G. Du Pré	C	2,000
		B. Disraeli	C	1,973
		Hon. C.C. Cavendish	L	1,403
		J. Lee	L	656

BUCKINGHAMSHIRE [201] (Cont.)
(Three Seats)

Election	Electors	Candidate	Party	Votes
1857	5,353	Hon. C.C. Cavendish	L	Unopp.
		B. Disraeli	C	Unopp.
		C.G. Du Pré	C	Unopp.
[Elevation of Cavendish to the Peerage — Lord Chesham]				
1857 (28/12)	5,353*	Hon. W.G. Cavendish	L	1,617
		C.J.B. Hamilton	C	1,454
[Appointment of Disraeli as Chancellor of the Exchequer]				
1858 (8/3)		B. Disraeli	C	Unopp.
1859	5,343	Hon. W.G. Cavendish	L	Unopp.
		B. Disraeli	C	Unopp.
		C.G. Du Pré	C	Unopp.
[Succession of Cavendish to the Peerage — Lord Chesham]				
1863 (29/12)	5,836	R.B. Harvey	C	2,311
		J. Lee	L	313
1865	6,126	B. Disraeli	C	Unopp.
		C.G. Du Pré	C	Unopp.
		R.B. Harvey	C	Unopp.
[Appointment of Disraeli as Chancellor of the Exchequer]				
1866 (13/7)		B. Disraeli	C	Unopp.
1868	7,894†	B. Disraeli	C	Unopp.
		C.G. Du Pré	C	Unopp.
		N.G. Lambert	L	Unopp.
1874	7,368	B. Disraeli	C	2,999
		Sir R.B. Harvey, Bt.	C	2,902
		N.G. Lambert	L	1,720
		W. Talley	C	151
[Appointment of Disraeli as Prime Minister and First Lord of the Treasury]				
1874 (17/3)		B. Disraeli	C	Unopp.
[Elevation of Disraeli to the Peerage — Earl of Beaconsfield]				
1876 (22/9)	7,273	Hon. T.F. Fremantle	C	2,725
		Hon. R.C.G. Carington	L	2,539
1880	8,114	Sir R.B. Harvey, Bt.	C	2,956
		Hon. T.F. Fremantle	C	2,790
		Hon. R.C.G. Carington	L	2,790
		F. Charsley	C	796

CAMBRIDGESHIRE [202]
(Three Seats)

Election	Electors	Candidate	Party	Votes
1832	6,435	†C.P. Yorke	C	3,693
		†R.G. Townley	L	3,261
		J.W. Childers	L	2,862
		†H.J. Adeane	L	2,850
1835	6,710	Hon. E.T. Yorke	C	3,871
		R.J. Eaton	C	3,261
		R.G. Townley	L	3,070
		J.W. Childers	L	2,979
1837	7,100	R.J. Eaton	C	Unopp.
		R.G. Townley	L	Unopp.
		Hon. E.T. Yorke	C	Unopp.
1841	7,400	J.P. Allix	C	Unopp.
		R.J. Eaton	C	Unopp.
		Hon. E.T. Yorke	C	Unopp.
1847	7,175	Lord George Manners	C	Unopp.
		R.G. Townley	L	Unopp.
		Hon. E.T. Yorke	C	Unopp.
1852	6,989	E. Ball	C	Unopp.
		Lord George Manners	C	Unopp.
		Hon. E.T. Yorke	C	Unopp.
1857	6,298	E. Ball	C	2,780
		H.J. Adeane	L	2,616
		Hon. E.T. Yorke	C	2,483
		Lord George Manners	C	2,127
1859	7,157	H.J. Adeane	L	Unopp.
		E. Ball	C	Unopp.
		Hon. E.T. Yorke	C	Unopp.
[Resignation of Ball]				
1863 (14/2)		Lord George Manners	C	Unopp.
1865	7,060	Lord George Manners	C	Unopp.
		Viscount Royston	C	Unopp.
		R. Young	L	Unopp.
[Appointment of Royston as Comptroller of H.M. Household]				
1866 (17/7)		Viscount Royston	C	Unopp.
1868	9,512†	Lord George Manners	C	3,998
		Viscount Royston	C	3,874
		H.B.W. Brand	L	3,300
		R. Young	L	3,290

Election	Electors	Candidate	Party	Votes
[Succession of Royston to the Peerage — Earl of Hardwicke]				
1874 (3/1)		Hon. E.C. Yorke	C	Unopp.
1874	10,104	H.B.W. Brand	L	Unopp.
		Lord George Manners	C	Unopp.
		Hon. E.C. Yorke	C	Unopp.
[Death of Manners]				
1874 (5/10)		B.B.H. Rodwell	C	Unopp.
[Death of Yorke]				
1879 (30/1)		E. Hicks	C	Unopp.
1880	10,023	H.B.W. Brand	L	Unopp.
		E. Hicks	C	Unopp.
		B.B.H. Rodwell	C	Unopp.
[Resignation of Rodwell]				
1881 (7/9)		J.R. Bulwer	C	Unopp.
[Elevation of Brand to the Peerage — Viscount Hampden]				
1884 (21/3)	10,003	A.J. Thornhill	C	3,915
		T. Coote	L	2,812

Note:—

1868-1880: Brand was Speaker of the House of Commons from February 1872 until February 1884

CHESHIRE, EASTERN [203]

(Two Seats)

Election	Electors	Candidate	Party	Votes
1868	6,276	E.C. Egerton	C	Unopp.
		W.J. Legh	C	Unopp.
[Death of Egerton]				
1869 (6/10)	6,276	W.C. Brooks	C	2,908
		Sir E.W. Watkin	L	1,815
1874	6,492	W.C. Brooks	C	Unopp.
		W.J. Legh	C	Unopp.
1880	6,849	W.C. Brooks	C	3,424
		W.J. Legh	C	3,310
		G.B. Worthington	L	2,032
		T.A. Bazley	L	1,947

CHESHIRE, MID [204]

(Two Seats)

Election	Electors	Candidate	Party	Votes
1868	7,158	Hon. W. Egerton	C	3,063
		G.C. Legh	C	3,056
		Hon. J.B.L. Warren	L	2,452
[Resignation of Legh]				
1873 (10/3)	7,801	E. Leigh	C	3,508
		G.W. Latham	L	2,118
1874	8,050	Hon. W. Egerton	C	Unopp.
		E. Leigh	C	Unopp.
[Death of Leigh]				
1876 (18/7)		P.E. Warburton	C	Unopp.
1880	8,963	Hon. W. Egerton	C	3,868
		P.E. Warburton	C	3,700
		G.W. Latham	L	3,374
		V.K. Armitage	L	3,247
[Succession of Egerton to the Peerage — Lord Egerton]				
1883 (16/3)	9,915	Hon. A. de T. Egerton	C	4,214
		G.W. Latham	L	3,592

CHESHIRE, NORTHERN [205]
(Two Seats)

Election	Electors	Candidate	Party	Votes
1832	5,105	†E.J. Stanley	L	2,556
		W.T. Egerton	C	2,428
		J.R.D. Tollemache	L	1,516
1835	5,045	W.T. Egerton	C	Unopp.
		E.J. Stanley	L	Unopp.
1837	6,029	W.T. Egerton	C	Unopp.
		E.J. Stanley	L	Unopp.
1841	6,154	W.T. Egerton	C	2,782
		G.C. Legh	C	2,652
		E.J. Stanley	L	2,206
1847	7,188	W.T. Egerton	C	Unopp.
		E.J. Stanley	L	Unopp.
[Stanley called to the House of Lords as Lord Eddisbury]				
1848 (8/6)	7,188*	G.C. Legh	C	3,060
		F.D.P. Astley	L	2,419
1852	7,494	W.T. Egerton	C	Unopp.
		G.C. Legh	C	Unopp.
1857	6,693	W.T. Egerton	C	Unopp.
		G.C. Legh	C	Unopp.
[Resignation of Egerton]				
1858 (7/8)		W. Egerton	C	Unopp.
1859	6,504	Hon. W. Egerton	C	Unopp.
		G.C. Legh	C	Unopp.
1865	6,026	Hon. W. Egerton	C	Unopp.
		G.C. Legh	C	Unopp.

This constituency was divided in 1868.

Petition:—

1848: Dismissed

CHESHIRE, SOUTHERN [206]
(Two Seats)

Election	Electors	Candidate	Party	Votes
1832	5,130	†G. Wilbraham	L	2,661
		†Earl Grosvenor	L	2,406
		Sir P. de M.G. Egerton, Bt.	C	2,297
1835	6,343	Sir P. de M.G. Egerton, Bt.	C	Unopp.
		G. Wilbraham	L	Unopp.
1837	7,084	Sir P. de M.G. Egerton, Bt.	C	3,135
		G. Wilbraham	L	3,015
		E. Corbett	C	2,646
1841	7,645	Sir P. de M.G. Egerton, Bt.	C	3,110
		J. Tollemache	C	3,034
		G. Wilbraham	L	2,365
1847	8,735	Sir P. de M.G. Egerton, Bt.	C	Unopp.
		J. Tollemache	C	Unopp.
1852	8,117	Sir P. de M.G. Egerton, Bt.	C	Unopp.
		J. Tollemache	C	Unopp.
1857	7,068	Sir P. de M.G. Egerton, Bt.	C	Unopp.
		J. Tollemache	C	Unopp.
1859	6,949	Sir P. de M.G. Egerton, Bt.	C	Unopp.
		J. Tollemache	C	Unopp.
1865	6,826	Sir P. de M.G. Egerton, Bt.	C	Unopp.
		J. Tollemache	C	Unopp.

This constituency was divided in 1868.

CHESHIRE, WESTERN [207]
(Two Seats)

Election	Electors	Candidate	Party	Votes
1868	8,894	Sir P. de M.G. Egerton, Bt.	C	Unopp.
		J. Tollemache	C	Unopp.
[Resignation of Tollemache]				
1872 (17/2)		W.F. Tollemache	C	Unopp.
1874	10,169	Sir P. de M.G. Egerton, Bt.	C	Unopp.
		W.F. Tollemache	C	Unopp.
1880	11,097	Sir P. de M.G. Egerton, Bt.	C	4,773
		Hon. W.F. Tollemache	C	4,637
		W.C. West	L	4,009
		C. Crompton	L	3,785
[Death of Egerton]				
1881 (25/4)	12,270	H.J. Tollemache	C	4,800
		J. Tomkinson	L	4,418

Petition:—

1880: Withdrawn

CORNWALL, EASTERN [208]

(Two Seats)

Election	Electors	Candidate	Party	Votes
1832	4,462	Sir W. Molesworth, Bt.	L	Unopp.
		W.L.S. Trelawny	L	Unopp.
1835	4,392	Sir W. Molesworth, Bt.	L	Unopp.
		Sir W.L.S. Trelawny, Bt.	L	Unopp.
1837	5,469	Lord Eliot	C	2,430
		Sir R.H. Vivian, Bt.	L	2,294
		Sir W.L.S. Trelawny, Bt.	L	2,250
1841	6,076	Lord Eliot	C	3,006
		W. Rashleigh	C	2,807
		J.S. Trelawny	L	1,647
[Appointment of Eliot as Chief Secretary to the Lord Lieutenant of Ireland]				
1841 (22/9)		Lord Eliot	C	Unopp.
[Succession of Eliot to the Peerage — Earl St. Germans]				
1845 (20/2)		W.H.P. Carew	C	Unopp.
1847	6,270	W.H.P. Carew	C	Unopp.
		T.J.A. Robartes	L	Unopp.
1852	5,694	T.J.A. Robartes	L	2,609
		N. Kendall	C	1,996
		W.H.P. Carew	C	1,979
1857	6,261	N. Kendall	C	Unopp.
		T.J.A. Robartes	L	Unopp.
1859	6,240	N. Kendall	C	Unopp.
		T.J.A. Robartes	L	Unopp.
1865	5,781	N. Kendall	C	Unopp.
		T.J.A. Robartes	L	Unopp.
1868	8,701	Sir J.S. Trelawny, Bt.	L	Unopp.
		E.W.B. Willyams	L	Unopp.
1874	8,982	Sir J.C. Rashleigh, Bt.	L	3,395
		J. Tremayne	C	3,276
		W.H.P. Carew	C	3,099
		R. Kelly	L	2,978

(Two Seats)

Election	Electors	Candidate	Party	Votes
1880	9,150	Hon. T.C.A. Robartes	L	4,018
		W.C. Borlase	L	3,883
		J. Tremayne	C	3,033
		D. Collins	C	2,403

[Succession of Robartes to the Peerage — Lord Robartes]

Election	Electors	Candidate	Party	Votes
1882 (3/4)	9,484	C.T.D. Acland	L	3,720
		J. Tremayne	C	3,520

CORNWALL, WESTERN [209]
(Two Seats)

Election	Electors	Candidate	Party	Votes
1832	3,353	†Sir C. Lemon, Bt.	L	Unopp.
		†E.W.W. Pendarves	L	Unopp.
1835	3,612	Sir C. Lemon, Bt.	L	Unopp.
		E.W.W. Pendarves	L	Unopp.
1837	4,928	Sir C. Lemon, Bt.	L	Unopp.
		E.W.W. Pendarves	L	Unopp.
1841	5,040	Lord Boscawen-Rose	C	Unopp.
		E.W.W. Pendarves	L	Unopp.
[Succession of Boscawen-Rose to the Peerage — Earl of Falmouth]				
1842 (16/2)		Sir C. Lemon, Bt.	L	Unopp.
1847	5,259	Sir C. Lemon, Bt.	L	Unopp.
		E.W.W. Pendarves	L	Unopp.
1852	4,649	Sir C. Lemon, Bt.	L	Unopp.
		E.W.W. Pendarves	L	Unopp.
[Death of Pendarves]				
1853 (18/7)		M. Williams	L	Unopp.
1857	4,542	R. Davey	L	Unopp.
		M. Williams	L	Unopp.
[Death of Williams]				
1858 (5/7)		J. St.Aubyn	L	Unopp.
1859	4,897	R. Davey	L	Unopp.
		J. St.Aubyn	L	Unopp.
1865	4,615	R. Davey	L	Unopp.
		J. St.Aubyn	L	Unopp.
1868	8,168†	J. St.Aubyn	L	Unopp.
		A.P. Vivian	L	Unopp.
1874	7,494	Sir J. St.Aubyn, Bt.	L	Unopp.
		A.P. Vivian	L	Unopp.
1880	6,987	Sir J. St.Aubyn, Bt.	L	Unopp.
		A.P. Vivian	L	Unopp.

CUMBERLAND, EASTERN [210]

(Two Seats)

Election	Electors	Candidate	Party	Votes
1832	4,035	†W. Blamire	L	Unopp.
		†Sir J.R.G. Graham, Bt.	L	Unopp.
1835	3,992	W. Blamire	L	Unopp.
		Sir J.R.G. Graham, Bt.	L	Unopp.
[Resignation of Blamire on appointment as Chief Commissioner for the Commutation of Tithes]				
1836 (2/9)		W. James	L	Unopp.
1837	4,638	F. Aglionby	L	2,294
		W. James	L	2,124
		Sir J.R.G. Graham, Bt.	C	1,605
[Death of Aglionby]				
1840 (20/7)		Hon. C.W.G. Howard	L	Unopp.
1841	4,842	Hon. C.W.G. Howard	L	2,086
		W. James	L	1,988
		W.W. Stephenson	C	1,906
1847	5,348	Hon. C.W.G. Howard	L	Unopp.
		W. Marshall	L	Unopp.
1852	5,351	Hon. C.W.G. Howard	L	2,375
		W. Marshall	L	2,255
		T. Salkeld	C	1,964
1857	5,693	Hon. C.W.G. Howard	L	Unopp.
		W. Marshall	L	Unopp.
1859	5,582	Hon. C.W.G. Howard	L	Unopp.
		W. Marshall	L	Unopp.
1865	5,455	Hon. C.W.G. Howard	L	Unopp.
		W. Marshall	L	Unopp.
1868	6,694	W.N. Hodgson	C	2,626
		Hon. C.W.G. Howard	L	2,546
		W. Marshall	L	2,397
1874	7,225	Hon. C.W.G. Howard	L	2,943
		W.N. Hodgson	C	2,629
		Sir R.C. Musgrave, Bt.	C	2,622
[Death of Hodgson]				
1876 (28/4)	7,323	E.S. Howard	L	2,939
		Sir R.C. Musgrave, Bt.	C	2,783

CUMBERLAND, EASTERN [210] (Cont.)
(Two Seats)

Election	Electors	Candidate	Party	Votes
[Death of Howard]				
1879 (25/4)		G.J. Howard	L	Unopp.
1880	7,798	Sir R.C. Musgrave, Bt.	C	3,161
		E.S. Howard	L	3,083
		G.J. Howard	L	3,039
[Death of Musgrave]				
1881 (28/2)	7,928	G.J. Howard	L	3,071
		J. Lowther	C	3,041

CUMBERLAND, WESTERN [211]
(Two Seats)

Election	Electors	Candidate	Party	Votes
1832	3,848	†Viscount Lowther	C	1,875
		E. Stanley	C	1,693
		H. Curwen	L	1,510
[Lowther elects to sit for Westmorland]				
1833 (25/3)	3,848	S. Irton	C	1,682
		F. Aglionby	L	1,601
1835	4,149	E. Stanley	C	1,899
		S. Irton	C	1,883
		F. Aglionby	L	1,581
1837	4,437	S. Irton	C	Unopp.
		E. Stanley	C	Unopp.
1841	4,031	S. Irton	C	Unopp.
		E. Stanley	C	Unopp.
1847	4,042	H. Lowther	C	Unopp.
		E. Stanley	C	Unopp.
1852	4,144	S. Irton	C	Unopp.
		H. Lowther	C	Unopp.
1857	4,389	H. Wyndham	C	1,848
		H. Lowther	C	1,825
		W. Lawson	L	1,554
1859	4,780	H. Lowther	C	Unopp.
		H. Wyndham	C	Unopp.
[Death of Wyndham]				
1860 (27/8)		Hon. P.S. Wyndham	C	Unopp.
1865	4,602	H. Lowther	C	Unopp.
		Hon. P.S. Wyndham	C	Unopp.
1868	5,676	H. Lowther	C	Unopp.
		Hon. P.S. Wyndham	C	Unopp.
[Succession of Lowther to the Peerage — Earl of Lonsdale]				
1872 (26/3)		Lord Muncaster	C	Unopp.
1874	6,034	Hon. P.S. Wyndham	C	2,532
		Lord Muncaster	C	2,520
		J.W.B. Dykes	L	1,786
		D. Ainsworth	L	1,771

CUMBERLAND, WESTERN [211] (Cont.)
(Two Seats)

Election	Electors	Candidate	Party	Votes
1880	7,496	D. Ainsworth	L	3,178
		Hon. P.S. Wyndham	C	2,686
		Lord Muncaster	C	2,624

DERBYSHIRE, EASTERN [212]

(Two Seats)

Election	Electors	Candidate	Party	Votes
1868	5,107	Hon. F. Egerton	L	2,089
		Hon. H. Strutt	L	2,032
		W.G. Turbutt	C	1,999
		W. Overend	C	1,970
1874	4,836	Hon. F. Egerton	L	2,206
		F. Arkwright	C	2,116
		W. Fowler	C	2,067
		Hon. H. Strutt	L	2,017
1880	6,173	A. Barnes	L	3,119
		Hon. F. Egerton	L	3,063
		F. Arkwright	C	2,577
		W.G. Turbutt	C	2,303

DERBYSHIRE, NORTHERN [213]
(Two Seats)

Election	Electors	Candidate	Party	Votes
1832	4,370	†Lord Cavendish	L	3,388
		†T. Gisborne	L	2,385
		Sir G. Sitwell, Bt.	C	1,183
[Succession of Cavendish to the Peerage — Earl of Burlington]				
1834 (27/5)		Hon. G.H. Cavendish	L	Unopp.
1835	4,175	Hon. G.H. Cavendish	L	Unopp.
		T. Gisborne	L	Unopp.
1837	5,527	Hon. G.H. Cavendish	L	2,816
		W. Evans	L	2,422
		G. Arkwright	C	1,983
1841	5,757	Hon. G.H. Cavendish	L	Unopp.
		W. Evans	L	Unopp.
1847	5,601	Hon. G.H. Cavendish	L	Unopp.
		W. Evans	L	Unopp.
1852	5,315	Hon. G.H. Cavendish	L	Unopp.
		W. Evans	L	Unopp.
[Resignation of Evans]				
1853 (22/7)	5,219	W.P. Thornhill	L	1,680
		T.W. Evans	L	1,195
1857	5,336	Hon. G.H. Cavendish *(Lord George Cavendish)*	L	Unopp.
		W.P. Thornhill	L	Unopp.
1859	5,380	Lord George Cavendish	L	Unopp.
		W.P. Thornhill	L	Unopp.
1865	5,055	Lord George Cavendish	L	Unopp.
		W. Jackson	L	Unopp.
1868	6,231†	Lord George Cavendish	L	2,903
		A.P. Arkwright	C	2,698
		W. Jackson	L	2,637
1874	6,594	A.P. Arkwright	C	Unopp.
		Lord George Cavendish	L	Unopp.
1880	6,985	Lord Edward Cavendish	L	3,416
		J.F. Cheetham	L	3,183
		A.P. Arkwright	C	2,936
		W. Sidebottom	C	2,718

Petition:— 1868: Withdrawn

DERBYSHIRE, SOUTHERN [214]
(Two Seats)

Election	Electors	Candidate	Party	Votes
1832	5,541	†Hon. G.J.V. Vernon	L	3,036
		†Lord Waterpark	L	2,839
		Sir R. Gresley, Bt.	C	1,952
1835	5,359	Sir G. Crewe, Bt.	C	2,517
		Sir R. Gresley, Bt.	C	2,495
		Hon. G.J.V. Vernon	L	1,951
		Lord Waterpark	L	1,910
1837	6,575	Sir G. Crewe, Bt.	C	Unopp.
		F. Hurt	C	Unopp.
1841	6,807	E.M. Mundy	C	3,234
		C.R. Colvile	C	3,209
		M. Gisborne	L	2,403
		Lord Waterpark	L	2,325
1847	7,272	C.R. Colvile	C	Unopp.
		E.M. Mundy	C	Unopp.
[Death of Mundy]				
1849 (23/3)		W. Mundy	C	Unopp.
1852	7,099	C.R. Colvile	C	Unopp.
		W. Mundy	C	Unopp.
1857	7,102	T.W. Evans	L	3,922
		C.R. Colvile	L	3,350
		S.W. Clowes	C	2,105
		Lord Stanhope	C	1,972
1859	7,147	T.W. Evans	L	3,536
		W. Mundy	C	3,185
		A.H. Vernon	L	3,184
1865	7,976	T.W. Evans	L	3,891
		C.R. Colvile	L	3,650
		W. Mundy	C	3,619
1868	7,833†	R. Smith	C	3,594
		Sir T. Gresley, Bt.	C	3,582
		C.R. Colvile	L	3,375
		T.W. Evans	L	3,443
[Death of Gresley]				
1869 (16/1)	7,833*	H. Wilmot	C	3,511
		T.W. Evans	L	3,478

DERBYSHIRE, SOUTHERN [214] (Cont.)
(Two Seats)

Election	Electors	Candidate	Party	Votes
1874	8,179	Sir H. Wilmot, Bt.	C	3,934
		T.W. Evans	L	3,773
		R. Smith	C	3,572
1880	8,934	T.W. Evans	L	Unopp.
		Sir H. Wilmot, Bt.	C	Unopp.

DEVON, EASTERN [215]

(Two Seats)

Election	Electors	Candidate	Party	Votes
1868	9,933	Sir L. Palk, Bt.	C	4,034
		Lord Courtenay	C	4,016
		C.J. Wade	L	3,457
[Resignation of Courtenay]				
1870 (9/4)		J.H. Kennaway	C	Unopp.
1874	10,246	Sir J.H. Kennaway, Bt.	C	Unopp.
		Sir L. Palk, Bt.	C	Unopp.
1880	10,416	Sir J.H. Kennaway, Bt.	C	4,501
		W.H. Walrond	C	4,457
		J.B. Sterling	L	3,487
[Appointment of Walrond as a Lord Commissioner of the Treasury]				
1885 (4/7)		W.H. Walrond	C	Unopp.

DEVON, NORTHERN [216]
(Two Seats)

Election	Electors	Candidate	Party	Votes
1832	5,368	†Viscount Ebrington	L	Unopp.
		Hon. N. Fellowes	L	Unopp.
1835	6,236	Viscount Ebrington	L	Unopp.
		Hon. N. Fellowes	L	Unopp.
1837	7,757	Sir T.D. Acland, Bt. (Senr.)	C	Unopp.
		Viscount Ebrington	L	Unopp.
[Ebrington called to the House of Lords as Lord Fortescue]				
1839 (18/3)	7,871*	L.W. Buck	C	3,720
		J.W. Buller	L	3,240
1841	8,869	Sir T.D. Acland, Bt. (Senr.)	C	Unopp.
		L.W. Buck	C	Unopp.
1847	8,597	Sir T.D. Acland, Bt. (Senr.)	C	Unopp.
		L.W. Buck	C	Unopp.
1852	8,064	Sir T.D. Acland, Bt. (Senr.)	C	Unopp.
		L.W. Buck	C	Unopp.
1857	7,264	J.W. Buller	L	3,652
		Hon. C.H.R. Trefusis	C	2,322
		Sir S.H. Northcote, Bt.	C	2,105
1859	8,764	J.W. Buller	L	Unopp.
		Hon. C.H.R. Trefusis	C	Unopp.
[Death of Buller]				
1865 (1/4)		T.D. Acland	L	Unopp.
1865	8,746	T.D. Acland	L	Unopp.
		Hon. C.H.R. Trefusis	C	Unopp.
[Succession of Trefusis to the Peerage — Lord Clinton]				
1866 (9/5)		Sir S.H. Northcote, Bt.	C	Unopp.
[Appointment of Northcote as President of the Board of Trade]				
1866 (14/7)		Sir S.H. Northcote, Bt.	C	Unopp.
[Appointment of Northcote as Secretary of State for India]				
1867 (18/3)		Sir S.H. Northcote, Bt.	C	Unopp.

DEVON, NORTHERN [216] (Cont.)

(Two Seats)

Election	Electors	Candidate	Party	Votes
1868	9,260†	Sir S.H. Northcote, Bt.	C	3,967
		T.D. Acland	L	3,898
		J.W. Walrond	C	3,520
1874	9,829	Sir T.D. Acland, Bt. (Junr.)	L	Unopp.
		Sir S.H. Northcote, Bt.	C	Unopp.

[Appointment of Northcote as Chancellor of the Exchequer]

Election	Electors	Candidate	Party	Votes
1874 (18/3)		Sir S.H. Northcote, Bt.	C	Unopp.
1880	9,496	Sir T.D. Acland, Bt. (Junr.)	L	Unopp.
		Sir S.H. Northcote, Bt.	C	Unopp.

[Resignation of Northcote on appointment as First Lord of the Treasury and elevation to the Peerage – Earl of Iddesleigh]

Election	Electors	Candidate	Party	Votes
1885 (2/7)		J.C.M. Stevens	C	Unopp.

DEVON, SOUTHERN [217]

(Two Seats)

Election	Electors	Candidate	Party	Votes
1832	7,453	†Lord John Russell	L	3,782
		J.C. Bulteel	L	3,684
		Sir J.B.Y. Buller, Bt.	C	3,217
1835	8,160	Sir J.B.Y. Buller, Bt.	C	Unopp.
		Lord John Russell	L	Unopp.
[Appointment of Russell as Secretary of State for the Home Department]				
1835 (7/5)	8,160	M.E.N. Parker	C	3,755
		Lord John Russell	L	3,128
1837	10,775	Sir J.B.Y. Buller, Bt.	C	4,974
		M.E.N. Parker	C	4,671
		J.C. Bulteel	L	3,744
1841	10,783	Sir J.B.Y. Buller, Bt.	C	Unopp.
		Lord Courtenay	C	Unopp.
1847	10,411	Sir J.B.Y. Buller, Bt.	C	Unopp.
		Lord Courtenay	C	Unopp.
[Resignation of Courtenay]				
1849 (13/2)		Sir R. Lopes, Bt.	C	Unopp.
1852	9,569	Sir J.B.Y. Buller, Bt.	C	Unopp.
		Sir R. Lopes, Bt.	C	Unopp.
[Death of Lopes]				
1854 (14/2)		L. Palk	C	Unopp.
1857	9,625	Sir J.B.Y. Buller, Bt.	C	Unopp.
		L. Palk	C	Unopp.
[Elevation of Buller to the Peerage — Lord Churston]				
1858 (6/8)		S.T. Kekewich	C	Unopp.
1859	9,466	S.T. Kekewich	C	Unopp.
		L. Palk	C	Unopp.
1865	9,592	S.T. Kekewich	C	Unopp.
		Sir L. Palk, Bt.	C	Unopp.
1868	8,047†	Sir L.M. Lopes, Bt.	C	3,234
		S.T. Kekewich	C	3,233
		Viscount Ambereley	L	2,694

DEVON, SOUTHERN [217] (Cont.)
(Two Seats)

Election	Electors	Candidate	Party	Votes
[Death of Kekewich]				
1873 (17/6)		J.C. Garnier	C	Unopp.
1874	8,350	J.C. Garnier	C	Unopp.
		Sir L.M. Lopes, Bt.	C	Unopp.
[Appointment of Lopes as a Civil Lord of the Admiralty]				
1874 (19/3)		Sir L.M. Lopes, Bt.	C	Unopp.
1880	7,982	J.C. Garnier	C	Unopp.
		Sir L.M. Lopes, Bt.	C	Unopp.
[Resignation of Garnier]				
1884 (14/8)		J. Tremayne	C	Unopp.

DORSET [218]
(Three Seats)

Election	Electors	Candidate	Party	Votes
1832	5,632	†Lord Ashley	C	Unopp.
		†W.J. Bankes	C	Unopp.
		†Hon. W.F.S. Ponsonby	L	Unopp.
1835	5,679	Lord Ashley	C	Unopp.
		Hon. W.F.S. Ponsonby	L	Unopp.
		H.C. Sturt	C	Unopp.
1837	6,263	Lord Ashley	C	Unopp.
		Hon. J.G.C.F. Strangways	L	Unopp.
		H.C. Sturt	C	Unopp.
1841	6,870	Lord Ashley	C	Unopp.
		G. Bankes	C	Unopp.
		H.C. Sturt	C	Unopp.
[Resignations of Ashley and Sturt]				
1846 (19/2)		J. Floyer	C	Unopp.
		H.K. Seymer	C	Unopp.
1847	6,275	G. Bankes	C	Unopp.
		J. Floyer	C	Unopp.
		H.K. Seymer	C	Unopp.
[Appointment of Bankes as Judge-Advocate General]				
1852 (9/3)		G. Bankes	C	Unopp.
1852	5,690	G. Bankes	C	Unopp.
		J. Floyer	C	Unopp.
		H.K. Seymer	C	Unopp.
[Death of Bankes]				
1856 (26/7)		H.G. Sturt	C	Unopp.
1857	5,621	Hon. W.H.B. Portman	L	2,430
		H.G. Sturt	C	2,197
		H.K. Seymer	C	2,177
		J. Floyer	C	2,159
1859	6,639	Hon. W.H.B. Portman	L	Unopp.
		H.K. Seymer	C	Unopp.
		H.G. Sturt	C	Unopp.
[Resignation of Seymer]				
1864 (27/2)		J. Floyer	C	Unopp.

DORSET [218] (Cont.)
(Three Seats)

Election	Electors	Candidate	Party	Votes
1865	6,203	J. Floyer	C	Unopp.
		Hon. W.H.B. Portman	L	Unopp.
		H.G. Sturt	C	Unopp.
1868	7,443†	J. Floyer	C	Unopp.
		Hon. W.H.B. Portman	L	Unopp.
		H.G. Sturt	C	Unopp.
1874	7,293	J. Floyer	C	Unopp.
		Hon. W.H.B. Portman	L	Unopp.
		H.G. Sturt	C	Unopp.
[Elevation of Sturt to the Peerage — Lord Alington]				
1876 (5/2)	7,142	Hon. E.H.T. Digby	C	3,060
		R. Fowler	C	1,866
1880	7,522	Hon. E.H.T. Digby	C	Unopp.
		J. Floyer	C	Unopp.
		Hon. W.H.B. Portman	L	Unopp.

DURHAM, NORTHERN [219]
(Two Seats)

Election	Electors	Candidate	Party	Votes
1832	4,267	H. Lambton	L	2,558
		†Sir H. Williamson, Bt. (Senr.)	L	2,182
		E.R.G. Braddyll	C	1,676
1835	4,772	H. Lambton	L	Unopp.
		Sir H. Williamson, Bt. (Senr.)	L	Unopp.
1837	5,170	H. Lambton	L	2,358
		Hon. H.T. Liddell	C	2,323
		Sir W. Chaytor, Bt.	L	2,062
1841	5,824	H. Lambton	L	Unopp.
		Hon. H.T. Liddell	C	Unopp.
1847	6,472	Viscount Seaham	C	Unopp.
		R.D. Shafto	L	Unopp.
1852	6,631	Viscount Seaham	C	Unopp.
		R.D. Shafto	L	Unopp.
[Succession of Seaham to the Peerage — Earl Vane]				
1854 (1/4)		Lord Adolphus Vane *(Vane-Tempest)*	C	Unopp.
1857	5,847	R.D. Shafto	L	Unopp.
		Lord Adolphus Vane-Tempest	C	Unopp.
1859	5,863	R.D. Shafto	L	Unopp.
		Lord Adolphus Vane-Tempest	C	Unopp.
[Death of Vane-Tempest]				
1864 (28/6)		Sir H. Williamson, Bt. (Junr.)	L	Unopp.
1865	6,042	Sir H. Williamson, Bt. (Junr.)	L	2,888
		R.D. Shafto	L	2,689
		Hon. G.W. Barrington	C	2,210
1868	10,576†	G. Elliot	C	4,649
		Sir H. Williamson, Bt. (Junr.)	L	4,011
		I.L. Bell	L	3,822
1874	10,760	I.L. Bell	L	4,364
		C.M. Palmer	L	4,327
		G. Elliot	C	4,011
		R.L. Pemberton	C	3,501

DURHAM, NORTHERN [219] (Cont.)
(Two Seats)

Election	Electors	Candidate	Party	Votes
[Election declared void on petition]				
1874 (22/6)	10,760	C.M. Palmer	L	4,256
		Sir G. Elliot, Bt.	C	4,254
		I.L. Bell	L	4,104
1880	13,165	J. Joicey	L	6,233
		C.M. Palmer	L	5,901
		Sir G. Elliot, Bt.	C	5,092
[Death of Joicey]				
1881 (7/9)	13,233	Sir G. Elliot, Bt.	C	5,548
		J. Laing	L	4,896

Petitions: —

1874: Void election

1874: (22/6) Dismissed

DURHAM, SOUTHERN [220]
(Two Seats)

Election	Electors	Candidate	Party	Votes
1832	4,336	J. Pease	L	2,273
		J. Bowes	L	2,218
		R.D. Shafto	L	1,841
1835	4,454	J. Bowes	L	Unopp.
		J. Pease	L	Unopp.
1837	4,980	J. Bowes	L	Unopp.
		J. Pease	L	Unopp.
1841	4,820	Lord Harry Vane	L	2,547
		J. Bowes	L	2,483
		J. Farrer	C	1,739
1847	5,783	J. Farrer	C	Unopp.
		Lord Harry Vane	L	Unopp.
1852	5,616	J. Farrer	C	Unopp.
		Lord Harry Vane	L	Unopp.
1857	5,565	H. Pease	L	2,570
		Lord Harry Vane	L	2,542
		J. Farrer	C	2,091
1859	6,681	J. Farrer	C	Unopp.
		H. Pease	L	Unopp.
1865	7,263	J.W. Pease	L	3,401
		C.F. Surtees	C	3,211
		F.E.B. Beaumont	L	2,925
1868	9,352†	J.W. Pease	L	4,319
		F.E.B. Beaumont	L	4,024
		C.F. Surtees	C	3,714
		Hon. G.R.H. Russell	C	3,206
1874	10,159	J.W. Pease	L	4,792
		F.E.B. Beaumont	L	4,461
		Viscount Castlereagh	C	3,887
1880	11,592	J.W. Pease	L	5,930
		Hon. F.W. Lambton	L	5,912
		C.F. Surtees	C	4,044

Petitions: —

1868: Withdrawn

1874: Withdrawn

ESSEX, EASTERN [221]
(Two Seats)

Election	Electors	Candidate	Party	Votes
1868	6,564	J. Round	C	2,861
		S.B.R. Brise	C	2,816
		Sir T.B. Western, Bt.	L	2,224
		Sir T.N. Abdy, Bt.	L	2,134
1874	6,453	S.B.R. Brise	C	Unopp.
		J. Round	C	Unopp.
1880	6,380	J. Round	C	2,691
		S.B.R. Brise	C	2,561
		C.P. Wood	L	2,369
[Resignation of Brise]				
1883 (25/8)		Hon. C.H. Strutt	C	Unopp.

ESSEX, NORTHERN [222]
(Two Seats)

Election	Electors	Candidate	Party	Votes
1832	5,163	Sir J.T. Tyrell, Bt.	C	2,448
		†A. Baring	C	2,280
		†C.C. Western	L	2,244
		T. Brand	L	1,840
1835	5,351	A. Baring	C	Unopp.
		Sir J.T. Tyrell, Bt.	C	Unopp.

[Elevation of Baring to the Peerage — Lord Ashburton]

Election	Electors	Candidate	Party	Votes
1835 (4/5)	5,351	J.P. Elwes	C	2,406
		J. Disney	L	1,357
1837	5,899	C.G. Round	C	Unopp.
		Sir J.T. Tyrell, Bt.	C	Unopp.
1841	5,771	C.G. Round	C	Unopp.
		Sir J.T. Tyrell, Bt.	C	Unopp.
1847	5,461	Sir J.T. Tyrell, Bt.	C	2,472
		W. Beresford	C	2,292
		J.G. Rebow	L	1,555
		F.G.F. Harrison	L	36

[Appointment of Beresford as Secretary at War]

Election	Electors	Candidate	Party	Votes
1852 (9/3)		W. Beresford	C	Unopp.
1852	5,715	Sir J.T. Tyrell, Bt.	C	2,412
		W. Beresford	C	2,334
		T.B. Lennard	L	833
1857	5,553	W. Beresford	C	Unopp.
		C. Du Cane	C	Unopp.
1859	5,510	W. Beresford	C	Unopp.
		C. Du Cane	C	Unopp.
1865	4,904	C. Du Cane	C	2,081
		Sir T.B. Western, Bt.	L	1,931
		W. Beresford	C	1,881

[Appointment of Du Cane as a Civil Lord of the Admiralty]

Election	Electors	Candidate	Party	Votes
1866 (16/7)		C. Du Cane	C	Unopp.

This constituency was divided in 1868.

Petition: —

1847: Withdrawn

ESSEX, SOUTHERN [223]
(Two Seats)

Election	Electors	Candidate	Party	Votes
1832	4,488	R.W.H. Dare	C	2,088
		Sir T.B. Lennard, Bt.	L	1,538
		†Hon. W.P.T.L. Wellesley	L	1,432
1835	4,655	R.W.H. Dare	C	2,212
		T.W. Bramston	C	2,118
		C.E. Branfill	L	1,010
[Death of Dare]				
1836 (9/6)	5,286	G. Palmer	C	2,103
		C.E. Branfill	L	1,527
1837	5,547	T.W. Bramston	C	2,511
		G. Palmer	C	2,260
		C.E. Branfill	L	1,550
1841	5,632	T.W. Bramston	C	2,310
		G. Palmer	C	2,230
		R.G. Alston	L	583
1847	5,326	T.W. Bramston	C	2,158
		Sir E.N. Buxton, Bt.	L	1,729
		W.B. Smijth	C	1,694
1852	5,819	T.W. Bramston	C	2,651
		Sir W.B. Smijth, Bt.	C	2,457
		Sir E.N. Buxton, Bt.	L	1,803
1857	6,169	T.W. Bramston	C	2,332
		R.B. Wingfield *(Baker)*	L	2,119
		Sir W.B. Smijth, Bt.	C	2,102
1859	6,669	T.W. Bramston	C	2,896
		J.W.P. Watlington	C	2,704
		R.B.W. Baker	L	2,245
1865	7,338	H.J. Selwin *(Ibbetson)*	C	2,817
		Lord Eustace Cecil	C	2,710
		R.B.W. Baker	L	2,382
1868	7,127†	R.B.W. Baker	L	Unopp.
		A. Johnston	L	Unopp.
1874	8,713	T.C. Baring	C	3,646
		W.T. Makins	C	3,528
		R.B.W. Baker	L	2,735
		A. Johnston	L	2,728
1880	11,950	T.C. Baring	C	4,841
		W.T. Makins	C	4,726
		E.N. Buxton	L	4,324
		E.L. Lyell	L	4,147

ESSEX, WESTERN [224]
(Two Seats)

Election	Electors	Candidate	Party	Votes
1868	5,479	Lord Eustace Cecil	C	Unopp.
		H.J.S. Ibbetson	C	Unopp.
1874	5,889	Lord Eustace Cecil	C	Unopp.
		Sir H.J.S. Ibbetson, Bt.	C	Unopp.
1880	5,732	Sir H.J.S. Ibbetson, Bt.	C	2,664
		Lord Eustace Cecil	C	2,397
		Sir T.F. Buxton, Bt.	L	1,772

GLOUCESTERSHIRE, EASTERN [225]

(Two Seats)

Election	Electors	Candidate	Party	Votes
1832	6,437	†Sir B.W. Guise, Bt.	L	3,311
		†Hon. H.G.F. Moreton	L	3,184
		C.W. Codrington	C	2,672
[Death of Guise]				
1834 (14/8)	6,569	C.W. Codrington	C	2,779
		C.H.T. Leigh	L	2,709
1835	6,521	C.W. Codrington	C	Unopp.
		Hon. A.H. Moreton	L	Unopp.
1837	7,598	C.W. Codrington	C	Unopp.
		Hon. A.H. Moreton	L	Unopp.
1841	7,971	Hon. F.W. Charteris	C	Unopp.
		C.W. Codrington	C	Unopp.
[Resignation of Charteris]				
1846 (27/2)		Marquess of Worcester	C	Unopp.
1847	7,803	C.W. Codrington	C	Unopp.
		Marquess of Worcester	C	Unopp.
1852	7,986	C.W. Codrington	C	Unopp.
		Marquess of Worcester	C	Unopp.
[Succession of Worcester to the Peerage – Duke of Beaufort]				
1854 (9/1)	7,906	Sir M.H.H. Beach, Bt.	C	3,363
		E. Holland	L	2,344
[Death of Beach]				
1854 (19/12)		R.S. Holford	C	Unopp.
1857	7,891	C.W. Codrington	C	Unopp.
		R.S. Holford	C	Unopp.
1859	7,816	C.W. Codrington	C	Unopp.
		R.S. Holford	C	Unopp.
[Death of Codrington]				
1864 (12/7)		Sir M.E.H. Beach, Bt.	C	Unopp.
1865	7,515	Sir M.E.H. Beach, Bt.	C	Unopp.
		R.S. Holford	C	Unopp.

GLOUCESTERSHIRE, EASTERN [225] (Cont.)
(Two Seats)

Election	Electors	Candidate	Party	Votes
1868	8,858†	Sir M.E.H. Beach, Bt.	C	Unopp.
		R.S. Holford	C	Unopp.
[Resignation of Holford]				
1872 (11/3)		J.R. Yorke	C	Unopp.
1874	9,157	Sir M.E.H. Beach, Bt.	C	Unopp.
		J.R. Yorke	C	Unopp.
[Appointment of Beach as Chief Secretary to the Lord Lieutenant of Ireland]				
1874 (17/3)		Sir M.E.H. Beach, Bt.	C	Unopp.
1880	8,579	Sir M.E.H. Beach, Bt.	C	Unopp.
		J.R. Yorke	C	Unopp.
[Appointment of Beach as Chancellor of the Exchequer]				
1885 (1/7)		Sir M.E.H. Beach, Bt.	C	Unopp.

GLOUCESTERSHIRE, WESTERN [226]

(Two Seats)

Election	Electors	Candidate	Party	Votes
1832	6,521	Hon. G.C.G.F. Berkeley	L	3,153
		Hon. A.H. Moreton	L	2,996
		Lord Robert Somerset	C	2,962
1835	6,473	Hon. G.C.G.F. Berkeley	L	Unopp.
		Marquess of Worcester	C	Unopp.
[Succession of Worcester to the Peerage — Duke of Beaufort]				
1836 (2/1)		R.B. Hale	C	Unopp.
1837	6,936	Hon. G.C.G.F. Berkeley	L	Unopp.
		R.B. Hale	C	Unopp.
1841	7,875	Hon. G.C.G.F. Berkeley	L	Unopp.
		R.B. Hale	C	Unopp.
1847	7,601	R.B. Hale	C	4,240
		Hon. G.C.G.F. Berkeley	L	2,744
		C.L.G. Berkeley	L	2,123
1852	8,635	R.N.F. Kingscote	L	3,528
		R.B. Hale	C	2,946
		Hon. G.C.G.F. Berkeley	C	2,166
1857	9,250	R.N.F. Kingscote	L	Unopp.
		J. Rolt	C	Unopp.
1859	9,167	R.N.F. Kingscote	L	Unopp.
		J. Rolt	C	Unopp.
[Appointment of Kingscote as a Groom in Waiting to Her Majesty]				
1859 (7/7)		R.N.F. Kingscote	L	Unopp.
1865	9,368	R.N.F. Kingscote	L	Unopp.
		J. Rolt	C	Unopp.
[Appointment of Rolt as Attorney-General]				
1866 (15/11)		Sir J. Rolt	C	Unopp.
[Resignation of Rolt on appointment as a Judge of the Court of Appeal in Chancery]				
1867 (25/7)	9,368*	E.A. Somerset	C	3,649
		Hon. C.P.F. Berkeley	L	3,553
1868	11,463	R.N.F. Kingscote	L	4,985
		S.S. Marling	L	4,862
		E.A. Somerset	C	4,394

Election	Electors	Candidate	Party	Votes
1874	11,632	Hon. R.E.S. Plunkett	C	4,553
		R.N.F. Kingscote	L	4,344
		Hon. C.P.F. Berkeley	L	4,317
1880	12,162	R.N.F. Kingscote	L	5,316
		Lord Moreton	L	5,164
		Hon. R.E.S. Plunkett	C	4,640

[Resignation of Kingscote on appointment as Commissioner of Woods, Forests, and Land Revenues]

1885	12,802*	B.St.J. Ackers	C	4,837
(12/3)		Sir W. Marling	L	4,426

HAMPSHIRE, NORTHERN [227]
(Two Seats)

Election	Electors	Candidate	Party	Votes
1832	2,424	†C.S. Lefevre	L	1,111
		J.W. Scott	L	1,082
		†Marquess of Douro	C	723
		W. Long	C	701
1835	2,694	J.W. Scott	L	Unopp.
		C.S. Lefevre	L	Unopp.
1837	3,616	Sir W. Heathcote, Bt.	C	Unopp.
		C.S. Lefevre	L	Unopp.
1841	3,668	Sir W. Heathcote, Bt.	C	Unopp.
		C.S. Lefevre	L	Unopp.
1847	3,411	Sir W. Heathcote, Bt.	C	Unopp.
		C.S. Lefevre	L	Unopp.
[Resignation of Heathcote]				
1849 (6/4)	3,303	M. Portal	C	1,199
		W. Shaw	C	868
1852	3,596	M. Portal	C	Unopp.
		C.S. Lefevre	L	Unopp.
1857	3,149	W.W.B. Beach	C	1,419
		G. Sclater *(Booth)*	C	1,365
		D.W. Carleton	L	869
1859	3,649	W.W.B. Beach	C	Unopp.
		G.S. Booth	C	Unopp.
1865	4,185	W.W.B. Beach	C	1,844
		G.S. Booth	C	1,724
		Sir H.B.P.St.J. Mildmay	L	1,493
1868	5,744	W.W.B. Beach	C	Unopp.
		G.S. Booth	C	Unopp.
1874	6,033	W.W.B. Beach	C	Unopp.
		G.S. Booth	C	Unopp.
[Appointment of Booth as President of the Local Government Board]				
1874 (14/3)		G.S. Booth	C	Unopp.
1880	5,783	W.W.B. Beach	C	Unopp.
		G.S. Booth	C	Unopp.

Note:- 1837–1852: Lefevre was Speaker of the House of Commons from May 1839 until March 1857

HAMPSHIRE, SOUTHERN [228]
(Two Seats)

Election	Electors	Candidate	Party	Votes
1832	3,143	†Viscount Palmerston	L	1,627
		†Sir G.T. Staunton, Bt.	L	1,542
		†J.W. Fleming	C	1,266
1835	3,785	J.W. Fleming	C	1,746
		H.C. Compton	C	1,689
		Viscount Palmerston	L	1,504
		Sir G.T. Staunton, Bt.	L	1,450
1837	5,598	J.W. Fleming	C	2,388
		H.C. Compton	C	2,371
		Sir G.T. Staunton, Bt.	L	2,080
		Sir J.A. Ommanney	L	1,962
1841	5,794	H.C. Compton	C	Unopp.
		J.W. Fleming	C	Unopp.
[Resignation of Fleming]				
1842 (23/8)		Lord Charles Wellesley	C	Unopp.
1847	5,812	H.C. Compton	C	Unopp.
		Lord Charles Wellesley	C	Unopp.
1852	5,694	Lord William Cholmondeley	C	Unopp.
		H.C. Compton	C	Unopp.
1857	5,525	Hon. R.H. Dutton	C	Unopp.
		Sir J.C. Jervoise, Bt.	L	Unopp.
1859	5,865	Hon. R.H. Dutton	C	Unopp.
		Sir J.C. Jervoise, Bt.	L	Unopp.
1865	5,677	H.H. Fane	C	Unopp.
		Sir J.C. Jervoise, Bt.	L	Unopp.
1868	8,135	W.F. Cowper *(Temple)*	L	2,797
		Lord Henry Scott	C	2,756
		C. Milward	L	2,726
		J.C. Garnier	C	2,716
1874	9,578	Lord Henry Scott	C	3,878
		W.F.C. Temple	L	2,946
		C. Swanston	L	2,382
1880	10,162	F. Compton	C	Unopp.
		Lord Henry Scott	C	Unopp.

Election	Electors	Candidate	Party	Votes
[Resignation of Scott]				
1884 (23/6)	10,296	Sir F.W.J. Fitz Wygram, Bt.	C	4,209
		W.H. Deverell	L	2,772

Petition: —

1868: Withdrawn

HEREFORDSHIRE [229]
(Three Seats)

Election	Electors	Candidate	Party	Votes
1832	5,013	†E.T. Foley	C	Unopp.
		†K. Hoskins	L	Unopp.
		†Sir R. Price, Bt.	L	Unopp.
1835	4,970	K. Hoskins	L	3,012
		E.T. Foley	C	2,802
		Sir R. Price, Bt.	L	2,657
		E. Poole	C	1,964
1837	7,216	E.T. Foley	C	Unopp.
		K. Hoskins	L	Unopp.
		Sir R. Price, Bt.	L	Unopp.
1841	7,365	T.B.M. Baskerville	C	Unopp.
		J. Bailey	C	Unopp.
		K. Hoskins	L	Unopp.
1847	7,345	J. Bailey	C	Unopp.
		F.R. Haggitt *(F.R.W. Prosser)*	C	Unopp.
		G.C. Lewis	L	Unopp.
[Death of Bailey] 1850 (18/10)		T.W. Booker	C	Unopp.
1852	6,972	J.K. King	C	3,167
		T.W. Booker *(Blakemore)*	C	3,143
		Hon. C.S.B. Hanbury	C	3,030
		G.C. Lewis	L	2,836
1857	7,330	Sir H.G. Cotterell, Bt.	L	3,352
		T.W.B. Blakemore	C	2,822
		J.K. King	C	2,771
		Hon. C.S.B. Hanbury	C	2,475
[Death of Blakemore] 1858 (18/12)		Lord William Graham	C	Unopp.
1859	7,722	Lord William Graham	C	Unopp.
		J.K. King	C	Unopp.
		H.F.St.J. Mildmay	L	Unopp.
1865	7,179	Sir J.R. Bailey, Bt.	C	Unopp.
		M. Biddulph	L	Unopp.
		J.K. King	C	Unopp.
1868	9,528	Sir H.G.D. Croft, Bt.	C	3,351
		Sir J.R. Bailey, Bt.	C	3,341
		M Biddulph	L	2,273
		T. Blake	L	1,878

HEREFORDSHIRE [229] (Cont.)
(Three Seats)

Election	Electors	Candidate	Party	Votes
1874	8,977	Sir J.R. Bailey, Bt.	C	Unopp.
		M. Biddulph	L	Unopp.
		D.P. Peploe	C	Unopp.
1880	8,222	Sir J.R. Bailey, Bt.	C	3,077
		M. Biddulph	L	2,769
		T. Duckham	L	2,726
		D.P. Peploe	C	2,527

Petition:—

1852: Withdrawn

HERTFORDSHIRE [230]
(Three Seats)

Election	Electors	Candidate	Party	Votes
1832	4,245	†Sir J.S. Sebright, Bt.	L	2,154
		†N. Calvert	L	2,141
		†Viscount Grimston	C	2,074
		R. Alston	L	2,007
1835	4,520	R. Alston	L	Unopp.
		Viscount Grimston	C	Unopp.
		A. Smith (Senr.)	C	Unopp.
1837	5,137	R. Alston	L	Unopp.
		Viscount Grimston	C	Unopp.
		A. Smith (Senr.)	C	Unopp.
1841	5,409	Viscount Grimston	C	2,585
		Hon. G.D. Ryder	C	2,552
		A. Smith (Senr.)	C	2,525
		R. Alston	L	1,732
[Succession of Grimston to the Peerage — Earl of Verulam]				
1846 (8/1)		T.P. Halsey	C	Unopp.
1847	5,591	T. Brand *(Trevor)*	L	Unopp.
		T.P. Halsey	C	Unopp.
		Sir H. Meux, Bt.	C	Unopp.
1852	5,779†	T.P. Halsey	C	2,225
		Sir H. Meux, Bt.	C	2,219
		Sir E.G.E.L.B. Lytton, Bt.	C	2,190
		Hon. T. Trevor	L	2,043
		C.W. Puller	L	1,890
		G.J. Bosanquet	L	1,868
[Death of Halsey]				
1854 (24/5)	5,752	A. Smith (Junr.)	C	2,205
		C.W. Puller	L	2,151
1857	6,061	Sir E.G.E.L.B. Lytton, Bt.	C	Unopp.
		Sir H. Meux, Bt.	C	Unopp.
		C.W. Puller	L	Unopp.
[Appointment of Lytton as Secretary of the State for the Colonies]				
1858 (8/6)		Sir E.G.E.L.B. Lytton, Bt.	C	Unopp.
1859	6,190	Sir E.G.E.L.B. Lytton, Bt.	C	Unopp.
		C.W. Puller	L	Unopp.
		A. Smith (Junr.)	C	Unopp.

(Three Seats)

Election	Electors	Candidate	Party	Votes
[Death of Puller]				
1864 (14/3)	5,742	H.E. Surtees	C	2,274
		Hon. H.F. Cowper	L	2,026
1865	6,228	Hon. H.F. Cowper	L	2,537
		Sir E.G.E.L.B. Lytton, Bt.	C	2,485
		H.E. Surtees	C	2,478
		A. Smith (Junr.)	C	2,447
[Elevation of Lytton to the Peerage — Lord Lytton]				
1866 (23/7)		A. Smith (Junr.)	C	Unopp.
1868	9,423†	Hon. H.F. Cowper	L	3,693
		H.R. Brand	L	3,625
		A. Smith (Junr.)	C	3,396
		H.E. Surtees	C	3,356
1874	9,809	T.F. Halsey	C	4,499
		A. Smith (Junr.)	C	4,498
		Hon. H.F. Cowper	L	2,974
		H.R. Brand	L	2,964
1880	10,050	Hon. H.F. Cowper	L	Unopp.
		T.F. Halsey	C	Unopp.
		A. Smith (Junr.)	C	Unopp.

HUNTINGDONSHIRE [231]
(Two Seats)

Election	Electors	Candidate	Party	Votes
1832	2,647	†Viscount Mandeville (1)	C	Unopp.
		†J.B. Rooper	L	Unopp.
1835	2,653	Viscount Mandeville (1)	C	Unopp.
		J.B. Rooper	L	Unopp.
1837	2,805	E. Fellowes	C	1,392
		G. Thornhill	C	1,332
		J.B. Rooper	L	990
1841	3,054	E. Fellowes	C	Unopp.
		G. Thornhill	C	Unopp.
1847	3,074	E. Fellowes	C	Unopp.
		G. Thornhill	C	Unopp.
[Death of Thornhill]				
1852 (11/6)		Viscount Mandeville (2)	C	Unopp.
1852	2,852	E. Fellowes	C	Unopp.
		Viscount Mandeville (2)	C	Unopp.
[Succession of Mandeville to the Peerage — Duke of Manchester]				
1855 (23/10)		J. Rust	C	Unopp.
1857	2,918	J. Rust	C	1,192
		*E. Fellowes	C	1,106
		**J.M. Heathcote	L	1,106
1859	3,024	E. Fellowes	C	1,404
		Lord Robert Montagu	C	1,314
		J.M. Heathcote	L	1,068
1865	2,999	E. Fellowes	C	Unopp.
		Lord Robert Montagu	C	Unopp.
[Appointment of Montagu as Vice-President of the Committee of the Privy Council for Education]				
1867 (25/3)		Lord Robert Montagu	C	Unopp.
1868	3,748	E. Fellowes	C	Unopp.
		Lord Robert Montagu	C	Unopp.
1874	3,592	E. Fellowes	C	1,648
		Sir H.C. Pelly, Bt.	C	1,482
		Lord Douglas Gordon	L	1,192

HUNTINGDONSHIRE [231] (Cont.)

(Two Seats)

Election	Electors	Candidate	Party	Votes
[Death of Pelly]				
1877 (30/6)	3,748	Viscount Mandeville (3)	C	1,468
		Hon. W.H.W. Fitzwilliam	L	1,410
1880	3,955	W.H. Fellowes	C	1,786
		Lord Douglas Gordon	L	1,617
		Viscount Mandeville (3)	C	1,596

Petitions:—

1837: Withdrawn

1857: Treble return. On scrutiny the poll was found to have been Rust 1,191; Fellowes 1,105; Heathcote 1,104. Fellowes was therefore declared duly elected. (Fellowes and Heathcote only).

ISLE OF WIGHT [232]

Election	Electors	Candidate	Party	Votes
1832	1,167	Sir R.G. Simeon, Bt.	L	712
		A.G. Campbell	C	112
1835	1,167*	Sir R.G. Simeon, Bt.	L	483
		G.H. Ward	C	337
1837	1,167*	Hon. W.H.A.A'C. Holmes	C	628
		Hon. C.D. Pelham	L	560
1841	1,167*	Hon. W.H.A.A'C. Holmes	C	Unopp.
1847	1,167*	J. Simeon	L	476
		T.W. Fleming	C	373
[Resignation]				
1851 (29/5)	1,650*	E. Dawes	L	565
		A.S. Hamond	C	519
1852	1,650*	F.V. Harcourt	C	681
		E. Dawes	L	593
1857	1,949	C.C. Clifford	L	730
		T.W. Fleming	C	610
1859	2,038	C.C. Clifford	L	756
		F.V. Harcourt	C	694
1865	2,315*	Sir J. Simeon, Bt.	L	786
		Sir C. Locock, Bt.	C	710
1868	3,807†	Sir J. Simeon, Bt.	L	1,353
		A.D.R.W.B. Cochrane	C	1,118
[Death]				
1870 (13/6)	3,807*	A.D.R.W.B. Cochrane	C	1,317
		G. Moffatt	L	1,282
1874	4,084*	A.D.R.W.B. Cochrane	C	1,614
		Hon. A.E.M. Ashley	L	1,605
1880	4,954	Hon. A.E.M. Ashley	L	1,986
		B.T. Cotton	C	1,973

Petition:—

1874: Withdrawn

KENT, EASTERN [233]
(Two Seats)

Election	Electors	Candidate	Party	Votes
1832	7,026	J.P. Plumptre	L	3,476
		Sir E. Knatchbull, Bt.	C	3,344
		Sir W.R. Cosway	L	2,627
		Sir W.P.H. Courtenay	L	4
1835	7,087	Sir E. Knatchbull, Bt.	C	Unopp.
		J.P. Plumptre	C	Unopp.
1837	7,293	Sir E. Knatchbull, Bt.	C	3,607
		J.P. Plumptre	C	3,029
		T. Rider	L	2,205
1841	7,553	Sir E. Knatchbull, Bt.	C	Unopp.
		J.P. Plumptre	C	Unopp.
[Appointment of Knatchbull as Paymaster-General]				
1841 (20/9)		Sir E. Knatchbull, Bt.	C	Unopp.
[Resignation of Knatchbull]				
1845 (3/3)		W. Deedes	C	Unopp.
1847	7,323	W. Deedes	C	Unopp.
		J.P. Plumptre	C	Unopp.
[Resignation of Plumptre]				
1852 (16/2)	7,119	Sir B.W. Bridges, Bt.	C	2,480
		Sir E.C. Dering, Bt.	L	2,289
1852	7,119	Sir E.C. Dering, Bt.	L	3,063
		W. Deedes	C	2,879
		Sir B.W. Bridges, Bt.	C	2,356
1857	8,000	Sir B.W. Bridges, Bt.	C	2,379
		Sir E.C. Dering, Bt.	L	2,358
		W. Deedes	C	2,216
		E.A. Acheson	L	127
[Resignation of Dering]				
1857 (10/12)		W. Deedes	C	Unopp.
1859	8,312	Sir B.W. Bridges, Bt.	C	Unopp.
		W. Deedes	C	Unopp.
[Death of Deedes]				
1863 (5/1)	7,092	Sir E.C. Dering, Bt.	L	2,777
		Sir N.J. Knatchbull, Bt.	C	2,690

(Two Seats)

Election	Electors	Candidate	Party	Votes
1865	8,250	Sir B.W. Bridges, Bt.	C	3,208
		Sir E.C. Dering, Bt.	L	3,195
		Sir N.J. Knatchbull, Bt.	C	2,919
[Elevation of Bridges to the Peerage — Lord Fitzwalter]				
1868 (2/5)	8,250*	E.L. Pemberton	C	3,606
		H.J. Tufton	L	3,109
1868	13,107	E.L. Pemberton	C	5,231
		Hon. G.W. Milles	C	5,104
		H.J. Tufton	L	4,685
		Sir J. Croft, Bt.	L	4,579
1874	12,605	Hon. G.W. Milles	C	5,424
		E.L. Pemberton	C	5,405
		Sir H.J. Tufton, Bt.	L	4,308
[Succession of Milles to the Peerage — Lord Sondes]				
1875 (27/1)		Sir W. Knatchbull, Bt.	C	Unopp.
[Resignation of Knatchbull]				
1876 (26/7)		W. Deedes	C	Unopp.
1880	13,169	A.A. Douglas	C	5,541
		E.L. Pemberton	C	5,473
		E.F. Davis	L	4,959

KENT, MID [234]
(Two Seats)

Election	Electors	Candidate	Party	Votes
1868	8,723	W.H. Dyke	C	3,251
		Viscount Holmesdale	C	3,248
		Lord John Hervey	L	2,872
		F.S. Head	L	2,868
1874	8,905	W.H. Dyke	C	3,710
		Viscount Holmesdale	C	3,542
		Sir D.L. Salomons, Bt.	L	2,956
1880	8,763	Sir W.H. Dyke, Bt.	C	4,056
		Sir E. Filmer, Bt.	C	3,783
		E. Cazalet	L	3,318
		H.W. Elphinstone	L	3,020
[Resignation of Filmer]				
1884 (15/5)		Hon. J.S.G. Hardy	C	Unopp.
[Appointment of Dyke as Chief Secretary to the Lord Lieutenant of Ireland]				
1885 (2/7)		Sir W.H. Dyke, Bt.	C	Unopp.

KENT, WESTERN [235]
(Two Seats)

Election	Electors	Candidate	Party	Votes
1832	6,678	†T.L. Hodges	L	3,364
		†T. Rider	L	3,100
		Sir W.R.P. Geary, Bt.	C	2,518
1835	6,850	Sir W.R.P. Geary, Bt.	C	2,558
		T.L. Hodges	L	2,092
		T. Rider	L	2,007
1837	8,432	Sir W.R.P. Geary, Bt.	C	3,584
		T.L. Hodges	L	3,334
		Sir E. Filmer, Bt.	C	3,229
[Resignation of Geary]				
1838 (5/3)		Sir E. Filmer, Bt.	C	Unopp.
1841	9,089	Sir E. Filmer, Bt.	C	Unopp.
		Viscount Marsham	C	Unopp.
[Succession of Marsham to the Peerage — Earl of Romney]				
1845 (25/4)		T. Austen	C	Unopp.
1847	9,489	Sir E. Filmer, Bt.	C	3,219
		T.L. Hodges	L	3,127
		T. Austen	C	3,082
1852	9,379	Sir E. Filmer, Bt.	C	3,247
		W.M. Smith	C	3,193
		T.L. Hodges	L	2,652
[Death of Filmer]				
1857 (16/2)	8,949	C.W. Martin	L	3,557
		Sir W.B. Riddell	C	3,149
1857	8,949	C.W. Martin	L	3,896
		J. Whatman	L	3,578
		W.M. Smith	C	3,171
1859	8,948	Viscount Holmesdale	C	3,769
		Sir E. Filmer, Bt.	C	3,684
		C.W. Martin	L	3,584
		J. Whatman	L	3,460
1865	9,811	Viscount Holmesdale	C	4,133
		W.H. Dyke	C	4,054
		Sir J. Lubbock, Bt.	L	3,896
		W. Angerstein	L	3,861

KENT, WESTERN [235] (Cont.)
(Two Seats)

Election	Electors	Candidate	Party	Votes
1868	8,828†	C.H. Mills	C	3,440
		J.G. Talbot	C	3,378
		Sir J. Lubbock, Bt.	L	3,323
		W. Angerstein	L	3,196
1874	11,973	Sir C.H. Mills, Bt.	C	5,295
		J.G. Talbot	C	5,227
		A. Hamilton	L	3,391
		E. Marjoribanks	L	3,346
[Resignation of Talbot in order to contest Oxford University]				
1878 (15/5)		Viscount Lewisham	C	Unopp.
1880	14,873	Sir C.H. Mills, Bt.	C	6,413
		Viscount Lewisham	C	5,986
		H.M. Bompas	L	4,857
		J. May	C	977
[Appointment of Lewisham as Vice-Chamberlain of H.M. Household]				
1885 (6/7)		Viscount Lewisham	C	Unopp.

Petition:—

1859: Withdrawn

LANCASHIRE, NORTHERN [236]

(Two Seats)

Election	Electors	Candidate	Party	Votes
1832	6,593	J.W. Patten	C	Unopp.
		†Hon. E.G.S. Stanley	L	Unopp.

[Appointment of Stanley as Secretary of State for War and the Colonies]

1833 (12/4)		Hon. E.G.S. Stanley *(Lord Stanley)*	L	Unopp.
1835	6,581	J.W. Patten	C	Unopp.
		Lord Stanley	L	Unopp.
1837	9,691	J.W. Patten	C	Unopp.
		Lord Stanley	C	Unopp.
1841	10,031	J.W. Patten	C	Unopp.
		Lord Stanley	C	Unopp.

[Appointment of Stanley as Secretary of State for War and the Colonies]

1841 (21/9)		Lord Stanley	C	Unopp.

[Stanley called to the House of Lords as Lord Stanley of Bickerstaffe]

1844 (20/9)		J.T. Clifton	C	Unopp.
1847	11,846	J. Heywood	L	Unopp.
		J.W. Patten	C	Unopp.
1852	12,297	J. Heywood	L	Unopp.
		J.W. Patten	C	Unopp.
1857	12,352	Lord Cavendish *(Marquess of Hartington)*	L	Unopp.
		J.W. Patten	C	Unopp.
1859	12,183	Marquess of Hartington	L	Unopp.
		J.W. Patten	C	Unopp.

[Appointment of Hartington as a Civil Lord of the Admiralty]

1863 (24/3)		Marquess of Hartington	L	Unopp.
1865	13,006	Marquess of Hartington	L	Unopp.
		J.W. Patten	C	Unopp.

[Appointment of Hartington as Secretary of State for the War Department]

1866 (28/2)		Marquess of Hartington	L	Unopp.

Election	Electors	Candidate	Party	Votes
[Appointment of Patten as Chancellor of the Duchy of Lancaster]				
1867 (1/7)		J.W. Patten	C	Unopp.
1868	14,399†	Hon. F.A. Stanley	C	6,832
		J.W. Patten	C	6,681
		Marquess of Hartington	L	5,296
1874	14,690	J.W. Patten	C	Unopp.
		Hon. F.A. Stanley	C	Unopp.
[Elevation of Patten to the Peerage — Lord Winmarleigh]				
1874 (26/3)		T.H. Clifton	C	Unopp.
[Appointment of Stanley as Secretary of State for the War Department]				
1878 (8/4)		Hon. F.A. Stanley	C	Unopp.
1880	17,057	Hon. F.A. Stanley	C	8,172
		R.J. Feilden	C	7,505
		T. Storey	L	6,500
[Appointment of Stanley as Secretary of State for the Colonies]				
1885 (2/7)		Hon. F.A. Stanley	C	Unopp.

LANCASHIRE, NORTH-EASTERN [237]
(Two Seats)

Election	Electors	Candidate	Party	Votes
1868	8,649	J.M. Holt	C	3,612
		J.P.C. Starkie	C	3,594
		U.J.K. Shuttleworth	L	3,463
		W. Fenton	L	3,441
1874	10,250	J.M. Holt	C	4,578
		J.P.C. Starkie	C	4,488
		Sir J.P.K. Shuttleworth, Bt.	L	4,401
		Lord Edward Cavendish	L	4,297
1880	12,991	Marquess of Hartington	L	6,682
		F.W. Grafton	L	6,513
		W.F. Ecroyd	C	5,231
		J.P.C. Starkie	C	5,185

[Appointment of Hartington as Secretary of State for India]

Election	Electors	Candidate	Party	Votes
1880 (17/5)		Marquess of Hartington	L	Unopp.

LANCASHIRE, SOUTHERN [238]
(Two seats until 1861; three seats from 1861)

Election	Electors	Candidate	Party	Votes
1832	10,039	G.W. Wood	L	5,694
		Viscount Molyneux	L	5,575
		Sir T. Hesketh, Bt.	C	3,082
1835	11,519	Lord Francis Egerton	C	5,620
		Hon. R.B. Wilbraham	C	4,729
		Viscount Molyneux	L	4,629
		G.W. Wood	L	4,394
1837	17,754	Lord Francis Egerton	C	7,822
		Hon. R.B. Wilbraham	C	7,645
		E. Stanley	L	6,576
		C. Towneley	L	6,047
1841	18,178	Lord Francis Egerton	C	Unopp.
		Hon. R.B. Wilbraham	C	Unopp.
[Death of Wilbraham]				
1844 (24/5)	18,521*	W. Entwisle	C	7,571
		W. Brown	L	6,973
[Elevation of Egerton to the Peerage — Earl of Ellesmere]				
1846 (21/7)		W. Brown	L	Unopp.
1847	23,630	W. Brown	L	Unopp.
		Hon. C.P. Villiers	L	Unopp.
[Villiers elects to sit for Wolverhampton]				
1847 (20/12)		A. Henry	L	Unopp.
1852	21,196	W. Brown	L	Unopp.
		J. Cheetham	L	Unopp.
1857	20,460	W. Brown	L	Unopp.
		J. Cheetham	L	Unopp.
1859	19,433	Hon. A.F. Egerton	C	7,470
		W.J. Leigh	C	6,983
		J. Cheetham	L	6,835
		J.P. Heywood	L	6,763
[Third seat created]				
1861 (19/8)	19,433*	C. Turner	C	9,714
		J. Cheetham	L	8,898

LANCASHIRE, SOUTHERN [238] (Cont.)
(Two seats until 1861; three seats from 1861)

Election	Electors	Candidate	Party	Votes
1865	21,555	Hon. A.F. Egerton	C	9,171
		C. Turner	C	8,806
		W.E. Gladstone	L	8,786
		W.J. Leigh	C	8,476
		H.Y. Thompson	L	7,703
		J.P. Heywood	L	7,653

This constituency was divided in 1868.

LANCASHIRE, SOUTH-EASTERN [239]
(Two Seats)

Election	Electors	Candidate	Party	Votes
1868	19,340	Hon. A.F. Egerton	C	8,290
		J.S. Henry	C	8,012
		F. Peel	L	7,024
		H.Y. Thompson	L	6,953
1874	21,427	Hon. A.F. Egerton	C	9,187
		E. Hardcastle	C	9,015
		P. Rylands	L	7,464
		J.E. Taylor	L	7,453
1880	26,037	R, Leake	L	11,313
		W. Agnew	L	11,291
		Hon. A.F. Egerton	C	10,569
		E. Hardcastle	C	10,419

LANCASHIRE, SOUTH-WESTERN [240]
(Two Seats)

Election	Electors	Candidate	Party	Votes
1868	21,261	R.A. Cross	C	7,729
		C. Turner	C	7,676
		W.E. Gladstone	L	7,415
		H.R. Grenfell	L	6,939
1874	22,729	R.A. Cross	C	Unopp.
		C. Turner	C	Unopp.
[Appointment of Cross as Secretary of State for the Home Department]				
1874 (19/3)		R.A. Cross	C	Unopp.
[Death of Turner]				
1875 (6/11)		J.I. Blackburne	C	Unopp.
1880	26,054	R.A. Cross	C	11,420
		J.I. Blackburne	C	10,905
		W. Rathbone	L	9,666
		Hon. H.H. Molyneux	L	9,207
[Appointment of Cross as Secretary of State for the Home Department]				
1885 (1/7)		Sir R.A. Cross	C	Unopp.

LEICESTERSHIRE, NORTHERN [241]

(Two Seats)

Election	Electors	Candidate	Party	Votes
1832	3,658	Lord Robert Manners	C	2,093
		†C.M. Phillipps	L	1,661
		W.A. Johnson	L	720
1835	3,806	Lord Robert Manners	C	Unopp.
		C.M. Phillipps	L	Unopp.
[Death of Manners]				
1835 (29/12)		Lord Charles Manners	C	Unopp.
1837	4,160	E.B. Farnham	C	Unopp.
		Lord Charles Manners	C	Unopp.
1841	4,211	E.B. Farnham	C	Unopp.
		Lord Charles Manners	C	Unopp.
1847	4,177	E.B. Farnham	C	Unopp.
		Lord Charles Manners	C	Unopp.
1852	4,097	E.B. Farnham	C	Unopp.
		Marquess of Granby	C	Unopp.
[Succession of Granby to the Peerage — Duke of Rutland]				
1857 (2/3)		Lord John Manners	C	Unopp.
1857	3,890	Lord John Manners	C	1,787
		E.B. Farnham	C	1,733
		C.H. Frewen	C	1,250
[Appointment of Manners as First Commissioner of Works and Public Buildings]				
1858 (8/3)		Lord John Manners	C	Unopp.
1859	4,330	Lord John Manners	C	2,220
		E.B. Hartopp	C	1,954
		C.H. Frewen	C	1,433
1865	4,767	Lord John Manners	C	2,305
		E.B. Hartopp	C	1,854
		C.H. Frewen	C	1,599
[Appointment of Manners as First Commissioner of Works and Public Buildings]				
1866 (14/7)		Lord John Manners	C	Unopp.

LEICESTERSHIRE, NORTHERN [241] (Cont.)
(Two Seats)

Election	Electors	Candidate	Party	Votes
1868	6,348	Lord John Manners	C	3,296
		S.W. Clowes	C	3,092
		C.H. Frewen	C	1,750
		Lord George Manners	C	9
1874	5,968	Lord John Manners	C	2,978
		S.W. Clowes	C	2,568
		H. Packe	L	1,997
[Appointment of Manners as Postmaster-General]				
1874 (20/3)		Lord John Manners	C	Unopp.
1880	6,619	Lord John Manners	C	3,213
		E.S. Burnaby	C	2,991
		H. Packe	L	2,651
[Death of Burnaby]				
1883 (18/6)		Hon. M. Curzon	C	Unopp.
[Appointment of Manners as Postmaster-General]				
1885 (2/7)		Lord John Manners	C	Unopp.

Petition:—

1859: Dismissed

LEICESTERSHIRE, SOUTHERN [242]
(Two Seats)

Election	Electors	Candidate	Party	Votes
1832	4,125	E. Dawson	L	Unopp.
		H. Halford	C	Unopp.
1835	4,244	H. Halford	C	Unopp.
		T.F. Turner	C	Unopp.
[Resignation of Turner]				
1836 (18/2)		C.W. Packe	C	Unopp.
1837	4,603	H. Halford	C	Unopp.
		C.W. Packe	C	Unopp.
1841	4,903	H. Halford	C	2,638
		C.W. Packe	C	2,622
		T. Gisborne	L	1,213
		E. Cheney	L	1,196
1847	5,448	Sir H. Halford, Bt.	C	Unopp.
		C.W. Packe	C	Unopp.
1852	5,131	Sir H. Halford, Bt.	C	Unopp.
		C.W. Packe	C	Unopp.
1857	5,205	Viscount Curzon	C	Unopp.
		C.W. Packe	C	Unopp.
1859	5,259	Viscount Curzon	C	Unopp.
		C.W. Packe	C	Unopp.
1865	6,283	Viscount Curzon	C	Unopp.
		C.W. Packe	C	Unopp.
[Death of Packe]				
1867 (30/11)	6,283*	T.T. Paget	L	2,302
		A. Pell	C	2,263
1868	8,308	Viscount Curzon	C	3,196
		A. Pell	C	3,111
		T.T. Paget	L	2,861
[Succession of Curzon to the Peerage — Earl Howe]				
1870 (13/6)	8,308*	W.U. Heygate	C	3,292
		T.T. Paget	L	2,585

LEICESTERSHIRE, SOUTHERN [242] (Cont.)
(Two Seats)

Election	Electors	Candidate	Party	Votes
1874	8,489	A. Pell	C	3,583
		W.U. Heygate	C	3,269
		T.T. Paget	L	2,883
1880	9,022	T.T. Paget	L	3,685
		A. Pell	C	3,453
		W.U. Heygate	C	3,175

LINCOLNSHIRE, PARTS OF KESTEVEN AND HOLLAND [243]

(Two Seats)

Election	Electors	Candidate	Party	Votes
1832	7,956	H. Handley	L	Unopp.
		†G.J. Heathcote	L	Unopp.
1835	7,694	H. Handley	L	Unopp.
		G.J. Heathcote	L	Unopp.
1837	8,100	H. Handley	L	Unopp.
		G.J. Heathcote	L	Unopp.
1841	8,914	C. Turnor	C	4,581
		Sir J. Trollope, Bt.	C	4,562
		H. Handley	L	2,948
1847	9,226	Lord Burghley	C	Unopp.
		Sir J. Trollope, Bt.	C	Unopp.
[Appointment of Trollope as President of the Poor Law Board]				
1852 (12/3)		Sir J. Trollope, Bt.	C	Unopp.
1852	8,554	Lord Burghley	C	Unopp.
		Sir J. Trollope, Bt.	C	Unopp.
1857	8,287	Sir J. Trollope, Bt.	C	4,020
		A. Wilson	C	3,636
		G.H. Packe	L	3,188
1859	9,435	G.H. Packe	L	Unopp.
		Sir J. Trollope, Bt.	C	Unopp.
1865	9,260	G.H. Packe	L	Unopp.
		Sir J. Trollope, Bt.	C	Unopp.
[Elevation of Trollope to the Peerage – Lord Kesteven]				
1868 (29/4)		W.E. Welby	C	Unopp.

This constituency was divided in 1868.

LINCOLNSHIRE, PARTS OF LINDSEY [244]
(Two Seats)

Election	Electors	Candidate	Party	Votes
1832	9,134	†Hon. C.A.W. Pelham	L	6,561
		†Sir W.A. Ingilby, Bt.	L	4,751
		Sir R. Sheffield, Bt.	C	4,056
1835	8,872	Hon. C.A.W. Pelham *(Lord Worsley)*	L	4,489
		T.G. Corbett	C	4,450
		Sir W.A. Ingilby, Bt.	L	3,984
1837	10,063	R.A. Christopher	C	Unopp.
		Lord Worsley	L	Unopp.
1841	10,280	Lord Worsley	L	5,401
		R.A. Christopher	C	4,522
		Hon. C.H. Cust	C	3,819
[Succession of Worsley to the Peerage — Earl of Yarborough]				
1847 (12/1)		Sir M.J. Cholmeley, Bt.	L	Unopp.
1847	11,424	Sir M.J. Cholmeley, Bt.	L	Unopp.
		R.A. Christopher	C	Unopp.
[Appointment of Christopher as Chancellor of the Duchy of Lancaster]				
1852 (13/3)		R.A. Christopher	C	Unopp.
1852	11,677	R.A. Christopher *(R.A.C.N. Hamilton)*	C	5,585
		J.B. Stanhope	C	5,579
		Sir M.J. Cholmeley, Bt.	L	4,777
1857	12,435	Sir M.J. Cholmeley, Bt.	L	Unopp
		J.B. Stanhope	C	Unopp
1859	12,401	Sir M.J. Cholmeley, Bt.	L	Unopp
		J.B. Stanhope	C	Unopp
1865	12,372	Sir M.J. Cholmeley, Bt.	L	Unopp
		J.B. Stanhope	C	Unopp

This constituency was divided in 1868.

LINCOLNSHIRE, MID [245]

(Two Seats)

Election	Electors	Candidate	Party	Votes
1868	8,694	W.C. Amcotts	L	Unopp.
		H. Chaplin	C	Unopp.
1874	8,549	H. Chaplin	C	Unopp.
		Hon. E. Stanhope	C	Unopp.
1880	8,822	H. Chaplin	C	Unopp.
		Hon. E. Stanhope	C	Unopp.

[Appointments of Chaplin as Chancellor of the Duchy of Lancaster and Stanhope as Vice-President of the Committee of the Privy Council for Education]

1885 (1/7)		H. Chaplin	C	Unopp.
		Hon. E. Stanhope	C	Unopp.

LINCOLNSHIRE, NORTHERN [246]
(Two Seats)

Election	Electors	Candidate	Party	Votes
1868	9,436	Sir M.J. Cholmeley, Bt.	L	Unopp.
		R. Winn	C	Unopp.
1874	10,117	Sir J.D. Astley, Bt.	C	Unopp.
		R. Winn	C	Unopp.
[Appointment of Winn as a Lord Commissioner of the Treasury]				
1874 (16/3)		R. Winn	C	Unopp.
1880	10,639	R. Laycock	L	4,159
		R. Winn	C	3,949
		Sir J.D. Astley, Bt.	C	3,865
[Death of Laycock]				
1881 (3/9)	11,061	J. Lowther	C	4,200
		G. Tomline	L	3,729
[Elevation of Winn to the Peerage — Lord St. Oswald]				
1885 (13/7)	10,435*	H.J. Atkinson	C	4,052
		Sir H.M.M. Thompson, Bt.	L	2,872

LINCOLNSHIRE, SOUTHERN [247]
(Two Seats)

Election	Electors	Candidate	Party	Votes
1868	10,476	W.E. Welby	C	4,514
		E. Turnor	C	4,078
		G.H. Packe	L	2,714
		J. Taylor	L	3
1874	11,020	E. Turnor	C	Unopp.
		W.E. Welby *(Gregory)*	C	Unopp.
1880	10,710	J.C. Lawrance	C	4,518
		Sir W.E.W. Gregory, Bt.	C	4,290
		C. Sharpe	L	3,583

[Resignation of Gregory]

1884 (29/2)		Hon. M.E.G.F. Hatton	C	Unopp.

MIDDLESEX [248]
(Two Seats)

Election	Electors	Candidate	Party	Votes
1832	6,939	†J. Hume	L	3,238
		†G. Byng	L	3,033
		†Sir C. Forbes, Bt.	C	1,494
		Sir J.S. Lillie	L	1,004
1835	8,005	G. Byng	L	3,505
		J. Hume	L	3,096
		T. Wood	C	2,707
1837	12,817	G. Byng	L	4,796
		T. Wood	C	4,582
		J. Hume	L	4,380
		H. Pownall	C	4,273
1841	13,915	G. Byng	L	Unopp.
		T. Wood	C	Unopp.
(Death of Byng)				
1847 (3/2)		Lord Robert Grosvenor	L	Unopp.
1847	13,781	Lord Robert Grosvenor	L	4,944
		R.B. Osborne	L	4,175
		T. Wood	C	3,458
1852	14,610	Lord Robert Grosvenor	L	5,241
		R.B. Osborne	L	4,390
		Marquess of Blandford	C	4,258
1857	14,977	R.C. Hanbury	L	5,426
		Lord Robert Grosvenor	L	5,327
		Viscount Chelsea	C	2,928
[Elevation of Grosvenor to the Peerage — Lord Ebury]				
1857 (3/9)		Hon. G.H.C. Byng	L	Unopp.
1859	15,171	R.C. Hanbury	L	3,678
		Hon. G.H.C. Byng *(Viscount Enfield)*	L	3,618
		J. Haig	C	1,147
1865	14,847	Viscount Enfield	L	Unopp.
		R.C. Hanbury	L	Unopp.
[Death of Hanbury]				
1867 (15/4)		H. Labouchere	L	Unopp.
1868	25,196†	Lord George Hamilton	C	7,850
		Viscount Enfield	L	6,487
		H. Labouchere	L	6,397

Election	Electors	Candidate	Party	Votes
1874	25,071	Lord George Hamilton	C	10,343
		O.E. Coope	C	9,867
		Viscount Enfield	L	5,623
		F. Lehmann	L	5,192

[Appointment of Hamilton as Vice-President of the Committee of the Privy Council for Education]

1878 (12/4)		Lord George Hamilton	C	Unopp.

1880	30,707	Lord George Hamilton	C	12,904
		O.E. Coope	C	12,328
		H.J. Gladstone	L	8,876

[Appointment as Hamilton as First Lord of the Admiralty]

1885 (3/7)		Lord George Hamilton	C	Unopp.

Petition:—

 1852: Withdrawn (Osborne only)

NORFOLK, EASTERN [249]

(Two Seats)

Election	Electors	Candidate	Party	Votes
1832	7,041	W.H. Windham	L	3,304
		Hon. G.T. Keppel	L	3,261
		†N.W. Peach	C	2,960
		†Lord Henry Cholmondeley	C	2,852
1835	7,281	E. Wodehouse	C	3,482
		Lord Walpole	C	3,196
		W.H. Windham	L	3,076
		R.H. Gurney	L	2,866
1837	8,343	E. Wodehouse	C	3,654
		H.N. Burroughes	C	3,523
		W.H. Windham	L	3,237
		R.H. Gurney	L	2,978
1841	8,556	E. Wodehouse	C	3,495
		H.N. Burroughes	C	3,434
		Sir W.J.H.B. Folkes, Bt.	L	1,378
1847	8,638	H.N. Burroughes	C	Unopp.
		E. Wodehouse	C	Unopp.
1852	8,216	H.N. Burroughes	C	Unopp.
		E. Wodehouse	C	Unopp.
[Resignation of Wodehouse]				
1855 (17/7)		H.J. Stracey	C	Unopp.
1857	7,755	Sir E.N. Buxton, Bt.	L	Unopp.
		C.A. Windham	L	Unopp.
[Death of Buxton]				
1858 (1/7)	7,755*	Hon. W.C.W. Coke	L	2,933
		Sir H.J. Stracey, Bt.	C	2,720
1859	7,776	Hon. W.C.W. Coke	L	Unopp.
		E. Howes	C	Unopp.
1865	7,939	E. Howes	C	3,100
		C.S. Read	C	2,985
		Sir T.P. Beauchamp, Bt.	L	2,150
		Hon. W.C.W. Coke	L	1,994

This constituency was divided in 1868.

Petitions: —

1832: Withdrawn

1837: Withdrawn

NORFOLK, NORTHERN [250]
(Two Seats)

Election	Electors	Candidate	Party	Votes
1868	6,432	Hon. F. Walpole	C	2,630
		Sir E.H.K. Lacon, Bt.	C	2,563
		E.R. Wodehouse	L	2,235
		R.T. Gurdon	L	2,078
1874	6,325	Sir E.H.K. Lacon, Bt.	C	Unopp.
		Hon. F. Walpole	C	Unopp.
[Death of Walpole]				
1876 (24/4)	6,231	J. Duff	C	2,302
		Sir T.F. Buxton, Bt.	L	2,192
[Death of Duff]				
1879 (23/1)	6,474	E. Birkbeck	C	2,742
		Sir T.F. Buxton, Bt.	L	2,252
1880	6,519	E. Birkbeck	C	Unopp.
		Sir E.H.K. Lacon, Bt.	C	Unopp.

Petition:—

1868: Dismissed

NORFOLK, SOUTHERN [251]
(Two Seats)

Election	Electors	Candidate	Party	Votes
1868	7,709	C.S. Read	C	3,097
		E. Howes	C	3,053
		H.L. Hudson	L	1,679
[Death of Howes]				
1871 (17/4)	7,719	Sir R.J. Buxton, Bt.	C	2,868
		R.T. Gurdon	L	2,547
1874	7,667	C.S. Read	C	3,146
		Sir R.J. Buxton, Bt.	C	3,010
		R.T. Gurdon	L	2,699
1880	7,412	Sir R.J. Buxton, Bt.	C	2,917
		R.T. Gurdon	L	2,906
		C.S. Read	C	2,905

NORFOLK, WESTERN [252]
(Two Seats)

Election	Electors	Candidate	Party	Votes
1832	4,396	Sir J. Astley, Bt.	L	Unopp.
		†Sir W.J.H.B. Folkes, Bt.	L	Unopp.
1835	4,633	Sir W.J.H.B. Folkes, Bt.	L	2,299
		Sir J. Astley, Bt.	L	2,134
		W. Bagge	C	1,880
1837	7,258	W. Bagge	C	3,178
		W.L.W. Chute	C	2,877
		Sir W.J.H.B. Folkes, Bt.	L	2,838
		Sir J. Astley, Bt.	L	2,713
1841	7,559*	W. Bagge	C	Unopp.
		W.L.W. Chute	C	Unopp.
1847	7,516	W. Bagge	C	3,113
		Hon. E.K.W. Coke	L	3,052
		A. Hamond (Senr.)	L	2,935
		H.L.S. Le Strange	C	2,676
1852	7,827	W. Bagge	C	3,421
		G.W.P. Bentinck	C	3,143
		A. Hamond (Senr.)	L	1,973
1857	7,179	G.W.P. Bentinck	C	Unopp.
		B. Gurdon	L	Unopp.
1859	6,941	G.W.P. Bentinck	C	Unopp.
		B. Gurdon	L	Unopp.
1865	6,534	W. Bagge	C	2,710
		Hon. T. de Grey	C	2,611
		Sir W. Jones, Bt.	L	2,133
		B. Gurdon	L	2,088
1868	7,062†	Sir W. Bagge, Bt.	C	Unopp.
		Hon. T. de Grey	C	Unopp.
[Succession of Grey to the Peerage — Lord Walsingham]				
1871 (8/2)		G.W.P. Bentinck	C	Unopp.
1874	6,647	Sir W. Bagge, Bt.	C	Unopp.
		G.W.P. Bentinck	C	Unopp.
[Death of Bagge]				
1880 (8/3)		W.A.T. Amherst	C	Unopp.

NORFOLK, WESTERN [252] (Cont.)
(Two Seats)

Election	Electors	Candidate	Party	Votes
1880	6,471	W.A.T. Amherst	C	2,671
		G.W.P. Bentinck	C	2,233
		A. Hamond (Junr.)	L	2,104
[Resignation of Bentinck]				
1884 (21/2)		C.S. Read	C	Unopp

Petition: —

1852: Withdrawn

NORTHAMPTONSHIRE, NORTHERN [253]
(Two Seats)

Election	Electors	Candidate	Party	Votes
1832	3,363	Viscount Milton	L	1,562
		†Lord Brudenell	C	1,541
		W. Hanbury	L	1,455
		T. Tyron	C	1,269
[Succession of Milton to the Peerage — Earl Fitzwilliam]				
1833 (9/3)		Viscount Milton	L	Unopp.
1835	3,552	Lord Brudenell	C	Unopp.
		Viscount Milton	L	Unopp.
[Death of Milton]				
1835 (21/12)	3,627	T.P. Maunsell	C	1,841
		W. Hanbury	L	1,247
1837	3,757	T.P. Maunsell	C	1,842
		Viscount Maidstone	C	1,801
		Viscount Milton	L	1,404
1841	4,166	T.P. Maunsell	C	Unopp.
		A.S. O'Brien *(Stafford)*	C	Unopp.
1847	4,065	T.P. Maunsell	C	Unopp.
		A.S.O'B. Stafford	C	Unopp.
1852	3,900	A.S.O'B. Stafford	C	562
		T.P. Maunsell	C	560
		Hon. G.W. Fitzwilliam	L	34
1857	3,800	Lord Burghley	C	Unopp.
		A.S.O'B. Stafford	C	Unopp.
[Death of Stafford]				
1857 (16/12)	3,800*	G.W. Hunt	C	1,461
		F.H. Vernon	L	1,119
1859	3,777	Lord Burghley	C	1,849
		G.W. Hunt	C	1,831
		F.H. Vernon	L	1,344
1865	4,016	Lord Burghley	C	Unopp.
		G.W. Hunt	C	Unopp.
[Appointment of Burghley as Treasurer of H.M. Household]				
1866 (14/7)		Lord Burghley	C	Unopp.

(Two Seats)

Election	Electors	Candidate	Party	Votes
[Succession of Burghley to the Peerage — Marquess of Exeter]				
1867 (13/2)		S.G. Stopford	C	Unopp.
[Appointment of Hunt as Chancellor of the Exchequer]				
1868 (7/3)		G.W. Hunt	C	Unopp.
1868	5,310†	G.W. Hunt	C	Unopp.
		S.G. Stopford *(Sackville)*	C	Unopp.
1874	5,215	G.W. Hunt	C	Unopp.
		S.G.S. Sackville	C	Unopp.
[Appointment of Hunt as First Lord of the Admiralty]				
1874 (18/3)		G.W. Hunt	C	Unopp.
[Death of Hunt]				
1877 (15/8)	5,033	Lord Burghley	C	2,261
		E.W. Edgell	L	1,475
1880	5,833	Hon. C.R. Spencer	L	2,425
		Lord Burghley	C	2,405
		S.G.S. Sackville	C	2,316

NORTHAMPTONSHIRE, SOUTHERN [254]
(Two Seats)

Election	Electors	Candidate	Party	Votes
1832	4,425	†Viscount Althorp (Senr.)	L	Unopp.
		W.R. Cartwright	C	Unopp.
1835	4,463	W.R. Cartwright	C	Unopp.
		Sir C. Knightley, Bt.	C	Unopp.
1837	4,626	W.R. Cartwright	C	Unopp.
		Sir C. Knightley, Bt.	C	Unopp.
1841	4,589	W.R. Cartwright	C	2,436
		Sir C. Knightley, Bt.	C	2,324
		Earl of Euston	L	925
[Resignation of Cartwright]				
1846 (24/2)		R.H.R.H. Vyse	C	Unopp.
1847	4,729	Sir C. Knightley, Bt.	C	2,272
		R.H.R.H. Vyse	C	2,064
		Lord Henley	L	1,460
1852	4,568	R.H.R.H. Vyse	C	1,833
		R. Knightley	C	1,833
		J. Houghton	L	164
1857	4,675	Viscount Althorp (Junr.)	L	2,107
		R. Knightley	C	1,932
		R.H.R.H. Vyse	C	1,593
[Succession of Althorp to the Peerage —Earl Spencer]				
1858 (20/2)	4,675*	H. Cartwright	C	1,983
		Lord Henley	L	1,899
1859	4,955	H. Cartwright	C	Unopp.
		R. Knightley	C	Unopp.
1865	5,293	Sir R. Knightley, Bt.	C	2,206
		H. Cartwright	C	2,092
		Lord Frederick Fitzroy	L	2,054
1868	6,338†	Sir R. Knightley, Bt.	C	2,522
		F.W. Cartwright	C	2,505
		Lord Frederick Fitzroy	L	2,305
1874	6,029	F.W. Cartwright	C	Unopp.
		Sir R. Knightley, Bt.	C	Unopp.

NORTHAMPTONSHIRE, SOUTHERN [254] (Cont.)

(Two Seats)

Election	Electors	Candidate	Party	Votes
1880	6,093	F.W. Cartwright	C	Unopp.
		Sir R. Knightley, Bt.	C	Unopp.
[Death of Cartwright]				
1881 (15/2)		P. Phipps	C	Unopp.

NORTHUMBERLAND, NORTHERN [255]
(Two Seats)

Election	Electors	Candidate	Party	Votes
1832	2,322	†Viscount Howick	L	Unopp.
		Lord Ossulston	C	Unopp.
1835	2,367	Viscount Howick	L	Unopp.
		Lord Ossulston	C	Unopp.
[Appointment of Howick as Secretary at War]				
1835 (1/5)		Viscount Howick	L	Unopp.
1837	2,786	Viscount Howick	L	Unopp.
		Lord Ossulston	C	Unopp.
1841	2,756	Lord Ossulston	C	1,216
		A.J.B. Cresswell	C	1,163
		Viscount Howick	L	1,101
1847	3,030	Sir G. Grey, Bt.	L	1,366
		Lord Ossulston	C	1,247
		Lord Lovaine	C	1,237
1852	3,111	Lord Lovaine	C	1,414
		Lord Ossulston	C	1,335
		Sir G. Grey, Bt.	L	1,300
1857	3,296	Lord Lovaine	C	Unopp.
		Lord Ossulston	C	Unopp.
[Appointment of Lovaine as a Civil Lord of the Admiralty]				
1858 (11/3)		Lord Lovaine	C	Unopp.
[Appointment of Lovaine as Vice-President of the Board of Trade]				
1859 (10/3)		Lord Lovaine	C	Unopp.
1859	3,280	Lord Lovaine	C	Unopp.
		Sir M.W. Ridley, Bt.	C	Unopp.
1865	3,109	Lord Henry Percy	C	Unopp.
		Sir M.W. Ridley, Bt.	C	Unopp.
1868	3,612	Earl Percy	C	Unopp.
		M.W. Ridley	C	Unopp.
1874	3,480	Earl Percy	C	Unopp.
		M.W. Ridley	C	Unopp.

NORTHUMBERLAND, NORTHERN [255] (Cont.)
(Two Seats)

Election	Electors	Candidate	Party	Votes
[Appointment of Percy as Treasurer of H.M. Household]				
1874 (17/3)		Earl Percy	C	Unopp.
1880	4,376	Earl Percy	C	2,163
		Sir M.W. Ridley, Bt.	C	2,001
		J. Clay	L	1,509

NORTHUMBERLAND, SOUTHERN [256]

(Two Seats)

Election	Electors	Candidate	Party	Votes
1832	5,192	†T.W. Beaumont	L	2,537
		M. Bell	C	2,441
		†W. Ord	L	2,351
1835	5,042	T.W. Beaumont	L	Unopp.
		M. Bell	C	Unopp.
1837	5,070	M. Bell	C	Unopp.
		C. Blackett	L	Unopp.
1841	5,369	M. Bell	C	Unopp.
		S.C.H. Ogle	L	Unopp.
1847	5,295	M. Bell	C	Unopp.
		S.C.H. Ogle	L	Unopp.
1852	5,369	W.B. Beaumont	L	2,306
		Hon. H.G. Liddell	C	2,132
		G. Ridley	L	2,033
1857	5,608	W.B. Beaumont	L	Unopp.
		Hon. H.G. Liddell	C	Unopp.
1859	5,522	W.B. Beaumont	L	Unopp.
		Hon. H.G. Liddell	C	Unopp.
1865	5,511	W.B. Beaumont	L	Unopp.
		Hon. H.G. Liddell	C	Unopp.
1868	6,862†	W.B. Beaumont	L	Unopp.
		Hon. H.G. Liddell	C	Unopp.
1874	6,698	W.B. Beaumont	L	Unopp.
		Hon. H.G. Liddell *(Lord Eslington)*	C	Unopp.
[Succession of Eslington to the Peerage — Earl of Ravensworth]				
1878 (18/4)	7,415	*E. Ridley	C	2,912
		**A.H.G. Grey	L	2,912
1880	8,800	A.H.G. Grey	L	3,896
		W.B. Beaumont	L	3,694
		E. Ridley	C	3,622

Petitions:—

1832: Withdrawn (Bell only)

1878: Double return. As the result of a recount the figures were found to be Ridley, 2,909; Grey, 2,903. Petitions against both candidates were withdrawn and Ridley was declared duly elected.

NOTTINGHAMSHIRE, NORTHERN [257]
(Two Seats)

Election	Electors	Candidate	Party	Votes
1832	2,889	†Viscount Lumley	L	1,680
		†T. Houldsworth	C	1,372
		J.G.C. Gardiner	L	1,171
1835	3,379	T. Houldsworth	C	Unopp.
		Viscount Lumley	L	Unopp.
[Succession of Lumley to the Peerage — Earl of Scarborough]				
1835 (31/3)		H.G. Knight	C	Unopp.
1837	3,410	T. Houldsworth	C	1,698
		H.G. Knight	C	1,572
		G.S. Foljambe	L	1,478
1841	3,721	T. Houldsworth	C	Unopp.
		H.G. Knight	C	Unopp.
[Death of Knight]				
1846 (6/3)	3,650*	Lord Henry Bentinck	C	1,742
		Earl of Lincoln	C	217
1847	3,910	Lord Henry Bentinck	C	Unopp.
		T. Houldsworth	C	Unopp.
1852	3,996	Lord Henry Bentinck	C	Unopp.
		Lord Robert Clinton	L	Unopp.
1857	4,028	Lord Robert Clinton	L	Unopp.
		J.E. Denison	L	Unopp.
1859	4,062	Lord Robert Clinton	L	Unopp.
		J.E. Denison	L	Unopp.
1865	4,065	Lord Edward Clinton	L	Unopp.
		J.E. Denison	L	Unopp.
1868	5,205	J.E. Denison	L	Unopp.
		F.C. Smith	C	Unopp.
[Elevation of Denison to the Peerage — Viscount Ossington]				
1872 (26/2)	5,448	Hon. G.E.M. Monckton	C	2,580
		R. Laycock	L	1,524
1874	6,297	Hon. G.E.M. Monckton *(Viscount Galway)*	C	Unopp.
		F.C. Smith	C	Unopp.

NOTTINGHAMSHIRE, NORTHERN [257] (Cont.)
(Two Seats)

Election	Electors	Candidate	Party	Votes
1880	6,699	C.G.S. Foljambe	L	2,814
		Viscount Galway	C	2,745
		H.F. Bristowe	L	2,735
		W.E. Denison	C	2,646

Note: —

1857–1868 Denison was Speaker of the House of Commons from April 1857 until February 1872

NOTTINGHAMSHIRE, SOUTHERN [258]

(Two Seats)

Election	Electors	Candidate	Party	Votes
1832	3,170	†J.E. Denison	L	Unopp.
		Earl of Lincoln	C	Unopp.
1835	3,432	J.E. Denison	L	Unopp.
		Earl of Lincoln	C	Unopp.
1837	3,389	Earl of Lincoln	C	Unopp.
		L. Rolleston	C	Unopp.
1841	3,629	Earl of Lincoln	C	Unopp.
		L. Rolleston	C	Unopp.
[Appointment of Lincoln as Commissioner of Woods, Forests, Land Revenues, Works, and Buildings]				
1841 (20/9)		Earl of Lincoln	C	Unopp.
[Appointment of Lincoln as Chief Secretary to the Lord Lieutenant of Ireland]				
1846 (27/2)	3,469*	T.B.T. Hildyard	C	1,736
		Earl of Lincoln	C	1,049
1847	3,692	T.B.T. Hildyard	C	Unopp.
		L. Rolleston	C	Unopp.
[Resignation of Rolleston]				
1849 (17/4)		R. Bromley	C	Unopp.
[Death of Bromley]				
1851 (17/2)	3,482	W.H. Barrow	C	1,493
		Viscount Newark	C	1,482
1852	3,801	W.H. Barrow	C	Unopp.
		Viscount Newark	C	Unopp.
1857	3,654	W.H. Barrow	C	Unopp.
		Viscount Newark	C	Unopp.
1859	3,602	W.H. Barrow	C	Unopp.
		Viscount Newark	C	Unopp.
[Succession of Newark to the Peerage — Earl Manvers]				
1860 (18/12)		Lord Stanhope	C	Unopp.
1865	3,427	W.H. Barrow	C	Unopp.
		Lord Stanhope	C	Unopp.

NOTTINGHAMSHIRE, SOUTHERN [258] (Cont.)

(Two Seats)

Election	Electors	Candidate	Party	Votes
[Succession of Stanhope to the Peerage — Earl of Chesterfield]				
1866 (18/6)		T.B.T. Hildyard	C	Unopp.
1868	4,846	W.H. Barrow	C	Unopp.
		T.B.T. Hildyard	C	Unopp.
1874	4,978	T.B.T. Hildyard	C	Unopp.
		G. Storer	C	Unopp.
1880	4,879	G. Storer	C	2,491
		T.B.T. Hildyard	C	2,227
		S.B. Bristowe	L	1,445

OXFORDSHIRE [259]

(Three Seats)

Election	Electors	Candidate	Party	Votes
1832	4,721	†G.G.V. Harcourt	L	Unopp.
		Lord Norreys	C	Unopp.
		†R. Weyland	L	Unopp.
1835	4,716	G.G.V. Harcourt	C	Unopp.
		Lord Norreys	C	Unopp.
		R. Weyland	L	Unopp.
1837	5,253	Lord Norreys	C	3,002
		G.G.V. Harcourt	C	2,885
		T.A.W. Parker	C	2,767
		T. Stonor	L	1,458
1841	5,809	G.G.V. Harcourt	C	Unopp.
		J.W. Henley	C	Unopp.
		Lord Norreys	C	Unopp.
1847	5,384	G.G.V. Harcourt	C	Unopp.
		J.W. Henley	C	Unopp.
		Lord Norreys	C	Unopp.
[Appointment of Henley as President of the Board of Trade]				
1852 (10/3)		J.W. Henley	C	Unopp.
1852	5,198	J.W. Henley	C	2,328
		J.S. North	C	2,218
		G.G.V. Harcourt	C	1,313
		Lord Norreys	C	681
1857	5,119	G.G.V. Harcourt	L	Unopp.
		J.W. Henley	C	Unopp.
		J.S. North	C	Unopp.
[Appointment of Henley as President of the Board of Trade]				
1858 (6/3)		J.W. Henley	C	Unopp.
1859	5,123	G.G.V. Harcourt	L	Unopp.
		J.W. Henley	C	Unopp.
		J.S. North	C	Unopp.
[Death of Harcourt]				
1862 (3/2)	5,010	J.W. Fane	C	1,909
		Sir H.W. Dashwood, Bt.	L	1,722
1865	5,798	J.W. Fane	C	Unopp.
		J.W. Henley	C	Unopp.
		J.S. North	C	Unopp.

OXFORDSHIRE [259] (Cont.)
(Three Seats)

Election	Electors	Candidate	Party	Votes
1868	7,663†	W.C. Cartwright	L	Unopp.
		J.W. Henley	C	Unopp.
		J.S. North	C	Unopp.
1874	7,554	W.C. Cartwright	L	Unopp.
		J.W. Henley	C	Unopp.
		J.S. North	C	Unopp.
[Resignation of Henley]				
1878 (5/2)		E.W. Harcourt	C	Unopp.
1880	7,495	W.C. Cartwright	L	Unopp.
		E.W. Harcourt	C	Unopp.
		J.S. North	C	Unopp.

Petition:—

1837: Withdrawn (Norreys and Parker only)

RUTLANDSHIRE [260]
(Two Seats)

Election	Electors	Candidate	Party	Votes
1832	1,296	†Sir G. Heathcote, Bt.	L	Unopp.
		†Sir G.N. Noel, Bt.	C	Unopp.
1835	1,264	Sir G. Heathcote, Bt.	L	Unopp.
		Sir G.N. Noel, Bt.	C	Unopp.
1837	1,325	Sir G. Heathcote, Bt.	L	Unopp.
		Sir G.N. Noel, Bt.	C	Unopp.
[Death of Noel]				
1838 (13/3)		Hon. W.M. Noel	C	Unopp.
[Resignation of Noel]				
1840 (28/1)		Hon. C.G. Noel	L	Unopp.
1841	1,557	G.J. Heathcote	L	767
		Hon. W.H. Dawnay	C	676
		Hon. C.G. Noel	L	664
[Resignation of Dawnay]				
1846 (14/2)		G. Finch	C	Unopp.
1847	1,887	G.J. Heathcote	C	Unopp.
		Hon. G.J. Noel	C	Unopp.
1852	1,876	Sir G.J. Heathcote, Bt.	L	Unopp.
		Hon. G.J. Noel	C	Unopp.
[Elevation of Heathcote to the Peerage — Lord Aveland]				
1856 (4/3)		Hon. G.H. Heathcote	L	Unopp.
1857	1,822	Hon. G.H. Heathcote	L	Unopp.
		Hon. G.J. Noel	C	Unopp.
1859	1,810	Hon. G.H. Heathcote	L	Unopp.
		Hon. G.J. Noel	C	Unopp.
1865	1,774	Hon. G.H. Heathcote	L	Unopp.
		Hon. G.J. Noel	C	Unopp.
[Appointment of Noel as a Lord Commissioner of the Treasury]				
1866 (14/7)		Hon. G.J. Noel	C	Unopp.

(Two Seats)

Election	Electors	Candidate	Party	Votes
[Succession of Heathcote to the Peerage — Lord Aveland]				
1867 (23/11)		G.H. Finch	C	Unopp.
1868	2,200	G.H. Finch	C	Unopp.
		Hon. G.J. Noel	C	Unopp.
1874	1,950	G.H. Finch	C	Unopp.
		Hon. G.J. Noel	C	Unopp.
[Appointment of Noel as First Commissioner of Works and Public Buildings]				
1876 (17/8)		Hon. G.J. Noel	C	Unopp.
1880	1,736	G.H. Finch	C	Unopp.
		Hon. G.J. Noel	C	Unopp.
[Resignation of Noel]				
1883 (1/9)	1,768	J.W. Lowther	C	860
		J.W.D. Handley	L	194

Petition:—

1841: Withdrawn (Dawnay only)

SHROPSHIRE, NORTHERN [261]
(Two Seats)

Election	Electors	Candidate	Party	Votes
1832	4,682	†Sir R. Hill, Bt.	C	2,981
		J. Cotes	L	2,117
		W.O. Gore	C	2,045
1835	4,653	W.O. Gore	C	Unopp.
		Sir R. Hill, Bt.	C	Unopp.
1837	4,910	W.O. Gore	C	Unopp.
		Sir R. Hill, Bt.	C	Unopp.
1841	5,075	W.O. Gore	C	Unopp.
		Sir R. Hill, Bt.	C	Unopp.
[Succession of Hill to the Peerage — Viscount Hill]				
1843 (16/1)		Viscount Clive	C	Unopp.
1847	4,876	Viscount Clive	C	Unopp.
		W.O. Gore	C	Unopp.
[Succession of Clive to the Peerage — Earl of Powis]				
1848 (16/2)		J.W. Dod	C	Unopp.
1852	4,685	J.W. Dod	C	Unopp.
		W.O. Gore	C	Unopp.
1857	4,227	J.W. Dod	C	Unopp.
		Hon. R.C. Hill	C	Unopp.
1859	4,110	J.R.O. Gore	C	Unopp.
		Hon. R.C. Hill	C	Unopp.
1865	5,315	Hon. C.H. Cust	C	Unopp.
		J.R.O. Gore	C	Unopp.
[Resignation of Cust]				
1866 (17/8)		Hon. A.W.B. Cust	C	Unopp.
[Succession of Cust to the Peerage — Earl Brownlow]				
1867 (14/3)		Viscount Newport	C	Unopp.
1868	7,611	J.R.O. Gore	C	3,602
		Viscount Newport	C	3,403
		R.G. Jebb	L	2,412

SHROPSHIRE, NORTHERN [261] (Cont.)
(Two Seats)

Election	Electors	Candidate	Party	Votes
1874	7,557	J.R.O. Gore	C	Unopp.
		Viscount Newport	C	Unopp.

[Elevation of Gore to the Peerage — Lord Harlech]

Election	Electors	Candidate	Party	Votes
1876 (3/2)	7,342	S. Leighton	C	2,737
		C.S. Mainwaring	C	2,700
1880	7,729	S. Leighton	C	Unopp.
		Viscount Newport	C	Unopp.

SHROPSHIRE, SOUTHERN [262]
(Two Seats)

Election	Electors	Candidate	Party	Votes
1832	2,791	Earl of Darlington	C	642
		†Hon. R.H. Clive	C	573
		T. Whitmore	C	20
1835	2,852	Hon. R.H. Clive	C	Unopp.
		Earl of Darlington	C	Unopp.
1837	3,240	Hon. R.H. Clive	C	Unopp.
		Earl of Darlington	C	Unopp.
1841	3,831	Hon. R.H. Clive	C	Unopp.
		Earl of Darlington	C	Unopp.
[Succession of Darlington to the Peerage — Duke of Cleveland]				
1842 (3/3)		Viscount Newport	C	Unopp.
1847	3,678	Hon. R.H. Clive	C	Unopp.
		Viscount Newport	C	Unopp.
[Appointment of Newport as Vice-Chamberlain of H.M. Household]				
1852 (23/3)		Viscount Newport	C	Unopp.
1852	3,571	Hon. R.H. Clive	C	Unopp.
		Viscount Newport	C	Unopp.
[Death of Clive]				
1854 (8/2)		Hon. R. Clive *(Hon. R.W. Clive)*	C	Unopp.
1857	3,183	Viscount Newport	C	Unopp.
		Hon. R.W. Clive	C	Unopp.
[Appointment of Newport as Vice-Chamberlain of H.M. Household]				
1858 (9/3)		Viscount Newport	C	Unopp.
1859	3,380	Viscount Newport	C	Unopp.
		Hon. R.W. Clive	C	Unopp.
[Death of Clive]				
1859 (14/9)		Sir B. Leighton, Bt. (Senr.)	C	Unopp.
[Succession of Newport to the Peerage — Earl of Bradford]				
1865 (12/4)		Hon. P.E. Herbert	C	Unopp.

Election	Electors	Candidate	Party	Votes
1865	4,170	R.J. More	L	1,819
		Hon. P.E. Herbert	C	1,669
		Sir B. Leighton, Bt. (Senr.)	C	1,388
[Appointment of Herbert as Treasurer of H.M. Household]				
1867 (8/3)		P.E. Herbert	C	Unopp.
1868	5,847	P.E. Herbert	C	2,703
		E. Corbett	C	2,514
		R.J. More	L	2,161
1874	5,710	E. Corbett	C	Unopp.
		Sir P.E. Herbert	C	Unopp.
[Death of Herbert]				
1876 (3/11)		J.E. Severne	C	Unopp.
[Resignation of Corbett]				
1877 (10/8)		Sir B. Leighton, Bt. (Junr.)	C	Unopp.
1880	5,690	Sir B. Leighton, Bt. (Junr.)	C	2,491
		J.E. Severne	C	2,216
		R.J. More	L	2,149
		J.W.H. Davenport	L	1,634

SOMERSET, EASTERN [263]
(Two Seats)

Election	Electors	Candidate	Party	Votes
1832	8,996	†W.G. Langton	L	4,249
		W.P. Brigstock	L	4,003
		†W. Miles	C	3,603
[Death of Brigstock]				
1834 (3/2)		W. Miles	C	Unopp.
1835	9,107	W.G. Langton	L	Unopp.
		W. Miles	C	Unopp.
1837	9,561	W.G. Langton	L	Unopp.
		W. Miles	C	Unopp.
1841	9,807*	W.G. Langton	L	Unopp.
		W. Miles	C	Unopp.
[Death of Langton]				
1847 (10/4)		W. Pinney	L	Unopp.
1847	9,655	W. Miles	C	Unopp.
		W. Pinney	L	Unopp.
1852	10,140	W. Miles	C	4,643
		W.F. Knatchbull	C	4,309
		A.H. Elton	L	2,984
1857	10,592	W.F. Knatchbull	C	Unopp.
		W. Miles	C	Unopp.
1859	10,644	W.F. Knatchbull	C	Unopp.
		Sir W. Miles, Bt.	C	Unopp.
1865	11,867	R.N. Grenville	C	Unopp.
		R.H. Paget	C	Unopp.
1868	8,795†	R.S. Allen	C	3,887
		R. Bright	C	3,848
		A.D. Hayter	L	2,704
		W. Pinney	L	2,656
1874	8,435	R.S. Allen	C	Unopp.
		R. Bright	C	Unopp.
[Death of Bright]				
1878 (20/3)		P.J.W. Miles	C	Unopp.

Election	Electors	Candidate	Party	Votes
[Resignation of Allen]				
1879 (19/3)		Lord Brooke	C	Unopp.
1880	8,360	Lord Brooke	C	Unopp.
		Sir P.J.W. Miles, Bt.	C	Unopp.

SOMERSET, MID [264]
(Two Seats)

Election	Electors	Candidate	Party	Votes
1868	8,364	R.H. Paget	C	3,692
		R.N. Grenville	C	3,636
		F. Tagart	L	2,151
		E.A. Freeman	L	2,018
1874	8,571	R.N. Grenville	C	Unopp.
		R.H. Paget	C	Unopp.
[Resignation of Grenville]				
1878 (19/3)		W.S.G. Langton	C	Unopp.
1880	8,470	W.S.G. Langton	C	Unopp.
		R.H. Paget	C	Unopp.
[Resignation of Langton]				
1885 (4/3)		J.K.D.W. Digby	C	Unopp.

SOMERSET, WESTERN [265]
(Two Seats)

Election	Electors	Candidate	Party	Votes
1832	7,884	†E.A. Sanford	L	4,815
		C.J.K. Tynte	L	4,299
		B. Escott	C	1,449
1835	7,658	E.A. Sanford	L	3,770
		C.J.K. Tynte	L	3,586
		B. Escott	C	2,766
1837	8,854	T.D. Acland	C	3,883
		E.A. Sanford	L	3,556
		F.H. Dickinson	C	3,524
		C.J.K. Tynte	L	3,458
1841	9,035*	T.D. Acland	C	Unopp.
		F.H. Dickinson	C	Unopp.
1847	8,433	C.A. Moody	C	3,603
		Sir A. Hood, Bt.	C	3,311
		Hon. P.P. Bouverie	L	2,783
		B. Escott	L	2,624
[Death of Hood]				
1851 (10/4)		W.H.P.G. Langton	C	Unopp.
1852	8,210	W.H.P.G. Langton	C	Unopp.
		C.A. Moody	C	Unopp.
1857	7,323	W.H.P.G. Langton	C	Unopp.
		C.A. Moody	C	Unopp.
1859	7,750	Sir A.B.P.F.A. Hood, Bt.	C	Unopp.
		C.A. Moody	C	Unopp.
[Resignation of Moody]				
1863 (17/2)		W.H.P.G. Langton	C	Unopp.
1865	8,632	Sir A.B.P.F.A. Hood, Bt.	C	Unopp.
		W.H.P.G. Langton	C	Unopp.
1868	7,671†	Hon. A.W.A.N. Hood	C	Unopp.
		W.H.P.G. Langton	C	Unopp.
[Death of Langton]				
1874 (12/1)		V.H. Lee	C	Unopp.

SOMERSET, WESTERN [265] (Cont.)
(Two Seats)

Election	Electors	Candidate	Party	Votes
1874	7,774†	Hon. A.W.A.N. Hood	C	Unopp
		V.H. Lee *(V.H.V. Lee)*	C	Unopp.
1880	8,291	V.H.V. Lee	C	3,186
		M.F. Bisset	C	3,136
		C.T.D. Acland	L	2,967
[Resignation of Lee]				
1882 (26/4)		E.J. Stanley	C	Unopp.
[Resignation of Bisset]				
1884 (18/2)	9,431	C.I. Elton	C	3,757
		Viscount Kilcoursie	L	2,995

STAFFORDSHIRE, EASTERN [266]
(Two Seats)

Election	Electors	Candidate	Party	Votes
1868	9,658	M.A. Bass	L	3,885
		J.R. McClean	L	3,675
		J. Hartley	C	2,972
[Death of McClean]				
1873 (8/8)	9,402	S.C. Allsopp	C	3,630
		J. Jaffray	L	2,693
1874	9,484	S.C. Allsopp	C	Unopp.
		M.A. Bass	L	Unopp.
1880	10,799	M.A. Bass	L	4,809
		H. Wiggin	L	4,617
		S.C. Allsopp	C	3,552
		Sir J. Hardy, Bt.	C	3,306

STAFFORDSHIRE, NORTHERN [267]
(Two Seats)

Election	Electors	Candidate	Party	Votes
1832	8,756	Sir O. Mosley, Bt.	L	4,777
		E. Buller	L	4,595
		J.D.W. Russell	C	3,387
1835	8,717	E. Buller	L	Unopp.
		Sir O. Mosley, Bt.	L	Unopp.
1837	9,540	Hon. W.B. Baring	C	4,332
		E. Buller	L	3,182
		Sir O. Mosley, Bt.	L	2,351
1841	10,282	C.B. Adderley	C	Unopp.
		J.D.W. Russell	C	Unopp.
1847	9,438	C.B. Adderley	C	4,092
		Viscount Brackley	C	4,076
		E. Buller	L	3,353
[Resignation of Brackley]				
1851 (22/2)		S. Child	C	Unopp.
1852	9,546	C.B. Adderley	C	Unopp.
		S. Child	C	Unopp.
1857	9,536	C.B. Adderley	C	4,112
		S. Child	C	3,865
		E. Buller	L	3,020
[Appointment of Adderley as Vice-President of the Committee of the Privy Council for Education]				
1858 (8/3)		C.B. Adderley	C	Unopp.
1859	10,859	C.B. Adderley	C	Unopp.
		Viscount Ingestre	C	Unopp.
1865	10,703	E. Buller *(E.M. Buller)*	L	4,628
		C.B. Adderley	C	4,416
		Viscount Ingestre	C	4,053
1868	10,261†	C.B. Adderley	C	Unopp.
		Sir E.M. Buller, Bt.	L	Unopp.
1874	10,104	Sir C.B. Adderley	C	Unopp.
		C.M. Campbell	C	Unopp.
[Appointment of Adderley as President of the Board of Trade]				
1874 (23/3)		Sir C.B. Adderley	C	Unopp.

STAFFORDSHIRE, NORTHERN [267] (Cont.)
(Two Seats)

Election	Electors	Candidate	Party	Votes
[Elevation of Adderley to the Peerage — Lord Norton]				
1878 (24/4)		R.W. Hanbury	C	Unopp.
1880	10,974	W.Y. Craig	L	4,821
		H.T. Davenport	C	4,333
		R.W. Hanbury	C	3,764

Petitions:—

1847: Withdrawn

1857: Withdrawn

STAFFORDSHIRE, SOUTHERN [268]
(Two Seats)

Election	Electors	Candidate	Party	Votes
1832	3,107	†E.J. Littleton	L	Unopp.
		†Sir J. Wrottesley, Bt.	L	Unopp.

[Appointment of Littleton as Chief Secretary to the Lord Lieutenant of Ireland]

1833	3,107	E.J. Littleton	L	439
(7/6)		Viscount Ingestre	C	6
1835	3,990	E.J. Littleton	L	Unopp.
		Sir J. Wrottesley, Bt.	L	Unopp.

[Elevation of Littleton to the Peerage — Lord Hatherton]

1835	3,990	Sir F.L.H. Goodricke, Bt.	C	1,776
(23/5)		Hon. G. Anson	L	1,553
1837	7,871	Hon. G. Anson	L	3,173
		Viscount Ingestre	C	3,126
		R. Dyott	C	3,046
		Sir J. Wrottesley, Bt.	L	2,993
1841	8,798	Hon. G. Anson	L	Unopp.
		Viscount Ingestre	C	Unopp.

[Appointment of Anson as Clerk of the Ordnance]

1846		Hon. G. Anson	L	Unopp.
(17/7)				
1847	8,545	Hon. G. Anson	L	Unopp.
		Viscount Ingestre	C	Unopp.

[Succession of Ingestre to the Peerage — Earl Talbot]

1849		Viscount Lewisham	C	Unopp.
(19/2)				
1852	10,116	Hon. G. Anson	L	Unopp.
		Viscount Lewisham	C	Unopp.

[Resignation of Anson]

1853		Hon. E.R. Littleton	L	Unopp.
(15/8)				

[Succession of Lewisham to the Peerage — Earl of Dartmouth]

1854	9,933	Lord Paget *(Earl of Uxbridge)*	L	4,328
(8/2)		Viscount Ingestre	C	2,769
1857	11,202	H.J.W.H. Foley	L	Unopp.
		W.O. Foster	L	Unopp.

STAFFORDSHIRE, SOUTHERN [268] (Cont.)
(Two Seats)

Election	Electors	Candidate	Party	Votes
1859	11,375	H.J.W.H. Foley	L	Unopp.
		W.O. Foster	L	Unopp.
1865	10,841	H.J.W.H. Foley	L	Unopp.
		W.O. Foster	L	Unopp.

This constituency was divided in 1868.

STAFFORDSHIRE, WESTERN [269]
(Two Seats)

Election	Electors	Candidate	Party	Votes
1868	9,942	S. Child	C	3,909
		H.F.M. Ingram	C	3,773
		W.O. Foster	L	3,295
		H.J.W.H. Foley	L	3,244
[Death of Ingram]				
1871 (13/6)		F. Monckton	C	Unopp.
1874	10,365	A.S. Hill	C	Unopp.
		F. Monckton	C	Unopp.
1880	11,288	A.S. Hill	C	4,123
		F. Monckton	C	3,967
		Sir W.R. Anson, Bt.	L	3,564
		J.H. Renton	L	3,344

SUFFOLK, EASTERN [270]
(Two Seats)

Election	Electors	Candidate	Party	Votes
1832	4,265	Lord Henniker	C	2,030
		R.N. Shawe	L	1,990
		Sir C.B. Vere	C	1,784
1835	5,034	Lord Henniker	C	2,452
		Sir C.B. Vere	C	2,321
		R.N. Shawe	L	2,029
1837	6,278	Lord Henniker	C	Unopp.
		Sir C.B. Vere	C	Unopp.
1841	6,915	Lord Henniker	C	3,279
		Sir C.B. Vere	C	3,178
		R.A.S. Adair	L	1,787
[Death of Vere]				
1843 (18/4)	6,786	Lord Rendlesham	C	2,952
		R.A.S. Adair	L	1,818
[Resignation of Henniker]				
1846 (19/2)		E.S. Gooch	C	Unopp.
1847	6,673	E.S. Gooch	C	Unopp.
		Lord Rendlesham	C	Unopp.
[Death of Rendlesham]				
1852 (1/5)		Sir F. Kelly	C	Unopp.
1852	6,343	Sir E.S. Gooch, Bt.	C	Unopp.
		Sir F. Kelly	C	Unopp.
[Death of Gooch]				
1856 (26/12)		Lord Henniker	C	Unopp.
1857	5,907	Lord Henniker	C	Unopp.
		Sir F. Kelly	C	Unopp.
[Appointment of Kelly as Attorney-General]				
1858 (6/3)		Sir F. Kelly	C	Unopp.
1859	5,837	Lord Henniker	C	2,677
		Sir F. Kelly	C	2,517
		R.A.S. Adair	L	1,883

Election	Electors	Candidate	Party	Votes
1865	6,769	Lord Henniker	C	Unopp.
		Sir F. Kelly	C	Unopp.

[Elevation of Henniker to a U.K. Peerage — Lord Hartismere; and resignation of Kelly on appointment as Chief Justice of the Court of the Exchequer]

1866 (25/7)		Hon. J.M.H. Major	C	Unopp.
		Sir E.C. Kerrison, Bt.	C	Unopp.

[Resignation of Kerrison]

1867 (20/2)	6,769*	F.S. Corrance	C	2,489
		R.A.S. Adair	L	2,120

1868	9,024†	Hon. J.M.H. Major	C	3,650
		F.S. Corrance	C	3,620
		R.A.S. Adair	L	3,321
		T.S. Western	L	3,045

[Succession of Major to the Peerage — Lord Hartismere]

1870 (1/6)	9,024*	Viscount Mahon	C	3,456
		Sir R.A.S. Adair	L	3,285

1874	9,484	Lord Rendlesham	C	4,136
		Viscount Mahon	C	3,896
		G. Tomline	L	3,014

[Appointment of Mahon as a Lord Commissioner of the Treasury]

1874 (20/3)		Viscount Mahon	C	Unopp.

[Succession of Mahon to the Peerage — Earl Stanhope]

1876 (24/2)	9,558	F.St.J.N. Barne	C	3,659
		C. Easton	L	2,708

1880	9,635	Lord Rendlesham	C	4,239
		F.St.J.N. Barne	C	3,618
		R.L. Everett	L	3,504

SUFFOLK, WESTERN 271]
(Two Seats)

Election	Electors	Candidate	Party	Votes
1832	3,326	†C. Tyrrell	L	1,832
		Sir H. Parker, Bt.	L	1,664
		H.S. Waddington	C	1,272
1835	3,731	H. Wilson	L	1,723
		R. Rushbrooke	C	1,655
		H. Logan	C	1,509
		J.T. Hales	L	1,350
1837	4,959	H. Logan	C	2,217
		R. Rushbrooke	C	2,173
		Sir H.E. Bunbury, Bt.	L	1,560
		H. Wilson	L	1,505
[Death of Logan]				
1838 (7/5)		H.S. Waddington	C	Unopp.
1841	5,091*	R. Rushbrooke	C	Unopp.
		H.S. Waddington	C	Unopp.
[Death of Rushbrooke]				
1845 (7/7)		P. Bennet	C	Unopp.
1847	4,913†	P. Bennet	C	Unopp.
		H.S. Waddington	C	Unopp.
1852	4,379	P. Bennet	C	Unopp.
		H.S. Waddington	C	Unopp.
1857	4,084	P. Bennet	C	Unopp.
		H.S. Waddington	C	Unopp.
1859	4,172	Earl Jermyn	C	1,958
		W. Parker	C	1,379
		P. Bennet	C	1,300
[Succession of Jermyn to the Peerage — Marquess of Bristol]				
1864 (8/12)		Lord Augustus Hervey	C	Unopp.
1865	4,269	Lord Augustus Hervey	C	Unopp.
		W. Parker	C	Unopp.
1868	5,583†	W. Parker	C	2,500
		Lord Augustus Hervey	C	2,389
		C. Lamport	L	1,705

SUFFOLK, WESTERN [271] (Cont.)
(Two Seats)

Election	Electors	Candidate	Party	Votes
1874	5,949	Lord Augustus Hervey	C	Unopp.
		W. Parker	C	Unopp.
[Death of Hervey]				
1875 (17/6)	5,811	F.M. Wilson	C	2,780
		C. Easton	L	1,061
[Death of Wilson]				
1875 (4/10)		T. Thornhill	C	Unopp.
1880	5,700	W. Biddell	C	Unopp.
		T. Thornhill	C	Unopp.

SURREY, EASTERN [272]
(Two Seats)

Election	Electors	Candidate	Party	Votes
1832	3,150	†J.I. Briscoe	L	1,643
		A.W. Beauclerk	L	1,155
		J.T. Allen	C	835
		J. Lainson	L	244
1835	3,537	R. Alsager	C	1,578
		A.W. Beauclerk	L	1,324
		J.I. Briscoe	L	1,200
1837	5,531	R. Alsager	C	2,176
		H. Kemble	C	2,155
		Hon. P.J.L. King	L	1,865
		J. Angerstein	L	1,823
[Death of Alsager]				
1841 (8/2)	6,222	E. Antrobus	C	2,635
		T. Alcock	L	1,436
1841	6,222	E. Antrobus	C	Unopp.
		H. Kemble	C	Unopp.
1847	6,028	T. Alcock	L	Unopp.
		Hon. P.J.L. King	L	Unopp.
1852	6,618	T. Alcock	L	2,508
		Hon. P.J.L. King	L	2,500
		E. Antrobus	C	2,064
		A. Cleasby	C	1,928
1857	7,191	T. Alcock	L	Unopp.
		Hon. P.J.L. King	L	Unopp.
1859	7,350	T. Alcock	L	2,953
		Hon. P.J.L. King	L	2,926
		A. Cleasby	C	2,050
1865	9,913	Hon. P.J.L. King	L	3,495
		C. Buxton	L	3,424
		H.W. Peek	C	3,333
		Hon. W. Brodrick	C	3,226
1868	10,932†	Hon. P.J.L. King	L	4,162
		C. Buxton	L	3,941
		W. Hardman	C	3,537
		J. Lord	C	3,459
[Death of Buxton]				
1871 (26/8)	12,960	J. Watney	C	3,912
		Hon. G.W.G.L. Gower	L	2,749

SURREY, EASTERN [272] (Cont.)
(Two Seats)

Election	Electors	Candidate	Party	Votes
1874	14,468	J. Watney	C	5,673
		W. Grantham	C	5,579
		Hon. P.J.L. King	L	4,292
		J.P. Gassiot	L	4,015
1880	18,969	W. Grantham	C	8,104
		J. Watney	C	8,006
		W.F. Robinson	L	5,978
		G.W. Medley	L	5,928

Petition:—

1852: Withdrawn

SURREY, MID [273]
(Two Seats)

Election	Electors	Candidate	Party	Votes
1868	10,565	H.W. Peek	C	4,487
		Hon. W. Brodrick	C	4,412
		J. Goldsmid	L	3,152
		C.H. Robarts	L	3,090
		T.M. Nelson	L	7
[Succession of Brodrick to the Peerage — Viscount Middleton]				
1870 (17/10)		Sir R. Baggallay	C	Unopp.
1874	14,645	Sir R. Baggallay	C	Unopp.
		H.W. Peek	C	Unopp.
[Appointment of Baggallay as Solicitor-General]				
1874 (16/3)		Sir R. Baggallay	C	Unopp.
[Resignation of Baggallay on appointment as a Judge of the Court of Appeal]				
1875 (24/11)		Sir J.J.T. Lawrence, Bt.	C	Unopp.
1880	20,433	Sir H.W. Peek, Bt.	C	8,475
		Sir J.J.T. Lawrence, Bt.	C	8,303
		S.J. Stern	L	5,770
		J.N. Higgins	L	5,727
[Resignation of Peek]				
1884 (23/6)	26,804	Sir J.W. Ellis, Bt.	C	7,645
		S.J. Stern	L	4,949

SURREY, WESTERN [274]
(Two Seats)

Election	Electors	Candidate	Party	Votes
1832	2,912	†W.J. Denison	L	1,517
		J. Leech	L	1,427
		G.H. Sumner	C	1,198
1835	2,967	W.J. Denison	L	1,488
		C. Barclay	C	1,316
		H.L. Long	L	1,285
1837	3,688	W.J. Denison	L	1,586
		Hon. G.J. Perceval	C	1,578
		H.L. Long	L	1,543
[Succession of Perceval to the Peerage — Lord Arden]				
1840 (31/7)		J. Trotter	C	Unopp.
1841	3,993	W.J. Denison	L	Unopp.
		J. Trotter	C	Unopp.
1847	3,778	W.J. Denison	L	Unopp.
		H. Drummond	C	Unopp.
[Death of Denison]				
1849 (27/9)	3,651	W.J. Evelyn	C	1,144
		R.W. Edgell	L	988
1852	3,897	W.J. Evelyn	C	1,646
		H. Drummond	C	1,610
		C.B. Challoner	L	1,385
1857	3,920	J.I. Briscoe	L	1,439
		H. Drummond	C	1,386
		H. Currie	C	1,204
1859	3,958	J.I. Briscoe	L	Unopp.
		H. Drummond	C	Unopp.
[Death of Drummond]				
1860 (10/3)		G. Cubitt	C	Unopp.
1865	4,081	J.I. Briscoe	L	Unopp.
		G. Cubitt	C	Unopp.
1868	6,708†	G. Cubitt	C	3,000
		J.I. Briscoe	L	2,826
		F. Pennington	L	1,757

SURREY, WESTERN [274] (Cont.)
(Two Seats)

Election	Electors	Candidate	Party	Votes
[Death of Briscoe]				
1870 (8/9)		L. Steere	C	Unopp.
1874	7,314	G. Cubitt	C	Unopp.
		L. Steere	C	Unopp.
1880	7,779	Hon. W.St.J.F. Brodrick	C	Unopp.
		G. Cubitt	C	Unopp.

SUSSEX, EASTERN [275]

(Two Seats)

Election	Electors	Candidate	Party	Votes
1832	3,437	†Hon. C.C. Cavendish	L	2,388
		†H.B. Curteis	L	1,941
		G. Darby	C	668
1835	3,811	Hon. C.C. Cavendish	L	Unopp.
		H.B. Curteis	L	Unopp.
1837	4,799	G. Darby	C	2,256
		Hon. C.C. Cavendish	L	1,793
		A.E. Fuller	C	1,749
		H.B. Curteis	L	1,619
1841	5,356	G. Darby	C	2,398
		A.E. Fuller	C	2,367
		J.V. Shelley	L	995
[Resignation of Darby on appointment as a Commissioner of Inclosures]				
1846 (3/2)		C.H. Frewen	C	Unopp.
1847	5,723	A.E. Fuller	C	Unopp.
		C.H. Frewen	C	Unopp.
1852	5,298	A.E. Fuller	C	2,155
		C.H. Frewen	C	1,974
		J.G. Dodson	L	1,637
[Resignation of Frewen]				
1857 (7/3)	6,114	Viscount Pevensey	C	2,302
		J.G. Dodson	L	2,234
1857	6,114	J.G. Dodson	L	2,524
		Viscount Pevensey	C	2,447
		W.H.F. Cavendish	L	2,286
		A.E. Fuller	C	2,216
1859	6,401	J.G. Dodson	L	Unopp.
		Viscount Pevensey	C	Unopp.
1865	6,670	J.G. Dodson	L	2,821
		Lord Edward Cavendish	L	2,647
		W.W. Burrell	C	2,463
		Hon. R.C.E. Abbot	C	2,316
1868	9,380†	J.G. Dodson	L	3,611
		G.B. Gregory	C	3,581
		M.D. Scott	C	3,560
		Lord Edward Cavendish	L	3,470
1874	10,141	G.B. Gregory	C	Unopp.
		M.D. Scott	C	Unopp.

SUSSEX, EASTERN [275] (Cont.)
(Two Seats)

Election	Electors	Candidate	Party	Votes
1880	10,214	G.B. Gregory	C	4,526
		M.D. Scott	C	4,396
		A. Donovan	L	2,982
		J. Pearson	L	2,863

SUSSEX, WESTERN [276]
(Two Seats)

Election	Electors	Candidate	Party	Votes
1832	2,365	†Lord John Lennox	L	Unopp.
		†Earl of Surrey	L	Unopp.
1835	2,408	Lord John Lennox	L	Unopp.
		Earl of Surrey	L	Unopp.
1837	3,152	Lord John Lennox	L	1,291
		Earl of Surrey	L	1,267
		H. Wyndham (1)	C	1,049
1841	3,618	Earl of March	C	Unopp.
		C. Wyndham	C	Unopp.
[Resignation of Wyndham]				
1847 (2/2)		R. Prime	C	Unopp.
1847	3,488	Earl of March	C	Unopp.
		R. Prime	C	Unopp.
1852	3,257	Earl of March	C	Unopp.
		R. Prime	C	Unopp.
[Resignation of Prime]				
1854 (13/2)		H. Wyndham (2)	C	Unopp.
1857	2,941	Earl of March	C	Unopp.
		H. Wyndham (2)	C	Unopp.
[Appointment of March as President of the Poor Law Board]				
1859 (9/3)		Earl of March	C	Unopp.
1859	2,853	Earl of March	C	Unopp.
		Hon. H. Wyndham (2)	C	Unopp.
[Succession of March to the Peerage — Duke of Richmond]				
1860 (27/12)		W.B. Barttelot	C	Unopp.
1865	2,607	W.B. Barttelot	C	Unopp.
		Hon. H. Wyndham (2)	C	Unopp.
1868	3,672†	W.B. Barttelot	C	Unopp.
		Hon. H. Wyndham (2)	C	Unopp.

SUSSEX, WESTERN [276] (Cont.)
(Two Seats)

Election	Electors	Candidate	Party	Votes
[Succession of Wyndham to the Peerage — Lord Leconfield]				
1869 (17/4)		Earl of March	C	Unopp.
1874	3,865	W.B. Barttelot	C	Unopp.
		Earl of March	C	Unopp.
1880	3,886	Sir W.B. Barttelot, Bt.	C	Unopp.
		Earl of March	C	Unopp.

WARWICKSHIRE, NORTHERN [277]
(Two Seats)

Election	Electors	Candidate	Party	Votes
1832	3,730	Sir J.E.E. Wilmot, Bt.	C	2,237
		†W.S. Dugdale	C	1,666
		D. Heming	L	1,573
1835	4,779	Sir J.E.E. Wilmot, Bt.	C	2,600
		W.S. Dugdale	C	2,513
		A.F. Gregory	L	1,854
1837	6,632	W.S. Dugdale	C	3,326
		Sir J.E.E. Wilmot, Bt.	C	2,768
		Sir G. Skipwith, Bt.	L	2,292
		C.H. Bracebridge	L	1,787
1841	6,785	W.S. Dugdale	C	Unopp.
		Sir J.E.E. Wilmot, Bt.	C	Unopp.
[Resignation of Wilmot on appointment as Governor of Tasmania]				
1843 (10/3)		C.N. Newdegate	C	Unopp.
1847	6,371	C.N. Newdegate	C	2,915
		R. Spooner	C	2,451
		Hon. W.H. Leigh	L	2,278
1852	7,002	C.N. Newdegate	C	2,950
		R. Spooner	C	2,822
		Hon. F.K. Craven	L	2,038
		Sir T.G. Skipwith, Bt.	L	2,021
1857	6,832	C.N. Newdegate	C	Unopp.
		R. Spooner	C	Unopp.
1859	6,871	C.N. Newdegate	C	Unopp.
		R. Spooner	C	Unopp.
[Death of Spooner]				
1864 (13/12)		W.D. Bromley	C	Unopp.
1865	6,710	C.N. Newdegate	C	3,159
		W.D. Bromley *(Davenport)*	C	2,873
		G.F. Muntz	L	2,408
1868	10,266†	C.N. Newdegate	C	4,547
		W.B. Davenport	C	4,377
		G.F. Muntz	L	3,411
		E.F. Flower	L	3,322

(Two Seats)

Election	Electors	Candidate	Party	Votes
1874	10,200	C.N. Newdegate	C	4,672
		W.B. Davenport	C	4,322
		G.F. Muntz	L	3,189
1880	11,789	W.B. Davenport	C	Unopp.
		C.N. Newdegate	C	Unopp.
[Death of Davenport]				
1884 (3/7)	11,993	P.A. Muntz	C	5,282
		A.C. Corbett	L	3,538

WARWICKSHIRE, SOUTHERN [278]
(Two Seats)

Election	Electors	Candidate	Party	Votes
1832	2,550	†Sir G. Skipwith, Bt.	L	1,396
		Sir G. Philips, Bt.	L	1,121
		E.J. Shirley	C	1,108
1835	2,901	Sir J. Mordaunt, Bt.	C	Unopp.
		E.R.C. Sheldon	L	Unopp.
[Death of Sheldon]				
1836 (1/7)	3,997	E.J. Shirley	C	1,885
		Sir G. Skipwith, Bt.	L	1,360
1837	4,304	Sir J. Mordaunt, Bt.	C	Unopp.
		E.J. Shirley	C	Unopp.
1841	4,261	Sir J. Mordaunt, Bt.	C	Unopp.
		E.J. Shirley	C	Unopp.
[Death of Mordaunt]				
1845 (5/11)		Lord Brooke	C	Unopp.
1847	4,066	Lord Brooke	C	Unopp.
		E.J. Shirley	C	Unopp.
[Resignation of Shirley]				
1849 (7/6)		Lord Guernsey	C	Unopp.
1852	3,980	Lord Brooke	C	Unopp.
		Lord Guernsey	C	Unopp.
[Succession of Brooke to the Peerage — Earl of Warwick]				
1853 (3/12)		E.P. Shirley	C	Unopp.
1857	3,522	E.B. King	L	Unopp.
		E.P. Shirley	C	Unopp.
1859	3,470	Sir C. Mordaunt, Bt.	C	Unopp.
		E.P. Shirley	C	Unopp.
1865	3,517	H.C. Wise	C	1,585
		Sir C. Mordaunt, Bt.	C	1,517
		Viscount Duncan	L	1,321
1868	6,205	H.C. Wise	C	2,581
		J. Hardy	C	2,501
		Sir R. Hamilton, Bt.	L	2,472
		Lord Hyde	L	2,453

Election	Electors	Candidate	Party	Votes
1874	6,340	Earl of Yarmouth	C	2,832
		Sir J.E.E. Wilmot, Bt.	C	2,801
		Sir R.N.C. Hamilton, Bt.	L	2,170
[Appointment of Yarmouth as Comptroller of H.M. Household]				
1879 (21/2)		Earl of Yarmouth	C	Unopp.
1880	6,429	Sir J.E.E. Wilmot, Bt.	C	2,644
		Hon. G.H.C. Leigh	L	2,550
		Earl of Yarmouth	C	2,507
[Death of Leigh]				
1884 (10/11)	6,590	S.S. Lloyd	C	3,095
		Lord William Compton	L	1,919

Petition:—

1868: Withdrawn (Hardy only)

WESTMORLAND [279]
(Two Seats)

Election	Electors	Candidate	Party	Votes
1832	4,392	†Viscount Lowther	C	2,052
		†Hon. H.C. Lowther	C	1,948
		†J. Barham	L	1,611
1835	4,644	Hon. H.C. Lowther	C	Unopp.
		Viscount Lowther	C	Unopp.
1837	4,775	Viscount Lowther	C	Unopp.
		Hon. H.C. Lowther	C	Unopp.
1841	4,384	Viscount Lowther	C	Unopp.
		Hon. H.C. Lowther	C	Unopp.
[Appointment of Lowther as Postmaster-General and called to the House of Lords as Lord Lowther]				
1841 (22/9)		W. Thompson	C	Unopp.
1847	4,078	Hon. H.C. Lowther	C	Unopp.
		W. Thompson	C	Unopp.
1852	4,062	Hon. H.C. Lowther	C	Unopp.
		W. Thompson	C	Unopp.
[Death of Thompson]				
1854 (31/3)		Earl of Bective	C	Unopp.
1857	4,168	Earl of Bective	C	Unopp.
		Hon. H.C. Lowther	C	Unopp.
1859	4,214	Earl of Bective	C	Unopp.
		Hon. H.C. Lowther	C	Unopp.
1865	4,237	Earl of Bective	C	Unopp.
		Hon. H.C. Lowther	C	Unopp.
[Death of Lowther]				
1868 (8/1)		W. Lowther	C	Unopp.
1868	5,240	Earl of Bective	C	Unopp.
		W. Lowther	C	Unopp.
[Succession of Bective to the Peerage — Marquess of Headfort]				
1871 (21/2)		Earl of Bective	C	Unopp.

WESTMORLAND [279] (Cont.)
(Two Seats)

Election	Electors	Candidate	Party	Votes
1874	5,177	Earl of Bective	C	Unopp.
		Hon. W. Lowther	C	Unopp.
1880	5,442	Earl of Bective	C	2,641
		Hon. W. Lowther	C	2,522
		Sir H.J. Tufton, Bt.	L	1,963

WILTSHIRE, NORTHERN [280]
(Two Seats)

Election	Electors	Candidate	Party	Votes
1832	3,614	P. Methuen	L	1,835
		†Sir J.D. Astley, Bt.	L	1,683
		J. Edridge	L	403
1835	3,560	W. Long	L	Unopp.
		P. Methuen	L	Unopp.
1837	5,068	Sir F. Burdett, Bt.	C	2,365
		W. Long	C	2,197
		P. Methuen	L	1,876
1841	5,241	Sir F. Burdett, Bt.	C	Unopp.
		W. Long	C	Unopp.
[Death of Burdett]				
1844 (12/2)		T.H.S. Sotheron	C	Unopp.
1847	5,165	W. Long	C	Unopp.
		T.H.S. Sotheron	C	Unopp.
1852	4,955	W. Long	C	Unopp.
		T.H.S. Sotheron *(Estcourt)*	C	Unopp.
1857	4,400	T.H.S.S. Estcourt	C	Unopp.
		W. Long	C	Unopp.
[Appointment of Estcourt as President of the Poor Law Board]				
1858 (5/3)		T.H.S.S. Estcourt	C	Unopp.
[Appointment of Estcourt as Secretary of State for the Home Department]				
1859 (8/3)		T.H.S.S. Estcourt	C	Unopp.
1859	4,417	T.H.S.S. Estcourt	C	Unopp.
		W. Long	C	Unopp.
[Resignation of Estcourt]				
1865 (20/3)		Lord Charles Bruce	L	Unopp.
1865	5,146	Lord Charles Bruce	L	2,151
		R.P. Long	C	1,911
		Sir G.S. Jenkinson, Bt.	C	1,373
1868	6,857	Sir G.S. Jenkinson, Bt.	C	2,769
		Lord Charles Bruce	L	2,600
		J.T. Schonberg	L	2,016

WILTSHIRE, NORTHERN [280] (Cont.)
(Two Seats)

Election	Electors	Candidate	Party	Votes
1874	7,152	G.T.J.B. Estcourt *(G.T.J.S. Estcourt)*	C	3,195
		Sir G.S. Jenkinson, Bt.	C	3,129
		Lord Charles Bruce	L	2,358
1880	7,249	W.H. Long	C	3,090
		G.T.J.S. Estcourt	C	2,836
		G.P. Fuller	L	2,784

WILTSHIRE, SOUTHERN [281]
(Two Seats)

Election	Electors	Candidate	Party	Votes
1832	2,540	†J. Benett	L	Unopp.
		Hon. S. Herbert	C	Unopp.
1835	2,448	J. Benett	L	Unopp.
		Hon. S. Herbert	C	Unopp.
1837	2,962	J. Benett	L	Unopp.
		Hon. S. Herbert	C	Unopp.
1841	2,280	J. Benett	L	Unopp.
		Hon. S. Herbert	C	Unopp.
[Appointment of Herbert as Secretary at War]				
1845 (15/2)		Hon. S. Herbert	C	Unopp.
1847	2,710	J. Benett	C	Unopp.
		Hon. S. Herbert	C	Unopp.
1852	3,256	Hon. S. Herbert	C	1,550
		W. Wyndham	L	1,304
		R.P. Long	C	1,074
[Appointment of Herbert as Secretary at War]				
1853 (11/1)		Hon. S. Herbert	C	Unopp.
[Appointment of Herbert as Secretary of State for the Colonies]				
1855 (15/2)		Hon. S. Herbert	C	Unopp.
1857	3,239	Hon. S. Herbert	L	1,517
		W. Wyndham	L	1,445
		Lord Henry Thynne	C	1,269
1859	3,437	Hon. S. Herbert	L	Unopp.
		Lord Henry Thynne	C	Unopp.
[Appointment of Herbert as Secretary of State for the War Department]				
1859 (29/6)		Hon. S. Herbert	L	Unopp.
[Elevation of Herbert to the Peerage — Lord Herbert of Lea]				
1861 (14/2)		F.T.A.H. Bathurst	C	Unopp.
1865	3,343	Lord Henry Thynne	C	1,576
		T.F. Grove	L	1,427
		F.T.A.H. Bathurst	C	1,270

WILTSHIRE, SOUTHERN [281] (Cont.)

(Two Seats)

Election	Electors	Candidate	Party	Votes
1868	3,810†	T.F. Grove	L	Unopp.
		Lord Henry Thynne	C	Unopp.
1874	3,938	Lord Henry Thynne	C	2,115
		Viscount Folkestone	C	1,977
		Sir T.F. Grove, Bt.	L	1,048
[Appointment of Thynne as Treasurer of H.M. Household]				
1876 (4/1)		Lord Henry Thynne	C	Unopp.
1880	3,789	Viscount Folkestone	C	Unopp.
		Lord Henry Thynne	C	Unopp.
[Appointment of Folkestone as Treasurer of H.M. Household]				
1885 (3/7)		Viscount Folkestone	C	Unopp.

WORCESTERSHIRE, EASTERN [282]
(Two Seats)

Election	Electors	Candidate	Party	Votes
1832	5,161	W.C. Russell	L	2,576
		T.H. Cookes	L	2,517
		J.S. Pakington (Senr.)	C	1,916
1835	5,164	E. Holland	L	2,254
		T.H. Cookes	L	2,192
		H. St. Paul	C	2,145
1837	5,995	H. St. Paul	C	2,595
		J. Barneby	C	2,528
		E. Holland	L	2,175
		J.H.H. Foley	L	2,168
1841	6,367	J. Barneby	C	Unopp.
		J.A. Taylor	C	Unopp.
[Death of Barneby]				
1847 (11/1)		G. Rushout	C	Unopp.
1847	6,269	J.H.H. Foley	L	Unopp.
		G. Rushout	C	Unopp.
1852	6,515	J.H.H. Foley	L	Unopp.
		G. Rushout	C	Unopp.
1857	6,065	J.H.H. Foley	L	Unopp.
		G. Rushout	C	Unopp.
[Succession of Rushout to the Peerage — Lord Northwick]				
1859 (24/2)	5,983	Hon. F.H.W.G. Calthorpe	L	2,304
		J.S. Pakington (Junr.)	C	1,965
1859	5,983	Hon. F.H.W.G. Calthorpe	L	Unopp.
		J.H.H. Foley	L	Unopp.
[Death of Foley]				
1861 (20/12)		H.F. Vernon	L	Unopp.
1865	6,875	Hon. F.H.W.G. Calthorpe	L	Unopp.
		H.F. Vernon	L	Unopp.
[Succession of Calthorpe to the Peerage — Lord Calthorpe]				
1868 (1/6)	6,875*	Hon. C.G. Lyttelton	L	2,688
		W. Laslett	C	2,429

WORCESTERSHIRE, EASTERN [282] (Cont.)
(Two Seats)

Election	Electors	Candidate	Party	Votes
1868	10,313†	R.G. Amphlett	C	4,108
		Hon. C.G. Lyttelton	L	4,093
		R.B. Martin	L	3,789
1874	11,039	H. Allsopp	C	4,421
		T.E. Walker	C	4,159
		Hon. C.G. Lyttelton	L	3,508
		A. Albright	L	2,831
		W. Laslett	C	55
1880	12,000	W.H. Gladstone	L	4,879
		G.W. Hastings	L	4,833
		Sir R. Temple, Bt.	C	4,417
		H. Allsopp	C	4,258

Petition: —

1835: Withdrawn (Cookes only)

WORCESTERSHIRE, WESTERN [283]
(Two Seats)

Election	Electors	Candidate	Party	Votes
1832	3,122	†Hon. T.H. Foley	L	Unopp.
		Hon. H.B. Lygon	C	Unopp.
[Succession of Foley to the Peerage — Lord Foley]				
1833 (16/5)	3,122	H.J. Winnington	L	1,369
		J.S. Pakington	C	1,278
1835	4,127	Hon. H.B. Lygon	C	1,945
		H.J. Winnington	L	1,938
		J.S. Pakington	C	1,773
1837	4,654	Hon. H.B. Lygon	C	Unopp.
		H.J. Winnington	L	Unopp.
1841	4,577	F.W. Knight	C	Unopp.
		Hon. H.B. Lygon	C	Unopp.
1847	4,357	F.W. Knight	C	Unopp.
		Hon. H.B. Lygon	C	Unopp.
1852	4,135	F.W. Knight	C	Unopp.
		Hon. H.B. Lygon	C	Unopp.
[Succession of Lygon to the Peerage — Earl Beauchamp]				
1853 (28/2)		Viscount Elmley	C	Unopp.
1857	4,015	Viscount Elmley	C	Unopp.
		F.W. Knight	C	Unopp.
1859	3,910	Viscount Elmley	C	Unopp.
		F.W. Knight	C	Unopp.
[Succession of Elmley to the Peerage — Earl Beauchamp]				
1863 (26/10)		Hon. F. Lygon	C	Unopp.
1865	5,221	F.W. Knight	C	Unopp.
		Hon. F. Lygon	C	Unopp.
[Succession of Lygon to the Peerage — Earl Beauchamp]				
1866 (24/3)		W.E. Dowdeswell	C	Unopp.
1868	6,311†	W.E. Dowdeswell	C	Unopp.
		F.W. Knight	C	Unopp.

WORCESTERSHIRE, WESTERN [283] (Cont.)
(Two Seats)

Election	Electors	Candidate	Party	Votes
1874	6,177	W.E. Dowdeswell	C	2,910
		F,W. Knight	C	2,554
		G.W. Hastings	L	1,540
[Resignation of Dowdeswell]				
1876 (8/7)		Sir E.A.H. Lechmere, Bt.	C	Unopp.
1880	6,962	Sir E.A.H. Lechmere, Bt.	C	2,975
		F.W. Knight	C	2,913
		H.R. Willis	L	1,231

Petition: —

1880: Dismissed

YORKSHIRE, EAST RIDING [284]
(Two Seats)

Election	Electors	Candidate	Party	Votes
1832	5,559	R. Bethell	C	Unopp.
		†P.B. Thompson	L	Unopp.
1835	5,140	R. Bethell	C	Unopp.
		P.B. Thompson	L	Unopp.
1837	7,180	R. Bethell	C	3,592
		H. Broadley	C	3,257
		P.B. Thompson	L	2,985
1841	7,640	H. Broadley	C	Unopp.
		Lord Hotham	C	Unopp.
1847	7,740	H. Broadley	C	Unopp.
		Lord Hotham	C	Unopp.
[Death of Broadley]				
1851 (7/10)		Hon. A. Duncombe	C	Unopp.
[Appointment of Duncombe as a Lord Commissioner of the Admiralty]				
1852 (9/3)		Hon. A. Duncombe	C	Unopp.
1852	7,538	Hon. A. Duncombe	C	Unopp.
		Lord Hotham	C	Unopp.
1857	7,382	Hon. A. Duncombe	C	Unopp.
		Lord Hotham	C	Unopp.
1859	7,221	Hon. A. Duncombe	C	Unopp.
		Lord Hotham	C	Unopp.
1865	7,400	Hon. A. Duncombe	C	Unopp.
		Lord Hotham	C	Unopp.
1868	10,827†	C. Sykes	C	6,299
		W.H.H. Broadley	C	5,587
		B.B. Haworth	L	2,603
1874	10,722†	W.H.H. Broadley	C	Unopp.
		C. Sykes	C	Unopp.
1880	10,414	C. Sykes	C	4,927
		W.H.H. Broadley	C	4,527
		Hon. H.J.L. Wood	L	3,707

YORKSHIRE, NORTH RIDING [285]
(Two Seats)

Election	Electors	Candidate	Party	Votes
1832	9,539	Hon. W. Duncombe	C	4,885
		E.S. Cayley	L	3,287
		†J.C. Ramsden	L	2,895
		M. Stapylton	L	602
1835	9,545	Hon. W. Duncombe	C	4,656
		E.S. Cayley	L	4,490
		J. Walker	C	3,841
1837	11,738	E.S. Cayley	L	Unopp.
		Hon. W. Duncombe	C	Unopp.
1841	11,361	E.S. Cayley	L	Unopp.
		Hon. W. Duncombe	C	Unopp.
[Succession of Duncombe to the Peerage — Lord Feversham]				
1841 (21/9)		Hon. O. Duncombe	C	Unopp.
1847	11,881	E.S. Cayley	L	Unopp.
		Hon. O. Duncombe	C	Unopp.
1852	11,319	E.S. Cayley	L	Unopp.
		Hon. O. Duncombe	C	Unopp.
1857	12,238	Hon. O. Duncombe	C	5,259
		E.S. Cayley	L	4,641
		Hon. J.C. Dundas	L	4,185
1859	13,479	E.S. Cayley	L	Unopp.
		Hon. W.E. Duncombe	C	Unopp.
[Death of Cayley]				
1862 (17/3)	13,367	W.J.S. Morritt	C	5,507
		F.A. Milbank	L	5,041
1865	15,438	F.A. Milbank	L	6,585
		Hon. W.E. Duncombe	C	6,362
		W.J.S. Morritt	C	5,889
[Succession of Duncombe to the Peerage — Lord Feversham]				
1867 (4/3)		Hon. O. Duncombe	C	Unopp.
1868	19,205†	Hon. O. Duncombe	C	7,689
		F.A. Milbank	L	7,429
		E.S. Cayley	C	1,721

YORKSHIRE, NORTH RIDING [285] (Cont.)
(Two Seats)

Election	Electors	Candidate	Party	Votes
1874	19,558	Viscount Helmsley	C	Unopp.
		F.A. Milbank	L	Unopp.
1880	20,484	Viscount Helmsley	C	Unopp.
		F.A. Milbank	L	Unopp.
[Death of Helmsley]				
1882	20,047	Hon. G.C. Dawnay	C	8,135
(26/1)		S. Rowlandson	L	7,749

Petition: —

1865: Withdrawn

YORKSHIRE, WEST RIDING [286]

(Two Seats)

Election	Electors	Candidate	Party	Votes
1832	18,056	†Viscount Morpeth	L	Unopp
		†G. Strickland	L	Unopp.
1835	18,061	Viscount Morpeth	L	Unopp.
		Sir G. Strickland, Bt.	L	Unopp.
[Appointment of Morpeth as Chief Secretary to the Lord Lieutenant of Ireland]				
1835 (6/5)	18,061	Viscount Morpeth	L	9,066
		Hon. J.S. Wortley	C	6,259
1837	29,346	Viscount Morpeth	L	12,576
		Sir G. Strickland, Bt.	L	11,892
		Hon. J.S. Wortley	C	11,489
1841	31,215	Hon. J.S. Wortley	C	13,165
		E.B. Denison	C	12,780
		Viscount Milton	L	12,080
		Viscount Morpeth	L	12,031
[Succession of Wortley to the Peerage — Lord Wharncliffe]				
1846 (4/2)		Viscount Morpeth	L	Unopp.
[Appointment of Morpeth as First Commissioner of Woods, Forests, Land Revenues, Works, and Buildings]				
1846 (18/7)		Viscount Morpeth	L	Unopp.
1847	36,165	R. Cobden	L	Unopp.
		Viscount Morpeth	L	Unopp.
[Succession of Morpeth to the Peerage — Earl of Carlisle]				
1848 (11/12)	35,280	E.B. Denison	C	14,743
		Sir C.E. Eardley, Bt.	L	11,795
1852	37,319	R. Cobden	L	Unopp.
		E.B. Denison	C	Unopp.
1857	37,513	E.B. Denison	C	Unopp.
		Viscount Goderich	L	Unopp.
[Succession of Goderich to the Peerage — Earl of Ripon]				
1859 (21/2)		Sir J.W. Ramsden, Bt.	L	Unopp.
1859	36,645	Sir J.W. Ramsden, Bt.	L	15,978
		F. Crossley	L	15,401
		Hon. J.A.S. Wortley	C	13,636

This constituency was divided in 1865.

YORKSHIRE (West Riding), EASTERN [287]
(Two Seats)

Election	Electors	Candidate	Party	Votes
1868	18,494	C.B. Denison	C	7,437
		J. Fielden	C	7,135
		H.S. Thompson	L	7,047
		I. Holden	L	6,867
1874	19,882	C.B. Denison	C	8,240
		J. Fielden	C	8,077
		Sir J.W. Ramsden, Bt.	L	7,285
		I. Holden	L	7,218
1880	21,640	Sir A. Fairbairn	L	9,518
		Sir J.W. Ramsden, Bt.	L	9,406
		C.B. Denison	C	8,341
		Viscount Lascelles	C	8,157

YORKSHIRE (West Riding), NORTHERN [288]
(Two Seats)

Election	Electors	Candidate	Party	Votes
1865	22,792	Lord Frederick Cavendish	L	Unopp.
		Sir F. Crossley, Bt.	L	Unopp.
1868	16,918†	Lord Frederick Cavendish	L	Unopp.
		Sir F. Crossley, Bt.	L	Unopp.
[Death of Crossley]				
1872 (3/2)	17,084	F.S. Powell	C	6,961
		I. Holden	L	6,917
[Appointment of Cavendish as a Lord Commissioner of the Treasury]				
1873 (27/8)		Lord Frederick Cavendish	L	Unopp.
1874	20,130	Lord Frederick Cavendish	L	8,681
		M. Wilson	L	8,598
		F.S. Powell	C	7,820
		W. Fison	C	7,725
1880	21,840	Lord Frederick Cavendish	L	10,818
		Sir M. Wilson, Bt.	L	10,732
		S.C. Lister	C	7,140
		F.S. Powell	C	7,096
[Appointment (prior to his assasination in Dublin on May 6) of Cavendish as Chief Secretary to the Lord Lieutenant of Ireland]				
1882 (20/5)	22,138	I. Holden	L	9,892
		Hon. A.E.G. Hardy	C	7,865

YORKSHIRE (West Riding), SOUTHERN [289]
(Two Seats)

Election	Electors	Candidate	Party	Votes
1865	17,903	Viscount Milton	L	7,258
		H.F. Beaumont	L	6,975
		C.B. Denison	C	6,884
		W.T.W.S. Stanhope	C	6,819
1868	19,908†	Viscount Milton	L	8,110
		H.F. Beaumont	L	7,943
		W.T.W.S. Stanhope	C	7,935
		L.R. Starkey	C	7,621
[Resignation of Milton]				
1872 (8/7)		W.T.W.S. Stanhope	C	Unopp
1874	22,358	W.T.W.S. Stanhope	C	9,705
		L.R. Starkey	C	9,639
		W.H. Leatham	L	8,265
		H.F. Beaumont	L	8,148
1880	26,329	Hon. W.H.W. Fitzwilliam	L	11,385
		W.H. Leatham	L	11,181
		W.T.W.S. Stanhope	C	10,391
		L.R. Starkey	C	10,020

Petition:—

1868: Dismissed

WALES and MONMOUTHSHIRE —— BOROUGHS

BEAUMARIS DISTRICT of BOROUGHS [290]
(Beaumaris, Amlwch, Holyhead, Llangefni)

Election	Electors	Candidate	Party	Votes
1832	329	F. Paget	L	Unopp.
1835	218	F. Paget	L	Unopp.
1837	323	F. Paget	L	Unopp.
1841	298	F. Paget	L	Unopp.
1847	335	Lord George Paget	L	Unopp.
1852	459	Lord George Paget	L	Unopp.
1857	473	Hon. W.O. Stanley	L	Unopp.
1859	521	Hon. W.O. Stanley	L	Unopp.
1865	558	Hon. W.O. Stanley	L	Unopp.
1868	1,944†	Hon. W.O. Stanley	L	941
		M. Lloyd	L	650
1874	2,048	M. Lloyd	L	947
		T.L.H. Lewis	C	344
		E.H. Verney	L	255
1880	2,581	M. Lloyd	L	Unopp.

BRECON [291]

Election	Electors	Candidate	Party	Votes
1832	242	J.L.V. Watkins	L	110
		†C.M.R. Morgan	C	104
1835	309	C.M.R. Morgan	C	Unopp.
1837	339	C,M.R. Morgan	C	156
		J.L. Lloyd	L	102
1841	331	C.M.R. Morgan	C	Unopp.
1847	304	J.L.V. Watkins	L	Unopp.
1852	336	C.R. Morgan	C	159
		J.L.V. Watkins	L	122
[Death]				
1854 (6/2)		J.L.V. Watkins	L	Unopp.
1857	323	J.L.V. Watkins	L	Unopp.
1859	302	J.L.V. Watkins	L	Unopp.
1865	281	J.L.V. Watkins	L	Unopp.
[Death]				
1866 (27/2)		Earl of Brecknock	L	Unopp.
[Succession to the Peerage — Marquess of Camden]				
1866 (3/10)	281	H. Gwyn	C	128
		Lord Alfred Churchill	C	102
1868	814	H. Gwyn	C	372
		H.P. Price	L	357
[Election declared void on petition]				
1869 (24/4)	814	Lord Hyde	L	391
		Lord Claud Hamilton	C	328
[Succession to the Peerage — Earl of Clarendon]				
1870 (19/7)	814*	J.P.W.G. Holford	C	372
		H.P. Price	L	338

Election	Electors	Candidate	Party	Votes
1874	843	J.P.W.G. Holford	C	374
		W.V. Morgan	L	353
1880	880	C. Flower	L	438
		J.P.W.G. Holford	C	379

Petitions: —

1868: Void election

1869: Withdrawn

1870: Dismissed. A further petition was lodged in 1871 alleging bribery, treating and undue influence after the 1870 by-election but this was also dismissed

CAERNARVON DISTRICT of BOROUGHS [292]
(Caernarvon, Bangor, Conway, Criccieth, Nevin, Pwllheli)

Election	Electors	Candidate	Party	Votes
1832	855	†**/*Sir C. Paget	L	410
		*/**O.J.E. Nanney	C	363
1835	917	L.P.J. Parry	L	378
		O.J.E. Nanney	C	350
1837	1,099	W.B. Hughes	C	405
		C.H. Paget	L	385
1841	1,021	W.B. Hughes	C	416
		Lord George Paget	L	387
1847	888	W.B. Hughes	C	Unopp.
1852	861	W.B. Hughes	C	369
		R. Davies	L	276
1857	919	W.B. Hughes	C	Unopp.
1859	929	C.G. Wynne *(Finch)*	C	380
		W.B. Hughes	L	328
1865	1,070	W.B. Hughes	L	Unopp.
1868	3,376†	W.B. Hughes	L	1,601
		Hon. T.J. Wynn	C	1,051
1874	3,833	W.B. Hughes	L	Unopp.
1880	4,157	W.B. Hughes	L	Unopp.
[Death] 1882 (30/3)	4,223	T.L.D.J. Parry	L	2,037
		R.S. Parry	L	596

Petitions:—

1832: Election of Paget declared void. Nanney duly elected. Returning Officer had included tendered votes cast at Pwllheli and when these were deducted the figures became Nanney 352 and Paget 343. A further petition was then lodged against Nanney and Paget was duly elected after scrutiny.

1835: Withdrawn

CARDIFF DISTRICT of BOROUGHS [293]
(Cardiff, Cowbridge, Llantrisant)

Election	Electors	Candidate	Party	Votes
1832	687	J. Nicholl	C	342
		Lord James Stuart	L	191
1835	672	J. Nicholl	C	Unopp.
[Appointed a Lord Commissioner of the Treasury]				
1835 (20/3)		J. Nicholl	C	Unopp.
1837	635	J. Nicholl	C	Unopp.
1841	765*	J. Nicholl	C	Unopp.
[Appinted Judge-Advocate General]				
1841 (17/9)		J. Nicholl	C	Unopp.
1847	797	J. Nicholl	C	Unopp.
1852	968	W. Coffin	L	490
		J. Nicholl	C	464
1857	1,640	J.F.D.C. Stuart	L	Unopp.
1859	1,793	J.F.D.C. Stuart	L	Unopp.
1865	2,072	J.F.D.C. Stuart	L	Unopp.
1868	5,388†	J.F.D.C. Stuart	L	2,501
		H.S. Giffard	C	2,055
1874	6,656	J.F.D.C. Stuart	L	2,780
		H.S. Giffard	C	2,771
1880	8,350	E.J. Reed	L	3,831
		A.E. Guest	C	3,383

CARDIGAN DISTRICT of BOROUGHS [294]
(Cardigan, Aberystwyth, Adpar, Lampeter)

Election	Electors	Candidate	Party	Votes
1832	1,030	†P. Pryse	L	Unopp.
1835	899	P. Pryse	L	Unopp.
1837	920	P. Pryse	L	Unopp.
1841	832	**J.S. Harford	C	226
		*P. Pryse	L	163
1847	761	P. Pryse	L	Unopp.
[Death]				
1849	657	P. Pryse *(Loveden)*	L	299
(12/2)		J.S. Harford	C	291
1852	849	P. Loveden	L	299
		J.I. Jones	C	282
[Death]				
1855	849*	J.L. Davies	C	298
(24/2)		J. Evans	L	286
1857	837	E.L. Pryse	L	Unopp.
1859	673	E.L. Pryse	L	Unopp.
1865	685	E.L. Pryse	L	Unopp.
1868	1,561†	Sir T.D. Lloyd, Bt.	L	Unopp.
1874	1,946	D. Davies	L	Unopp.
1880	2,280	D. Davies	L	Unopp.

Petition:—

1841: Double return. The poll books for two polling stations at Aberystwyth had been lost or stolen in transit to the Returning Officer who decided that in the circumstances it was best to return both candidates. The Committee accepted evidence that the polling at Aberystwyth had resulted Pryse 142 and Harford 59 making the totals, Pryse 305 and Harford 285. They declared the election of Harford void and found that Pryse was duly elected (Harford only).

CARMARTHEN DISTRICT of BOROUGHS [295]
(Carmarthen, Llanelly)

Election	Electors	Candidate	Party	Votes
1832	684	Hon. W.H. Yelverton	L	302
		†J. Jones	C	295
1835	773	D. Lewis	C	304
		Hon. W.H. Yelverton	L	268
1837	786	D. Morris	L	333
		D. Lewis	C	287
1841	938	D. Morris	L	Unopp.
1847	991	D. Morris	L	Unopp.
1852	849	D. Morris	L	Unopp.
1857	799	D. Morris	L	Unopp.
1859	823	D. Morris	L	Unopp.
[Death]				
1864 (31/10)		W. Morris	L	Unopp.
1865	884	W. Morris	L	Unopp.
1868	3,286†	J.S.C. Stepney	L	1,892
		M.D. Treherne	C	595
1874	4,494	C.W. Nevill	C	1,654
		E.A.A.K.C. Stepney	L	1,481
[Resignation]				
1876 (14/8)		E.A.A.K.C. Stepney	L	Unopp.
[Resignation]				
1878 (11/5)		B.T. Williams	L	Unopp.
1880	5,369	B.T. Williams	L	1,935
		J.J. Jenkins	L	1,825
[Resignation on appointment as a County Court Judge]				
1882 (7/1)		J.J. Jenkins	L	Unopp.

DENBIGH DISTRICT of BOROUGHS [296]
(Denbigh, Holt, Ruthin, Wrexham)

Election	Electors	Candidate	Party	Votes
1832	1,131	J. Madocks	L	Unopp.
1835	987	W. Jones	C	490
		J. Madocks	L	242
1837	909	W. Jones	C	411
		R.M. Biddulph	L	338
1841	944	T. Mainwaring	C	365
		R.M. Biddulph	L	309
1847	841	F.R. West	C	Unopp.
1852	858	F.R. West	C	362
		W.L. Foulkes	L	288
1857	861	T. Mainwaring	C	364
		J. Maurice	L	302
1859	852	T. Mainwaring	C	Unopp.
1865	903	T. Mainwaring	C	Unopp.
1868	2,785†	C.J.W. Williams	L	1,319
		T. Mainwaring	C	944
1874	2,879	C.J.W. Williams	L	1,238
		Hon. G.T. Kenyon	C	1,208
1880	3,071	Sir R.A. Cunliffe, Bt.	L	1,424
		Hon. G.T. Kenyon	C	1,409

Petition: —

1837: Withdrawn

FLINT DISTRICT of BOROUGHS [297]

(Flint, Caergwyle, Caerwys, Holywell, Mold, Overton, Rhuddlan, St. Asaph)

Election	Electors	Candidate	Party	Votes
1832	1,359	†Sir S.R. Glynne, Bt.	L	Unopp.
1835	1,067	Sir S.R. Glynne, Bt.	L	Unopp.
1837	1,297	C.W.D. Dundas	L	591
		R.J. Mostyn	C	393
1841	1,006	Sir R.B.W. Bulkeley, Bt.	L	Unopp.
1847	840	Sir J. Hanmer, Bt.	C	Unopp.
1852	819	Sir J. Hanmer, Bt.	L	386
		R.P. Warren	C	267
1857	783	Sir J. Hanmer, Bt.	L	Unopp.
1859	741	Sir J. Hanmer, Bt.	L	Unopp.
1865	689	Sir J. Hanmer, Bt.	L	Unopp.
1868	3,279†	Sir J. Hanmer, Bt.	L	Unopp.
[Elevation to the Peerage — Lord Hanmer]				
1872 (16/10)		Sir R.A. Cunliffe, Bt.	L	Unopp.
1874	3,628	P.E. Eyton	L	1,076
		C.G.H.R. Conwy	C	1,072
		Sir R.A. Cunliffe, Bt.	L	772
[Death]				
1878 (5/7)	3,707	J. Roberts	L	1,636
		P.P. Pennant	C	1,511
1880	3,794	J. Roberts	L	2,039
		P.P. Pennant	C	1,468

HAVERFORDWEST DISTRICT of BOROUGHS [298]
(Haverfordwest, Fishguard, Narberth)

Election	Electors	Candidate	Party	Votes
1832	723	†Sir R.B.P. Philipps, Bt.	L	Unopp.
1835	538	W.H. Scourfield	C	241
		J.H. Peel	L	125
1837	706	Sir R.B.P. Philipps, Bt.	L	247
		W.H. Scourfield	C	165
1841	722	Sir R.B.P. Philipps, Bt.	L	Unopp.
1847	667	J. Evans	L	Unopp.
1852	682	J.H. Philipps	C	297
		J. Evans	L	203
1857	740	J.H. Philipps	C	258
		W. Rees	L	256
1859	777	J.H. Philipps *(Scourfield)*	C	Unopp.
1865	669	J.H. Scourfield	C	314
		Hon. W. Edwardes	L	222
1868	1,526	Hon. W. Edwardes *(Lord Kensington)*	L	638
		S. Pitman	C	497
[Appointed a Groom in Waiting to Her Majesty]				
1873 (26/11)	1,592	Lord Kensington	L	609
		X. de C.R. Peel	C	558
1874	1,357	Lord Kensington	L	Unopp.
[Election declared void on petition]				
1874 (12/6)		Lord Kensington	L	Unopp.
1880	1,543	Lord Kensington	L	686
		E.D.T. Cropper	C	522
[Appointed Comptroller of H.M. Household]				
1880 (12/5)		Lord Kensington	L	Unopp.

Petition: —

1874: Void election

MERTHYR TYDFIL [299]
(One seat until 1868; two seats from 1868)

Election	Electors	Candidate	Party	Votes
1832	502	J.J. Guest	L	Unopp.
1835	561	J.J. Guest	L	Unopp.
1837	582	J.J. Guest	L	309
		J.B. Bruce	C	135
1841	776	Sir J.J. Guest, Bt.	L	Unopp.
1847	822	Sir J.J. Guest, Bt.	L	Unopp.
1852	938	Sir J.J. Guest, Bt.	L	Unopp.
[Death]				
1852 (14/12)		H.A. Bruce	L	Unopp.
1857	1,263	H.A. Bruce	L	Unopp.
1859	1,349	H.A. Bruce	L	800
		C.M. Elderton	L	106
[Appointed Vice-President of the Committee of the Privy Council for Education]				
1864 (25/4)		H.A. Bruce	L	Unopp.
1865	1,387	H.A. Bruce	L	Unopp.
1868	14,577†	H. Richard	L	11,683
		R. Fothergill	L	7,439
		H.A. Bruce	L	5,776
1874	15,429	H. Richard	L	7,606
		R. Fothergill	L	6,908
		T. Halliday	L/Lab	4,912
1880	14,259	H. Richard	L	8.033
		C.H. James	L	7,526
		W.T. Lewis	C	4,445

Petition:—

1841: Withdrawn

MONMOUTH DISTRICT of BOROUGHS [300]
(Monmouth, Newport, Usk)

Election	Electors	Candidate	Party	Votes
1832	899	†B. Hall	L	393
		†Marquess of Worcester	C	355
1835	1,088	B. Hall	L	428
		J. Bailey	C	424
1837	1,169	R.J. Blewitt	L	440
		J. Bailey	C	386
1841	1,268	R.J. Blewitt	L	476
		W. Edwards	Ch	0
1847	1,420	R.J. Blewitt	L	Unopp.
[Resignation]				
1852 (3/4)	1,676	C. Bailey	C	764
		W.S. Lindsay	L	529
1852	1,676	C. Bailey	C	Unopp.
1857	1,744	C. Bailey	C	Unopp.
1859	1,745	C. Bailey	C	Unopp.
1865	2,087	C. Bailey	C	Unopp.
1868	3,771†	Sir J.W. Ramsden, Bt.	L	1,618
		S. Homfray	C	1,449
1874	4,702	T. Cordes	C	2,090
		H.D. Pochin	L	1,447
1880	5,090	E.H. Carbutt	L	2,258
		T. Cordes	C	2,197

Petitions:—

1835: Dismissed

1852: (3/4) Withdrawn

MONTGOMERY DISTRICT of BOROUGHS [301]
(Montgomery, Llanfyllin, Llanidloes, Machynlleth, Newtown, Welshpool)

Election	Electors	Candidate	Party	Votes
1832	723	D. Pugh	C	335
		J. Edwards	L	321
[Election declared void on petition]				
1833	723	J. Edwards	L	331
(8/4)		P. Corbett	C	321
1835	899	J. Edwards	L	Unopp.
1837	1,037	J. Edwards	L	472
		P. Corbett	C	443
1841	995	Hon. H. Cholmondeley	C	464
		Sir J. Edwards, Bt.	L	437
1847	982	**Hon. H. Cholmondeley	C	389
		*D. Pugh	C	389
1852	1,003	D. Pugh	C	435
		G.H. Whalley	L	300
1857	927	D. Pugh	C	Unopp.
1859	900	D. Pugh	C	Unopp.
[Death]				
1861		J.S.W. Johnson	C	Unopp.
(4/5)				
[Death]				
1863	933	Hon.C.D.R.H. Tracy	L	439
(20/8)		C.V. Pugh	C	330
1865	965	Hon. C.D.R.H. Tracy	L	437
		T.L. Hampton	C	372
1868	2,559	Hon. C.D.R.H. Tracy	L	Unopp.
1874	2,839	Hon. C.D.R.H. Tracy	L	Unopp.
[Succession to the Peerage — Lord Sudeley]				
1877	2,914	Hon. F.S.A.H. Tracy	L	1,447
(17/5)		Viscount Castlereagh	C	1,118

Election	Electors	Candidate	Party	Votes
1880	3,120	Hon. F.S.A.H. Tracy	L	1,572
		P. Jones	C	1,211

Petitions:—

1832: Void election

1833: Dismissed

1847: Double return. A petition was lodged against Cholmondeley but was withdrawn after he decided not to defend his claim to the seat and allow Pugh to be declared duly elected.

PEMBROKE DISTRICT of BOROUGHS [302]
(Pembroke, Milford, Tenby, Wiston)

Election	Electors	Candidate	Party	Votes
1832	1,208	†H.O. Owen	C	Unopp.
1835	1,168	H.O. Owen	C	Unopp.
1837	1,152	H.O. Owen	C	Unopp.
[Resignation]				
1838 (20/2)		Sir J.R.G. Graham, Bt.	C	Unopp.
1841	1,134	Sir J. Owen, Bt.	C	282
		H.O. Owen	C	184
		J.M. Child	L	95
1847	952	Sir J. Owen, Bt.	C	Unopp.
1852	951	Sir J. Owen, Bt.	C	Unopp.
1857	810	Sir J. Owen, Bt.	L	Unopp.
1859	914	Sir J. Owen, Bt.	L	Unopp.
[Death]				
1861 (22/2)	896*	Sir H.O. Owen, Bt.	L	342
		T.C. Meyrick	C	257
1865	1,433	Sir H.O. Owen, Bt.	L	668
		B. Hardwicke	C	304
1868	3,028†	T.C. Meyrick	C	1,419
		Sir H.O. Owen, Bt.	L	1,049
1874	3,146	E.J. Reed	L	1,339
		T.C. Meyrick	C	1,310
1880	3,338	H.G. Allen	L	1,462
		T.C. Meyrick	C	1,429

Petitions: —

1868: Withdrawn
1874: Withdrawn

RADNOR DISTRICT of BOROUGHS [303]

(New Radnor, Cefnllys, Knighton, Knucklas, Presteign, Rhayader)

Election	Electors	Candidate	Party	Votes
1832	529	†R. Price	C	Unopp.
1835	517	R. Price	C	Unopp.
1837	551	R. Price	C	Unopp.
1841	500*	R. Price	C	Unopp.
1847	462	Sir T.F. Lewis, Bt.	L	Unopp.
1852	484	Sir T.F. Lewis, Bt.	L	Unopp.
[Death]				
1855 (8/2)		Sir G.C. Lewis, Bt.	L	Unopp.
[Appointed Chancellor of the Exchequer]				
1855 (5/3)		Sir G.C. Lewis, Bt.	L	Unopp.
1857	447	Sir G.C. Lewis, Bt.	L	Unopp.
1859	407	Sir G.C. Lewis, Bt.	L	Unopp.
[Appointed Secretary of State for the Home Department]				
1859 (27/6)		Sir G.C. Lewis, Bt.	L	Unopp.
[Death]				
1863 (25/4)		R.G. Price	L	Unopp.
1865	443	R.G. Price	L	Unopp.
1868	841	R.G. Price	L	Unopp.
[Resignation]				
1869 (25/2)	841	Marquess of Hartington	L	546
		G.H. Phillips	C	175
1874	968	Marquess of Hartington	L	612
		G.W. Cockburn	C	162

Election	Electors	Candidate	Party	Votes
1880	945	Marquess of Hartington	L	Unopp.

[Elects to sit for Lancashire, North-Eastern]

Election	Electors	Candidate	Party	Votes
1880 (17/5)	945	S.C.E. Williams	L	458
		C.E.T. Otway	C	390

[Resignation]

Election	Electors	Candidate	Party	Votes
1884 (30/10)		C.C. Rogers	L	Unopp.

SWANSEA DISTRICT of BOROUGHS [304]
(Swansea, Aberavon, Kenfig, Loughor, Neath)

Election	Electors	Candidate	Party	Votes
1832	1,307	J.H. Vivian	L	Unopp.
1835	1,303	J.H. Vivian	L	Unopp.
1837	1,349	J.H. Vivian	L	Unopp.
1841	1,287	J.H. Vivian	L	Unopp.
1847	1,563	J.H. Vivian	L	Unopp.
1852	1,694	J.H. Vivian	L	Unopp.
[Death]				
1855 (27/2)		L.L. Dillwyn	L	Unopp.
1857	1,901	L.L. Dillwyn	L	Unopp.
1859	1,921	L.L. Dillwyn	L	Unopp.
1865	1,967	L.L. Dillwyn	L	Unopp.
1868	7,543†	L.L. Dillwyn	L	Unopp.
1874	12,476	L.L. Dillwyn	L	5,215
		C. Bath	C	2,708
1880	13,631	L.L. Dillwyn	L	Unopp.

WALES and MONMOUTHSHIRE ---- COUNTIES

ANGLESEY [305]

Election	Electors	Candidate	Party	Votes
1832	1,187	†Sir R.B.W. Bulkeley, Bt.	L	Unopp.
1835	1,155	Sir R.B.W. Bulkeley, Bt.	L	Unopp.
[Resignation]				
1837 (23/2)	1,450	Hon. W.O. Stanley	L	693
		O.J.A.F. Metrick	C	586
1837	1,450	Hon. W.O. Stanley	L	Unopp.
1841	2,434	Hon. W.O. Stanley	L	Unopp.
1847	2,465	Sir R.B.W. Bulkeley, Bt.	L	Unopp.
1852	2,577	Sir R.B.W. Bulkeley, Bt.	L	Unopp.
1857	2,310	Sir R.B.W. Bulkeley, Bt.	L	Unopp.
1859	2,258	Sir R.B.W. Bulkeley, Bt.	L	Unopp.
1865	2,352	Sir R.B.W. Bulkeley, Bt.	L	Unopp.
1868	3,496†	R. Davies	L	Unopp.
1874	3,173	R. Davies	L	1,636
		R.L.M.W. Bulkeley	C	793
1880	3,171	R. Davies	L	1,394
		G.P. Rayner	C	1,085

BRECONSHIRE [306]

Election	Electors	Candidate	Party	Votes
1832	1,668	†T. Wood	C	Unopp.
1835	1,897	T. Wood	C	Unopp.
1837	2,295	T. Wood	C	1,222
		J.P.G. Holford	L	570
1841	2,830	T. Wood	C	Unopp.
1847	2,548	J. Bailey	C	Unopp.
1852	2,779	Sir J. Bailey, Bt.	C	Unopp.
1857	2,609	Sir J. Bailey, Bt.	C	Unopp.
[Death]				
1858 (28/12)		G.C. Morgan	C	Unopp.
1859	2,688	Hon. G.C. Morgan	C	Unopp.
1865	2,409	Hon. G.C. Morgan	C	Unopp.
1868	3,644	Hon. G.C. Morgan	C	Unopp.
1874	3,574	Hon. G.C. Morgan	C	1,594
		W.F. Maitland	L	1,036
[Succession to the Peerage — Lord Tredegar]				
1875 (22/5)	4,256	W.F. Maitland	L	1,710
		H. Gwyn	C	1,607
1880	4,195	W.F. Maitland	L	1,810
		Hon. A.J. Morgan	C	1,550

CAERNARVONSHIRE [307]

Election	Electors	Candidate	Party	Votes
1832	1,688	T.A. Smith	C	Unopp.
1835	1,642	T.A. Smith	C	Unopp.
1837	1,791	J.R.O. Gore	C	Unopp.
1841	2,162	Hon. E.G.D. Pennant	C	Unopp.
1847	2,117	Hon. E.G.D. Pennant	C	Unopp.
1852	1,913	Hon. E.G.D. Pennant	C	Unopp.
1857	2,060	Hon. E.G.D. Pennant	C	Unopp.
1859	2,116	Hon. E.G.D. Pennant	C	Unopp.
1865	2,190	Hon. E.G.D. Pennant	C	Unopp.
[Elevation to the Peerage — Lord Penrhyn]				
1866 (14/8)		Hon. G.S.G.D. Pennant	C	Unopp.
1868	4,852†	T.L.D.J. Parry	L	1,968
		Hon. G.S.G.D. Pennant	C	1,815
1874	6,286	Hon. G.S.G.D. Pennant	C	2,750
		T.L.D.J. Parry	L	2,318
1880	6,652	C.J.W. Williams	L	3,303
		Hon. G.S.G.D. Pennant	C	2,206
[Resignation on appointment as a Judge of the Queen's Bench Division of the High Court of Justice]				
1880 (2/12)	6,652	W. Rathbone	L	3,180
		H.J.E. Nanney	C	2,151

CARDIGANSHIRE [308]

Election	Electors	Candidate	Party	Votes
1832	1,184	†W.E. Powell	C	Unopp.
1835	1,352	W.E. Powell	C	Unopp.
1837	1,788	W.E. Powell	C	Unopp.
1841	2,060	W.E. Powell	C	Unopp.
1847	2,278	W.E. Powell	C	Unopp.
1852	2,235	W.E. Powell	C	Unopp.
[Resignation]				
1854 (22/2)		Earl of Lisburne	C	Unopp.
1857	2,723	Earl of Lisburne	C	Unopp.
1859	2,586	W.T.R. Powell	C	1,070
		A.H.S. Davies	C	928
1865	3,520	Sir T.D. Lloyd, Bt.	L	1,510
		D. Davies	L	1,149
1868	5,115†	E.M. Richards	L	2,074
		E.M. Vaughan	C	1,918
1874	4,438	T.E. Lloyd	C	1,850
		E.M. Richards	L	1,635
1880	4,882	L.P. Pugh	L	2,406
		T.E. Lloyd	C	1,605

CARMARTHENSHIRE [309]

(Two Seats)

Election	Electors	Candidate	Party	Votes
1832	3,887	Hon. G.R.R. Trevor	C	1,853
		E.H. Adams	L	1,638
		†Sir J.H. Williams, Bt.	L	1,504
1835	4,227	Hon. G.R.R. Trevor	C	2,204
		Sir J.H. Williams, Bt.	L	1,939
		J. Jones	C	1,851
1837	5,125	Hon. G.R.R. Trevor	C	2,486
		J. Jones	C	2,173
		Sir J.H. Williams, Bt.	L	2,068
1841	5,614	J. Jones	C	Unopp.
		Hon. G.R.R. Trevor	C	Unopp.
[Death of Jones]				
1842 (27/12)		D.A.S. Davies	C	Unopp.
1847	5,261	D.A.S. Davies	C	Unopp.
		Hon. G.R.R. Trevor	C	Unopp.
[Succession of Trevor to the Peerage – Lord Dynevor]				
1852 (13/5)		D. Jones	C	Unopp.
1852	4,791	D.A.S. Davies	C	Unopp.
		D. Jones	C	Unopp.
1857	4,272	D.A.S. Davies	C	Unopp.
		D. Jones	C	Unopp.
[Death of Davies]				
1857 (12/6)		D. Pugh	C	Unopp.
1859	4,491	D. Jones	C	Unopp.
		D. Pugh	C	Unopp.
1865	4,833	D. Jones	C	Unopp.
		D. Pugh	C	Unopp.
1868	8,026†	E.J. Sartoris	L	3,280
		J. Jones	C	2,942
		H.L. Puxley	C	2,828
		D. Pugh	C	1,340

CARMARTHENSHIRE [309] (Cont.)

(Two Seats)

Election	Electors	Candidate	Party	Votes
1874	8,161	Viscount Emlyn	C	3,389
		J. Jones	C	3,261
		W.R.H. Powell	L	2,799
		E.J. Sartoris	L	2,331
1880	8,593	W.R.H. Powell	L	4,101
		Viscount Emlyn	C	3,030
		J. Jones	C	2,712

DENBIGHSHIRE [310]
(Two Seats)

Election	Electors	Candidate	Party	Votes
1832	3,401	†Sir W.W. Wynn, Bt.	C	2,528
		†R.M. Biddulph	L	1,479
		†Hon. L. Kenyon	C	1,291
1835	3,395	Sir W.W. Wynn, Bt.	C	2,378
		Hon. W. Bagot	C	1,512
		R.M. Biddulph	L	1,256
1837	3,689	Hon. W. Bagot	C	Unopp.
		Sir W.W. Wynn, Bt.	C	Unopp.
[Death of Wynn]				
1840 (30/1)		Hon. H. Cholmondeley	C	Unopp.
1841	4,024	Hon. W. Bagot	C	Unopp.
		Sir W.W. Wynn, Bt.	C	Unopp.
[Appointment of Wynn as Steward of the Queen's Lordships and Manors of Bromfield and Yale]				
1845 (7/5)		Sir W.W. Wynn, Bt.	C	Unopp.
1847	3,939	Sir W.W. Wynn, Bt.	C	2,055
		Hon. W. Bagot	C	1,530
		R.M. Biddulph	L	1,394
1852	3,901	Sir W.W. Wynn, Bt.	C	2,135
		R.M. Biddulph	L	1,611
		Hon. W. Bagot	C	1,532
1857	4,506	R.M. Biddulph	L	Unopp.
		Sir W.W. Wynn, Bt.	C	Unopp.
1859	4,508	R.M. Biddulph	L	Unopp.
		Sir W.W. Wynn, Bt.	C	Unopp.
1865	5,333	R.M. Biddulph	L	Unopp.
		Sir W.W. Wynn, Bt.	C	Unopp.
1868	7,623†	Sir W.W. Wynn, Bt.	C	3,355
		G.O. Morgan	L	2,720
		R.M. Biddulph	L	2,412
1874	7,323	G.O. Morgan	L	Unopp.
		Sir W.W. Wynn, Bt.	C	Unopp.

DENBIGHSHIRE [310] (Cont.)

(Two Seats)

Election	Electors	Candidate	Party	Votes
1880	7,469	G.O. Morgan	L	Unopp.
		Sir W.W. Wynn, Bt.	C	Unopp.

[Appointment of Morgan as Judge-Advocate General]

1880 (14/5)		G.O. Morgan	L	Unopp.

[Death of Wynn]

1885 (27/5)		Sir H.L.W.W. Wynn, Bt.	C	Unopp.

FLINTSHIRE [311]

Election	Electors	Candidate	Party	Votes
1832	1,271	†Hon. E.M.L. Mostyn	L	Unopp.
1835	1,344	Hon. E.M.L. Mostyn	L	Unopp.
1837	2,189	Sir S.R. Glynne, Bt.	C	945
		Hon. E.M.L. Mostyn	L	905
1841	2,963	**Hon. E.M.L. Mostyn	L	1,234
		*Sir S.R. Glynne, Bt.	C	1,192
1847	3,141	Hon. E.M.L. Mostyn	L	Unopp.
1852	2,912	Hon. E.M.L. Mostyn	L	1,276
		E. Peel	C	910
[Succession to the Peerage — Lord Mostyn]				
1854 (8/5)		Hon. T.E.M.L.L. Mostyn	L	Unopp.
1857	2,840	Hon. T.E.M.L.L. Mostyn	L	1,171
		Sir S.R. Glynne, Bt.	C	876
1859	2,896	Hon. T.E.M.L.L. Mostyn	L	Unopp.
[Death]				
1861 (30/5)	2,887*	Lord Richard Grosvenor	L	1,168
		H.R. Hughes	C	868
1865	2,998	Lord Richard Grosvenor	L	Unopp.
1868	4,150†	Lord Richard Grosvenor	L	Unopp.
[Appointed Vice-Chamberlain of H.M. Household]				
1872 (2/3)		Lord Richard Grosvenor	L	Unopp.
1874	3,907	Lord Richard Grosvenor	L	Unopp.
1880	4,794	Lord Richard Grosvenor	L	Unopp.

Petitions:—

1837: Withdrawn

1841: Election of Mostyn declared void. Glynne duly elected after scrutiny

GLAMORGANSHIRE [312]

(Two Seats)

Election	Electors	Candidate	Party	Votes
1832	3,680	L.W. Dillwyn	L	Unopp.
		†C.R.M. Talbot	L	Unopp.
1835	3,611	L.W. Dillwyn	L	Unopp.
		C.R.M. Talbot	L	Unopp.
1837	4,373	Viscount Adare	C	2,009
		C.R.M. Talbot	L	1,794
		J.J. Guest	L	1,590
1841	5,384	Viscount Adare	C	Unopp.
		C.R.M. Talbot	L	Unopp.
1847	5,775	Viscount Adare *(Earl of Dunraven)*	C	Unopp.
		C.R.M. Talbot	L	Unopp.
[Resignation of Dunraven]				
1851 (25/2)		Sir G. Tyler	C	Unopp.
1852	6,424	C.R.M. Talbot	L	Unopp.
		Sir G. Tyler	C	Unopp.
1857	6,356	C.R.M. Talbot	L	3,161
		H.H. Vivian	L	3,002
		N.V.E. Vaughan	C	2,088
1859	6,600	C.R.M. Talbot	L	Unopp.
		H.H. Vivian	L	Unopp.
1865	6,759	C.R.M. Talbot	L	Unopp.
		H.H. Vivian	L	Unopp.
1868	11,329†	C.R.M. Talbot	L	Unopp.
		H.H. Vivian	L	Unopp.
1874	10,006	H.H. Vivian	L	4,100
		C.R.M. Talbot	L	4,040
		Sir I.B. Guest, Bt.	C	3,355
1880	12,811	C.R.M. Talbot	L	Unopp.
		H.H. Vivian	L	Unopp.

MERIONETHSHIRE [313]

Election	Electors	Candidate	Party	Votes
1832	580	†Sir R.W. Vaughan, Bt.	C	Unopp.
1835	698	Sir R.W. Vaughan, Bt.	C	Unopp.
[Resignation]				
1836 (27/6)	785	R. Richards Sir W. Wynne	C L	501 150
1837	1,336	R. Richards	C	Unopp.
1841	1,306	R. Richards	C	Unopp.
1847	1,180	R. Richards	C	Unopp.
1852	1,006	W.W.E. Wynne	C	Unopp.
1857	1,126	W.W.E. Wynne	C	Unopp.
1859	1,091	W.W.E. Wynne D. Williams	C L	389 351
1865	1,527	W.R.M. Wynne D. Williams	C L	610 579
1868	3,185	D. Williams	L	Unopp.
[Death]				
1870 (17/1)	3,187*	S. Holland C.J. Tottenham	L C	1,610 963
1874	3,335	S. Holland	L	Unopp.
1880	3,571	S. Holland A.M. Dunlop	L C	1,860 1,074

Petitions: —

1836: Withdrawn

1859: Withdrawn

MONMOUTHSHIRE [314]

(Two Seats)

Election	Electors	Candidate	Party	Votes
1832	3,738	†Lord Granville Somerset	C	Unopp.
		†W.A. Williams	L	Unopp.
1835	3,714	Lord Granville Somerset	C	Unopp.
		W.A. Williams	L	Unopp.
1837	4,347	Lord Granville Somerset	C	Unopp.
		W.A. Williams	L	Unopp.
[Resignation of Williams]				
1841 (9/2)		C.O.S. Morgan	C	Unopp.
1841	4,393	C.O.S. Morgan	C	Unopp.
		Lord Granville Somerset	C	Unopp.
[Appointment of Somerset as Chancellor of the Duchy of Lancaster]				
1841 (24/9)		Lord Granville Somerset	C	Unopp.
1847	5,286	C.O.S. Morgan	C	2,334
		Lord Granville Somerset	C	2,230
		E.A. Somerset	C	2,187
[Death of Somerset]				
1848 (24/3)		E.A. Somerset	C	Unopp.
1852	4,973	C.O.S. Morgan	C	Unopp.
		E.A. Somerset	C	Unopp.
1857	5,099	C.O.S. Morgan	C	Unopp.
		E.A. Somerset	C	Unopp.
1859	5,073	C.O.S. Morgan	C	Unopp.
		E.A. Somerset	C	Unopp.
[Resignation of Somerset]				
1859 (1/7)		P.G.H. Somerset	C	Unopp.
1865	4,909	C.O.S. Morgan	C	Unopp.
		P.G.H. Somerset	C	Unopp.
1868	7,971†	C.O.S. Morgan	C	3,761
		P.G.H. Somerset	C	3,525
		H.M. Clifford	L	2,338

MONMOUTHSHIRE [314] (Cont.)

(Two Seats)

Election	Electors	Candidate	Party	Votes
[Resignation of Somerset]				
1871 (4/3)		Lord Henry Somerset	C	Unopp.
1874	7,630	Hon. F.C. Morgan	C	Unopp.
		Lord Henry Somerset	C	Unopp.
[Appointment of Somerset as Comptroller of H.M. Household]				
1874 (17/3)		Lord Henry Somerset	C	Unopp.
1880	8,518	Hon. F.C. Morgan	C	3,529
		J.A. Rolls	C	3,294
		Hon. G.C. Brodrick	L	3,019
		C.M. Warmington	L	2,927

Petition:—

1847: Withdrawn on death of respondent. (Somerset only)

MONTGOMERYSHIRE [315]

Election	Electors	Candidate	Party	Votes
1832	2,525	†C.W.W. Wynn	C	Unopp.
1835	2,737	C.W.W. Wynn	C	Unopp.
1837	2,819	C.W.W. Wynn	C	Unopp.
1841	2,936	C.W.W. Wynn	C	Unopp.
1847	3,214	C.W.W. Wynn	C	Unopp.
[Death]				
1850 (11/10)		H.W.W. Wynn	C	Unopp.
1852	2,986	H.W.W. Wynn	C	Unopp.
1857	2,872	H.W.W. Wynn	C	Unopp.
1859	2,723	H.W.W. Wynn	C	Unopp.
[Death]				
1862 (14/7)	2,675	C.W.W. Wynn	C	1,269
		Hon. S.C.G.H. Tracy	L	959
1865	3,339	C.W.W. Wynn	C	Unopp.
1868	4,810	C.W.W. Wynn	C	Unopp.
1874	5,014	C.W.W. Wynn	C	Unopp.
1880	5,291	S. Rendal	L	2,232
		C.W.W. Wynn	C	2,041

PEMBROKESHIRE [316]

Election	Electors	Candidate	Party	Votes
1832	3,700	†Sir J. Owen, Bt.	C	Unopp.
1835	3,664	Sir J. Owen, Bt.	C	Unopp.
1837	3,706	Sir J. Owen, Bt.	C	Unopp.
1841	3,663	Viscount Emlyn	C	Unopp.
1847	3,479	Viscount Emlyn	C	Unopp.
1852	3,132	Viscount Emlyn	C	Unopp.
1857	2,784	Viscount Emlyn	C	Unopp.
1859	2,700	Viscount Emlyn	C	Unopp.
[Succession to the Peerage — Earl Cawdor]				
1861 (19/1)	2,809*	G.L. Phillips	C	1,194
		H.O. Owen	L	979
1865	3,797	G.L. Phillips	C	Unopp.
[Death]				
1866 (26/11)		J.B. Bowen	C	Unopp.
1868	4,690†	J.H. Scourfield	C	Unopp.
1874	4,621	J.H. Scourfield	C	Unopp.
[Death]				
1876 (28/6)	4,541	J.B. Bowen	C	1,882
		W. Davies	L	1,608
1880	5,052	W. Davies	L	2,185
		C.E.G. Philipps	C	1,737

RADNORSHIRE [317]

Election	Electors	Candidate	Party	Votes
1832	1,046	†T.F. Lewis	C	Unopp.
1835	1,074	W. Wilkins	L	483
		Sir J.B. Walsh, Bt.	C	456
1837	1,944	W. Wilkins	L	Unopp.
[Death]				
1840 (10/6)		Sir J.B. Walsh, Bt.	C	Unopp.
1841	2,067	Sir J.B. Walsh, Bt.	C	973
		Lord Harley	L	504
1847	1,943	Sir J.B. Walsh, Bt.	C	Unopp.
1852	1,802	Sir J.B. Walsh, Bt.	C	Unopp.
1857	1,662	Sir J.B. Walsh, Bt.	C	Unopp.
1859	1,656	Sir J.B. Walsh, Bt.	C	Unopp.
1865	1,597	Sir J.B. Walsh, Bt.	C	Unopp.
[Elevation to the Peerage — Lord Ormathwaite]				
1868 (28/4)		Hon. A. Walsh	C	Unopp.
1868	2,216	Hon. A. Walsh	C	Unopp.
1874	2,431	Hon. A. Walsh	C	889
		R.G. Price	L	832
		G.A. Haig	L	100
1880	2,434	Sir R.G. Price, Bt.	L	1,137
		R.B.R. Mynors	C	800

SCOTLAND ––– BURGHS

ABERDEEN [318]

Election	Electors	Candidate	Party	Votes
1832	2,024	A. Bannerman	L	Unopp.
1835	2,098	A. Bannerman	L	938
		Sir A. Farquhar	C	372
1837	2,110	A. Bannerman	L	Unopp.
1841	2,189*	A. Bannerman	L	780
		W. Innes	C	513
		R. Lowery	Ch	30
1847	3,364	A.D. Fordyce	L	918
		W.H. Sykes	L	422
1852	4,547	G. Thompson	L	682
		Sir A.L. Hay	L	478
1857	2,346	W.H. Sykes	L	1,035
		J.F. Leith	L	849
1859	3,442	W.H. Sykes	L	Unopp.
1865	3,996	W.H. Sykes	L	Unopp.
1868	8,312	W.H. Sykes	L	Unopp.
[Death]				
1872 (29/6)	13,996	J.F. Leith	L	4,392
		J.W. Barclay	L	2,615
		J. Shaw	C	704
1874	14,585	J.F. Leith	L	3,910
		J. Shaw	C	2,724
1880	14,184	J. Webster	L	7,505
		J. Shaw	C	3,139

AYR DISTRICT of BURGHS [319]
(Ayr, Campbeltown, Inveraray, Irvine, Oban)

Election	Electors	Candidate	Party	Votes
1832	631	†T.F. Kennedy	L	375
		J. Taylor	L	164
		J. Cruickshanks	C	33
[Resignation]				
1834 (3/3)	701	Lord James Stuart	L	305
		J. Taylor	L	213
1835	848	Lord James Stuart	L	339
		A. Johnston	L	323
1837	1,030	Lord James Stuart	L	368
		A. Johnston	L	355
1841	1,097*	Lord James Stuart	L	Unopp.
1847	1,051	Lord James Stuart	L	Unopp.
1852	1,039	E.H.J. Craufurd	L	338
		A.T. Boyle	C	329
1857	1,136	E.H.J. Craufurd	L	Unopp.
1859	1,203	E.H.J. Craufurd	L	Unopp.
1865	1,340	E.H.J. Craufurd	L	567
		A.H. Oswald	L	501
1868	2,565	E.H.J. Craufurd	L	1,116
		J. Anderson	L	1,025
1874	4,092	Sir W.J.M. Cuninghame, Bt.	C	1,697
		E.H.J. Craufurd	L	1,683
1880	4,297	R.F.F. Campbell	L	2,303
		Sir W.J.M. Cuninghame, Bt.	C	1,420

Petition: —

1874: Withdrawn

DUMFRIES DISTRICT of BURGHS [320]
(Dumfries, Annan, Kirkcudbright, Lochmaben, Sanquhar)

Election	Electors	Candidate	Party	Votes
1832	967	M. Sharpe	L	488
		D. Hannay	L	370
1835	999	M. Sharpe	L	422
		D. Hannay	L	370
1837	1,050	M. Sharpe	L	Unopp.
1841	977*	W. Ewart	L	402
		Sir A.H. Johnstone, Bt.	L	342
1847	892	W. Ewart	L	Unopp.
1852	881	W. Ewart	L	Unopp.
1857	882	W. Ewart	L	506
		J. Hannay	C	185
1859	966	W. Ewart	L	432
		G.G. Walker	C	403
1865	1,124	W. Ewart	L	540
		C. Kennedy	L	384
1868	2,353	R. Jardine	L	1,125
		E. Noel	L	1,083
1874	2,833	E. Noel	L	1,420
		M.C. Yorstoun	C	1,122
1880	2,931	E. Noel	L	1,700
		W. Gordon	C	872
		T.E.D. Byrne	C	54

DUNDEE [321]

(One seat until 1868; two seats from 1868)

Election	Electors	Candidate	Party	Votes
1832	1,622	G.S. Kinloch	L	852
		D.C. Guthrie	L	593
[Death]				
1833 (17/4)		Sir H.B. Parnell, Bt.	L	Unopp.
1835	1,751	Sir H.B. Parnell, Bt.	L	Unopp.
[Appointment of Parnell as Paymaster-General of the Land Forces and Treasurer of the Navy]				
1835 (6/5)		Sir H.B. Parnell, Bt.	L	Unopp.
1837	2,214	Sir H.B. Parnell, Bt.	L	633
		J. Gladstone	C	381
1841	2,739*	G. Duncan	L	577
		J.B. Smith	L	445
1847	2,635	G. Duncan	L	Unopp.
1852	3,190	G. Duncan	L	Unopp.
1857	2,343	Sir J. Ogilvy, Bt.	L	1,092
		G. Armitstead	L	847
1859	2,317	Sir J. Ogilvy, Bt.	L	Unopp.
1865	3,039	Sir J. Ogilvy, Bt.	L	Unopp.
1868	14,798	G. Armitstead	L	7,738
		Sir J. Ogilvy, Bt.	L	7,661
		J.A. Guthrie	L	3,548
		H.W. Scott	L	2,085
[Resignation of Armitstead]				
1873 (7/8)	16,652	J. Yeaman	L	5,297
		E. Jenkins	L	4,010
		J.F. Stephen	L	1,086
1874	17,814	J. Yeaman	L	6,595
		E. Jenkins	L	6,048
		Sir J. Ogilvy, Bt.	L	4,401
		J.M.D. Meiklejohn	L	2,231
		J.A.L. Gloag	C	573
1880	14,566	G. Armistead	L	9,168
		F. Henderson	L	6,750
		J. Yeaman	C	4,993

EDINBURGH [322]
(Two Seats)

Election	Electors	Candidate	Party	Votes
1832	6,048	†F. Jeffrey	L	4,035
		J. Abercromby	L	3,850
		F.H. Blair	C	1,519
[Resignation of Jeffrey on appointment as a Senator of the College of Justice — Lord Jeffrey]				
1834 (2/6)	6,512	Sir J. Campbell	L	1,932
		J. Learmouth	C	1,401
		J. Aytoun	L	480
[Appointment of Abercromby as Master of the Mint]				
1834 (23/6)		J. Abercromby	L	Unopp.
1835	7,862	J. Abercromby	L	2,963
		Sir J. Campbell	L	2,858
		Lord Ramsay	C	1,716
		J. Learmouth	C	1,608
[Appointment of Campbell as Attorney-General]				
1835 (30/4)		Sir J. Campbell	L	Unopp.
1837	9,640	J. Abercromby	L	Unopp.
		Sir J. Campbell	L	Unopp.
[Elevation of Abercromby to the Peerage — Lord Dunfermline]				
1839 (4/6)		T.B. Macaulay	L	Unopp.
[Appointment of Macaulay as Secretary at War]				
1840 (23/1)		T.B. Macaulay	L	Unopp.
1841	5,346*	W.G. Craig	L	Unopp.
		T.B. Macaulay	L	Unopp.
[Appointment of Craig as a Lord Commissioner of the Treasury]				
1846 (13/7)		W.G. Craig	L	Unopp.
[Appointment of Macaulay as Paymaster-General]				
1846 (15/7)	6,118*	T.B. Macaulay	L	1,735
		Sir C.E. Smith *(Eardley)*, Bt.	L	832
1847	7,114	C. Cowan	L	2,063
		W.G. Craig	L	1,854
		T.B. Macaulay	L	1,477
		P. Blackburn	C	980

Election	Electors	Candidate	Party	Votes
[Disqualification of Cowan who at the time of his election held a Government contract]				
1847 (15/12)		C. Cowan	L	Unopp.
1852	6,230	T.B. Macaulay	L	1,872
		C. Cowan	L	1,754
		D. McLaren	L	1,559
		Hon. T.C. Bruce	C	1,065
		A. Campbell	L	625
[Resignation of Macaulay]				
1856 (9/2)	8,297*	A. Black	L	2,429
		F.B. Douglas	L	1,786
1857	8,297	A. Black	L	Unopp.
		C. Cowan	L	Unopp.
1859	8,347	A. Black	L	Unopp.
		J. Moncreiff	L	Unopp.
[Appointment of Moncreiff as Lord Advocate]				
1859 (28/6)		J. Moncreiff	L	Unopp.
1865	10,343	D. McLaren	L	4,354
		J. Moncreiff	L	4,148
		A. Black	L	3,797
		J. Miller	L	3,723
1868	20,779	D. McLaren	L	Unopp.
		J. Miller	L	Unopp.
1874	24,832	D. McLaren	L	11,431
		J. Cowan	L	8,749
		J. Miller	L	6,218
		J.H.A. Macdonald	C	5,713
1880	28,524	D. McLaren	L	17,807
		J. Cowan	L	17,301
		J.H.A. Macdonald	C	5,651
[Resignation of McLaren]				
1881 (28/1)	28,644	J. McLaren	L	11,390
		E. Jenkins	L	3,940
[Resignation of McLaren on appointment as a Senator of the College of Justice — Lord McLaren]				
1881 (24/8)		T.R. Buchanan	L	Unopp.

EDINBURGH [322] (Cont.)
(Two Seats)

Election	Electors	Candidate	Party	Votes
[Resignation of Cowan]				
1882	29,252	S.D. Waddy	L	8,455
(4/11)		J.H. Renton	L	7,718

Note: —

1835—1837	Abercromby was Speaker of the House of Commons from February 1835 until May 1839

ELGIN DISTRICT of BURGHS [323]
(Elgin, Banff, Cullen, Inverurie, Kintore, Peterhead)

Election	Electors	Candidate	Party	Votes
1832	776	A.L. Hay	L	350
		H. Mackenzie	C	225
		A. Morrison	L	123
[Appointed Clerk of the Ordnance]				
1834 (30/6)		A.L. Hay	L	Unopp.
1835	812	A.L. Hay	L	384
		W. Brodie	C	264
[Appointed Clerk of the Ordnance]				
1835 (2/5)		A.L. Hay	L	Unopp.
1837	858	Sir A.L. Hay	L	Unopp.
[Resignation on appointment as Governor of Bermuda]				
1838 (13/2)		Hon. F. Maule	L	Unopp.
1841	857	Sir A.L. Hay	L	311
		T.A. Duff	C	297
1847	862	G.S. Duff	L	242
		A. Bannerman	C	192
		Sir A.L. Hay	L	147
1852	988	G.S. Duff	L	Unopp.
1857	967	G.S. Duff	L	Unopp.
[Resignation]				
1857 (19/12)		M.E.G. Duff	L	Unopp.
1859	969	M.E.G. Duff	L	Unopp.
1865	1,059	M.E.G. Duff	L	Unopp.
1868	2,962	M.E.G. Duff	L	Unopp.
1874	3,501	M.E.G. Duff	L	Unopp.
1880	3,806	M.E.G. Duff	L	2,082
		J.M. Maclean	C	764

Election	Electors	Candidate	Party	Votes
[Resignation on appointment as Governor of Madras]				
1881 (15/7)		A. Asher	L	Unopp.
[Appointed Solicitor-General for Scotland]				
1881 (27/8)		A. Asher	L	Unopp.

Petition:—

1841: Withdrawn

FALKIRK DISTRICT of BURGHS [324]
(Falkirk, Airdrie, Hamilton, Lanark, Linlithgow)

Election	Electors	Candidate	Party	Votes
1832	969	†W.D. Gillon	L	505
		Hon. C.A. Murray	L	361
1835	1,046	W.D. Gillon	L	Unopp.
1837	1,177	W.D. Gillon	L	Unopp.
1841	1,369*	W. Baird	C	484
		W.D. Gillon	L	433
[Resignation]				
1846 (2/5)	1,332*	Earl of Lincoln	C	506
		J. Wilson	L	495
1847	1,437	Earl of Lincoln	C	522
		W.S. Boyd	L	491
[Succession to the Peerage – Duke of Newcastle]				
1851 (14/2)	1,749	J. Baird	C	590
		G. Loch	L	544
1852	1,905	J. Baird	C	579
		J. Anderson	L	529
1857	1,473	J. Merry	L	770
		G. Baird	C	491
[Election declared void on petition]				
1857 (8/8)		J.G.C. Hamilton	L	Unopp.
1859	1,540	J. Merry	L	Unopp.
1865	1,510	J. Merry	L	683
		Sir F.J. Halliday	C	419
1868	4,704	J. Merry	L	1,724
		E. Horsman	L	16
1874	5,165	J. Ramsay	L	2,583
		A. Baird	C	1,958
[Disqualification of Ramsay who at the time of his election held a Government contract]				
1874 (26/3)		J. Ramsay	L	Unopp.

Election	Electors	Candidate	Party	Votes
1880	5,333	J. Ramsay	L	3,270
		W.B. McTaggart	C	1,140

Petitions: —

1851: Withdrawn

1857: Void election

GLASGOW [325]

(Two seats until 1868; three seats from 1868]

Election	Electors	Candidate	Party	Votes
1832	6,989	J. Ewing	L	3,214
		J. Oswald	L	2,838
		Sir D.K. Sandford	L	2,168
		J. Crawfurd	L	1,850
		J. Douglas	L	1,340
		†J. Dixon	L	995
1835	7,922	J. Oswald	L	3,832
		C. Dunlop	L	3,267
		J. Ewing	C	2,297
[Resignation of Dunlop]				
1836 (17/2)	8,819	Lord William Bentinck	L	1,995
		G. Mills	L	903
[Resignation of Oswald]				
1837 (27/5)	8,676	J. Dennistoun	L	3,049
		R. Monteith	C	2,298
1837	8,676	Lord William Bentinck	L	2,767
		J. Dennistoun	L	2,743
		J. Campbell	C	2,124
		R. Monteith	C	2,090
[Resignation of Bentinck]				
1839 (24/6)		J. Oswald	L	Unopp.
1841	8,241*	J. Oswald	L	2,776
		J. Dennistoun	L	2,728
		J. Campbell	C	2,416
		G. Mills	Ch	355
1847	9,589	J. MacGregor	L	2,193
		A. Hastie	L	2,081
		W. Dickson	L	1,814
		J. Dennistoun	L	1,745
1852	15,502	A. Hastie	L	3,209
		J. MacGregor	L	3,140
		P. Blackburn	C	1,681
		Viscount Melgund	L	354
[Resignation of MacGregor]				
1857 (6/3)	18,118	W. Buchanan	L	5,792
		J. Merry	L	2,943
1857	18,118	W. Buchanan	L	7,060
		R. Dalglish	L	6,765
		A. Hastie	L	5,044

GLASGOW [325] (Cont.)

(Two seats until 1868; three seats from 1868)

Election	Electors	Candidate	Party	Votes
1859	18,611	W. Buchanan	L	Unopp.
		R. Dalglish	L	Unopp.
1865	16,819	W. Graham	L	8,171
		R. Dalglish	L	6,713
		J. Ramsay	L	5,832
1868	47,854	R. Dalglish	L	18,287
		W. Graham	L	18,062
		G. Anderson	L	17,803
		Sir G. Campbell, Bt.	C	10,820
1874	54,374	C. Cameron	L	18,455
		G. Anderson	L	17,902
		A. Whitelaw	C	14,134
		J. Hunter	C	12,533
		A. Crum	L	7,453
		Hon. F.E. Kerr	L	4,444
		J.C. Bolton	L	169
[Death of Whitelaw]				
1879 (16/7)		C. Tennant	L	Unopp.
1880	57,920	G. Anderson	L	24,016
		C. Cameron	L	23,658
		R.T. Middleton	L	23,360
		W. Pearce	C	11,622
		Sir J. Bain	C	11,071
[Resignation of Anderson on appointment as Master of the Mint at Melbourne, Australia]				
1885 (12/3)		T. Russell	L	Unopp.

GREENOCK [326]

Election	Electors	Candidate	Party	Votes
1832	985	R. Wallace	L	493
		J. Fairrie	L	262
1835	1,170	R. Wallace	L	Unopp
1837	1,065	R. Wallace	L	401
		J. Smith	C	202
1841	1,113*	R. Wallace	L	406
		Sir T.J. Cochrane	C	309
[Resignation]				
1845 (18/4)	1,165*	W. Baine	L	350
		A.M. Dunlop	L	344
1847	1,089	Viscount Melgund	L	456
		A.M. Dunlop	L	315
1852	1,164	A.M. Dunlop	L	470
		Sir J.D.H. Elphinstone, Bt.	C	254
1857	1,405	A.M. Dunlop	L	Unopp
1859	1,524	A.M. Dunlop	L	Unopp
1865	1,871	A.M. Dunlop	L	Unopp
1868	6,223	J.J. Grieve	L	2,962
		W.D. Christie	L	2,092
1874	6,330	J.J. Grieve	L	Unopp
[Resignation]				
1878 (25/1)	7,446	J. Stewart	L	2,183
		Sir J. Fergusson, Bt.	C	2,124
		D. Currie	L	1,648
		W.D.S. Moncrieff	L	108
1880	7,203	J. Stewart	L	3,351
		J. Scott	C	2,162
[Resignation]				
1884 (28/11)	7,641*	T. Sutherland	L	3,548
		J. Scott	C	2,417

Petition:—

1868: Dismissed

HADDINGTON DISTRICT of BURGHS [327]
(Haddington, Dunbar, Jedburgh, Lauder, North Berwick)

Election	Electors	Candidate	Party	Votes
1832	545	†R. Steuart	L	Unopp.
1835	601	R. Steuart	L	Unopp.
[Appointed a Lord Commissioner of the Treasury]				
1835 (2/5)		R. Steuart	L	Unopp.
1837	635	R. Steuart	L	268
		Sir T.B. Hepbun, Bt.	C	237
1841	650*	J.M. Balfour	C	273
		R. Steuart	L	264
1847	775	Sir H.R.F. Davie, Bt.	L	Unopp.
1852	642	Sir H.R.F. Davie, Bt.	L	312
		A.C. Swinton	C	185
1857	741	Sir H.R.F. Davie, Bt.	L	Unopp.
1859	657	Sir H.R.F. Davie, Bt.	L	Unopp.
1865	698	Sir H.R.F. Davie, Bt.	L	Unopp.
1868	1,477	Sir H.R.F. Davie, Bt.	L	Unopp.
1874	1,753	Sir H.R.F. Davie, Bt.	L	Unopp.
[Resignation]				
1878 (3/8)	1,840	Lord William Hay	L	881
		Sir J.G. Suttie, Bt.	C	651
[Succession to the Peerage — Marquess of Tweeddale]				
1879 (26/2)	1,846	Sir D. Wedderburn, Bt.	L	921
		J.H.A. Macdonald	C	723
1880	1,896	Sir D. Wedderburn, Bt.	L	1,019
		J.F. Houston	C	607
[Resignation]				
1882 (24/8)	1,839	A.C. Sellar	L	833
		W.S.S. Karr	C	544

HAWICK DISTRICT of BURGHS [328]
(Hawick, Galashiels, Selkirk)

Election	Electors	Candidate	Party	Votes
1868	3,335	G.O. Trevelyan	L	Unopp.

[Appointed a Civil Lord of the Admiralty]

1869 (4/1)		G.O. Trevelyan	L	Unopp.
1874	3,729	G.O. Trevelyan	L	Unopp.
1880	4,920	G.O. Trevelyan	L	3,518
		J.T.S. Elliot	C	553

[Appointed Chief Secretary to the Lord Lieutenant of Ireland]

1882 (18/5)		G.O. Trevelyan	L	Unopp.

INVERNESS DISTRICT of BURGHS [329]

(Inverness, Forres, Fortrose, Nairn)

Election	Electors	Candidate	Party	Votes
1832	715	J. Baillie	C	250
		J. Stewart	L	243
		†C.L.C. Bruce	C	192
		R. Fraser	L	6
[Death]				
1833 (17/5)	715	C.L.C. Bruce	C	357
		J. Stewart	L	290
1835	757	C.L.C. Bruce	C	344
		E. Ellice	L	340
1837	699	R. Macleod	L	336
		J.J.R. Mackenzie	C	317
[Resignation]				
1840 (4/3)	757	J. Morrison	L	353
		J. Fraser	C	307
1841	757*	J. Morrison	L	Unopp.
1847	771	A. Matheson	L	280
		R.H. Kennedy	L	199
1852	825	A. Matheson	L	Unopp.
1857	854	A. Matheson	L	382
		A. Campbell	C	335
1859	874	A. Matheson	L	410
		A. Campbell	C	307
1865	1,022	A. Matheson	L	Unopp.
1868	1,995	A.W. Mackintosh	L	Unopp.
1874	2,419	C.F. Mackintosh	L	1,134
		A.W. Mackintosh	L	879
		A. Mackintosh	C	16
1880	2,990	C.F. Mackintosh	L	Unopp.

KILMARNOCK DISTRICT of BURGHS [330]
(Kilmarnock, Dumbarton, Port Glasgow, Renfrew, Rutherglen)

Election	Electors	Candidate	Party	Votes
1832	1,155	J. Dunlop	L	535
		J. Campbell	L	528
1835	1,261	J. Bowring	L	520
		J. Dunlop	L	276
		R. Downie	C	153
1837	1,451	J.C. Colquhoun	C	509
		J. Bowring	L	438
1841	1,262*	A. Johnston	L	490
		J.C. Colquhoun	C	479
[Death]				
1844 (29/5)	1,289*	Hon. E.P. Bouverie	L	389
		H.T. Prinsep	C	379
		H. Vincent	Ch	98
1847	1,243	Hon. E.P. Bouverie	L	Unopp.
1852	1,380	Hon. E.P. Bouverie	L	558
		J.A. Campbell	C	302
[Appointed Vice-President of the Board of Trade]				
1855 (7/4)		Hon. E.P. Bouverie	L	Unopp.
[Appointed President of the Poor Law Board]				
1855 (16/8)		Hon. E.P. Bouverie	L	Unopp.
1857	1,414	Hon. E.P. Bouverie	L	Unopp.
1859	1,449	Hon. E.P. Bouverie	L	Unopp.
1865	1,645	Hon. E.P. Bouverie	L	Unopp.
1868	6,531	Hon. E.P. Bouverie	L	2,892
		E. Chadwick	L	1,148
		R. Thomson	L	999
1874	8,020	J.F. Harrison	L	3,316
		Hon. E.P. Bouverie	L	3,019
1880	7,700	J.D. Peddie	L	3,320
		J.N. Cuthbertson	C	2,005
		R.M. Kerr	L	1,384

Petition:— 1844: Withdrawn

KIRKCALDY DISTRICT of BURGHS [331]
(Kirkcaldy, Burntisland, Dysart, Kinghorn)

Election	Electors	Candidate	Party	Votes
1832	507	†R. Ferguson	L	Unopp.
1835	539	J. Fergus	L	Unopp.
1837	641	R. Ferguson	L	Unopp.
[Death]				
1841 (27/1)	657*	R. Ferguson	L	218
		J. Bowring	L	131
1841	657*	R. Ferguson	L	Unopp.
1847	896	R. Ferguson	L	Unopp.
1852	786	R. Ferguson	L	Unopp.
1857	728	R. Ferguson	L	Unopp.
1859	777	R. Ferguson	L	312
		W.G.G.V.V. Harcourt	L	294
[Resignation]				
1862 (25/7)		R.S. Aytoun	L	Unopp.
1865	816	R.S. Aytoun	L	Unopp.
1868	3,160	R.S. Aytoun	L	Unopp.
1874	3,766	R. Reid	L	1,967
		J.T. Oswald	C	1,228
[Death]				
1875 (23/4)	3,811	Sir G. Campbell	L	1,811
		W.J. Harker	L	1,171
1880	4,465	Sir G. Campbell	L	2,763
		C. Scott	C	59

LEITH DISTRICT of BURGHS [332]
(Leith, Musselburgh, Portobello)

Election	Electors	Candidate	Party	Votes
1832	1,624	J.A. Murray	L	Unopp.
[Appointed Lord Advocate]				
1834 (2/6)	1,618	J.A. Murray	L	686
		W. Aitchison	C	449
1835	1,838	J.A. Murray	L	Unopp.
[Appointed Lord Advocate]				
1835 (8/5)	1,838	J.A. Murray	L	727
		Sir D. Milne	C	423
1837	2,171	J.A. Murray	L	Unopp.
[Resignation on appointment as a Senator of the College of Justice — Lord Murray]				
1839 (29/4)		A. Rutherfurd	L	Unopp.
1841	1,732*	A. Rutherfurd	L	Unopp.
[Appointed Lord Advocate]				
1846 (9/7)		A. Rutherfurd	L	Unopp.
1847	1,888	A. Rutherfurd	L	Unopp.
[Resignation on appointment as a Senator of the College of Justice — Lord Rutherfurd]				
1851 (14/4)		J. Moncreiff	L	Unopp.
1852	2,027	J. Moncreiff	L	643
		T.W. Henerson	C	407
[Appointed Lord Advocate]				
1853 (4/1)		J. Moncreiff	L	Unopp.
1857	1,973	J. Moncreiff	L	821
		W. Miller	L	701
1859	2,139	W. Miller	L	904
		R.A. Macfie	L	746
1865	2,672	W. Miller	L	Unopp.

Election	Electors	Candidate	Party	Votes
1868	6,223	R.A. Macfie	L	2,916
		W. Miller	L	2,319
1874	8,248	D.R. Macgregor	L	4,489
		R.A. Macfie	L	1,945
[Resignation]				
1878 (29/1)	9,739	A. Grant	L	4,929
		C.W. Tennant	C	1,788
1880	10,333	A. Grant	L	Unopp.

MONTROSE DISTRICT of BURGHS [333]
(Montrose, Arbroath, Brechin, Forfar, Inverbervie)

Election	Electors	Candidate	Party	Votes
1832	1,494	†H. Ross	L	796
		P. Chalmers	L	535
1835	1,551	P. Chalmers	L	Unopp.
1837	1,636	P. Chalmers	L	Unopp.
1841	1,403*	P. Chalmers	L	Unopp.
[Resignation]				
1842 (16/4)		J. Hume	L	Unopp.
1847	1,178	J. Hume	L	532
		D. Greenhill	L	231
1852	1,586	J. Hume	L	Unopp.
[Death]				
1855 (9/3)	1,586*	W.E. Baxter	L	478
		Sir J. Ogilvy, Bt.	L	434
1857	1,575	W.E. Baxter	L	Unopp.
1859	1,651	W.E. Baxter	L	Unopp.
1865	1,806	W.E. Baxter	L	Unopp.
1868	6,337	W.E. Baxter	L	3,199
		W.M. Macdonald	C	1,027
1874	7,891	W.E. Baxter	L	3,333
		W.M. Macdonald	C	1,875
1880	8,343	W.E. Baxter	L	Unopp.

PAISLEY [334]

Election	Electors	Candidate	Party	Votes
1832	1,242	Sir J. Maxwell, Bt.	L	775
		J. McKerrell	C	180
[Resignation]				
1834 (24/3)	1,261	Sir D.K. Sandford	L	542
		J. Crawfurd	L	509
		J.E. Gordon	C	29
1835	1,510	A.G. Speirs	L	661
		H. Ross	C	477
[Resignation]				
1836 (17/3)	1,465	A. Hastie	L	680
		J. Aytoun	L	529
1837	1,610	A. Hastie	L	Unopp.
1841	1,324*	A. Hastie	L	157
		W. Thomason	Ch	0
1847	1,060	A. Hastie	L	Unopp.
1852	1,342	A. Hastie	L	406
		W.T. Haly	L	374
1857	1,305	A. Hastie	L	611
		H.E.C. Ewing	L	524
		C.F.F. Wordsworth	Ch	4
[Death]				
1857 (11/12)	1,349	H.E.C. Ewing	L	767
		W.T. Haly	L	98
1859	1,370	H.E.C. Ewing	L	Unopp.
1865	1,361	H.E.C. Ewing	L	Unopp.
1868	3,264	H.E.C. Ewing	L	1,576
		A.C. Campbell	C	921
		A. Kintrea	L	421
1874	5,083	W. Holms	L	Unopp.
1880	4,979	W. Holms	L	Unopp.
[Resignation]				
1884 (18/2)	5,688	S. Clark	L	3,049
		Lord Ernest Hamilton	C	1,806

PERTH [335]

Election	Electors	Candidate	Party	Votes
1832	780	L. Oliphant	L	458
		Lord James Stuart	L	205
1835	874	L. Oliphant	L	Unopp.
1837	900	Hon. A.F. Kinnaird	L	355
		Sir J.P.M. Threipland	C	188
[Resignation]				
1839 (19/8)		D. Greig	L	9
		L. Oliphant	L	0
1841	1,082*	F. Maule	L	356
		W.F. Black	C	227
[Appointed Secretary at War]				
1846 (11/7)		F. Maule	L	Unopp.
1847	1,030	F. Maule	L	Unopp.
[Appointed President of the Board of Control for the Affairs of India]				
1852 (9/2)		F. Maule	L	Unopp.
[Succession to the Peerage — Lord Panmure]				
1852 (15/5)	1,034	Hon. A.F. Kinnaird	L	325
		C. Gilpin	L	225
1852	1,034	Hon. A.F. Kinnaird	L	Unopp.
1857	947	Hon. A.F. Kinnaird	L	Unopp.
1859	966	Hon. A.F. Kinnaird	L	Unopp.
1865	982	Hon. A.F. Kinnaird	L	Unopp.
1868	2,801	Hon. A.F. Kinnaird	L	Unopp.
1874	3,863	Hon. A.F. Kinnaird	L	1,648
		C. Scott	C	940
[Succession to the Peerage — Lord Kinnaird]				
1878 (29/1)	4,224	C.S. Parker	L	2,206
		A. Mackie	C	855

Election	Electors	Candidate	Party	Votes
1880	4,000	C.S. Parker	L	2,315
		D.R. Williamson	C	774

ST. ANDREWS DISTRICT of BURGHS [336]

(St. Andrews, Anstruther Easter, Anstruther Wester, Crail, Cupar, Kilrenny, Pittenweem)

Election	Electors	Candidate	Party	Votes
1832	621	†A. Johnston	L	331
		Sir R.A. Anstruther, Bt.	C	200
1835	669	A. Johnston	L	Unopp.
1837	694	E. Ellice	L	290
		D.M. Makgill	C	261
1841	835*	E. Ellice	L	366
		G. Makgill	C	258
1847	768	E. Ellice	L	Unopp.
1852	680	E. Ellice	L	Unopp.
1857	714	E. Ellice	L	357
		F.B. Douglas	L	202
1859	742	E. Ellice	L	Unopp.
1865	839	E. Ellice	L	Unopp.
1868	1,847	E. Ellice	L	Unopp.
1874	2,108	E. Ellice	L	Unopp.
1880	2,542	S. Williamson	L	1,258
		J.L. Bennet	L	892

STIRLING DISTRICT of BURGHS [337]
(Stirling, Culross, Dunfermline, Inverkeithing, Queensferry South)

Election	Electors	Candidate	Party	Votes
1832	956	Lord Dalmeny	L	492
		†J. Johnston	L	366
1835	1,060	Lord Dalmeny	L	418
		J. Crawfurd	L	345
[Appointed a Civil Lord of the Admiralty]				
1835 (5/5)		Lord Dalmeny	L	Unopp.
1837	1,241	Lord Dalmeny	L	455
		T.P. Thompson	L	2
1841	1,141*	Lord Dalmeny	L	438
		J. Aytoun	L	420
1847	1,125	J.B. Smith	L	345
		A.C.R.G. Maitland	L	312
		A. Alison	L	156
1852	1,097	Sir J. Anderson	L	431
		J. Miller	L	411
1857	1,149	Sir J. Anderson	L	Unopp.
1859	1,224	J. Caird	L	Unopp.
1865	1,262	L. Oliphant	L	Unopp.
[Resignation]				
1868 (30/4)	1,257*	J. Ramsay	L	565
		H. Campbell	L	494
1868	4,372	H. Campbell *(Bannerman)*	L	2,201
		J. Ramsay	L	1,682
1874	4,779	H.C. Bannerman	L	Unopp.
1880	4,807	H.C. Bannerman	L	2,906
		Sir J.R.G. Maitland, Bt.	C	132
[Appointed Chief Secretary to the Lord Lieutenant of Ireland]				
1884 (31/10)		H.C. Bannerman	L	Unopp.

WICK DISTRICT of BURGHS [338]
(Wick, Cromarty, Dingwall, Dornoch, Kirkwall, Tain)

Election	Electors	Candidate	Party	Votes
1832	366	†J. Loch	L	Unopp.
1835	571	J. Loch	L	Unopp.
1837	680	J. Loch	L	Unopp.
1841	742*	J. Loch	L	270
		G. Dempster	C	189
1847	690	J. Loch	L	Unopp.
1852	699	S. Laing	L	233
		J. Loch	L	202
1857	635	Lord John Hay	L	318
		A.M. Shaw	L	213
1859	657	S. Laing	L	Unopp.
[Resignation on appointment as a Member of the Council of India]				
1860 (1/12)		Viscount Bury	L	Unopp.
1865	793	S. Laing	L	Unopp.
1868	1,673	G. Loch	L	851
		S. Laing	L	635
[Resignation]				
1872 (28/2)	1,439	J. Pender	L	704
		R. Reid	L	498
1874	1,793	J. Pender	L	857
		J. Bryce	L	730
1880	1,754	J. Pender	L	Unopp.

Petition:—

1868: Withdrawn

WIGTOWN DISTRICT of BURGHS [339]

(Wigtown, New Galloway, Stranraer, Whithorn)

Election	Electors	Candidate	Party	Votes
1832	316	†E. Stewart	L	159
		J. McTaggart	L	137
1835	362	J. McTaggart	L	224
		J. Douglas	L	82
1837	380	J. McTaggart	L	151
		Sir A. Agnew, Bt.	L	116
1841	393*	J. McTaggart	L	157
		P.V. Agnew	C	129
1847	382	Sir J. McTaggart, Bt.	L	Unopp.
1852	400	Sir J. McTaggart, Bt.	L	140
		J. Caird	C	139
1857	694	Sir W. Dunbar, Bt.	L	Unopp.
1859	505	Sir W. Dunbar, Bt.	L	Unopp.
[Appointed a Lord Commissioner of the Treasury]				
1859 (27/6)		Sir W. Dunbar, Bt.	L	Unopp.
[Resignation on appointment as a Commissioner for Auditing the Public Accounts]				
1865 (15/4)		G. Young	L	Unopp.
1865	518	G. Young	L	Unopp.
1868	966	G. Young	L	484
		R.V. Agnew	C	364
[Appointed Solicitor-General for Scotland]				
1869 (4/1)		G. Young	L	Unopp.
1874	1,176	**M.J. Stewart	C	522
		*G. Young	L	520
[Resignation on appointment as a Senator of the College of Justice — Lord Young]				
1874 (15/6)	1,176	M.J. Stewart	C	525
		A. Smith	L	517

Election	Electors	Candidate	Party	Votes
1880	1,391	J. McLaren	L	650
		M.J. Stewart	C	638
[Appointed Lord Advocate]				
1880 (20/5)	1,391	M.J. Stewart	C	656
		J. McLaren	L	633
[Election declared void on petition]				
1880 (2/8)	1,391	Sir J.C.D. Hay, Bt.	C	636
		G. McMicking	L	620

Petitions:—

1852: Dismissed

1874: Election of Stewart declared void. Young duly elected after scrutiny. Scrutiny resulted: Young 515; Stewart 514. By the time the petition had been heard, Young had been appointed a Judge, thus vacating the seat.

1874: (15/6) Dismissed

1880: (20/5) Void election

SCOTLAND ––– COUNTIES

ABERDEENSHIRE [340]

Election	Electors	Candidate	Party	Votes
1832	2,271	†Hon. W. Gordon	C	1,183
		Sir M. Bruce, Bt.	L	1,002
1835	2,657	Hon. W. Gordon	C	Unopp.
1837	2,996	Hon. W. Gordon	C	1,220
		Sir T. Burnett, Bt.	L	807
1841	3,181*	Hon. W. Gordon	C	Unopp.
[Appointed a Lord Commissioner of the Admiralty]				
1841 (21/9)		Hon. W. Gordon	C	Unopp.
1847	3,694	Hon. W. Gordon	C	Unopp.
1852	4,022	Hon. W. Gordon	C	Unopp.
[Resignation]				
1854 (22/8)		Lord Haddo	L	Unopp.
1857	4,682	Lord Haddo	L	Unopp.
1859	4,952	Lord Haddo	L	Unopp.
[Succession to the Peerage — Earl of Aberdeen]				
1861 (13/2)	4,928*	W. Leslie	C	851
		Hon. A.H. Gordon	L	665
1865	4,384	W. Leslie	C	Unopp.
[Resignation]				
1866 (15/5)	4,447	W.D. Fordyce	L	2,175
		Sir J.D.H. Elphinstone, Bt.	C	1,088

This constituency was divided in 1868.

ABERDEENSHIRE, EASTERN [341]

Election	Electors	Candidate	Party	Votes
1868	4,297	W.D. Fordyce	L	Unopp.
1874	4,371	W.D. Fordyce	L	Unopp.
[Death]				
1875	4,499	Hon. Sir A.H. Gordon	C	1,903
(24/12)		G. Hope	L	1,558
1880	4,788	Hon. Sir A.H. Gordon	L	Unopp.

ABERDEENSHIRE, WESTERN [342]

Election	Electors	Candidate	Party	Votes
1868	4,081	W. McCombie	L	Unopp.
1874	3,954	W. McCombie	L	2,401
		E. Ross	C	326
[Resignation]				
1876 (12/5)	3,899	Lord Douglas Gordon	L	2,343
		T. Innes	C	813
1880	4,155	R. Farquharson	L	2,390
		Sir W. Forbes, Bt.	C	1,042

ARGYLL [343]

Election	Electors	Candidate	Party	Votes
1832	995	J.H. Callander	L	Unopp
1835	1,084	W.F. Campbell	L	Unopp
1837	1,666	W.F. Campbell	L	712
		A. Campbell	C	462
1841	1,600*	A. Campbell	C	Unopp
[Resignation]				
1843 (8/9)		D. McNeill	C	Unopp
1847	1,889	D. McNeill	C	Unopp
[Resignation on appointment as a Senator of the College of Justice — Lord Colonsay]				
1851 (6/6)		Sir A.I. Campbell, Bt.	C	Unopp
1852	2,156	Sir A.I. Campbell, Bt.	C	Unopp
1857	2,256	A.S. Finlay	L	Unopp
1859	2,294	A.S. Finlay	L	Unopp
1865	1,914	A.S. Finlay	L	Unopp
[Resignation]				
1868 (3/3)		Marquess of Lorne	L	Unopp
1868	2,870	Marquess of Lorne	L	Unopp
1874	3,018	Marquess of Lorne	L	Unopp
[Resignation on appointment as Governor-General of Canada]				
1878 (31/8)	3,133	Lord Colin Campbell	L	1,462
		J.W. Malcolm	C	1,107
1880	3,299	Lord Colin Campbell	L	1,457
		J.W. Malcolm	C	1,191

AYRSHIRE [344]

Election	Electors	Candidate	Party	Votes
1832	3,150	R.A. Oswald	L	2,152
		†W. Blair	C	324
1835	3,171	R.A. Oswald	L	Unopp.
[Resignation]				
1835 (3/7)	3,171	J. Dunlop	L	1,435
		Sir J.A. Cathcart, Bt.	C	829
1837	3,985	J. Dunlop	L	1,559
		Viscount Kelburne	C	1,370
[Death]				
1839 (1/5)	4,242	Viscount Kelburne	C	1,758
		J. Campbell	L	1,296
		H. Craig	Ch	46
1841	4,274*	Viscount Kelburne	C	Unopp.
[Succession to the Peerage — Earl of Glasgow]				
1843 (3/8)		A.H. Oswald	C	Unopp.
1847	4,305	A.H. Oswald	C	Unopp.
1852	3,823	J.H. Blair	C	1,301
		E. Cardwell	L	1,200
[Death]				
1854 (30/12)	3,823*	Sir J. Fergusson, Bt.	C	1,510
		A.H. Oswald	L	1,381
1857	3,976	Lord James Stuart	L	1,663
		Sir J. Fergusson, Bt.	C	1,458
1859	3,939	Lord James Stuart	L	Unopp.
[Death]				
1859 (31/10)	4,072	Sir J. Fergusson, Bt.	C	1,687
		J. Campbell	L	1,641
1865	4,642	Sir J. Fergusson, Bt.	C	Unopp.

This constituency was divided in 1868.

AYRSHIRE, NORTHERN [345]

Election	Electors	Candidate	Party	Votes
1868	3,219	W. Finnie	L	1,397
		R. Montgomerie	C	1,322
1874	3,407	R. Montgomerie	C	1,562
		W. Finnie	L	1,301
1880	3,642	R.W.C. Patrick	C	1,636
		J.B. Balfour	L	1,581

AYRSHIRE, SOUTHERN [346]

Election	Electors	Candidate	Party	Votes
1868	3,370	Sir D. Wedderburn, Bt.	L	1,416
		C. Alexander	C	1,391
1874	3,547	C. Alexander	C	Unopp.
1880	3,865	C. Alexander	C	1,830
		Hon. N. de C. Dalrymple	L	1,583

BANFFSHIRE [347]

Election	Electors	Candidate	Party	Votes
1832	498	G. Ferguson	C	295
		T. Gordon	L	128
1835	525	G. Ferguson	C	Unopp.
1837	685	J. Duff	L	292
		G. Ferguson	C	214
1841	717*	J. Duff	L	316
		Viscount Reidhaven	C	273
1847	833	J. Duff	L	Unopp.
1852	813	J. Duff *(Earl of Fife)*	L	327
		H.M. Grant	C	301
1857	927	Earl of Fife	L	Unopp.
[Resignation]				
1857 (30/6)		L.D. Gordon *(Duff)*	L	Unopp.
1859	905	L.D.G. Duff	L	Unopp.
[Resignation]				
1861 (1/5)		R.W.D. Abercromby *(Duff)*	L	Unopp.
1865	1,062	R.W. Duff	L	Unopp.
1868	2,291	R.W. Duff	L	Unopp.
1874	2,418	R.W. Duff	L	Unopp.
1880	2,649	R.W. Duff	L	Unopp.
[Appointed a Lord Commissioner of the Treasury]				
1882 (19/6)		R.W. Duff	L	Unopp.

BERWICKSHIRE [348]

Election	Electors	Candidate	Party	Votes
1832	1,053	C. Marjoribanks	L	478
		†Hon. A. Maitland	C	410
[Death]				
1834 (13/1)		Sir H.P.H. Campbell, Bt.	C	Unopp.
1835	1,071	Sir H.P.H. Campbell, Bt.	C	507
		Sir F. Blake, Bt.	L	324
1837	1,244	Sir H.P.H. Campbell, Bt.	C	Unopp.
1841	1,319*	Sir H.P.H. Campbell, Bt.	C	Unopp.
1847	1,238	Hon. F. Scott	C	Unopp.
1852	1,073	Hon. F. Scott	C	Unopp.
1857	1,102	Hon. F. Scott	C	394
		D. Robertson	L	305
1859	1,201	D. Robertson	L	461
		Sir J. Marjoribanks	C	428
1865	1,247	D. Robertson	L	Unopp.
1868	1,580	D. Robertson	L	Unopp.
[Elevation to the Peerage – Lord Marjoribanks]				
1873 (30/6)	1,595	W. Miller	L	623
		Lord Dunglass	C	609
1874	1,652	Hon. R.B. Hamilton	C	748
		W. Miller	L	674
1880	1,830	E. Marjoribanks	L	939
		Hon. R.B. Hamilton	C	671

BUTE [349]

Election	Electors	Candidate	Party	Votes
1832	279	C. Stuart	C	Unopp.
[Resignation]				
1833 (4/9)		Sir W. Rae, Bt.	C	Unopp.
1835	310	Sir W. Rae, Bt.	C	Unopp.
1837	345	Sir W. Rae, Bt.	C	Unopp.
1841	380*	Sir W. Rae, Bt.	C	134
		H. Dunlop	L	72
[Appointed Lord Advocate]				
1841 (23/9)		Sir W. Rae, Bt.	C	Unopp.
[Death]				
1842 (1/12)		Hon. J.A.S. Wortley	C	Unopp.
[Appointed Judge-Advocate General]				
1846 (7/2)		Hon. J.A.S. Wortley	C	Unopp.
1847	410	Hon. J.A.S. Wortley	C	Unopp.
1852	491	Hon. J.A.S. Wortley	C	Unopp.
[Appointed Solicitor-General]				
1857 (12/2)		Hon. J.A.S. Wortley	L	Unopp.
1857	489	Hon. J.A.S. Wortley	L	Unopp.
1859	479	D. Mure	C	138
		J. Lamont	L	129
[Resignation on appointment as a Senator of the College of Justice — Lord Mure]				
1865 (16/2)	513	Hon. G.F. Boyle	C	205
		J. Lamont	L	190
1865	513	J. Lamont	L	203
		Hon. G.F. Boyle	C	192
1868	1,073	C. Dalrymple	C	527
		J.W. Burns	L	362

Election	Electors	Candidate	Party	Votes
1874	1,113	C. Dalrymple	C	Unopp.
1880	1,311	T. Russell	L	568
		C. Dalrymple	C	551

[Disqualification of Russell who at the time of his election held a Government contract]

1880 (6/7)	1,311	C. Dalrymple	C	585
		T. Russell	L	540

[Appointed a Lord Commissioner of the Treasury]

1885 (3/7)		C. Dalrymple	C	Unopp.

Petition:—

1880: Withdrawn

CAITHNESS [350]

Election	Electors	Candidate	Party	Votes
1832	221	†G. Sinclair	L	Unopp.
1835	246	G. Sinclair	L	Unopp.
1837	333	Sir G. Sinclair, Bt.	C	129
		G. Traill	L	106
1841	420*	G. Traill	L	Unopp.
1847	571	G. Traill	L	Unopp.
1852	642	G. Traill	L	147
		J.G.T. Sinclair	L	106
1857	779	G. Traill	L	Unopp.
1859	789	G. Traill	L	Unopp.
1865	512	G. Traill	L	Unopp.
1868	1,005	G. Traill	L	512
		J. Horne	C	237
[Resignation]				
1869 (26/8)	1,005	Sir J.G.T. Sinclair, Bt.	L	432
		J.C. Traill	L	360
1874	1,126	Sir J.G.T. Sinclair, Bt.	L	452
		W. Kidston	C	439
1880	1,263	Sir J.G.T. Sinclair, Bt.	L	696
		A. Henerson	C	369

CLACKMANNANSHIRE and KINROSS-SHIRE [351]

Election	Electors	Candidate	Party	Votes
1832	879	†C. Adam	L	527
		R. Bruce	C	196
1835	990	C. Adam	L	447
		R. Bruce	C	285
[Appointed a Lord Commissioner of the Admiralty]				
1835 (4/5)		C. Adam	L	Unopp.
1837	1,181	Sir C. Adam	L	Unopp.
1841	1,272*	Hon. G.R. Abercromby	L	Unopp.
[Resignation]				
1842 (18/2)		W. Morison	L	Unopp.
1847	1,373	W. Morison	L	Unopp.
[Death]				
1851 (9/6)	1,385	J. Johnstone	L	328
		W.P. Adam	L	263
1852	1,658	J. Johnstone	L	Unopp.
1857	1,836	Viscount Melgund	L	Unopp.
1859	1,932	W.P. Adam	L	Unopp.
[Appointed a Lord Commissioner of the Treasury]				
1865 (20/4)		W.P. Adam	L	Unopp.
1865	1,162	W.P. Adam	L	Unopp.
1868	1,802	W.P. Adam	L	Unopp.
[Appointed a Lord Commissioner of the Treasury]				
1869 (6/1)		W.P. Adam	L	Unopp.
1874	1,896	W.P. Adam	L	943
		J.R. Haig	C	468

Election	Electors	Candidate	Party	Votes
1880	2,084	W.P. Adam	L	1,150
		J.R. Haig	C	458

[Appointed First Commissioner of Works and Public Buildings]

1880 (14/5)		W.P. Adam	L	Unopp.

[Resignation on appointment as Governor of Madras]

1880 (1/12)		J.B. Balfour	L	Unopp.

DUMFRIESSHIRE [352]

Election	Electors	Candidate	Party	Votes
1832	1,123	†J.J.H. Johnstone (Senr.)	C	Unopp.
1835	1,374	J.J.H. Johnstone (Senr.)	C	Unopp.
1837	1,461	J.J.H. Johnstone (Senr.)	C	Unopp.
1841	1,912*	J.J.H. Johnstone (Senr.)	C	Unopp.
1847	2,485	Viscount Drumlanrig	C	Unopp.
1852	2,520	Viscount Drumlanrig	C	Unopp.
[Appointed Comptroller of H.M. Household]				
1853 (12/1)		Viscount Drumlanrig	C	Unopp.
[Succession to the Peerage — Marquess of Queensberry]				
1857 (12/2)		J.J.H. Johnstone (Senr.)	C	Unopp.
1857	2,702	J.J.H. Johnstone (Senr.)	C	Unopp.
1859	3,192	J.J.H. Johnstone (Senr.)	C	Unopp.
1865	2,097	G.G. Walker	C	Unopp.
1868	2,989	Sir S.H. Waterlow	L	1,100
		G.G. Walker	C	1,056
[Disqualification of Waterlow who at the time of his election held a Government contract]				
1869 (31/3)	2,989	G.G. Walker	C	1,117
		Sir S.H. Waterlow	L	1,081
1874	3,130	J.J.H. Johnstone (Junr.)	C	1,453
		R. Jardine	L	1,315
1880	3,379	R. Jardine	L	1,577
		G.G. Walker	C	1,505

Petition:—

1868: Withdrawn

DUNBARTONSHIRE [353]

Election	Electors	Candidate	Party	Votes
1832	927	J.C. Colquhoun	L	422
		Sir J. Colquhoun, Bt.	L	375
1835	999	A. Dennistoun	L	436
		A. Smollett	C	399
1837	1,139	Sir J. Colquhoun, Bt.	L	452
		A. Smollett	C	411
1841	1,212*	A. Smollett	C	Unopp.
1847	1,288	A. Smollett	C	536
		T.C. Robertson	L	294
1852	1,314	A. Smollett	C	Unopp.
1857	1,348	A. Smollett	C	Unopp.
1859	1,379	P.B. Smollett	C	490
		W.C. Bontine	L	399
1865	1,597	*P.B. Smollett	C	574
		**J. Stirling	L	574
1868	2,156	A.O. Ewing	C	Unopp.
1874	2,265	A.O. Ewing	C	995
		J.W. Burns	L	942
1880	2,976	A.O. Ewing	C	1,333
		J.W. Burns	L	1,324

Petitions:—

1865: Double return. A petition was lodged against Stirling but was withdrawn after he decided not to defend his claim to the seat and allow Smollett to be declared duly elected.

1880: Withdrawn

EDINBURGHSHIRE [354]

Election	Electors	Candidate	Party	Votes
1832	1,298	Sir J.H. Dalrymple, Bt.	L	601
		†Sir G. Clerk, Bt.	C	536
1835	1,376	Sir G. Clerk, Bt.	C	565
		W.G. Craig	L	534
1837	1,682	W.G. Craig	L	703
		Sir G. Clerk, Bt.	C	661
1841	2,315*	W.R. Ramsay	C	Unopp.
[Resignation]				
1845 (25/6)		Sir J. Hope, Bt.	C	Unopp.
1847	2,185	Sir J. Hope, Bt.	C	Unopp.
1852	2,017	Sir J. Hope, Bt.	C	Unopp.
[Death]				
1853 (25/6)		Earl of Dalkeith	C	Unopp.
1857	1,960	Earl of Dalkeith	C	Unopp.
1859	1,974	Earl of Dalkeith	C	Unopp.
1865	1,656	Earl of Dalkeith	C	Unopp.
1868	2,489	Sir A.C.R.G. Maitland, Bt.	L	1,146
		Earl of Dalkeith	C	905
1874	2,672	Earl of Dalkeith	C	1,194
		Lord William Hay	L	1,059
1880	3,260	W.E. Gladstone	L	1,579
		Earl of Dalkeith	C	1,368
[Appointed Prime Minister, First Lord of the Treasury and Chancellor of the Exchequer]				
1880 (10/5)		W.E. Gladstone	L	Unopp.

ELGINSHIRE and NAIRNSHIRE [355]

Election	Electors	Candidate	Party	Votes
1832	642	†Hon. F.W. Grant	C	Unopp.
1835	690	Hon. F.W. Grant	C	Unopp.
1837	727	Hon. F.W. Grant	C	Unopp.
[Resignation]				
1840 (25/4)		C.L.C. Bruce	C	Unopp.
1841	750*	C.L.C. Bruce	C	372
		Sir A. Duff	L	173
1847	718	C.L.C. Bruce	C	Unopp.
1852	683	C.L.C. Bruce	C	Unopp.
1857	870	C.L.C. Bruce	C	Unopp.
1859	946	C.L.C. Bruce	C	Unopp.
1865	863	C.L.C. Bruce	C	Unopp.
1868	1,580	Hon. J.O. Grant	C	Unopp.
1874	1,693	Viscount Macduff	L	829
		Hon. J.O. Grant	C	619
[Succession to the Peerage — Earl of Fife]				
1879 (18/9)	1,884	Sir G.M. Grant, Bt.	L	959
		H.F.A. Brodie	C	701
1880	1,891	Sir G.M. Grant, Bt.	L	Unopp.

FIFE [356]

Election	Electors	Candidate	Party	Votes
1832	2,185	J.E. Wemyss	L	Unopp.
1835	2,309	J.E. Wemyss	L	1,051
		J. Lindsay	C	584
1837	2,720	J.E. Wemyss	L	1,086
		Hon. J. Bruce	C	567
1841	2,967*	J.E. Wemyss	L	Unopp.
1847	2,444	J. Fergus	L	834
		J. Balfour	C	768
1852	3,211	J. Fergus	L	Unopp.
1857	3,389	J. Fergus	L	Unopp.
1859	4,056	J.H.E. Wemyss	L	1,087
		Lord Loughborough	C	850
[Death] 1864 (19/4)		Sir R. Anstruther, Bt.	L	Unopp.
1865	2,725	Sir R. Anstruther, Bt.	L	Unopp.
1868	4,206	Sir R. Anstruther, Bt.	L	1,837
		J.B. Kinnear	L	1,127
1874	4,358	Sir R. Anstruther, Bt.	L	1,859
		Sir F.W. Hamilton	C	1,230
1880	4,767	Hon. R.P. Bruce	L	2,421
		J.T. Oswald	C	1,373

FORFARSHIRE [357]

Election	Electors	Candidate	Party	Votes
1832	1,241	†Hon. D.G. Hallyburton	L	Unopp.
1835	1,421	Hon. D.G. Hallyburton *(Lord Douglas Hallyburton)*	L	625
		Hon. J.S. Wortley	C	446
1837	1,790	Lord Douglas Hallyburton	L	Unopp.
1841	1,979	Lord John Gordon *(Gordon-Hallyburton)*	L	Unopp.
1847	2,540	Lord John Gordon-Hallyburton	L	Unopp.
1852	2,873	Hon. L. Maule	L	Unopp.
[Appointed Surveyor-General of the Ordnance]				
1853 (25/2)		Hon. L. Maule	L	Unopp.
[Death]				
1854 (11/10)		Viscount Duncan	L	Unopp.
[Appointed a Lord Commissioner of the Treasury]				
1855 (10/3)		Viscount Duncan	L	Unopp.
1857	3,288	Viscount Duncan	L	Unopp.
1859	3,421	Viscount Duncan	L	Unopp.
[Succession to the Peerage — Earl of Camperdown]				
1860 (1/2)		Hon. C. Carnegie	L	Unopp.
1865	2,108	Hon. C. Carnegie	L	Unopp.
1868	3,379	Hon. C. Carnegie	L	Unopp.
[Resignation on appointment as Inspector of Constabulary for Scotland]				
1872 (16/12)	3,603	J.W. Barclay	L	1,481
		Sir J.H. Ramsay, Bt.	C	1,128
1874	3,619	J.W. Barclay	L	Unopp.
1880	3,634	J.W. Barclay	L	Unopp.

HADDINGTONSHIRE [358]

Election	Electors	Candidate	Party	Votes
1832	617	†J. Balfour	C	271
		Sir D. Baird, Bt.	L	232
1835	649	R. Ferguson	L	268
		J.T. Hope	C	231
1837	718	Lord Ramsay	C	299
		R. Ferguson	L	208
[Succession to the Peerage – Earl of Dalhousie]				
1838 (14/4)		Sir T.B. Hepburn, Bt.	C	Unopp.
1841	740*	Sir T.B. Hepburn, Bt.	C	Unopp.
1847	694	Hon. F.W. Charteris	C	271
		Sir D. Baird, Bt.	L	136
1852	716	Hon. F.W. Charteris	C	Unopp.
[Appointed a Lord Commissioner of the Treasury]				
1853 (11/1)		Hon. F.W. Charteris *(Lord Elcho)*	C	Unopp.
1857	715	Lord Elcho	C	Unopp.
1859	680	Lord Elcho	C	Unopp.
1865	666	Lord Elcho	C	285
		G. Hope	L	159
1868	895	Lord Elcho	C	405
		Lord William Hay	L	340
1874	924	Lord Elcho	C	Unopp.
1880	1,040	Lord Elcho	C	469
		T.R. Buchanan	L	425
[Succession to the Peerage – Earl of Wemyss and March]				
1883 (7/2)	1,071	Lord Elcho	C	492
		R.B. Finlay	L	400

Election	Electors	Candidate	Party	Votes
1832	669	†C. Grant	L	257
		J.N. McLeod	C	210
1835	717	C. Grant	L	260
		J.N. McLeod	C	253
[Appointed Secretary of State for War and the Colonies and elevation to the Peerage — Lord Glenelg]				
1835 (15/5)	717	A.W. Chisholm	C	268
		J.M. Grant	L	240
1837	753	A.W. Chisholm	C	303
		J.M. Grant	L	249
[Resignation]				
1838 (12/6)		F.W. Grant	C	Unopp.
[Death]				
1840 (31/3)		H.J. Baillie	C	Unopp.
1841	789*	H.J. Baillie	C	Unopp.
1847	817	H.J. Baillie	C	Unopp.
1852	908	H.J. Baillie	C	Unopp.
1857	827	H.J. Baillie	C	Unopp.
1859	884	H.J. Baillie	C	Unopp.
1865	878	H.J. Baillie	C	336
		Sir G.M. Grant, Bt.	L	297
1868	1,661	D. Cameron	C	Unopp.
1874	1,724	D. Cameron	C	Unopp.
[Appointed a Groom in Waiting to Her Majesty]				
1874 (19/3)		D. Cameron	C	Unopp.
1880	1,851	D. Cameron	C	808
		Sir K.S. Mackenzie, Bt.	L	779

Petitions:— 1835: Lapsed on death of petitioner 1835: (15/5) Dismissed

KINCARDINESHIRE [360]

Election	Electors	Candidate	Party	Votes
1832	763	†Hon. H. Arbuthnott	C	388
		T. Burnett	L	269
1835	844	Hon. H. Arbuthnott	C	Unopp.
1837	906	Hon. H. Arbuthnott	C	Unopp.
1841	914*	Hon. H. Arbuthnott	C	Unopp.
1847	808	Hon. H. Arbuthnott	C	Unopp.
1852	951	Hon. H. Arbuthnott	C	Unopp.
1857	997	Hon. H. Arbuthnott	C	Unopp.
1859	1,021	Hon. H. Arbuthnott	C	Unopp.
1865	987	J.D. Nicol	L	490
		Sir T. Gladstone, Bt.	C	288
1868	1,731	J.D. Nicol	L	Unopp.
[Death]				
1872 (10/12)		Sir G. Balfour	L	Unopp.
1874	1,767	Sir G. Balfour	L	941
		J.B. Nicolson	C	533
1880	1,838	Sir G. Balfour	L	1,037
		D. Sinclair	C	500

KIRKCUDBRIGHTSHIRE [361]

Election	Electors	Candidate	Party	Votes
1832	1,059	†R.C. Fergusson	L	Unopp.
[Appointed Judge-Advocate General]				
1834 (3/7)		R.C. Fergusson	L	Unopp.
1835	1,079	R.C. Fergusson	L	Unopp.
[Appointed Judge-Advocate General]				
1835 (2/5)		R.C. Fergusson	L	Unopp.
1837	1,119	R.C. Fergusson	L	Unopp.
[Death]				
1838 (31/12)		A. Murray	L	Unopp.
1841	1,332*	A. Murray	L	672
		W. Maxwell	C	249
[Death]				
1845 (20/8)	1,349*	T. Maitland	L	486
		J. McDouall	C	344
[Appointed Solicitor-General]				
1846 (17/7)		T. Maitland	L	Unopp.
1847	1,351	T. Maitland	L	Unopp.
[Resignation on appointment as a Senator of the College of Justice — Lord Dundrennan]				
1850 (20/2)		J. Mackie (Senr.)	L	Unopp.
1852	1,326	J. Mackie (Senr.)	L	Unopp.
1857	1,312	J. Mackie (Junr.)	L	365
		G. Maxwell	L	332
1859	1,573	J. Mackie (Junr.)	L	Unopp.
1865	1,353	J. Mackie (Junr.)	L	Unopp.

Election	Electors	Candidate	Party	Votes
[Death]				
1868 (30/1)		W.H. Maxwell	L	Unopp.
1868	1,940	W.H. Maxwell	L	932
		R. Hannay	L	703
1874	1,996	J. Maitland	L	835
		H.G.M. Stewart	C	831
1880	2,204	J.M.H. Maxwell	L	982
		H.G.M. Stewart	C	961

LANARKSHIRE [362]

Election	Electors	Candidate	Party	Votes
1832	2,705	J. Maxwell	L	1,555
		R.G. Buchanan	C	615
		A.G. Hamilton	L	30
1835	3,030	J. Maxwell	L	1,251
		A.M. Lockhart	C	1,117
1837	3,654	A.M. Lockhart	C	1,486
		Hon. C.A. Murray	L	1,485
1841	3,964*	W. Lockhart	C	Unopp.
1847	3,687	W. Lockhart	C	Unopp.
1852	3,471	W. Lockhart	C	Unopp.
[Death]				
1857 (5/1)		A.D.R.W.B. Cochrane	C	Unopp.
1857	3,124	Sir T.E. Colebrooke, Bt.	L	1,233
		A.D.R.W.B. Cochrane	C	1,197
1859	3,826	Sir T.E. Colebrooke, Bt.	L	Unopp.
1865	5,183	Sir T.E. Colebrooke, Bt.	L	Unopp.

This constituency was divided in 1868.

Petitions: —

1837: Withdrawn

1857: Withdrawn

LANARKSHIRE, NORTHERN [363]

Election	Electors	Candidate	Party	Votes
1868	5,458	Sir T.E. Colebrooke, Bt.	L	Unopp.
1874	7,217	Sir T.E. Colebrooke, Bt.	L	Unopp.
1880	10,324	Sir T.E. Colebrooke, Bt.	L	Unopp.

LANARKSHIRE, SOUTHERN [364]

Election	Electors	Candidate	Party	Votes
1868	2,871	J.G.C. Hamilton	L	1,328
		Sir N.M. Lockhart, Bt.	C	1,107
1874	3,214	Sir W.C.J.C. Anstruther, Bt.	C	1,347
		J.G.C. Hamilton	L	1,326
1880	3,666	J.G.C. Hamilton	L	1,808
		Sir W.C.J.C. Anstruther, Bt.	C	1,430

LINLITHGOWSHIRE [365]

Election	Electors	Candidate	Party	Votes
1832	600	†Hon. Sir A. Hope	C	267
		†J.J.H. Vere	L	253
1835	692	Hon. J. Hope	C	Unopp.
1837	725	Hon. J. Hope	C	329
		Hon. R.F. Greville	L	191
[Resignation]				
1838 (14/6)	734	Hon. C. Hope	C	330
		J. Johnston	L	210
1841	686	Hon. C. Hope	C	Unopp.
[Appointed a Commissioner of Greenwich Hospital]				
1841 (20/10)		Hon. C. Hope	C	Unopp.
[Resignation on appointment as Governor of the Isle of Man]				
1845 (22/8)		W. Baillie	C	Unopp.
1847	596	G. Dundas	C	Unopp.
1852	502	G. Dundas	C	Unopp.
1857	427	G. Dundas	C	Unopp.
[Resignation on appointment as Lieutenant-Governor of Prince Edward Island]				
1859 (5/2)		C. Baillie	C	Unopp.
1859	425	W.F. Hamilton	L	Unopp.
1865	813	P. McLagan	L	Unopp.
1868	1,226	P. McLagan	L	600
		J. Pender	L	385
1874	1,198	P. McLagan	L	Unopp.
1880	1,232	P. McLagan	L	747
		J.P.B. Robertson	C	256

Petition:—

1832: Dismissed

ORKNEY and SHETLAND [366]

Election	Electors	Candidate	Party	Votes
1832	272	†G. Traill	L	107
		S. Laing (Senr.)	C	96
		R. Hunter	L	9
1835	298	T. Balfour	C	114
		G. Traill	L	84
1837	476	F. Dundas	L	Unopp.
1841	526*	F. Dundas	L	Unopp.
1847	599	A. Anderson	L	209
		F. Dundas	L	183
1852	651	F. Dundas	L	227
		J. Inglis	C	194
1857	615	F. Dundas	L	Unopp.
1859	621	F. Dundas	L	Unopp.
1865	685	F. Dundas	L	Unopp.
1868	1,486	F. Dundas	L	715
		H.B. Riddell	C	446
[Death]				
1873 (11/1)	1,537	S. Laing (Junr.)	L	646
		Sir P. Tait	L	621
1874	1,618	S. Laing (Junr.)	L	Unopp.
1880	1,704	S. Laing (Junr.)	L	896
		G.R. Badenoch	C	578

PEEBLESSHIRE [367]

Election	Electors	Candidate	Party	Votes
1832	307	†Sir J. Hay, Bt.	C	Unopp.
1835	354	Sir J. Hay, Bt.	C	Unopp.
1837	690	W.F. Mackenzie	C	251
		A.G. Carmichael	L	245
1841	863*	W.F. Mackenzie	C	Unopp.
[Appointed a Lord Commissioner of the Treasury]				
1845 (5/5)		W.F. Mackenzie	C	Unopp.
1847	718	W.F. Mackenzie	C	240
		A.G. Carmichael	L	163
1852	542	Sir G.G. Montgomery, Bt.	C	Unopp.
1857	394	Sir G.G. Montgomery, Bt.	C	Unopp.
1859	407	Sir G.G. Montgomery, Bt.	C	Unopp.
1865	499	Sir G.G. Montgomery, Bt.	C	Unopp.
[Appointed a Lord Commissioner of the Treasury]				
1866 (24/7)		Sir G.G. Montgomery, Bt.	C	Unopp.

This constituency was combined with Selkirkshire in 1868.

Petition:—

1847: Dismissed

PEEBLESSHIRE and SELKIRKSHIRE [368]

Election	Electors	Candidate	Party	Votes
1868	889	Sir G.G. Montgomery, Bt.	C	361
		Sir J. Murray, Bt.	L	358
1874	1,026	Sir G.G. Montgomery, Bt.	C	Unopp.
1880	1,136	C. Tennant	L	516
		Sir G.G. Montgomery, Bt.	C	484

Election	Electors	Candidate	Party	Votes
1832	3,180	Earl of Ormelie	L	1,666
		†Sir G. Murray	C	1,093
[Succession to the Peerage — Marquess of Breadalbane]				
1834 (5/5)	3,425	Sir G. Murray	C	1,464
		R. Graham	L	1,268
1835	3,689	Hon. F. Maule	L	1,453
		Sir G. Murray	C	1,371
1837	4,452	Viscount Stormont	C	1,495
		Hon. F. Maule	L	1,379
[Succession to the Peerage — Earl of Mansfield]				
1840 (9/3)	4,224	H.H. Drummond	C	1,586
		G.D. Stewart	L	1,128
1841	4,224*	H.H. Drummond	C	Unopp.
1847	4,187	H.H. Drummond	C	Unopp.
1852	4,938	W. Stirling	C	Unopp.
1857	3,415	W. Stirling	C	Unopp.
1859	3,368	W. Stirling	C	Unopp.
1865	3,448	W. Stirling *(Maxwell)*	C	Unopp.
1868	4,876	C.S. Parker	L	2,046
		Sir W.S. Maxwell, Bt.	C	1,767
1874	5,505	Sir W.S. Maxwell, Bt.	C	2,554
		C.S. Parker	L	2,060
[Death]				
1878 (4/2)	5,613	H.E.S.H.D. Moray	C	2,439
		Hon. A.W.F. Greville	L	2,255
1880	5,918	D. Currie	L	2,764
		H.E.S.H.D. Moray	C	2,472

RENFREWSHIRE [370]

Election	Electors	Candidate	Party	Votes
1832	1,347	†Sir M.S. Stewart, Bt.	L	700
		R.S. Bontine	L	412
1835	1,480	Sir M.S. Stewart, Bt.	L	528
		G. Houstoun	C	460
		W. Dixon	L	230
[Death]				
1837 (30/1)	1,979	G. Houstoun	C	811
		Sir J. Maxwell, Bt.	L	637
1837	1,979	G. Houstoun	C	821
		H. Stewart	L	704
1841	2,289*	P.M. Stewart	L	959
		W. Mure (Senr.)	C	945
[Death]				
1846 (9/12)		W. Mure (Senr.)	C	Unopp.
1847	2,306	W. Mure (Senr.)	C	Unopp.
1852	2,450	W. Mure (Senr.)	C	Unopp.
[Resignation]				
1855 (14/5)		Sir M.R.S. Stewart, Bt.	C	Unopp.
1857	2,649	Sir M.R.S. Stewart, Bt.	C	Unopp.
1859	2,877	Sir M.R.S. Stewart, Bt.	C	Unopp.
1865	2,276	A.A. Speirs	L	938
		Sir M.R.S. Stewart, Bt.	C	836
1868	3,571	A.A. Speirs	L	Unopp.
[Death]				
1869 (25/1)		H.A. Bruce	L	Unopp.
[Elevation to the Peerage — Lord Aberdare]				
1873 (13/9)	4,385	A.C. Campbell	C	1,855
		W. Mure (Junr.)	L	1,677

Election	Electors	Candidate	Party	Votes
1874	4,572	W. Mure (Junr.)	L	1,991
		A.C. Campbell	C	1,903
1880	6,038	W. Mure (Junr.)	L	2,815
		A.C. Campbell	C	2,341
[Death]				
1880 (30/11)		A. Crum	L	Unopp.

Petition:—

1874: Dismissed

ROSS and CROMARTY [371]

Election	Electors	Candidate	Party	Votes
1832	516	†J.A.S. Mackenzie	L	272
		H.A.J. Munro	C	148
1835	594	J.A.S. Mackenzie	L	241
		T. Mackenzie	C	200
[Resignation on appointment as Governor of Ceylon]				
1837 (18/4)	754	T. Mackenzie	C	307
		W. Mackenzie	L	196
1837	754	T. Mackenzie	C	Unopp.
1841	713*	T. Mackenzie	C	Unopp.
1847	827	J. Matheson	L	Unopp.
1852	832	Sir J. Matheson, Bt.	L	288
		G.W.H. Ross	C	218
1857	825	Sir J. Matheson, Bt.	L	Unopp.
1859	851	Sir J. Matheson, Bt.	L	Unopp.
1865	933	Sir J. Matheson, Bt.	L	Unopp.
1868	1,564	A. Matheson	L	Unopp.
1874	1,559	A. Matheson	L	Unopp.
1880	1,664	A. Matheson	L	Unopp.
[Resignation]				
1884 (22/8)	1,721	R.C.M. Ferguson	L	717
		A.R. Mackenzie	C	334
		R. Macdonald	Crf	248

ROXBURGHSHIRE [372]

Election	Electors	Candidate	Party	Votes
1832	1,321	Hon. G. Elliot	L	624
		Lord John Scott	C	532
		Sir W.F. Elliot	L	12
1835	1,674	Lord John Scott	C	757
		Hon. G. Elliot	L	681
1837	1,932	Hon. J.E. Elliot	L	803
		Hon. F. Scott	C	759
1841	2,277*	Hon. F. Scott	C	830
		Hon. J.E. Elliot	L	748
1847	2,091	Hon. J.E. Elliot	L	Unopp.
1852	2,033	Hon. J.E. Elliot	L	Unopp.
1857	1,650	Hon. J.E. Elliot	L	Unopp.
1859	1,663	Sir W. Scott, Bt.	L	Unopp.
1865	1,639	Sir W. Scott, Bt.	L	Unopp.
1868	1,664†	Sir W. Scott, Bt.	L	750
		Lord Schomberg Kerr	C	610
[Resignation]				
1870 (2/3)		Marquess of Bowmont	L	Unopp.
1874	1,813	Sir G.H.S. Douglas, Bt.	C	789
		Marquess of Bowmont	L	762
1880	1,978	Hon. A.R.D. Elliot	L	859
		Sir G.H.S. Douglas, Bt.	C	849

Petition:—

1837: Dismissed

SELKIRKSHIRE [373]

Election	Electors	Candidate	Party	Votes
1832	281	R. Pringle	L	133
		†A. Pringle	C	124
1835	423	A. Pringle	C	206
		R. Pringle	L	175
1837	561	A. Pringle	C	262
		R. Pringle	L	215
1841	612*	A. Pringle	C	Unopp.
[Appointed a Lord Commissioner of the Treasury]				
1841 (21/9)		A. Pringle	C	Unopp.
[Resignation on appointment as Clerk of Sasines]				
1846 (12/2)		A.E. Lockhart	C	223
		J.N. Murray	L	0
1847	622	A.E. Lockhart	C	Unopp.
1852	497	A.E. Lockhart	C	Unopp.
1857	362	A.E. Lockhart	C	Unopp.
1859	361	A.E. Lockhart	C	Unopp.
[Resignation]				
1861 (1/8)	361*	Lord Henry Scott	C	158
		Hon. W.J.G. Napier	L	136
1865	502	Lord Henry Scott	C	227
		Hon. W.J.G. Napier	L	196

This constituency was combined with Peeblesshire in 1868.

STIRLINGSHIRE [374]

Election	Electors	Candidate	Party	Votes
1832	1,787	Hon. C.E. Fleeming	L	995
		W. Forbes	C	465
1835	1,948	W. Forbes	C	779
		Hon. C.E. Fleeming	L	759
1837	2,105	**W. Forbes	C	859
		*Hon. G.R. Abercromby	L	858
1841	2,323*	W. Forbes	C	1,019
		Sir M. Bruce, Bt.	L	895
1847	2,398	W. Forbes	C	Unopp.
1852	2,431	W. Forbes	C	Unopp.
[Death]				
1855 (5/3)		P. Blackburn	C	Unopp.
1857	1,973	P. Blackburn	C	Unopp.
[Appointed a Lord Commissioner of the Treasury]				
1859 (14/3)		P. Blackburn	C	Unopp.
1859	1,900	P. Blackburn	C	Unopp.
1865	1,943	J.E. Erskine	L	726
		P. Blackburn	C	692
1868	2,751	J.E. Erskine	L	Unopp.
1874	2,837	Sir W. Edmondstone, Bt.	C	1,171
		Sir W.C.C. Bruce, Bt.	L	1,127
1880	3,328	J.C. Bolton	L	1,606
		Sir W. Edmondstone, Bt.	C	1,246

Petition:—

1837: Election of Forbes declared void. Abercromby duly elected after scrutiny

SUTHERLAND [375]

Election	Electors	Candidate	Party	Votes
1832	84	†R. Macleod	L	Unopp.
1835	108	R. Macleod	L	Unopp.
1837	128	Hon. W. Howard	C	Unopp.
[Resignation]				
1840 (8/4)		D. Dundas	L	Unopp.
1841	137*	D. Dundas	L	Unopp.
[Appointed Solicitor-General]				
1846 (28/7)		D. Dundas	L	Unopp.
1847	184	Sir D. Dundas	L	Unopp.
[Appointed Judge-Advocate General]				
1849 (5/6)		Sir D. Dundas	L	Unopp.
1852	207	Marquess of Stafford	L	Unopp.
1857	264	Marquess of Stafford	L	Unopp.
1859	298	Marquess of Stafford	L	Unopp.
[Succession to the Peerage — Earl of Sutherland]				
1861 (27/3)		Sir D. Dundas	L	Unopp.
1865	180	Sir D. Dundas	L	Unopp.
[Resignation]				
1867 (27/5)		Lord Ronald Leveson-Gower	L	Unopp.
1868	358	Lord Ronald Leveson-Gower	L	Unopp.
1874	324	Marquess of Stafford	L	Unopp.
1880	326	Marquess of Stafford	L	Unopp.

WIGTOWNSHIRE [376]

Election	Electors	Candidate	Party	Votes
1832	845	†Sir A. Agnew, Bt. (Senr.)	L	Unopp.
1835	875	Sir A. Agnew, Bt. (Senr.)	L	340
		J. Blair	C	228
		J. Douglas	L	58
1837	838	J. Blair	C	362
		A. Murray	L	314
1841	1,039*	J. Dalrymple	L	403
		J. Blair	C	397
1847	1,095	J. Dalrymple	L	Unopp.
1852	1,272	J. Dalrymple *(Viscount Dalrymple)*	L	Unopp.
[Resignation]				
1856 (9/2)		Sir A. Agnew, Bt. (Junr.)	L	Unopp.
1857	1,357	Sir A. Agnew, Bt. (Junr.)	L	Unopp.
1859	1,464	Sir A. Agnew, Bt. (Junr.)	L	Unopp.
1865	1,087	Sir A. Agnew, Bt. (Junr.)	L	484
		Lord Garlies	C	456
1868	1,517	Lord Garlies	C	719
		Sir A. Agnew, Bt. (Junr.)	L	652
[Succession to the Peerage — Earl of Galloway]				
1873 (24/2)	1,549	R.V. Agnew	C	713
		Viscount Dalrymple	L	656
1874	1,553	R.V. Agnew	C	Unopp.
1880	1,657	Sir H.E. Maxwell, Bt.	C	768
		Viscount Dalrymple	L	722

Petition:—

1841: Withdrawn

UNIVERSITIES ---- ENGLAND, SCOTLAND

CAMBRIDGE UNIVERSITY [377]

(Two Seats)

Election	Electors	Candidate	Party	Votes
1832	2,319	†H. Goulburn	C	Unopp.
		†C.M. Sutton	C	Unopp.
1835	2,319*	H. Goulburn	C	Unopp.
		Sir C.M. Sutton	C	Unopp.
[Elevation of Sutton to the Peerage — Viscount Canterbury]				
1835 (21/3)		Hon. C.E. Law	C	Unopp.
1837	2,613	H. Goulburn	C	Unopp.
		Hon. C.E. Law	C	Unopp.
1841	2,873	H. Goulburn	C	Unopp.
		Hon. C.E. Law	C	Unopp.
[Appointment of Goulburn as Chancellor of the Exchequer]				
1841 (15/9)		H. Goulburn	C	Unopp.
1847	3,800	Hon. C.E. Law	C	1,486
		H. Goulburn	C	1,189
		Viscount Feilding	C	1,147
		J.G.S. Lefevre	L	860
[Death of Law]				
1850 (4/10)		L.T. Wigram	C	Unopp.
1852	4,063	H. Goulburn	C	Unopp.
		L.T. Wigram	C	Unopp.
[Death of Goulburn]				
1856 (11/2)	4,552	S.H. Walpole	C	886
		Hon. G. Denman	L	419
1857	4,552	S.H. Walpole	C	Unopp.
		L.T. Wigram	C	Unopp.
[Appointment of Walpole as Secretary of State for the Home Department]				
1858 (4/3)		S.H. Walpole	C	Unopp.
1859	4,566	C.J. Selwyn	C	Unopp.
		S.H. Walpole	C	Unopp.
1865	5,184*	C.J. Selwyn	C	Unopp.
		S.H. Walpole	C	Unopp.

(Two Seats)

Election	Electors	Candidate	Party	Votes
[Appointment of Walpole as Secretary of State for the Home Department]				
1866 (11/7)		S.H. Walpole	C	Unopp.
[Appointment of Selwyn as Solicitor-General]				
1867 (22/7)		C.J. Selwyn	C	Unopp.
[Resignation of Selwyn on appointment as a Judge of the Court of Appeal in Chancery]				
1868 (24/2)	5,184*	A.J.B.B. Hope	C	1,931
		A. Cleasby	C	1,400
1868	5,435	A.J.B.B. Hope	C	Unopp.
		S.H. Walpole	C	Unopp.
1874	5,855	A.J.B.B. Hope	C	Unopp.
		S.H. Walpole	C	Unopp.
1880	6,161	A.J.B.B. Hope	C	Unopp.
		S.H. Walpole	C	Unopp.
[Resignation of Walpole]				
1882 (28/11)	6,371	H.C. Raikes	C	3,491
		J. Stuart	L	1,301

Note:—

1832—1835 Sutton was Speaker of the House of Commons from June 1817 until February 1835

LONDON UNIVERSITY [378]

Election	Electors	Candidate	Party	Votes
1868	1,160	R. Lowe	L	Unopp.
[Appointed Chancellor of the Exchequer]				
1868 (21/12)		R. Lowe	L	Unopp.
1874	1,485	R. Lowe	L	Unopp.
1880	1,947	R. Lowe	L	1,014
		E. Charles	C	535
[Elevation to the Peerage — Viscount Sherbrooke]				
1880 (3/6)		Sir J. Lubbock, Bt.	L	Unopp.

OXFORD UNIVERSITY [379]
(Two Seats)

Election	Electors	Candidate	Party	Votes
1832	2,496	†T.G.B. Estcourt	C	Unopp.
		†Sir R.H. Inglis, Bt.	C	Unopp.
1835	2,496*	T.G.B. Estcourt	C	Unopp.
		Sir R.H. Inglis, Bt.	C	Unopp.
1837	2,496*	T.G.B. Estcourt	C	Unopp.
		Sir R.H. Inglis, Bt.	C	Unopp.
1841	2,496*	T.G.B. Estcourt	C	Unopp.
		Sir R.H. Inglis, Bt.	C	Unopp.
1847	3,300	Sir R.H. Inglis, Bt.	C	1,700
		W.E. Gladstone	C	997
		C.G. Round	C	824
1852	3,474	Sir R.H. Inglis, Bt.	C	1,369
		W.E. Gladstone	C	1,108
		R.B. Marsham	C	758
[Appointment of Gladstone as Chancellor of the Exchequer]				
1853 (20/1)	3,357	W.E. Gladstone	C	1,022
		D.M. Perceval	C	898
[Resignation of Inglis]				
1854 (7/2)		Sir W. Heathcote, Bt.	C	Unopp.
1857	3,538	W.E. Gladstone	C	Unopp.
		Sir W. Heathcote, Bt.	C	Unopp.
[Appointment of Gladstone as Lord High Commissioner to the Ionian Islands]				
1859 (12/2)		W.E. Gladstone	C	Unopp.
1859	3,623	W.E. Gladstone	C	Unopp.
		Sir W. Heathcote, Bt.	C	Unopp.
[Appointment of Gladstone as Chancellor of the Exchequer]				
1859 (1/7)	3,623	W.E. Gladstone	L	1,050
		Marquess of Chandos	C	859
1865	3,755*	Sir W. Heathcote, Bt.	C	3,236
		G. Hardy	C	1,904
		W.E. Gladstone	L	1,724
[Appointment of Hardy as President of the Poor Law Board]				
1866 (12/7)		G. Hardy	C	Unopp.

(Two Seats)

Election	Electors	Candidate	Party	Votes
[Appointment of Hardy as Secretary of State for the Home Department]				
1867 (20/5)		G. Hardy	C	Unopp.
1868	4,190	G. Hardy	C	Unopp.
		J.R. Mowbray	C	Unopp.
1874	4,659	G. Hardy	C	Unopp.
		J.R. Mowbray	C	Unopp.
[Appointment of Hardy as Secretary of State for the War Department]				
1874 (14/3)		G. Hardy	C	Unopp.
[Elevation of Hardy to the Peerage — Viscount Cranbrook]				
1878 (17/5)	5,026	J.G. Talbot	C	2,687
		H.J.S. Smith	L	989
1880	5,033	J.R. Mowbray	C	Unopp.
		J.G. Talbot	C	Unopp.

Election	Electors	Candidate	Party	Votes
1868	4,368	J. Moncreiff	L	2,067
		E.S. Gordon	C	2,020
[Resignation on appointment as Lord Justice Clerk — Lord Moncreiff]				
1869 (22/11)	4,368*	E.S. Gordon	C	2,120
		A. Smith	L	1,616
1874	4,776	E.S. Gordon	C	Unopp.
[Appointed Lord Advocate]				
1874 (14/3)		E.S. Gordon	C	Unopp.
[Resignation on appointment as a Lord of Appeal — Lord Gordon of Drumearn]				
1876 (14/11)	5,389	W. Watson	C	2,392
		A. Kirkwood	L	1,788
1880	5,969	J.A. Campbell	C	2,520
		A. Asher	L	2,139

Election	Electors	Candidate	Party	Votes
1868	4,880	L. Playfair	L	2,322
		A.C. Swinton	C	2,067
[Appointed Postmaster-General]				
1873 (4/12)		L. Playfair	L	Unopp.
1874	4,861	L. Playfair	L	Unopp.
1880	5,966	L. Playfair	L	2,522
		E.R. Bickersteth	C	2,448

TABLES

Table 1

CANDIDATES AT GENERAL ELECTIONS

	1832	1835	1837	1841
ENGLAND	716	658	700	655
WALES	40	40	45	41
SCOTLAND	98	85	84	78
IRELAND	175	156	158	136
UNIVERSITIES	8	6	7	6
UNITED KINGDOM	**1,037**	**945**	**994**	**916**

	1847	1852	1857	1859
ENGLAND	625	670	618	617
WALES	35	42	36	36
SCOTLAND	71	74	68	61
IRELAND	138	159	148	140
UNIVERSITIES	11	7	8	6
UNITED KINGDOM	**880**	**952**	**878**	**860**

	1865	1868	1874	1880
ENGLAND	667	747	743	764
WALES	37	49	55	54
SCOTLAND	68	90	97	103
IRELAND	142	140	176	170
UNIVERSITIES	8	13	9	12
UNITED KINGDOM	**922**	**1,039**	**1,080**	**1,103**

Table 2

MEMBERS ELECTED AT GENERAL ELECTIONS

	1832		1835		1837	
	C	L	C	L	C	L
ENGLAND	117	347	200	264	238	226
WALES	14	18	17	15	19	13
SCOTLAND	10	43	15	38	20	33
IRELAND	28	75	35	68	30	73
UNIVERSITIES	6	0	6	0	6	0
UNITED KINGDOM	**175**	**483**	**273**	**385**	**313**	**345**
	1841		**1847**		**1852**	
	C	L	C	L	C	L
ENGLAND	277	187	238	224[1]	244	216
WALES	21	11	20	12	20	12
SCOTLAND	22	31	20	33	20	33
IRELAND	41	62	40	63	40	63
UNIVERSITIES	6	0	6	0	6	0
UNITED KINGDOM	**367**	**291**	**324**	**332**	**330**	**324**
	1857		**1859**		**1865**	
	C	L	C	L	C	L
ENGLAND	185	275	208	252	212	252
WALES	17	15	17	15	14	18
SCOTLAND	14	39	13	40	11	42
IRELAND	42	61	53	50	45	58
UNIVERSITIES	6	0	6	0	6	0
UNITED KINGDOM	**264**	**390**	**297**	**357**	**288**	**370**
	1868		**1874**		**1880**	
	C	L	C	L	C	L
ENGLAND	211	244	280	171	196	255
WALES	10	23	14	19	4	29
SCOTLAND	7	51	18	40	6	52
IRELAND	37	66	31	70	23	78
UNIVERSITIES	6	3	7	2	7	2
UNITED KINGDOM	**271**	**387**	**350**	**302**	**236**	**416**

Notes:—

This table should only be regarded as approximately correct. For an explanation of the difficulties in deciding to which party an MP belonged, see Introductory Notes (Party Designations). The figures given above reflect the state of parties after the double and treble returns (see Appendix 4) had been decided but prior to the changes caused by other types of election petitions.

The figures for Conservatives includes Liberal Conservative (Peelites) in 1847, 1852, 1857 and 1859. See Introductory Notes (Liberal Conservatives).

The figures for Liberals in Ireland includes Repealers in 1832, 1841 and 1847; Irish Confederate in 1847; Independent Opposition in 1857; Home Rulers in 1874 and 1880.

The figures for Liberals in Great Britain in 1874 and 1880 includes Liberal/Labour.

[1] Including one Chartist

Table 3

ELECTORATE

	1832	1835	1837	1841
ENGLAND	609,772	625,193	741,250	777,312
WALES	41,763	42,426	49,706	54,653
SCOTLAND	64,447	72,778	84,302	83,632
IRELAND	90,068	98,402	122,073	96,870
UNIVERSITIES	6,888	6,915	7,209	7,469
UNITED KINGDOM	**812,938**	**845,714**	**1,004,540**	**1,019,936**

	1847	1852	1857	1859
ENGLAND	828,385	857,764	878,803	900,059
WALES	55,251	54,858	55,686	56,033
SCOTLAND	88,792	98,967	100,206	105,608
IRELAND	124,825	163,546	191,345	200,242
UNIVERSITIES	8,827	9,237	9,790	9,889
UNITED KINGDOM	**1,106,080**	**1,184,372**	**1,235,830**	**1,271,831**

	1865	1868	1874	1880
ENGLAND	970,096	1,873,368	2,097,296	2,338,809
WALES	61,656	127,385	137,143	149,841
SCOTLAND	105,069	231,376	271,240	293,581
IRELAND	202,683	223,400	222,622	229,204
UNIVERSITIES	10,639	22,184	23,336	28,615
UNITED KINGDOM	**1,350,143**	**2,477,713**	**2,751,637**	**3,040,050**

Note:— The above figures include an unknown number of duplicate entries and should only be regarded as approximately correct. See Introductory Notes (Electorate) for an explanation of the difficulties in obtaining accurate figures.

Table 4

UNCONTESTED CONSTITUENCIES

The figures within brackets indicate the number of seats which were uncontested.

	1832	1835	1837	1841
ENGLAND	66 (113)	101 (177)	78 (140)	116 (209)
WALES	20 (22)	20 (22)	15 (17)	20 (24)
SCOTLAND	16 (16)	23 (23)	21 (22)	28 (29)
IRELAND	21 (34)	30 (47)	32 (53)	45 (69)
UNIVERSITIES	2 (4)	3 (6)	2 (4)	3 (6)
UNITED KINGDOM	**125 (189)**	**177 (275)**	**148 (236)**	**212 (337)**

	1847	1852	1857	1859
ENGLAND	134 (241)	95 (169)	123 (214)	129 (238)
WALES	25 (27)	18 (21)	24 (27)	24 (28)
SCOTLAND	37 (37)	33 (33)	37 (38)	43 (45)
IRELAND	39 (63)	22 (32)	29 (45)	38 (62)
UNIVERSITIES	0 (0)	2 (4)	2 (4)	3 (6)
UNITED KINGDOM	**235 (368)**	**170 (259)**	**215 (328)**	**237 (379)**

	1865	1868	1874	1880
ENGLAND	102 (182)	59 (100)	69 (126)	35 (66)
WALES	23 (27)	13 (14)	10 (12)	8 (10)
SCOTLAND	37 (37)	25 (26)	22 (22)	12 (12)
IRELAND	32 (55)	40 (67)	11 (18)	9 (15)
UNIVERSITIES	1 (2)	3 (5)	6 (9)	3 (6)
UNITED KINGDOM	**195 (303)**	**140 (212)**	**118 (187)**	**67 (109)**

Table 5

THE ILLITERATE VOTE[1]

Year	England	Wales	Scotland	Ireland	Total
1874†					
1880	27,490	2,136	†	5,312	34,938

1 Voters who were illiterate, or incapacitated by blindness or other physical cause, could have their ballot papers marked for them by Presiding Officers at polling stations.

† No figures available.

Source: House of Commons Papers, 1883 (327) liv, 293

Table 6

SPOILT BALLOT PAPERS

Year	England	Wales	Scotland	Ireland	Total
1874†					
1880	7,905	531	1,797	1,551	11,784[1]

1 No figures available from 17 constituencies.

† No figures available.

Source: House of Commons Papers, 1881 (25), lxxiv, 285

Table 7

SEATS IN THE HOUSE OF COMMONS

	1832–68[1]	1868–85[2]
London Boroughs	18	22
English Boroughs	304	263
English Counties	142	170
ENGLAND	**464**	**455**
Welsh Boroughs	15	16
Welsh Counties	17	17
WALES	**32**	**33**
Scottish Burghs	23	26
Scottish Counties	30	32
SCOTLAND	**53**	**58**
Irish Boroughs	39	39
Irish Counties	64	64
IRELAND	**103**	**103**
THE UNIVERSITIES[3]	**6**	**9**
UNITED KINGDOM	**658**	**658**

1 In 1844 Sudbury (2 seats) was disfranchised reducing the number of Members to 656. In 1852 St. Albans (2 seats) was disfranchised reducing the number of Members to 654. By the Appropriation of Seats (Sudbury and St. Albans) Act, 1861 (24 & 25 Vict., c. 112) two of these seats were allocated immediately to Birkenhead and Lancashire, Southern, and the remaining two seats were given to Yorkshire, West Riding from the Dissolution of Parliament in 1865. The number of Members was thus restored to 656 in 1861 and 658 in 1865.

2 In 1870 Beverley (2 seats), Bridgwater (2 seats), Cashel (1 seat) and Sligo (1 seat) were disfranchised reducing the number of Members to 652. In June 1885, Macclesfield (2 seats) and Sandwich (2 seats) were disfranchised reducing the number of Members to 648.

3 Of the University seats, four (five from 1868) were in England, two (from 1868) in Scotland, and two in Ireland.

Table 8

GENERAL ELECTION TIME–TABLE

Year	Parliament Dissolved	First Member Returned	Last Member Returned	Parliament Assembled
1832	December 3	December 8	January 15 (1833)	January 29
1835	December 29 (1834)	January 5	February 9	February 19
1837	July 17	July 22	August 18	November 15
1841	June 23	June 28	July 17	August 19
1847	July 23	July 28	September 1	November 18
1852	July 1	July 6	August 3	November 4
1857	March 21	March 26	April 20	April 30
1859	April 23	April 28	May 20	May 31
1865	July 6	July 10	July 29	February 1 (1866)
1868	November 11	November 16	December 8	December 10
1874	January 26	January 30	February 17	March 5
1880	March 24	March 30	April 27	April 29

Table 9

CONTESTED AND UNCONTESTED BY–ELECTIONS

From	Contested	%	Uncontested	%	Total[1]
1832–1835	35	60.3	23	39.7	58
1835–1837	47	52.8	42	47.2	89
1837–1841	48	45.7	57	54.3	105
1841–1847	62	26.8	169	73.2	231
1847–1852	73	42.4	99	57.6	172
1852–1857	98	45.0	120	55.0	218
1857–1859	24	26.7	66	73.3	90
1859–1865	102	46.2	119	53.8	221
1865–1868	45	31.9	96	68.1	141
1868–1874	104	59.1	72	40.9	176
1874–1880	123	63.7	70	36.3	193
1880–1885	99	51.3	94	48.7	193
Total	**860**	**45.6**	**1,027**	**54.4**	**1,887**

[1] There was an average of 36 by-elections each year between 1832 and 1885.

Table 10

REASONS FOR BY-ELECTIONS

Cause of Vacancy	Total	%
Acceptance of office which vacated seat and necessitated re-election	508[1]	26.9
Resignation	489	25.9
Death	449	23.8
Unseated as the result of an election petition	165	8.7
Succession to the Peerage	150	8.0
Elevation to the Peerage	54	2.9
Resignation in order to contest another constituency	32	1.7
Decision to seek re-election on changing party allegiance or for other reason	15	0.8
Elected for more than one constituency	12[2]	0.6
Disqualification as a Member of the House of Commons	8[3]	0.4
Creation of additional seats in the House of Commons during a Parliament	2	0.1
Expulsion from the House of Commons	2[4]	0.1
Unseated for having voted in the House of Commons before taking the Oath	1[5]	0.1

1 Under the provisions of the Succession to the Crown Act, 1707 and a number of subsequent Acts, MPs appointed to certain ministerial and legal offices were required to seek re-election. Of these by-elections only 77 were contested.

2 See Appendix 3.

3 Namely:— C. Cowan, Edinburgh, 1847 (government contract); W.S. O'Brien, Limerick County, 1849 (convicted of high treason); Sir S.H. Waterlow, Dumfriesshire, 1868 (government contract); J.O'D. Rossa, Tipperary County, 1870 (serving a term of life imprisonment); J. Ramsay, Falkirk Burghs, 1874 (government contract); J. Mitchel, Tipperary County, 1875 (convicted felon and alien); T. Russell, Bute, 1880 (government contract); M. Davitt, Meath County, 1882 (serving a term of 15 years imprisonment).

4 Namely: J. Sadleir, Tipperary County, 1857; C. Bradlaugh, Northampton, 1882.

5 Namely: C. Bradlaugh, Northampton, 1881.

Table 11

ANALYSIS OF CONSTITUENCIES

1832–1868[1]

	4 Members	3 Members	2 Members	1 Member	Total
London Boroughs	1	0	7	0	8
English Boroughs	0	0	126	52	178
English Counties	0	7	60	1	68
ENGLAND	**1**	**7**	**193**	**53**	**254**
Welsh Boroughs	0	0	0	15	15
Welsh Counties	0	0	4	9	13
WALES	**0**	**0**	**4**	**24**	**28**
Scottish Burghs	0	0	2	19	21
Scottish Counties	0	0	0	30	30
SCOTLAND	**0**	**0**	**2**	**49**	**51**
Irish Boroughs	0	0	6	27	33
Irish Counties	0	0	32	0	32
IRELAND	**0**	**0**	**38**	**27**	**65**
THE UNIVERSITIES	**0**	**0**	**3**	**0**	**3**
UNITED KINGDOM	**1**	**7**	**240**	**153**	**401**

1868–1885[2]

	4 Members	3 Members	2 Members	1 Member	Total
London Boroughs	1	0	9	0	10
English Boroughs	0	4	80	91	175
English Counties	0	7	74	1	82
ENGLAND	**1**	**11**	**163**	**92**	**267**
Welsh Boroughs	0	0	1	14	15
Welsh Counties	0	0	4	9	13
WALES	**0**	**0**	**5**	**23**	**28**
Scottish Burghs	0	1	2	19	22
Scottish Counties	0	0	0	32	32
SCOTLAND	**0**	**1**	**2**	**51**	**54**
Irish Boroughs	0	0	6	27	33
Irish Counties	0	0	32	0	32
IRELAND	**0**	**0**	**38**	**27**	**65**
THE UNIVERSITIES	**0**	**0**	**3**	**3**	**6**
UNITED KINGDOM	**1**	**12**	**211**	**196**	**420**

1 For details of the changes which took place between 1832 and 1868 see Table 7, footnote[1]

2 For details of the changes which took place between 1868 and 1885 see Table 7, footnote[2]

Table 12

ELECTION PETITIONS

General Elections	Void Elections[1]	Undue Elections[2]	Elections upheld[3]	Petitions withdrawn[4]	Total
1832	7	10	23	8	48
1835	5	7	9	13	34
1837	1	13	40	31	85
1841	11	14	11	36	72
1847	17	1	11	22	51
1852	31	2	29	60	122
1857	8	1	24	39	72
1859	11	0	23	26	60
1865	14	2	19	34	69
1868	21	1	43	36	101
1874	17	2	8	9	36
1880	18	0	15	20	53
Total	**161**	**53**	**255**	**334**	**803**
By-Elections					
1832–35	1	1	3	1	6
1835–37	0	4	4	2	10
1837–41	5	2	10	1	18
1841–47	4	2	6	8	20
1847–52	6	1	4	10	21
1852–57	4	1	7	15	27
1857–59	1	0	0	2	3
1859–65	2	1	6	11	20
1865–68	2	1	2	3	8
1868–74	5	2	8	4	19
1874–80	6	1	5	3	15
1880–85	4	1	3	0	8
Total	**40**	**17**	**58**	**60**	**175**

[1] A 'void' election was one in which the result was quashed and a new writ issued or in the case of 'double' and 'treble returns', the election of one member was found to be void.

[2] An 'undue' election was one in which the Committee or Court found the successful candidate not duly elected and ruled that another candidate was entitled to be declared elected.

[3] An election 'upheld' was one in which the Committee or Court dismissed the petition and found the Member duly elected.

[4] A 'withdrawn' petition includes a number of cases in which petitions lapsed due to a legal technicality or the Dissolution of Parliament. Also included in this category are some instances of petitioners failing to appear for the hearing. Petitions which were withdrawn after a hearing or trial commenced are not included in this category but are treated as elections upheld.

Sources: *Journals of the House of Commons*
O'Malley and Hardcastle's Reports on Election Petitions, Vols: 1, 2, 3, 4
House of Lords Record Office
Public Record Office
Royal Courts of Justice

APPENDICES

Appendix 1

REPRESENTATION OF IRISH CONSTITUENCIES 1832–1880

The following chart gives the party representation in each Irish constituency from the General Election of 1832 until the General Election of 1880.

BOROUGHS

CONSTITUENCY	1832	1835	1837	1841	1847	1852
ARMAGH	L	L	L	L	L	C
ATHLONE	L	C	L	C	C	L
BANDON	C	C	C	C	C	C
BELFAST	L	C	L	C	L	C
[two seats]	L	L	L	C	C	C
CARLOW	R	C	L	L	L	L
CARRICKFERGUS	C	C	C	C	C	C
CASHEL	R	L	L	L	R	L
CLONMEL	R	L	L	L	R	L
COLERAINE	C	L	C	C	C	C
CORK	R	C	L	L	R	L
[two seats]	R	C	L	R	R	L
DOWNPATRICK	C	C	C	C	C	C
DROGHEDA	R	L	L	L	L	L
DUBLIN	R	L	L	C	C	C
[two seats]	R	L	L	C	R	C
DUNDALK	L	L	L	L	R	L
DUNGANNON	C	C	C	C	C	C
DUNGARVAN	L	L	L	L	L	L
ENNIS	R	L	L	L	R	L
ENNISKILLEN	C	C	C	C	C	C
GALWAY	R	L	L	R	R	L
[two seats]	R	L	L	R	R	L
KILKENNY	R	L	L	R	R	L
KINSALE	L	C	L	L	C	L
LIMERICK	R	L	L	R	R	L
[two seats]	R	L	L	L	R	L
LISBURN	C	C	C	C	C	C
LONDONDERRY	L	L	L	L	L	L
MALLOW	R	L	L	L	L	L
NEW ROSS	R	L	L	L	R	L
NEWRY	C	L	C	C	C	L
PORTARLINGTON	C	C	C	C	L	C
SLIGO	L	L	L	R	R	L
TRALEE	R	L	C	R	R	L
WATERFORD	R	L	L	C	R	L
[two seats]	C	L	L	C	R	L
WEXFORD	R	L	L	L	R	L
YOUGHAL	R	L	L	L	Conf	C

BOROUGHS

CONSTITUENCY	1857	1859	1865	1868	1874	1880
ARMAGH	C	C	C	C	C	C
ATHLONE	Ind Op	L	L	L	HR	L
BANDON	C	C	C	L	L	C
BELFAST	C	C	C	C	C	C
[two seats]	C	C	C	L	C	C
CARLOW	C	L	L	L	HR	HR
CARRICKFERGUS	C	C	C	C	C	C
CASHEL	L	L	L	L	–	–
CLONMEL	L	L	L	L	HR	HR
COLERAINE	C	C	C	C	L	C
CORK	L	L	L	L	HR	HR
[two seats]	L	L	L	L	HR	HR
DOWNPATRICK	L	C	C	C	C	C
DROGHEDA	L	L	L	L	HR	HR
DUBLIN	C	C	C	C	C	HR
[two seats]	C	C	L	L	HR	L
DUNDALK	L	L	L	L	HR	L
DUNGANNON	C	C	C	C	L	L
DUNGARVAN	Ind Op	L	L	L	HR	HR
ENNIS	L	L	L	L	HR	HR
ENNISKILLEN	C	C	C	C	C	C
GALWAY	L	C	L	L	HR	HR
[two seats]	L	L	L	L	HR	HR
KILKENNY	Ind Op	L	L	L	HR	HR
KINSALE	L	L	L	L	HR	HR
LIMERICK	L	L	L	L	HR	HR
[two seats]	L	L	L	L	HR	HR
LISBURN	L	C	C	C	C	C
LONDONDERRY	L	L	C	L	C	C
MALLOW	L	C	L	L	HR	L
NEW ROSS	C	C	C	L	HR	HR
NEWRY	L	C	C	L	L	C
PORTARLINGTON	C	C	L	C	C	C
SLIGO	L	C	L	C	–	–
TRALEE	L	L	L	L	L	HR
WATERFORD	Ind Op	C	L	L	HR	HR
[two seats]	C	L	L	L	HR	HR
WEXFORD	L	L	L	L	HR	HR
YOUGHAL	L	L	L	L	HR	HR

REPRESENTATION OF IRISH CONSTITUENCIES 1832-1880

COUNTIES

CONSTITUENCY	1832	1835	1837	1841	1847	1852
ANTRIM	C	C	C	C	C	C
[two seats]	L	L	C	C	C	C
ARMAGH	L	L	L	L	L	L
[two seats]	C	C	C	C	C	C
CARLOW	R	C	L	C	C	L
[two seats]	L	C	L	C	C	C
CAVAN	C	C	C	C	C	C
[two seats]	C	C	C	C	C	C
CLARE	R	L	L	R	C	L
[two seats]	R	L	L	R	R	L
CORK	R	L	L	R	R	L
[two seats]	L	L	L	R	R	L
DONEGAL	C	C	C	C	C	C
[two seats]	C	C	C	C	C	C
DOWN	C	C	C	C	C	C
[two seats]	L	L	C	C	C	C
DUBLIN	R	L	L	C	C	C
[two seats]	L	L	L	C	C	C
FERMANAGH	C	C	C	C	C	C
[two seats]	C	C	C	C	C	C
GALWAY	L	L	L	L	R	L
[two seats]	C	L	L	L	C	L
KERRY	R	L	L	L	C	L
[two seats]	R	L	C	R	R	C
KILDARE	R	L	L	L	L	L
[two seats]	L	L	L	L	C	L
KILKENNY	R	L	L	L	R	L
[two seats]	R	L	L	R	R	L
KING'S	R	L	L	L	L	L
[two seats]	L	L	L	L	L	L
LEITRIM	L	L	L	L	L	C
[two seats]	L	L	L	L	L	L
LIMERICK	L	L	L	L	L	L
[two seats]	L	L	L	L	Conf	L
LONDONDERRY	C	C	C	C	C	C
[two seats]	C	C	C	C	C	C
LONGFORD	R	C	L	R	R	L
[two seats]	R	C	L	R	R	L
LOUTH	R	L	L	L	L	L
[two seats]	R	L	L	L	L	L
MAYO	L	L	L	R	L	L
[two seats]	L	L	L	R	R	L
MEATH	R	L	L	R	L	L
[two seats]	R	L	L	R	R	L
MONAGHAN	C	C	C	C	L	C
[two seats]	L	L	L	L	C	C
QUEEN'S	R	C	C	C	L	C
[two seats]	C	C	L	C	C	L
ROSCOMMON	L	L	L	L	L	L
[two seats]	R	L	L	R	L	L

REPRESENTATION OF IRISH CONSTITUENCIES 1832-1880

CONSTITUENCY	1832	1835	1837	1841	1847	1852
SLIGO	C	C	C	C	C	C
[two seats]	C	C	C	C	C	L
TIPPERARY	L	L	L	L	R	L
[two seats]	R	L	L	L	R	L
TYRONE	C	C	C	C	C	C
[two seats]	C	C	C	C	C	C
WATERFORD	R	L	L	L	R	L
[two seats]	L	L	L	L	R	L
WESTMEATH	L	L	L	L	R	L
[two seats]	R	L	L	L	L	L
WEXFORD	L	L	L	L	R	L
[two seats]	L	L	L	L	R	C
WICKLOW	L	L	L	C	C	C
[two seats]	L	L	L	L	L	L

CONSTITUENCY	1857	1859	1865	1868	1874	1880
ANTRIM	C	C	C	C	C	C
[two seats]	C	C	C	C	C	C
ARMAGH	C	C	C	C	C	L
[two seats]	C	C	C	C	C	C
CARLOW	C	C	C	C	C	HR
[two seats]	C	C	C	C	C	HR
CAVAN	C	C	C	C	HR	HR
[two seats]	C	C	L	L	HR	HR
CLARE	L	C	L	L	HR	HR
[two seats]	Ind Op	L	C	C	HR	HR
CORK	L	L	L	L	HR	HR
[two seats]	L	L	C	L	HR	HR
DONEGAL	C	C	C	C	C	L
[two seats]	C	C	C	C	C	L
DOWN	C	C	C	C	C	C
[two seats]	C	C	C	C	L	C
DUBLIN	C	C	C	C	C	C
[two seats]	C	C	C	C	C	C
FERMANAGH	C	C	C	C	C	C
[two seats]	C	C	C	C	C	C
GALWAY	L	L	L	L	HR	HR
[two seats]	L	L	L	L	HR	HR
KERRY	L	L	L	L	HR	L
[two seats]	L	L	L	L	L	HR
KILDARE	L	L	L	L	HR	HR
[two seats]	L	L	L	L	L	HR
KILKENNY	L	L	L	L	HR	HR
[two seats]	Ind Op	L	L	L	HR	HR
KING'S	L	C	C	L	HR	HR
[two seats]	L	L	L	L	HR	HR
LEITRIM	C	L	C	L	HR	C
[two seats]	Ind Op	C	L	C	C	HR
LIMERICK	L	L	L	L	HR	HR
[two seats]	L	C	L	L	HR	HR
LONDONDERRY	C	C	C	C	L	L
[two seats]	L	C	C	C	L	L
LONGFORD	L	L	L	L	HR	HR
[two seats]	L	L	L	L	HR	HR

REPRESENTATION OF IRISH CONSTITUENCIES 1832-1880

CONSTITUENCY	1857	1859	1865	1868	1874	1880
LOUTH	L	L	L	L	HR	HR
[two seats]	C	L	L	L	HR	HR
MAYO	C	L	C	C	HR	HR
[two seats]	Ind Op	C	L	L	HR	HR
MEATH	Ind Op	L	L	L	HR	HR
[two seats]	Ind Op	L	L	L	HR	HR
MONAGHAN	C	C	C	C	C	L
[two seats]	C	C	L	C	C	L
QUEEN'S	C	C	C	L	HR	HR
[two seats]	L	L	L	L	HR	HR
ROSCOMMON	L	L	L	L	HR	HR
[two seats]	L	C	L	L	HR	HR
SLIGO	C	C	C	L	C	HR
[two seats]	C	C	C	C	HR	HR
TIPPERARY	Ind Op	L	L	L	HR	HR
[two seats]	L	L	L	L	HR	HR
TYRONE	C	C	C	C	C	C
[two seats]	C	C	C	C	C	L
WATERFORD	L	L	L	L	C	L
[two seats]	L	C	C	L	HR	HR
WEATMEATH	Ind Op	L	L	L	HR	HR
[two seats]	L	L	L	L	HR	HR
WEXFORD	Ind Op	L	C	L	HR	HR
[two seats]	L	C	L	L	HR	HR
WICKLOW	L	C	C	C	HR	HR
[two seats]	C	L	L	L	C	HR

UNIVERSITY

	1832	1835	1837	1841	1847	1852
DUBLIN	C	C	C	C	C	C
[two seats]	C	C	C	C	C	C
	1857	**1859**	**1865**	**1868**	**1874**	**1880**
DUBLIN	C	C	C	C	C	C
[two seats]	C	C	C	C	C	C

Source:— *Parliamentary Election Results in Ireland, 1801-1922* by Brian M. Walker (Royal Irish Academy, Dublin, forthcoming).

Appendix 2

BOROUGHS DISFRANCHISED FOR CORRUPTION

Borough	Date	Transferred to	Act
Sudbury	29/7/44	Suffolk, Western	7 & 8 Vict., c. 53
St. Albans	3/5/52	Hertfordshire	15 Vict., c. 9
Great Yarmouth	11/11/68	Norfolk, Northern Suffolk, Eastern	30 & 31 Vict., c. 102
Lancaster	11/11/68	Lancashire, Northern	30 & 31 Vict., c. 102
Reigate	11/11/68	Surrey, Mid	30 & 31 Vict., c. 102
Totnes	11/11/68	Devon, Southern	30 & 31 Vict., c. 102
Beverley	4/7/70	Yorkshire, East Riding	33 & 34 Vict., c. 21
Bridgwater	4/7/70	Somerset, Western	33 & 34 Vict., c. 21
Cashel	1/8/70	Tipperary County	33 & 34 Vict., c. 38
Sligo	1/8/70	Sligo County	33 & 34 Vict., c. 38
Macclesfield	25/6/85	Cheshire, Eastern	48 & 49 Vict., c. 23
Sandwich	25/6/85	Kent, Eastern	48 & 49 Vict., c. 23

Appendix 3

DOUBLE AND TREBLE ELECTIONS

The following is a list of double and treble elections at each General Election, i.e. where a candidate was elected for more than one constituency and had to choose which constituency he wished to represent.

The constituency prefixed with an asterisk is the one which the MP chose to represent.

1832

Viscount Lowther (C)	Cumberland, Western *Westmorland
C.P. Thomson (L)	Dover *Manchester

1841

D. O'Connell (R)	*Cork County Meath County

1847

R. Cobden (L)	Stockport *Yorkshire, West Riding
J. O'Connell (R)	Kilkenny City *Limerick City
Hon. C.P. Villiers (L)	Lancashire, Southern *Wolverhampton

1865

G. Hardy (C)	Leominster *Oxford University

1874

P. Callan (HR)	*Dundalk Louth County

1880

W.E. Gladstone (L)	*Edinburghshire Leeds
Marquess of Hartington (L)	Radnor Boroughs *Lancashire, North-Eastern
C.S. Parnell (HR)	*Cork City Mayo County Meath County

Appendix 4

DOUBLE AND TREBLE RETURNS

Prior to the passing of the Ballot Act in 1872, a Returning Office had no right to give a casting vote in the event of candidates polling the same number of votes. His duty was to return all candidates polling equal votes although they were not allowed to take their seats in the House of Commons until after election petitions had been decided. From 1872, a Returning Officer, *if a registered elector in the constituency,* could give a casting vote if the votes were equal.

GENERAL ELECTIONS

1841	Thetford Cardigan Boroughs[1]
1847	Montgomery Boroughs
1852	Knaresborough[2]
1857	Huntingdonshire
1859	Aylesbury
1865	Dunbartonshire
1868	Horsham
1874	Athlone

BY-ELECTIONS

1839	Totnes
1878	Northumberland, Southern

[1] This double return was due to the loss of poll books and not to equal votes.

[2] Treble return. Three candidates in a two-member constituency polled equal votes.

Appendix 5

BRITISH GOVERNMENTS AND PRIME MINISTERS, 1830–1885

Date[1]	Government	Prime Minister	Party
22 November 1830	Liberal	Earl Grey	Liberal
16 July 1834	Liberal	Viscount Melbourne	Liberal
17 November 1834	Conservative	Duke of Wellington	Conservative
10 December 1834	Conservative	Sir Robert Peel	Conservative
18 April 1835	Liberal	Viscount Melbourne	Liberal
30 August 1841	Conservative	Sir Robert Peel	Conservative
30 June 1846	Liberal	Lord John Russell	Liberal
23 February 1852	Conservative	Earl of Derby	Conservative
19 December 1852	Coalition	Earl of Aberdeen	Liberal
6 February 1855	Liberal	Viscount Palmerston	Liberal
20 February 1858	Conservative	Earl of Derby	Conservative
12 June 1859	Liberal	Viscount Palmerston	Liberal
29 October 1865	Liberal	Earl Russell[2]	Liberal
28 June 1866	Conservative	Earl of Derby	Conservative
27 February 1868	Conservative	Benjamin Disraeli	Conservative
3 December 1868	Liberal	William Ewart Gladstone	Liberal
20 February 1874	Conservative	Benjamin Disraeli (Earl of Beaconsfield)	Conservative
23 April 1880	Liberal	William Ewart Gladstone	Liberal
23 June 1885	Conservative	Marquess of Salisbury	Conservative

[1] The date of the kissing of hands as given in Handbook of British Chronology (F.M. Powicke and E.B. Fryde, 2nd edition, 1961).

[2] Formerly Lord John Russell.

Appendix 6

REASONS FOR HOLDING GENERAL ELECTIONS

1832: To elect a new Parliament subsequent to the passing of the First (Electoral) Reform Act.

1835: Viscount Melbourne resigned as Prime Minister and was succeeded by Sir Robert Peel who immediately asked for a Dissolution.

1837: Death of William IV.

1841: Request by the Prime Minister for a Dissolution after a defeat in the House of Commons.

1847: Request by the Prime Minister for a Dissolution on Parliament nearing the end of its statutory term of seven years.

1852: Lord John Russell resigned as Prime Minister after a defeat in the House of Commons. He was succeeded by the Earl of Derby who four months later requested a Dissolution.

1857: Request by the Prime Minister for a Dissolution after a defeat in the House of Commons.

1859: Request by the Prime Minister for a Dissolution after a defeat in the House of Commons.

1865: Request by the Prime Minister for a Dissolution on Parliament nearing the end of its statutory term of seven years.

1868: To elect a new Parliament subsequent to the passing of the Second (Electoral) Reform Act.

1874: Request by the Prime Minister for a Dissolution on Parliament nearing the end of its statutory term of seven years.

1880: Request by the Prime Minister for a Dissolution on Parliament nearing the end of its statutory term of seven years.

SELECT BIBLIOGRAPHY

The year of publication is given at the end of each entry and the original place of publication is London except where otherwise stated.

CONSTITUENCY HISTORY and/or ELECTION RESULTS

Albery (W.), *A Parliamentary History of the Ancient Borough of Horsham, 1295–1885.* (1927).

Aspinall (A.) & others, *Parliament Through Seven Centuries: Reading and its M.P.'s.* (1962).

Bean (W.W.), *The Parliamentary Representation of the Six Northern Counties of England, 1603–1886.* (Hull, 1890).

Bealey (F.), Blondel (J.) & McCann (W.P.), *Constituency Politics: A Study of Newcastle-under-Lyme.* (1965).

Beaven (A.B.), *Bristol Lists: Municipal and Miscellaneous.* (Bristol, 1899).

The Aldermen of the City of London: Henry III to 1912. (2 volumes, 1908–13).

Bennett (R.), *A Record of Elections: Parliamentary and Municipal – For Liverpool, Birkenhead, Bootle, South and South-West Lancashire, 1832–1878.* (Liverpool, 1880).

Breese (E.), *Calendars of Gwynedd.* (1873).

Caunt (G.), *Essex in Parliament.* (Chelmsford, 1969).

Davis (R.W.), *Political Change and Continuity 1760–1885: A Buckinghamshire Study.* (Newton Abbot, 1972).

Dobson (W.), *History of the Parliamentary Representation of Preston.* (Second edition, 1868).

Donald (J), *Past Parliamentary Elections in Greenock.* (Greenock, 1933).

Edwards (E.), *Parliamentary Elections of the Borough of Shrewsbury from 1283–1859.* (Shrewsbury, 1859).

Ferguson (R.S.), *Cumberland and Westmorland M.P.'s: from the Restoration to the Reform Bill of 1867.* (1871).

Hill (G.), *The Electoral History of the Borough of Lambeth since its Enfranchisement in 1832.* (1879).

Hills (W.H.),*The Parliamentary History of the Borough of Lewes, 1295–1885.* (Lewes, 1908).

Humberstone (T.L.), *University Representation.* (1951).

James (C.), *M.P. for Dewsbury.* (Brighouse, 1970).

Jones (R.A.), *Members of Parliament for Andover, 1295–1885.* (Andover, 1972).

Kemp (T.) & Beaven (A.B.), *A List of Members of Parliament for Warwick (and for Warwick and Leamington from 1885).* (Warwick, 1912).

Klieneberger (H.R.), *Durham Elections: A list of material relating to Parliamentary Elections in Durham, 1675–1874.* (Durham, 1956).

Lawrance (W.T.), *Parliamentary Representation of Cornwall, 1295–1885.* (Truro, 1925).

Olney (R.J.), *Lincolnshire Politics, 1832–1885.* (1973).

Park (G.R.), *Parliamentary Representation of Yorkshire, 1290–1886.* (Hull, 1886).

Pink (W.D.) & Beaven (A.B.), *The Parliamentary History of Lancashire (County and Borough), 1258–1885.* (1889).

Shedden (Sir Lewis), *The Parliamentary History of Kilmarnock.* (Kilmarnock, 1929).

Smith (F.F.), *Rochester in Parliament, 1295–1933.* (1933).

Smith (H.S.), *The Parliamentary Representation of Yorkshire.* (1854)

Smith (J.E.), *The Parliamentary Representation of Surrey from 1290–1924.* (1927).

Snell (F.J.), *Palmerston's Borough (Tiverton).* (1894).

Weyman (H.T.), *The Members of Parliament for Ludlow.* (? 1895).

Shropshire and Shrewsbury Members of Parliament. (Transactions of the Shropshire Archaeological Society, Volumes X, XI, XIII). (Shrewsbury, 1925–30).

Whitley (T.W.), *The Parliamentary Representation of the City of Coventry from the earliest times to the present day.* (Coventry, 1894).

Wilkie (T.), *The Representation of Scotland.* (Paisley, 1895).

Wilks (G.), *The Barons of the Cinque Ports and the Parliamentary Representation of Hythe.* (Folkestone, 1892).

Williams (W.R.), *The Parliamentary History of the Principality of Wales, 1541–1895.* (Brecknock, 1895).

The Parliamentary History of the County of Hereford, 1213–1896. (Brecknock, 1896).

The Parliamentary History of the County of Worcester, 1213–1897. (Hereford, 1897).

The Parliamentary History of the County of Gloucester, 1213–1898. (Hereford, 1898).

The Parliamentary History of the County of Oxford, 1213–1899. (Brecknock, 1899).

THE REFORM ACTS

Brock (M.), *The Great Reform Act (1832).* (1973).

Jones (A.), *The Politics of Reform 1884.* (1972). (Cambridge, 1972).

Smith (F.B.), *The Making of the Second Reform Bill (1867).* (1966).

MISCELLANEOUS

Acland (J.), *The Imperial Poll Book of All Elections 1832–1869.* (Second edition, 1869).

Chambers (J.D.), *A Complete Dictionary of the Law and Practice of Elections.* (1837).

Crosby (G.), *Crosby's Parliamentary Record.* (Fourth edition, Leeds, 1849).

Dod (C.R.), *Parliamentary Companion* (Annually (various editors), 1833–85. Two (New Parliament) editions in 1841, 1847, 1852, 1857, 1859, 1865, 1880).

Electoral Facts from 1832 to 1853. (Second edition 1853 and reprinted (edited by H.J. Hanham) with introduction and bibliographical guide, Brighton, 1972).

Drake (M.), *Introduction to Historical Psephology.* (Milton Keynes, 1974).

King (P.S.), *Guide to the House of Commons.* (Editions for 1857, 1859 and 1868 located but possibly published annually during this period).

Lloyd (T.), *The General Election of 1880.* (1968).

McCalmont (F.H.), *The Parliamentary Poll Book of All Elections.* (Seventh edition, 1910 and reprinted with introduction and additional material by J. Vincent and M. Stenton, Brighton, 1971).

Saunders (W.), *The New Parliament 1880.* (1880).

Smith (H.S.), *The Parliaments of England from 1717 to 1847.* (Three volumes, 1844–50 and reprinted (edited by F.W.S. Craig) with introduction and additional material, Chichester, 1973).

Stenton (M.), *Who's Who of British Members of Parliament: Volume 1– 1832-1885.* (Hassocks, 1976).

The New House of Commons. Collated or reprinted from The Times. (1880).

Vincent (J.R.), *Pollbooks: How Victorians Voted.* (1968).

INDEX TO CANDIDATES

This index lists the names of all candidates at General Elections from 1832 until 1880 and at intervening by-elections up to November 1885. The number or numbers following the name of each candidate indicate the constituency reference number which is given, after the name of the constituency, at the top of each page. It does *not* refer to the folio number which appears in small type at the foot of each page.

Owing to the lack of biographical information which is available about many of the candidates during this period, there is no doubt that some errors must have occurred. Every entry has been verified as far as possible but compiling an index of this size is complicated by changes in surname by deed poll, the adoption of additional surnames and by the acquirement of courtesy titles.

The Editor would appreciate notification of any corrections which would improve future reprints of this volume.

A

Abbot, Hon. R.C.E., 60, 275
Abdy, Sir T.N., Bt., 109, 113, 221
Abdy, Sir W.N., Bt., 113
Abercromby, Hon. G.R., 351, 374
Abercromby, J., 322
Abercromby, R.W.D., see Duff, R.W.
Abrahams, I., 59, 63
Acheson, E.A., 233
Ackers, B. St. J., 73, 226
Ackers, J., 108
Acland, C.T.D., 208, 265
Acland, J., 96
Acland, Sir Thomas Dyke, Bt., (Senr.), 216
Acland, Sir Thomas Dyke, Bt., (Junr.), 25, 216, 265
A'Court, C.H.W., 191
A'Court, E.H., 167
Acton, J., 190
Acton, Sir J.E.E.D., Bt., 31
Adair, H.E., 92
Adair, Sir R.A.S., 41, 42, 270
Adam, Sir C., 351
Adam, W.P. 351
Adams, E.H., 309
Adams, Sir G.P. 174
Adams, J., 164, 182
Adams, W.H., 29
Adare, Viscount, see Dunraven, Earl of
Adderley, Sir C.B., 267
Addington, Hon. W.W., 59, 134
Addison, H.R., 68, 158
Adeane, H.J., 202
Aglionby, F., 210, 211
Aglionby, H.A., 52
Agnew, Sir Andrew, Bt., (Senr.), 339, 376
Agnew, Sir Andrew, Bt., (Junr.), 376
Agnew, P.V., 339
Agnew, R.V., 339, 376
Agnew, W., 239
Ainsworth, D., 211
Ainsworth, P., 28
Aitchison, W., 332
Akroyd, E., 80, 89
Albright, A., 282
Alcock, T., 108, 272
Aldam, W., 100
Aldridge, J., 88
Alexander, C., 346
Alexander, G.W., 177
Alexander, R., 197
Alford, Viscount, 199

Alison, A., 337
Allan, Sir H.M.H., Bt., (formerly Havelock), 164, 166
Allcard, W., 181
Allcroft, J.D., 196
Allen, H.G., 302
Allen, J.T., 272
Allen, L.B., 8
Allen, R., 25
Allen, R.S., 263
Allen, W.S., 122
Allix, J.P., 202
Allott, J., 153
Allsopp, G.H., 64
Allsopp, H., 282
Allsopp, S.C., 168, 266
Alsager, R., 272
Alston, R., 230
Alston, R.G., 39, 223
Althorp, Viscount (1), 254
Althorp, Viscount (2), 254
Ambereley, Viscount, 100, 128, 217
Ambrose, W., 161
Amcotts, W.C., 245
Amery, Sir J.H.H., Bt., 173
Amherst, W.A.T., 252
Amphlett, R.P., 103, 282
Anderson, A., 366
Anderson, G., 325
Anderson, Sir James, 337
Anderson, James, 319, 324
Andover, Viscount (1), 114
Andover, Viscount (2), 114
Andrews, R., 156
Angerstein, J., 4, 272
Angerstein, W., 4, 235
Annesley, Earl, 76
Anson, Viscount, 104
Anson, Hon. A.H.A., 23, 104
Anson, Sir George, 104
Anson, Hon. George, 78, 163, 268
Anson, Sir W.R., Bt., 269
Anstey, T.C., 20
Anstruther, Sir R., Bt., 356
Anstruther, Sir R.A., Bt., 336
Anstruther, Sir W.C.J.C., Bt., 364
Antrobus, Sir E., Bt., 191, 272
Apsley, Lord, 50
Arbuthnot, G., 85
Arbuthnot, W., 72
Arbuthnott, Hon. H., 360
Arcedeckne, A., 82
Arch, J., 191
Arkell, J., 55
Arkwright, A.P., 213
Arkwright, F., 212
Arkwright, G., 102, 213
Arkwright, R., 102
Armitage, B., 148
Armitage, Sir E., 148
Armitage, V.K., 204
Armitstead, G., 321
Armstrong, J., 98
Armstrong, R.B., 98
Arnold, A., 90, 148
Arundel and Surrey, Earl of (formerly Lord Fitzalan), 13
Ashbury, J.L., 34
Asher, A., 323, 380
Ashley, Lord (1), 19, 218
Ashley, Lord (2), 55, 96
Ashley, Hon. A.E.M., 136, 232
Ashley, Hon. J.A., 149
Ashworth, H., 148
Aspinall, J.T.W., 51
Assheton, R., 51
Astell, J.H., 14, 41
Astell, R.W., 33
Astell, W., 199
Astley, F.D.P., 205
Astley, Sir J., Bt., 252
Astley, Sir John Dugdale, Bt. (1), 280
Astley, Sir John Dugdale, Bt.,(2), 246
Atcherley, D.F., 198
Atherley, A., 156
Atherton, Sir W., 66
Athlumney, Lord (formerly Sir W.M. Somerville, Bt.), 42, 185
Atkins, H., 155
Atkinson, H.J., 96, 246
Attenborough, R., 139
Attwood, C.M., 123
Attwood, G. de B., 179
Attwood, J., 82
Attwood, M., 189
Attwood, M.W., 2, 4, 166
Attwood, T., 25
Aubyn, Sir J. St., Bt., see St. Aubyn
Aubyn, W.N.M. St., see St. Aubyn
Austen, H.A.C., 79
Austen, T., 235
Austin, A., 61, 168
Aylmer, J.E.E., 112
Ayrton, A.S., 9
Aytoun, J., 123, 322, 334, 337
Aytoun, R.S., 331

B

Babbage, C., 3
Backhouse, E., 56
Badcock, H., 168
Badenoch, G.R., 366
Badnall, R., 122
Bagehot, W., 32
Baggallay, Sir R., 85, 273
Bagge, Sir W., Bt., 252
Bagnall, C., 179, 188
Bagot, Hon. W., 310
Bagshaw, J., 82, 94, 165
Bagshaw, R.J., 78, 82
Bahr, G.W., 138
Bailey, C., 300
Bailey, Sir Joseph, Bt., 196, 306
Bailey, Joseph, 165, 229, 300
Bailey, Sir J.R., Bt., 229
Bailey, L.R., 166
Bailey, S., 153
Baillie, C., 365
Baillie, H., 33

Baillie, H.D., 87
Baillie, H.J., 359
Baillie, H.S., 150
Baillie, J., 329
Baillie, J.E., 35
Baillie, W., 365
Bain, Sir J., 325
Bainbridge, E.T., 168
Bainbridge, G., 126
Baine, W., 326
Baines, Edward, (Senr.), 100
Baines, Edward, (Junr.), 100
Baines, M.T., 96, 100
Baird, A., 324
Baird, Sir D., Bt., 358
Baird, G., 324
Baird, J., 324
Baird, W., 324
Baker, E., 191
Baker, R.B.W. (formerly Wingfield), 223
Baker, S., 164
Baldock, E.H., 155
Baldwin, C., 6
Baldwin, C.B., 174
Baldwin, E., 23
Baldwin, J., 65
Balfour, A.J., 86
Balfour, Sir G., 360
Balfour, James, 358
Balfour, John, 356
Balfour, J.B., 345, 351
Balfour, J.M., 327
Balfour, J.S., 167
Balfour, T., 366
Ball, E., 202
Bankes, G., 187, 218
Bankes, H.H.N., 33
Bankes, W.J., 218
Banks, G., 30
Banks, W., 43
Bannerman, Alexander (1), 318
Bannerman, Alexander (2), 323
Bannerman, H.C. (formerly Campbell) 337
Barber, W., 80
Barbour, G., 31
Barclay, A.C., 168
Barclay, C., 274
Barclay, D., 166
Barclay, J.W., 318, 357
Barham, J., 93, 279
Baring, Viscount, 192
Baring, A., 222
Baring, Hon. A.H., 171
Baring, Hon. F., 171
Baring, Sir F,T., Bt., 137
Baring, H.B., 117
Baring, T., 2, 78, 90
Baring, T.C., 223
Baring, T.G., 131
Baring, Hon. W.B., 158, 171, 192, 267
Barkley, C.F., 198
Barkly, H., 102
Barnard, E.G., 4
Barnard, T., 20
Barne, F. St. J.N., 270
Barneby, J., 64, 282
Barnes, A., 212
Barnes, Sir E., 165
Barnes, R.E., 147
Barnes, T., 28, 38
Barnett, C.J., 112
Barnett, E.W., 63
Barnett, H., 195
Barran, J., 100
Barrington, Viscount (1), 200
Barrington, Viscount (2) (formerly Hon. G.W. Barrington), 36, 70, 219
Barrington, F.L., 66, 162
Barrington, Hon. G., 166
Barrington, Hon. G.W. see Barrington, Viscount (2)
Barrow, W.H., 258
Bartlett, E.A., 70
Bartley, G.C.F., 5
Barttelot, Sir W.B., Bt., 276
Baskerville, T.B.M., 229
Bass, H.A., 167
Bass, M.A., 158, 266
Bass, M.T., 58
Bassett, F., 199
Bassett, J., 84
Bates, E., 134
Bateson, S.S., 92
Bateson, Sir T., Bt., 59
Bath, C., 304
Bathurst, A.A., 50
Bathurst, F.T.A.H., 281
Baxter, R., 96
Baxter, W.E., 333
Bayford, A.F., 16, 126, 151
Bayntun, S.A., 198
Bazley, Sir T., Bt., 116
Bazley, T.A., 203
Beach, Sir M.E.H., Bt., 225
Beach, Sir M.H.H., Bt., 225
Beach, W.W.B., 227
Beadon, W., 168
Beale, S., 58
Beales, E., 9
Beauchamp, Sir T.P., Bt., 249
Beauclerk, A.W., 272
Beaumont, A.H., 123
Beaumont, F.E.B., 220
Beaumont, H.F., 289
Beaumont, S.A., 123, 177
Beaumont, T.W., 256
Beaumont, W.B., 256
Beauvoir, Sir J.E. de, see de Beauvoir
Beckett, Sir J., Bt., 67, 100
Beckett, W., 100, 142
Bective, Earl of (1), 279
Bective, Earl of (2), 279
Bedford, J., 140
Beecroft, G.S., 100
Bell, C., 2, 17
Bell, H., 161
Bell, I.L., 81, 219
Bell, Jacob, 7, 77, 146
Bell, James, 79
Bell, John (1), 54, 153

Bell, John (2), 172
Bell, M., 256
Bell, W.M., 179
Benbow, J., 65, 194
Benett, J., 281
Bennet, J.L., 336
Bennet, P., 271
Bennett, Sir J., 4, 113
Bennett, J.M., 116
Benson, R., 52
Benson, R.A., 139, 185
Bentall, E.H., 113
Bentinck, Lord George, 95
Bentinck, G.A.F.C., 168, 189
Bentinck, G.W.P., 93, 252
Bentinck, Lord Henry, 257
Bentinck, Lord William, 325
Benyon, R., 200
Beresford, Sir J.P., Bt., 44
Beresford, Marcus (1), 21
Beresford, Marcus (2), 8
Beresford, W., 82, 222
Beresford, Hon. W.H., 91, 146
Berkeley, Hon. C.F., 45
Berkeley, C.L.G., 45, 68
Berkeley, Hon. C.P.F., 73, 226
Berkeley, F.H.F., 35
Berkeley, Hon. F.W.F., 45
Berkeley, Hon. G.C.G.F., 226
Berkeley, Sir G.H.F., 60
Berkeley, G.L.G., 226
Berkeley, Sir M.F.F., 73
Bernal, Ralph (1), 144, 187
Bernal, Ralph (2), see Osborne, R.B.
Bernard, T.T., 16
Best, J., 94
Best, Hon. T., 144
Best, Hon. W.S., 18, 152
Bethell, Sir Richard, 16, 152, 194
Bethell, Richard, 284
Betts, E.L., 112
Bevan, R.C.L., 2
Bevan, T., 75
Bewes, T.B., 134
Bickersteth, E.R., 381
Biddell, W., 271
Biddulph, M., 229
Biddulph, R., 85
Biddulph, R.M., 296, 310
Bigge, C.J., 123
Biggs, J., 101
Biggs, R.H.W., 169
Biggs, W., 124
Bignold, Sir S., 127
Bingham, P., 156
Birch, Sir T.B., Bt., 107
Birkbeck, E., 250
Birkin, R., 128
Birley, H., 116
Biron, R.J., 42
Bish, T., 102
Bisset, M.F., 265
Black, A., 322
Black, W.F., 335
Blackburn, P., 322, 325, 374
Blackburne, J., 89
Blackburne, John Ireland (1), 181
Blackburne, John Ireland (2), 240
Blackett, C., 123, 256
Blackett, J.F.B., 123
Blackiston, J., 110
Blackstone, W.S., 178
Blackwood, Hon. P., 134
Blair, F.H., 322
Blair, J., 376
Blair, J.H., 344
Blair, S., 28
Blair, W., 344
Blake, Sir F., Bt., 21
Blake, T., 102, 229
Blake, W.J., 124
Blakely, T.A., 169
Blakemore, R., 85, 184
Blakemore, T.W.B. (formerly Booker), 229
Blamire, W., 210
Blandford, Marquess of (1), 195
Blandford, Marquess of (2), 195, 248
Blencowe, J.G., 103
Blewitt, R.J., 300
Blount, E., 88
Blount, W., 158, 174
Blunt, Sir C.R., Bt., 103
Blunt, Sir C.W., Bt., 103
Bodkin, W.H., 144
Bolckow, H.W.F., 118
Boldero, H.G., 48, 127
Bolitho, J.B., 147
Bolling, W., 28
Bolton, J.C., 325, 374
Bompas, H.M., 156, 235
Bonar, T., 136
Bonham, F.R., 82
Bonham, Sir S.G., Bt., 107
Bontine, R.S., 370
Bontine, W.C., 353
Booker, T,W., see Blakemore, T.W.B.
Boord, T.W., 4
Booth, G.S., (formerly Sclater), 227
Boringdon, Viscount, 174
Borlase, W.C., 208
Borthwick, A., 68
Borthwick, P., 68, 131, 147
Bosanquet, G.J., 230
Boscawen-Rose, Lord, 209
Boss, J.G., 125
Botfield, B., 108
Bourke, Hon. H.L., 52
Bourke, Hon. R., 95
Bourne, James, 68
Bourne, John, 158
Bourne, R., 95
Bousfield, N.G.P., 19
Bouverie, Hon. D.P., 149
Bouverie, Hon. E.P., 106, 149, 200, 330
Bouverie, Hon. P.P., 59, 200, 265
Bovill, W., 79
Bowen, E.E., 86
Bowen, J.B., 316
Bower, J., 100
Bower, R.H., 115

Bowes, J., 220
Bowlby, R., 157
Bowles, T., 11
Bowles, T.G., 17, 56
Bowles, W., 99
Bowmont, Marquess of, 372
Bowring, E.A., 69
Bowring, J., 26, 28, 330, 331
Bowyer, G., 139
Box, P., 36
Boycott, W., 94
Boyd, W.S., 324
Boyle, A.T., 319
Boyle, Sir C., 71
Boyle, Hon. G.F., 349
Boyle, Hon. R.E., 71
Boyle, Hon. W.G., 71
Bracebridge, C.H., 277
Brackley, Viscount, 122, 267
Braddyll, E.R.G., 219
Bradlaugh, C., 126
Bradshaw, J., 21, 42
Braidley, B., 116
Braine, G.T., 134
Bramston, T.W., 223
Brand, Hon. H.B.W., 103, 202
Brand, H.R., 164, 230
Brand, Hon. T., see Trevor, Hon. T.
Branfill, C.E., 223
Brassey, H.A., 150
Brassey, T., 24, 60, 83, 150
Brecknock, Earl of, 291
Bremridge, R., 18
Brennan, E.J., 73
Brett, R.B., 131
Brett, W.B., 84, 143
Brewer, W., 53
Bridgeman, Hon. F.C., 28, 158, 167
Bridges, Sir B.W., Bt., 150, 233
Bridges, M., 71, 163, 185
Bridson, T.R., 28
Briggs, J., 69
Briggs, R., 80
Briggs, W.E., 26
Bright, B.H., 129
Bright, Sir C.T., 4
Bright, Jacob, 116
Bright, John, 25, 66, 116
Bright, R., 263
Brigstock, W.P., 263
Brinckman, T.H., 42
Brinton, J., 94
Brisco, M., 83
Briscoe, J.I., 186, 272, 274
Brise, S.B.R., 221
Bristow, A.R., 94
Bristowe, H.F., 67, 257
Bristowe, S.B., 121, 258
Broadhurst, H., 163, 197
Broadley, H., 284
Broadley, W.H.H., 284
Broadwood, H., 32
Broadwood, T., 88
Brocklehurst, J., 111
Brocklehurst, W.C., 111
Brockman, E.D., 91
Brodie, H.F.A., 355
Brodie, W., 323
Brodie, W.B., 149
Brodrick, Hon. G.C., 195, 314
Brodrick, Hon. W., 272, 273
Brodrick, Hon, W. St. J.F., 274
Brogden, A., 78, 183
Broke, H.G., 92
Bromley, R., 258
Bromley, T., 128
Bromley, W.D., see Devenport, W.B.
Brooke, Lord (1), 278
Brooke, Lord (2), 263
Brooke, E., 166
Brooke, T., 89
Brooker, C., 34
Brooks, J., 28
Brooks, R., 187
Brooks, W.C., 203
Brotherton, J., 148
Brougham, J., 93
Brougham, W., 8, 100
Brown, A.H., 185
Brown, H., 170
Brown, J., 96, 115
Brown, J.C., 88
Brown, W., 238
Browne, U., 14
Browne, W.J., 1
Brownrigg, J.S., 29
Bruce, Lord, see Elgin, Earl of
Bruce, Lord Charles, 117, 280
Bruce, C.L.C., 329, 355
Bruce, Lord Ernest, 117
Bruce, G., 72, 123
Bruce, Lord Henry, 117
Bruce, H.A., 299, 370
Bruce, Hon. J., 356
Bruce, J.B., 299
Bruce, Sir M., Bt., 340, 374
Bruce, R., 351
Bruce, Hon. R.P., 356
Bruce, Hon. T.C., 84, 137, 322
Bruce, Sir W.C.C., Bt., 374
Bruce, W.D., 83
Brudenell, Lord, 253
Bruges, W.H.L., 19, 59
Bryce, J., 9, 338
Brymer, W.E., 62
Buchanan, R.C., 362
Buchanan, T.R., 322, 358
Buchanan, W., 325
Buck, G.S. see Stucley, Sir G.S., Bt.
Buck, L.W., 216
Buckingham, J.S., 153
Buckley, A., 15
Buckley, Sir Edmund, Bt., 122
Buckley, Edmund, 122
Buckley, E.P., 149
Buckley, N., 159
Bulkeley, Sir R.B.W., Bt., 297, 305
Bulkeley, R.L.M.W., 305
Bulkeley, T., 193
Buller, Sir A.W., 60, 84, 106

Buller, C., 106
Buller, E., see Buller, Sir E.M., Bt.
Buller, Sir E.M., Bt. (formerly E. Buller), 158, 267
Buller, Sir J.B.Y., Bt., 217
Buller, J.W., 69, 216
Bulpett, W.W., 192
Bulteel, J.C., 217
Bulwer, Sir E.G.E.L., Bt., see Lytton Sir E.G.E.L.B., Bt.
Bulwer, Sir H.L.E., 7, 54, 167
Bulwer, J.R., 92, 202
Bunbury, C.J.F., 39
Bunbury, E.H., 39
Bunbury, Sir H.E., Bt., 271
Burdett, Sir F., Bt., 10, 280
Burdon, W.W., 187
Burge, W., 129
Burghersh, Lord, 109
Burghley, Lord (1), 243, 253
Burghley, Lord (2), 253
Burke, E.H., 49
Burke, U.R., 40
Burnaby, E.S., 241
Burnaby, F.G., 25
Burnett, Sir Thomas, Bt., 340
Burnett, Thomas, 360
Burns, J.W., 349, 353
Burr, D.H.D., 11, 85, 149
Burrell, Sir C.M., Bt., 154
Burrell, Sir P., Bt., 154
Burrell, Sir W.W., Bt., 154, 275
Burroughes, H.N., 249
Burt, T., 120
Burton, H., 22
Burton, J.R., 9, 194
Burton, L.A., 114
Bury, Viscount, 21, 63, 127, 164, 338
Busfeild, William, (1), 30
Busfeild, William (2) see Ferrand, W.B.
Buszard, M.C., 160
Butler, Hon. C.L., 42, 96
Butler, C.S., 5, 9
Butler, Sir E., 156
Butler, S., 48
Butt, C.P., 156, 167
Butt, G.M., 187
Butt, I., 82
Buxton, C., 112, 124, 272
Buxton, Sir Edward North, Bt., 223, 249
Buxton, Edward North, 223
Buxton, F.W., 12
Buxton, Sir R.J., Bt., 39, 251
Buxton, S.C., 29, 132
Buxton, Sir Thomas Fowell, Bt., 10, 95, 224, 250
Buxton, Thomas Fowell, 187
Byng, G., 248
Byng, Hon. G.H.C., see Enfield, Viscount (2)
Byng, Hon. G.S., see Enfield, Viscount (1)
Byng, Sir J., 136
Byrne, T.E.D., 320

C

Cabbell, B.B., 7, 29, 146
Cabbell, T., 6
Cadogan, Hon. F.W., 31, 55, 158
Caine, W.S., 107, 151
Caird, J., 57, 337, 339
Calcraft, J.H., 180
Calcraft, J.H.M., 180
Calcraft, W.M., 180
Callander, J.H., 343
Callender, W.R., 116
Calley, T., 55
Calmady, C.B., 134
Calthorpe, Hon. A.C.G., 25
Calthorpe, Hon. F.G., 39
Calthorpe, Hon. F.H.W.G., 282
Calthorpe, Hon. S.G., 83
Calvert, F., 16
Calvert, N., 230
Cameron, C., 325
Cameron, Donald (1), 197
Cameron, Donald (2), 359
Cameron, G., 49
Campbell, A., 322, 329, 343
Campbell, A.C., 334, 370
Campbell, A.G., 232
Campbell, A.H., 99
Campbell, Sir A.I., Bt., 343
Campbell, Lord Colin, 343
Campbell, C.M., 163, 267
Campbell, Sir George, Bt., 325
Campbell, Sir George, 331
Campbell, H., see Bannerman, H.C.
Campbell, Sir H.P.H., Bt., 348
Campbell, James (1), 330, 344
Campbell, James (2), 325
Campbell, James (3), 102
Campbell, Sir John, 65, 322
Campbell, James Alexander, 380
Campbell, James Archibald, 330
Campbell, J.H., see Wyndham, J.H.C.
Campbell, R., 84, 97
Campbell, R.F.F., 319
Campbell, R.J.R., 187
Campbell, Walter Frederick, 343
Campbell, Hon. William Frederick, 41, 82, 168
Candlish, J., 166
Cane, C. Du, see Du Cane
Canning, Hon. C.J., 182
Canning, Sir S., 95
Cantelupe, Viscount, 84, 103
Capper, C., 150
Carbutt, E.H., 300
Carden, Sir R.W., 7, 18, 73, 139, 146
Cardwell, E., 51, 107, 130, 344
Carew, W.H.P., 106, 208
Cargill, W.W., 21, 168
Carington, Hon. C.R., 197
Carington, Hon. R.C.G., 201
Carington, Hon. W.H.P., 197
Carleton, D.W., 227
Carmichael, A.G., 367
Carnac, Sir James Rivett, Bt., 150
Carnac, Sir John Rivett, Bt., 110

Carne, W., 131
Carnegie, Hon. C., 357
Carnegie, Hon. S.T., 158
Carpenter, G.W., 21
Carpenter, W., 77
Carr, H., 27
Carruthers, D., 96
Carson, J.S., 197
Carstairs, P., 123
Carter, John Bonham (1), 137
Carter, John Bonham (2), 192
Carter, R.M., 100
Carter, S., 54, 169
Carter, W.P., 47
Cartwright, F.W., 254
Cartwright, H., 254
Cartwright, W.C., 259
Cartwright, W.R., 254
Castlereagh, Viscount, 220, 301
Cathcart, Sir J.A., Bt., 344
Cattley, M., 8
Caulfeild, J., 11
Caulfeild, J.M., 151
Causton, R.K., 53
Cave, S., 154
Cave, T., 18
Cavendish, Lord (1), 213
Cavendish, Lord (2), see Hartington, Marquess of
Cavendish, Hon. C.C., 201, 275
Cavendish, Lord Edward, 213, 237, 275
Cavendish, Lord Frederick, 288
Cavendish, Lord George (formerly Hon. G.H. Cavendish), 213
Cavendish, Hon. G.H., see Cavendish Lord George
Cavendish, H.F.C., 58
Cavendish, Hon. R., 36
Cavendish, W.G., 132, 201
Cavendish, W.H.F., 275
Cawley, C.E., 148
Cayley, Edward Stillingfleet (1), 285
Cayley, Edward Stillingfleet (2), 285
Cayley, Sir G., Bt., 151
Cayley, G.A., 142
Cayley, G.J., 151
Cazalet, E., 234
Cecil, Lord Eustace, 223, 224
Cecil, Lord Robert, see Cranborne, Viscount
Chadwick, D., 111
Chadwick, E., 68, 330
Challis, T., 3
Challoner, C.B., 274
Chalmers, P., 333
Chamberlain, J., 25, 153
Chambers, G.H., 35
Chambers, M., 4, 20, 60
Chambers, Sir T., 7, 86
Champneys, Sir T.S.M., 71
Chandos, Marquess of (1), 201
Chandos, Marquess of (2), 36, 379
Chaplin, E., 105
Chaplin, H., 245
Chaplin, T., 160
Chaplin, W.J., 149
Chapman, A., 188
Chapman, J., 76, 149
Chapman, T., 188
Chapman, W., 176
Charles, E., 378
Charles, R., 124
Charlesworth, J.C.D., 177
Charley, Sir W.T., 92, 148
Charlton, E.L., 108
Charlton, T.B., 128
Charsley, F., 197, 201
Charteris, Hon. F.W., see Elco, Lord (1)
Chawner, R.C., 158
Chaytor, Sir W., Bt., 166, 219
Chaytor, W.R.C., 66
Cheetham, J., 89, 148, 238
Cheetham, J.F., 213
Chelsea, Viscount (1), 63, 139, 248
Chelsea, Viscount, (2), 19, 38
Cheney, E., 242
Chester, J., 175
Chetwode, Sir J., Bt., 36
Chetwynd, W.F., 158
Chichester, A., 87
Chichester, C., 173
Chichester, Sir J.P.B., Bt., 18
Child, J.M., 302
Child, S., 267, 269
Childers, H.C.E., 135
Childers, J.W., 115, 202
Ching, W., 44
Chisholm, A.W., 359
Chitty, J.W., 130
Cholmeley, Sir H.A.H., Bt., 74
Cholmeley, Sir M.J., Bt., 74, 244, 246
Cholmondeley, Lord Henry, 249
Cholmondeley, Hon. Hugh, 301, 310
Cholmondeley, Lord William, 228
Christie, W.D., 41, 187, 326
Christie, W.L., 103
Christopher, R.A., see Hamilton, R.A.C.N.
Christy, S., 122
Churchill, Lord Alfred, 195, 291
Churchill, Lord Charles, 195
Churchill, C.H., 105
Churchill, Lord John, 195
Churchill, Lord Randolph, 195
Chute, W.L.W., 252
Claneboye, Lord Dufferin and, see Dufferin and Claneboye
Clark, S., 334
Clark, T., 153
Clarke, E.G., 8, 134
Clarke, J.C., 11
Clarke, T.C., 136
Clay, James, 22, 96
Clay, John, 255
Clay, Sir W., Bt., 9
Clayden, P.W., 128
Clayton, R.R., 16
Clayton, Sir W.R., Bt., 77
Cleasby, A., 272, 377
Clement, W.J., 155
Clerk, Sir G., Bt., 63, 160, 354

Clifford, C.C., 124, 232
Clifford, H.M., 85, 314
Clifton, J.T., 132, 138, 236
Clifton, Sir R.J., Bt., 128
Clifton, T.H., 236
Clinton, Lord Arthur, 121
Clinton, Lord Charles, 67, 150
Clinton, Lord Edward, 257
Clinton, Lord Robert, 257
Clinton, Lord Thomas Pelham-, see Pelham-Clinton
Clive, Viscount (1), 108
Clive, Viscount (2), 261
Clive, E.B., 85
Clive, E.H., 85
Clive, G., 85
Clive, Hon. G.H.W.W., 108
Clive, H., 108
Clive, H.B., 108
Clive, Hon. R., see Clive, Hon. R.W.
Clive, Hon. R.H., 108, 262
Clive, Hon. R.W. (formerly Hon. R. Clive), 108, 262
Clowes, S.W., 214, 241
Cobbett, J.M., 47, 54, 129
Cobbett, J.P., 38
Cobbett, W., 116, 129
Cobbold, J.C., 92
Cobbold, J.P., 92
Cobbold, T.C., 92
Cobden, R., 89, 143, 161, 286
Cochrane, A.D.R.W.B., 33, 87, 156, 232, 362
Cochrane, C., 10
Cochrane, Sir T.J., 10, 92, 326
Cockburn, Sir A.J.E., 156
Cockburn, Sir G., 4, 134, 137, 142
Cockburn, G.W., 303
Cockburn, J.P., 87
Cockerell, Sir C., Bt., 68
Cocks, T.S., 140
Coddington, W., 26
Codrington, C.W., 225
Codrington, Sir E., 60
Codrington, Sir W.J., 4, 10, 103
Coffin, W., 293
Cohen, A., 8, 103
Coke, Hon. E.K.W., 252
Coke, Hon. W.C.W., 249
Colbeck, W.H., 61
Colborne, N.W.R., 184
Colborne, Hon. W.N.R., 141
Cole, H.T., 131
Colebrooke, Sir T.E., Bt., 168, 362, 363
Coleridge, Sir J.D., 69
Coles, H.B., 12
Collett, W.R., 29, 105
Collier, J., 134
Collier, R., 99
Collier, Sir R.P., 134
Collings, J., 92
Collingwood, G.L.N., 144
Collins, D., 208
Collins, T., 29, 58, 97
Collins, W., 182
Colman, J.J., 127
Colquhoun, Sir J., Bt., 353
Colquhoun, J.C., 122, 330, 353
Colvile, Sir C., 58
Colvile, C.R., 58, 214
Colville, A., 78
Commerell, Sir J.E., 156
Compton, F., 228
Compton, H.C., 228
Compton, Lord William (1), 96
Compton, Lord William (2), 278
Coningham, W., 10, 34
Coningsby, R., 4
Conwy, C.G.H.R., 297
Conygham, Lord Albert, see Denison, Lord Albert
Cooke, C.E.B., 141
Cooke, G.W., 7, 53
Cooke, W.H., 179
Cookes, T.H., 282
Cookson, J.C.F., 151
Coope, O.E., 9, 78, 248
Cooper, Hon. A.H.A., 62
Cooper, C.P., 42
Coote, T., 202
Copeland, W.T., 163
Corbett, A.C., 277
Corbett, Edward, 126, 262
Corbett, Edwin, 206
Corbett, J., 64
Corbett, P., 301
Corbett, T.G., 244
Cordes, T., 300
Cornish, J., 174
Corrance, F.S., 270
Cossham, H., 48, 61, 128
Cosway, Sir W.R., 233
Cotes, C.C., 155
Cotes, J., 261
Cother, W., 73
Cotterell, Sir H.G., Bt., 229
Cotton, B.T., 232
Cotton, W.J.R., 2, 8
Coulson, J.B., 123
Coulthart, J.R., 15
Courtauld, G., 113
Courtenay, Lord (1), 217
Courtenay, Lord (2), 69, 215
Courtenay, P., 32
Courtenay, Sir W.P.H. *(soidisant)* (J.M. Thom), 42, 233
Courtney, L.H., 106
Cowan, C., 322
Cowen, Joseph (1), 123
Cowen, Joseph (2), 123
Cowper, Hon. H.F., 167, 230
Cowper, Hon. W.F., see Temple, Hon. W.F.C.
Cox, E.W., 168, 170
Cox, J.C., 19, 61
Cox, W., 3
Cox, W.T., 58
Craig, H., 344
Craig, W.G., 322, 354
Craig, W.Y., 267
Cranborne, Viscount (formerly Lord Robert Cecil), 160
Craufurd, E.H.J., 319

Craven, Hon. F.K., 146, 277
Crawford, R., 155
Crawford, R.W., 2, 82
Crawford, W., 2, 34
Crawford, W.S., 143
Crawfurd, J., 138, 325, 334, 337
Crawley, S., 20
Cremer, W.R., 182
Cresswell, A.J.B., 255
Cresswell, C., 107
Crewe, Sir G., Bt., 214
Creyke, R., 198
Cripps, J., 50
Cripps, W., 50
Croft, Sir H.G.D., Bt., 229
Croft, Sir J., Bt., 233
Crompton, Charles (1), 124, 138
Crompton, Charles (2), 207
Crompton, J.S., 142
Crompton, S., 172
Crook, J., 28
Cropper, E.D.T., 298
Cropper, J., 93
Crosland, T.P., 89
Cross, J.K., 28
Cross, Sir R.A., 138, 240
Crosse, T.B., 190
Crossley, Sir F., Bt., 80, 286, 288
Crossley, J., 80
Croston, J., 111
Crowder, R.B., 106, 192
Cruickshanks, J., 319
Crum, A., 325, 370
Cubitt, G., 274
Cubitt, W., 2, 12
Cuninghame, Sir W.J.M., Bt., 319
Cunliffe, J.C.P., 23
Cunliffe, Sir R.A., Bt., 296, 297
Curling, J., 12, 59
Currie, D., 326, 369
Currie, E.H., 9
Currie, H., 79, 274
Currie, J., 86
Currie, R., 2, 126
Curteis, E.B., 145
Curteis, H.B., 145, 275
Curteis, H.M., 145
Curteis, W.C., 106
Curwen, H., 211
Curzon, Viscount, 242
Curzon, Hon. F., 58
Curzon, Hon. M., 241
Cust, Hon. A.W.B., 261
Cust, Hon. C.H., 244, 261
Cust, H.F.C., 74
Cuthbert, W., 123
Cuthbertson, J.N., 330

D

Dakin, A.T., 171
Dalbiac, Sir J.C., 142
Dalglish, R., 325
Dalkeith, Earl of, 354
Dalmeny, Lord, 337
Dalrymple, Viscount (1) (formerly J. Dalrymple), 376
Dalrymple, Viscount (2), 376
Dalrymple, Sir A.J., Bt., 34
Dalrymple, C., 349
Dalrymple, D., 19
Dalrymple, J., see Dalrymple, Viscount (1)
Dalrymple, Sir J.H., Bt., 354
Dalrymple, Hon. N. de C., 346
Damer, Hon. G.L.D., 62
Daniel, W.T.S., 167
Darby, G., 275
Dare, R.W.H., 223
Darlington, Earl of, 262
Darwin, F., 142
Dashwood, F., 144, 155
Dashwood, Sir G.H., Bt., 197, 201
Dashwood, Sir H.W., Bt., 259
Daubeney, H., 19
Davenport, E.D., 161, 181
Davenport, E.G., 147
Davenport, H.T., 122, 163, 267
Davenport, J., 163
Davenport, J.W.H., see Handley, J.W.D.
Davenport, W.B. (formerly Bromley), 277
Davey, H., 49
Davey, R., 209
Davie, Sir H.R.F., Bt., 327
Davie, J.D.F., 18
Davies, A.H.S., 308
Davies, D., 294, 308
Davies, D.A.S., 309
Davies, J.L., 294
Davies, K., 85
Davies, R., 292, 305
Davies, T.H.H., 196
Davies, William (1), 108
Davies, William (2), 316
Davis, E.F., 233
Davison, J.R., 66
Dawes, E., 232
Dawkins, W.G., 174
Dawnay, Hon. G.C., 285
Dawnay, Hon. L.P., 172, 198
Dawnay, Hon. W.H., 260
Dawson, E., 242
Dawson, G.R., 60
Deakin, James Henry (Senr.), 99
Deakin, James Henry (Junr.), 99
Deane, J.P., 130
de Beauvoir, Sir J.E., 193
Deedes, William (1), 233
Deedes, William (2), 233
Deering, J.P., 16
de Ferrières, Baron, 45
de Grey, Earl, 142
de Grey, Hon. T., 252
De Horsey, S.H., 122
Dempster, G., 338
Denison, Lord Albert (formerly Lord Albert Conygham), 42
Denison, C.B., 287, 289
Denison, E., 121
Denison, E.B., 286
Denison, J.E., 115, 257, 258

Denison, W.B., 67
Denison W.E., 128, 257
Denison, Hon. W.H.F., 22, 151
Denison. W.J., 274
Denman, Hon. G., 173, 377
Denman, Hon. J., 116
Dennistoun, A., 353
Dennistoun, J., 325
Dent, J., 174
Dent, J.D., 97, 151
Dering, Sir E.C., Bt., 233
de Rothschild, Baron, F.J., 16
de Rothschild, Baron L.N., 2
de Rothschild, Baron M.A., 91
de Rothschild, Sir N.M., Bt., 16
Desart, Earl of, 92
Deverell, W.H., 228
de Wilton, Viscount Grey, see Grey de Wilton
de Worms, Baron (formerly H. Worms), 4, 150
D'Eyncourt, C., (formerly Tennyson), 6
Dick, Q., 16, 113
Dickinson, B.B., 173
Dickinson, F.H., 265
Dickinson, S.S., 164
Dickson, A.G., 63
Dickson, L.S., 5, 7, 127
Dickson, P., 176
Dickson, S.A., 96, 139
Dickson, W., 325
Digby, Hon. E.H.T., 218
Digby, J.K.D.W., 264
Dilke, A.W., 123
Dilke, Sir C.W., Bt., 1, 178
Dillwyn, L.L., 304
Dillwyn, L.W., 312
Dimsdale, C.J., 86
Dimsdale, R., 86
Dingley, J., 99
Disney, J., 82, 222
Disraeli, B., 112, 155, 168, 197, 201
Divett, E., 69
Dixon, G., 25
Dixon, John, 43
Dixon, Joseph, 325
Dixon, W., 370
Dod, J.W., 261
Dodd, G., 112
Dodds, J., 162
Dodson, J.G., 46, 151, 275
Donaldson, S.A., 82
Donkin, Sir R.S., 21, 150
Donovan, A., 275
Dorington, J.E., 164
Dottin, A.R., 156
Douglas, A.A., 233
Douglas, Sir C.E., 17, 66, 182
Douglas, F.B., 322, 336
Douglas, Sir G.H.S., Bt., 372
Douglas, Sir H., Bt., 107
Douglas, J., 325, 339, 376
Douglas, J.D.S., 144
Doulton, F., 6, 140
Douro, Marquess of, 127, 227
Dowdeswell, W., 170
Dowdeswell, W.E., 170, 283
Downie, R., 330
Drax, J.S.W.S.E., 180
Drewe, E.S., 32
Drinkwater, H.C., 99
Drumlanrig, Viscount, 352
Drummond, H., 274
Drummond, H.H., 369
Duberley, J., 90
Du Cane, C., 113, 222
Duckham, T., 229
Duckworth, Sir J.T.B., Bt., 69
Duckworth, S., 101
Duff, Sir A., 355
Duff, G.S., 323
Duff, James (1), see Fife, Earl of
Duff, James, (2), 250
Duff, L.D.G. (formerly Gordon), 347
Duff, M.E.G., 323
Duff, R.W. (formerly Abercromby), 347
Duff, T.A., 323
Dufferin and Claneboye, Lord, 44
Duffield, T., 11
Dugdale, J., 148
Dugdale, W.S., 277
Duke, Sir J., Bt., 2, 29
Dumas, F.K., 34
Dunbar, Sir W., Bt., 339
Duncan, Viscount, (1), 19, 38, 156, 357
Duncan, Viscount (2), 278
Duncan, F., 3, 66, 120
Duncan, G., 321
Duncannon, Viscount (1), 128
Duncannon, Viscount (2) (formerly Hon. J.G.B. Ponsonby), 58
Duncombe, Hon. Arthur, 67, 100, 284
Duncombe, Arthur, 151
Duncombe, Hon. O., 285
Duncombe, T.S., 3, 86
Duncombe, Hon. W., 285
Duncombe, Hon. W.E., 67, 285
Duncuft, J., 129
Dundas, Lord (formerly Hon. T. Dundas), 141, 198
Dundas, C.W.D., 297
Dundas, Sir D., 375
Dundas, F., 366
Dundas, G., 365
Dundas, Hon. John Charles (Senr.), 141, 198
Dundas, Hon. John Charles (Junr.), 141, 285
Dundas, J.W.D., 4, 59
Dundas, L., 141
Dundas, R.A., see Hamilton, R.A.C.N.
Dundas, Hon. Sir R.L., 141
Dundas, Hon. T., see Dundas, Lord
Dungannon, Viscount (formerly Hon. A. Trevor), 66
Dungarvan, Viscount, 71
Dunglass, Lord, 348
Dunlop, Alexander Milne, 313
Dunlop, Alexander Murray, 326
Dunlop, C., 325
Dunlop, H., 349
Dunlop, J., 330, 344

Dunn, A., 8
Dunn, J., 57, 174
Dunraven, Earl of (formerly Viscount Adare), 312
Du Pré, C.G., 201
Durham, Sir P.C.H., 59
Dutton, Hon. R.H., 50, 149, 228
Dyke, Sir W.H. Bt., 234, 235
Dykes, F.L.B., 52
Dykes, J.W.B., 211
Dyott, R., 104, 268

E

Eagle, F.K., 39
Eagle, W., 28, 128
Eardley, Sir C.E., Bt. (formerly Smith), 135, 286, 322
Earle, R.A., 21, 113
Earp, T., 121
East, E.G.C., 200
East, Sir J.B., Bt., 192
Easthope, Sir John, Bt., 31, 101, 103, 156
Easthope, John, 170
Eastnor, Viscount (1), 140
Eastnor, Viscount (2), 140
Easton, C., 70, 270, 271
Eastwick, E.B., 131
Eaton, H.W., 54
Eaton, R.J., 202
Eaton, W.M., 111
Ebrington, Viscount (1), 216
Ebrington, Viscount (2), 7, 18, 134
Ebrington, Viscount (3), 173
Eccles, W., 26
Eckersley, N., 190
Ecroyd, W.F., 43, 138, 237
Edge, S.R., 122
Edgell, E.W., 253
Edgell, R.W., 274
Edmondstone, Sir W., Bt., 374
Edridge, J., 280
Edwardes, Hon. W., see Kensington, Lord
Edwards, C., 42, 193
Edwards, Sir Henry, Bt., 22, 80
Edwards, Henry, 187
Edwards, Sir J., Bt., 301
Edwards, J.P., 149, 175
Edwards, W., 300
Egerton, Hon. A. de T., 204
Egerton, Hon. A.F., 190, 238, 239
Egerton, E.C., 46, 111, 203
Egerton, Lord Francis, 238
Egerton, Hon. Francis, 212
Egerton, Sir P. de M.G., Bt., 206, 207
Egerton, Hon. W., 204, 205
Egerton, W.T., 205
Elcho, Lord (1) (formerly Hon. F.W. Charteris), 225, 358
Elcho, Lord (2), 358
Elderton, C.M., 299
Elgin, Earl of (formerly Lord Bruce), 156
Eliot, Lord (1), 27, 208
Eliot, Lord (2), 55, 60
Elley, Sir J., 193
Ellice, A., 82
Ellice, Edward (1), 54
Ellice, Edward (2), 89, 329, 336
Elliot, Hon. A.R.D., 372
Elliot, Sir George, Bt., 219
Elliot, Hon. George, 372
Elliot, George, 44
Elliot, G.W., 125
Elliot, Hon. J.E., 372
Elliot, J.T.S., 328
Elliot, Sir W.F., 372
Ellis, C.W.J., 27
Ellis, Hon. H., 105
Ellis, John (1), 101
Ellis, John (2), 98
Ellis, Sir J.W., Bt., 273
Ellis , W., 101
Elmley, Viscount, 283
Elphinstone, H., 83, 103, 107
Elphinstone, H.W., 234
Elphinstone, Sir J.D.H., Bt., 137, 326, 340
Elton, Sir A.H., Bt., 19, 263
Elton, C.I., 265
Elwes, J.P., 222
Emlyn, Viscount (1), 316
Emlyn, Viscount (2), 309
Emmens, S.H., 180
Enfield, Viscount (1) (formerly Hon. G.S. Byng), 44, 136
Enfield, Viscount (2) (formerly Hon. G.H.C. Byng), 169, 248
Engledue, J.R., 156
Entwisle, J., 143
Entwisle, W., 116, 238
Epps, J., 126
Erle, W., 130
Erskine, J.E., 374
Escott, B., 10, 45, 134, 192, 265
Eslington, Lord (formerly Hon. H.G. Liddell), 256
Estcourt, G.T.J.B. see Estcourt, G.T.J.S.
Estcourt, G.T.J.S. (formerly G.T.J.B. Estcourt), 280
Estcourt, J.B.B., 59
Estcourt, T.G.B., 379
Estcourt, T.H.S.B., see Estcourt, T.H.S.S.
Estcourt, T.H.S.S. (formerly Estcourt, T.H.S.B. and Sotheron, T.H.S.), 59, 280
Etwall, R., 12
Euston, Earl of (Senr.), 171, 254
Euston, Earl of (Junr.), 171
Evans, Sir G. De L., 10, 145
Evans, J., 294, 298
Evans, J.C., 158
Evans, S., 25
Evans, T.W., 158, 213, 214
Evans, W., 101, 213
Evans, W.H., 18
Evelyn, W.J., 79, 274
Everett, R.L., 270
Ewart, J.C., 107
Ewart, W., 7, 107, 190, 320
Ewing, A.O., 353
Ewing, H.E.C., 334
Ewing, J., 325

Eykyn, R., 168, 193
Eyncourt, C.T.D', see D'Eyncourt
Eyre, H., 67, 121
Eyston, C., 178
Eyton, P.E., 297

F

Fairbairn, Sir A., 97, 100, 287
Fairrie, J., 326
Faithful, G., 34
Fancourt, C. St. J., 18
Fane, H.H., 228
Fane, J.W., 259
Farebrother, C., 6
Farnham, E.B., 241
Farquhar, Sir A., 318
Farquhar, Sir W.M.T., Bt., 86
Farquharson, J.R., 27
Farquharson, R., 342
Farrand, R., 158
Farrer, J., 220
Faulkner, D., 128
Fawcett, H., 5, 34, 41
Fawcett, J.H., 52
Fazakerley, J.N., 132
Fector, J.M., 63, 112
Feilden, H.M., 26
Feilden, J., 26
Feilden, M.J., 26
Feilden, R.J., 236
Feilden, W., 26
Feilding, Viscount, 377
Fellowes, E., 231
Fellowes, H.A.W., 12
Fellowes, I.N., 12
Fellowes, Hon. N., 216
Fellowes, W.H., 231
Fenton, J., 143
Fenton, L., 89
Fenton, W., 46, 237
Fenwick, E.M., 98
Fenwick, H., 66, 166
Fereday, D., 194
Fergus, J., 331, 356
Ferguson, G., 347
Ferguson, J., 43
Ferguson, Robert (1), 331, 358
Ferguson, Robert (2), 331
Ferguson, Robert (3), 43
Ferguson, Sir R.C., 128
Ferguson, R.C.M., 371
Fergusson, Sir J., Bt., 71, 150, 326 344
Fergusson, J.A., 132
Fergusson, R.C., 361
Fergusson, W.F., 193
Fermoy, Lord, 7
Fernley, G.A., 161
Ferrand, W., 132
Ferrand, W.B. (formerly Busfeild), 16, 30, 54, 60, 97
Ferrières, Baron de, see de Ferrières
Ffolkes, Sir W.H.B., Bt., 95
Field, E., 34, 121
Fielden, John, 129
Fielden, Joshua, 287
Fife, Earl of (formerly J. Duff), 347
Figgins, J., 155
Fildes, J., 76
Filmer, Sir Edmund, Bt., (1), 235
Filmer, Sir Edmund, Bt., (2), 234, 235
Finch, C.G.W. (formerly Wynne), 292
Finch, F., 104, 179
Finch, G., 160, 260
Finch, G.H., 260
Finlay, A.S., 343
Finlay, R.B., 358
Finnie, W., 345
Firth, J.F.B., 1
Fison, W., 288
Fitzalan, Lord, see Arundel and Surrey, Earl of
Fitzgerald, W.R.S.V., 88
Fitzharris, Viscount, 137, 191
Fitzmaurice, Lord Edmond, 40
Fitzmaurice, Hon. W.E., 201
Fitzroy, Lord Charles, 39
Fitzroy, Lord Frederick, 171, 254
Fitzroy, Hon. H., 103, 126
Fitzroy, Lord James, 171
Fitzroy, R., 66
Fitzwilliam, Hon. C.W.W., 115
Fitzwilliam, Hon. G.W., 132, 141, 253
Fitzwilliam, Hon. W.C.W., see Milton, Viscount (1)
Fitzwilliam, Hon. W.H.W., 231, 289
Fitzwilliam, Hon. W.J.W., 132
Fitz Wygram, Sir F.W.J., Bt., 228
Fleeming, Hon. C.E., 374
Fleetwood, Sir P.H., Bt., 138
Fleming, J., 18, 60
Fleming, J.W., 228
Fleming, T.W., 192, 232
Fletcher, Sir H., Bt., 88
Fletcher, I., 52
Fletcher, W., 52
Flower, C., 291
Flower, E.F., 54, 277
Flower, Sir J., Bt., 171
Floyer, J., 218
Foley, E.T., 229
Foley, H.J.W.H., 268, 269
Foley, J.H.H., 64, 282
Foley, Hon. T.H., 283
Foljambe, C.G.S., 257
Foljambe, F.J.S., 67
Foljambe, G.S., 257
Folkes, Sir W.J.H.B., Bt., 249, 252
Folkestone, Viscount, 281
Follett, B.S., 32, 50
Follett, R.B., 104
Follett, Sir, W.W., 69
Fooks, J., 34
Forbes, Sir C., Bt., 248
Forbes, J., 65, 138
Forbes, J.S., 63
Forbes, Sir William, Bt., 342
Forbes, William, 374
Fordwich, Viscount, 42

Fordyce, A.D., 318
Fordyce, W.D., 340, 341
Forester, C.T.W., 185
Forester, Hon. G.C.W., 185
Forlonge, W., 127
Forman, T.S., 32
Forster, Sir C., Bt., 179
Forster, C.S., 179
Forster, J., 21
Forster, M., 21
Forster, R., 72
Forster, W.E., 30, 100
Forsyth, W., 7, 19, 41
Fort, J., 51
Fort, Richard (1), 51
Fort, Richard (2), 51
Fortescue, Hon. D.F., 12
Fortescue, Hon. J.W., 18
Forwood, A.B., 107
Foster, J.F.L., 131
Foster, R., 41
Foster, T.C., 153
Foster, W.H., 31
Foster, W.O., 268, 269
Fothergill, R., 299
Foulkes, W.L., 296
Fowler, H.H., 194
Fowler, J.A., 170
Fowler, R., 218
Fowler, R.N., 2, 131
Fowler, William (1), 41, 126
Fowler, William (2), 212
Fox, C.J., 144
Fox, C.R., 9, 150, 164, 169
Fox, G.L., 22
Fox, S.W.L., 22, 84, 92
Fox, W.J., 129
Frankland, Sir R., Bt., 172
Frankland, Sir W.A., Bt., 172
Franklyn, G.W., 136
Fraser, J., 329
Fraser, R., 329
Fraser, W., 91
Fraser, Sir W.A., Bt., 18, 82, 94, 108
Freake, C.J., 1
Freeland, H.W., 47
Freeman, E.A., 264
Freestun, W.L., 187
Fremantle, Sir Thomas Francis, Bt., 36
Fremantle, Hon. Thomas Francis, 35, 180, 201
French, J.T.W., 150
Freshfield, C.K., 63
Freshfield, J.W., 2, 29, 58, 131, 197
Frewen, C.H., 101, 145, 241, 275
Fripp, W., 35
Frost, Sir T.G., 46
Fry, L., 35
Fry, T., 56
Fryer, R., 194
Fuller, A.E., 275
Fuller, G.P., 280
Fyler, G., 157
Fyler, T.B., 54
Fytche, A., 145

G

Galloway, A., 63
Gallwey, Sir W.P., Bt., 172
Galway, Viscount (1), 67
Galway, Viscount (2) (formerly Hon. G.E.M. Monckton), 257
Gambier, C.S., 78
Gamble, R.W., 80, 143
Gard, R.S., 69, 87
Gardiner, J.G.C., 257
Gardner, J.A., 45
Gardner, J.D. (formerly Earl of Leicester and John Townshend), 27
Gardner, J.T.A., 45
Gardner, R., 101
Gardner, R.R., 193
Garfit, T., 29
Garlies, Lord, 376
Garnett, W., 148
Garnett, W.J., 98
Garnier, J.C., 217, 228
Garth, R., 79
Garvagh, Lord, 140
Gaselee, S., 32, 130, 137
Gaskell, C.G.M., 97, 135, 185
Gaskell, D., 177
Gaskell, J.M., 185
Gaskell, W.P., 45
Gassiot, J.P., 272
Geach, C., 54
Geary, Sir W.R.P., Bt., 235
Geissler, G., 147
German, J., 138
Gervis, G.W.T. (formerly Tapps), 49
Gibb, W., 28, 161
Gibbons, S.J., 2
Gibbs, A.G.H., 11
Gibbs, F.W., 47, 86
Gibbs, H.P., 42
Gibson, T.M., 15, 41, 92, 116
Giffard, Sir H.S., 88, 99, 293
Gifford, Earl of, 174
Giles, A., 156
Gill, T., 134
Gill, W.J., 5, 128
Gillon, W.D., 324
Gilpin, C., 126, 335
Gilpin, R.T., 199
Gipps, H.P., 42
Gisborne, M., 214
Gisborne, T., 92, 94, 124, 128, 174, 213, 242
Gisborne, T.G., 174
Gladstone, H.J., 100, 248
Gladstone, J., 321
Gladstone, J.H., 198
Gladstone, J.N., 59, 92, 179
Gladstone, R., 98
Gladstone, Sir T., Bt., 92, 101, 132, 360
Gladstone, W.E., 4, 100, 116, 121, 238, 240, 354, 379
Gladstone, W.H., 46, 188, 282
Glass, Sir R.A., 23
Gloag, J.A.L., 321

Glover, E.A., 22, 42
Glyn, E.L., 108
Glyn, G.C., 93
Glyn, G.G., 152
Glyn, Hon. H.C., 44
Glyn, Hon. S.C., 152
Glynne, Sir S.R., Bt., 297, 311
Goddard, A., 55
Goddard, A.L., 55
Goderich, Viscount, 89, 96, 286
Godson, A.F., 182
Godson, R., 94
Godwin, J.V., 30
Goldney, G., 48
Goldsmid, A., 127
Goldsmid, F.D., 34, 87
Goldsmid, F.H., 78, 139
Goldsmid, Sir I.L., Bt., 22
Goldsmid, Sir J., Bt., 34, 50, 87, 144, 150, 273
Gompertz, H., 135
Gooch, Sir D., Bt., 55
Gooch, Sir E.S., Bt., 270
Goodman, Sir G., 100
Goodman, N., 132
Goodricke, Sir F.L.H., Bt., 158, 268
Goodson, J., 78
Gordon, Hon. Sir Alexander Hamilton, 341
Gordon, Hon. Arthur Hamilton, 22, 106, 340
Gordon, C.W., 21
Gordon, Lord Douglas, 231, 342
Gordon, E.S., 171, 380
Gordon, Lord John, see Gordon-Hallyburton
Gordon, J.A., 158
Gordon, J.E., 128, 334
Gordon, Sir J.W., Bt., 124
Gordon, L.D., see Duff, L.D.G.
Gordon, R., 55, 193
Gordon, T., 347
Gordon, Hon. William, 340
Gordon, William, 1, 320
Gordon-Hallyburton, Lord John (formerly Lord John Gordon), 357
Gordon-Lennox, Lord Alexander, 154
Gordon-Lennox, Lord George, 110
Gordon-Lennox, Lord Henry, 47
Gore, J.R.O., 261, 307
Gore, M., 18, 59
Gore, W.O., 261
Goring, C., 154
Goring, H.D., 154
Gorst, J.E., 41, 44, 83
Goshen, G.J., 2, 142
Goulburn, E., 43, 92, 101
Goulburn, H., 377
Gourley, E.T., 166
Gowan, W., 157
Gower, Hon. E.F.L., 27, 58, 163
Gower, G.W.G.L., 140, 272
Gower, Lord Ronald Leveson-, see Leveson-Gower
Grafton, F.W., 237
Graham, J., 175
Graham, Sir J.R.G., Bt., 43, 62, 142, 210, 302
Graham, R., 369
Graham, Lord William, 74, 229
Graham, William (1), 325
Graham, William (2), 16
Granby, Marquess of, 160, 241
Granger, T.C., 66
Grant, Albert, 94
Grant, Andrew, 332
Grant, Sir A.C., Bt., 41, 76, 87
Grant, Charles, 359
Grant, Sir Colquhoun, 136
Grant, Corrie, 195
Grant, D., 7
Grant, Hon. Francis William, 355
Grant, Francis William, 359
Grant, Sir G.M., Bt., 355, 359
Grant, H.M., 347
Grant, J.M., 359
Grant, Hon. J.O., 355
Grant, R., 3
Grantham, W., 272
Graves, S.R., 107
Gray, C.W., 32
Gray, W., 28
Greaves, E., 182
Green, A., 52
Green, E., 135, 177
Green, W., 132
Greenall, Sir G., Bt., 181
Greenall, P., 190
Greenaway, C., 102
Greene, B.B., 82
Greene, E., 39
Greene, J.B., 101
Greene, J.G.J., 191
Greene, T., 98
Greenhill, D., 333
Greening, E.O., 80
Greenwood, J., 142
Greg, R.H., 111, 116
Greg, W.R., 98
Gregory, A.F., 160, 277
Gregory, G.B., 275
Gregory, J., 174
Gregory, Sir W.E., Bt. (formerly Welby), 74, 243, 247
Gregson, S., 98, 110
Greig, D., 335
Greig, W., 122
Grenfell, C.P., 138, 190
Grenfell, C.W., 150, 193
Grenfell, H.R., 18, 46, 110, 163, 175, 240
Grenfell, W.H., 149
Grenville, R.N. (formerly Neville), 193, 263 264
Gresley, Sir R., Bt., 214
Gresley, Sir T., Bt., 214
Greville, Hon. A.W.F., 62, 369
Greville, Hon. Sir C.J., 182
Greville, Hon. R.F., 365
Grey, Earl de, see de Grey
Grey, A.H.G., 256
Grey, Hon. C., 197
Grey, Sir C.E., 176
Grey, Hon. F.W., 60
Grey, Sir George, Bt., 60, 120, 255

Grey, Sir George, 121
Grey, R.W., 106, 176
Grey, Hon. T. de, see de Grey
Grey de Wilton, Viscount, 19, 187
Gridley, H.G., 22, 187
Grieve, J.J., 326
Griffith, C.D., 59, 200
Griffith, G., 23
Griffiths, E., 85
Griffiths, S., 194
Griffits, J.O., 77
Grimsditch, T., 111
Grimston, Viscount, 230
Grimston, Hon. E.H., 146
Gronow, R.H., 158
Grosvenor, Earl (1), 206
Grosvenor, Earl (2), 46
Grosvenor, Hon. N., 46
Grosvenor, Lord Richard, 311
Grosvenor, Lord Robert, 46, 248
Grosvenor, Hon. R.W., 10
Grote, G., 2
Grove, Sir T.F., Bt., 281
Grundy, E., 38
Grylls, S.M., 84
Guernsey, Lord, 278
Guest, A.E., 136, 293
Guest, Sir I.B., Bt., 35, 136, 312
Guest, Sir J.J., Bt., 299, 312
Guest, M.J., 180
Guinness, R.S., 18
Guise, Sir B.W., Bt., 225
Gully, J., 135
Gully, W.C., 189
Gunter, R., 97
Gurdon, B., 252
Gurdon, R.T., 250, 251
Gurney, J.H., 95
Gurney, R., 156
Gurney, R.H., 127, 249
Gurney, S., 131
Guthrie, D.C., 321
Guthrie, J.A., 321
Gwyn, H., 18, 131, 291, 306

H

Hackblock, W., 140
Haddo, Lord, 340
Hadfield, G., 30, 153
Haggitt, F.R., see Prosser, F.R.W.,
Haig, G.A., 317
Haig, J., 6, 248
Haig, J.R., 351
Halcomb, J., 63, 182
Hale, R.B., 226
Hales, J.T., 271
Halford, Sir H., Bt., 242
Haliburton, T.C., 99
Hall, A.W., 130
Hall, Sir B., Bt., 7, 300
Hall, James, 168
Hall, John, 36
Hall, Richard, 105
Hall, Robert, 100
Hall, W., 195
Hallett, F.C.H., 150
Hallewell, E.G., 45
Halliday, Sir F.J., 324
Halliday, T., 299
Hallyburton, Lord Douglas (formerly Hon. D.G. Hallyburton), 357
Hallyburton, Hon. D.G. , see Hallyburton, Lord Douglas
Hallyburton, Lord John Gordon-, see Gordon-Hallyburton
Halse, J., 147
Halsey, T.F., 230
Halsey, T.P., 230
Haly, W.T., 136, 334
Hambro, C.J.T., 187
Hamilton, A., 235
Hamilton, A.G., 362
Hamilton, Lord Claud, 95, 107, 291
Hamilton, C.J.B., 16, 201
Hamilton, Lord Ernest, 334
Hamilton, E.W.T., 149
Hamilton, Sir F.W., 356
Hamilton, Lord George, 248
Hamilton, H.B.H., 157
Hamilton, J.G.C., 324, 364
Hamilton, Sir J.J., Bt., 7, 165
Hamilton, Sir R., Bt., 278
Hamilton, R.A.C.N. (formerly R.A. Christopher and R.A. Dundas), 92, 244
Hamilton, Hon. R.B., 348
Hamilton, Sir R.N.C., Bt., 278
Hamilton, W.F., 365
Hamilton, W.J., 124
Hammond, F.G., 4
Hamond, A. (Senr.), 127, 252
Hamond, A. (Junr.), 252
Hamond, A.S., 232
Hamond, C.F., 123
Hampden, R., 77, 109
Hampton, T.L., see Lewis T.L.H.
Hanbury, Hon. C.S.B., see Lennox, Hon. C.S.B.H.K.
Hanbury, R.C., 248
Hanbury, R.W., 138, 167, 178, 267
Hanbury, W., 253
Handley, B., 29
Handley, H., 243
Handley, J., 121
Handley, J.W.D. (formerly J.W.H. Davenport), 260, 262
Handley, P.H., 121
Handley, W.F., 121
Hankey, A., 91
Hankey, J.A., 29
Hankey, T., 29, 132
Hanmer, H., 16
Hanmer, Sir J., Bt., 96, 155, 297
Hannay, D., 320
Hannay, J., 320
Hannay, R., 361
Hannen, J., 154
Harben, H., 127
Harbord, Hon. E.V., 127
Harcourt, E.V., 112

Harcourt, E.W., 259
Harcourt, F.V., 232
Harcourt, G.G.V., 259
Harcourt, G.S., 201
Harcourt, Sir W.G.G.V.V., 58, 130, 331
Hardaker, J., 30
Hardcastle, E., 239
Hardcastle, J.A., 39, 53
Hardinge, Sir H., 99
Hardman, H., 38
Hardman, W., 272
Hardwicke, B., 302
Hardy, Hon. A.E.G., 42, 288
Hardy, G., 30, 102, 379
Hardy, Sir John, Bt., 17, 57, 119, 134, 266, 278
Hardy, John, 30
Hardy, J.S., see Hardy, Hon. J.S.G.
Hardy, Hon. J.S.G. (formerly J.S. Hardy), 145, 234
Hardy, Reginald, 19
Hardy, Robert, 196
Hare, S.V., 35
Harford, J.S., 294
Harford, S., 34, 103
Hargreaves, W., 26
Harker, W.J., 331
Harland, W.C., 66
Harley, Lord, 317
Harney, G.J., 173
Harper, E., 34
Harris, A., 30, 93
Harris, D., 4
Harris, Hon. E.A.J., 49
Harris, J., 68
Harris, J.D., 101
Harris, J.Q., 122
Harris, R., 101
Harris, W.J., 136
Harrison, B., 8
Harrison, C., 23
Harrison, F.G.F., 222
Harrison, J.F., 330
Harrop, J., 15
Hart, R., 126
Hartington, Marquess of (formerly Lord Cavendish (2)), 236, 237, 303
Hartland, F.D.D., 68, 85
Hartley, James, 166
Hartley, John, 266
Hartopp, E.B., 241
Harvey, D.W., 8, 53
Harvey, Sir R.B., Bt., 201
Harvey, R.J.H., 171
Hastie, Alexander, 325
Hastie, Archibald, 334
Hastings, G.W., 22, 282, 283
Hatchell, J., 193
Hatton, Hon. M.E.G.F., 121, 247
Havelock, Sir H.M., Bt., see Allan, Sir H.M.H., Bt.
Havens, W.R., 53
Hawes, B., 6
Hawkes, H., 167
Hawkes, M.L., 70
Hawkes, T., 65
Hawkins, H., 18
Hawkins, J.H., 124
Hawkins, W.W., 53
Hawkshaw, J., 12, 109
Haworth, B.B., 284
Hay, Sir A.L., 318, 323
Hay, Lord John (1), 193
Hay, Lord John (2), 142, 338
Hay, Sir John, Bt., 367
Hay, Sir J.C.D., Bt., 160, 173, 177, 339
Hay, Lord William, 168, 327, 354, 358
Hayne, C.S., 57
Hayter, Sir A.D., Bt., 19, 85, 184, 193, 263
Hayter, Sir W.G., Bt., 184
Head, F.F., 62
Head, F.S., 234
Headlam, T.E., 123
Headley, Lord, 7
Heald, J., 129, 161
Healey, T.P., 163
Heath, D.W., 128
Heath, R., 163
Heathcoat, J., 173
Heahcote, Sir G., Bt., 260
Heathcote, G.H., 29, 260
Heathcote, Sir G.J., Bt., 243, 260
Heathcote, J.M., 231
Heathcote, R.E., 163
Heathcote, Sir W., Bt., 227, 379
Hector, C.J., 133
Helmsley, Viscount, 285
Helps, T.W., 15
Heming, D., 277
Henderson, A., 350
Henderson, F., 321
Henderson, J., 66
Henderson, T.W., 332
Henderson, W., 27
Heneage, Edward (1), 76
Heneage, Edward (2), 76
Heneage, G.F., 76, 105
Heneage, G.H.W., 59
Henley, Lord, 32, 126, 254
Henley, J.W., 259
Henly, T.L., 40
Henniker, Lord, 270
Henry, A., 238
Henry, J.S., 239
Henry, M., 116, 195
Hepburn, Sir T.B., Bt., 327, 358
Herbert, Hon. A.E.W.M., 124, 128, 200
Herbert, Hon. P.E., 108, 262
Herbert, Hon. Sidney (1), 281
Herbert, Hon. Sidney (2), 191
Herbert, Sir T., 57
Hermon, E., 138
Heron, Sir R., Bt., 132
Herries, J.C., 82, 92, 160
Herschell, F., 66
Hervey, Lord Alfred, 34, 39
Hervey, Lord Augustus, 271
Hervey, Lord Francis, 39
Hervey, Lord George, 18

Hervey, Lord John, 19, 234
Hesketh, Sir T., Bt., 238
Hesketh, Sir T.G., Bt., see Hesketh, Sir T.G.F., Bt.
Hesketh, Sir T.G.F., Bt. (formerly Sir T.G. Hesketh, Bt.), 109, 138
Heygate, W.U., 33, 101, 160, 242
Heywood, A., 116
Heywood, J., 236
Heywood, J.P., 238
Heyworth, L., 58
Hibbert, J.T., 26, 41, 129
Hick, J., 28
Hickman, A., 194
Hicks, E., 202
Higgins, J.N., 68, 273
Higgins, M., 186
Higgins, W.B., 199
Hildyard, E., 112
Hildyard, R.C., 189
Hildyard, T.B.T., 258
Hill, A.S., 54, 194, 269
Hill, C., 126
Hill, Sir D.St.L., 82
Hill, J.D.H., 54
Hill, Lord Marcus, 68
Hill, M.D., 96
Hill, Sir R., Bt., 261
Hill, Hon. R.C., 261
Hill, T.R., 196
Hinchingbrooke, Viscount, 90
Hinde, J.H., (formerly Hodgson), 123
Hindley, C., 15, 181
Hindmarch, J., 102
Hingley, B., 65
Hoare, Sir H.A., Bt., 1, 193
Hoare, J., 96, 116
Hoare, P.M., 156
Hoare, R., 46
Hobhouse, Sir A., 10
Hobhouse, H.W., 3, 19, 85, 182
Hobhouse, Sir J.C., Bt., 10, 35, 82, 128
Hobhouse, T.B., 16, 92, 105, 121, 144
Hodges, T.L., 235
Hodges, T.T., 42, 144
Hodgkinson, G., 121
Hodgson, F., 18
Hodgson, J., see Hinde, J.H.
Hodgson, K.D., 33, 35, 131
Hodgson, R., 21, 123, 176
Hodgson, W.N., 43, 210
Hogg, J.M., see Hogg, Sir J.M.M., Bt.
Hogg, Sir J.M.M., Bt., 19, 175
Hogg, Sir J.W., Bt., 22, 87
Holbech, H., 17
Holden, A., 97
Holden, I., 97, 287, 288
Holdsworth, J., 177
Holford, J.P.G., 306
Holford, J.P.W.G., 291
Holford, R.S., 225
Holker, Sir J., 138
Holland, E., 68, 225, 282
Holland, Sir H.T., Bt., 119
Holland, S., 313
Hollond, J.R., 34
Hollond, R., 83
Holloway, G., 164
Hollway, J.H., 29
Holmes, W., 21, 92, 158
Holmes, Hon. W.H.A.A'C., 232
Holmesdale, Viscount, 234, 235
Holms, J., 5
Holms, W., 334
Holroyd, G.F., 126
Holt, G.F., 74
Holt, J., 18
Holt, J.M., 237
Holyoake, F., 194
Home, D.M., 21
Homer, J.J., 5
Homfray, S., 300
Hood, Sir A., Bt., 265
Hood, Sir A.B.P.F.A., Bt., 265
Hood, Hon. A.W.A.N., 265
Hope, Hon. Sir A., 365
Hope, A.J.B., see Hope, A.J.B.B.
Hope, A.J.B.B. (formerly A.J.B. Hope), 112, 163, 377
Hope, Hon. C., 365
Hope, G., 341, 358
Hope, G.W., 63, 156, 187, 193
Hope, H.T., 7, 73
Hope, Hon. James, 365
Hope, Sir John, Bt., 354
Hope, J.T., 116, 358
Hopkins, W.R.J., 118
Hopkinson, E., 158
Hopwood, C.H., 161
Hopwood, J.T., 51
Hornby, E.G., 181
Hornby, E.K., 26
Hornby, J., 26
Hornby, Sir P., 109
Hornby, W.H., 26
Horne, J., 350
Horne, Sir W., 7
Horsey, S.H. De, see De Horsey
Horsfall, T.B., 58, 107
Horsman, E., 52, 106, 164, 324
Hoskins, K., 229
Hoskyns, C.W., 85
Hotham, Lord, 102, 284
Houghton, J., 16, 199, 254
Houldsworth, T., 257
Houldsworth, W.H., 116
Houston, J.F., 327
Houstoun, G., 370
Howard, Lord, 152
Howard, Hon. C.W.G., 210
Howard, Lord Edward, 13, 88, 138, 154
Howard, Hon. E.G.G., 120
Howard, E.S., 210
Howard, Hon. F.G., 120
Howard, F.J., 31
Howard, G.J., 210
Howard, Hon. H.T., 55
Howard, J., 20, 199
Howard, Hon. J.K., 114
Howard, J.M., 6
Howard, P.H., 43
Howard, Sir R., Bt., 68

Howard, Hon. W., 375
Howell, D., 99
Howell, G., 16, 158
Howes, E., 249, 251
Howick, Viscount, 166, 255
Hoy, J.B., 156
Hoyle, W., 61
Hubback, J., 21
Hubbard, E., 36
Hubbard, J.G., 2, 36
Hubbard, W.E., 154
Huddleston, J.W., 42, 94, 127, 155, 196
Hudson, C.D., 122
Hudson, G., 166
Hudson, H.L., 251
Hudson, J.G.B., 11, 103
Hudson, T., 68
Hugessen, E.H.K., 150
Huggins, T., 111
Hughes, H.R., 311
Hughes, T., 6, 7, 71
Hughes, W.B., 292
Hughes, W.H., 130
Humberston, P.S., 46
Hume, J., 100, 248, 333
Humfrey, L.C., 105, 126
Humphery, J., 8
Humphery, W.H., 12
Hunt, F.S., 7
Hunt, G.W., 126, 253
Hunt, H., 138
Hunter, J., 325
Hunter, R., 366
Hurst, Robert Henry (Senr.), 88
Hurst, Robert Henry (Junr.), 88
Hurt, F., 214
Hussey, A., 149
Hussey, T., 109
Hutchins, E.J., 110, 131, 136, 156
Hutchinson, A.K., 9
Hutchinson, J.D., 80
Hutt, Sir W., 72, 96
Hutton, G.M., 76
Hutton, J., 125
Hyde, Lord, 278, 291
Hyett, W.H., 164

I

Ibbetson, Sir H.J.S., Bt. (formerly Selwin), 92, 223, 224
Ilderton, S., 176
Illingworth, A., 30, 97
Ince, H.B., 83
Inderwick, F.A., 50, 63, 145
Ingestre, Viscount (1), 86, 268
Ingestre, Viscount (2), 158, 160, 267, 268
Ingham, R., 157
Ingilby, Sir W.A., Bt., 244
Inglis, J., 160, 366
Inglis, Sir R.H., Bt., 379
Ingram, H., 29
Ingram, H.F.M., 269
Ingram, W.J., 29
Innes, T., 342
Innes, W., 318
Inverurie, Lord, 1
Ireland, T.J., 23
Irton, S., 211
Irving, J., 51, 136
Isaac, S., 128
Isaacson, F.W., 183

J

Jackson, Sir H.M., Bt., 24, 54
Jackson, R.W., 81
Jackson, W., 122, 213
Jackson, W.L., 100
Jaffray, J., 266
James, C.H., 299
James, E., 116
James, E.J., 7
James, Sir H., 168
James, W., 43, 210
James, Sir W.C., Bt., 96
James, W.H., 72
James, W.M., 58
Jardine, R., 14, 320, 352
Jardine, W., 14
Jebb, R.G., 261
Jeffrey, F., 322
Jenkins, D.J., 82, 131
Jenkins, E., 175, 321, 322
Jenkins, J.J., 295
Jenkins, R., 155
Jenkinson, Sir G.S., Bt., 128, 280
Jermyn, Earl (1), 39
Jermyn, Earl (2), 271
Jerningham, H.E.H., 21
Jerningham, Hon. H.V.S., 135
Jervis, H.J.W., 82
Jervis, Sir John, 46
Jervis, John, 88
Jervis, S., 33
Jervoise, Sir J.C., Bt., 228
Jessel, G., 63
Jeune, F.H., 53
Jocelyn, Viscount, 95, 100
Johns, J.W., 125
Johnson, E., 69
Johnson, J., 2, 134
Johnson, J.G., 69
Johnson, J.S.W., 301
Johnson, R.W., 12
Johnson, W.A., 89, 129, 241
Johnston, Alexander, 319, 330
Johnston, Andrew (1), 336
Johnston, Andrew (2), 223
Johnston, J., 337, 365
Johnstone, Sir A.H., Bt., 320
Johnstone, Sir F.G., Bt., 187
Johnstone, Sir F.J.W., Bt., 187
Johnstone, H.A.M.B., 42
Johnstone, Hon. H.B., 42
Johnstone, Sir H.V.B., Bt., 151, 172
Johnstone, J., 351
Johnstone, John James Hope (1), 352
Johnstone, John James Hope (2), 352
Johnstone, Sir J.V.B., Bt., 151
Johnstone, P.F.C., 110
Joicey, J., 219

Jolliffe, Hon. H.H., 184
Jolliffe, Sir W.G.H., Bt., 133
Jolliffe, Hon. W.S.H., 133
Jones, D., 165, 309
Jones, E., 178
Jones, E.B.A., 64
Jones, E.C., 80, 116, 128
Jones, G.F., 154
Jones, John (1), 295, 309
Jones, John (2), 309
Jones, Joseph, 129
Jones, J.I., 294
Jones, L.G., 7
Jones, P., 301
Jones, T.M., 29, 54
Jones, Sir Willoughby, Bt., 45, 252
Jones, Wilson, 296

K

Kane, J., 118
Karr, W.S.S., 144, 327
Karslake, E.K., 53
Karslake, Sir J.B., 12, 69, 90
Kay, E.E., 51
Kay, J., 148
Keane, D., 22
Kearsley, J.H., 190
Kearsley, R., 142
Keating, Sir H.S., 139
Kekewich, A., 54
Kekewich, S.T., 106, 217
Kelburne, Viscount, 344
Kelk, J., 82
Kelly, Sir F., 41, 82, 92, 109, 270
Kelly, R., 208
Kemble, F., 2
Kemble, H., 272
Kemp, Thomas Reid, 103
Kemp, Thomas Richardson, 79
Kendall, N., 208
Kenealy, A.L., 81
Kenealy, E.V.H., 163, 183
Kennard, A.S., 73, 149
Kennard, C.J., 149
Kennard, E.H., 22, 110
Kennard, H.M., 124
Kennard, R.W., 124
Kennaway, Sir J.H., Bt., 215
Kennedy, C., 320
Kennedy, J., 173
Kennedy, R.H., 329
Kennedy, T.F., 319
Kensington, Lord (formerly Hon. W. Edwardes), 298
Kenyon, Hon. G.T., 296
Kenyon, Hon. L., 310
Keppel, Hon. G.T., 95, 110, 249
Keppel, Hon. Sir H., 137
Ker, H.C.B., 127
Kerr, Hon. F.E., 325
Kerr, R.M., 132, 330
Kerr, Lord Schomberg, 372
Kerrison, Sir E., Bt., 70
Kerrison, Sir E.C., Bt., 70, 270
Kerry, Earl of, 40
Kershaw, J., 161
Key, Sir J., Bt., 2
Kidston, W., 350
Kiell, G.M., 1
Kilcoursie, Viscount, 168, 265
King, E.B., 182, 278
King, G.S., 141
King, J., 92
King, J.K., 229
King, Hon. P.J.L., 272
Kinglake, A.W., 32
Kinglake, J.A., 144, 184
Kingscote, R.N.F., 226
Kinloch, G.S., 321
Kinnaird, Hon. A.F., 335
Kinnear, J.B., 356
Kintrea, A., 334
Kirkwood, A., 380
Kitching, A.G., 114
Knatchbull, Sir E., Bt., 233
Knatchbull, Sir N.J., Bt., 233
Knatchbull, Sir W., Bt., 233
Knatchbull, W.F., 263
Knight, F.W., 283
Knight, H.G., 257
Knight, J.L., 41
Knight, W., 82
Knightley, Sir C., Bt., 254
Knightley, Sir R., Bt., 254
Knowles, A., 28
Knowles, Sir F., 169
Knowles, J., 28
Knowles, T., 190
Knox, B.W., 77

L

Labouchere, Henry (1), 168
Labouchere, Henry (2), 126, 128, 193, 248
Lacon, Sir E.H.K., Bt., 78, 250
Lacy, H.C., 27
Laffan, R.M., 147
Laing, J., 219
Laing, Samuel (Senr.), 366
Laing, Samuel (Junr.), 338, 366
Lainson, J., 272
Laird, J., 24
Lambert, N.G., 201
Lambton, Hon. F.W., 220
Lambton, H., 219
Lamont, J., 349
Lamont, N., 184
Lamport, C., 39, 271
Lancaster, J., 190
Lane, R.S., 134
Lang, J., 150
Langdale, Hon. C., 22, 97
Lange, D.A., 119
Langford, Lord, 160
Langley, J.B., 4
Langmead, J., 173
Langston, J.H., 130
Langton, W.G., 263
Langton, W.H.G., 35
Langton, W.H.P.G., 265
Langton, W.S.G., 264

Langworthy, E.R., 148
Larpent, Sir G.G. de H., Bt., 2, 108, 128
Lascelles, Viscount (1), 170
Lascelles, Viscount (2), 287
Lascelles, Hon. E., 125, 142
Lascelles, Hon. E.W., 125
Lascelles, W.S.S., 97, 177
Laslett, W., 196, 282
Latham, G.W., 204
Laurie, J., 18
Laurie, R.P., 42
Laverton, A., 186
Law, Hon. C.E., 377
Lawley, Hon. B., 46, 185
Lawley, Hon. B.R., 135
Lawley, Hon. F.C., 22
Lawrance, J.C., 132, 247
Lawrence, E., 98
Lawrence, Sir J.C., Bt., 6
Lawrence, Sir J.J.T., Bt., 73, 273
Lawrence, W., 2
Lawson, A., 97
Lawson, A.S., 97
Lawson, Sir W., Bt., 43, 211
Layard, A.H., 8, 16, 198
Laycock, R., 128, 246, 257
Lea, G.H., 94
Lea, J., 158
Lea, T., 94
Leach, G., 60
Leader, J.T., 10, 32
Leader, N.P., 82
Leake, R., 239
Learmonth, A., 53
Learmouth, J., 322
Leatham, E.A., 89
Leatham, W.H., 177, 289
Lechmere, Sir E.A.H., Bt., 170, 283
Lee, H., 148, 156
Lee, J., 16, 201
Lee, J.L., 184
Lee, R.N., 168
Lee, V.H., see Lee V.H.V.
Lee, V.H.V. (formerly V.H. Lee), 265
Lee, W., 112
Lee, W.H., 177
Leech, J., 274
Leeke, Sir H.J., 63
Leeman, G., 198
Leeman, J.J., 198
Lees, F.R., 100, 126, 142
Lees, J.F., 129
Lees, N., 84
Lees, T.E., 129
Lees, W.N., 73
Leese, J.F., 138
Lefevre, C.S., 227
Lefevre, G.J.S., 139, 192
Lefevre, J.G.S., 133, 377
Legard, Sir C., Bt., 127, 151
Legh, G.C., 204, 205
Legh, W.J., 203
Lehmann, F., 68, 248
Leicester, Earl of, see Gardner, J.D.
Leigh, C.H.T., 225
Leigh, E., 204
Leigh, Hon. G.H.C., 278
Leigh, J.W.B., 101
Leigh, R., 144
Leigh, Hon. W.H., 277
Leigh, W.J., 238
Leighton, Sir Baldwin, Bt. (Senr.), 262
Leighton, Sir Baldwyn, Bt. (Junr.), 262
Leighton, S., 23, 261
Leith, J.F., 318
Le Marchant, Sir D., Bt., 82, 196
Lemon, Sir C., Bt., 209
Lempriere, C., 192
Lendrick, W.E., 126
Lennard, Sir T.B., Bt., 113, 222, 223
Lennox, Lord Alexander Gordon- see Gordon-Lennox
Lennox, Lord Arthur, 47, 78
Lennox, Hon. C.S.B.H.K. (formerly Hon. C.S.B. Hanbury), 102, 229
Lennox, Lord George Gordon- see Gordon-Lennox
Lennox, Lord Henry Gordon- see Gordon-Lennox
Lennox, Lord John, 276
Lennox, Lord William, 95
Leslie, Hon. G.W., 83
Leslie, W., 340
Lester, B.L., 136
Le Strange, H.L.S, 252
Lethbridge, Sir T.B., Bt., 32
Leveson, Lord, 104, 120
Leveson-Gower, Lord Ronald, 375
Levett, T.J., 104
Levick, J., 196
Lewin, Sir G.A., 97
Lewin, M., 198
Lewin, S., 136
Lewis, D., 295
Lewis, E.D., 118
Lewis, Sir G.C., Bt., 132, 229, 303
Lewis, J.D., 60, 130
Lewis, J.H., 7, 27, 96
Lewis, Sir T.F., Bt., 303, 317
Lewis, T.L.H. (formerly Hampton), 290, 301
Lewis, W., 112
Lewis, W.D., 117, 127, 135, 150
Lewis, W.T., 299
Lewisham, Viscount (1), 268
Lewisham, Viscount (2), 235
Ley, E., 147
Liardet, J.E., 4
Liddell, Hon. A.F.O., 72
Liddell, Hon H.G., see Eslington, Lord
Liddell, Hon. H.T., 107, 157, 219
Lillie, Sir J.S., 95, 248
Lincoln, Earl of (1), 257, 258, 324
Lincoln, Earl of (2), 121, 128
Lindsay, Lord, 190
Lindsay, Hon. C.H., 11
Lindsay, H.H., 150
Lindsay, Hon. James, 190
Lindsay, James, 356
Lindsay, R.J.L., 200

Lindsay, W.A., 37, 89
Lindsay, W.S., 57, 166, 176, 300
Lisburne, Earl of, 308
Lister, E.C., 30
Lister, S.C., 288
Lister, W.C., 30
Listowel, Earl of, 146
Littledale, I., 189
Littleton, E.J., 268
Littleton, Hon. E.R., 179, 268
Lloyd, J.H., 161
Lloyd, J.L., 291
Lloyd, M., 290
Lloyd, S.S., 25, 134, 278
Lloyd, T., 18, 23
Lloyd, Sir T.D., Bt., 294, 308
Lloyd, T.E., 308
Loch, G., 116, 324, 338
Loch, J., 338
Locke, John, 8, 83
Locke, Joseph, 87
Locke, W., 59
Lockhart, A.E., 373
Lockhart, A.M., 362
Lockhart, J.I., 16, 126
Lockhart, Sir N.M., Bt., 364
Lockhart, W., 362
Lockwood, F., 95, 198
Locock, Sir C., Bt., 232
Loder, R., 154
Loftus, Viscount, 73, 195
Loftus, Lord Henry, 103
Logan, H., 271
Long, H.L., 79, 274
Long, R.P., 48, 280, 281
Long, W., 227, 280
Long, W.H., 280
Loosemore, R.F., 173
Lopes, H.C., 71, 99
Lopes, Sir L.M., Bt., 186, 217
Lopes, Sir R., Bt., 186, 217
Lord, J., 58, 272
Lorne, Marquess of, 343
Loughborough, Lord (1), 76
Loughborough, Lord (2), 356
Lovaine, Lord, 69, 255
Loveden, P. (formerly Pryse), 294
Lovell, P.A., 114
Lowe, R., 40, 94, 378
Lowery, R., 318
Lowther, Viscount, 211, 279
Lowther, H., 211
Lowther, Hon. H.C., 279
Lowther, J., 198, 210, 246
Lowther, J.H., 198
Lowther, J.W., 260
Lowther, Hon. W., 279
Loyd, S.J., 116
Loyd, W.J., 145
Lubbock, Sir J., Bt., 112, 235, 378
Lucas, M.P., 112
Luce, C.R., 114
Luce, T., 114
Lucraft, B., 3, 9
Lumley, Viscount, 257
Lush, J.A., 149
Lushington, C., 10, 14
Lushington, C.M., 42, 127
Lushington, G., 11
Lushington, S., 9
Lushington, S.R., 42
Lusk, Sir A., Bt., 3
Lyall, G., 2, 189
Lycett, Sir F., 106, 147, 196
Lyell, E.L., 223
Lygon, Hon. F., 170, 283
Lygon, Hon. H.B., 283
Lymington, Viscount, 18
Lyon, W., 7, 42, 103, 154
Lysley, W.J., 48
Lyttelton, Hon. C.G., 282
Lyttelton, Hon. S., 23
Lytton, Sir E.G.E.L.B., Bt. (formerly Bulwer), 105, 230

M

Maberly, W.L., 11, 44
MacAlister, A., 5
McArthur, A., 101
McArthur, W., 6, 135
Macaulay, K., 41
Macaulay, T.B., 100, 322
McClean, J.R., 266
McCombie, W., 342
McCorquodale, G., 190
McCrea, H.C., 80
McCullagh, W.T., 78
Macdonald, A., 158
Macdonald, J.H.A., 322, 327
Macdonald, R., 371
Macdonald, W.M., 21, 145, 333
McDouall, J., 361
McDouall, P.M., 43, 126
Macduff, Viscount, 355
McEnteer, T., 113
Macfie, R.A., 332
McGeachy, F.A., 35, 87
McGrath, P., 58
Macgregor, D.R., 332
McGregor, James, 17, 150
MacGregor, John, 325
McIntyre, A.J., 196
MacIver, D., 24
Mackay, T.M., 156
Mackenzie, A.R., 371
Mackenzie, H., 323
Mackenzie, J.A.S., 371
Mackenzie, J.J.R., 329
Mackenzie, J.T., 126, 174
Mackenzie, Sir K.S., Bt., 359
Mackenzie, T., 371
Mackenzie, W., 371
Mackenzie, W.D., 139
Mackenzie, W.F., 58, 107, 367
McKerrell, J., 334
Mackie, A., 335
Mackie, James, 361
Mackie, John, 361
Mackie, R.B., 177

Mackillop, J., 156
Mackinnon, C., 92
Mackinnon, L.B., 145
Mackinnon, William Alexander (Senr.), 110, 145
Mackinnon, William Alexander (Junr.), 110, 145
Mackintosh, A., 329
Mackintosh, A.W., 329
Mackintosh, C.F., 329
Mackworth, Sir D., Bt., 58, 107
McLagan, P., 365
McLaren, C.B.B., 158
McLaren, D., 322
McLaren, J., 21, 322, 339
Maclean, D., 130
Maclean, J.M., 323
McLeod, J.N., 359
Macleod, R., 329, 375
Macliver, P.S., 134
McMicking, G., 339
McMinnies, J.G., 181
MacNab, Sir A., Bt., 34
McNeill, D., 343
McTaggart, Sir J., Bt., 339
McTaggart, W.B., 324
Maddock, J.F., 46
Maddock, Sir T.H., 144
Madocks, J., 296
Magniac, C., 20, 147
Mahon, Viscount (1), 86
Mahon, Viscount (2), 4, 102, 270
Maidstone, Viscount, 10, 41, 253
Mainwaring, C.S., 261
Mainwaring, T., 296
Mainwaring, Hon. W.F.B.M., 127
Maitland, Hon. A., 348
Maitland, Sir A.C.R.G., Bt., 337, 354
Maitland, J., 361
Maitland, Sir J.R.G., Bt., 337
Maitland, T., 361
Maitland, W.F., 306
Majendie, L.A., 42
Major, Hon. J.M.H., 270
Makgill, D.M., 336
Makins, W.T., 94, 223
Malcolm, Sir J., 43
Malcolm, J.W., 29, 343
Malcolm, N., 130
Malet, Sir A.C., Bt., 117
Malgarini, F.L., 46
Malins, R., 178
Maltby, E.H., 90
Mandeville, Viscount (1), 231
Mandeville, Viscount (2), 10, 23, 231
Mandeville, Viscount (3), 231
Mangles, C.E., 124, 156
Mangles, J., 79
Mangles, R.D., 79
Manners, Lord Charles, 241
Manners, Lord George, 202, 241
Manners, Lord John, 2, 53, 107, 121, 241
Manners, Lord Robert, 241
Mansell, J.C., 32
Mappin, F.T., 67
March, Earl of (1), 276
March, Earl of (2), 276
Marchant, Sir D. Le, Bt., see Le Marchant
Marcy, W.N., 23
Mare, C.J., 134
Marjoribanks, C., 348
Marjoribanks, Sir D.C., Bt., 21
Marjoribanks, E., 235, 348
Marjoribanks, Sir J., 348
Marjoribanks, S., 91
Markham, C., 126
Markham, W., 142
Marlay, C.B., 74
Marling, S.S., 164, 226
Marling, Sir W., 226
Marriott, W.T., 34
Marryat, F., 9
Marryat, J., 150
Marsh, M.H., 149
Marshall, J., 100
Marshall, J.G., 100
Marshall, W., 43, 210
Marsham, Viscount, 235
Marsham, R.B., 379
Marshman, J.C., 7, 82, 92
Marsland, H., 161
Marsland, T., 161
Marten, A.G., 41, 128
Martin, C.W., 112, 124, 235
Martin, F.O., 127
Martin, James, 170
Martin, John, 170
Martin, P.W., 144
Martin, R.B., 2, 170, 282
Martin, R.M., 33
Martin, S., 135
Martin, T.M., 32
Marton, G., 98
Martyn, C.C., 156
Maskelyne, M.H.N.S., 55
Mason, B., 15
Mason, G.M., 163
Mason, H., 15
Mason, W., 67
Massey, W.N., 107, 124, 148, 173
Master, Thomas William Chester (Senr.), 50
Master, Thomas William Chester (Junr.), 50
Masterman, J., 2
Matheson, A., 329, 371
Matheson, Sir, J., Bt., 14, 371
Matheson, T., 14
Mathew, G.B., 152
Mattinson, M.W., 43
Maule, Hon. F., 323, 335, 369
Maule, Hon. L., 357
Maunsell, T.P., 253
Maurice, J., 296
Maxfield, W., 76
Maxse, F.A., 9, 156
Maxwell, G., 361
Maxwell, Sir H.E., Bt., 376
Maxwell, Sir John, Bt., 334, 370
Maxwell, John, 362
Maxwell, Sir J.H., 4, 60
Maxwell, J.M.H., 361
Maxwell, Hon. M.C., 22
Maxwell, W., 361

Maxwell, W.H., 361
Maxwell, Sir W.S. Bt., (formerly Stirling), 369
May, J., 235
Mayhew, W., 53
Mayne, J.D., 131
Mayne, J.T., 48, 174
Mayo, Earl of (formerly Lord Naas), 52
Medley, G.W., 272
Meiklejohn, J.M.D., 321
Melgund, Viscount, 91, 144, 325, 326, 351
Meller, W., 158
Mellor, J., 54, 78, 128, 182
Mellor, J.W., 74
Mellor, T.W., 15
Melly, G., 138, 163
Melville, J., 109
Merewether, C.G., 126
Merry, J., 324, 325
Merryweather, M., 91
Methuen, P., 280
Metrick, O.J.A.F., 305
Meux, Sir H., Bt., 230
Meyrick, A.W.H., 85, 113
Meyrick, T.C., 302
Miall, E., 8, 17, 30, 80, 143, 169
Michell, W., 27
Middleton, Sir A.E., Bt. (formerly Monck), 66
Middleton, R.T., 325
Milbank, F.A., 285
Mildmay, Sir H.B.P.St.J., Bt., 227
Mildmay, H.F.St.J., 112, 229
Mildmay, H.St.J., 96, 113, 156
Mildmay, P.St.J., 192
Miles, C.W., 114
Miles, J.W., 35
Miles, P.J., 35
Miles, Sir P.J.W., Bt., 263
Miles, P.W.S., 35
Miles, Sir W., Bt., 263
Mill, J.S., 10
Miller, J., 322, 337
Miller, T.J., 53, 113
Miller, W., 332, 348
Miller, W.H., 21, 122
Milles, Hon. G.W., 233
Milligan, R., 30
Mills, A., 69, 168
Mills, Sir C.H., Bt., 125, 235
Mills, G., 325
Mills, J., 144
Mills, J.R., 3, 100, 197
Mills, R., 183
Mills, T., 139, 174
Milne, Sir D., 332
Milner, Sir F.G., Bt., 198
Milner, W.M.E., 198
Milnes, R.M., 135
Milton, Viscount (1) (formerly Hon. W.C.W. Fitzwilliam), 115, 253
Milton, Vicount, (2), 115, 253, 286
Milton, Viscount (3), 289
Milward, C., 49, 228
Mitcalfe, H., 176
Mitchell, A., 21
Mitchell, G., 144
Mitchell, T.A., 33
Mitford, P., 161
Mitford, W.T., 119
Moffat, G., 14, 57, 87, 92, 156, 232
Molesworth, G.B.G.F.R.P., 26
Molesworth, Sir W., Bt., 8, 100, 208
Molyneux, Viscount, 238
Molyneux, Hon. H.H., 240
Monck, Viscount, 65, 137
Monck, Sir A.E., Bt., see Middleton, Sir A.E., Bt.
Monckton, F., 269
Monckton, Hon. G.E.M., see Galway, Viscount (2)
Moncreiff, J., 322, 332, 380
Moncrieff, W.D.S., 326
Money, G.H., 144
Monk, C.J., 55, 73
Monson, Hon. E.J., 140
Monson, Hon. W.J., 140
Montagu, Lord Robert, 231
Monteith, R., 23, 325
Montgomerie, R., 345
Montgomery, Sir G.G., Bt., 367, 368
Monypenny, T.G., 145
Moody, C.A., 265
Moor, H., 34
Moore, J., 6, 140
Moore, J.B., 96, 105, 107, 110, 113
Moore, R.R.R., 83
Moorsom, R., 188
Moray, H.E.S.H.D., 369
Mordaunt, Sir C., Bt., 278
Mordaunt, Sir J., Bt., 278
More, R.J., 262
Moreton, Lord (1), 164
Moreton, Lord (2), 226
Moreton, Hon. A.H., 225, 226
Moreton, Hon. H.G.F., 225
Morgan, Hon. A.J., 306
Morgan, C.M.R., 291
Morgan, C.O.S., 314
Morgan, C.R., 291
Morgan, Hon. F.C., 314
Morgan, G., 36
Morgan, Hon. G.C., 306
Morgan, G.O., 310
Morgan, W.V., 291
Morison, W., 351
Morley, A., 128
Morley, J., 10, 26, 123
Morley, S., 35, 128
Morne, Viscount Newry and, see Newry and Morne
Morpeth, Viscount, 286
Morris, D., 295
Morris, J., 107
Morris, William (1), 295
Morris, William (2), 55
Morrison, Alexander, 323
Morrison, Alfred, 178
Morrison, J., 92, 165, 329
Morrison, W., 2, 134
Morritt, W.J.S., 285

Mosley, Sir O., Bt., 267
Moss, J.E.E., 49
Moss, R., 192
Mostyn, Hon. E.M.L., 104, 311
Mostyn, R.J., 297
Mostyn, Hon. T.E.M.L.L., 311
Motte, R.S., 91
Mottershead, T., 138
Mowatt, F., 41, 131
Mowbray, J.R., 66, 379
Mowbray, R.G.C., 188
Mulgrave, Earl of, 151
Mullings, J.R., 50
Muncaster, Lord, 211
Mundella, A.J., 153
Mundy, E.M., 214
Mundy, W., 214
Munro, H.A.J., 371
Muntz, George Frederick (1), 25
Muntz, George Frederick (2), 277
Muntz, P.A., 277
Muntz, P.H., 25
Murch, J., 19
Mure, D., 349
Mure, William (Senr.), 370
Mure, William (Junr.), 370
Murphy, T., 7
Murray, A., 361, 376
Murray, Hon. C.A., 7, 324, 362
Murray, C.J., 83
Murray, C.R.S., 201
Murray, Sir G., 10, 116, 369
Murray, Sir J., Bt., 368
Murray, J.A., 332
Murray, J.N., 373
Murray, T.L., 22
Murray, W., 122
Murrough, J.P., 26, 33, 119
Musgrave, Sir R.C., Bt., 210
Muskett, G.A., 146
Mynors, R.B.R., 317

N

Naas, Lord, see Mayo, Earl of
Naghten, A.R., 192
Nanney, H.J.E., 307
Nanney, O.J.E., 292
Napier, Sir C., 4, 6, 7, 8, 78, 137
Napier, Hon. W.J.G., 373
Neale, Sir H.B., Bt., 110
Neate, C., 130
Neeld, A.W., 55
Neeld, Sir John, Bt., 48, 55
Neeld, Joseph, 48
Nelson, T.M., 273
Nevill, C.W., 295
Neville, R., see Grenville, R.N.,
Newark, Viscount (1), 67
Newark, Viscount (2), 258
Newdegate, C.N., 277
Newport, Viscount (1), 262
Newport, Viscount (2), 261
Newry and Morne, Viscount, 155
Newton, A., 142
Newton, W., 9, 92
Nicholl, J., 293
Nicholson, J., 194
Nicholson, R., 83
Nicholson, T., 92
Nicholson, W., 133
Nicholson, W.N., 121
Nicol, J.D., 360
Nicol, W., 63
Nicoll, D., 71
Nicolson, J.B., 360
Nightingale, E., 12
Nisbet, R.P., 48
Noble, J., 101
Noel, Hon. C.G., 260
Noel, E., 320
Noel, Hon. G.J., 260
Noel, Sir G.N., Bt., 260
Noel, Hon. W.M., 260
Norreys, Lord, 11, 259
Norris, J.F., 137, 191
Norris, J.T., 11
North, F., 83
North, J.S., 259
Northcote, H.S., 69
Northcote, Sir S.H., Bt., 65, 160, 216
Northmore, T., 18
Norton, Hon. C.F., 79
Norton, J., 164
Norton, T., 110, 139
Norwood, C.M., 96
Nugent, Lord, 16, 156
Nugent, A., 91
Nurse, M., 127

O

Oakeley, R.B., 155
Oakes, J.H.P., 39
Oastler, R., 89
O'Brien, A.S., see Stafford, A.S.O'B.
O'Connor, F., 128, 129
Odger, G., 8
Ogilvy, Sir J., Bt., 321, 333
Ogle, S.C.H., 256
Oliphant, Laurence (1), 335,
Oliphant, Laurence (2), 337
Oliveira, B., 135, 139
O'Malley, E.L., 20
O'Malley, P.F., 3
Ommanney, Sir J.A., 228
Onslow, D.R., 79
Onslow, G.J.H.M.E., 79
Ord, W., 123, 256
Ord, W.H., 124
Ormelie, Earl of, 369
Osborn, S., 24
Osborne, R.B. (formerly Bernal), 63, 106, 128, 197, 248
Ossulston, Lord, 255
Oswald, A.H., 187, 319, 344
Oswald, J., 325
Oswald, J.T., 331, 356
Oswald, R.A., 344
Otway, A.J., 44, 144, 158, 176

Otway, C.E.T., 303
Overend, W., 135, 153, 212
Owen, Sir E.W.C.R., 150
Owen, Sir H.O., Bt., 302, 316
Owen, Sir J., Bt., 302, 316
Owen, R., 7

P

Packe, C.W., 242
Packe, G.H., 121, 243, 247
Packe, H., 241
Padmore, R., 196
Padwick, H., 32
Paget, Lord, see Uxbridge, Earl of
Paget, Lord Alfred, 104
Paget, Sir Charles, 292
Paget, Charles, 128
Paget, Lord Clarence, 150, 156
Paget, C.H., 292
Paget, F., 290
Paget, Lord George, 290, 292
Paget, R.H., 263, 264
Paget, T.T., 242
Paget, Lord William, 12
Pakington, John Slaney, 282
Pakington, Sir John Somerset, Bt., 64, 282, 283
Palk, Sir L., Bt., 215, 217
Palliser, W., 60, 168
Palmer, C., 19
Palmer, C.F., 139
Palmer, C.M., 157, 219
Palmer, Geoffrey, 101
Palmer, George (1), 157, 223
Palmer, George (2), 139
Palmer, John Hinde, 6, 105
Palmer, John Horsley, 2, 14
Palmer, Robert, 200
Palmer, Sir Roundell, 134, 141
Palmerston, Viscount, 107, 173, 228
Pankhurst, R.M., 116
Papillon, P.O., 53
Parbury, G., 112
Parker, C.S., 335, 369
Parker, C.W., 76
Parker, Sir H., Bt., 271
Parker, Sir H.W., 4
Parker, James, 101
Parker, John, 153
Parker, M.E.N., 217
Parker, R.T., 138
Parker, T.A.W., 259
Parker, W., 271
Parkyns, Sir T.G.A., Bt., 7
Parnell, Sir H.B., Bt., 321
Parratt, H.M., 140
Parrott, J., 174
Parry, J.H., 3, 127
Parry, Sir L.P.J., 155, 292
Parry, R.S., 292
Parry, T., 29
Parry, T.L.D.J., 292, 307
Pashley, R., 95
Patrick, R.W.C., 345
Patten, J.W., 236
Pateshall, E., 85
Pattison, J., 2
Patton, G., 32
Paul, Sir H.D.C.St., Bt., see St. Paul
Paul, H.St., see St. Paul
Paull, H., 147
Paxton, Sir J., 54
Payne, Sir P., Bt., 199
Payne, W., 2
Peach, N.W., 249
Peacocke, G.M.W., see Sandford, G.M.W.
Peacocke, W., 110
Pearce, W., 325
Pearson, C., 6
Pearson, James, 190
Pearson, John, 275
Pease, A., 188
Pease, H., 220
Pease, J., 220
Pease, Joseph Walker, 96
Pease, Joseph Whitwell, 220
Pechell, Sir G.R.B., Bt., 34
Pechell, Sir S.J.B., Bt., 193
Peddie, J.D., 330
Peek, Sir H.W., Bt., 272, 273
Peel, A., 60
Peel, A.W., 54, 182
Peel, Edmund (1), 122
Peel, Edmund (2), 311
Peel, F., 38, 102, 239
Peel, John, 167
Peel, Jonathan (1), 90
Peel, Jonathan (2), 45, 51
Peel, J.H., 298
Peel, Sir Robert, Bt., (1), 167
Peel, Sir Robert, Bt., (2), 75, 90, 167
Peel, W.Y., 167
Peel, X. de C.R., 298
Pelham, Lord, 103
Pelham, Hon. C.A.W., see Worsley, Lord (1)
Pelham, Hon. C.D., 232
Pelham, Hon. D.A., 29
Pelham, J.C., 155
Pelham-Clinton, Lord Thomas, 42
Pell, A., 242
Pell, J., 170
Pellatt, A., 35
Pelly, Sir H.C., Bt., 231
Pemberton, E.L., 233
Pemberton, H.W., 154
Pemberton, R.L., 219
Pemberton, T., 142
Pendarves, E.W.W., 209
Pendarves, W.C., 147
Pender, J., 174, 338, 365
Penleaze, J.S., 156
Pennant, Hon. E.G.D., 307
Pennant, Hon. G.S.G.D., 307
Pennant, P.P., 297
Pennington, F., 161, 274
Penrhyn, E., 152
Penruddocke, J.H., 191
Peploe, D.P., 229
Pepys, Sir C.C., 115
Perceval, C.G.J., 119

Perceval, D.M., 3, 379
Perceval, Hon. G.J., 274
Percy, Earl, 255
Percy, Lord Algernon, 10
Percy, Lord Henry, 255
Percy, Hon. J.W., 99
Perfect, R., 103
Perfitt, T.W., 3
Perkins, Sir F., 156
Perry, Sir T.E., 44, 60, 107, 112
Peter, W., 27
Pethick, W., 99
Peto, Sir S.M., Bt., 3, 35, 127
Petre, Hon. E.R., 33, 198
Pevensey, Viscount, 275
Peyton, H., 195
Phibbs, R., 155
Philipps, G.E.G., 316
Philipps, J.H., see Scourfield, J.H.
Philipps, Sir R.B.P., Bt., 298
Philips, Sir G., Bt., 278
Philips, G.R., 94, 136
Philips, M., 116
Philips, R.N., 38
Phillimore, J.G., 102
Phillimore, R.J., 54, 169
Phillipps, C.M., 241
Phillips, G.H., 303
Phillips, G.L., 316
Phillips, W., 3
Phillpotts, J., 73
Phinn, T., 19, 60
Phipps, Hon. C.B., 105, 151
Phipps, C.N.P., 186
Phipps, C.P., 186
Phipps, Hon. E., 188
Phipps, J.L., 186
Phipps, P., 126, 254
Pickard, W., 190
Picton, J.A., 101
Pigot, Sir R., Bt., 31
Pigott, F., 139, 192
Pigott, G., 139
Pilcher, J., 8
Pilkington, J., 26
Pim, B.C.T., 75, 174
Pinney, W., 109, 263
Pirie, J., 2
Pitman, S., 298
Planta, J., 83
Platt, J., 129
Playfair, L., 381
Plimsoll, S., 58, 107
Plowden, W.H.C., 124, 128
Plumptre, J.P., 233
Plumridge, J.H., 131
Plunkett, Hon. R.E.S., 226
Pochin, H.D., 158, 300
Pocock, W.W., 79
Pole, E.S.C., 58
Polhill, F., 20
Pollen, Sir J.W., Bt., 12
Pollington, Viscount (1), 135
Pollington, Viscount (2), 135
Pollock, Sir F., 90
Pomfret, R.C., 145
Ponsonby, Hon. A.G.J., 50, 164
Ponsonby, Hon. C.F.A.C., 50, 136
Ponsonby, Hon. J.G.B., see Duncannon, Viscount (2)
Ponsonby, Hon. W.F.S., 218
Pook, W., 4
Poole, E., 229
Pope, J.B., 96
Pope, S., 28, 163
Portal, M., 227
Portal, W.S., 137, 192
Portman, E.B., 7
Portman, Hon. W.H.B., 152, 218
Potter, E., 43
Potter, G., 132
Potter, Sir J., 116
Potter, J.G., 26
Potter, Richard (1), 190
Potter, Richard (2), 73
Potter, T.B., 143
Potts, G., 18
Poulter, J.S., 152
Powell, F.S., 41, 116, 159, 190, 288
Powell, J.J., 73, 187
Powell, W., 114
Powell, W.E., 308
Powell, W.R.H., 309
Powell, W.T.R., 308
Powerscourt, Viscount, 19
Powlett, Lord William, 108, 147
Pownall, H., 3, 248
Powys, P.L., 124
Poyntz, W.S., 14, 119
Praed, C.T., 147
Praed, H.B.M., 53
Praed, J.B., 201
Praed, W.M., 16, 78, 147
Praed, W.T., 147
Pratt, D., 110
Preston, T.H., 135
Price, E.P., 153
Price, G.E., 60
Price, H.P., 291
Price, Richard, 303
Price, Sir Robert, Bt., 85, 229
Price, Sir R.G., Bt., 303, 317
Price, S.G., 150
Price, W.E., 170
Price, W.P., 73
Prime, R., 276
Pringle, A., 373
Pringle, R., 373
Prinsep, H.T., 18, 53, 57, 63, 82, 330
Pritchard, J., 31
Probyn, J.W., 59, 77
Prosser, F.R.W. (formerly Haggitt), 229
Protheroe, E., 35, 80
Pryme, G., 41
Pryse, E.L., 294
Pryse, P., see Loveden, P.
Pugh, C.V., 301
Pugh, David (1), 301
Pugh, David (2), 309
Pugh, L.P., 308

Puleston, J.H., 60
Puller, C.W., 230
Pulley, J., 85
Pulsford, R., 85
Purvis, T., 66
Pusey, P., 200
Puxley, H.L., 309

R

Rae, Sir W., Bt., 349
Raikes, H., 58
Raikes, H.C., 46, 58, 60, 138, 377
Ralli, P., 33, 178
Ramsay, Lord (1), 322, 358
Ramsay, Lord (2), 107
Ramsay, Sir A., Bt., 143
Ramsay, J., 324, 325, 337
Ramsay, Sir J.H., Bt., 357
Ramsay, W.R., 354
Ramsbottom, J., 193
Ramsden, J.C., 115, 285
Ramsden, Sir J.W., Bt., 91, 168, 286, 287, 300
Randolph, C.W., 3
Rankin, J., 102
Raper, J.H., 132
Raphael, A., 135, 146
Rapley, D., 52
Rashleigh, Sir J.C., Bt., 208
Rashleigh, W., 208
Ratcliff, D.R., 68
Rathbone, W., 107, 240, 307
Rawlinson, Sir H.C., 71, 140
Rawson, H., 148
Rawson, W., 65
Rayner, G.P., 305
Raynham, Viscount, 167
Read, C.S., 249, 251, 252
Rebow, J.G., 53, 222
Reed, C., 5, 147
Reed, E.J., 96, 293, 302
Reed, J.H., 3, 11, 106
Rees, W., 298
Reid, G.A., 193
Reid, Sir J.R., Bt., 63
Reid, R., 331, 338
Reid, R.T., 85
Reidhaven, Viscount, 347
Rendel, S., 315
Rendlesham, Lord (1), 270
Rendlesham, Lord (2), 270
Rennie, G., 22, 92
Renton, J.C., 21
Renton, J.H., 269, 322
Repton, G.W.J., 146, 182
Ricardo, D., 164
Ricardo, J.L., 163
Ricardo, O., 196
Ricardo, S., 94, 174, 193
Rice, E.R., 63
Rice, T.S., 41
Rich, H., 97, 141
Richard, H., 299
Richards, A.B., 142
Richards, E.M., 87, 308
Richards, H.C., 126
Richards, J., 8, 97
Richards, R., 313
Richardson, G.G., 140
Richardson, Thomas (1), 81
Richardson, Thomas (2), 88
Richardson, T.S., 68
Rickford, W., 16
Riddell, H.B., 366
Riddell, Sir W.B., 235
Rider, T., 233, 235
Ridler, W., 45
Ridley, E., 256
Ridley, G., 123, 256
Ridley, Sir Matthew White, Bt., (1), 123
Ridley, Sir Matthew White, Bt., (2), 255
Ridley, Sir Matthew White, Bt., (3), 255
Riley, J., 122
Ripley, H.W., 30
Rippon, C., 72
Ritchie, C.T., 9
Robartes, Hon. T.C.A., 208
Robartes, T.J.A., 208
Robarts, A.W., 112
Robarts, C.H., 273
Roberts, C.H.C., 150
Roberts, H., 182
Roberts, John, 297
Roberts, Julius, 149
Roberts, W.H., 141
Roberts, W.P., 26
Robertson, D., 348
Robertson, H., 155
Robertson, J.P.B., 365
Robertson, P.F., 83
Robertson, T.C., 353
Robinson, A., 32, 155
Robinson, E.S., 35
Robinson, G.R., 9, 136, 196
Robinson, Sir R.S., 167
Robinson, T., 73
Robinson, W.F., 272
Roden, W.S., 163
Rodwell, B.B.H., 202
Roe, T., 58
Roebuck, J.A., 19, 153
Rogers, C.C., 303
Rogers, J.E.T., 8, 151
Rogers, J.J., 84
Rogers, T., 200
Rolfe, Sir R.M., 131
Rolleston, L., 258
Rolls, J.A., 314
Rolt, Sir J., 33, 160, 226
Rolt, P., 4
Romaine, W.G., 44
Romer, R., 34
Romilly, E., 108
Romilly, F., 7, 42
Romilly, Sir J., 33, 60
Rooker, A., 134
Rooper, J.B., 231
Rose, Lord Boscawen-, see Boscawen-Rose
Rose, Sir G.H., 49

Rose, G.P., 136
Rose, W.A., 124, 156
Ross, A.H., 112
Ross, C., 126
Ross, C.C., 147
Ross, E., 342
Ross, G.W.H., 371
Ross, H., 333, 334
Ross, T., 122
Rotch, B., 97
Rothwell, P., 28
Rothschild, Baron F.J. de, see de Rothschild
Rothschild, Baron L.N. de, see de Rothschild
Rothschild, Baron M.A. de, see de Rothschild
Rothschild, Sir N.M. de, Bt., see de Rothschild
Round, C.G., 222, 379
Round, James, 221
Round, John, 113
Roundell, C.S., 51, 74
Roupell, W., 6
Rous, Hon. H.J., 10
Rowlandson, S., 285
Rowley, Sir C., 137
Rowley, G.F., 29
Rowley, Hon. R.T., 82
Royds, C., 143
Royston, Viscount, 202
Rufford, F., 196
Rumbold, C.E., 78
Rummens, J., 169
Rundle, J., 169
Rushbrooke, R., 271
Rushout, G., 68, 282
Rushton, T.L., 28
Russell, Lord, see Tavistock, Marquess of (1)
Russell, Lord Arthur (formerly A.J.E. Russell), 169
Russell, A.J.E., see Russell, Lord Arthur
Russell, Lord Charles, 199
Russell, Sir Charles, Bt., 10, 200
Russell, Charles, 139
Russell, Lord Cosmo, 41
Russell, Lord Edward, 169
Russell, Hon. E.S., 169
Russell, F.C.H., 199
Russell, Hon. G.R.H., 220
Russell, G.W.E., 16
Russell, Lord John, 2, 164, 217
Russell, J.D.W., 267
Russell, T., 325, 349
Russell, Sir W., Bt., 63, 127
Russell, W.C., 282
Russell, W.H., 1
Rust, J., 231
Ruston, J., 105
Rutherfurd, A., 332
Rutson, A.O., 125
Ryder, Hon. F.D., 46, 163
Ryder, Hon. G.D., 230
Ryder, G.R., 149
Rylands, P., 37, 181, 239
Ryle, J., 111

S

Sackville, S.G.S. (formerly Stopford), 126, 253
Sadler, M.T., 89, 100
Sadler, S.A., 118
St. Aubyn, Sir J., Bt., 209
St. Aubyn, W.N.M., 84
St. Paul, H., 282
St. Paul, Sir H.D.C., Bt., 65
Salisbury, E.D., 98
Salisbury, E.G., 46
Salkeld, T., 210
Salmon, H.T., 122
Salomons, D., 4, 112, 154
Salomons, Sir D.L., Bt., 234
Salt, Thomas, 158
Salt, Titus, 30
Salter, I., 114
Salwey, H., 108
Samuda, J.D'A., 9, 169
Samuelson, B., 17
Samuelson, H.B., 45, 71
Samuelson, J., 24
Sandars, G., 177
Sandars, J., 23, 60, 78
Sandeman, A.G., 139
Sanderson, R., 53
Sanderson, T.K., 177
Sandford, Sir D.K., 325, 334
Sandford, G.M.W. (formerly Peacocke), 82, 113
Sandon, Viscount (1), 107
Sandon, Viscount (2), 104, 107, 158
Sandwith, H., 7
Sandys, T.M., 46
Sanford, E.A., 265
Sankey, W.V., 7
Sartoris, A., 178
Sartoris, E.J., 131, 309
Saunders, J.E., 4
Saunders, W.A.F., 93, 98
Savage, I., 136
Sawle, C.B.G., 27
Sayle, P., 76
Scales, M., 2
Scarlett, Sir J., 127
Scarlett, Hon. Sir J.Y., 37, 79
Scarlett, Hon. R.C., 88, 127
Schenley, E.W.H., 57
Schneider, H.W., 98, 127
Schofield, W.W., 143
Scholefield, J., 25
Scholefield, W., 25
Schonberg, J.T., 280
Schreiber, C., 45, 136
Sclater, G., see Booth, G.S.
Scobell, G.T., 19
Scoble, A.R., 155
Scott, A.J., 192
Scott, C., 331, 335
Scott, E., 112
Scott, Sir E.D., Bt., 104
Scott, Hon. F., 348, 372
Scott, Lord Henry, 228, 373
Scott, H.W., 321
Scott, James, 88
Scott, Lord John, 372

Scott, John, 326
Scott, J.W., 227
Scott, M.D., 275
Scott, R., 179
Scott, Sir W., Bt., 372
Scourfield, J.H. (formerly Philipps), 298, 316
Scourfield, W.H., 298
Scovell, G., 8
Scrope, G.P., 164
Seaham, Viscount, 219
Seale, Sir J.H., Bt., 57
Sebright, Sir J.S., Bt., 230
Seddon, P.K., 76
Seely, Charles (1), 105, 124
Seely, Charles (2), 128
Sellar, A.C., 60, 327
Selwin, H.J., see Ibbetson, Sir H.J.S., Bt.
Selwyn, C.J., 377
Sergeant, C.E., 27
Severne, J.E., 108, 262
Seymer, H.K., 218
Seymour, Lord, 174
Seymour, A., 149, 174
Seymour, Sir H.B., 119
Seymour, H.D., 136, 152
Seymour, Sir M., 60
Seymour, William Digby (1), 96
Seymour, William Digby (2), 96, 128, 156, 162, 166
Shackleton, R., 26
Shadwell, W.D.L., 83
Shafto, R.D., 219, 220
Sharpe, C., 247
Sharpe, M., 320
Shaw, A.M., 338
Shaw, James, 318
Shaw, John, 135
Shaw, R., 37
Shaw, T., 80
Shaw, W., 227
Shawe, R.N., 270
Shee, W., 7, 163
Sheffield, Sir R., Bt., 244
Shelburne, Earl of, 40
Sheldon, E.R.C., 278
Shelley, Sir J.V., Bt., 10, 32, 275
Shenstone, F.S., 65
Sheppard, T., 71
Sheppard, W., 153
Sheridan, H.B., 65
Sheridan, R.B., 32, 62, 152, 163
Sherriff, A.C., 196
Shield, H., 41
Shipton, G., 8
Shirley, E.J., 278
Shirley, E.P., 278
Shute, C.C., 34
Shuttleworth, Sir J.P.K., Bt., 237
Shuttleworth, Sir U.J.K., Bt., 54, 83, 237
Sibthorp, C.D.W., 105
Sibthorp, G.T.W., 105
Sidebottom, J., 159
Sidebottom, T.H., 159
Sidebottom, W., 213
Sidney, T., 100, 158, 196
Simeon, Sir J., Bt., 232
Simeon, Sir R.G., Bt., 232
Simon, J., 61
Simonds, W.B., 192
Simpson, C., 104
Simpson, W., 197
Simpson, W.S., 107, 138
Sinclair, D., 360
Sinclair, Sir G., Bt., 80, 350
Sinclair, Sir J.G.T., Bt., 350
Sitwell, Sir G., Bt., 213
Sitwell, Sir G.R., Bt., 151
Skipwith, Sir G., Bt., 277, 278
Skipwith, Sir T.G., Bt., 277
Slade, Sir A.F.A., Bt., 103, 168
Slade, F.W., 35, 41, 149
Slagg, J., 116
Slaney, R.A., 155
Slater, W., 43
Sleigh, B.W.A., 4
Sleigh, W.C., 6, 71, 89, 121
Sleigh, W.W., 158
Sloper, S.F.K., 59
Smee, A., 144
Smethurst, R., 177
Smijth, Sir W.B., Bt., 223
Smith, Abel (Senr.), 230
Smith, Abel (Junr.), 230
Smith, Archibald, 380
Smith, Augustus (1), 175
Smith, Augustus (2), 339
Smith, B., 127, 165
Smith, Sir C.E., Bt., see Eardley, Sir C.E., Bt.
Smith, E.C., 45
Smith, E.T., 20
Smith, F.C., 257
Smith, G., 197
Smith, G.R., 197, 201
Smith, H.J.S., 379
Smith, H.S., 110
Smith, James, 326
Smith, Jervoise, 131
Smith, John (1), 201
Smith, John (2), 149
Smith, J.A., 47
Smith, J.B., 26, 161, 179, 321, 337
Smith, Sir J.M.F., 44
Smith, M.E., 175
Smith, M.T., 197
Smith, R., 214
Smith, Hon. R.J., 197
Smith, R.V., 126
Smith, S., 107
Smith, S.G., 16
Smith, T., 138
Smith, T.A., 307
Smith, T.B.C., 142
Smith, T.C., 12
Smith, T.E., 63, 176
Smith, William Abel, 165
Smith, William Adams, 65
Smith, W.H., 10
Smith, W.M., 235
Smollett, A., 353
Smollett, P.B., 41, 353
Smyth, Sir G.H., Bt., 53
Smyth, J.G., 198

Smyth, T.J., 19
Smythe, Hon. G.A.F.P.S., 42
Sombre, D.O.D., 165
Somerset, E.A., 226, 314
Somerset, Lord Granville, 314
Somerset, Lord Henry, 314
Somerset, P.G.H., 314
Somerset, Lord Robert, 50, 226
Somerton, Viscount, 191
Somerville, Sir W.M., Bt., see Athlumney, Lord
Somes, Joseph (1), 57, 78
Somes, Joseph (2), 96
Sotheron, T.H.S., see Estcourt, T.H.S.S.
Spalding, J.E., 86
Spankie, R., 3, 38
Spark, H.K., 56
Spearman, H.J., 66
Speirs, A., 141
Speirs, A.A., 370
Speirs, A.G., 334
Spencer, Hon. C.R., 253
Spencer, Hon. F., 119
Spinks, F.L., 129
Spinks, T., 102
Spooner, R., 25, 277
Spry, Sir S.T., 27
Stafford, Marquess of (1), 375
Stafford, Marquess of (2), 375
Stafford, A.S.O'B. (formerly O'Brien), 253
Standish, C.S., 190
Stanford, J.F., 139
Stanford, V.F.B., 152
Stanhope, Lord, 214, 258
Stanhope, Hon. E., 245
Stanhope, J.B., 244
Stanhope, Hon. L., 9
Stanhope, Hon. P.J., 63
Stanhope, R.H., 63
Stanhope, W.T.W.S., 289
Staniland, M., 29
Stanley, Lord (1) (formerly Hon. E.G.S. Stanley), 236
Stanley, Lord (2) (formerly Hon. E.H. Stanley), 7, 95, 98
Stanley, Edward (1), 211
Stanley, Edward (2), 238
Stanley, Hon. E.G.S., see Stanley, Lord (1)
Stanley, Hon. E.H., see Stanley, Lord (2)
Stanley, Edward James, 265
Stanley, Edward John, 205
Stanley, Hon. E.L., 129
Stanley, Hon. F.A., 138, 236
Stanley, Hon. H.T., 138
Stanley, Hon. J.C., 112
Stanley, W.M., 135
Stanley, Hon. W.O., 46, 290, 305
Stansfeld, J., 80
Stansfield, W.R.C., 89
Stanton, A.J., 164
Stanton, J.T., 164
Stanton, W.H., 164
Stanton, W.J., 164
Stapleton, A.G., 25
Stapleton, J., 21
Stapleton, M.T., 141
Stapylton, H.M., 172
Stapylton, M., 285
Starkey, J., 89
Starkey, L.R., 289
Starkie, J.P.C., 237
Starkie, Le G.N., 51
Starkie, T., 41
Staunton, Sir G.T., Bt., 137, 228
Staveley, T.K., 142
Steble, R.F., 151
Steel, J., 52
Steere, L., 274
Stephen, G., 129, 187
Stephen, J.F., 82, 321
Stephens, F.H., 147
Stephens, H.L., 147
Stephens, J.R., 15
Stephens, S.L., 165
Stephenson, R., 188
Stephenson, W.W., 210
Stepney, E.A.A.K.C., 295
Stepney, J.S.C., 295
Sterling, J.B., 106, 215
Stern, S.J., 273
Steuart, A., 41
Steuart, R., 327
Stevens, J.C.M., 216
Stevenson, J.C., 157
Steward, A.B., 189
Stewart, A., 110
Stewart, C., 131
Stewart, E., 339
Stewart, G.D., 369
Stewart, H., 4, 370
Stewart, H.G.M., 361
Stewart, James (1), 18, 87
Stewart, James (2), 326
Stewart, John (1), 110
Stewart, John (2), 329
Stewart, M.J., 339
Stewart, Sir M.R.S., Bt., 370
Stewart, Sir M.S., Bt., 370
Stewart, P.M., 98, 370
Stirling, Sir James, 44
Stirling, James, 353
Stirling, W., see Maxwell, Sir W.S., Bt.
Stitt, S., 24
Stocks, M., 80
Stocks, S., 111
Stone, W.H., 3, 44, 137
Stonor, T., 130, 259
Stopford, S.G., see Sackville, S.G.S.
Storer, G., 258
Storey, S., 166
Storey, T., 236
Storks, Sir H.K., 53, 142
Stormont, Viscount, 127, 369
Strachey, Sir H.J., Bt., 78, 127, 249
Straight, D., 155
Strange, H.L.S. Le, see Le Strange
Strangways, Hon. J.G.C.F., 40, 218
Stratton, G., 17
Strickland, Sir G., Bt., 138, 286
Strutt, Hon. C.H., 221
Strutt, E., 13, 54, 58, 128
Strutt, Hon. H., 21, 212
Stuart, C., 349

Stuart, Lord Dudley, 7, 13
Stuart, H., 20
Stuart, Lord James, 293, 319, 335, 344
Stuart, James, 5, 377
Stuart, John, 39, 121
Stuart, J.F.D.C., 293
Stuart, William (Senr.), 199
Stuart, William (Junr.), 20, 199
Stucley, Sir G.S., Bt. (formerly Buck), 18, 69
Sturch, W.J., 71
Sturge, J., 25, 100, 128
Sturgeon, C., 97, 128
Sturt, C.N., 62
Sturt, H.C., 218
Sturt, H.G., 62, 218
Style, Sir T.C., Bt., 151
Sugden, Sir E.B., 41, 142
Summers, W., 159
Sumner, G.H., 274
Surrey, Earl of, 276
Surrey, Earl of Arundel and, see Arundel and Surrey
Surtees, C.F., 220
Surtees, H.E., 230
Surtees, W.E., 132
Sutcliffe, W., 19
Sutherland, T., 326
Suttie, Sir J.G., Bt., 327
Sutton, Sir C.M., 377
Sutton, J.H.M., 121
Sutton, Hon. J.H.T.M., 41, 82
Swainson, C., 138
Swanston, C., 228
Swinburne, Sir J., Bt., 104
Swinton, A.C., 327, 381
Sykes, C., 22, 284
Sykes, J., 22
Sykes, W.H., 318
Symons, G.S., 60
Symons, J.C., 164

T

Tagart, F., 264
Tait, Sir P., 366
Talbot, C.R.M., 312
Talbot, Lord Edmund, 37
Talbot, G.F., 158
Talbot, J.G., 94, 114, 235, 379
Talbot, Hon. R.A.J., 158
Talbot, W.H.F., 48
Talfourd, T.N., 139
Talley, W., 201
Tancred, H.W., 17
Tapps, G.W., see Gervis, G.W.T.
Tavistock, Marquess of (1) (formerly Lord Russell), 169
Tavistock, Marquess of (2), 199
Tawney, H., 17
Tayleur, W., 32
Taylor, C., 165
Taylor, H., 176
Taylor, James (1), 143
Taylor, James (2), 18
Taylor, John (1), 319
Taylor, John (2), 247
Taylor, J.A., 282
Taylor, J.E., 239
Taylor, M.A., 165
Taylor, P.A., 101, 123
Taylor, S.W., 59
Teed, T., 178
Teignmouth, Lord, 7
Tempest, Lord Adolphus Vane-, see Vane-Tempest
Tempest, Lord Ernest Vane-, see Vane-Tempest
Tempest, J.P., 100
Temple, C., 3, 59, 155
Temple, Sir R., Bt., 282
Temple, Hon. W.F.C. (formerly Cowper), 86, 228
Tennant, C., 325, 368
Tennant, C.W., 332
Tennant, R., 100, 132
Tennyson, C., see D'Eyncourt, C.T.
Thackeray, W.M., 130
Thesiger, Sir F., 11, 121, 160, 195
Thicknesse, R., 190
Thicknesse, R.A., 190
Thom, J.N., see Courtenay, Sir W.P.H.
Thomas, M.D., see Treherne, M.D.
Thomason, W., 334
Thomasson, J.P., 28
Thompson, A.C.M., 59
Thompson, A.G., 52
Thompson, C., 19, 189
Thompson, George (1), 9, 156
Thompson, George (2), 318
Thompson, Sir H.M.M., Bt., 97, 246
Thompson, H.S., 97, 188, 287
Thompson, H.Y., 138, 238, 239
Thompson, M.W., 30
Thompson, P.B., 284
Thompson, T.C., 66, 166
Thompson, T.E.P., 9
Thompson, T.P., 7, 30, 45, 96, 112, 138, 166, 337
Thompson, W., 166, 279
Thomson, C.P., 63, 116
Thomson, R., 330
Thornbury, G., 92
Thorneley, J., 153
Thornely, T., 107, 194
Thorneycroft, T., 194
Thornhill, A.J., 202
Thornhill, G., 231
Thornhill, T., 271
Thornhill, W.P., 213
Thornton, F. Du P., 54, 133
Thorold, J.H., 74
Threipland, Sir J.P.M., 335
Throckmorton, N., 31
Throckmorton, R.G., 200
Thruston, C.A., 83
Thurlow, T.L., 79
Thwaites, D., 26
Thynne, Lord Edward, 71
Thynne, Lord Henry, 281
Tice, W., 49
Tidmas, W., 92
Tillett, J.H., 127
Tipping, W., 161
Tite, W., 18, 19
Todd, J.R., 53, 87
Tollemache, Hon. A.G., 74

Tollemache, Hon. F.J., 74
Tollemache, H.J., 207
Tollemache, J., 206, 207
Tollemache, J.R.D., 205
Tollemache, Hon. W.F., 207
Tomes, J., 182
Tomkinson, J., 207
Tomline, G., 76, 82, 155, 165, 246, 270
Tomlinson, W.E.M., 138
Tooke, W., 139, 175
Torr, J., 107
Torrens, R., 28
Torrens, Sir R.R., 41
Torrens, W.T.M., 3
Tottenham, C.J., 313
Tower, C., 201
Tower, C.T., 82
Towneley, C., 130, 238
Towneley, J., 22
Townley, R.G., 202
Townsend, J., 4
Townshend, Lord Charles, 167
Townshend, Lord James, 84
Townshend, John (1), 167
Townshend, John (2), see Gardner, J.D.
Tracy, Hon. C.D.R.H., 301
Tracy, C.H., 170
Tracy, Hon. F.S.A.H., 301
Tracy, H.H., 31
Tracy, Hon. S.C.G.H., 315
Traill, G., 350, 366
Traill, J.C., 350
Treeby, J.W., 109
Trefusis, Hon. C.H.R., 216
Treherne, M.D. (formerly Thomas), 54, 295
Trelawny, Sir J.S., Bt., 20, 34, 106, 169, 208
Trelawny, Sir W.L.S., Bt., 208
Tremayne, A., 175
Tremayne, J., 208, 217
Trench, Sir F.W., 151
Trevelyan, G.O., 176, 328
Trevor, Hon. A., see Dungannon, Viscount
Trevor, Hon. G.R.R., 309
Trevor, Hon. T. (formerly Brand), 103, 222, 230
Tristram, T.H., 81
Trollope, A., 22
Trollope, Sir J., Bt., 243
Trotter, H.J., 21, 176
Trotter, J., 274
Troubridge, Sir E.T., Bt., 150
Trueman, C., 84
Truscott, Sir F.W., 65, 75
Tucker, H., 55
Tucker, S., 139
Tudway, R.C., 184
Tufnell, H., 53, 60, 92
Tufton, Sir H.J., Bt., 233, 279
Tulk, C.A., 136
Tullamore, Lord, 131
Tunno, E.R., 12
Turbutt, W.G., 212
Turner, C., 107, 238, 240
Turner, E., 175
Turner, F.C.P., 20
Turner, G.J., 54
Turner, J.A., 116
Turner, M.M., 65, 121, 136, 164
Turner, R., 74
Turner, T.F., 242
Turner, William (1), 26
Turner, William (2), 146
Turnor, C., 243
Turnor, E., 74, 247
Turton, T.E.M., 165
Tuxford, G.P., 29
Twells, P., 2
Twelvetrees, H., 7
Twiss, H., 33, 39, 128
Twistleton, Hon. E.T.B., 41
Twyford, H.R., 124
Tyler, Sir G., 312
Tyler, Sir H.W., 82
Tynte, C.J.K., 32, 265
Tynte, C.K.K., 32
Tyrell, Sir J.T., Bt., 222
Tyron, T., 253
Tyrrell, C., 271

U

Uffington, Viscount, 200
Urquhart, D., 153, 158
Uxbridge, Earl of (formerly Lord Paget), 268

V

Valletort, Viscount, 134
Vance, J., 42
Vanderbyl, P., 32, 78
Van de Weyer, V.W.B., 193
Vane, Lord Adolphus, see Vane-Tempest
Vane, Lord Harry, 83, 220
Vane, H.M., 201
Vane-Tempest, Lord Adolphus (formerly Lord Adolphus Vane), 66, 219
Vane-Tempest, Lord Ernest, 162
Vansittart, A., 193
Vansittart, A.A., 156
Vansittart, G.H., 200
Vansittart, W., 193
Vaughan, E.M., 308
Vaughan, J.E., 184
Vaughan, N.V.E., 312
Vaughan, Sir R.W., Bt., 313
Veasey, C., 90
Venables, W., 2
Vere, Sir C.B., 270
Vere, J.J.H., 365
Vereker, Hon. C.S., 78
Verner, R.N., 82
Verney, E.H., 77, 137, 290
Verney, Sir H., Bt., 20, 36
Vernon, A.H., 214
Vernon, F.H., 253
Vernon, G.E.H., 121
Vernon, G.H., 67
Vernon, Hon. G.J.V., 214
Vernon, H.F., 282
Vernon, L.V., 44, 200
Vickers, S., 178
Vigors, W.R., 84

Villiers, Viscount, 50, 87, 187
Villiers, C.P., 194, 238
Villiers, Hon. F.J.R., 144
Villiers, F.M., 42, 165
Villiers, Hon. F.W.C., 187
Vincent, Sir F., Bt., 146
Vincent, H., 17, 92, 134, 169, 198, 330
Vivian, A.P., 209
Vivian, Hon. C.C., 27
Vivian, E., 147
Vivian, H.H., 175, 312
Vivian, Hon. J.C.W., 27, 131, 175
Vivian, J.E., 175
Vivian, J.H., 304
Vivian, Sir R.H., Bt., 175, 208
Vogel, Sir J., 131
Vyner, R.A., 142
Vyse, R.H.R.H., 193, 254
Vyvyan, E.R., 31
Vyvyan, Sir R.R., Bt., 35, 84

W

Waddington, D., 82, 113
Waddington, H.S., 271
Waddy, S.D., 18, 153, 322
Wade, C.J., 215
Wait, W.K., 73
Waithman, R., 2
Wakefield, D., 6
Wakley, T., 3
Walcott, J.E., 49
Walker, G.G., 320, 352
Walker, J., 285
Walker, J.R., 22
Walker, O.O., 38, 148
Walker, R., 38
Walker, T.E., 183, 282
Walker, W.C., 63
Wall, C.B., 79, 149
Wallace, R., 326
Wallis, C.W., 119
Walmsley, Sir J., 28, 101, 107
Walpole, Lord, 249
Walpole, Hon. F., 95, 250
Walpole, S.H., 119, 377
Walrond, J.W., 173, 216
Walrond, W.H., 215
Walsh, Hon. A., 102, 317
Walsh, Sir J.B., Bt., 136, 165, 317
Walter, E., 139
Walter, John (Senr.), 128
Walter, John (Junr.), 8, 128, 200
Walters, R., 22, 72, 166
Walton, A.A., 163
Warburton, G.D., 82
Warburton, H., 33, 93
Warburton, P.E., 204
Ward, G.H., 232
Ward, H.G., 146, 153
Ward, T.A., 153
Ward, W., 2
Wardlaw, J., 112
Waring, C., 136
Warmington, C.M., 314
Warner, E., 127
Warner, H.J.L., 42
Warner, J.H.B., 83, 101
Warre, J.A., 83, 142
Warren, Hon. J.B.L., 204
Warren, R.P., 297
Warren, S., 119
Warton, C.N., 33
Wason, R., 92
Waterhouse, S., 135
Waterlow, Sir S.H., Bt., 8, 75, 112, 352
Waterman, A., 65
Waterpark, Lord, 104, 214
Waters, R.E.C., 127
Watkin, A.M., 76
Watkin, Sir E.W., Bt., 69, 78, 91, 161, 203
Watkins, J.L.V., 291
Watlington, J.W.P., 223
Watney, J., 272
Watson, Hon. R., 42, 132
Watson, W., 380
Watson, W.H., 96, 123
Waugh, E., 52
Wawn, J.T., 157
Way, A.E., 19
Webb, C.L., 5, 27
Webb, E., 73
Webster, J., 318
Webster, R.E., 23, 99
Webster, R.G., 52
Wedderburn, Sir D., Bt., 327, 346
Wedgwood, J., 163
Weeding, T., 21
Weguelin, C., 63
Weguelin, T.M., 156, 194
Weir, T., 54
Welby, G.E., 74
Welby, W.E., see Gregory, Sir W.E.W., Bt.
Wellesley, Lord Charles, 144, 193, 228
Wellesley, H., 12
Wellesley, Hon. W.P.T.L., 223
Wells, E., 178
Wells, W., 22, 132
Wemyss, J.E., 356
Wemyss, J.H.E., 356
Wentworth, T.V., 16
West, F.R., 296
West, H.W., 92
West, J., 161
West, J.T., 16
West, W.C., 110, 207
Western, C.C., 222
Western, Sir T.B., Bt., 221, 222
Western, T.S., 113, 270
Westhead, J.P., see Westhead, J.P.B.
Westhead, J.P.B. (formerly J.P. Westhead), 97, 198
Westropp, H., 32
Wethered, T.O., 77
Wetherell, Sir C., 25, 130
Weyland, R., 259
Whalley, George Hammond, 132, 301
Whalley, George Hampden, 132
Whalley, Sir S.St.S.B., 7
Whalley, W., 51
Wharton, J.L., 66
Whateley, W., 19, 157
Whatley, T.D., 50

Whatman, J., 112, 235
Wheelhouse, W.St.J., 100
Whetham, Sir C., 33
Whitbread, S., 20
Whitbread, W.H., 20
White, A., 166
White, J., 34, 134
White, Hon. L., 94
White, W.F., 112
Whitehead, S.T., 129
Whitehorne, J.C., 111
Whitehurst, J.C., 27
Whitelaw, A., 325
Whitley, E., 107
Whitmore, H., 31
Whitmore, T., 262
Whitmore, T.C., 31
Whitmore, W.W., 194
Whittle, J., 190
Whitwell, J., 93
Whitworth, B., 158
Wickham, H.W., 30
Wickham, J.W.D.T., 71
Wiggin, H., 266
Wigney, I.N., 34
Wigram, J., 102
Wigram, L.T., 377
Wilberforce, W., 30, 96, 168
Wilbraham, G., 206
Wilbraham, Hon. R.B., 238
Wilde, J.P., 101, 132
Wilde, Sir T., 121, 196
Wilkins, C., 68, 198
Wilkins, W., 317
Wilkinson, J.J., 17, 127
Wilkinson, W.A., 6, 140, 166
Wilks, J., 29, 146
Willans, W., 89
Willans, W.H., 71
Willcox, B.M., 156
Williams, A.J., 24
Williams, B.B., 145
Williams, B.T., 295
Williams, C.H., 18
Williams, C.J.W., 296, 307
Williams, D., 313
Williams, E.L., 17
Williams, E.W.B., 175
Williams, Sir F.M., Bt., 175
Williams, G., 15
Williams, John (1), 35
Williams, John (2), 111
Williams, Sir J.H., Bt., 309
Williams, M., 209
Williams, O.L.C., 77
Williams, Robert (Senr.), 62
Williams, Robert (Junr.), 62
Williams, S.C.E., 303
Williams, T.P., 77
Williams, Walter, 194
Williams, William, 6, 54
Williams, W.A., 314
Williams, Sir W.F., Bt., 40
Williamson, D.R., 335
Williamson, Sir Hedworth, Bt. (Senr.), 166, 219
Williamson, Sir Hedworth, Bt. (Junr.), 219
Williamson, J.W., 72
Williamson, S., 336
Willis, H.R., 283
Willis, W., 53
Willoughby, Sir H.P., Bt., 68, 122, 126, 136
Willoughby, J.P., 102
Wills, M., 82
Wills, W.H., 54
Willyams, E.W.B., 175, 208
Willyams, H., 175
Wilmot, Sir H., Bt., 214
Wilmot, Sir John Eardley Eardley, Bt. (1), 277
Wilmot, Sir John Eardley Eardley, Bt. (2), 278
Wilshere, W., 78
Wilson, A., 243
Wilson, C.H., 96
Wilson, F.M., 271
Wilson, H., 271
Wilson, I., 118
Wilson, James, 60, 186
Wilson, John, 324
Wilson, J.W.H., 42
Wilson, Sir M., Bt., 51, 288
Wilson, T., 2
Wilton, Viscount Grey de, see Grey de Wilton
Windham, C.A., 249
Windham, W.H., 249
Wingfield, Sir C.J., 75
Wingfield, J.H.L., 132
Wingfield, R.B., see Baker, R.B.W.
Winn, C., 22
Winn, R., 246
Winnington, H.J., 283
Winnington, Sir T.E., Bt., 23
Winterbotham, H.S.P., 164
Winterton, W., 101
Wire, D.W., 4, 29
Wise, H.C., 278
Wise, J.A., 122, 158
Wodehouse, E., 249
Wodehouse, E.R., 19, 95, 250
Wolff, Sir H.D., 49, 62, 137
Wolseley, Sir C., Bt., 116, 158
Wood, B., 8, 96, 173
Wood, Sir C., Bt., 80, 142
Wood, C.A., 29
Wood, C.P., 221
Wood, D.E., 66
Wood, G.W., 93, 238
Wood, Hon. H.J.L., 284
Wood, James, 15
Wood, Joseph, 89
Wood, Sir M., Bt., 2
Wood, Thomas (1), 306
Wood, Thomas (2), 248
Wood, Western, 2
Wood, William, 135
Wood, Sir W.P., 130
Woodall, W., 163
Woodd, B.T., 97
Woods, H., 190
Woolf, S., 135
Woolley, J., 18
Worcester, Marquess of (1), 226, 300

Worcester, Marquess of (2), 225
Wordsworth, C.F.F., 334
Worley, H.T., 146
Worms, Baron de, see de Worms
Worms, H., see de Worms, Baron
Worsley, Lord (1) (formerly Hon. C.A.W. Pelham), 244
Worsley, Lord (2), 76
Worsley, Sir W.C., Bt., 115, 188
Worthington, G.B., 203
Worthington, W.H., 167
Wortley, Hon. A.H.P.S.S., 87
Wortley, C.B.S., 153
Wortley, Hon. J.A.S., 80, 286, 349
Wortley, Hon. J.F.S., 153
Wortley, Hon. J.S., 286, 357
Wrangham, D.C., 165
Wraxall, Sir W.L., Bt., 164
Wren, W., 178, 190
Wrenfordsley, H.T., 132
Wright, C.I., 128
Wright, J.S., 128
Wright, P.L., 113
Wrightson, W.B., 125
Wrottesley, Sir J., Bt., 268
Wroughton, P., 200
Wyld, J., 3, 27
Wylie, A.C., 187
Wylie, J.W.S., 85
Wyndham, C., 276
Wyndham, Hon. Henry, 276
Wyndham, Henry, 52, 211, 276
Wyndham, J.H.C. (formerly Campbell), 149
Wyndham, Hon. P.S., 211
Wyndham, Wadham, 149
Wyndham, William, 281
Wynn, Charles Watkin Williams (1), 315
Wynn, Charles Watkin Williams (2), 315
Wynn, Sir H.L.W.W., Bt., 310
Wynn, H.W.W., 315
Wynn, Hon. T.J., 292
Wynn, Sir Watkin Williams, Bt. (1), 310
Wynn, Sir Watkin Williams, Bt. (2), 310
Wynne, C.G., see Finch, C.G.W.
Wynne, Sir W., 313
Wynne, W.R.M., 313
Wynne, W.W.E., 313
Wyvill, M., 141

Y

Yardley, Sir W., 108
Yarmouth, Earl of, 278
Yates, E., 17
Yates, J.A., 28
Yeaman, J., 321
Yelverton, Hon. W.H., 295
Yorke, C.P., 202
Yorke, Hon. E.C., 202
Yorke, Hon. E.T., 202
Yorke, H.G.R., 198
Yorke, J.R., 170, 225
Yorstoun, M.C., 320
Young, A.W., 78, 84
Young, Sir George, Bt., 48, 134
Young, George, 339
Young, G.A., 7
Young, G.F., 151, 176
Young, R., 95, 202
Young, W.J., 81
Young, Sir W.L., Bt., 201

INDEX TO CONSTITUENCIES

This index shows the constituency reference number which is given, following the name of the constituency, at the top of each page. It does *not* refer to the folio number which appears in small type at the foot of each page. The index has been extensively cross-indexed for ease of reference.

The names of borough constituencies are followed, within brackets, by the name of the administrative county in which they were either entirely or mainly situated. The only exceptions are boroughs which bear the same name as the county. This information will allow readers to collate election results on a county basis.

For those who may wish to compare the 1832–1885 constituencies with those of post-1885, it should be noted that the following counties have changed their names during this century: Angus (formerly Forfarshire), East Lothian (formerly Haddingtonshire), Hampshire (formerly Southamptonshire), Midlothian (formerly Edinburghshire), Moray (formerly Elginshire), West Lothian (formerly Linlithgowshire).

The following abbreviations have been used:

Beds.	Bedfordshire
Berks.	Berkshire
Bucks.	Buckinghamshire
Glam.	Glamorganshire
Glos.	Gloucestershire
Hants.	Hampshire
Herts.	Hertfordshire
Lancs.	Lancashire
Lincs.	Lincolnshire
Middx.	Middlesex
Mon.	Monmouthshire
Northants.	Northamptonshire
Notts.	Nottinghamshire
Oxon.	Oxfordshire
Salop.	Shropshire
Staffs.	Staffordshire
Wilts.	Wiltshire
Worcs.	Worcestershire
Yorks.	Yorkshire

A

Aberavon, see Swansea Boroughs
ABERDEEN, 318
ABERDEEN and GLASGOW UNIVERSITIES, 380
ABERDEENSHIRE, 340
  Eastern, 341
  Western, 342
Aberystwyth, see Cardigan Boroughs
ABINGDON (Berks.), 11
Adpar, see Cardigan Boroughs
Airdrie, see Falkirk Burghs
Amlwch, see Beaumaris Boroughs
ANDOVER (Hants.), 12
ANGLESEY, 305
Annan, see Dumfries Burghs
Anstruther, see St. Andrews Burghs
Arbroath, see Montrose Burghs
ARGYLL, 343
ARUNDEL (Sussex), 13
ASHBURTON (Devon), 14
ASHTON-UNDER-LYNE (Lancs.), 15
AYLESBURY (Bucks.), 16
AYR DISTRICT of BURGHS, 319
AYRSHIRE, 344
  Northern, 345
  Southern, 346

B

BANBURY (Oxon.), 17
Banff, see Elgin Burghs
BANFFSHIRE, 347
Bangor, see Caernarvon Boroughs
BARNSTAPLE (Devon), 18
BATH (Somerset), 19
BEAUMARIS DISTRICT of BOROUGHS (Anglesey), 290
BEDFORD, 20
BEDFORDSHIRE, 199
BERKSHIRE, 200
BERWICK-UPON-TWEED (Northumberland), 21
BERWICKSHIRE, 348
BEVERLEY (Yorks.), 22
BEWDLEY (Worcs.), 23
BIRKENHEAD (Cheshire), 24
BIRMINGHAM (Warwickshire), 25
BLACKBURN (Lancs.), 26
BODMIN (Cornwall), 27
BOLTON (Lancs.), 28
Bolton-Le-Moors, see Bolton
Border Burghs, see Hawick Burghs
BOSTON (Lincs.), 29
BRADFORD (Yorks.), 30
Brechin, see Montrose Burghs
BRECON, 291
BRECONSHIRE, 306
BRIDGNORTH (Salop.), 31
BRIDGWATER (Somerset), 32
BRIDPORT (Dorset), 33
BRIGHTON (Sussex), 34
BRISTOL (Glos./Somerset), 35
BUCKINGHAM, 36
BUCKINGHAMSHIRE, 201
BURNLEY (Lancs.), 37
Burntisland, see Kirkcaldy Burghs
BURY (Lancs.), 38
BURY ST. EDMUNDS (Suffolk), 39
BUTE, 349

C

Caergwyle, see Flint Boroughs
CAERNARVON DISTRICT of BOROUGHS, 292
CAERNARVONSHIRE, 307
Caerwys, see Flint Boroughs
CAITHNESS, 350
CALNE (Wilts.), 40
CAMBRIDGE, 41
CAMBRIDGE UNIVERSITY, 377
CAMBRIDGESHIRE, 202
Campbeltown, see Ayr Burghs
CANTERBURY (Kent), 42
CARDIFF DISTRICT of BOROUGHS (Glam.), 29
CARDIGAN DISTRICT of BOROUGHS, 294
CARDIGANSHIRE, 308
CARLISLE (Cumberland), 43
CARMARTHEN DISTRICT of BOROUGHS, 295
CARMARTHENSHIRE, 309
Carnarvon, see Caernarvon
Cefnllys, see Radnor Boroughs
CHATHAM (Kent), 44
CHELSEA (Middx.), 1
CHELTENHAM (Glos.), 45
CHESHIRE
  Eastern, 203
  Mid, 204
  Northern, 205
  Southern, 206
  Western, 207
CHESTER, 46
CHICHESTER (Sussex), 47
CHIPPENHAM (Wilts.), 48
Chipping Wycombe, see Wycombe
CHRISTCHURCH (Hants.), 49
CIRENCESTER (Glos.), 50
CITY OF LONDON (Middx.), 2
CLACKMANNANSHIRE and KINROSS-SHIRE, 351
CLITHEROE (Lancs.), 51
COCKERMOUTH (Cumberland), 52
COLCHESTER (Essex), 53
Conway, see Caernarvon Boroughs
CORNWALL
  Eastern, 208
  Western, 209
COVENTRY (Warwickshire), 54
Cowbridge, see Cardiff Boroughs
Crail, see St. Andrews Burghs
Criccieth, see Caernarvon Boroughs
CRICKLADE (Wilts.), 55
Cromarty (Burgh), see Wick Burghs
Cromarty (County), see Ross and Cromarty
Cullen, see Elgin Burghs
Culross, see Stirling Burghs
CUMBERLAND
  Eastern, 210
  Western, 211
Cupar, see St. Andrews Burghs

D

DARLINGTON (Durham), 56
DARTMOUTH (Devon), 57
DENBIGH DISTRICT of BOROUGHS, 296
DENBIGHSHIRE, 310
DERBY, 58
DERBYSHIRE
  Eastern, 212
  Northern, 213
  Southern, 214
DEVIZES (Wilts.), 59
DEVON
  Eastern, 215
  Northern, 216
  Southern, 217
DEVONPORT (Devon), 60
DEWSBURY (Yorks.), 61
Dingwall, see Wick Burghs
DORCHESTER (Dorset), 62
Dornoch, see Wick Burghs
DORSET, 218
DOVER (Kent), 63
DROITWICH (Worcs.), 64
DUDLEY (Worcs.), 65
Dumbarton, see Kilmarnock Burghs
Dumbartonshire, see Dunbartonshire
DUMFRIES DISTRICT of BURGHS, 320
DUMFRIESSHIRE, 352
Dunbar, see Haddington Burghs
DUNBARTONSHIRE, 353
DUNDEE (Forfarshire), 321
Dunfermline, see Stirling Burghs
DURHAM, 66
DURHAM
  Northern, 219
  Southern, 220
Dysart, see Kirkcaldy Burghs

E

EAST RETFORD (Notts.), 67
EDINBURGH, 322
EDINBURGH and ST. ANDREWS UNIVERSITIES, 381
EDINBURGHSHIRE, 354
ELGIN DISTRICT of BURGHS, 323
ELGINSHIRE and NAIRNSHIRE, 355
ESSEX
  Eastern, 221
  Northern, 222
  Southern, 223
  Western, 224
EVESHAM (Worcs.), 68
EXETER (Devon), 69
EYE (Suffolk), 70

F

FALKIRK DISTRICT of BURGHS (Stirlingshire), 324
Falmouth, see Penryn and Falmouth
FIFE, 356
FINSBURY (Middx.), 3
Fishguard, see Haverfordwest Boroughs
FLINT DISTRICT of BOROUGHS, 297
FLINTSHIRE, 311
Forfar, see Montrose Burghs
FORFARSHIRE, 357
Forres, see Inverness Burghs
Fortrose, see Inverness Burghs
FROME (Somerset), 71

G

Galashiels, see Hawick Burghs
GATESHEAD (Durham), 72
GLAMORGANSHIRE, 312
GLASGOW (Lanarkshire), 325
Glasgow University, see Aberdeen and Glasgow Universities
GLOUCESTER, 73
GLOUCESTERSHIRE
  Eastern, 225
  Western, 226
GRANTHAM (Lincs.), 74
GRAVESEND (Kent), 75
GREAT GRIMSBY (Lincs.), 76
GREAT MARLOW (Bucks.), 77
GREAT YARMOUTH (Norfolk), 78
GREENOCK (Renfrewshire), 326
GREENWICH (Kent), 4
Grimsby, see Great Grimsby
GUILDFORD (Surrey), 79

H

HACKNEY (Middx.), 5
HADDINGTON DISTRICT of BURGHS, 327
HADDINGTONSHIRE, 358
HALIFAX (Yorks.), 80
Hamilton, see Falkirk Burghs
HAMPSHIRE
  Northern, 227
  Southern, 228
HARTLEPOOLS, THE (Durham), 81
HARWICH (Essex), 82
HASTINGS (Sussex), 83
HAVERFORDWEST DISTRICT of BOROUGHS (Pembrokeshire), 298
HAWICK DISTRICT of BURGHS (Roxburghshire), 328
HELSTON (Cornwall), 84
HEREFORD, 85
HEREFORDSHIRE, 229
HERTFORD, 86
HERTFORDSHIRE, 230
Holland, see Lincolnshire
Holt, see Denbigh Boroughs
Holyhead, see Beaumaris Boroughs
Holywell, see Flint Boroughs
HONITON (Devon), 87
HORSHAM (Sussex), 88
HUDDERSFIELD (Yorks.), 89
Hull, see Kingston upon Hull
HUNTINGDON, 90
HUNTINGDONSHIRE, 231
HYTHE (Kent), 91

I

Inveraray, see Ayr Burghs
Inverbervie, see Montrose Burghs

Inverkeithing, see Stirling Burghs
INVERNESS DISTRICT of BURGHS, 329
INVERNESS-SHIRE, 359
Inverurie, see Elgin Burghs
IPSWICH (Suffolk), 92
Irvine, see Ayr Burghs
ISLE of WIGHT, 232

J

Jedburgh, see Haddington Burghs

K

KENDAL (Westmorland), 93
Kenfig, see Swansea Boroughs
KENT
    Eastern, 233
    Mid, 234
    Western, 235
Kesteven, see Lincolnshire
KIDDERMINSTER (Worcs.), 94
KILMARNOCK DISTRICT of BURGHS (Ayrshire), 330
Kilrenny, see St. Andrews Burghs
KINCARDINESHIRE, 360
Kinghorn, see Kirkcaldy Burghs
KING'S LYNN (Norfolk), 95
KINGSTON UPON HULL (Yorks.), 96
Kintore, see Elgin Burghs
KIRKCALDY DISTRICT of BURGHS (Fife), 331
Kirkcudbright, see Dumfries Burghs
KIRKCUDBRIGHTSHIRE, 361
Kirkwall, see Wick Burghs
KNARESBOROUGH (Yorks.), 97
Knighton, see Radnor Boroughs
Knucklas, see Radnor Boroughs

L

LAMBETH (Surrey), 6
Lampeter, see Cardigan Boroughs
Lanark, see Falkirk Burghs
LANARKSHIRE, 362
    Northern, 363
    Southern, 364
LANCASHIRE
    Northern, 236
    North-Eastern, 237
    Southern, 238
    South-Eastern, 239
    South-Western, 240
LANCASTER, 98
Lauder, see Haddington Burghs
LAUNCESTON (Cornwall), 99
LEEDS (Yorks.), 100
LEICESTER, 101
LEICESTERSHIRE
    Northern, 241
    Southern, 242
LEITH DISTRICT of BURGHS (Edinburghshire), 332
LEOMINSTER (Herefordshire), 102
LEWES (Sussex), 103
LICHFIELD (Staffs.), 104
LINCOLN, 105
LINCOLNSHIRE
    Parts of Kesteven and Holland, 243
    Parts of Lindsey, 244
    Mid, 245
    Northern, 246
    Southern, 247
Lindsey, see Lincolnshire
Linlithgow, see Falkirk Burghs
LINLITHGOWSHIRE, 365
LISKEARD (Cornwall), 106
LIVERPOOL (Lancs.), 107
Llanelly, see Carmarthen Boroughs
Llanfyllin, see Montgomery Boroughs
Llangefni, see Beaumaris Boroughs
Llanidloes, see Montgomery Boroughs
Llantrisant, see Cardiff Boroughs
Lochmaben, see Dumfries Burghs
London, City of, see City of London
LONDON UNIVERSITY, 378
Loughor, see Swansea Boroughs
LUDLOW (Salop.), 108
LYME REGIS (Dorset), 109
LYMINGTON (Hants.), 110
Lynn Regis, see King's Lynn

M

MACCLESFIELD (Cheshire), 111
Machynlleth, see Montgomery Boroughs
MAIDSTONE (Kent), 112
MALDON (Essex), 113
MALMESBURY (Wilts.), 114
MALTON (Yorks.), 115
MANCHESTER (Lancs.), 116
MARLBOROUGH (Wilts.), 117
Marlow, see Great Marlow
MARYLEBONE (Middx.), 7
Melcombe Regis, see Weymouth and Melcombe Regis
MERIONETHSHIRE, 313
MERTHYR TYDFIL (Glam.), 299
MIDDLESBROUGH (Yorks.), 118
MIDDLESEX, 248
MIDHURST (Sussex), 119
Milford, see Pembroke Boroughs
Mold, see Flint Boroughs
MONMOUTH DISTRICT of BOROUGHS, 300
MONMOUTHSHIRE, 314
MONTGOMERY DISTRICT of BOROUGHS, 301
MONTGOMERYSHIRE, 315
MONTROSE DISTRICT of BURGHS (Forfarshire), 333
MORPETH (Northumberland), 120
Musselburgh, see Leith Burghs

N

Nairn, see Inverness Burghs
Nairnshire, see Elginshire and Nairnshire
Narberth, see Haverfordwest Boroughs
Neath, see Swansea Boroughs
Nevin, see Caernarvon Boroughs
NEWARK-ON-TRENT (Notts.), 121
NEWCASTLE-UNDER-LYME (Staffs.), 122
NEWCASTLE UPON TYNE (Northumberland), 12

New Galloway, see Wigtown Burghs
New Malton, see Malton
NEWPORT (Isle of Wight), 124
Newport, see Monmouth Boroughs
New Radnor, see Radnor
New Sarum, see Salisbury
New Shoreham, see Shoreham
Newtown, see Montgomery Boroughs
New Windsor, see Windsor
New Woodstock, see Woodstock
NORFOLK
  Eastern, 249
  Northern, 250
  Southern, 251
  Western, 252
NORTHALLERTON (Yorks.), 125
NORTHAMPTON, 126
NORTHAMPTONSHIRE
  Northern, 253
  Southern, 254
North Berwick, see Haddington Burghs
Northern Burghs, see Wick Burghs
North Shields, see Tynemouth and North Shields
NORTHUMBERLAND
  Northern, 255
  Southern, 256
NORWICH (Norfolk), 127
NOTTINGHAM, 128
NOTTINGHAMSHIRE
  Northern, 257
  Southern, 258

O

Oban, see Ayr Burghs
OLDHAM (Lancs.), 129
ORKNEY and SHETLAND, 366
Overton, see Flint Boroughs
OXFORD, 130
OXFORD UNIVERSITY, 379
OXFORDSHIRE, 259

P

PAISLEY (Renfrewshire), 334
PEEBLESSHIRE, 367
PEEBLESSHIRE and SELKIRKSHIRE, 368
PEMBROKE DISTRICT of BOROUGHS, 302
PEMBROKESHIRE, 316
PENRYN and FALMOUTH (Cornwall), 131
PERTH, 335
PERTHSHIRE, 369
PETERBOROUGH (Northants.), 132
Peterhead, see Elgin Burghs
PETERSFIELD (Hants.), 133
Pittenweem, see St. Andrews Burghs
PLYMOUTH (Devon), 134
PONTEFRACT (Yorks.), 135
POOLE (Dorset), 136
Port Glasgow, see Kilmarnock Burghs
Portobello, see Leith Burghs
PORTSMOUTH (Hants.), 137
Presteign, see Radnor Boroughs
PRESTON (Lancs.), 138
Pwllheli, see Caernarvon Boroughs

Q

Queensferry, see Stirling Burghs

R

RADNOR DISTRICT of BOROUGHS, 303
RADNORSHIRE, 317
READING (Berks.), 139
REIGATE (Surrey), 140
Renfrew, see Kilmarnock Burghs
RENFREWSHIRE, 370
Retford, see East Retford
Rhayader, see Radnor Boroughs
Rhuddlan, see Flint Boroughs
RICHMOND (Yorks.), 141
RIPON (Yorks.), 142
ROCHDALE (Lancs.), 143
ROCHESTER (Kent), 144
ROSS and CROMARTY, 371
ROXBURGHSHIRE, 372
Rutherglen, see Kilmarnock Burghs
Ruthin, see Denbigh Boroughs
RUTLANDSHIRE, 260
RYE (Sussex), 145

S

ST. ALBANS (Herts.), 146
ST. ANDREWS DISTRICT of BURGHS (Fife), 336
St. Andrews University, see Edinburgh and St. Andrews Universities
St. Asaph, see Flint Boroughs
ST. IVES (Cornwall), 147
SALFORD (Lancs.), 148
SALISBURY (Wilts.), 149
SANDWICH (Kent), 150
Sanquhar, see Dumfries Burghs
SCARBOROUGH (Yorks.), 151
Selkirk, see Hawick Burghs
SELKIRKSHIRE, 373
Selkirkshire, see Peeblesshire and Selkirkshire
SHAFTESBURY (Dorset), 152
SHEFFIELD (Yorks.), 153
Shetland, see Orkney and Shetland
SHOREHAM (Sussex), 154
SHREWSBURY (Salop.), 155
SHROPSHIRE
  Northern, 261
  Southern, 262
SOMERSET
  Eastern, 263
  Mid, 264
  Western, 265
SOUTHAMPTON (Hants.), 156
SOUTH SHIELDS (Durham), 157
SOUTHWARK (Surrey), 8
STAFFORD, 158
STAFFORDSHIRE
  Eastern, 266
  Northern, 267
  Southern, 268
  Western, 269

STALYBRIDGE (Cheshire/Lancs.), 159
STAMFORD (Lincs.), 160
STIRLING DISTRICT of BURGHS, 337
STIRLINGSHIRE, 374
STOCKPORT (Cheshire), 161
STOCKTON-ON-TEES (Durham), 162
STOKE-ON-TRENT (Staffs.), 163
Stranraer, see Wigtown Burghs
STROUD (Glos.), 164
SUDBURY (Suffolk), 165
SUFFOLK
Eastern, 270
Western, 271
SUNDERLAND (Durham), 166
SURREY
Eastern, 272
Mid, 273
Western, 274
SUSSEX
Eastern, 275
Western, 276
SUTHERLAND, 375
SWANSEA DISTRICT of BOROUGHS (Glam.), 304

T

Tain, see Wick Burghs
TAMWORTH (Staffs./Warwickshire), 167
TAUNTON (Somerset), 168
TAVISTOCK (Devon), 169
Tenby, see Pembroke Boroughs
TEWKESBURY (Glos.), 170
THETFORD (Norfolk), 171
THIRSK (Yorks.), 172
TIVERTON (Devon), 173
TOTNES (Devon), 174
TOWER HAMLETS (Middx.), 9
TRURO (Cornwall), 175
TYNEMOUTH and NORTH SHIELDS (Northumberland), 176

U

Universities, see Aberdeen and Glasgow, Cambridge, Edinburgh and St. Andrews, London, Oxford
Usk, see Monmouth Boroughs

W

WAKEFIELD (Yorks.), 177
WALLINGFORD (Berks.), 178
WALSALL (Staffs.), 179
WAREHAM (Dorset), 180
WARRINGTON (Lancs.), 181
WARWICK, 182
WARWICKSHIRE
Northern, 277
Southern, 278
WEDNESBURY (Staffs.), 183
WELLS (Somerset), 184
Welshpool, see Montgomery Boroughs
WENLOCK (Salop.), 185
WESTBURY (Wilts.), 186
WESTMINSTER (Middx.), 10
WESTMORLAND, 279
WEYMOUTH and MELCOMBE REGIS (Dorset), 187
WHITBY (Yorks.), 188
WHITEHAVEN (Cumberland), 189
Whithorn, see Wigtown Burghs
WICK DISTRICT of BURGHS (Caithness), 338
WIGAN (Lancs.), 190
Wight, Isle of, see Isle of Wight
WIGTOWN DISTRICT of BURGHS, 339
WIGTOWNSHIRE, 376
WILTON (Wilts.), 191
WILTSHIRE
Northern, 280
Southern, 281
WINCHESTER (Hants.), 192
WINDSOR (Berks.), 193
Wiston, see Pembroke Boroughs
WOLVERHAMPTON (Staffs.), 194
WOODSTOCK (Oxon.), 195
WORCESTER, 196
WORCESTERSHIRE
Eastern, 282
Western, 283
Wrexham, see Denbigh Boroughs
WYCOMBE (Bucks.), 197

Y

Yarmouth, see Great Yarmouth
YORK, 198
YORKSHIRE (EAST RIDING), 284
YORKSHIRE (NORTH RIDING), 285
YORKSHIRE (WEST RIDING), 286
Eastern, 287
Northern, 288
Southern, 289

Z

Zetland, see Shetland

INDEX TO PLACES OF ELECTION

In each county constituency, one town was designated as the 'place of election' at which nominations were made and the result was declared. The following index will assist readers in tracing local newspapers published in the principal town of the constituency.

ENGLAND

Bedfordshire	Bedford
Berkshire	Abingdon
Buckinghamshire	Aylesbury
Cambridgeshire	Cambridge
Cheshire, Eastern	Macclesfield
Cheshire, Mid	Knutsford
Cheshire, Northern	Knutsford
Cheshire, Southern	Chester
Cheshire, Western	Chester
Cornwall, Eastern	Bodmin
Cornwall, Western	Truro
Cumberland, Eastern	Carlisle
Cumberland, Western	Cockermouth
Derbyshire, Eastern	Chesterfield
Derbyshire, Northern	Bakewell
Derbyshire, Southern	Derby
Devon, Eastern	Exeter
Devon, Northern	South Molton (Barnstaple 1868–)
Devon, Southern	Exeter (Plymouth 1868–)
Dorset	Dorchester
Durham, Northern	Durham
Durham, Southern	Darlington
Essex, Eastern	Colchester
Essex, Northern	Braintree
Essex, Southern	Chelmsford (Brentwood 1868–)
Essex, Western	Chelmsford
Gloucestershire, Eastern	Gloucester
Gloucestershire, Western	Dursley
Hampshire, Northern	Winchester
Hampshire, Southern	Southampton
Herefordshire	Hereford
Hertfordshire	Hertford
Huntingdonshire	Huntingdon
Isle of Wight	Newport
Kent, Eastern	Canterbury
Kent, Mid	Maidstone
Kent, Western	Maidstone (Sevenoaks 1868–)
Lancashire, Northern	Lancaster
Lancashire, North-Eastern	Blackburn
Lancashire, Southern	Newton
Lancashire, South-Eastern	Manchester
Lancashire, South-Western	Liverpool
Leicestershire, Northern	Loughborough
Leicestershire, Southern	Leicester
Lincolnshire, Kesteven and Holland	Sleaford
Lincolnshire, Lindsey	Lincoln
Lincolnshire, Mid	Lincoln
Lincolnshire, Northern	Brigg
Lincolnshire, Southern	Spalding
Middlesex	Brentford
Norfolk, Eastern	Norwich
Norfolk, Northern	Aylsham
Norfolk, Southern	Norwich
Norfolk, Western	Swaffham
Northamptonshire, Northern	Kettering
Northamptonshire, Southern	Northampton
Northumberland, Northern	Alnwick
Northumberland, Southern	Hexham
Nottinghamshire, Northern	Mansfield
Nottinghamshire, Southern	Newark-on-Trent
Oxfordshire	Oxford
Rutlandshire	Oakham
Shropshire, Northern	Shrewsbury
Shropshire, Southern	Church Stretton
Somerset, Eastern	Wells (Bath 1868–)
Somerset, Mid	Wells
Somerset, Western	Taunton
Staffordshire, Eastern	Lichfield
Staffordshire, Northern	Stafford (Stoke-on-Trent 1868–)
Staffordshire, Southern	Lichfield
Staffordshire, Western	Stafford
Suffolk, Eastern	Ipswich
Suffolk, Western	Bury St. Edmunds
Surrey, Eastern	Croydon
Surrey, Mid	Kingston upon Thames

ENGLAND (Cont.)

Surrey, Western	Guildford
Sussex, Eastern	Lewes
Sussex, Western	Chichester
Warwick, Northern	Coleshill
Warwick, Southern	Warwick
Westmorland	Appleby
Wiltshire, Northern	Devizes
Wiltshire, Southern	Salisbury
Worcestershire, Eastern	Droitwich
Worcestershire, Western	Worcester
Yorkshire, East Riding	Beverley
Yorkshire, North Riding	York
Yorkshire, West Riding	Wakefield
Yorkshire (West Riding), Eastern	Leeds
Yorkshire (West Riding), Northern	Bradford
Yorkshire (West Riding), Southern	Wakefield

WALES

Anglesey	Beaumaris
Breconshire	Brecon
Caernarvonshire	Caernarvon
Cardiganshire	Cardigan
Carmarthenshire	Carmarthen
Denbighshire	Denbigh
Flintshire	Flint
Glamorganshire	Bridgend
Merionethshire	Harlech
Monmouthshire	Monmouth
Montgomeryshire	Montgomery
Pembrokeshire	Haverfordwest
Radnorshire	Radnor (or Presteign)

SCOTLAND

Aberdeenshire	Aberdeen
Aberdeenshire, Eastern	Peterhead
Aberdeenshire, Western	Aberdeen
Argyll	Inveraray
Ayrshire	Ayr
Ayrshire, Northern	Kilmarnock
Ayrshire, Southern	Ayr
Banffshire	Banff
Berwickshire	Duns
Bute	Rothesay
Caithness	Wick
Clackmannanshire and Kinross-shire	Dollar
Dumfriesshire	Dumfries
Dunbartonshire	Dumbarton
Edinburghshire	Edinburgh
Elginshire and Nairnshire	Forres
Fife	Cupar
Forfarshire	Forfar
Haddingtonshire	Haddington
Inverness-shire	Inverness
Kincardineshire	Stonehaven
Kirkcudbrightshire	Kirkcudbright
Lanarkshire	Lanark
Lanarkshire, Northern	Hamilton
Lanarkshire, Southern	Lanark
Linlithgowshire	Linlithgow
Orkney and Shetland	Kirkwall
Peeblesshire	Peebles
Peebleshire and Selkirkshire	Peebles
Perthshire	Perth
Renfrewshire	Renfrew
Ross and Cromarty	Dingwall
Roxburghshire	Jedburgh
Selkirkshire	Selkirk
Stirlingshire	Stirling
Sutherland	Dornoch
Wigtownshire	Wigtown